**W9-BHG-576**

*Reference*
*Library of*

# AMERICAN

# WOMEN

# *Reference Library of*

## AMERICAN

## WOMEN

VOLUME **I**

*A-F*

Distributed exclusively by:
African American Publications

*Editor:* Jennifer Mossman
*Managing Editor:* Neil Walker
*Senior Editor:* Terrie M. Rooney
*Contributing Editor:* Frank V. Castronova
*Associate Editor:* Catt Slovey

*Permissions Manager:* Susan M. Trosky
*Permissions Specialist:* Margaret Chamberlain

*Production Director:* Mary Beth Trimper
*Production Manager:* Evi Seoud

*Art Director:* Cynthia Baldwin
*Cover Design:* Michelle DiMercurio

While every effort has been made to ensure the reliability of the information presented in this publication, Gale Research does not guarantee the accuracy of the data contained herein. Gale accepts no payment for listing; and inclusion in the publication of any organization, agency, institution, publication, service, or individual does not imply endorsement of the editors or publisher. Errors brought to the attention of the publisher and verified to the satisfaction of the publisher will be corrected in future editions.

This publication is a creative work fully protected by all applicable copyright laws, as well as by misappropriation, trade secret, unfair competition, and other applicable laws. The authors and editors of this work have added value to the underlying factual material herein through one or more of the following: unique and original selection, coordination, expression, arrangement, and classification of the information. All rights to this publication will be vigorously defended.

Copyright © 1999
Gale Research
27500 Drake Rd.
Farmington Hills, MI 48331-3535

All rights reserved including the right of reproduction in whole or in part in any form.

ISBN 0-7876-3864-1 (complete set)
ISBN 0-7876-3865-X (Volume 1)
ISBN 0-7876-3866-8 (Volume 2)
ISBN 0-7876-3867-6 (Volume 3)
ISBN 0-7876-3868-4 (Volume 4)

Printed in 2000
Printed in the United States of America

*For Mary Motz my love, my friend, my wife, mother of my children John and Sam, in my heart the finest American woman. Love John.*

# CONTENTS

Introduction ............................................................................... ix

Acknowledgments ........................................................................ xi

Historical Chronology ................................................................. xix

Biographies:

Volume I (A-F) ............................................................................. 1

Volume II (G-M) ...................................................................... 237

Volume III (N-Z) ..................................................................... 489

Volume IV (International) ......................................................... 743

Indexes:

Name ...................................................................................... A-1

Nationality .............................................................................. B-1

Occupation ............................................................................. C-1

# INTRODUCTION

One hundred fifty years ago, in 1848, a bold and courageous civil rights movement began when the first Women's Rights Convention was held in Seneca Falls, New York. Since then, women have made great gains in many parts of the world. Having begun the twentieth century without the right to vote or to receive a university education in the United States, we end with most legal and institutional barriers removed. The same degree of progress has been made in other nations as well.

The contributions of many women have only recently been acknowledged. Their biographies offer fascinating and inspiring glimpses at centuries of mostly unsung heroines. The *Reference Library of American Women* provides a unique, comprehensive source for biographical information on 650 women who have gained international recognition for their enduring contributions to human culture and society. To meet the needs of students and researchers, the first three volumes are devoted to American women while the fourth volume expands coverage to include notable women from around the globe.

## Scope

Entries in the four-volume series have been culled from Gale's extensive biographical database. Both contemporary and historic figures covering a wide range of occupations or fields of endeavor can be found. Featured are such renowned twentieth-century women as Mother Teresa, Diana, Princess of Wales, poet laureate Maya Angelou, Supreme Court Justice Ruth Bader Ginsburg, and artist Maya Ying Lin. Important historic figures include Queen Elizabeth I, Cleopatra, Joan of Arc, Pocahontas, Marie Antoinette, and Madame Curie. Biographical information can be found for the many social or political activists who have organized movements to improve the quality of our lives. Others have made major contributions to the arts, business, education, journalism, religion, or science.

## Format

Arranged alphabetically, each authoritative article begins with a brief descriptive paragraph that provides a capsule identification and a statement of the woman's significance. Birth and death years are included. Often this is all the information required. Without scanning a lengthy article, this useful feature allows you to determine at a glance whether you need to read further. For example:

> *The social worker and agency administrator Grace Abbott (1878-1939) awakened many Americans to the responsibility of government to help meet the special problems of immigrants and of children.*

Should you decide to continue, the essays that follow are generally about 800 words in length and offer a substantial treatment of the women's lives. Some proceed chronologically, while others confine biographical data to a few paragraphs and then move on to a consideration of the subject's life work. When very few biographical facts are known, the article is necessarily devoted to an analysis of the subject's contribution to society and culture.

Following the essay is a "Further Reading" section and, when applicable, a list of additional sources providing more recent biographical works. Bibliographic citations contain books, periodicals, and Internet addresses for World Wide Web pages. This feature is especially helpful to students, who are frequently required to consult multiple sources when compiling a report or preparing a classroom presentation.

## Additional Features

•**Images.**  Portraits accompany many of the articles and provide an authentic likeness or representation of the biographee.  Of the historic figures there are depictions from coins, engravings, and sculptures; of the moderns there are many photographs.

•**Historical Chronology**. To further enhance the reference value of this authoritative set, you can also find a chronology of people, places, and events that changed women's history.

•**Indexes.** Three indexes have been included to help researchers identify women by name, nationality, and field of endeavor.

## A Valuable Resource

Many community programs, ceremonies, and activities are being planned to commemorate the 150th anniversary of the Women's Rights Movement. Biographical information on internationally renowned women is sure to be in high demand. The *Reference Library of American Women* can meet this need by presenting lively and informative essays on 650 women whose contributions have earned them a place in the annals of human history.

# ACKNOWLEDGMENTS

Photographs and illustrations appearing in *Reference Library of American Women* were received from the following sources:

Abbott, Berenice, photograph. AP/Wide World Photos. Reproduced by permission.

Abzug, Bella, photograph by Ted Cowell. AP/Wide World Photos. Reproduced by permis sion.

Addams, Jane, photograph. The Library of Congress.

Albright, Madeline, photograph. AP/Wide World Photos. Reproduced by permission.

Alcott, Louisa May, photograph. Concord Free Public Library.

Allen, Florence, photograph. The Library of Congress.

Allen, Paula Gunn, photograph. AP/Wide World Photos. Reproduced by permission.

Allende, Isabel, photograph. Archive Photos. Reproduced by permission.

Anderson, Marian, photograph by Carl Van Vechten. The Library of Congress.

Angelou, Maya, photograph. AP/Wide World Photos. Reproduced by permission.

Anthony, Susan B., photograph. The Library of Congress.

Arden, Elizabeth, photograph. The Library of Congress.

Arendt, Hannah, photograph. The Library of Congress.

Ashrawi, Hanan, photograph. AP/Wide World Photos. Reproduced by permission.

Aung San Suu Kyi, photograph. AP/Wide World Photos. Reproduced by permission.

Austen, Jane, watercolor drawing by Cassandra Austen.

Baca-Barragan, Polly, photograph. AP/Wide World Photos. Reproduced by permission.

Baez, Joan, photograph. The Library of Congress.

Baker, Ella, photograph. AP/Wide World Photos. Reproduced by permission.

Baker, Josephine, photograph by Carl Van Vechten. The Library of Congress.

Balch, Emily Greene, photograph. The Library of Congress.

Ball, Lucille, photograph. The Library of Congress.

Bandaranaike, Sirimavo, photograph. The Library of Congress.

Barton, Clara, photograph. National Archives and Records Administration.

Bates, Katherine Lee, drawing. The Library of Congress.

Battle, Kathleen, photograph. AP/Wide World Photos. Reproduced by permission.

Beard, Mary Ritter, photograph. The Library of Congress.

Beecher, Catherine E., photograph. Corbis-Bettmann. Reproduced by permission.

Berry, Mary Frances, photograph. AP/Wide World Photos. Reproduced by permission.

Bethune, Mary McLeod, photograph by Carl Van Vechten. The Library of Congress.

Bhutto, Benazir, photograph by B. K. Bangash. AP/Wide World Photos. Reproduced by permission.

Bishop, Elizabeth, photograph by J.L. Castel. The Library of Congress.

Blackwell, Elizabeth, photograph. The Library of Congress.

Blanding, Sarah Gibson, photograph. The Library of Congress.

Bloomer, Amelia Jenks, engraving. The Library of Congress.

Bloor, Ella Reeve, photograph. The Library of Congress.

Blume, Judy, photograph. AP/Wide World Photos. Reproduced by permission.

Booth, Evangeline, photograph. The Library of Congress.

Borgia, Lucrezia, engraving. The Library of Congress.

Bourgeoys, Marguerite, photograph. Archive Photos. Reproduced by permission.

Bourke-White, Margaret, photograph by Alan M. Fern. The Library of Congress.

Boxer, Barbara, photograph. AP/Wide World Photos. Reproduced by permission.

Braun, Carol Moseley, photograph by Barry Thumma. AP/Wide World Photos. Reproduced by permission.

Brice, Fanny, photograph. The Library of Congress.

Bronte, Charlotte, painting. Archive Photos. Reproduced by permission.

Bronte, Emily, painting by Bramwell Bronte.

Brooks, Gwendolyn, photograph. The Library of Congress.

Brothers, Dr. Joyce, photograph. Archive Photos. Reproduced by permission.

Brown, Rachel Fuller, photograph. The Library of Congress.

Browner, Carol, photograph. AP/Wide World Photos. Reproduced by permission

Browning, Elizabeth Barrett, print. Archive Photos. Reproduced by permission.

Brownmiller, Susan, photograph. AP/Wide World Photos. Reproduced by permission.

Buck, Pearl S., photograph. International Portrait Gallery. Reproduced by permission.

Burke, Selma, photograph. The Library of Congress.

Byrne, Jane, photograph by Laurence Agron. Archive Photos. Reproduced by permission.

Calamity Jane, photograph. Archive Photos/American Stock. Reproduced by permission.

Caldicott, Helen, photograph. AP/Wide World Photos. Reproduced by permission.

Caldwell, Sarah, photograph. The Library of Congress.

Callas, Maria, photograph. The Library of Congress.

Capriati, Jennifer, photograph. AP/Wide World Photos. Reproduced by permission.

Caraway, Sen. Hattie W., painting. The Library of Congress.

Carnegie, Hattie, photograph. The Library of Congress.

Carson, Rachel, photograph. The Library of Congress.

Cassatt, Mary, photograph. Archive Photos. Reproduced by permission.

Catherine of Aragon as Mary Magdalen, 15th century, painting. Archive Photos. Reproduced by permission.

Catherine the Great, painting. The Library of Congress.

Catt, Carrie Chapman, photograph. The Library of Congress.

Chanel, Gabrielle "Coco," photograph. Archive Photos. Reproduced by permission.

Chavez, Linda, photograph. AP/Wide World Photos. Reproduced by permission.

Chicago, Judy, photograph. AP/Wide World Photos. Reproduced by permission.

Child, Julia, photograph. AP/Wide World Photos. Reproduced by permission.

Child, Lydia Maria, photograph. The Library of Congress.

Chinn, May Edward, photograph. AP/Wide World Photos. Reproduced by permission.

Chisholm, Shirley, photograph. AP/Wide World Photos. Reproduced by permission.

Chopin, Kate, photograph.

Christie, Agatha, photograph. The Library of Congress.

Chung, Connie, photograph. AP/Wide World Photos. Reproduced by permission.

Ciller, Tansu, photograph. Archive Photos. Reproduced by permission.

Cisneros, Sandra, photograph by Dana Tynan. AP/Wide World Photos. Reproduced by permission.

Claiborne, Liz, photograph by Mark Peterson. Reuters/Archive Photos. Reproduced by permission.

Clapp, Margaret, photograph. Archive Photos. Reproduced by permission.

Cleopatra VII, illustration. The Library of Congress.

Cline, Patsy, photograph. Archive Photos/Frank Driggs Collection. Reproduced by permission.

Clinton, Hillary Rodham, photograph. AP/Wide World Photos. Reproduced by permission.

Cochran, Jacqueline, photograph. Archive Photos. Reproduced by permission.

Collins, Eileen, photograph. AP/Wide World Photos. Reproduced by permission.

Collins, Marva, photograph. AP/Wide World Photos. Reproduced by permission.

Comnena, Anna, illustration. The Library of Congress.

Corazon, Aquino, photograph. AP/Wide World Photos. Reproduced by permission.

Cori, Gerty T., photograph. The Library of Congress.

Crandall, Prudence, photograph. The Library of Congress.

Curie, Marie, photograph. The Library of Congress.

Cushman, Charlotte, photograph. The Library of Congress.

Dandridge, Dorothy, photograph. AP/Wide World Photos. Reproduced by permission.

Davis, Bette, photograph. Archive Photos. Reproduced by permission.

de Beauvoir, Simon, photograph. AP/Wide World Photos. Reproduced by permission.

De Mille, Agnes, photograph. Archive Photos. Reproduced by permission.

Dee, Ruby, photograph. The Library of Congress.

Deer, Ada, photograph. AP/Wide World Photos. Reproduced by permission.

Devlin, Bernadette, photograph. Archive Photos. Reproduced by permission.

Diana, Princess of Wales, photograph. Archive Newsphotos/Press Association. Reproduced by permission.

Dickinson, Emily, painting. The Library of Congress.

Doi, Takako, photograph. AP/Wide World Photos. Reproduced by permission.

Dole, Elizabeth, photograph. Archive Photos/Gates. Reproduced by permission.

Doolittle, Hilda, photograph. The Library of Congress.

Dorr, Rheta Childe, photograph. The Library of Congress.

Dove, Rita, photograph. AP/Wide World Photos. Reproduced by permission.

Duncan, Isadora, photograph. Archive Photos/ Popperfoto. Reproduced by permission.

Dunham, Katherine, photograph. The Library of Congress.

Earhart, Amelia, photograph. Archive Photos. Reproduced by permission.

Earle, Sylvia A., photograph. AP/Wide World Photos. Reproduced by permission.

Edelman, Marian Wright, photograph. AP/Wide World Photos. Reproduced by permission.

Eisenhower, Mamie Dodd, photograph. Archive Photos. Reproduced by permission.

Eleanor of Aquitaine, drawing. Archive Photos/ Popperfoto. Reproduced by permission.

Elion, Gertrude Belle, photograph. AP/Wide World Photos. Reproduced by permission.

Eliot, George, drawing. The Library of Congress.

Elizabeth I, painting. The Library of Congress.

Elizabeth II, Queen of England, photograph. The Library of Congress.

Ephron, Nora, photograph. AP/Wide World Photos. Reproduced by permission.

Evers-Williams, Myrlie, photograph. AP/Wide World Photos. Reproduced by permission.

Farrell, Susan, photograph by Mike Davis. Archive Photos/Camera Press. Reproduced by permission.

Ferber, Edna, photograph. The Library of Congress.

Ferraro, Geraldine, photograph. Archive Photos. Reproduced by permission.

Fiske, Minnie M., photograph. The Library of Congress.

Flynn, Elizabeth, photograph. The Library of Congress.

Fonda, Jane, photograph. Archive Photos. Reproduced by permission.

Fossey, Dian, photograph. AP/Wide World Phots. Reproduced by permission.

Frank, Anne, photograph. The Library of Congress.

Frankenthaler, Helen, photograph. AP/Wide World Photos. Reproduced by permission.

Franklin, Aretha, photograph. AP/Wide World Photos. Reproduced by permission.

Fraser, Antonia, photograph. Archive Photos. Reproduced by permission.

Freud, Anna, photograph. AP/Wide World Photos. Reproduced by permission.

Friedan, Betty, photograph. The Library of Congress.

Fry, Elizabeth Gurney, painting. The Library of Congress.

Fuller, Margaret, painting by John Plumbe. The Library of Congress.

Gage, Matilda J., engraving. The Library of Congress.

Gandhi, Indira, photograph. The Library of Congress.

Garbo, Greta, photograph. The Museum of Modern Art/Film Stills Archive. The Library of Congress.

Garland, Judy, photograph. Archive Photos. Reproduced by permission.

Gaskell, Elizabeth C., illustration. The Library of Congress.

Gayle, Helene, photograph. AP/Wide World Photos. Reproduced by permission.

Gibson, Althea, photograph by Carl Van Vechten. The Library of Congress.

Gilbreth, Lillian, photograph. AP/Wide World Photos. Reproduced by permission.

Glasgow, Ellen, photograph. The Library of Congress.

Goeppert-Mayer, Maria, photograph. The Library of Congress.

Goldberg, Whoopi, photograph. AP/Wide World Photos. Reproduced by permission.

Goodall, Jane, photograph. The Library of Congress.

Goodman, Ellen, photograph. AP/Wide World Photos. Reproduced by permission.

Gordeeva, Ekaterina, photograph. AP/Wide World Photos. Reproduced by permission.

Gordon, Pamela with Lord Waddington, photograph. AP/Wide World Photos. Reproduced by permission.

Graham, Katherine, photograph. The Library of Congress.

Graham, Martha, photograph. The Library of Congress.

Graves, Nancy, photograph. AP/Wide World Photos. Reproduced by permission.

Green, Constance M., photograph. The Library of Congress.

Green, Edith S., photograph. The Library of Congress.

Greer, Germaine, photograph. Archive Photos. Reproduced by permission.

Grimke, Sarah, engraving. The Library of Congress.

Grossinger, Jennie, photograph. Archive Photos. Reproduced by permission.

Guisewite, Cathy, photograph. AP/Wide World Photos. Reproduced by permission.

Hagen, Uta, photograph by Neal Boenzi. New York Times Co./Archive Photos. Reproduced by permission.

Hale, Sarah Josepha, photograph. New York Public Library Picture Collection.

Hamer, Fannie Lou, photograph. The Library of Congress.

Hamilton, Alice, photograph. The Library of Congress.

Hansen, Julia B., photograph. The Library of Congress.

Harjo, Suzan Shown, photograph. AP/Wide World Photos. Reproduced by permission.

Harriman, Pamela, photograph by Steve Jaffe. Reuters/Archive Photos. Reproduced by permission.

Harris, Barbara, photograph. AP/Wide World Photos. Reproduced by permission.

Harris, Patricia Roberts, photograph. AP/Wide World. Reproduced by permission.

Hayes, Helen, photograph. Archive Photos. Reproduced by permission.

Hayworth, Rita, photograph. AP/Wide World Photos. Reproduced by permission.

Head, Edith, photograph. AP/Wide World Photos. Reproduced by permission.

Healy, Bernadine, photograph. AP/Wide World Photos. Reproduced by permission.

Heckler, Margaret O., photograph. The Library of Congress.

Hellman, Lillian, photograph. AP/Wide World Photos. Reproduced by permission.

Hepburn, Audrey, photograph. Archive Photos. Reproduced by permission

Hepburn, Katharine, photograph. AP/Wide World Photos. Reproduced by permission.

Hepworth, Dame Barbara, photograph. Express Newspaper/Archive Photos. Reproduced by permission.

Higgins, Marguerite, photograph. The Library of Congress.

Hill, Anita, photograph. AP/Wide World Photos. Reproduced by permission.

Hills, Carla Anderson, photograph. The Library of Congress.

Hobby, Oveta Culp, photograph. Women in Military Service for America Memorial Foundation, Inc.

Hodgkin, Dorothy, photograph. Archive Photos. Reproduced by permission.

Holiday, Billie, photograph by Carl Van Vechten. The Library of Congress.

Holm, Hanya, photograph. Archive Photos/LDE. Reproduced by permission.

Hopper, Grace, photograph. The Library of Congress.

Horne, Lena, photograph. Archive Photos. Reproduced by permission.

Horner, Matina S., photograph. The Library of Congress.

Hurston, Zora Neale, photograph by Carl Van Vechten. The Library of Congress.

Hyman, Libbie Henrietta, photograph. The Library of Congress.

Ibarruri, Dolores, photograph. Archive Photos/Camera Press LTD. Reproduced by permission.

Ireland, Patricia, photograph. AP/Wide World Photos. Reproduced by permission.

Isabella I, engraving. The Library of Congress.

Jackson, Helen, photograph. The Library of Congress.

Jackson, Shirley Ann, photograph. AP/Wide World Photos. Reproduced by permission.

Jemison, Mae C., photograph. AP/Wide World Photos. Reproduced by permission.

Joan of Arc, sculpture. The Library of Congress.

Johnson, Betsey, photograph. AP/Wide World Photos. Reproduced by permission.

Johnson, Virginia, photograph. AP/Wide World Photos. Reproduced by permission.

Joliot-Curie, Frederic, photograph. The Library of Congress.

Jordan, June, photograph. AP/Wide World Photos. Reproduced by permission.

Joy Adamson, photograph. Archive Photos. Reproduced by permission.

Karan, Donna, photograph. Archive Photo/Jason Trigg. Reproduced by permission.

Karle, Isabella L., photograph. AP/Wide World Photos. Reproduced by permission.

Kassebaum, Nancy Landon, photograph. Archive Photo/Consolidated. Reproduced by permission.

Keller, Helen, photograph. AP/Wide World Photos. Reproduced by permission.

Kellor, Frances, photograph. The Library of Congress.

King, Billie Jean, photograph. Archive Photos. Reproduced by permission.

King, Coretta Scott, photograph. AP/Wide World Photos. Reproduced by permission.

Kirkpatrick, Jeane, photograph. Archive Photos. Reproduced by permission.

Kreps, Juanita, photograph. Archive Photos. Reproduced by Permission

Kubler-Ross, Elisabeth, photograph. AP/Wide World Photos. Reproduced by permission.

Kunin, Madeline, photograph. AP/Wide World Photos. Reproduced by permission.

Lange, Dorothea, photograph. The Library of Congress.

Lauder, Estee, photograph. AP/Wide World Photos. Reproduced by permission.

Leakey, Mary, Louise Robbins, photograph. AP/Wide World Photos. Reproduced by permission.

Lease, Mary E., photograph. The Library of Congress.

Leibovitz, Annie, photograph. AP/Wide World Photos. Reproduced by permission.

Levi-Montalcini, Rita, photograph. AP/Wide World Photos. Reproduced by permission.

Liliuokalani, painting. Archive Photos. Reproduced by permission.

Lin, Maya, photograph. AP/Wide World Photos. Reproduced by permission.

Lindbergh, Anne Morrow, photograph. The Library of Congress.

Livia, illustration. The Library of Congress.

Long, Irene D., photograph. National Archives and Records Adminisrration.

Lonsdale, Kathleen, photograph. AP/Wide World Photos. Reproduced by permission.

Lorde, Audre, photograph. The Library of Congress.

Loren, Sophia, photograph. Archive Photos. Reproduced by permission.

Love, Susan, photograph. AP/Wide World Photos. Reproduced by permission.

Lowell, Josephine, drawing. The Library of Congress.

Luce, Clare Boothe, photograph by Carl Van Vechten. The Library of Congress.

Luxemburg, Rosa, photograph. The Library of Congress.

Lyon, Mary, photograph. The Library of Congress.

Madison, Mrs. James (Dolly), photograph by Stuart Gilbert. National Archives and Records Administration.

Mandela,Winnie, photograph. AP/Wide World Photos. Reproduced by permission.

Mankiller, Wilma, photograph. AP/Wide World Photos. Reproduced by permission.

Mansfield, Katherine, photograph. Corbis-Bettmann. Reproduced by permission.

Marcos, Imelda, photograph by Tom Gates. Archive Photos. Reproduced by permission.

Marie Antoinette, painting. The Library of Congress.

Marshall, Paule, photograph. AP/Wide World Photos. Reproduced by permission.

Martin, Agnes, photograph. Archive Photos/Christopher Felver. Reproduced by permission.

Martin, Lynn, photograph. AP/Wide World Photos. Reproduced by permission.

Martin, Mary, photograph. The Library of Congress/ Corbis-Bettmann. Reproduced by permission.

Martinez, Vilma S., photograph. AP/Wide World Photos. Reproduced by permission.

Mary I, drawing. Archive Photos/Popperfoto. Reproduced by permissions.

McCarthy, Mary, photograph. The Library of Congress.

McDaniels, Hattie, Fay Bainter, photograph. AP/Wide World Photos. Reproduced by permission.

Mcmillan, Terry, photograph. AP/Wide World Photos. Reproduced by permission.

McQueen, Butterfly, photograph. Archive Photos. Reproduced by permission.

Mead, Margaret, photograph. AP/Wide World Photos. Reproduced by permission.

Meitner, Lise, photograph. The Library of Congress.

Menchu, Rigoberta, photograph by Daniel Hernandez. AP/Wide World Photos. Reproduced by permission.

Mikulski, Barbara, photograph. Archive Photos/Consolidated. Reproduced by permission.

Millay, Edna St.Vincent, photograph by Carl Van Vechten. The Library of Congress.

Mistral, Gabriels, photograph. The Library of Congress.

Mitchell, Maria , photograph. The Library of Congress.

Monroe, Marilyn, photograph. Archive Photos. Reproduced by permission.

Montessori, Maria, illustration. The Library of Congress.

Moore, Marianne, photograph. AP/Wide World Photos. Reproduced by permission.

Morgan, Robin, photograph. AP/Wide World Photos. Reproduced by permission.

Morrison, Toni, Photograph. AP/Wide World Photos. Reproduced by permission.

Moses, Grandma, photograph. AP/Wide World Photos. Reproduced by permission.

Mother Teresa, photograph. AP/Wide World Photos. Reproduced by permission.

Motley, Constance Baker, photograph. AP/Wide World Photos. Reproduced by permission.

Muldowney, Shirley"Cha Cha," photograph. AP/Wide World Photos. Reproduced by permission.

Nation, Carrie, photograph. Archive Photos. Reproduced by permission.

Natividad, Irene, photograph. AP/Wide World Photos. Reproduced by permission.

Navratilova, Martina, photograph. AP/Wide World Photos. Reproduced by permission.

Naylor, Gloria, photograph. AP/Wide World Photos. Reproduced by permission.

Nevelson, Louise, photograph. AP/Wide World Photos. Reproduced by permission.

Nin, Anais, photograph. AP/Wide World Photos. Reproduced by permission.

Noether, Amalie Emmy, photograph. Archive Photos. Reproduced by permission.

Norman, Jessye, photograph. AP/Wide World Photos. Reproduced by permission.

Novello, Antonia, photograph. AP/Wide World Photos. Reproduced by permission.

O'Connor, Sandra Day, photograph. AP/Wide World Photos. Reproduced by permission.

O'Keeffe, Georgia, photograph by Carl Van Vechten. The Library of Congress.

Oakley, Annie, photograph. Archive Photos. Reproduced by permission.

Oates, Joyce Carol, photograph. AP/Wide World Photos. Reproduced by permission.

Ochoa, Ellen, photograph. U. S. National Aeronautics and Space Administration (NASA).

Owen, Ruth Bryan, photograph. AP/Wide World Photos. Reproduced by permission.

Pandit, Vijaya Lakshmi, photograph. Archive Photos. Reproduced by permission.

Parker, Dorothy, photograph. AP/Wide World Photos. Reproduced by permission.

Parks, Rosa, photograph. AP/Wide World Photos. Reproduced by permission.

Patrick, Ruth, photograph. AP/Wide World Photos. Reproduced by permission.

Perkins, Frances, photograph. Archive Photos. Reproduced by permission.

Peron, Eva, photograph. The Library of Congress.

Picasso, Paloma, photograph. AP/Wide World Photos. Reproduced by permission.

Plath, Sylvia, photograph. AP/Wide World Photos. Reproduced by permission.

Pocahontas, line drawing. International Portrait Gallery.

Porter, Katherine Anne, photograph by Paul Porter. AP/Wide World Photos. Reproduced by permission.

Potter, Beatrix, photograph. AP/Wide World Photos. Reproduced by permission.

Price, Leontyne, photograph by Carl Van Vechten. The Library of Congress.

Queen Victoria, photograph. Archive Photos/Popperfoto. Reproduced by permission

Rankin, Jeannette, photograph. AP/Wide World Photos. Reproduced by permission.

Ray, Dr. Dixie Lee, photograph. AP/Wide World Photos. Reproduced by permission.

Redgrave, Vanessa, photograph. AP/Wide World Photos. Reproduced by permission.

Reno, Janet, photograph. AP/Wide World Photos. Reproduced by permission.

Rice, Anne, photograph. AP/Wide World Photos. Reproduced by permission.

Rich, Adrienne, photograph. AP/Wide World Photos. Reproduced by permission.

Richier, Germaine, photograph. Archive Photos/Archive France. Reproduced by permission.

Ride, Sally, photograph. U.S. National Aeronautics and Space Administration (NASA).

Riefenstahl, Leni, photograph. AP/Wide World Photos. Reproduced by permission.

Rivlin, Alice, photograph. Archive Photos. Reproduced by permission.

Robinson, Harriet H., photograph. The Library of Congress.

Robinson, Mary, photograph. AP/Wide World Photos. Reproduced by permission.

Rogers, Edith Nourse, photograph. UPI/Corbis-Bettmann. Reproduced by permission.

Rohde, Ruth, photograph. The Library of Congress.

Roosevelt, Eleanor, photograph. The Library of Congress

Ros-Lehtinen, Ileana, photograph. The Library of Congress.

Ross, Betsy, painting. National Archives and Records Administration.

Ross, Diana, photograph. AP/Wide World Photos. Reproduced by permission.

Rudkin, Margaret, photograph. Archive Photos. Reproduced by permission.

Rudolph, Wilma, photograph. AP/Wide World Photos. Reproduced by permission.

Russell, Elizabeth S., photograph. AP/Wide World

Photos. Reproduced by permission.

Sabin, Florence Rena, sketch. The Library of Congress.

Sand, George, photograph. Archive Photos. Reproduced by permission.

Sanger, Margaret, photograph. AP/Wide World Photos. Reproduced by permission.

Sarandon, Susan, photograph. Archive Photos. Reproduced by permission.

Schiess, Betty, photograph. AP/Wide World Photos. Reproduced by permission.

Schlafly, Phyllis, photograph. AP/Wide World Photos. Reproduced by permission.

Schroeder, Patricia, photograph. The Library of Congress.

Seibert, Dr. Florence B., photograph. The Library of Congress.

Selena, photograph. Archive Photos/Hernandez. Reproduced by permission.

Seton, Elizabeth, drawing. Archive Photos. Reproduced by permission.

Sexton, Anne, photograph. AP/Wide World Photos. Reproduced by permission.

Siebert, Muriel F., photograph. AP/Wide World Photos. Reproduced by permission.

Silkwood, Karen, photograph. AP/Wide World Photos. Reproduced by permission.

Sills, Beverly, photograph by Carl Van Vechten. The Library of Congress.

Smith, Bessie, photograph. New York Public Library.

Smith, Lillian, photograph. The Library of Congress.

Smith, Margaret Chase, photograph. AP/Wide World Photos. Reproduced by permission.

Snowe, Olympia, photograph. Archive Photos/Consolidated. Reproduced by permission.

Sogourner Truth, drawing. Frank Leslie's Illustrated Weekly, December 25, 1869.

Sontag, Susan, photograph. AP/Wide World Photos. Reproduced by permission.

St. Denis, Ruth, photograph. Archive Photos. Reproduced by permission.

Stanton, Elizabeth Cady, engraving. National Archives and Records Administration.

Steel, Dawn, photograph by Darlene Hammond. Archive Photos. Reproduced by permission.

Steele, Danielle, photograph. AP/Wide World Photos. Reproduced by permission.

Stein, Gertrude, photograph by Carl Van Vechten. The Library of Congress.

Steinem, Gloria, photograph. AP/Wide World Photos. Reproduced by permission.

Stone, Lucy, photograph. Library of Congress.

Stowe, Harriet Beecher, photograph. National Archives and Records Administration.

Streisand, Barbra, photograph. AP/Wide World Photos. Reproduced by permission.

Suzman, Helen, photograph. AP/Wide World Photos. Reproduced by permission.

Tallchief, Maria, photograph. The Library of Congress.

Tan, Amy Ruth, photograph. Archive Photos. Reproduced by permission.

Tarbell, Ida M., photograph. AP/Wide World Photos. Reproduced by permission.

Taussig, Helen, B., photograph. AP/Wide World Photos. Reproduced by permission.

Taylor, Elizabeth, photograph. Archive Photos. Reproduced by permission.

Tereshkova, Valentina, photograph. The Library of Congress.

Thatcher, Margaret, photograph. AP/Wide World Photos. Reproduced by permission.

Trotter, Mildred, photograph. AP/Wide World Photos. Reproduced by permission.

Tubman, Harriet, photograph. The Library of Congress.

Tucker, C. Delores, photograph. AP/Wide World Photos. Reproduced by permission.

Turner, Tina, photograph. AP/Wide World Photos. Reproduced by permission.

Vaughan, Sarah, photograph. AP/Wide World Photos. Reproduced by permission.

Velazquez, Nydia, photograph. AP/Wide World Photos. Reproduced by permission.

Von Furstenberg, Diane, photograph. Archive Photos/Express Newspaper. Reproduced by permission.

vos Savant, Marilyn, photograph. AP/Wide World Photos. Reproduced by permission.

Wald, Lillian, photograph. Archive Photos. Reproduced by permission.

Walker, Alice, photograph. AP/Wide World Photos. Reproduced by permission.

Walters, Barbara, photograph. Archive Photos. Reproduced by permission.

Warren, Mercy Otis, photograph. Archive Photos. Reproduced by permission.

Waters, Maxine, photograph. AP/Wide World Photos. Reproduced by permission.

Wattleton, Faye, photograph. AP/Wide World Photos. Reproduced by permission.

Wauneka, Annie D., photograph. AP/Wide World Photos. Reproduced by permission.

Webb, Beatrice, photograph. Hulton-Deutsch Collection/Corbis-Bettmann. Reproduced by permission.

Welty, Eudora, photograph. AP/Wide World Photos. Reproduced by permission.

Westwood, Vivienne, photograph. Archive Photos/Propperfoto. Reproduced by permission.

Wexler, Nancy, photograph. The Library of Congress.

Wharton, Edith, photograph. The Library of Congress.

Wheatley, Phillis, engraving. The Library of Congress.

Whitman, Christie, photograph. AP/Wide World Photos. Reproduced by permission.

Whitmire, Kathy, photograph. AP/Wide World Photos. Reproduced by permission.

Widnall, Sheila, photograph. AP/Wide World Photos. Reproduced by permission.

Willard, Emma, photograph. Archive Photos. Reproduced by permission.

Willard, Frances, photograph. Archive Photos. Reproduced by permission.

Winfrey, Oprah, photograph. AP/Wide World Photos. Reproduced by permission.

Wong, Anna May, photograph by Carl Van Vechten. The Library of Congress.

Woodhull, Victoria, drawing. The Library of Congress.

Wright, Frances, photograph. Archive Photos. Reproduced by permission.

Yalow, Rosalyn S., photograph. The Library of Congress.

Yard, Molly, photograph. Archive Photos. Reproduced by permission.

Zaharias, Babe Didriksen, photograph. AP/Wide World Photos. Reproduced by permission.

# HISTORICAL CHRONOLOGY

**40,000 B.C.** Modern *Homo Sapiens* well-established in Europe.

**25,000 B.C.** Earliest known oil lamps in France.

**24,000 B.C.** Sculptured clay figurines in Europe.

**11,000 B.C.** Small bands of hunters make their way across the Bering Sea Land Bridge from Siberia.

**10,000 B.C.** Bow and arrow in use in Europe (earliest known use).

**9000 B.C.** Jericho established; among earliest known towns.

**9000 B.C.** Earliest fired pottery in Japan (Jomon period).

**8500 B.C.** Sheep are domesticated in Near East.

**8350 B.C.** Cold-hammered copper in use in Turkey.

**7000 B.C.** Copper-casting in Near East.

**3000 B.C.** Oldest pottery in New World. Colombia.

**3000 B.C.** First bronze artifacts in Middle East.

**2570 B.C.** Queen Nefertari rules in Egypt calling herself "God's wife."

**2500 B.C.** Pyramid construction begins in Egypt.

**2500 B.C.** Beginnings of Indus River civilization in India.

**1490 B.C.** Queen Hatsheput rules in Egypt, claiming rights of pharaoh.

**1360 B.C.** Queen Nefertiti rules in Egypt.

**1200 B.C.** Fu Hao, woman warrior in China, leads military expeditions.

**1180 B.C.** Spartan Queen Helen kidnapped by Paris.

**1150 B.C.** Deborah leads Israel in victory over the invading Canaanites.

**c.1000 B.C.** First extensive use of wool clothing (Scandinavia).

**1000 B.C.** Earliest rotary hand mills for grain in Middle East.

**776 B.C.** First recorded Olympiad in Greece.

**750 B.C.** Assyrian Empire establishes world's first highway system.

**C.625 B.C.** Spartan woman are the most independent of all in the ancient world; Sappho, Greek poetess, flourishes on the island of Lesbos.

**563 B.C.** Beginning of Buddhism in India.

**C.400 B.C.** Peak of classical Greece.

**C. 400 B.C.** Democritus introduces concept of atom.

**250 B.C.** Cultivation of locally domesticated plants begins in present-day northeastern United States.

**C. 240 B.C.** Initial phases of construction of Great Wall of China.

**226 B.C.** Colossus of Rhodes destroyed by earthquake.

**51 B.C.** Cleopatra VII is queen of Egypt.

**C. 30 A.D.** Crucifixion of Jesus of Nazareth; Christian faith established.

**64 A.D.** Burning of Rome.

**267 A.D.** Queen Zenobia leads independence movement for Palmyra (present-day Syria).

**330 A.D.** Constantinople founded at Byzantium.

**C. 400 A.D.** Invention of stern post rudder in northern Europe.

**C. 570 A.D.** Muhammad, founder of Islam, is born.

**592 A.D.** Empress Gemmei orders the writing of the *Kojiki,* first national history of Japan.

**700 A.D.** *Beowulf written* in northern Europe.

**700 A.D.** Polynesian Triangle (Hawaii, Easter Island, New Zealand) now settled.

**725 A.D.** Earliest known mechanical clock.

**c. 800 A.D.** First porcelain produced in China.

**800 A.D.** Charlemagne, king of Franks, proclaimed Holy Roman Emperor by pope.

**900 A.D.** Agriculture is commonly practiced in most areas. Maize becomes a major crop.

**910 A.D.** First paper currency (China).

**969 A.D.** Cairo, Egypt, founded.

**C. 1000 A.D.** Arabic numerals begin to replace Roman numerals in Europe.

**C. 1000 A.D.** Japanese author Murasaki Shikibu writes *The Tale of Genji,* generally considered the world's first novel.

**1138** Byzantine princess Anna Comnena, early woman historian, writes the *Alexiad,* a 15-volume historical work.

**1157** Hojo Masako is influential woman in medieval Japan.

**1174** Eleanor of Aquitaine is influential woman in twelfth century Europe.

**1215** Magna Carta limits royal power in England.

**c.1250** Earliest development of cannons in Europe.

**c.1300** Invention of spinning wheel.

**c.1300** Beginning of Renaissance in Italy.

**1342** Chinese Empress Ma is born.

**c.1350** Cast-metal type developed in Korea.

**1431** Joan of Arc burned at the stake.

**1470** Queen Isabella creates unified Spain with her husband Ferdinand.

**1492** Queen Isabella approves the expedition to America led by Christopher Columbus; they touch ground in the Bahamas.

**1497** Vasco da Gama rounds the Cape of Good Hope.

**c.1500** Beginnings of empirical science in Europe.

**c.1503** Leonardo da Vinci paints the *Mona Lisa.*

**1507** German mapmaker Martin Waldseemuller, after reading Amerigo Vespucci's descriptions of the New World, names it America after him.

**1512** Michelangelo completes painting of the Sistine chapel ceiling.

**1513** Juan Ponce de Le n discovers Florida. Vasco Nunez de Balboa crosses Panama and sights the Pacific Ocean.

**1517** Protestant Reformation begins when Martin Luther posts his "Ninety-Five Theses" on Nurenberg, Germany, church door.

**1519** Hernan Cortez lands in Mexico.

**1520** First circumnavigation of globe by Ferdinand Magellan's crew.

**1521** Maria von Habsburg becomes queen of Hungary and Bohemia.

**1525** Martin Luther translates Bible into German; Luther marries former nun Katherine von Bora.

**1536** John Calvin publishes the *Institutes of the Christian Religion.*

**1541** Coronado discovers Mississippi River.

**1542** Portuguese traders reach Japan.

**1542** Copernicus formulates theory of suncentered solar system.

**1553** Queen Mary I tries to reestablish Roman Catholicism in England.

**1584** Sir Walter Raleigh discovers Roanoke Island and names land Virginia, after Queen Elizabeth.

**1587** Mary, Queen of Scots is executed.

**1597** Shakespeare's *Romeo and Juliet.*

**1605** Cervantes' *Don Quixote.*

**1607** Jamestown, Virginia, the first English colony in the New World, is founded.

**1609** Galileo builds first effective telescope.

**1618** Thirty Years' War.

**1620** Pilgrims and others arrive in Plymouth, Massachusetts, aboard the *Mayflower.*

**1630** Taj Mahal is constructed in Agra, India, as a memorial to emperor Shah Jahan's favorite wife, Mumataz Mahal.

**1642** Pascal builds early mechanical calculating device.

**c. 1648** Margaret Brent of Maryland is first American woman to demand right to vote.

**1654** Antoni van Leeuwenhoek invents microscope.

**1655** Lady Deborah Moody of Long Island becomes first American woman to vote.

**1665** Great plague in London kills 68,000 people.

**1665** First microscope-based description of living cells (Hooks).

**1670** Newton develops the principles of calculus.
**1687** Newton formulates law of gravity.

**1688** Aphra Behn's novel *Oroonoko* published.

**1700** Rise of modern national states in Europe.

**1702** Queen Anne's War.

**1717** Halley shows that solar system moves through space.

**1729** J. S. Bach's *St. Matthew Passion.*

**c. 1738** Eliza Lucas Pinckney, first woman agriculturist in America, develops cultivation of indigo in South Carolina.

**c. 1750** Beginning of the Industrial Revolution.

**1752** Benjamin Franklin proves lightning is electrical; develops lightning rod.

**1762** Catherine the Great becomes empress of Russia.

**1765** Scottish inventor James Watt develops first efficient steam engine.

**1769** Spinning machine patented.

**1774** Marie Antoinette becomes queen of France.

**1776** The American Revolution.

**1781** Immanuel Kant's *Critique of Pure Reason* published.

**1782** England recognizes United States independence.

**1787** Convention in Philadelphia writes United States Constitution.

**1787** Mozart's *Don Giovanni.*

**1788** United States Constitution ratified and takes effect.

**1789** French Revolution begins.

**1789** First United States presidential election results in victory for George Washington.

**1792** Mary Wollstonecraft's *A Vindication of the Rights of Woman* is published.

**1793** Eli Whitney invents cotton gin.

**1804** Napoleon crowns himself emperor.

**1808** Beethoven's *Fifth* and *Sixth Symphonies* performed.

**1813** Jane Austen's novel *Pride and Prejudice is* published.

**1833** Oberlin College (Ohio) becomes first coed college in U.S.

**1835** Morse invents the telegraph.

**1840s** Dorothea Dix lobbies for reform in treatment of mental illness in the United States.

**1842** Edgar Allan Poe writes his poem, "The Raven."

**1846** Potato famine in Ireland.

**1848** California Gold Rush.

**1848** *Communist Manifesto (Marx* and Engels) published.

**1848** Women's Rights Convention in Seneca Falls, New York. It produces the Declaration of Sentiments, patterned after the Declaration of Independence, calling for equal rights for women.

**1849** Elizabeth Blackwell becomes first American woman to receive medical degree.

**1850** World population reaches one billion.

**1850** Elizabeth Barrett Browning's *Sonnets from the Portuguese* published.

**1851** Taipei Revolution in China.

**1852** Harriet Beecher Stowe's *Uncle Tom's Cabin* is published.

**1854-60** Susan B. Anthony crusades for women's rights.

**1856** Sewing machine invented.

**1859** *On the Origin of Species* published by Charles Darwin.

**1860** Charles Dickens publishes *Great Expectations.*

**1860** Florence Nightingale publishes *Notes on Nursing,* the first textbook for nurses.

**1861** First transcontinental telegraph line.

**1861-65** American Civil War.

**1865** The first volume of Tolstoy's *War and Peace* is published.

**1869** Transcontinental railroad completed in United States.

**1869** National Woman Suffrage Association and American Woman Suffrage Association formed in the United States.

**1869** John Stuart Mill publishes *The Subjection of Women.*

**1874** Sophia Jex-Blake establishes the London School of Medicine for Women.

**1874** Women's Christian Temperance Union founded to fight alcohol abuse in the United States.

**1876** Alexander Graham Bell invents the telephone.

**1879** Belva Ann Lockwood becomes the first woman lawyer to practice before the U.S. Supreme Court.

**1882** American Red Cross is founded by Clara Barton.

**1883** Cosima Wagner, wife of composer Richard Wagner and daughter of Franz Liszt, becomes director of Bayreuth (Music) Festival in Germany.

**1885** Friedrich Nietzsche publishes *Beyond Good and Evil.*

**1890** Wounded Knee massacre.

**1893** New Zealand becomes the first nation to grant women the right to vote.

**1893** Mary Cassatt paints *The Boating Party.*

**1895** Discovery of X-rays by Abraham Roentgen.

**1898** Spanish-American War.

**1900** Sigmund Freud publishes *The Interpretation of Dreams.*

**1901** First trans-Atlantic radio transmission.

**1902** Australian women get the right to vote in all federal elections. Vida Goldstein runs for the senate there, becoming the first woman in the British Empire to run for a national office.

**1903** Orville and Wilbur Wright brothers fly first successful heavier-than-air aircraft.

**1903** Marie Curie is awarded Nobel Prize for Physics for discovery of radioactivity.

**1907** Chinese feminist and radical Qiu Jin is assassinated.

**1909** North Pole reached by Peary and Henson.

**1910** First Mother's Day celebrated in West Virginia.

**1911** First transcontinental flight.

**1911** Marie Curie is awarded second Nobel Prize for Chemistry for her discovery and isolation of pure radium.

**1913** Willa Cather publishes O *Pioneers.*

**1913** Stravinsky's *The Rite of Spring.*

**1915** 'Liner *Lusitania* is sunk by German Uboat.

**1915** Albert Einstein's *General Theory of Relativity.*

**1916** Margaret Sanger opens first birth control clinic.

**1917** Russian Revolution; Soviet women get the vote.

**1918** Canadian women get the vote.

**1919** Treaty of Versailles ends WWI.

**1920** League of Nations is established.

**1920** With the passage of the Nineteenth Amendment to the U.S. Constitution, American women get the vote.

**1921** Chinese Communist Party founded. Jinhyu Xiang, Chinese feminist revolutionary, is cofounder.

**1922** U.S.S.R. is established.

**1922** James Joyce's *Ulysses* published.

**1924** Stalin seizes power in Soviet Union.

**1924** Ichikawa Fusae organizes *Fusen Kakutoku Domei* (Women's Suffrage League) in Japan.

**1925** Nellie Tayloe Ross is elected first woman governor in U.S. (Wyoming).

**1927** Virginia Woolf publishes *To the Lighthouse.*

**1928** Margaret Mead publishes *Coming of Age in Samoa.*

**1928** Age of suffrage is lowered from 30 to 21 in Great Britain.

**1929** Collapse of stock market in the United States triggers world depression.

**1930** World population reaches two billion.

**1930** Kubushiro Ochimi organizes *Zen Nibon Fusen Taikai* (All-Japan Women's Suffrage Conference).

**1931** Margaret Sanger publishes *My Fight for Birth Control.*

**1932** Amelia Earhart becomes the first woman to fly across the Atlantic alone.

**1933** Frances Perkins becomes Secretary of Labor, first woman cabinet member in U.S. history.

**1934** Hitler assumes power in Germany.

*1939* World War II begins in Europe.

**1942** Atomic age begins with first controlled atomic chain reaction.

**1945** World War II ends.

**1946** Winston Churchill's "Iron Curtain" speech.

**1947** Radiocarbon (carbon-14) dating developed by Willard Libby.

**1947** British India partitioned into independent nations of India and Pakistan.

**1948** United Nations establishes State of Israel.

**1949** Communists establish People's Republic of China; women get the vote.

**1949** Simone de Beauvoir publishes *The Second Sex.*

**1950** In India, women over 21 get to vote.

**1950** North Korean Communist forces invade South Korea.

**1953** Mexican women get the vote.

**1954** *Brown v. Board of Education.*

**1957** Soviet satellite *Sputnik* is launched.

**1962** Rachel Carson publishes *Silent Spring.*

**1962** John Glenn is first American to orbit Earth.

**1963** Valentina Vladimirovna Nikolayeva Tereshkova becomes first woman in space.

**1963** Betty Friedan publishes *The Feminine Mystique.*

**1966** National Organization for Women (NOW) is founded in the United States.

**1966** Indira Gandhi becomes prime minister of India.

**1967** The Beatles release *Sgt. Pepper's Lonely Hearts Club Band.*

**1967** World's first successful human heart transplant.

*1968* Dr. Martin Luther King, Jr., is assassinated.

**1969** American astronaut Neil Armstrong becomes first person to set foot on the moon.

**1969** Golda Meir becomes prime minister of Israel.

**1969** Maya Angelou publishes *I Know Why the Caged Bird Sings.*

**1970** First "Earth Day."

**1973** *Roe* v. *Wade*

**1976** World population reaches four billion.

**1977** Smallpox eradicated.

**1979** Margaret Thatcher elected first woman prime minister of Great Britain.

**1979** Nuclear power plant accident at Three Mile Island in Pennsylvania.

**1980** Mount St. Helens erupts in Washington state.

**1981** Sandra Day O'Connor appointed first woman U. S. Supreme Court justice.

*1983* Sally Ride becomes the first American woman in space.

**1984** Geraldine Ferraro becomes first woman vice-presidential nominee of a major U.S. political party.

**1984** Kathryn Sullivan is first U.S. woman astronaut to walk in space.

**1986** Major nuclear power plant accident at Chernobyl in the Soviet Union.

**1986** Corazon Aquino elected president of Philippines.

**1988** Benazir Bhutto sworn in as prime minister of Pakistan

**1989** Exxon supertanker Valdez runs aground in Alaska.

**1989** Opening of Berlin Wall signifies end to the Cold War.

**1989** Tiannanmen Square massacre in Beijing.

**1989** Victoria Murden and Shirley Metz (American) become the first women to reach the South Pole overland.

**1993** Janet Reno named first U.S. attorney general.

**1994** United Nations Fourth World Conference on Women is held in Beijing, China.

# Berenice Abbott

**Berenice Abbott (1898–1991) was one of the most gifted American photographers of the 20th century.**

Berenice Abbott's work spanned more than 50 years of the twentieth century. At a time when "career women" were not only unconventional but controversial, she established herself as one of the nation's most gifted photographers. Her work is often divided into four categories: portraits of celebrated residents of 1920s Paris; a 1930s documentary history of New York City; photographic explorations of scientific subjects from the 1950s and 1960s; and a lifelong promotion of the work of French photographer Eugène Atget. As a woman and a serious artist, Abbott faced numerous obstacles, not least of which was denial of the recognition she was due. Only recently has the high quality of her work been adequately appreciated. As one writer put it, "She was a consummate professional and artist."

Abbott was born into a world of rigid social rules, especially for women, who were expected to accept without question certain cultural dictates about clothing, manners, proper education, and other areas of everyday life. Abbott was an independent and somewhat defiant girl who hated such arbitrary constraints. One of her earliest acts of "rebellion" was to change the spelling of her name; Bernice became Berenice. "I put in another letter," she told an interviewer, "made it sound better."

Abbott's childhood was not especially happy. Her parents divorced when she was young, and though Abbott remained with her mother, her brothers were sent to live with their father. She never saw them again. This was a severe blow and may partly explain why Abbott never married or had her own family. She said she never wed because "marriage is the finish for women who want to work," and in her era this was largely true.

## "Reinvented" herself in New York

At age 20 Abbott headed for New York City to "reinvent" herself, as one writer put it. She rented an apartment, studied journalism, drawing, and sculpture, and formed a circle of friends, many of whom were "bohemians" rebelling against the strict social rules of the day. Friends who remembered her from those days said Abbott was shy and "looked sort of forbidding." After three years Abbott had had her fill of New York and decided to go to Paris, something unmarried young women rarely did by themselves. In fact, that such a move was sure to generate controversy probably contributed to Abbott's decision to pursue it.

## Photography became her calling

In Paris Abbott studied sculpture, but she ultimately found it unsatisfying. In 1923 photographer Man Ray, whom she had known in New York, offered her a job as his assistant. Abbott knew nothing about photography but accepted the job. "I was glad to give up sculpture," she said. "Photography was much more interesting." She worked for Man Ray for three years, mastering photographic techniques sufficiently to earn commissions of her own. Indeed, her work became so successful that she decided she had finally found her calling and opened her own studio.

Photographic portraits had become quite fashionable in Paris, and Abbott gained a solid reputation. She photographed some of the most distinguished people of the day, including Irish writer James Joyce; French writer, artist, and

**1**

filmmaker Jean Cocteau; and Princess Eugènie Murat, granddaughter of French emperor Napoleon III. Her works have been called "astonishing in their immediacy and insight," revealing much of the personality of her sitters, especially women. Abbott herself commented that Man Ray's photographs of women made them "look like pretty objects"; she instead allowed their character to come through.

### Championed work of Eugène Atget

While her star was on the rise, Abbott "discovered" some pictures of Paris that she called "the most beautiful photographs ever made." She sought out the photographer, an aged, penniless man named Eugène Atget. For almost 40 years Atget had been making a poor living photographing buildings, monuments, and scenes of the city and selling the prints to artists and publishers. Abbott's keen eye detected the originality of these photos, and she befriended the old man. When Atget died in 1927, Abbott arranged to purchase all of his prints, glass slides, and negatives—more than a thousand items in all. She became obsessed with this massive collection, spending the next 40 years promoting and preserving Atget's work, arranging exhibitions, books, and sales of prints to raise money. She donated the collection to New York's Museum of Modern Art in 1968, by which time she had almost singlehandedly brought Atget from total obscurity to worldwide renown. Some critics have claimed that Abbott's devotion to Atget's works hampered her career. But she denied this, insisting, "It was my responsibility and I had to do it. I thought he was great and his work should be saved."

### Photographs documented New York City

Abbott's career took a new turn when she returned to New York in 1929. Inspired by Atget's work and by the excitement she felt in the air, she began a new project: photographing the city as no one ever had. She spent most of the 1930s lugging her camera around, shooting pictures of buildings, construction sites, billboards, fire escapes, and stables. Many of these sites disappeared during the 1930s as a huge construction boom in New York swept away the old buildings and mansions to make way for modern skyscrapers. Several of these photos were published in a 1939 book called *Changing New York*. In it Abbott wrote, "To make the portrait of a city is a life work and no one portrait suffices, because the city is always changing. Everything in the city is properly part of its story—its physical body of brick, stone, steel, glass, wood, its lifeblood of living, breathing men and women."

This task of documenting the city was not an easy one, especially for a woman. Abbott was "menaced by bums, heckled by suspicious crowds, and chased by policemen." Her most famous anecdote of the period came from her work in the rundown neighborhood known as the Bowery. A man asked her why a nice girl was visiting such a bad area. Abbott replied, "I'm not a nice girl. I'm a photographer." Finances presented further obstacles, and she spent her own money on the project until 1935, when the Federal Art Project of the Works Progress Administration began to sponsor her work. Until 1939 she was able to earn a salary of $35 a week and enjoyed the participation of an assistant. When funding ran out, however, she had to abandon the project.

### Took on scientific community

Abbott continued working during the 1940s and 1950s, though largely outside the spotlight. She became preoccupied during this period with scientific photography, hoping to record evidence of the laws of physics and chemistry, among other phenomena. She took courses in chemistry and electricity to expand her understanding. Again her iron determination served her well.

The scientific community looked on her efforts with suspicion, both because of its skepticism about photography's usefulness and its hostility toward women who ventured into the virtually all-male enclave of science. She spent years trying to convince scientists and publishers that texts and journals could be illustrated with photographs, fighting the conventional belief that drawings were sufficient. In all, as Abbott told an interviewer, the project was a minefield of sexism: "When I wanted to do a book on electricity, most scientists . . . insisted it couldn't be done. When I finally found a collaborator, his wife objected to his working with a woman. . . . The male lab assistants were treated with more respect than I was. You have no idea what I went through because I was a woman."

### Photographs showed beauty in science

Political events rescued Abbott when the Soviet Union launched the first space satellite in 1957, initiating the "space race." The U.S. government began a new push in the field of science. In 1958 Abbott was invited to join the

Massachusetts Institute of Technology's Physical Science Study Committee, which was charged with the task of improving high school science education. At last Abbott was vindicated in her insistence on the value of photography to science. Her biographer, Hank O'Neal, has said that her scientific photos were her best work. This is a subject of some debate, but many agree that she was able to uniquely demonstrate the beauty and grace in the path of a bouncing ball, the pattern of iron filings around a magnet, or the formation of soap bubbles.

In her later years Abbott did some photography around the country, in particular documenting U.S. Route I, a highway along the East Coast from Florida to Maine. During this project she fell in love with Maine and bought a small house in the woods of that state, where she lived for the rest of her life. As the popularity of photography grew in the 1970s and her life's work became recognized, Abbott was visited there by a string of admirers, photography students, and journalists. She became something of a legend in her own time, honored as a pioneer woman artist who conquered a male-dominated field thanks to "the vinegar of her personality and the iron of her character." But perhaps most importantly, students of the medium recognized the talent and artistry behind Abbot's work, among which reside some of the prize gems of twentieth-century photography.

### Further Reading

Abbott, Berenice, *Berenice Abbott,* Aperture Foundation, 1988.
Abbott, Berenice, *Berenice Abbott Photographs,* Smithsonian Institution Press, 1990.
O'Neal, Hank, *Berenice Abbott: American Photographer,* McGraw-Hill, 1982. □

# Grace Abbott

**The social worker and agency administrator Grace Abbott (1878-1939) awakened many Americans to the responsibility of government to help meet the special problems of immigrants and of children.**

Grace Abbott was born and raised in Grand Island, Nebraska. Her father was lieutenant-governor, and her mother was an abolitionist and suffragist. Grace received her bachelor's degree from Grand Island College in 1898 and taught for several years at Grand Island High School. She did graduate work in political science and in law at the University of Chicago, receiving a master's degree in 1909. The year before, greatly attracted to the pioneering social work of Jane Addams, she became a resident of Hull House in Chicago and collaborated effectively with Addams for over a decade.

She shared Addams' interest in the cause of world peace, and she worked effectively to advance women's suffrage. But very early she became preoccupied with the problem of immigrants. For over 20 years many Americans had been worried that the flood of immigrants—as many as a million in a single year—arriving from eastern and southern Europe constituted a severe threat to American life and institutions. These "new immigrants"—as they were called—seemed dangerously "different" in language, dress, religion, and their disposition to cluster in the cities (as most people in this era were also doing). Other Americans—like Addams and Abbott—believed that it was not the immigrants who were "new," but America—increasingly urban, industrial, impersonal; to them, the problem was how to help the newcomers find and maintain their families, get jobs, and learn to play a knowledgeable part in a democracy.

From 1908 to 1917 Abbott directed the Immigrants' Protective League in Chicago. Close personal contact with immigrants made her aware of how difficult it was for new arrivals from Poland, or Italy, or Russia to find the relatives or friends they depended on; how hard it was to get jobs that were not exploitative; and how tricky it was not to be abused by the political machines. A trip in 1911 to eastern Europe deepened her understanding of the needs and hopes of the immigrants. Abbott's point-of-view is eloquently summarized in her *The Immigrant and the Community* (1917). To Abbott, the "new immigrants" were every bit as desirable as additions to America as were the older arrivals. In modern American society, they needed help; and, while the states and local philanthropic organizations such as the Immigrants' Protective League could and should help, the federal government had an important role to play. It was wrong, she argued, to concentrate on restricting or excluding immigration; the government should plan how best to accommodate and integrate the newcomers. She was not successful in redirecting federal policy; the acts of 1921 and 1924 drastically reduced the number of new immigrants. But her writings and her work with the Immigrants' Protective League helped develop a more widespread and a more generous understanding of the difficulties the immigrants encountered.

### Work in the Children's Bureau

In 1912 Congress established the Children's Bureau in the recognition that children were entitled to special consideration in schools, in the workplace, in the courts, and even in the home. In 1916 Congress passed a law prohibiting the shipment in interstate commerce of products made by child labor. It remained for the Children's Bureau to make the law effective. Julia Lathrop, the first head of the bureau, in 1917 asked her friend Abbott to head up the child labor division. She proved to be an exceptionally able administrator. However, within a year the Supreme Court invalidated the law as an infringement upon the rights of the states to deal with child labor as they thought best. Abbott resigned and for the rest of her life worked to secure an amendment to the Constitution outlawing child labor. To her regret, this effort, too, was frustrated by states-rights feelings and by the concern that the amendment would jeopardize the rights of parents and churches to supervise the rearing of children.

After a brief period back in Illinois, Abbott returned to Washington in 1921 as the new head of the Children's Bureau. Probably her most important responsibility was to administer the Sheppard-Towner Act (1921), which extended federal aid to states that developed appropriate programs of maternal care. Abbott had been appalled to find that infant mortality was higher in the United States than in any country where records were kept, and she was convinced that the best way to reduce that mortality was to improve the health of the mother, before and after child-birth. The Supreme Court rejected protests against this dramatic extension of federal government responsibilities for social welfare. Abbott, while seeing to it that the over 3,000 centers across the country met federal standards, showed herself sensitive to the special concerns of localities. Though Congress terminated the program in 1929, the act, as administered by Abbott, was a pioneering federal program of social welfare.

Abbott never lost faith that the American people would, when properly informed and led, support enlightened welfare programs. She was optimistic that the New Deal of Franklin Roosevelt and of her old friend Frances Perkins would realize many of her dreams. She had the satisfaction of helping draft the Social Security Act of 1935 which, among other things, provided federal guarantees of aid to dependent children.

Ill health prompted her to resign in 1934. She became professor of public welfare at the University of Chicago, where her sister, Edith Abbott, was a dean. She lived with Edith until her death in 1939. Quiet and forceful, compassionate and efficient, singularly immune to cant or prejudice, Grace Abbott epitomized the enormous contribution made by her generation of women. She helped make America a more decent place.

### Further Reading

There is an excellent summary of Abbott's life in *Notable American Women* (1971). Edith Abbott wrote three helpful articles about her sister in *Social Service Review* (1939 and 1950). Grace Abbott's role is clearly indicated in Clarke A. Chambers, *Seedtime of Reform: American Social Service and Social Action, 1918-1933* (1963). Abbott wrote many reports, articles, and books. Among the most instructive are *The Immigrant and the Community* (1917) and two volumes of documents, with critical introductions, *The Child and the State* (1938).

### Additional Sources

Costin, Lela B., *Two sisters for social justice: a biography of Grace and Edith Abbott,* Urbana: University of Illinois Press, 1983. □

# Bella Stavisky Abzug

**Liberal lawyer and unconventional politician, Bella Stavisky Abzug (born 1920) works energetically for civil and women's rights. She served three terms as a New York Congresswoman.**

Bella Stavisky Abzug was born on July 24, 1920, in the Bronx, New York. She was the daughter of Emanuel and Esther Stavisky, Russian Jewish immigrants who owned a local meat market. During her youth she worked in her father's store until it failed in the 1920s and he turned to selling insurance. In 1930 her father died, which left her mother to support the family with his insurance money and jobs in local department stores. She attended an all-female high school in the west Bronx and eventually entered Hunter College, where she excelled as a student, earning her degree in 1942.

### Student Activist

Abzug was elected as president of her high school class and later as student body president at Hunter College. She taught Hebrew and Jewish history on the weekends and marched in protest against the spread of Nazism in Europe and against British and American neutrality during the Spanish Civil War. In World War II she joined the ranks of thousands of American women entering war production industries and worked in a shipbuilding factory. In 1944 she married Maurice Abzug, a stockbroker and novelist. They had two daughters.

By the time she entered Columbia Law School Bella's career as a litigation lawyer, politician, and activist was well along. At Columbia she was editor of the *Columbia Law Review*. After her graduation in 1947 she joined a firm that specialized in labor law, one of the most confrontational areas of law practice. In the 1950s she worked as a labor lawyer and represented civil rights workers. She launched a lifelong commitment to helping poor and oppressed people gain justice and a decent life in the days following World War II. During this time such commitments were viewed with suspicion as part of the "red scare." She defended many individuals, such as New York school teachers ac-

cused of subversive activities during the anti-communist crusade of Senator Joseph McCarthy.

## Civil Rights

In the early 1950s she was deeply involved in the early Civil Rights movement. While carrying her second child in 1962, she undertook a case to defend an African American man accused of raping a white woman with whom he had been having an affair. Although she ultimately lost the case, Abzug was able to delay the man's execution for two years by appealing the conviction twice to the Supreme Court. Her arguments in the case were nearly two decades ahead of their time, and the Warren and Burger Courts would eventually accept similar arguments made for guaranteeing a fair trial and prohibiting cruel and unusual punishment.

During the 1960s Abzug joined in the movement to ban nuclear testing. She helped to found the Woman's Strike for Peace organization, leading the organization in demonstrations that took place in New York and Washington, D.C. After the signing of the Nuclear Test Ban Treaty she helped to refocus the antinuclear movement into an antiwar movement as the U.S. became more deeply involved in the Vietnam War.

In the late 1960s Abzug struggled to forge a broad, progressive coalition across party lines to address the concerns of the poor, ethnic minorities, and women's groups in shaping a new national agenda. During these years she became active in the Democratic party, and after the insider fiasco at the Chicago Democratic Convention in 1968 she joined with other liberal Democrats to found the New Democratic Coalition.

## Elected to office

Running for office in 1970, supported by her ties to labor and a strong backing from the Jewish vote, Abzug was elected to the U.S. House of Representatives from New York City's 19th ward. During her first year in Congress she gained national attention by her bold and daring political initiatives on behalf of liberal causes, as well by wearing her wide, trademark hat within the halls of congress. On her first day in office she introduced a bill calling for the withdrawal of troops from Vietnam by July 4, 1971. Although conservative forces in Congress defeated the bill within a week, Abzug established herself immediately as an unconventional politician who would take on her opponents using a brusque and often confrontational style. During her tenure she co-authored the Freedom of Information and Privacy Acts, she was the first to call for President Nixon's impeachment in the 1970s, and she cast one of the first votes for the Equal Rights Amendment.

In 1972 redistricting eliminated Abzug's congressional district, and she decided to run in the 20th district against a popular liberal incumbent, William Fitz Ryan. She lost the primary, but Ryan died before the general election in November, and Abzug became the Democratic nominee. She won in the November election and served in the House until 1976 when she gave up her seat to run for the Senate, a race she lost to Daniel Patrick Moynihan. She then ran in the Democratic mayoral primary in New York, but was de-

feated by Edward Koch. Never one to give up, she told reporters who assumed she was finished with politics, "I'll thank you not to write my obituary."

## Continuing Activism

Abzug continued to make headlines fighting for peace and women's rights long after leaving office. President Jimmy Carter appointed her as co-chair of the National Advisory Committee for Women, but was apparently unprepared for the demands that the committee would make. When the committee met with President Carter, several of the members spoke to him about the cuts in social services and pointed out their negative impact on the nation's women. After that meeting Abzug was dismissed from the committee, an action that sparked the resignation of several members, including the other co-chair, and gave rise to a massive public outcry against Carter for the firing.

Throughout her long and controversial political career, Abzug has retained a place in the limelight with her characteristic sharp tongue and unconventional style. Her hats along with her defiance of codes of dress and demeanor have won her a reputation as a nonconformist. But above and beyond the flair of her personality, it is the issues she supports that are her deepest concern. As she wrote in the introduction to her autobiography, "I am not evoking a wild fantasy when I claim that I'm going to help organize a new political coalition of the women, the minorities and the young people, along with the poor, the elderly, the workers, and the unemployed, which is going to turn this country upside down and inside out."

Abzug continues to devote her energies to women's rights and reproductive freedom. As chair of New York City's Commission on the Status of Women she directs a National Parity Campaign to increase the number of women in elective office. In 1991, she presided over the Women's Congress for a Healthy Planet and her presence at the United Nations 4th Women's Conference in Beijing garnered considerable attention. She is also co-chair of the Women's Environmental Development Organization (WEDO), and as senior advisor to UNCED Secretary General Maurice Strong she successfully campaigned to incorporate key issues of the women's agenda into official statements approved at the Earth Summit.

## Further Reading

Bella Abzug has written her own autobiography, *Bella,* edited by Mel Ziegler and published by the Saturday Review Press in 1972. While it chronicles Abzug's political career up to that time, she remained in Congress four more years and was active later. There is a biography of her by Doris Faber, *Bella Abzug* (William Morrow, 1976). She is listed in *Political Profiles: The Nixon/Ford Years,* Facts on File, v. 5 (1979). She has also been written up in the *New York Times Biographical Service* in February and December, 1978. Numerous contemporary articles have appeared about her in publications such as *Time, Newsweek, The New Republic,* and *Life.* □

# Jane Addams

**As social worker, reformer, and pacifist, Jane Addams (1860-1935) was the "beloved lady" of American reform. She founded the most famous settlement house in American history, Hull House in Chicago.**

Jane Addams was born in Cedarville, Ill., on Sept. 6, 1860, the eighth child of a successful miller, banker, and landowner. She did not remember her mother, who died when Jane was 3 years old. She was devoted to and profoundly influenced by her father, an idealist and philanthropist of Quaker tendencies and a state senator of Illinois for 16 years.

Jane Addams attended Rockford Female Seminary in northern Illinois, from which she graduated in 1881. The curriculum was dominated by religion and the classics, but she developed an interest in the sciences and entered the Women's Medical College in Philadelphia. After 6 months, illness forced her to discontinue her studies permanently and undergo a spinal operation; she was never quite free of illness throughout her life.

## Finding a Career

During a long convalescence Addams fell into a deep depression, partly because of her affliction but also because of her sensitivity to the lot of women of her station in 19th-century America. Although intelligent middle-class women were frequently well educated, as Jane Addams was, society dictated a life of ornamental uselessness for them as wives and mothers within a masculine-dominated home. During a leisurely tour in Europe between 1883 and 1885 and winters spent in Baltimore in 1886 and 1887, Addams sought solace in religion. Only after a second trip to Europe in 1887-1888, however, when she visited Toynbee Hall, the famous settlement house in London, did she find a satisfactory outlet for her talents and energies.

Toynbee Hall was a social and cultural center in the slums of London's East End; it was designed to introduce young ministerial candidates to the world of England's urban poor. Jane Addams hit upon the idea of providing a similar opportunity for young middle-class American women, concluding "that it would be a good thing to rent a house in a part of the city where many primitive and actual needs are found, in which young women who had been given over too exclusively to study might restore a balance of activity along traditional lines and learn of life from life itself."

## Creation of Hull House

Hull House, in one of Chicago's most poverty-stricken immigrant slums, was originally envisioned as a service to young women desiring more than a homemaker's life. But it soon developed into a great center for the poor of the neighborhood, providing a home for working girls, a theater, a boys' club, a day nursery, and numerous other services. Thousands visited it annually, and Hull House was the source of inspiration for dozens of similar settlement houses in other cities. Its success catapulted Jane Addams into national prominence. She became involved in an attempt to remedy Chicago's corrupt politics, served on a mediation commission in the Pullman railroad strike of 1894, supported the right of labor to organize, and spoke and wrote widely on virtually every reform issue of the day, from woman's suffrage to pacifism.

Jane Addams served as an officer for innumerable reform groups, including the Progressive party and the Women's International League for Peace and Freedom (of which she was president in 1915), and she attended international peace congresses in a dozen European cities. Her books cover wide-ranging subjects: prostitution and woman's rights (*A New Conscience and an Ancient Evil,* 1912, and *The Long Road of Woman's Memory,* 1916), juvenile delinquency (*The Spirit of Youth and the City Streets,* 1909), and militarism in America (*Newer ideals of peace,* 1906). She received honorary degrees from a half dozen American universities and was an informal adviser to several American presidents. She died on May 21, 1935.

## Further Reading

Most of the biographies of Jane Addams are satisfactory. Her two autobiographical works are of great interest: *Twenty Years at Hull-House* (1910) and *The Second Twenty Years at Hull-House* (1930). *Jane Addams: A Centennial Reader* (1960) is the best book of selections from her writings and includes valuable introductions by other authors. John C. Farrell, *Beloved Lady: A History of Jane Addams' Ideas on Reform and Peace* (1967), provides a fascinating analysis of her ideas.

## Additional Sources

Addams, Jane, *The social thought of Jane Addams,* New York,
N.Y.: Irvington, 1982, 1965.
Hovde, Jane, *Jane Addams,* New York: Facts on File, 1989.
Levine, Daniel, *Jane Addams and the liberal tradition,* Westport,
Conn.: Greenwood Press, 1980, 1971. □

# Madeleine Korbel Albright

**A professor and foreign policy expert, Madeleine Korbel Albright (born 1937) was appointed by President Bill Clinton in 1992 to be the U.S. permanent representative to the United Nations and head of the U.S. delegation to that body. President Clinton was also responsible for her appointment as the Secretary of State in 1997.**

In filling the sensitive diplomatic post of ambassador to the United Nations (U.N.), President Clinton turned to a prominent Washington insider with an extensive background in academia together with strong political connections. Rewarding Madeleine Albright for her support of Democratic Party candidates and making her the second woman to serve as chief of mission at the United Nations, he also signaled the weight to be assigned to international frameworks in American foreign policy by making her a member of his cabinet.

Madeleine Korbel Albright was born on May 15, 1937, in Prague, the daughter of a Czech diplomat. At the age of 11 she came to the United States, joining her father, Josef Korbel, who was on an official assignment for his country at the U.N. but who then used the opportunity to seek political asylum in the United States for himself and his family.

Becoming a naturalized citizen, Albright pursued an academic career, starting with a B.A. from Wellesley College (1959). Pursuing graduate work at Columbia University, she received a master's degree in international affairs (1968), specializing in Soviet studies, and her Ph.D. in 1976.

Albright's subsequent career record highlights a combination of scholarly research and political activity. She was a coordinator for the unsuccessful presidential candidacy of Senator Edmund S. Muskie of Maine in 1976, later becoming his chief legislative assistant. In 1978 Albright was asked by one of her former professors at Columbia University, Zbigniew Brzezinski, National Security Adviser under President Carter, to join the National Security Council staff as a legislative liaison, where she remained until 1981. The following year was spent writing a book about the role of the press in bringing about political change in Poland in the period 1980 to 1982, a project conducted under a fellowship from the Woodrow Wilson Center for Scholars at the Smithsonian Institute.

Albright's next important career milestone came in 1982, when she joined the faculty of Georgetown University and expanded both her interests and personal contacts. As a research professor of international affairs and director of women students enrolled in the foreign service program at the university's School of Foreign Service, she taught undergraduate and graduate courses in international studies, U.S. foreign relations, Russian foreign policy, and central and eastern European politics. She was also instrumental in developing programs designed to enhance professional opportunities for women in international affairs. She also became affiliated with the Georgetown University Center for Strategic and International Studies as a senior fellow in Soviet and eastern European affairs. In October of 1989 she took over the presidency of the Center for National Policy, a Washington-based nonprofit research organization formed in 1981 as a Democratic think tank with a mandate to generate discussion and study about domestic and international issues. Having been divorced, she did all this while over the years raising three daughters by herself, and still found the time to be a board member on numerous institutes, national commissions, and civic organizations ranging from the Atlantic Institute, the Boards of Trustees of Wellesley College and of Williams College, and the National Democratic Institute for International Affairs to the Black Student Fund and the Washington Urban League.

Parallel with her research and teaching, Albright deepened her involvement in Democratic Party politics. She acted as an adviser to both Walter Mondale and Geraldine Ferraro during the 1984 presidential election year; and as an adviser to Michael S. Dukakis in 1988 when he failed in his bid to defeat Republican George Bush. She was more successful, however, in 1992, when she endorsed Arkansas Governor Bill Clinton's candidacy. During the campaign she served as his senior foreign policy adviser, and in the transition period as foreign policy liaison in the White House prior to her U.N. posting.

Based clearly on the strength of her personal views and familiarity with world politics, Ambassador Albright immediately became a presence to be reckoned with at the United Nations, especially since she also represented the world's most powerful country and largest contributor to the organization's activities and budget.

Already during the first year it became evident that she saw herself as a spokesperson to three different audiences: first, to the delegations assembled in debate at the New York headquarters, articulating the American position and preferences on global problems dominating the world organization's agenda; second, to President Clinton and his administration, formulating the stand of the U.S. government on U.N.-related topics; and third, to the American public, mobilizing support for policies pursued at, and through, the United Nations. Consequently, Madeleine Albright found herself involved simultaneously in political debate, maneuvering, and consultation in the U.N. arena over such controversial questions as peace-keeping, expanding the Security Council's membership to include possibly both Germany and Japan, and clarifying the precise authority and powers of Secretary-General Boutros-Ghali; in the U.S. policymaking process in Washington; and in the ongoing national debate over the direction of American foreign relations in the 1990s.

Madeleine Albright was nominated by President Clinton in 1996 for the position of Secretary of State. In 1997 the U.S. Senate unanimously confirmed her nomination. This appointment made Albright the first female to hold the position of Secretary of State. This designation also bestows her with the title of highest-ranking female within the United States government.

Shortly after her confirmation, Albright's Czech cousin revealed to reporters at the *Washington Post* that Albright's family were Czech Jews and not Catholics as she believed, and that three of her grandparents had perished in concentration camps. Albright stated that she was not totally surprised by the news and was quoted in *Newsweek* as saying, "I have been proud of the heritage that I have known about and I will be equally proud of the heritage that I have just been given." A few months later, Albright flew to Prague, toured the Old Jewish Cemetery and the Pinkas Synagogue, and was honored by the Czech president.

Meanwhile, in her diplomatic duties, she continued to play hardball. She made efforts to charm North Carolina Senator Jesse Helms, Chair of the Senate Foreign Relations Committee. She interrupted her world travels to tour his home state, speak at his alma mater, and give him a t-shirt inscribed with "Somebody at the State Department Loves Me." Her efforts paid off as Helms was persuaded to work on a measure where the U.S. would repay funds owed to the U.N.

Albright began a peace mission in the Middle East in the fall of 1997, first meeting with Israeli Prime Minister Benjamin Netanyahu in September to discuss Israeli-Palestinian relations. At a joint news conference, there appeared to be a wide gap between the goals of the Clinton administration and the Israeli government. Although Albright condemned terrorist activities, she also urged Netanyahu to make concessions. While in Jerusalem, she also visited the Hall of Remembrance at Yad Vashem, Israel's Holocaust Memorial.

She then conferred with Palestinian leader Yasser Arafat before addressing Jewish and Arab students in Jerusalem, and met with Syrian President Hafez al-Assad, Egyptian President Hosni Mubarek, King Fahd of Saudi Arabia, and King Hussein of Jordan. Albright vowed not to meet with Israeli and Palestinian leaders again until they were "ready to make the hard decisions."

## Further Reading

Madeleine Albright's views on foreign policy can be found in her writings, which include *Poland, the Role of the Press in Political Change* (1983); *The Role of the Press in Political Change: Czechoslovakia 1968* (1976); and *The Soviet Diplomatic Service: Profile of an Elite* (1968). Information regarding her appointment as Secretary of State may be viewed at http://secretary.state.gov. Also see *Time,* July 28, 1997; August 4, 1997; September 15, 1997; *Newsweek,* February 24, 1997; September 15, 1997; *U.S. News & World Report,* September 1, 1997; September 22, 1997. □

# Louisa May Alcott

**Louisa May Alcott (1832-1888) is one of America's best-known writers of juvenile fiction. She was also a reformer, working in the causes of temperance and woman's suffrage.**

Louisa May Alcott was born in Germantown, Pa., in 1832. She was the daughter of Bronson Alcott, the Concord transcendentalist philosopher and educator. She and her three sisters spent their childhood in poverty. However, they had as friends, and even as tutors, some of the most brilliant and famous men and women of the day, such as Henry David Thoreau, Ralph Waldo Emerson, Margaret Fuller, and Theodore Parker. This combination of intellectual plenty and physical want endowed Alcott with an ironical sense of humor. She soon realized that, if she or her sisters did not find ways to bring money into the home, the family would be doomed to permanent poverty.

In her early years Alcott worked at a variety of menial tasks to help financially. At 16 she wrote a book, *Flower Fables* (not published for 6 years), and she wrote a number of plays that were never produced. By 1860 she was publishing stories and poems in the *Atlantic Monthly*. During the Civil War she served as a nurse until her health failed, and her *Hospital Sketches* (1863) brought the first taste of widespread public attention.

The attention seemed to die out, however, when she published her first novel, *Moods,* in 1865, and she was glad to accept in 1867 the editorship of the juvenile magazine *Merry's Museum*. The next year she produced the first volume of *Little Women*, a cheerful and attractive account of her childhood, portraying herself as Jo and her sisters as Amy, Beth, and Meg. The book was an instant success, so in 1869 she produced the second volume. The resulting sales accomplished the goal she had worked toward for 25 years: the Alcott family was financially secure.

*Little Women* had set the direction, and Alcott continued a heavy literary production in the same vein. She wrote *An Old-fashioned Girl* (1870), *Little Men* (1871), and *Work* (1873), an account of her early efforts to help support the family. During this time she was active in the causes of temperance and woman's suffrage, and she also toured Europe. In 1876 she produced *Silver Pitchers*, a collection containing ''Transcendental Wild Oats,'' an account of her father's disastrous attempts to found a communal group at Fruitlands, Mass. In later life she produced a book almost every year and never wanted for an audience.

Alcott died on March 6, 1888, in Boston. She seems never to have become bitter about her early years or her dreamy, improvident father, but she did go so far as to say that a philosopher was like a man up in a balloon: he was safe as long as three women held the ropes on the ground.

### Further Reading

Ednah Cheney, ed., *Louisa May Alcott: Her Life, Letters, and Journals* (1889), is an early biography. Also of interest are Katharine S. Anthony, *Louisa May Alcott* (1938), and Marjorie M. Worthington, *Miss Alcott of Concord* (1958). A documented, full-length study of Miss Alcott's works is Madeleine B. Stern, *Louisa May Alcott* (1950). □

# Florence Ellinwood Allen

**Florence Ellinwood Allen (1884-1966) was a pioneering woman in the U.S. justice system, serving in a variety of roles in the legal profession previously filled only by men.**

Florence Ellinwood Allen was possibly the premiere pioneer female judge in United States history. In fact, any question that begins, ''Who was the first woman judge to . . .'' regardless as to how the question ends, the chances are good the answer is ''Florence Ellinwood Allen.'' She was Ohio's first female assistant county prosecutor, the first woman ever to preside over a first-degree murder trial, the first woman to pronounce a death sentence, the first woman to be elected to a Court of Appeals, and the first woman ever appointed to the U.S. Court of Appeals.

### Early Life and Education

Allen was born in Salt Lake City, the daughter of Clarence Emir Allen, a professor of classical languages at Western Reserve University in Cleveland. With her father coaching her, she became proficient in Greek and Latin by age seven and was preparing for college by age 13. As a teenager she attended a lecture by suffragist leader Susan B. Anthony. Subsequently, she became Anthony's protégé and a lifelong feminist activist.

She earned a bachelor of arts degree from Western Reserve in 1904, then studied music for two years in Europe with hopes of becoming a concert pianist. That career was derailed by a nerve injury, but upon returning to Cleveland in 1906 she became music critic for the Cleveland Plain Dealer, a job she held for three years.

Allen became interested in law early in the next decade, but would not be admitted to Western Reserve's law school because she was a woman. She attended the University of Chicago for one year before earning a law degree from New York University in 1913. She worked her way through N.Y.U. by serving as investigator for the New York League for the Protection of Immigrants and lecturing on music for the Board of Education.

### Legal Career

Allen overcame discrimination to be admitted to the Ohio bar in 1914 and established a law practice in Cleveland that specialized in women's legal problems. She worked as a volunteer counselor for the Legal Aid Society, worked for the Woman's Suffrage Party of Cleveland and became a leader in Ohio's state campaign for women's voting rights. She was appointed assistant prosecutor for Cuyahoga County in 1919.

In 1921 Allen was the first woman in American history to become judge of a Common Pleas Court when she was elected to the bench in Cuyahoga County. She tried 892 cases from that bench, including eight murder trials. There she developed a reputation as a "no-nonsense" jurist. She did not hesitate to sentence fellow judges to prison when they were caught in wrongdoing. In 1925 she presided over one of her most famous cases, the trial of Frank Motto, who had been accused of murdering two manufacturers in a payroll robbery. Motto was convicted and Allen returned a sentence of death. In 1926 Allen was the first woman to be appointed associate justice on the Ohio State Supreme Court. During the 1920s Allen cultivated a friendship with Eleanor Roosevelt, and in 1934 Mrs. Roosevelt convinced her husband, President Franklin D. Roosevelt, to appoint Allen as the first female judge on the U.S. Court of Appeals, making her the country's foremost female jurist. During her 25 years on the Court of Appeals she handled cases dealing with taxation, patents, personal injuries, forgeries, contracts, interstate commerce, labor laws, and conflicts between federal and state authority. One noted trial in 1937-38 concerned a suit filed by 18 private utility companies against the Tennessee Valley Authority. Judge Allen ruled that the statute creating the T.V.A. was constitutional, and the U.S. Supreme Court upheld the decision.

When Associate Justice George Sunderland retired from the U.S. Supreme Court in late 1937, Allen was widely regarded as a potential successor, but Roosevelt nominated Sen. Hugo Black of Alabama. In 1958, however, Allen became the first woman to serve as the chief judge of a federal appellate court, a position she held briefly until her retirement in 1959. Upon her retirement from active duty she was named a senior judge of the Sixth Circuit Court of Appeals, and worked on her memoirs, titled "To Do Justly." She broke a hip at the age of 81, and suffered ill health until her death one year later.

## Further Reading

Florence Ellinwood Allen, *To Do Justly* (Cleveland: Western Reserve University Press, 1965).

Beverly Blair Cook, Entry on Allen, in *Notable American Women: The Modern Period,* edited by Barbara Sicherman and Carol Hurd Green, with the assistance of Ilene Kantrov and Harriette Walker (Cambridge, Mass. & London: Harvard University Press, 1980), pp. 11-13. □

# Paula Gunn Allen

**As a scholar and literary critic, Paula Gunn Allen (born 1939) has worked to encourage the publication of Native American literature and to educate others about its themes, contexts, and structures. Having stated that her convictions can be traced back to the woman-centered structures of traditional Pueblo society, she is active in American feminist movements and in antiwar and antinuclear organizations.**

Paula Gunn Allen is one of the foremost scholars of Native American literature as well as a talented poet and novelist. She also collects and interprets Native American mythology. She describes herself as a "multicultural event," citing her Pueblo/Sioux/Lebanese/Scottish-American ancestry. Her father, E. Lee Francis, born of Lebanese parents at Seboyeta, a Spanish-Mexican land grant village north of Laguna Pueblo, spoke only Spanish and Arabic until he was ten. Due to the lack of a Marionite rite in the area, he was raised Roman Catholic. He owned the Cubero Trading Company and was Lieutenant Governor of New Mexico from 1967 through 1970. Her mother, Ethel, is Laguna Pueblo, Sioux, and Scots. She converted to Catholicism from Presbyterianism to marry Francis.

Allen's great-grandfather, the Scottish-born Kenneth Gunn, immigrated into the area in the 1800s and married her great-grandmother, Meta Atseye, whose Indian name was Corn Tassel. Meta had been educated at the Carlisle Indian School to be, as Allen says in her introduction to *Spider Woman's Granddaughters,* "a literate, modest, excruciatingly exacting maid for well-to-do white farmers' and ranchers' wives," but "became the farmer-rancher's wife instead." Her grandmother, half Laguna, half Scottish-American, Presbyterian, first married a Sioux (Ethel's father) and then remarried a German Jewish immigrant, Sidney Solomon Gottlieb. Her mother grew up speaking and writing both English and Mexican Spanish.

Allen was born in Albuquerque, New Mexico, and grew up in Cubero, New Mexico, a Spanish-Mexican land grant village abutting the Laguna and Acoma reservations and the Cibola National Forest. She attended mission schools in Cubero and San Fidel, but she did most of her schooling at a Sisters of Charity boarding school in Albuquerque, from which she graduated in 1957. Her 1983 novel *The Woman Who Owned the Shadows* and some of her poetry draws from this experience of being raised Catholic. However, Allen is well aware of the conflicting influences in her background: Catholic, Native American, Protestant, Jewish, and Marionite. In an interview with Joseph Bruchac for *Survival This Way,* Allen says: "Sometimes I get in a dialogue between what the Church taught me, the nuns taught me, and what my mother taught me, what my experience growing up where I grew up taught me. Often you can't reconcile them." Her novel speaks to this confusion as the main character attempts to sort through the varying influences to reclaim a Native American women's spiritual tradition. On her journey, her protagonist uses traditional Laguna Pueblo healing ceremonies as well as psychotherapy, the Iroquois story of Sky Woman, and the aid of a psychic Euro-American woman.

Allen received both her bachelor's degree in English (1966) and her Master of Fine Arts degree in creative writing (1968) from the University of Oregon after beginning her studies at Colorado Women's College. She had three children and is divorced. She received her doctorate in American studies with an emphasis on Native American literature (1975) from the University of New Mexico. Two other writers from Laguna Pueblo are related to Allen—a sister, Carol Lee Sanchez, and a cousin, Leslie Marmon Silko.

## Contributions to Native American Literary Scholarship

Allen is recognized as a major scholar, literary critic, and teacher of Native American literature. Her teaching positions include San Francisco State University, the University of New Mexico, Fort Lewis College in Durango, California, the University of California at Berkeley, and the University of California at Los Angeles, where she was a professor of English. Allen's 1983 *Studies in American Indian Literature: Critical Essays and Course Designs,* an important text in the field, has an extensive bibliography in addition to information on teaching Native American literatures. *The Sacred Hoop: Recovering the Feminine in American Indian Traditions,* published in 1986, contains her 1975 germinal essay "The Sacred Hoop: A Contemporary Perspective," which was one of the first to detail the ritual function of Native American literatures as opposed to Euro-American literatures. Allen's belief in the power of the oral tradition embodied in contemporary Native American literature to effect healing, survival, and continuance underlies all of her work.

Allen writes from the perspective of a Laguna Pueblo woman from a culture in which the women are held in high respect. The descent is matrilineal—women owned the houses, and the major deities are female. A major theme of Allen's work is delineation and restoration of this woman-centered culture. Her work abounds with the mythic dimensions of women's relationship to the sacred, as well as the plight of contemporary Native American women, many of whom have lost the respect formerly accorded to them.

Elaborating on the roles and power of Native American women, Allen's "Who Is Your Mother: Red Roots of White Feminism" was published in *Sinister Wisdom* in 1984. In this startling article, Allen articulated Native American contributions to democracy and feminism, countering a popular idea that societies in which women's power was equal to men's never existed. She also has been a major champion to restore the place of gay and lesbian Native Americans in the community. These ideas were first published in 1981 in a groundbreaking essay in *Conditions,* "Beloved Women: Lesbians in American Indian Cultures," and then reworked for the *Sacred Hoop.*

Allen says that her focus on women is intended to affect the consciousness of Euro-American women rather than men because, until the last ten years or so, the women in her culture were never considered weak, and she wants others to know that women were not held down in all cultures. Allen feels some ambivalence about the feminist movement because of this misunderstanding and the cultural chauvinism of Euro-American women, which has been personally hurtful to her and other Native women, but she admits that feminists provide the best audience for her work and have given her much support. In her family, the woman-centered tradition was so strong that her grandfather wanted to name her mother Susan B. Anthony.

Allen was awarded a National Endowment for the Arts Fellowship for Writing in 1978, and she received a postdoctoral fellowship grant from the Ford Foundation-National Research Council in 1984. Also at this time, she served as associate fellow at the Stanford Humanities Institute, coordinating the Gynosophic Gathering, A Woman Identified Worship Service, in Berkeley. She is active in the anti-nuclear and anti-war movements as well as the feminist movement. She won an American Book Award in 1990 for *Spider Woman's Granddaughters: Traditional Tales and Contemporary Writings by Native American Women,* which is an attempt to correct the lack of stories by and/or about Native Women in literature collections. In her 1991 *Grandmother of the Light: A Medicine Woman's Sourcebook,* Allen expands her interest in the ritual experience of women as exhibited in the traditional stories. She traces the stages in a woman's spiritual path using Native American stories as models for walking in the sacred way.

## Contributions to Native American Poetry

Besides her extensive work as a scholar, Allen is the author of numerous volumes of poetry. Because of her multicultural background, Allen can draw on varying poetic rhythms and structures, which emanate from such sources as country-western music, Pueblo corn dances, Catholic masses, Mozart, Italian opera, and Arabic chanting. In her work, a finely detailed sense of place resonates with landscapes from the city, the reservation, and the interior. She has been recognized by critics such as A. Lavonne Ruoff for her purity of language and emotional intensity.

Allen became interested in writing in high school when she discovered the work of Gertrude Stein, whom she read extensively and tried to copy. Other influences have been the Romantic poets, Shelley and Keats. Allen took up writing more seriously in college when she read Robert Creeley's *For Love* and discovered that he was teaching at the University of New Mexico, where she was a student. She took his poetry class, although she considered herself a prose writer at the time. Creeley introduced her to the work of the poets Charles Olson, Allen Ginsberg, and Denise Levertov—all of whom have been major influences on Allen. She left New Mexico to finish her bachelor's degree at the University of Oregon and studied with Ralph Salisbury, who was Cherokee, though she did not know it at the time. Feeling isolated and suicidal, Allen says that the presence of a Santee Sioux friend, Dick Wilson, and the discovery of N. Scott Momaday's *House Made of Dawn* made all the difference to her. Recent influences upon her work have been Adrienne Rich, Patricia Clark Smith, and E.A. Mares.

Allen's 1982 *Shadow Country* received an honorable mention from the National Book Award Before Columbus Foundation. Allen uses the theme of shadows—the not dark and not light—to bridge her experience of mixed heritage as she attempts to respond to the world in its variety. Allen's poetry has an infusion of spirits common to Native American literature, but represents not only her Native American heritage, but her multicultural heritage. She also uses her poetry to respond to personal events in her life, such as her mother's suffering with lupus ("Dear World" in *Shadow Country*) and the death of one of her twin sons ("On the Street: Monument" in *Shadow Country*). In the interview with Bruchac, Allen says, "My poetry has a haunted sense to it . . . a sorrow and grievingness in it that comes directly from being split, not in two but in twenty, and never being able to reconcile all the places that I am." Allen's multicultural vision allows her to mediate between her different worlds to make a rich contribution to Native American literature as a scholar, writer, and educator.

Allen continued to receive attention in the 1990s, having her work examined and critiqued in such publications as *The Journal of Homosexuality, The Explicator* and *Ariel.* Also, in 1996 she cowrote an anthology of nine stories about Native Americans for young readers titled *As Long As the Rivers Flow.*

## Further Reading

Aal, Katharyn Machan, "Writing as an Indian Woman: An Interview with Paula Gunn Allen," *North Dakota Quarterly,* spring 1989; 149-61.

Allen, Paula Gunn, "Beloved Woman: The Lesbians in American Indian Cultures," *Conditions,* 1981; 65-67.

Allen, Paula Gunn, "Who Is Your Mother? Red Roots of White Feminism," *Sinister Wisdom,* winter 1984; 34-46.

Ballinger, Franchot, and Brian Swann, "A *MELUS* Interview: Paula Gunn Allen," *MELUS,* summer 1983; 3-25.

Bataille, Gretchen M., and Kathleen Mullen Sands, *American Indian Women: Telling Their Lives,* Lincoln, Nebraska, University of Nebraska Press, 1984.

Bruchac, Joseph, "I Climb the Mesas in My Dreams: An Interview with Paula Gunn Allen," *Survival This Way: Interviews with American Indian Poets,* Tucson, Arizona, Sun Tracks and University of Arizona Press, 1987; 1-24.

Caputi, Jane, "Interview with Paula Gunn Allen," *Trivia, a Journal of Ideas,* fall 1990; 50-67.

Coltelli, Laura, *Winged Words: American Writers Speak,* Lincoln, Nebraska, University of Nebraska Press, 1990; 11-39.

Crawford, C.F., John F. William Balassi, and Annie O. Ersturox, "Paula Gunn Allen," in *This About Vision: Interviews with Southwestern Writers,* Albuquerque, University of New Mexico Press, 1990; 95-107.

Hanson, Elizabeth J., *Paula Gunn Allen,* Western Writers Series, Boise, Idaho, Boise State University, 1990.

Milton, John R., "Paula Gunn Allen (Laguna-Sioux-Lebanese)," *Four Indian Poets,* Vermillion, South Dakota, 1974.

Ruoff, A. LaVonne Brown, *American Indian Literatures: An Introduction, Bibliographic Review and Selected Bibliography,* New York, Modern Language Association, 1990; 92-4.

Ruoff, *Literatures of the American Indian,* New York, Chelsea House Publishers, 1991; 95-6.

Swann, Brian, and Arnold Krupat, editors, "Paula Gunn Allen, 'The Autobiography of a Confluence,'" *I Tell You Now: Autobiographical Essays by Native American Writers,* Lincoln, Nebraska, University of Nebraska Press, 1987; 141-54.

Van Dyke, Annette, "The Journey Back to Female Roots: A Laguna Pueblo Model," *Lesbian Texts and Contexts,* Karla Jay and Joanne Glasgow, editors, New York, New York University Press, 1990; 339-54.

Van Dyke, "Curing Ceremonies: The Novels of Leslie Marmon Silko and Paula Gunn Allen," *The Search for a Woman-Centered Spirituality,* New York, New York University Press, 1992.

Van Dyke, "Paula Gunn Allen," *Contemporary Lesbian Writers of the United States: A Bio-Bibliographical Critical Source-*

*book,* Sandra Pollack and Denise Knight, editors, Westport, Connecticut, Greenwood Press, 1993. □

# Julia Alvarez

**In her poetry and prose, Julia Alvarez (born 1950) has expressed her feelings about her immigration to the United States. She was born in New York City of Dominican parents, who returned to their native land with their newborn daughter. After her family's reimmigration to the United States when Alvarez was ten, she and her sisters struggled to find a place for themselves in their new world. Alvarez has used her dual experience as a starting point for the exploration of culture through writing.**

Alvarez's most notable work, *How the Garcia Girls Lost Their Accents,* fictionally discusses her life in the Dominican Republic and the United States and the hardships her family faced as immigrants. Apparently the culmination of many years of effort, the 15 stories which make up the novel offer entertaining insights for a wide variety of potential readers that includes both Hispanics and non-Hispanics.

## Background in the Dominican Republic

Reminiscing about her youth in an article in *American Scholar,* Alvarez wrote, "Although I was raised in the Dominican Republic by Dominican parents in an extended Dominican family, mine was an American childhood." Her family lived close to her mother's family. Life was somewhat communal; Alvarez and her sisters were brought up along with their cousins and supervised by her mother, maids, and many aunts. Although her own family was not as well off as some of their relatives, Alvarez did not feel inferior. Her father, a doctor who ran the nearby hospital, had met her mother while she was attending school in the United States. While such extravagances as shopping trips to America were beyond their financial means, Alvarez's family was highly influenced by American attitudes and goods. Alvarez and her sisters attended the American school, and for a special treat, ate ice cream from the American ice cream parlor. The entire extended family was obsessed with America; to the children, it was a fantasy land.

As Alvarez acknowledges in her article in *American Scholar,* her family's association with the United States may have saved her father's life. The members of her mother's family were respected because of their ties with America. Alvarez's uncles had attended Ivy League colleges, and her grandfather was a cultural attaché to the United Nations. The dictator of the Dominican Republic, Rafael Leonidas Trujillo Molina, could not victimize a family with such strong American ties. However, when Alvarez's father secretly joined the forces attempting to oust Trujillo, the police set up surveillance of his home. It was rumored that,

respected family or not, her father was soon to be apprehended. An American agent and the offer of a fellowship at a New York hospital helped the family escape the country. Describing the scene as their plane landed in the United States in *American Scholar,* Alvarez wrote, "All my childhood I had dressed like an American, eaten American foods, and befriended American children. I had gone to an American school and spent most of the day speaking and reading English. At night, my prayers were full of blond hair and blue eyes and snow. . . . All my childhood I had longed for this moment of arrival. And here I was, an American girl, coming home at last."

## American Experiences

Alvarez's homecoming was not what she had expected it to be. Although she was thrilled to be back in America, she would soon face homesickness, alienation, and prejudice. She missed her cousins, her family's large home, and the respect her family name demanded. Alvarez, her parents, and her sisters squeezed themselves and their possessions into a tiny apartment. As she related to *Brújula Compass,* the experience was like a crash: "The feeling of loss caused a radical change in me. It made me an introverted little girl." Alvarez became an avid reader, immersing herself in books and, eventually, writing.

Alvarez went on to college. She earned undergraduate and graduate degrees in literature and writing and became an English professor at Middlebury College in Vermont. She received grants from the National Endowment for the Arts and The Ingram Merrill Foundation in addition to a PEN Oakland/Josephine Miles Award for excellence in multicultural literature. She published several collections of poetry including *Homecoming,* which appeared in 1984, and by 1987 she was working on a collection of stories. When Alvarez published *How the Garcia Girls Lost Their Accents* in 1991, the novel received considerable attention. The past decade had seen a surge of ethnic novels, and *Garcia Girls* came to be known as an exemplary example of the genre.

## *How the Garcia Girls Lost Their Accents*

Rather than a straight narrative, *How the Garcia Girls Lost Their Accents* is a reverse- chronological order series of 15 interwoven stories chronicling four sisters and their parents. A comparison with Alvarez's article in *American Scholar* suggests that these stories are based on her own experience; like her family, the Garcia family is Dominican and displaced in America. Like Alvarez and her sisters, the Garcia girls struggle to adapt to their new environment and assimilate themselves into the American culture.

The first group of stories is dated "1989-1972." Thus, the novel's first story seems to be its ending. Entitled, "Antojos," which is Spanish for "cravings," this story is a memory of one of the sisters, Yolanda, and her return to the Dominican Republic as an adult. Yolanda—whose story ends the novel and who acts as Alvarez's alter ego—has secretly decided to make her home there, having found life in the United States unfulfilling. When she ignores the warnings of her wealthy relatives and drives into the country for the guava fruit she has been craving, she faces disappointment. She is regarded as an American despite her native roots, and although she finds her guavas, her romantic journey is marred by her feelings as an outsider. Alvarez ends this story ambiguously—similar to the rest of the stories. The attempts of Yolanda and her sisters to lead successful lives in the United States are presented more as memory fragments than stories with definite beginnings and endings.

The next story focuses on Sofia, the youngest of the girls. At this point, however, the four girls are women, with husbands and careers. The details of Sofia's break with her father over her decision to take a lover before marriage are presented, and the events at a birthday party she prepared for her father are recounted. Sofia cannot be totally forgiven, nor can she ever return to the Dominican Republic; in the process of becoming an American girl of the 1960s, she has gone beyond the moral limits imposed by her father, who personifies life in the old world.

The third story relates some background information as it reveals a mother's perceptions of her four girls. During a family gathering, Mami tells her favorite story about each of the girls, and the reader learns that Sandi spent time in a mental institution after almost starving herself to death. The fourth story about Yolanda reveals that she too had a mental breakdown of her own after a failed relationship, and in the next story she becomes the narrator. In "The Rudy Elmenhurst Story," Yolanda's tale of her reluctance to sleep with the dashing young man she loved because of his casual approach to the matter explains her ensuing trouble with men as well as her problems assimilating into American youth culture: "Catholic or not, I still thought it a sin for a guy to just barge in five years later with a bottle of expensive wine and assume you'd drink out of his hand. A guy who had ditched me, who had haunted my sexual awakening with a nightmare of self-doubt. For a moment as I watched him get in his car and drive away, I felt a flash of that old self-doubt."

The memories in the second section of the novel recall the years from 1960 to 1970. The girls are younger, and they are experiencing their first years as immigrants. Attempts they made to reconcile themselves to their new culture are challenged by their parents, who want their children to "mix with the 'right kind' of Americans," and the girls are threatened with having to spend time on the island, which they have come to dread. In this section, the girls save their sister from a macho cousin's imposition, a pervert exposes himself to Carla, and Yolanda sees snow for the first time and thinks it is fall-out from a nuclear bomb.

The final story in this section, "Floor Show," focuses on Sandi's perception of events as the family spends a scandalous evening with an American doctor and his drunkenly indiscreet wife in a Spanish restaurant. Sandi is shocked and upset when this woman kisses her father and later dances with the flamenco dancers that the young girl had so admired. Cautioned by her mother to behave at the important dinner, Sandi does as she is told and stays quiet until she is offered a flamenco doll by the American woman, who seems to understand her desire for it. "Sandi was not going to miss her chance. This woman had kissed her father. This woman had ruined the act of the beautiful dancers. The way

Sandi saw it, this woman owed her something." The woman gave Sandi something more than the doll; her smile "intimated the things Sandi was just beginning to learn, things that the dancers knew all about, which was why they danced with such vehemence, such passion."

In third and final section, "1960-1956," America is still a dream—the family is still on the island. The first story is divided into two parts and recalls the family's traumatic encounter with the *guardia,* or secret police, and their subsequent flight from their home. From that moment on, the tales regress to the girls' early memories of life in the huge family compound. Yolanda tells of the presents her grandmother brought the children from America and an ensuing encounter with her cousin, Sandi recalls her art lessons and the fright she had at the instructor's home, Carla remembers the mechanical bank her father brought her from F.A.O. Schwartz in New York and the maid who desperately wanted it.

Finally, Yolanda concludes the novel with one of her earliest memories—she stole a kitten from its mother and then abandoned it, even though she had been warned by a strange hunter: "To take it away would be a violation of its natural right to live." The mother cat haunted the girl until she left the island, and, as Yolanda confides in her narration, "There are still times I wake up at three o'clock in the morning and peer into the darkness. At that hour and in that loneliness, I hear her, a black furred thing lurking in the corners of my life, her magenta mouth opening, wailing over some violation that lies at the center of my art."

The praise Alvarez received for her first novel outweighed the criticism that a new novelist often encounters. The *New York Times Book Review* found that Alvarez "beautifully captured the threshold experience of the new immigrant, where the past is not yet a memory and the future remains an anxious dream." *Hispanic*'s critic wrote, "Well-crafted, although at times overly sentimental, these stories provide a glimpse into the making of another American family with a Hispanic surname." And the *Library Journal* reported, "Alvarez is a gifted, evocative storyteller of promise."

Alvarez's second novel, *In the Time of Butterflies,* was published in 1994. This work recounts the lives and tragic end of the Mirabel sisters—Patria, Minerva, and Maria Terese (Mate)—who were assassinated after visiting their imprisoned husbands during the last days of the Trujillo regime in the Dominican Republic. Each sister in turn relates her own aspect of the narrative, beginning with their childhood and gradually defining how they came to be involved in the liberation movement. Their story is framed by that of the surviving sister, Dedé, who adds her own tale of suffering to the memory of her martyred sisters. *In the Time of Butterflies* received a favorable reaction from reviewers, some of whom admired Alvarez's ability to express the wide range of emotions brought on by the revolution. For example, the reviewer for *Publishers Weekly* observed that "Alvarez captures the terrorized atmosphere of a police state, in which people live under the sword of terrible fear and atrocities cannot be acknowledged. As the sisters' energetic fervor turns to anguish, Alvarez conveys their courage and their desperation, and the full import of the tragedy." The novel was a finalist for the National Book Critics Award in 1994.

A collection of poems entitled *The Other Side/El Otro Lado,* was published in 1995. It deals with similar themes of biculturalism and the power of language. In the book's title poem a spirit conjuror commands Alvarez to serve her own people in the Dominican Republic. But in the end she returns "to the shore I've made up on the other side, to a life of choice, a life of words." Her next work, *Yo!,* published in 1997, is based on Yolanda, one of her characters from her first novel, *How the Garcia Girls Lost Their Accents.* Each section of the novel is told from different characters' perspectives, all of whom depict Yolanda as they see her in order to provide a complex portrait.

## Further Reading

*American Scholar,* Winter 1987, pp. 71-85.
*Atlanta Journal,* August 11, 1991, p. A13.
*Boston Globe,* May 26, 1991, p. A13.
*Brújula Compass* (Spanish-language; translation by Ronie-Richele Garcia- Johnson), January-February 1992, p. 16.
*Hispanic,* June 1991, p. 55.
*Los Angeles Times,* June 7, 1991, p. E4.
*Library Journal,* May 1, 1991, p. 102; August 1994, 123.
*Más,* (Spanish-language; translation by Ronie-Richele Garcia-Johnson), November-December 1991, p. 100.
*New York Times Book Review,* October 6, 1991, p. 14; July 16, 1995, p. 20.
*Nuestro,* November 1984, pp. 34 + ; March 1985, pp. 52 + ; January-February 1986, pp. 32 + .
*Publishers Weekly,* April 5, 1991, p. 133; July 11, 1994, p. 62.
*School Library Journal,* September 1991, p. 292.
*Washington Post,* June 20, 1991, p. D11. □

# Dorothy Andersen

**Dorothy Andersen (1901-1963) was the first medical researcher to recognize the disorder known as cystic fibrosis.**

Dorothy Andersen was the first medical researcher to recognize the disorder known as cystic fibrosis. She devoted much of her life to the further study of this disease, as well as to study of congenital defects of the heart. During World War II, Anderson was asked to develop a training program in cardiac embryology and anatomy for surgeons learning techniques of open-heart surgery.

Dorothy Hansine Andersen was born on May 15, 1901, in Asheville, North Carolina. She was the only child of Hans Peter Andersen and the former Mary Louise Mason. Hans Peter Andersen was a native of Denmark and was employed by the Young Men's Christian Association (YMCA) in Asheville. Andersen's mother was a descendent of Benning Wentworth, for whom the town of Bennington, Vermont, was named.

Andersen was forced to take responsibility for her own upbringing early in life. Her father died when she was

thirteen years old, leaving behind an invalid wife dependent on her daughter's care. They moved to Saint Johnsbury, Vermont, where Mary Andersen died in 1920. Her death left young Dorothy "with not a single close relative," according to biographer Libby Machol in *Notable American Women.*

Andersen put herself through Saint Johnsbury Academy and Mount Holyoke College before enrolling in the Johns Hopkins School of Medicine, from which she received her M.D. in 1926. While still a medical student, Andersen published in the journal *Contributions to Embryology* two scientific papers dealing with the reproductive system of the female pig. After graduating from Johns Hopkins, Andersen accepted a one-year position teaching anatomy at the Rochester School of Medicine. She then did her internship in surgery at the Strong Memorial Hospital in Rochester, New York. For medical students an internship is normally followed by a residency, which ultimately leads to certification as a physician. Andersen found, however, that she was unable to find a hospital that would allow her to do a residency in surgery or to work as a pathologist, her other major interest. The reason for this slight, according to Machol, was that Andersen was a woman.

Denied the opportunity to have a medical practice, Andersen turned instead to medical research. She took a job as research assistant in pathology at Columbia University's College of Physicians and Surgeons that allowed her to begin a doctoral program in endocrinology, the study of glands. She completed the course in 1935 and was granted the degree of doctor of medical science by Columbia University. From 1930 to 1935 Andersen also served as an instructor in pathology at the Columbia Medical School. Andersen later accepted an appointment as a pathologist at Babies Hospital of the Columbia-Presbyterian Medical Center in New York City, where she stayed for more than twenty years, eventually becoming chief of pathology in 1952. By 1958 she had become a full professor at the College of Physicians and Surgeons.

Andersen's research interests fell into two major categories. The first of these involved a long and careful study of congenital (existing from birth) heart problems based on the examination of infants who had died of cardiac conditions. She began that study during her first year at Babies Hospital and was still publishing her findings on the subject in the late 1950s. Andersen's experience with cardiac problems was put to use during World War II when she was asked to teach courses for physicians who wanted to learn how to conduct open-heart surgery.

The second area of research, for which Andersen is probably best known, evolved out of her discovery in 1935 of cystic fibrosis. That discovery came about during the postmortem examination of a child who had supposedly died of celiac disease, a nutritional disorder. According to Machol, "her researcher's sixth sense alerted, Dr. Andersen searched for similar cases in the autopsy files and in the literature." Eventually she realized that she had found a disease that had never been described in the medical literature, to which she gave the name cystic fibrosis. Cystic fibrosis is a congenital disease of the mucous glands and pancreatic enzymes that results in abnormal digestion and difficulty in breathing; it is believed to affect approximately one in fifteen hundred people. Over the next twenty-six years, Andersen was successful in developing diagnostic tests for cystic fibrosis but less successful in her efforts to treat and cure the disease.

Andersen died of lung cancer in New York City on March 3, 1963. A contributing factor may well have been her smoking habits. As Machol has written: "Ashes from the cigarette that usually dangled from the corner of her mouth were virtually a part of her costume." Among the honors Andersen received were the Mead Johnson Award for Pediatric Research in 1938, the Borden Award for Research in Nutrition from the American Academy of Pediatrics in 1948, the Elizabeth Blackwell Citation for Women in Medicine from the New York Infirmary in 1954, a citation for outstanding performance from Mount Holyoke College in 1952, and, posthumously, the distinguished service medal of the Columbia-Presbyterian Medical Center.

## Further Reading

Sicherman, Barbara, and Carol Hurd Green, editors, *Notable American Women, the Modern Period: A Biographical Dictionary*, Belknap Press, 1980, pp. 18-20.
*Journal of the American Medical Association*, "Andersen, Dorothy Hansine," May 25, 1963, p. 150.
Damrosch, Douglas S., "Dorothy Hansine Andersen," *Journal of Pediatrics*, October, 1964, pp. 477-479. □

# June Anderson

**An American opera singer, June Anderson (born 1953) specialized in roles from operas by Donizetti, Rossini, and Bellini that require *bel canto* singing, although she sang operas by many other composers.**

June Anderson was born in 1953 in Boston and raised in Connecticut. When she was 11 she began taking voice lessons at her mother's urging. At the age of 14 she performed in her first opera, *The Princess and the Pea* by Ernst Toch. At the age of 17 she sang the part of Gilda in *Rigoletto* and, in the same year, was a finalist in the Metropolitan Opera National Council Auditions. Although she was the youngest singer to be named a finalist at these auditions, she decided not to continue training for a professional career and instead went to Yale University where she majored in French and graduated *cum laude*. She then challenged herself to become a well-known singer in two years, and if she failed to do so, to enter law school.

It was at this point that she began working with the vocal coach Robert Leonard, with whom she studied for many years. He was able to depend on her hard work and high standards to develop excellent breath control, which allowed the natural quality of her voice to project itself unhampered by lack of support. His approach was to build a great voice over time and not to rush the process of growth. Anderson agreed with this approach and frequently declined offers to sing roles that she felt were not suited to her

vocal development even though they posed no technical difficulties for her. She worked hard to develop her voice, even though there were many discouraging moments, and as she said, ". . . without a touch of luck, hard work doesn't necessarily pay off." It did, however, and she became a member of the New York City Opera Company, with which she made her debut in 1978 as Queen of the Night in Mozart's *Magic Flute*.

There were many operas in which she sang while at the New York City Opera Company, including *Le coq d'or* by Rimsky-Korsakov, *Rigoletto* by Verdi, the role of Donna Elvira in Mozart's *Don Giovanni*, three different roles in *Les Contes d'Hoffmann* by Offenbach, *Il barbiere di Siviglia* by Rossini, *Giulio Cesare* by Handel, *La traviata* by Verdi, and a concert version of *I puritani* by Bellini. Although she received good reviews from New York critics, she felt that she was not being given the roles she felt ready for. As she put it, "I sang very few performances and covered just about everything for other singers!"

It was through the recommendation of Sherrill Milnes that Anderson was brought to the attention of Giovanni Lupetin, an agent for European opera houses. He arranged for her to sing in several provincial houses, where she was heard by Italo Gomez, the manager of La Fenice in Venice. He was so impressed by her voice that he offered to mount a production of her choice. Without hesitation she chose *La sonnambula* by Bellini, which she felt "was written for me." Anderson also signed a contract with La Scala, the opera house in Milan, to perform *La sonnambula* and with the opera house in Rome to perform *Semiramide* by Rossini.

## European Debuts

It was at this point that June Anderson decided to move to Italy as she perceived her career to be developing more rapidly abroad than at home. Once she had made her debut in the major houses of Italy (she was the first non-Italian to win the prestigious Bellini d'Oro prize), offers to record and to perform came from all over the world. She sang *Die Feen* by Wagner in Munich in 1983. Her strong lyric vocal quality meant that repertoire outside the difficult *bel canto* style was possible for her, but she selected her roles with care. She sang in Canada and on the West Coast in the same year, performing *I puritani* in Edmonton and *Il barbiere di Siviglia* in Seattle.

In 1984 she again sang *Il barbiere di Siviglia*, this time in New Orleans; then *La sonnambula* in Venice; *La fille du regiment* by Donizetti in Parma; *Lucia di Lammermore*, also by Donizetti, in Geneva. In 1985 she began to sing operas that were not in the standard repertoire. In Pittsburgh she sang Verdi's *La battaglia di Legnano*; in Paris, Meyerbeer's *Robert le diable*; she also sang two Handel operas, *Samson* in Chicago and *Giulio Cesare* in Washington, D.C.

Although her life was centered in Italy, Anderson was acclaimed internationally both for the quality of her singing and the intelligence and willingness to work for the sake of the music rather than for herself. As she put it, "I attack the music from the inside out."

The following year Anderson made her debut at Covent Garden where she sang *Semiramide* to critical praise. She returned in 1987 to sing Lucia in *Lucia di Lammermore*. Her desire to explore further the lesser known works of the *bel canto* composers led her to accept roles in *Beatrice di Tenda* by Bellini in Venice, *Maometto II* by Rossini for San Francisco, and *Armida* by Rossini at Aix-en-Provence. She did not confine herself totally to unusual operas, however. During the same period she sang two standard works by Verdi—*La traviata* in Santiago and *Rigoletto* for both Covent Garden and for her Metropolitan Opera debut in 1989.

## Recordings and Concerts

Throughout her career Anderson recorded and gave concert performances of several operas. By her own admission, the difficulties she encountered in finding adequately staged productions of *bel canto* operas caused her to consider whether she should increase the number of her recordings and concerts, avoiding the frustrations of the stage and permitting her to exert more control over the final result. In 1983 she presented Albinoni's *Il nasciemento dell' Aurora* in Vicenza and in Venice in concert form. In the same year she filled in for Monserrat Caballe in a concert performance of *Semiramide* at Carnegie Hall. That performance was very widely acclaimed, but resulted in no significant new offers for roles in the United States and was a contributing factor in her decision to move abroad to further her career. She returned to Carnegie Hall many times singing Handel's *Ariodante* and *Beatrice di Tenda* and Berlioz' *Nuits d'Ete*. She sang Bernstein's *Candide* in concert in London and planned to record the work.

Her recordings followed the thrust of her career, including some of the lesser known operas of the early Romantic period. She also recorded some of the French repertoire, which endeared her to the French, so much so that she was asked to perform in July of 1989 at the opening concert of Paris' new Opera Bastille. The French operas she recorded include Bizet's *La jolie fille de Perthe*, Adam's *Le postilion de longjumeau*, Auber's *La muette de portici*, and Halevy's *La juive*. In addition, she recorded Rossini's *Mose in Egito*, *Maometto II*, *Les soirees musicales*, *Il naciemento dell' Aurora*, and, for variety, Carl Orff's *Carmina burana* (a 20th-century work based on medieval Latin texts) and Bernstein's *Candide*.

Anderson's vocal qualities were admired by many critics on both sides of the Atlantic, even when her dramatic skills were not. She was compared to Joan Sutherland, Jennie Tourel, and Nellie Melba. Peter G. Davis in *New York* magazine wrote that her singing "shows off the clarity, evenness and facility of an agile voice with an easy upper extension." Words such as "creamy," "lush," "brilliant," and "assured" have been used to describe her voice. In her own words, she was "a big lyric (soprano) with high notes and agility."

After establishing herself as a prima donna in the United States and in Europe, June Anderson finally reached a level of achievement that placed her among the top international opera singers. Her special affinity for and ability to perform *bel canto* roles gave her career a direction and focus that served her well. The operas that require *bel canto* singing are written in a highly ornamented style that empha-

sizes the agility of the singer. The style flourished in the early Romantic period in Europe, particularly in Italy from about 1811 to 1843. Many singers find the unusual technical demands of the repertoire, particularly the high range and the rapid runs and ornaments, to exceed their ability to perform it well.

Throughout the 1990s, Anderson performed many roles for the first time, including Elena of *La Donna del Lago* in Milan (1992), Maria in *Mazeppa* at Carnegie Hall (1993), Desdemona in *Otello* in Los Angeles (1995), Rosalinde in *Die Fledermaus* at the Metropolitan Opera (1995), Giovanna in *Giovanna d'Arco* in Barcelona and New York (1996), and Tatiana in Tokyo (1996). In 1997 Anderson assumed the role of Norma the Druid priestess for the first time at Chicago's Lyric Opera and received many good reviews. John von Rhein of the *Chicago Tribune* gave Anderson credit for "not only taking on such a tough role at this stage of a comfortably settled career but—amazingly—pulling it off so well" and asserted that her first playing of Norma "had to be reckoned a qualified success."

Anderson's talent was not narrowly confined, however. She appeared in many operas outside of the *bel canto* repertoire. Whatever period of music she sang, her performances were of exceptional quality.

Although some of her critics characterized her as temperamental and moody, her reaction to the impression that people are terrified of her is laughter. She described herself to Kathy Petrere of the *New York Times* in a 1995 interview as "Jell-O with chilies. A really distinct flavor, but in the end it's Jell-O." She admitted to being a perfectionist who "can't stand it" when she made mistakes. Anderson also defined what she deemed most important in life as "friendships," and noted, "If I never sang another note in my life [my friends] would still be there." As she commented in the same interview, "Singing is my job, it's not who I am."

## Further Reading

Anderson has been reviewed frequently in magazines and articles. In the August 1986 issue of *Opera News* she appeared on the cover. In the *New York Times* on October 29, 1989, Walter Price wrote an article discussing her career and her debut at the Metropolitan Opera House. See also *Chicago Tribune* (February 7, 1997), *New York Times* (November 6, 1995; April 8, 1997), and *Opera News* (June 1997). Also see the June Anderson page online by Laurent Lacoquelle at http://pages.infinit.net/balza/junea.hmt. □

# Marian Anderson

**Marian Anderson (1902-1993) is remembered as one of the best American contraltos of all time. She was the first African American singer to perform at the White House and also the first African American to sing with New York's Metropolitan Opera.**

Marian Anderson was born in Philadelphia on Feb. 17, 1902, and was educated in the public schools. She displayed a remarkable flair for singing when very young. Local supporters provided funds for study with Agnes Reifsnider and, later, Giuseppe Boghetti. When Anderson was 23, she entered a competition and won first place over 300 other singers, gaining her an engagement with the New York Philharmonic at Lewisohn Stadium. Further sponsorships enabled her to continue her studies in the United States and, after winning the Rosenwald Fellowship, in Europe.

Following debuts in Berlin in 1930 and London in 1932, Anderson concertized in Scandinavia, Germany, South America, and the Soviet Union. In Salzburg, Austria, she gave a sensational performance at the Mozarteum with famous conductor Arturo Toscanini in the audience. Upon hearing her sing, Toscanini reportedly told her she had "a voice heard but once in a century."

## Return to the United States

At the end of her European tour, Anderson was an acclaimed sensation in the capitals of Europe, and American impresario Sol Hurok signed her to 15 concerts in the United States. On December 30, 1935, she opened her American tour at New York's Town Hall. The program was typical for Marian Anderson, consisting of songs by Handel, Schubert, Giuseppe Verdi, and Sibelius as well as several black spirituals. The performance was a resounding success, with critics welcoming her as a "new high priestess of song." In the words of a *New York Times* contributor, the

concert established her as "one of the great singers of our time."

Over the next several years Anderson sang for U.S. President Franklin Delano Roosevelt at the White House, and she returned to perform for King George VI and Queen Elizabeth of England during their 1939 visit to the United States. She made several cross country tours and soon was booking engagements two years in advance. In one year she covered 26,000 miles in the longest tour in concert history, giving 70 concerts in five months. After World War II ended, she again performed in major European cities. By 1950, it was estimated that she had performed before nearly 4 million listeners.

Marian Anderson's contralto voice was notable for its power and exceptionally dark texture, particularly in the lowest register. The high voice changed quality—not unusual in a contralto of prodigious range—but idiosyncracies never obliterated the fine musicality and sincere emotion that marked her performances.

## Victory Over Racial Discrimination

With Roland Hayes and Paul Robeson, Marian Anderson pioneered in winning recognition at home and abroad for black artists. In 1939, an incident involving the Daughters of the American Revolution did much to focus public attention on racism. The DAR denied Anderson use of their Constitution Hall in Washington, D.C. for an April concert. First Lady Eleanor Roosevelt resigned from the DAR in protest, and the U.S. government placed Lincoln Memorial at Anderson's disposal. Her concert there, on Easter morning, drew a live audience of 75,000, and millions more heard it over the radio.

In 1942 she established the Marian Anderson Award for talented young singers; among the recipients were Camilla Williams, Mattiwilda Dobbs, and Grace Bumbry. Anderson married Orpheus H. Fisher, a New York architect, in 1943.

In 1948 Anderson underwent a dangerous operation for the removal from her esophagus of a cyst that threatened to damage her voice. For two months she was not permitted to use her voice and was unsure if she would ever be able to sing again. When she was finally allowed to rehearse, her voice returned free of impairment. Following her recovery, Anderson made her first post-World War II tour of Europe, including stops in Scandinavia, Paris, London, Antwerp, Zurich, and Geneva.

## Her Operatic Debut

On Jan. 7, 1955, Anderson sang Ulrica in Verdi's *Un ballo in maschera* (*The Masked Ball*) at New York's Metropolitan Opera House, and she returned the following season in the same role. This was the first time an African American person had sung with the Metropolitan since it opened in 1883.

Over the years, Anderson continued to add to her accomplishments. She sang at the presidential inaugurations of Dwight D. Eisenhower and John F. Kennedy. In 1957, as an emissary of the State Department, Anderson made a concert tour of India and the Far East that was filmed by CBS-TV. In 1958 President Eisenhower appointed her a delegate to the 13th General Assembly of the United Nations. Anderson gave her farewell concert at Carnegie Hall on Easter Sunday in 1965.

Describing the range and quality of her voice, *New York Times* music critic Harold C. Schoenberg wrote: "Those who remember her at her height . . . can never forget that big resonant voice, with those low notes almost visceral in nature, and with that easy, unforced ascent to the top register. A natural voice, a hauntingly colorful one, it was one of the vocal phenomena of its time."

Marian Anderson's honors included a doctorate of music from Howard University (1938) and honorary degrees from more than 20 other American educational institutions. She received the Springarn Medal from the National Association for the Advancement of Colored People in 1939 and the Bok Award of $10,000 from her hometown of Philadelphia in 1941. In addition to decorations from many foreign governments, she was awarded the Presidential Medal of Freedom in 1963. At age 89, in 1991, Anderson was honored as the subject of a 60-minute documentary broadcast over public television. She died on April 8, 1993.

Renewed accolades abounded in 1997, the centenary year of Anderson's birth. The Marian Anderson Study Center at the University of Pennsylvania was erected to hold her archives. On February 27, the day that would have been her 100th birthday, Robert Shaw conducted a tribute concert at New York's Carnegie Hall, joined by signers including Jessye Norman, William Warfield, and Roberta Peters. At noon the following Saturday, a gala of spirituals and art songs took place at Union Baptist Church, at 19th and Fitzwater Streets in Philadelphia—the church where Anderson prayed and sang as a little girl.

### Further Reading

Information on Anderson can be found in the *Philadelphia Inquirer* (February 26, 1997); Hitchcock, H. Wiley, and Stanley Sadie, *The New Grove Dictionary of American Music* (Macmillan, 1986); Sims, Janet L., *Marian Anderson: An Annotated Bibliography and Discography* (Greenwood, 1981); and Tedards, Anne, *Marian Anderson* (1988). □

# Fannie Fern Phillips Andrews

**Fannie Fern Phillips Andrews (1867–1950) was an educator who fought endlessly for the promotion of peace studies through an international bureau of education.**

Fannie Fern Phillips Andrews was an educator who campaigned tirelessly for an international bureau of education to promote peace studies. Born in Lynn, Massachusetts, she was the daughter of a shoemaker father and a mother who was president of the Woman's Christian Temperance Union. Deciding at age three that she wanted to be a teacher, Andrews later attended Salem Normal School in Massachusetts and then taught for six years before receiving her degree in psychology and education from Radcliffe College in 1902. Her work in the public schools of Boston convinced her that students from different ethnic and economic backgrounds had to be taught to communicate and negotiate with each other. Her core belief that men who make war are spurred to conflict by their inability to understand one another's perspectives fueled her interest in "teaching peace".

### The American Peace League

In 1908 she founded the American Peace League, an organization which sought to promote peace by teaching the principles of "international justice" in American schools. She extended her influence by organizing the Boston School-Parent group and serving as president of the Boston Home and School Association from 1914-1918. Andrews campaigned nationally for her ideals, and by 1915 League branches had been established in forty states. She envisioned an international bureau of education which would promote understanding among nations. But the era just before the United States entered the World War was an inauspicious time to promote peace. Andrews, who eventually supported American involvement in the war, changed the name of the American Peace League to the American School Citizenship League in 1918, believing that the old title was too provocative during wartime.

### International Attention

Andrews and the League received serious consideration from the highest branches of government for her plan to create an international bureau of education. She was engaged in the final planning stages of a multi-national conference to consider the logistics of such an institution when World War I erupted. She had already caught the attention of President Woodrow Wilson , however, and in 1918 he picked Andrews to attend the Paris Peace Conference . There she lobbied for the emerging League of Nations to include in its covenant a provision for her dream of an international bureau of education, but she was unsuccessful. During the war she received a post-graduate degree in international affairs, never losing sight of her goal of an international school curriculum which would promote justice and understanding. Andrews maintained her dedication to promoting peace studies until her death, serving in the International Law Association, the World Peace Foundation, and the International Guild.

### Further Reading

J. McKeen Cattell, ed., *Leaders in Education: A Biographical Directory* (New York: The Science Press, 1932).
Alden Whitman, ed., *American Reformers* (New York: H. W. Wilson Co., 1985), pp. I22-123. □

# Maya Angelou

**Maya Angelou (born 1928)—author, poet, play-wright, stage and screen performer, and director—is best known for her autobiography, *I Know Why the Caged Bird Sings* (1970), which recalls a young African American woman's discovery of her self-confidence.**

Maya Angelou was born Marguerite Johnson on April 4, 1928, in St. Louis, Missouri. Growing up in rural Stamps, Arkansas, with her brother, Bailey, she lived with her pious grandmother, who owned a general store. She attended public schools in Arkansas and California, and became San Francisco's first female streetcar conductor. Later she studied dance with Martha Graham and drama with Frank Silvera, and went on to a career in theater. She appeared in *Porgy and Bess,* which toured 22 countries; on Broadway in *Look Away;* and in several off-Broadway plays, including *Cabaret for Freedom,* which she wrote in collaboration with Godfrey Cambridge.

During the early 1960s, Angelou lived in Egypt, where she was the associate editor of *The Arab Observer* in Cairo. During this time, she also contributed articles to *The Ghanaian Times* and was featured on the Ghanaian Broadcasting Corporation programming in Accra. During the mid-1960s, she became assistant administrator of the School of Music and Drama at the University of Ghana. She was the feature editor of the *African Review* in Accra from 1964 to 1966. During this time she served as northern coordinator for the Southern Christian Leadership Conference at the request of Dr. Martin Luther King, Jr.

When she returned to the United States, Angelou worked as writer-producer for 20th Century-Fox Television, from which her full-length feature film *Sisters, Sisters* received critical acclaim. In addition, she wrote the screenplays *Georgia, Georgia* and *All Day Long* along with the television scripts for *Sister, Sister* and the series premiere of *Brewster Place.* She wrote, produced, and hosted the NET public broadcasting series *Blacks! Blues! Black!* Angelou also costarred in the motion picture *How to Make an American Quilt* in 1995.

Angelou has taught at several American colleges and universities, including the University of California at Los Angeles, the University of Kansas, Wichita State University, and California State University at Sacramento. Since the early 1980s, she has been Reynolds Professor and writer-in-residence at Wake Forest University.

Angelou has been a prolific poet for decades. Her collections include *Just Give Me A Cool Drink of Water 'Fore I Die* (1971); *Oh Pray My Wings Are Going to Fit Me Well* (1975); *And Still I Rise* (1976), which was produced as a choreo-poem on Off-Broadway in 1979; and *Shaker, Why Don't You Sing* (1983) *Poems: Maya Angelou* (1986); *Life Doesn't Frighten Me,* illustrated by celebrated New York artist Jean Michel Basquiat (1993); *On the Pulse of the Morning* (1993), recited at Bill Clinton's first Presidential

Inauguration; *Soul Looks Back in Wonder* (1994); and *I Shall Not Be Moved* (1997), her first book of poetry in over 10 years.

Angelou's poetry is fashioned almost entirely of short lyrics and jazzy rhythms. Although her poetry has contributed to her reputation and is especially popular among young people, most commentators reserve their highest praise for her prose. Angelou's dependence on alliteration, her heavy use of short lines, and her conventional vocabulary has led several critics to declare her poetry superficial and devoid of her celebrated humor. Other reviewers, however, praise her poetic style as refreshing and graceful. They also laud Angelou for addressing social and political issues relevant to African Americans and for challenging the validity of traditional American values and myths. For example, Angelou directed national attention to humanitarian concerns with her poem "On the Pulse of the Morning," which she recited at the 1993 inauguration of President Bill Clinton. In this poem, Angelou calls for recognition of the human failings pervading American history and an renewed national commitment to unity and social improvement.

Although Angelou began her literary career as a poet, she is well known for her five autobiographical works, which depict sequential periods of her life. *I Know Why the Caged Bird Sings* (1970) is about Marguerite Johnson and her brother Bailey growing up in Arkansas. It chronicles Angelou's life up to age sixteen, providing a child's perspective of the perplexing world of adults. Although her grandmother instilled pride and confidence in her, her self-image was shattered when she was raped at the age of eight by her mother's boyfriend. Angelou was so devastated by the attack that she refused to speak for approximately five years. *I Know Why the Caged Bird Sings* concludes with Angelou having regained self-esteem and caring for her newborn son, Guy. In addition to being a trenchant account of an African American girl's coming-of-age, this work affords insights into the social and political tensions of the 1930s. Sidonie Ann Smith echoed many critics when she wrote: "Angelou's genius as a writer is her ability to recapture the texture of the way of life in the texture of its idioms, its idiosyncratic vocabulary and especially in its process of image-making."

Her next autobiographical work, *Gather Together in My Name,* (1974) covers the period immediately after the birth of her son Guy and depicts her valiant struggle to care for him as a single parent. *Singin' and Swingin' and Gettin' Merry Like Christmas* (1976) describes Angelou's stage debut and concludes with her return from the international tour of *Porgy and Bess. The Heart of A Woman* (1981) portrays the mature Angelou becoming more comfortable with her creativity and her success. *All God's Children Need Traveling Shoes* (1986) recalls her four-year stay in Ghana.

Widely celebrated by popular audiences and critics, Angelou has a long roster of recognitions, including: a nomination for National Book Award, 1970, for *I Know Why the Caged Bird Sings;* a Yale University fellowship, 1970; a Pulitzer Prize nomination, 1972, for *Just Give Me a Cool Drink of Water 'fore I Diiie;* an Antoinette Perry ("Tony") Award nomination from League of New York Theatres and Producers, 1973, for performance in *Look Away;* Rockefeller Foundation scholar in Italy, 1975; honorary degrees from Smith College, 1975, Mills College, 1975, Lawrence University, 1976, and Wake Forest University, 1977; a Tony Award nomination for best supporting actress, 1977, for *Roots;* and the North Carolina Award in Literature, 1987. In the 1970s she was appointed to the Bicentennial Commission by President Gerald Ford, and the National Commission on the Observance of International Women's Year by Jimmy Carter. She was also named Woman of the Year in Communications by *Ladies' Home Journal,* 1976; and named one of the top one hundred most influential women by *Ladies' Home Journal,* 1983.

Angelou's autobiographical works have an important place in the African American tradition of personal narrative, and they continue to garner praise for their honesty and moving sense of dignity. Although an accomplished poet and dramatist, Angelou is dedicated to the art of autobiography. Angelou explained that she is "not afraid of the ties [between past and present]. I cherish them, rather. It's the vulnerability . . . it's allowing oneself to be hypnotized. That's frightening because we have no defenses, nothing. We've slipped down the well and every side is slippery. And how on earth are you going to come out? That's scary. But I've chosen it, and I've chosen this mode as my mode."

## Further Reading

For biographical information, see the following periodical pieces: "*The African-American Scholar Interviews:* Maya Angelou," in the *African-American Scholar* (January/February 1977); "I Know Why the Caged Bird Sings," in *Ebony* (April 1970); and Mary Helen Washington, "Their Fiction Becomes Our Reality," in *African-American World* (August 1974). For critical information see: Estelle C. Jelinek, "In Search of the African-American Female Self: African-American Women's Autobiographies and Ethnicity," in *Women's Autobiography* (1980); Claudia Tate, *African-American Women Writers at Work* (1983); Carol E. Neubauer, "Displacement and Autobiographical Style in Maya Angelou's *The Heart of a Woman,*" in *African-American Literature Forum* (1983); and Mari Evans, "Maya Angelou" in *African-American Women Writers, 1950-1980* (1983).

Additional information can be found in "Maya-ness is Next to Godliness," in *GQ* (July 1995) and "Maya Angelou: A Celebrated Poet Issues a Call to Arms to the Nation's Artists," in *Mother Jones* (May/June 1995). □

# Susan Brownell Anthony

**Susan Brownell Anthony (1820-1906) was an early leader of the American woman's suffrage movement and pioneered in seeking other equalities for women. An active abolitionist, she campaigned for emancipation of the slaves.**

Susan B. Anthony was born on Feb. 15, 1820, in Adams, Mass., one of seven children. Her family had settled in Rhode Island in 1634. She attended Quaker schools and began teaching at the age of 15 for $1.50 a week plus board. When the family moved to Rochester, N.Y., in 1845, her brilliant father, Daniel Anthony, the dominant influence in her life, worked with important abolitionists. Frederick Douglass, William Lloyd Garrison, Wendell Phillips, and other guests at the Anthony farm helped form her strong views on abolition of slavery.

## Woman's Rights

Though her family attended the first Woman's Rights Convention held in Seneca Falls and Rochester, N.Y., in 1848, Anthony did not take up the cause of woman's rights until 1851, when male hostility to her temperance efforts convinced her that women must win the right to speak in public and to vote before anything else could be accomplished. Her lifelong friendship and partnership with Elizabeth Cady Stanton also began in 1851, as did her temporary doffing of corsets in favor of the revolutionary "bloomer" costume—which was women's first major dress reform in the movement. Anthony attended her first woman's-rights convention in 1852; from then until the end of the Civil War she campaigned from door to door, in legislatures, and in meetings for the two causes of abolition of slavery and of woman's rights. The New York State Married Woman's Property and Guardianship Law in 1860 was her first major legislative victory.

## Formation of Suffrage Movement

With the outbreak of the Civil War in 1861, woman's rights took second place. Susan Anthony organized the Women's National Loyal League, which mobilized the crucial petitions to force passage of the 13th Amendment to the Constitution to abolish slavery. In 1865 she began her battle in the content of the 14th and 15th Amendments, hoping to gain the franchise for women as well as for African American males. But her former male allies in the abolitionist struggle brushed her aside, saying the time was not yet ripe for woman's suffrage. Saddened but not deterred by this defeat, Anthony worked solely for woman's suffrage from this time to the end of her life, organizing the National Woman Suffrage Association with Stanton. The association's New York weekly, *The Revolution,* was created in 1868 to promote women's causes. After its bankruptcy in 1870, Anthony lectured throughout the nation for 6 years to pay its $10,000 debt.

In the 1872 presidential race Susan Anthony and 15 Rochester comrades became the first women ever to vote in a national election. That they were promptly arrested for their boldness did not dismay her, as she sought to test women's legal right to vote under the 14th Amendment by carrying the case to the U.S. Supreme Court. Her case was singled out for prosecution, and trial was set for 1873 in Rochester. Free on bail of $1,000, Anthony stumped the country with a carefully prepared legal argument, "Is It a Crime for a U.S. Citizen to Vote?" She lost her case, following some dubious legal maneuvering by the judge, but was

unfortunately barred from appealing to the Supreme Court when her sentence was not made binding.

## Later Years

Susan Anthony spent the rest of her life working for the Federal suffrage amendment—a strenuous effort that took her not only to Congress but to political conventions, labor meetings, and lyceums in every section of the country. Mindful of the nearly total omission of women from historical literature, in 1877 she forced herself to sit down with her colleagues to begin the monumental and invaluable *History of Woman Suffrage* in five volumes. She later worked with her biographer, Ida Husted Harper, on two of the three volumes of *The Life and Work of Susan B. Anthony,* which were drawn largely from her continuous scrapbooks (1838-1900), now in the Library of Congress, and her diaries and letters.

Up to just one month before her death in 1906, Anthony was still active: she attended her last suffrage convention and her eighty-sixth birthday celebration in Washington. She closed her last public speech with the words, "Failure is impossible." When she died in her Rochester home on March 13, only four states had granted the vote to women. Fourteen years later the suffrage amendment, the 19th, was added to the Constitution.

## Further Reading

The most complete work on Anthony is Ida Husted Harper, *The Life and Work of Susan B. Anthony* (3 vols., 1898-1908). Katharine Anthony, a distant relative and noted biographer, had access to Miss Anthony's diaries and wrote the best recent biography, *Susan B. Anthony: Her Personal History and Her Era* (1954). Alma Lutz, *Susan B. Anthony: Rebel, Crusader, Humanitarian* (1959) and *Created Equal: A Biography of Elizabeth Cady Stanton* (1940), which also contains considerable material on Anthony, are more solid accounts than Rheta Childe Dorr, *Susan B. Anthony: The Woman Who Changed the Mind of a Nation* (1928). □

# Virginia Apgar

**Medical instructor and researcher Virginia Apgar (1909-1974) revolutionized the field of perinatology—the care of infants around the time of birth—with her development of the Apgar Newborn Scoring System. Her method of rating a newborn's health in five major categories allows doctors to quickly establish if a child requires medical attention. Implementation of this basic practice throughout the United States and around the world resulted in a significant increase in infant survival rates.**

Virginia Apgar contributed to many areas of medicine during her career, including anesthesiology, infant care, and the study and prevention of birth defects. It was her work with new babies and mothers, however, that has left the greatest mark in the health sciences. She was the creator of the Apgar Newborn Scoring System, a method of evaluating the health of infants minutes after birth in order to ensure the delivery of proper care. Apgar also contributed to infant health through her discovery that some anesthetics given to women during childbirth had a negative effect on babies. Her findings led doctors across the country to revise their use of painkillers during labor. Later in her career, Apgar was a vital force in the March of Dimes organization, where she directed research efforts, raised money, and educated the public about birth defects. Her lifetime of energetic work resulted in standard medical procedures for mothers and babies that have prevented thousands of infant deaths.

## Specialized in New Medical Field

Apgar was born on June 7, 1909, in Westfield, New Jersey. Her childhood home contained a basement laboratory, where her father pursued scientific experiments with electricity and radio waves and built a telescope. Perhaps due to this atmosphere of curiosity and inquiry, Apgar set her sights on a scientific career in the field of medicine. After graduating from high school, she entered Mount Holyoke College with the intention of becoming a doctor. Although she received scholarships that helped to pay for her tuition, she still had to take a number of jobs to support herself through college. Despite the extra work, she graduated with a bachelor's degree in 1929.

Apgar's financial situation did not improve when she enrolled at the College of Physicians and Surgeons at Columbia University in New York City the following September. A month later, the stock market crashed, signaling the beginning of the decade of economic turmoil known as the Great Depression. Determined to stay in school, Apgar borrowed money in order to complete her course work. She emerged in 1933 with a medical degree and a fourth-place rank in her graduating class, but also with the burden of a large financial debt. Her high marks earned her a much sought-after internship in surgery at Columbia, but during this period of training Apgar began to consider how she could best support herself in the medical profession. She saw that even male surgeons had trouble finding work in New York City, and as a woman in what was then a male-dominated profession, she realized that her chances of success were even slimmer. She felt that she was more likely to be successful in the field of anesthesia.

Traditionally, nurses had been responsible for administering anesthesia, but at that time greater emphasis was being to be placed on the importance of anesthetics; doctors had begun entering the field in the hopes of making breakthroughs that would allow for improved surgery techniques. Women physicians, in particular, were encouraged to pursue medical anesthesiology, perhaps because it was still considered a female realm. So after finishing her internship at Columbia in 1935, Apgar began a two-year residency program in anesthesiology, during which time she studied not only at Columbia, but also at the University of Wisconsin in Madison and Bellevue Hospital in New York.

Apgar's choice of career did allow her to realize her goal of securing a job. She was hired as director of the anesthesia division at Columbia University in 1938. Her new position, however, proved to be a challenging one. She was the only person in the anesthesia area, leaving her with a heavy workload. In addition, she struggled to get surgeons to recognize the anesthesiologist as a fellow doctor, not a subordinate, and she fought against the policy that prevented anesthesiologists from being allowed to charge standard doctor's fees. Eventually, Apgar and her department began to receive more support and respect—she gradually increased the number of physicians in the division and won sufficient funding for the area and its employees in 1941, after threatening to quit her post if the school refused her requests. After World War II, anesthesiology began gaining more attention across the nation as an area of specialty and research, and Columbia University created a separate department of anesthesia for training physicians and conducting research. When the chair of the new department was selected in 1949, however, Apgar was passed over in favor of a male anesthesiologist. Instead, she was named a full professor in the department, making her the first woman to reach such a level at Columbia.

## Apgar Newborn Scoring System Developed

It was in this position as a teacher and researcher that Apgar would make her greatest contributions to medicine over the next decade. She began to focus her work in the area of anesthesia used during childbirth. Apgar realized that the period immediately following birth was a critical time for many infants; however, babies were usually not evaluated carefully by doctors, who were often more concerned with the welfare of the mother. Because of this lack of an organized examination, many life-threatening conditions were not identified in infants. To provide a quick and efficient means of determining which babies required special care, she devised a five-part test that scored a child's heart rate, respiration, muscle tone, color, and reflexes. The test, known as the Apgar Newborn Scoring System, was to be scored one minute after birth; the recommended timing of the test was later expanded to five and ten minutes as well. Although developed in 1949, a description of the system was not published until 1953. It eventually became a world-wide standard among physicians. A study by Apgar involving a dozen hospitals and more than 17,000 infants evaluated by the Apgar score proved that the testing method was a predictable indicator of a child's survival and rate of development.

Another victory for infant health was won with Apgar's research into the effects of anesthesia given to mothers during childbirth. Collaborating with pediatrician L. Stanley James and anesthesiologist Duncan Holaday, Apgar monitored the blood levels, blood gases, and pH levels of newborns whose mother received anesthesia during labor. These measurements, combined with the application of the Apgar score system, were designed to indicate to doctors what kinds of problems—such as a low oxygen level or a pH imbalance in the blood—needed to be addressed if a baby was doing poorly. To take such measurements and facilitate treatments, Apgar became the first person to place a catheter in the umbilical artery, now a standard practice in neonatal care. In the course of her research, Apgar found that the anesthesia cyclopropane had a noticeable negative effect on a baby's overall condition. Immediately ceasing her use of the gas for mothers in labor, other doctors across the country quickly followed suit after Apgar published her findings.

## Conducted Birth Defect Research

After a more than twenty-year career at Columbia, Apgar left her post as professor to earn a master of public health degree at Johns Hopkins University. Her new career took her to the March of Dimes organization in 1959, where she was hired as the head of the division on congenital birth defects. In 1969, she became the head of the March of Dimes research program; during her three-year stint in this role she changed the foundation's emphasis from the prevention of the crippling disease polio to a concentrated effort to prevent birth defects. In an effort to educate the public about the topic, she gave many lectures and cowrote a book titled *Is My Baby All Right?* in 1972. Apgar left her research position in 1973 to become vice president for medical affairs and a fund-raiser. She was a great success in both roles, increasing donations to the charity and channeling the new money into research on birth defects, resulting in better prevention and treatment of many conditions. At the same time, she held a research fellowship at Johns Hopkins University and a position as clinical professor at Cornell University, where she became the first U.S. medical professor to specialize in birth defects.

During her lifetime, Apgar made significant contributions to science not only in the laboratory, but also in the classroom. She instructed hundreds of doctors and left a lasting mark on the field of neonatal care. Apgar received a number of awards recognizing her role in medicine. She was honored with the Ralph Waters Medal from the American Society of Anesthesiologists and the Gold Medal of Columbia University, was named Woman of the Year for 1973 by *Ladies' Home Journal,* and was the recipient of four honorary degrees. In addition, a prize in her name was founded by the American Academy of Pediatrics and an academic chair was created in her honor at Mount Holyoke College.

Apgar, who never married, was unrelenting in her pursuit of knowledge. In her sixties, she began a course of study in genetics at Johns Hopkins University. She also found time, however, for a number of personal interests, including music, gardening, photography, and stamp collecting. On August 7, 1974, Apgar died in New York City at the age of 65. She was remembered as an honest and encouraging teacher who inspired numerous doctors in their medical practice and research. The modern fields of anesthesiology and neonatal care are greatly indebted to her pioneering work.

## Further Reading

For more information see Apgar, Virginia, and Joan Beck, *Is My Baby All Right?: A Guide to Birth Defects,* Trident Press, 1972; Calmes, Selma, "Virginia Apgar: A Woman Physician's Career in a Developing Specialty," *Journal of the American Medical Women's Association,* November/December, 1984, pp. 184-188; Diamonstein, Barbaralee, *Open Secrets: Ninety-four Women in Touch with Our Time,* Viking Press, 1972; Vare, Ehlie Ann, and Greg Ptacek, *Mothers of Invention: From the Bra to the Bomb—Forgotten Women and Their Unforgettable Ideas,* William Morrow, 1988. □

# Diane Nemerov Arbus

**The American photographer Diane Nemerov Arbus (1923-1971) specialized in photographs of nontraditional subjects, including gays, the physically challenged, circus performers, and nudists.**

Diane Arbus was born Diane Nemerov on March 14, 1923. The daughter of a wealthy New York businessman (the family owned Russeks department store on Fifth Avenue), Arbus led a pampered childhood. Being a member of a prominent New York family, she grew up with a strong sense of what was "acceptable" and what was "prohibited" in polite society. Her world was a protected one in which she never felt adversity, yet it seemed to her to be an unreal world. Ludicrous as it may seem, the sense of being "immune" from hardship was painful for her. An extremely shy child, Arbus was often fearful but told no one of her fantasies. Her closest relationship was with her older brother, Howard.

From the seventh through the twelfth grade Arbus attended Fieldstone School in the Riverdale section of the Bronx, a part of the Ethical Culture educational system. Here she became interested in myths, ritual, and public spectacle, ideas which would later inform her photography. At Fieldstone she also devoted much time and energy to art class—painting, sketching, and working in clay. During this period of her life Arbus and several of her friends began exploring New York on their own, getting off the subway in unfamiliar areas of Brooklyn or the Bronx, observing and following interesting or unusual passersby.

At the age of 14 Diane met Allan Arbus, a 19-year-old City College student who was employed in the art department at Russeks. It was love at first sight. Her parents disapproved, but this only served to heighten Diane's resolve to marry him as soon as she came of age. In many ways, Allan represented an escape from all that was restricting and oppressive in her family life. They were married in a rabbi's chambers on April 10, 1941, with only their immediate families present.

## Early Career as Fashion Photographer

To ease financial pressures, Allan supplemented his job at Russeks by working as a salesman and also by doing some fashion photography. Arbus became his assistant. During

World War II when Allan was sent to a photography school near Fort Monmouth, New Jersey, Arbus moved to nearby Red Bank and set up a darkroom in their bathroom. Allan taught her everything he was learning at the school. In May of 1944 Allan was transferred to another photography school, this time in Astoria, Queens. Then, late in 1944, he was sent to Burma. By this time Diane was pregnant with their first child, Doon, who was born April 3, 1945.

During the 1940s Arbus studied briefly under photographer Berenice Abbott. After Allan's discharge from the army, husband and wife teamed up as fashion photographers, working for Russeks and Bonwit Teller. Their first magazine assignment appeared in the May 1947 issue of *Glamour* and marked the beginning of a long association with Condé Nast publishing firm. Their trademark was to shoot models in action. Yet the Arbuses despised the shallowness of the fashion industry. Her real joy during this period was photographing friends and relatives; often she wore her camera around her neck at family meals.

On April 16, 1954, Arbus gave birth to her second daughter, Army. In addition to her fashion work with Allan, she photographed children—strangers in Spanish Harlem, the offspring of close friends, and, of course, Doon and Amy. Throughout the 1950s she also found herself increasingly attracted to nontraditional subjects, people on the fringes of normal society. This provided a release from the oppression she felt in the fashion world. During these years she also suffered from recurring bouts of depression.

In 1957 the couple decided to make a change. He continued to run their fashion studio, freeing her to photograph subjects of her own choice. She briefly attended Alexey Brodovitch's workshop at the New School and, on her own, made a detailed study of the history of photography. But Arbus found herself most drawn to the photographs of her contemporaries Louis Faurer and Robert Frank and, especially, to the unusual images of Lisette Model. In 1958 Arbus enrolled in a class Model was offering at the New School.

It was during this period of work with Model that Arbus decided what she really wanted to photograph was "the forbidden." She saw her camera as a sort of license that allowed her to be curious and to explore the lives of others. Gradually overcoming her shyness, she enjoyed going where she never had, entering the lives and homes of others and confronting that which had been off-limits in her own protected childhood.

## Career with a "Candid Camera"

Model taught her to be specific, that close scrutiny of reality produces something fantastic. An early project Arbus undertook involved photographing what she referred to as "freaks." She responded to them with a mixture of shame and awe. She always identified with her subjects in a personal way. Model once referred to Arbus' "specific subject matter" as "freaks, homosexuals, lesbians, cripples, sick people, dying people, dead people." Instead of looking away from such people, as does most of the public, Arbus looked directly at these individuals, treating them seriously and humanely. As a result, her work was always original and unique.

When Arbus and her husband separated in 1960, her work became increasingly independent. During that period she began her series of circus images, photographing midget clowns, tattooed men, and sideshow subjects. She frequented Hubert's Freak Museum at Broadway and 42nd Street, fascinated by what she saw. She returned again and again until her subjects knew and trusted her. She also frequented the Times Square area, getting to know the bag ladies and derelicts.

Arbus posed her subjects looking directly into the camera, just as she looked directly at them. She said, "I don't like to arrange things; I arrange myself." For her, the subject was always more important than the picture. She firmly believed that there were things which nobody would see unless she photographed them. Arbus created photo essays of these subjects which she sold to magazines such as *Esquire, Harper's Bazaar,* and *Infinity.*

In the early 1960s Arbus began to photograph another group, nudists. She frequented nudist camps in New Jersey and Pennsylvania, agreeing to go naked herself in order to gain her subjects' trust. This period, 1962 to 1964, was a particularly productive one for her. Among Arbus' many accomplishments during this time was winning her first Guggenheim fellowship, which allowed her to photograph "American rites and customs, contests, festivals. . . ."

Three of Arbus' pictures were included in John Szarkowski's 1965 show at the Museum of Modern Art (MOMA), "Recent Acquisitions"—one of two female impersonators back stage and two from her series on nudists. Viewers were shocked and often repelled by these frank images. A few years later her work was included, along with that of Garry Winogrand and Lee Friedlander, in Szarkowski's "New Documents" exhibition at the MOMA. The show, which opened March 6, 1967, marked the pinnacle of Arbus' career and included some 30 examples of her work. One critic called her "the wizard of odds." Another asserted that she catered "to the peeping Tom in all of us."

From 1966 on Arbus struggled with bouts of hepatitis which often left her weak and depressed. Then, in 1969, Allan Arbus formally divorced her, marrying Mariclare Costello; soon after, they moved to California. During this difficult period Arbus photographed many of the leading figures of the 1960s: F. Lee Bailey, Jacqueline Susann, Coretta Scott King. She also did some lecturing at Cooper Union, Parsons, and Rhode Island School of Design in addition to giving a master class at Westbeth, the artists' community in which she lived.

Arbus committed suicide in her New York apartment on July 26, 1971. Perhaps the words of her longtime friend, photographer Richard Avedon, provide the most fitting epithet: "Nothing about her life, her photographs, or her death was accidental or ordinary." Her unique vision, her personal style, and the range of her subject matter provided a seminal influence in 20th-century photography.

## Further Reading

The standard work on Arbus' photography is the Aperture monograph *Diane Arbus* (1972). Patricia Bosworth's *Diane Arbus, a Biography* (1984) provides a good overview of the photographer's life. In addition, *Magazine Work* (1984), edited by Doon Arbus and Marvin Israel, includes both Arbus' own words and essays by those closest to her. Arbus is also included in Anne Tucker's *The Woman's Eye* (1973) and is the subject of numerous magazine and newspaper critiques. □

# Mary Kay Wagner Ash

**Texas make-up tycoon Mary Kay (Wagner) Ash (born ca. 1916) parlayed her early training in direct sales into a multi-million-dollar, Dallas-based cosmetics firm.**

Although her choice of a cosmetics career was not unique, Mary Kay Ash proved incomparable at combining the skills she had acquired selling books door-to-door with her understanding of marketing to women. Successful beauty product entrepreneurs before her had proved this a lucrative field for women. A few, such as Madame C.J. Walker, Elizabeth Arden, and Helena Rubenstein, had "invented" a specialized product line and established highly effective sales networks. It was Mary Kay's reliance on women as in-home salespersons, her use of a signature color—pink—as part of the corporate identity, and her shrewd incorporation of premiums and incentives (such as pink Cadillacs and diamond jewelry) into company sales plans that brought her such astonishing financial success.

Clinging to the rather time-worn convention that "a lady never reveals her age," Ash withheld the exact year in which her May 12th birth occurred; it is estimated by those who have known her to be 1916. She was born to Edward and Lula Wagner in rural Hotwells, Texas, and proved to be an eager and dependable student throughout her school years. She was, as well, a mainstay of her family; after her mother left each day for work, Ash prepared her physically challenged father's meals. Her capabilities and intellect were not sufficient, however, to lift her out of the domestic sphere. Due to her family's limited resources Ash was unable to go to college, and at age 17 she married and would go on to have three children.

During an era when it was uncommon for married women with a family to work outside the home, Ash became an employee of Stanley Home Products, often conducting several demonstration "parties" each day at which she sold company products, mostly to homemakers much like herself. As did many parents, Ash sought to provide the best for her children, and she believed that the quickest way to do so was for her to excel at a job. Energetic and a quick learner, Ash found that direct sales suited her well. She rose at Stanley to unit manager, a post that she held from 1938 to 1952. Although she spent a year studying at the University of Houston, she gave up on academics to return to the stimulation of sales challenges.

Following a divorce from her husband soon after the close of World War II, Ash moved in 1952 from her job at Stanley Home Products to a similar sales slot at World Gift Company, where she remained for another 11 years. Throughout this time she was refining her theory of marketing and sales: provide a quality product, target that product at a specified market, and offer sales incentives not only to the sales force but to the customer as well. During her years at Stanley, Ash had developed effective techniques and strategies, and it was her belief that other women were able to do the same in selling. However, she had hit glass ceilings at both companies, and eventually quit, hoping to write a book about her techniques.

Instead, in 1963 she founded her own company, originally named "Beauty by Mary Kay," a venture based primarily on a special skin care cream to which she had purchased the manufacturing rights. Since Ash had endured several decades of gender discrimination in the predominately male world of commerce and industry, she was determined in her own firm to offer career opportunities to any woman who was willing to devote the energy and creativity required to sell Mary Kay cosmetics. Before long she had built an effective force of female sales representatives who—like their doggedly positive chief executive officer— were eager to prove they were capable of *any* job.

Ash's second husband had died in 1963, only weeks after her company was established. She relied heavily on her oldest son to guide and advise her throughout the start-up phase of her cosmetics company; three years later she married Melville J. Ash and assumed the name that is so well-known today.

A relentless optimist with evangelical leanings, Ash published a carefully laundered autobiography in 1981; in 1984 she wrote *Mary Kay on People Management,* a volume that expanded on the now-familiar God-and-family theory of business success for women; and in 1995, she released another text on working women, *Mary Kay— You Can Have It All.* Among the tenets that she held as basic to her success was her idea that women needed to place "God first, family second, and career third."

Despite her conservative views, conventional approach to combining family and job responsibilities, and ultrafeminine appearance, Mary Kay Ash was a tough business person with a veteran's knowledge of marketing and sales. After her "semi-retirement" she served for a time at the Hastings Center, a think tank in Briarcliff Manor, New York.

Her predilection for flashy pink Cadillacs, gold-plated dinnerware, and layers of make-up aside, Ash helped innumerable women to careers and to the financial security that derives from earning one's own money. Though her personal views may not be typical of other women who have strived for their civil rights, Mary Kay nevertheless encouraged and empowered legions of women. Through her belief in women's abilities and her willingness to give them a chance, she made the dream of self-sufficiency a reality for hundreds of thousands of women worldwide.

Mary Kay Cosmetics now employs over 475,000 beauty consultants in over 25 countries throughout the world. Mary Kay Ash became involved in cancer research through fund raising after her husband, Mel, died of cancer in 1980. In 1993, she was honored with the dedication of the Mary Kay Ash Center for Cancer Immunotherapy Research at St. Paul Medical Center in Dallas. In 1996 a new foundation was started to research cancers which have historically affected women, the foundation was named the Mary Kay Ash Charitable Foundation.

To date, her autobiography *Mary Kay* has sold over one million copies. In 1987 Ash became the chairman emeritus of Mary Kay Inc.

## Further Reading

Mary Kay Ash published an autobiography, *Mary Kay* (1981), providing an overview of her personal life and career as a cosmetics entrepreneur. She followed this in 1984 with *Mary Kay on People Management* and in 1995 with *Mary Kay— You Can Have It All* . See also *Contemporary Authors,* Volume 112 (Detroit: Gale, 1985). She also has been profiled in magazines, including portraits, in *People* (July 29, 1985) and *Fortune* (September 20, 1993).Additional information can be obtained from the Mary Kay Inc. web site at http://www.marykay.com. ☐

# B

## Polly Baca-Barragán

**Elected to the Colorado House of Representatives and, later, to the state senate, Polly Baca-Barragán (born 1943) was the first Hispanic woman elected to those offices. She remains active in politics working on behalf of Mexican Americans and dealing with housing issues.**

Polly Baca-Barragán is a pioneer in the growing field of Hispanic woman politics. A Colorado State Senator for 12 years, Baca-Barragán was the first woman chair of the House Democratic Caucus, and in 1985 she was elected chair of the Senate Democratic Caucus. She was the first and only minority woman to be elected to the Colorado Senate and the first Hispanic Woman to serve in leadership in any State Senate in the United States. A longtime activist at the local, regional, and national levels with civic groups, she is nationally known for her leadership skills and motivational presentations.

Baca-Barragán was born in Greeley, Colorado, in 1943. She is the daughter of Spanish Americans José Manuel, a former migrant farm worker, and Leda Sierra, a strong and fiercely independent woman. From her mother Polly learned that "a woman must be her own person, independent and able to care for herself," Baca-Barragán stated in a 1988 interview contributor Gloria Bonilla-Santiago.

### Encounters Racism as a Child

One of Baca-Barragán's early memories is from grade school, where she first began to notice racial discrimination. She and her family went to church and saw little girls inside in white dresses; somehow, Baca-Barragán knew she wanted to be seated with them. But the ushers came and told her family they had to sit on the side aisle because they were "Mexican Americans." The center aisles were reserved for the Anglos who went to that church. In her interview, Baca-Barragán recalled clearly the experience: "They assumed we were Mexican American from the other side of the tracks. They didn't want us there. My mother forced my father to move into a low-income, racially mixed neighborhood, but it was not the Spanish neighborhood. We called it the Spanish American colony because we were from Colorado and from the old Spanish families. My mother was the strength in my family."

At fourteen, Baca-Barragán's father was killed in an accident, and shortly after her mother died. She literally had to assume the role of an adult even though she had no role models. She raised her three younger brothers using common sense. She loved them and she did what she thought her mother would have done. Motivated by her neighbor, Baca-Barragán finished high school and won a scholarship to attend college. She recollected in her interview that she "wanted to go to Colorado State University and major in Physics. My chemistry teacher told me about Madame Curie and told me I couldn't succeed in public life because I was 'Mexican American,' but I could in the scientific field because they had to judge you by what you were. So that's what I decided to be, a physics major. The principal at that high school was very bigoted. She tried to discourage me from applying to the state university."

Although Baca-Barragán began university studies with a major in physics, she was soon drawn back to her ninth-grade desire to enter a field of power—law and politics. She plunged into campus politics, taking the vice presidency, and later the presidency, of the university Young Democ-

Caucus, and in 1985, she was elected chair of the Senate Democratic caucus. She was the first minority woman to be elected to the Colorado Senate and the first Hispanic woman to serve in leadership in any State Senate in the United States.

In her interview Baca-Barragán recalled a personal note Senator Edward Kennedy sent to her with his best personal wishes during her Legislative campaign, saying, "We need more representation of the Chicano community in public office as we need more women, and Polly's the best of both. . . . She will represent a progressive, bright, and effective addition to the state legislature, one who will speak for all the people of her district."

As a freshman legislator in the Colorado House of Representatives, Baca-Barragán broke an old rule of the seniority system which imposed a "watch and wait" attitude on first termers. In the 1975 session of the Colorado Legislature, she introduced nine House bills and carried six Senate bills in the House. Two of these House bills and three of Senate bills were passed by both houses and signed into law by the governor. Throughout her term she sponsored 201 more House bills and 57 additional Senate bills. Of these, 156 passed both houses and are now law. Some of her most notable bills are Senate Bill 118, providing for the protection of deposits of public monies held by the state and national banks (1986); Senate Bill 87, providing authority to the Colorado district courts to enforce foreign subpoenas, (1985); Senate Bill 139, concerning assessment of civil money penalties by the state banking board, (1985); House Bill 1117, continuing the short-term-loan revolving fund in the division of housing, (1985); House Bill 1336, regulating the operation of non state post-secondary institutions in Colorado by the Colorado Commission of Higher Education, and many others.

As the *Denver Post* summarized, Baca-Barragán was known in Colorado as "a democratic senator representing 63,000 Adams County resident. On the other hand, she is the Colorado politician who has the closest ties to the nation's Democratic Leadership in Washington, D.C. . . . In fact, Barragan, has better, more open links to the White House than Gov. Dick Lamm and other Democratic leaders in Colorado." Throughout her work Baca-Barragán won the respect of many leaders in the state of Colorado and nationally. By any standards, she must be judged a good policy maker.

Part of her success is attributable to her many volunteer and civic activities, which she has pursued throughout her career and which she views as a basic training ground for any politician. These activities included Chicano and minority activism, party politics, women's rights, professional and business development, and political and community organizing. Locally, she worked on the Board of Trustees of Labor's Community Agency, the Latin American Research and Service Agency, the Mile High United Way, and she has been on the Policy Advisory Council on the Division of the State Compensation Insurance Fund. On a broader scale, she served on the boards of the National Chicano Planning Council and Mexican American Legal Defense and Education Fund (MALDEF) and many others.

rats; she was also secretary for her freshman class. Active as a volunteer for congressional campaigns, Baca-Barragán was a student volunteer of the Viva Kennedy Clubs for John F. Kennedy and worked as an intern for the Colorado Democratic Party.

After receiving her B.A. in political science in 1962, Baca-Barragán was recruited to work as an editorial assistant for a trade union newspaper in Washington, D.C. Shortly after, she was recruited to work for President Lyndon Johnson's administration as a public information officer for a White House agency. Next she joined the national campaign staff of the late Senator Robert F. Kennedy in his bid for President of the United States in 1968. That same year she served as the director of research and information for the National Council of La Raza in Phoenix, Arizona, where she met her husband, Miguel Barragán, a Chicano activist and former priest. The marriage produced two children, Monica and Mike, before ending in divorce. A few years later, adding to a long list of "firsts," Polly became an assistant to the Chairman of the Democratic National Committee. Shortly after, she opened a public relations business in Adams County after returning to Colorado, where her professional experiences blossomed into her political career.

## Wins Election in Colorado

In 1974, Polly Baca-Barragán won Colorado's 34th district seat in the state's House of Representatives, and four years later she was elected to the Colorado State Legislature as the first Hispanic woman senator. In 1977, she was elected the first woman chair of the House Democratic

Baca-Barragán told the *Denver Post* that she is especially proud of her part in the founding of the National Congress of Hispanic American Citizens, better known as "El Congreso," the country's first and only full-time Latino lobby at the nation's Capitol. Her experience at the state legislative committee level reads like a Who's Who of committee assignments: Rules; Business Affairs and Labor; Finance; Local Government; Agriculture, National Resources and Energy; Transportation; School Finance; State Affairs; Health, Environment, Welfare and Institutions; Legislative Audit; and Education. Baca-Barragán's legislation, moreover, has always been people-oriented. For example, in 1986 Polly Baca-Barragán introduced innovative legislation to correct inequitable financial burdens on Colorado property tax-payers, while still providing quality education. In addition, she introduced legislation to protect public monies in state national banks. In 1980 and again in 1984, she was elected Co-Chair of the Democratic National Convention and chaired the Colorado delegation to the 1978 Democratic Mid-term Conference. Baca-Barragán also gladly shared her extensive foreign affairs experience as a participant and panelist to major international conferences in Columbia, Mexico, the USSR, Israel, Egypt, Lebanon, Canada, Belgium, and West Germany.

It was her track record of performance and success at the national level as Senator that motivated her to be a candidate for the U.S. Congress in 1986. In a personal interview for *Hispanic Women Breaking Ground and Barriers,* Baca-Barragán commented on the disappointment she felt after losing the race: "I've had two great pains in my life. The divorce was rejection by a male . . . but that's how I perceived it. The other was when I lost my race for Congress. This was rejection because I was an Hispanic woman. That's the only reason I lost that race. It's a great deal of pain. I don't know of a pain that is greater and that's why people don't take risks. It's a lack of confidence that you can't succeed or the willingness to withstand the rejection if you fail."

After the long campaign, Baca-Barragán retired from public office and became President of Sierra Baca Systems, a consulting firm specializing in program development and assessment, leadership training, issue analysis and motivational presentations. In addition, Baca-Barragán has frequently appeared as a political commentator on both television and radio. She is nationally known for her leadership skills and for breaking ground in the area of politics for Latinas in the United States.

In 1988, she was honored as one of the original 14 members to be inducted into the National Hispanic Hall of Fame and being listed in the World Who's Who of Women. Though Baca-Barragán has no political aspirations at present, she continues to be active with national civic groups and serves on a bipartisan Commission on National Political Conventions. More recently, Baca-Barragán has been devoting her time to heading up the Colorado Institute for Hispanic Education and Economic Empowerment, whose mission is to "create a pool of Hispanic leaders who are sensitive to cultural differences and gender issues, and who will jump on the fast track to leadership positions," according to Mercedes Olivera in *Vista.* "If we are to have social cohesiveness as a nation," Baca-Barragán related in *Vista,* "I feel strongly that we have to value the other people, their value system, culture, history. If we honor those differences, then we can look at the human thread that unites us all as human beings." □

# Joan Baez

**American folk singer Joan Baez (born 1941) was recognized for her non-violent, anti-establishment, and anti-war positions. She used her singing and speaking talents to denounce violations of human rights in a number of countries.**

By the age of 22, Joan Baez was already known as the "queen of folk singers." Her rich and varied early experiences contributed significantly to her later "anti-establishment" attitudes. Her father, Albert V. Baez, was a physicist who came to the United States from Mexico at a very early age, and her mother was of West-European descent. Joan inherited her father's dark complexion, and the occasional racial prejudice she suffered as a child probably led to her later involvement in the civil rights movement. Although as an adult she claimed not to share her parents' Quaker faith, it undoubtedly contributed to what some called her keen "social conscience."

One of three sisters, Baez was born on January 9, 1941, in Staten Island, New York. She was exposed to an intellectual atmosphere with classical music during her childhood, but rejected piano lessons in favor of the guitar and rock and roll.

Her father's research and teaching positions took the family to various American and foreign cities. She attended high school in Palo Alto, California, where she excelled in music more than in academic subjects. Shortly after her high school graduation in 1958, her family moved to Boston where Baez's interest in folk music surfaced after visiting a coffeeshop where amateur folk singers performed.

## From Boston Coffee Houses to Newport

She briefly attended Boston University where she made friends with several semi-professional folk singers from whom she learned much about the art. In addition to simple folk songs, she began to sing Anglo-American ballads, blues, spirituals, and songs from various countries. As she worked to develop her technique and repertoire, Baez began to perform professionally in Boston coffeehouses and quickly became a favorite of Harvard students. She was also noticed by other folk singers, including Harry Belafonte, who offered her a job with his singing group.

In the summer of 1959 she was invited to sing at the Newport (Rhode Island) Folk Festival. That performance made her a soaring phenomenon—especially to young people—and led to friendships with other important folk singers such as the Seeger family and Odetta. Although that

performance brought her offers to make recordings and concert tours, she decided to resume her Boston coffeeshop appearances.

After her second Newport appearance in 1960, Baez made her first album for Vanguard Records, simply labelled *Joan Baez,* which was an immediate success. She was then such a "hot item" that she could tell CBS what songs she would sing and what props she would use in her appearance. In the following years Baez sang to capacity crowds on American college campuses and concert halls and on several foreign tours. Her eight gold album and one gold single awards attested to her popularity as a singer.

Her soprano voice has been described as "so clear and so luminously sensual that it reminded everyone of their first loves." She had no need to take lessons to enhance her voice, which ranged over three octaves, but she needed practice in order to achieve command of the guitar.

### Politics a Source of Controversy

While many critics agreed that her untrained singing voice was unusually haunting, beautiful, and very soothing, they saw her spoken words, lifestyle, and actions as discordant and sometimes anti-American. In the turbulent 1960s, Baez became a center of controversy when she used her singing and speaking talents to urge non-payment of taxes used for war purposes and to urge men to resist the draft during the Vietnam War. She helped block induction centers and was twice arrested for such violations of the law. She had already studied, understood, and adopted non-

violent strategies as a way to effect changes where she perceived injustices to exist.

She was married to David Harris, a draft resister, in March 1968. She was pregnant with their son, Gabriel, in April 1969 and three months later saw her husband arrested for refusing induction into the military forces. (He spent the next 20 months in a federal prison in Texas.)

### Baez Creates A Stir Among American Left

In the early 1970s, Baez began to speak with less stridence and by the end of the decade had offended dozens of her former peace-activist allies, such as Jane Fonda and attorney William Kunstler, when she publicly denounced the atrocities in Vietnam's Communist "re-education" centers. As she had done in the case of Chile and Argentina (without public outcries from former associates), Baez called for human rights to be extended to those centers in post-war Vietnam. Although her position seemed similar to that of Western intellectuals, it nevertheless created a stir among the American left (some of whom called for her own re-education). When some asked what right any American had to criticize the Communist government for anything it was doing after what the United States had done to the Vietnamese, she responded: "The same right we have to help anyone anywhere who is a prisoner of conscience."

### Baez' Career Through the 1980s and '90s

In later years Baez' singing career faltered despite various attempts to revive it. Her 1985 effort featured a more conventional hairstyle and attire. Her supporters believed she would regain her prominence in the entertainment industry because her voice, although deeper, retained the same qualities which earlier made her so successful. Meanwhile, she was quite busy throughout the world as the head of the Humanitas International Human Rights Committee, which concentrated on distracting (in any possible non-violent way) those whom it believed exercised illegitimate power.

Baez has continued to make music and to influence younger performers. In 1987, Baez released *Recently,* her first studio solo album in eight years. She was nominated for a 1988 Best Contemporary Folk Recording Grammy Award for the song "Asimbonanga" from the album. Also in 1988, Baez recorded *Diamonds and Rust in the Bullring* in Bilbao, Spain. The album was released the following April. In 1990, Baez toured with the Indigo Girls and the threesome were recorded for a PBS video presentation, *Joan Baez In Concert.* In 1991, she released a compilation album, *Brothers In Arms,* featuring two new tracks. In 1993, two more Baez recordings were released: *Play Me Backwards,* consisting of new material; and *Rare, Live & Classic,* a retrospective of her career from 1958 to 1989, featuring 22 previously unreleased tracks. Another compilation CD, *Live At Newport,* containing previously unreleased performances from the 1963, 1964 and 1965 Newport Folk Festivals was released by Vanguard records in 1996. Baez released another solo album, *Gone from Danger,* in early 1997.

The singer's interest in politics and human rights has continued as well. In 1993, she was invited by Refugees

International to travel to Bosnia-Herzegovina in order to help bring attention to the suffering there. In September of that same year, Baez became the first major artist to perform in a professional concert on Alcatraz Island (the former Federal Penitentiary) in San Francisco to benefit her sister Mimi Farina's organization, Bread & Roses. She returned to the island for a second benefit in 1996 along with the Indigo Girls and Dar Williams. She has also supported the gay and lesbian cause, joining Janis Ian in a performance at the National Gay and Lesbian Task Force's *Fight the Right* fundraising event in San Francisco in 1995.

## Further Reading

Bits of biographical data about Joan Baez may be found in her book *Daybreak* (1968) and in *Coming Out* (1971), which she co-authored with husband, David Harris. The latter chronicles a brief period after Harris's release from prison for draft evasion. The best sources for additional information about her anti-war activities are news and popular periodicals from 1968 to 1977.

Baez's 1987 autobiography, *And A Voice To Sing With*, is an excellent source of information as well. Other current sources include the January 17, 1997 issue of *Goldmine* in which she is profiled in an extensive 14-page cover story by Bill Carpenter.

Baez can be found on the web at http://baez.woz.org and on the *A&E Biography* site at http://www.biography.com/find/find.html. □

# Florence Merriam Bailey

**Florence Merriam Bailey (1863-1948) wrote numerous works for a wide range of people interested in birding.**

A prominent ornithologist, Florence Merriam Bailey wrote numerous works for a wide range of people interested in birding. In addition to publishing technical guides for specialists in the field, Bailey was able to pique the interest of young people and novices through her informative and entertaining books.

The last of four children, Florence Augusta Merriam was born to Clinton Levi Merriam and Caroline Hart Merriam on August 8, 1863, in Locust Grove, a New York village in Lewis County. Merriam's mother was the daughter of County Judge Levi Hart. Her father, a merchant banker, retired about the time Merriam was born.

Merriam's love of nature was inspired by the natural setting of her family's home in the foothills of the Adirondack Mountains. It was also nurtured by her father and by her brother, Clinton, a physician and a naturalist, who eventually became the chief of the U.S. Biological Survey.

Because she planned to be a writer, Merriam attended the newly-opened Smith College in Northampton, Massachusetts, for four years as a special student. Although she left in 1886 without a degree, Smith awarded her one in 1921.

While at Smith, Merriam led nature groups into the countryside, founded one of the nation's first Audubon societies, and wrote articles on birds for *Audubon Magazine*.

The Audubon articles became the core of her first book, *Birds through an Opera Glass* (1889), which was part of a series for young people. The first book's entertaining style, enhanced by close observation and enthusiasm for the subjects, became Merriam's hallmark.

In addition to her love of nature, Merriam was also interested in people. During the summer of 1891 she worked a month at a Chicago school for working girls, and that same winter she worked in a working girl's club in New York City. Her social service was curtailed when she contracted tuberculosis, an illness that prompted Merriam to travel west in 1893 in search of a better climate in which to recover.

Life in a small Utah town led to Merriam's *My Summer in a Mormon Village* (1894), a description of everyday Mormon life. From Utah, Merriam traveled to Palo Alto, California, where she attended Stanford University for six months. In the spring of 1894, she visited Twin Oaks, an area of California, to take notes on birds, and then moved on to observe in the mountains of Arizona.

Her trip west had a profound influence on her career. *A Birding on a Bronco* (1896), her first big western bird book, written for beginners in ornithology, became one of the first popular American bird guides. Merriam's *Handbook of the Birds of the Western United States* (1902) complemented Frank Chapman's *Handbook of Birds of Eastern North America* (1895). The handbook became a standard reference book—informative, succinct, technical, and filled with illustrations of the area's hundreds of species.

*Birds of New Mexico* (1928), originally intended for inclusion in a Biological Survey report, became in Merriam's hands a comprehensive book for general use. It won her the Brewster Medal of the American Ornithologist's Union in 1931—she was the first woman to be thus honored. Two years later she received an honorary LL.D. from the University of New Mexico.

Both the handbook and the New Mexico volumes contain substantial contributions by biologist Vernon Bailey, who later became the chief naturalist of the U.S. Biological Survey. Merriam met Vernon at her brother's home in Washington, D.C., and married him on December 16, 1899. Shortly after their marriage, Vernon began a series of biological field trips to New Mexico, often accompanied by Florence. Over the years, each contributed to the other's books. Her New Mexico book and his *Mammals of New Mexico* (1931) are considered classics on western natural history.

Although Florence looked delicate, her arduous travels testified to her stamina and unflagging spirit. From one end of the country to the other, the Baileys journeyed by railroad, wagon, pack train, or on foot. Although the couple remained childless, Florence aimed to transmit her love of birds to young people. The subtitle of her fourth book, *Birds of Village and Field: A Bird Book for Beginners,* suggests that she had youngsters in mind.

When the Baileys were not away on a field trip, their home in Washington, D.C., was a gathering place for amateur and professional naturalists, young and old. Florence tirelessly promoted the Audubon Society of Washington, D.C., which she helped to found in 1887. She also directed and taught the society's program for teachers of nature studies.

The last major work of Florence Merriam Bailey, *Among the Birds in the Grand Canyon National Park* (1939), was published by the National Park Service just four years before her husband's death and nearly ten years before her own death on September 22, 1948, of myocardial degeneration. She is buried on the grounds of her childhood home in Locust Grove, New York.

In addition to Bailey's books, a tribute to her work in the West lives on in a resident of the higher mountains of southern California. A form of a chickadee, *Parus gambeli baileyae,* was named for her in 1908.

### Further Reading

Oehser, Paul H., "Bailey, Florence Augusta Merriam," in *Notable American Women: A Biographical Dictionary,* edited by Edward James, Belknap Press, 1971.

Welker, Robert H., "Bailey, Florence Augusta Merriam," in *Dictionary of American Biography,* Supplement Four, 1946-1950, edited by John Garraty and Edward James, Scribner, 1974. □

# Ella Josephine Baker

**American activist Ella Baker (1903-1986) was the consummate organizer and unsung brains behind many of the most effective African American civil rights and political organizations in the twentieth century.**

Ella Baker's democratic vision and grass-roots activism left an indelible imprint on African American civil rights and political movements in the twentieth-century. She was regarded as a brilliant strategist, a radical intellectual, and superb organizer. Her political legacy forever linked criticisms of racism and gender-based discrimination to criticisms of capitalism and social imperialism. She combined liberation rhetoric with direct activism, and developed strong internal structures that made organizational growth and progress possible. Baker was a proponent of the "under class," and believed "ordinary" people could become political leaders. An article in *Black Scholar* attributed her low profile in the civil rights movement to her preference of taking political directives from the poor and working class, rather than civil rights elites, some of whom marginalized her and the importance of her contributions. Baker considered herself a facilitator, rather than a leader and she believed in the strength and power of the common man to help themselves.

Political activism began shaping her life in Harlem during the Great Depression. She helped found and eventually became coordinator, and then director of the Young Negroes Cooperative League (YNCL), which organized stores and buying clubs to achieve economic self-sufficiency among the African American community. This experience, along with that of writing about New York City's African American domestics, deepened her understanding of the relationship between politics and economic exploitation of people according to gender, race, and class. She went on to establish a grass-roots field network for the National Association for the Advancement of Colored People (NAACP), becoming a national leader in the 1940s. She became the first director of the Southern Christian Leadership Conference (SCLC) in the 1950s and was a founder of and adviser to the Student Nonviolent Coordinating Committee (SNCC) in the 1960s. She worked well into her 70s with numerous political organizations to further social and racial justice. Baker was always striving to form a bridge among different socio-economic groups to foster communication and cooperation.

## A Heritage of Strength

Born in Norfolk, Virginia, and raised in Littleton, North Carolina, Ella Josephine Baker was the middle child of educated parents who were active participants in community life. *Black Scholar* describes her early years as somewhat protected and privileged. She was part of a close-knit racially proud family, whose ancestors had been community leaders with a southern African American tradition of

cooperating with and helping one another that was carried on by her family. They were not wealthy, but were able to send her to Shaw boarding school in Raleigh for high school—there was no secondary school in Littleton. She excelled academically, and continued her education at Shaw University, a conservative institution with a "classical" curriculum of literature, philosophy, foreign languages, and mathematics. Her sense of social justice began to form while she was a student; she led several protests against strict rules, such as not being allowed to wear silk stockings on campus. She majored in sociology, and graduated as valedictorian of the class of 1927.

## A Time of Testing

Full of energy, idealism, and possibilities, she rejected an offer to teach school realizing that mostly white school boards would control her future. Instead, on the eve of the Great Depression, she moved to New York City—worlds apart from the confines of university life. She was appalled by the suffering, poverty, and hunger, as well as the sense of desperation that hung over the streets of Harlem. Her first job was as a waitress. Rather than succumb to exploitation, she started organizing with others for jobs and helped found The Young Negroes Cooperative League (YNCL) as a means to help people save money and gain economic power by buying collectively. As a group organizer, she learned first-hand the devastation caused by the Depression. Elected to be the YNCL's first national director, she viewed the organization as a proving ground for communalism and interdependency. Such groups were branded as radical because they embraced socialism and some forms of communism; in fact, the YNCL resembled Baker's memory of the cooperative community environment in which she grew up. The YNCL was based on democratic principles, for men and women alike, and its leaders were drawn from the membership.

Throughout the 1930s Baker was involved in numerous organizations, but a few were particularly influential in her development as a social activist. One was the Workers Education Project, which was part of the Works Progress Administration (WPA). There, in addition to teaching subjects that enabled people to re-enter the workforce, she came in contact with left-wing activists and the growing union movement. Others, such as the Women's Day Workers and Industrial League, a union for domestic workers; the Harlem Housewives Cooperative; and the Harlem Young Women's Christian Association (YWCA), brought her in touch with her identity as an African American woman. She began to consider how social, political, and government structures exploited race, and refused to be classified as anything other than a "person." Even in marriage she did not assume her husband's last name, an act that was considered highly unusual in the 1930s. She commented, "I began to see that there were certain social forces over which the individual had very little control. It wasn't an easy lesson for me to learn, but I was able to learn it. It was out of that context that I began to explore; more in the area of ideology and the theory of social change. . . . I began to confront poverty, to identify to some extent with the unemployed. . ."

## Oppression on the Block

Baker had the opportunity to see people's lives from many different venues, including that of a reporter. In 1935 she co-authored with Marvel Cooke an exposé on the precarious situations of African-American domestic workers. Entitled "The Bronx Slave Market," the sexual and racial exploitation unique to African American women was described. Both writers posed as domestics looking for jobs in the "slave marts," auction blocks where day workers negotiated wages, as part of their research. With 15 million Americans without jobs and savings, the Depression intensified the poverty conditions tying African Americans to domestic service. Wages ranged from 15 to 30 cents an hour. In desperation, African Americans turned to the federal government for assistance, which although it provided a safety net for some, failed to include domestic work in most legislation—and did nothing to establish a basic wage. The dehumanizing experience of facing derision from "respectable" wage earners, as well as fraudulent employment agencies that bilked workers' wages, lead Baker to conclude that economic justice should be the primary objective in political struggles. According to *Black Scholar,* her labor activism placed "work" central to critiques of racism, classism, and sexism; and made the struggles against racism and sexism indispensable to dismantling economic oppression.

## Into the Mainstream

In 1940, Baker started working with the NAACP as a field secretary and from 1943-1946 as director of branches criss-crossing the south and establishing a vast network of contacts. Baker disagreed with the NAACP's reliance on legal approaches to combat discrimination, advocating instead a strategy that would involve the entire membership. Also impatient with the organization's bureaucracy, she resigned, but volunteered as president of the New York branch.

In the 1950s, her interests turned to the growing southern civil rights movement. Along with two friends, she founded In Friendship, an organization that raised money to help organizations, such as the Montgomery Improvement Association, which coordinated the bus boycott, as well as needy individuals who lost property in retribution for their participation. The advent of the Southern Christian Leadership Conference (SCLC), which was formed to maximize the momentum generated by the Montgomery boycott, rendered the smaller organization unnecessary. Baker joined the SCLC as its first director working along side Dr. Martin Luther King, Jr., even though they had differences of opinion on leadership issues. For two years she coordinated the SCLC's voter rights campaign, called Crusade for Citizenship, expanded grass-roots participation, and ran the office. Eventually, however, she resigned due to her strong belief that the organization was relying too heavily on King's persona to mobilize people.

Coincidentally, about the same time, students in Greensboro, North Carolina, led a successful desegregation sit-in. Baker immediately shifted her attention to maximizing this new activism among African-American students, and took a job with the local YWCA in order to be nearby and involved. Under her direction, a new independent youth organization, the Student Nonviolent Coordinating Committee (SNCC), was formed as an alternative to more politically moderate organizations. Egalitarian in structure, it was based on grass-roots democracy managed on a local level, which gave women, young people, and the poor a chance to become leaders. This organization epitomized Baker's philosophy of sharing knowledge and skills with others, which PBS later captured in a documentary, *Fundi: The Story of Ella Baker. Fundi* is a Swahili word meaning "one who hands down a craft from one generation to another."

*Black Scholar* noted that the SNCC distinguished itself by using mass direct-action tactics and by going into rural areas of the Deep South, where racism and violence were worst. The SNCC lead a wave of sit-in demonstrations throughout the South and became one of the most effective student movements in US history. It remained an independent organization, declining to become affiliated with the SCLC, a decision supported by Baker that reinforced her split with the SCLC.

Baker taught people not to be ashamed of their race, made them believe in themselves, and understand the power of unity. Behind the scenes and out of the limelight, she nurtured generations of African Americans to keep the spirit of freedom going. While she was content to work in supportive roles, she urged African American women to take up their struggle for equality. She explained the social environment of the 1950s and 1960s: "The movement . . . was carried largely by women, since it came out of church groups. It was sort of second nature to women to play a supportive role. . . . [I]t's true that the number of women who carried the movement is much larger than that of men. Black women have had to carry this role, and I think the younger women are insisting on an equal footing." Always a pioneer, Baker anticipated and encouraged the next wave of social activism in the 1970s and 1980s.

Baker's later years were spent advising countless organizations. She was an organizer who identified with all people, and who sought to create change by empowering people to act on their own behalf. Ella Baker died in New York, New York in 1986 and left behind a legacy that lived well beyond her eighty-three years.

### Further Reading

*Black Women in America,* edited by Darlene Clark Hine, Carlson Publishing, 1993.
*Notable Black American Women,* Gale, 1992.
*Papers of the Southern Christian Leadership Conference, 1954-1970,* University Publications of America, 1995.
*Black Scholar,* Fall, 1994.
*Journal of Black Studies,* May, 1996. □

# Josephine Baker

**Josephine Baker (1906-1975) was a Parisian dancer and singer, the most famous American expatriate in France.**

Josephine Baker was born in a poor, Black slum in East St. Louis, Illinois, on June 3, 1906, to 21-year-old Carrie MacDonald. Her mother hoped to be a music hall dancer; meanwhile, she was forced to take in laundry. She was of mixed ethnic background: Indian/Negro (as they would say in 1906) or Native American/African American (as we would say today). She descended from Apalachee Indians and Black slaves in South Carolina. Olive-skinned Eddie Carson, her father, was a vaudeville drummer and was not seen much by his daughter.

At the age of eight Josephine was hired out to a white woman as a maid; she was forced to sleep in the coal cellar with a pet dog and was scalded on the hands when she used too much soap in the laundry. At the age of ten she returned, thankfully, to school. "There is no Santa Claus," she said. "I'm Santa Claus." Josephine witnessed the cruel East St. Louis race riot of 1917. She moved from the St. Louis area at the age of 13 and emigrated out of the United States at 19. "That such a childhood produced an expatriate is not surprising," Phyllis Rose, one of her biographers, commented.

"Because I was born in a cold city, because I felt cold throughout my childhood . . . I always wanted to dance on

the stage," Josephine offered as explanation of why she was determined to be a dancer (in the first of her five autobiographies). From watching the dancers in a local vaudeville house she "graduated" to dancing in a touring show based in Philadelphia (where her grandmother lived) at age 16. She had already been married twice: to Willie Wells (for a few weeks in 1919) and to Will Baker (for a short time in 1921). She took her second husband's name as her own—Josephine Baker.

It is hard to discover true biographical facts, especially when it comes to show people. We know that Josephine joined the chorus line of the touring show of *Shuffle Along* in Boston in August 1922. The comedy was produced in Manhattan by a renowned African American songwriting team, Noble Sissle and Eubie Blake; it was the first all-Black Broadway musical. Subsequently, Josephine was in New York for the *Chocolate Dandies* (at the Cotton Club) and the floor show at the Plantation Club in Harlem (with Ethel Waters). She drew the attention of the audience (at the end of the chorus line) by clowning, mugging, and improvising. With her long legs, slim figure, and comic interludes, her special style as an entertainer evolved.

## Baker Goes to Paris

African American performers were established in France already in the 1920s. "Bricktop" (Ada Smith, with her signature red hair) had moved from Harlem to Paris, where she owned a locally famous nightclub on the rue Pigalle. Bricktop claimed to have taught Josephine personal grooming, clothes-sense, and even writing—everything—from the moment the younger woman's arrived in Paris in October 1925. This is an exaggeration. Josephine went to Paris for a top salary ($250 a week; more than twice what she was paid in New York) to gyrate at the Théâtre des Champs Elysées as a variety dancer in *La Revue Nègre*. With other African Americans, including jazz star Sidney Bechet, she introduced *le jazz hot* and went on to international fame on the wave of French intoxication for American jazz and exotic nudity.

The Parisian cultural scene was ready for things African in the 1920s. African American music had penetrated to such European classical composers as Debussy, Ravel, and Stravinsky since at least 1908. But Parisians became aware of jazz only in the 1920s (the first jazz band in Paris played in 1917). African art and sculpture was one of the influences on the Cubist movement and Art Deco. Josephine's oval head, resembling a temple sculpture, and lithe body, her "geometry" (according to *Dance Magazine*) was perfect for anything Cubist or in the Art Deco style.

She was the favorite of artists and left-intellectuals such as Picasso, Pirandello, Georges Roualt, Le Corbusier, e.e. cummings, Jean Cocteau, Aleksander Wat, and Ernest Hemingway (who thought she was "the most beautiful woman there is, there ever was, or ever will be," in hyperbole). But Josephine had not been to Africa and she knew nothing of the culture there, at that time. She had a relatively small repertoire of dance steps ("Charleston knock-knees for eight counts, camel-walk eight counts") and a small vocal repertoire, too (her keynote song, "J'ai deux amours,"

was repeated over and over again in various contexts); but the core materials were absolutely perfect with her body style and fitted to the era.

Josephine endured a breach-of-contract lawsuit about her abandoning *Le Revue Nègre* for a star billing at the *Folies-Bergère* in 1926. (The legal case was one of many in her life.) She was 20 when she was a sensation in the "jungle" banana dance: naked but for a string of rubber bananas around her waist. Soon banana-clad Josephine dolls were selling like hot cakes! Feet stomping, elbows flapping, knees bent, she would bump and grind a Charleston, puffing out her cheeks and crossing her eyes and always having a perpetual grin on her face (as stated by *American Heritage*). She was likened to a snake, a giraffe, and a hummingbird. Also, in 1926, she recorded her throaty voice for the first time. Magazine covers and posters added to her fame.

In December 1926 she opened her own nightclub in Pigalle called Chez Joséphine (later moved to rue Francois I, a more fashionable spot). She became a chic, affluent woman with expensive idiosyncracies, like parading her pet leopard down the elegant Champs Elysées. She went on a world tour for two years in 1928-1930, and received thousands of love letters. But back in France she said: "I don't want to live without Paris. . . . It's my country. . . . I want to be worthy of Paris." In addition she met, in the fall of 1926, Pepito Abatino, a Sicilian "count" who became her lover and manager (until about 1935, when they split up in anger, Abatino still loving her). In 1934 she took a title part in an operetta, a revival of Offenbach's *La Créole* at the Théâtre Marigny, opening in December for a six-month run. Josephine was in America with the *Ziegfeld Follies* in 1936 when Abatino died. While he was alive, Abatino helped Josephine evolve from a mere eccentric dancer to integrating her songs and speech and dance in performances; from being "the highest-paid chorus girl in vaudeville" to being "one of the high-paid stars in the world," in part by controlling her scripts and the first two volumes of her memoirs. Returning to the *Follies* in the 1930s, her photographs, 20 feet high, flanked the theater entrance. In France she was called simply "Joséphine" or "La Baker." In 1937 Josephine officially became a French citizen.

## A Heroine in World War II

She married Jean Lion, a French industrialist. She had a miscarriage in 1938, and Lion divorced her in 1940, during the early months of World War II. When Germany occupied Belgium, Josephine became a Red Cross nurse, watching over refugees. When Germany finally occupied France itself, she worked for the French Resistance as an underground courier, transmitting information "pinned inside her underwear" to Captain Jacques Abtey. In October 1940 she began complicated journeys from London to Pau in southwestern France, through Spain and Portugal, and to Rio de Janeiro, Brazil (where she had theatrical bookings), back to Marseilles. In December 1940 she had the leading role in the Marseilles municipal opera production of *La Créole*, but she was sued for breach of contract after leaving Algiers, Algeria in 1941. A mysterious near-fatal illness with peritonitis kept her in a Casablanca clinic from June 1941 to December 1942. It left Josephine weak, but not too weak to entertain troops in North Africa and the Middle East as a sublieutenant in the women's auxiliary of the Free French forces. She was awarded the Croix de Guerre and the Légion d'Honneur by General Charles de Gaulle and the Rosette of the Résistance.

After the war Josephine returned to her beloved Paris, regularly appearing in the *Follies*. In June 1947 she married Jo Bouillon, a jazz bandleader; after several miscarriages they separated in 1957. In 1950 at her 300-acre estate in the Dordogne (with a medieval chateau), Les Milandes, she began adopting orphaned babies of all races and religions. She retired to look after the estate and family in 1956, but soon debts amounting to $400,000 were accrued, and she was forced back into show business in 1959, in a musical autobiography called *Paris mes Amours,* which opened at the Olympia Theatre in Paris in May.

Josephine more than once looked back to her childhood in America disconsolately. She was in a bind which many find themselves in: bound to one country but in love with another. She could never forgive the United States for its racism. But her song (written by Vincent Scotto), *J'ai deux amours,* was a constant reminder: "I have two loves: my country and Paris." She visited America in the 1930s and 1940s and was disappointed. In 1951 her trip to New York was sullied by a racial incident at the Stork Club, where she was at first refused service. Walter Winchell, a columnist, linked her to communism (the "Communist conspiracy" was in the news, led by Senator J. McCarthy). In 1952 she told a reporter in Buenos Aires, Argentina: "The U.S. is not a free country. . . . They treat Negroes as though they were dogs." As late as 1955, on her return to the United States, she was questioned by immigration officials about her alleged anti-American sentiments.

President John F. Kennedy made a difference to America. Josephine returned in August 1963 to attend the civil rights march in Washington, D.C. In October of that year she made a trip to Manhattan to sing, dance, and "fight bias" (as *The New York Times* said). She flaunted her age: she said she was 60 (she was only 57), but she seemed ageless to reporters.

### Problems in Her "True" Home

In France there were also problems: she was evicted from her chateau with her adopted family in 1969. Princess Grace Kelly of Monte Carlo (who was also an American expatriate) and her husband, Prince Rainier, offered the Baker family a villa in Monaco. The Rainiers helped to put on the spectacle *Joséphine* in 1975, in which Josephine, aged 69, had a dozen costume changes and, with tears streaming down from sequined eyelids, "stole the show" once again.

Describing herself, Josephine Baker said "I have never really been a great artist. I have been a human being that has loved art, which is not the same thing. But I have loved and believed in art and the idea of universal brotherhood so much, that I have put everything I have into them, and I have been blessed." (*Ebony* report of interview in 1975.)

More than that, Josephine Baker pulled herself out of poverty and the trauma of humiliation and made herself an international star, principally due to her love of dancing.

She died in her sleep of a stroke on April 12, 1975, after 14 successful performances of *Joséphine.* The Roman Catholic funeral service was held at the Church of the Madeleine in Paris, which was, after all, her true home.

### Further Reading

There are five autobiographies of Josephine Baker: *Les Mémoires de Josephine Baker,* Vol. I (Paris, 1927); *Voyages et Aventures de Joséphine Baker* (with Marcel Sauvage), Vol. II (Paris, 1931); *Une Vie de Toutes Couleurs* (memories presented by André Rivollet), Vol. III (Grenoble, 1935); *Les Memoires de Josephine Baker* (collected and adapted by Marcel Sauvage), Vol. IV (Paris, 1949); and *Joséphine* (with Jo Bouillon and Jacqueline Cartier), Vol. V (Paris, 1976). Books about Baker include *Bricktop* (1983) by her friend Bricktop (with Jim Haskins), *Josephine Baker* (1988) by Bryan Hammond (personal collection) and Patrick O'Connor (theatrical biography), *Jazz Cleopatra* (1988) by Phyllis Rose, and *Josephine: The Hungry Heart* (1993) by Jean-Claude Baker (who called Josephine "Mother" although he was never legally adopted) and Chris Chase. Among the best articles are *Ebony* (June 1991), *Dance Magazine* (July 1989), *American Heritage* (November 1989), and *New Republic* (6 November 1989). □

# Sara Josephine Baker

**Sara Josephine Baker (1873–1945) was a physician working toward improving the public health care and reducing infant mortality rates substantially in New York City.**

Sara Josephine Baker was a pioneer in the field of public health and an activist in the women's movement. She was the first woman to receive a doctorate in public health. As the head of the Department of Health's newly created division of child hygiene, she reduced New York City's infant mortality rate to the lowest of all major cities worldwide. From 1922 to 1924 she represented the United States on the health committee of the League of Nations.

Born on November 15, 1873, in Poughkeepsie, New York, Baker was the daughter of affluent parents. Her Quaker father, Orlando Daniel Mosser Baker, was a lawyer and her mother was one of the first women to attend Vassar College. Baker's Quaker Aunt Abby stimulated her intellectually and instilled in her the courage to be a nonconformist. This background influenced her decision to enter medicine and establish innovative programs in preventive health, particularly in obstetrics (childbirth) and pediatrics (treatment of children).

### Becomes a doctor

When Baker was 16 years old both her father and brother died in a typhoid epidemic. Devastated, she abandoned plans for attending Vassar and decided to go directly to New York Women's Medical College. She was determined to become a doctor in order to help support her mother and sister. In 1898, after four years of intensive study, Baker graduated second in a class of 18. She interned, or gained practical experience in medicine, at the New England Hospital for Women and Children, an outpatient clinic serving residents in one of the worst slums in Boston, Massachusetts. Later she moved to New York City with her roommate and fellow intern, where they set up a practice near Central Park West. Unable to make ends meet, Baker took a job as a medical inspector for the New York City Department of Health. She examined sick children in schools and worked toward controlling the spread of contagious disease.

## Becomes first woman health official

In 1902 Baker was given the job of searching for sick infants in Hell's Kitchen. Located near the docks of Manhattan's West Side, Hell's Kitchen was a slum area where 1,500 children were dying each week of dysentery (a disease that causes severe diarrhea and dehydration). In 1908 the Department of Health established a division of child hygiene, with Baker as its director. She was the first woman in the United States to hold an executive position in a health department. There she shaped policies for innovative health reform and made preventive medicine and health education the responsibility of government. As Baker's program saved the lives of countless infants, she revolutionized pediatric health care in the United States and in other nations as well.

## Starts innovative projects

One of Baker's projects was establishing "milk stations" throughout the city, where nurses examined babies, dispensed low-cost, high-quality milk, and scheduled checkups. In 1911 alone 15 milk stations prevented more than 1,000 deaths, and the next year 40 more stations were opened. Another of Baker's programs was the training and licensing of midwives, or persons who assist women in childbirth. Since many immigrant women were used to midwifery, they were reluctant to allow their babies to be delivered by male doctors in hospitals. Midwives were often unqualified, however, and infant death rates were high. Baker instituted a mandatory licensing program with results so successful that she was able to demonstrate that rates of infection for home deliveries were lower than those for hospitals.

Baker also started a program called the Little Mothers League to train young girls in the care of babies, since many girls were put in charge of their younger siblings while their mothers worked. Through this program nurses instructed schoolgirls in the feeding, exercising, dressing, and general care of infants. An even more significant method of reducing infant mortality was a foster care system Baker founded to give orphaned babies a better environment than that available in institutions. Her efforts helped reduce death rates from one-half to one-third of infants born in a year. She also introduced the concept of prenatal care to prevent infant mortality during and following childbirth.

## Contributes to nation's public health system

Among Baker's other accomplishments were a school inspection system and the organization and streamlining of record-keeping procedures for health departments, which was adopted nationwide. She opened specialized clinics and instituted parent training by public health nurses. In 1912 she established the Federal Children's Bureau and made plans for creating a division of child hygiene in every state. Besides being a leader in the medical field, Baker was in the forefront of the fledgling women's movement. In 1915 she was invited by officials at the New York University (NYU) Medical School to lecture on child hygiene for a new course leading to a degree of doctor of public health. Since she did not have an actual degree in the field of public health herself, she offered to teach in return for the opportunity to earn the diploma. When Dean William Park turned down her request on the grounds that the medical school did not admit women, Baker refused the appointment.

Park searched in vain for a year for another instructor, finally giving up and admitting Baker and other women to the program. Baker's reception by some of the male students was hostile, but she continued teaching at NYU for 15 years. Along with five other women Baker founded the College Equal Suffrage League, an organization that campaigned for women's voting rights, and she marched in the first annual Fifth Avenue suffrage parade.

## Appointed League of Nations representative

During her term as U.S. representative on the health committee of the League of Nations from 1922 to 1924, Baker was appointed consulting director in maternity and child hygiene of the U.S. Children's Bureau. After retirement she participated in more than 25 committees devoted to improving children's health care. She also served a term as president of the American Medical Women's Association. Baker died of cancer on February 22, 1945, in New York City. Her work laid the foundation for preventive health procedures that saved the lives of hundreds of thousands of babies, resulting in an improvement in mortality rates from one in six in 1907 to one in 20 by 1943.

## Further Reading

Peavy, Linda, and Ursula Smith, *Women Who Changed Things*, Charles Scribner's Sons, 1983, p. 122.

Morantz-Sanchez, Regina Markell, *Sympathy and Science: Women Physicians in American Medicine*, Oxford University Press, 1985.

Morantz, Regina Markell, Cynthia Stodola Pomerleau, and Carol Fenichel, eds., *In Her Own Words: Oral Histories of Women Physicians*, Yale University Press, 1982, p. 30. □

# Emily Greene Balch

**Pacifist, political activist, college professor, and social reformer, Emily Greene Balch (1867-1961) dedi-**

**cated her life to humanitarian causes. In 1946 she shared the Nobel Peace Prize with John R. Mott.**

Emily Greene Balch was born in Jamaica Plain, Massachusetts, on January 8, 1867. Her father and mother, Ellen Noyes and Francis V. Balch, were educated Unitarians who raised their six children to cherish high moral and religious standards.

When selecting a college after attending Miss Catherine Ireland's School in Boston, Balch chose Bryn Mawr. Entering in 1886, she studied economics and graduated with an A.B. degree in 1889. The initial recipient of the European Fellowship at Bryn Mawr, she went first to New York City to work under social reformer Jacob Riis, then used her award to attend the Sorbonne. From 1890 to 1891 she applied herself to "the social question," and upon her return to the United States she worked in Boston with Charles W. Birtwell at the Children's Aid Society.

Now in her element, Balch became acquainted in 1892 with three other reform-minded women: Jane Addams, Katherine Coman, and Vida Scudder. That same year she helped found the Boston settlement Denison House, acting as its director for a brief time.

Following her social work experience, Balch turned to college teaching as a way to further advance the cause of reform. She prepared for this by studying at the University of Chicago, at Harvard University, and at the University of Berlin. In 1896 Balch joined Coman at Wellesley College as

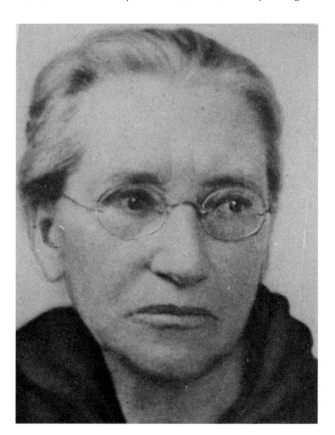

an assistant, teaching economics courses. She illustrated her lectures with her social work experiences and was highly regarded as an imaginative and dedicated teacher.

In 1902 Balch became president of the Women's Trade Union League of Boston, which she co-founded, and sat on a state commission organized to investigate minimum wages for women. In 1906 she announced her affinity for socialism and worked closely with others to advance its principles. These radical activities cost her the chance to move up quickly in the academic hierarchy at Wellesley.

Balch's research led to the publication of *Our Slavic Fellow Citizens* in 1910. She was appointed chairwoman of the economics and sociology department at Wellesley College in 1913. Two years later, in April 1915, she travelled to The Hague, where she was an American delegate to the International Congress of Women. The 42-member delegation included such notables as Addams, Alice Hamilton, and Louis Lochner.

Balch was on leave from Wellesley between 1916 and 1918. During that period she became active in pacifism and was connected with such groups as the American Union Against Militarism and the Women's Peace Party. Because of her outspoken views and radical behavior, renewal of Balch's contract at Wellesley was denied in 1919. That same year she accompanied another delegation to the International Congress of Women. While there, she was elected secretary-treasurer of the newly-formed Women's International League for Peace and Freedom (WILPF), which had Addams as its president.

Balch relied heavily on her spiritual convictions during these years and in 1921 joined the London Society of Friends. She dedicated herself to the success of the League of Nations, helping to ensure that the interests of smaller nations and of women and children were upheld.

By 1922, due to poor health, Balch resigned as secretary-treasurer of the WILPF, although she continued to work for the group on a voluntary basis. She travelled to Haiti with a commission established by Herbert Hoover in 1930 to investigate conditions in that occupied nation. Hoover subsequently removed U.S. troops from Haiti on the basis of the commission's report.

In 1935 Wellesley College invited Balch to speak at an Armistice Day program, ending its public disapproval of the former faculty member.

Balch worked tirelessly on behalf of world peace and in 1939 published *Refugees as Assets,* urging the United States to admit refugees from Nazis out of respect for humanitarian principles. After Pearl Harbor in 1941, Balch advocated support for Japanese-Americans held in U.S. detention camps.

Balch won the Nobel Peace Prize in 1946, an award she shared with John R. Mott, international Young Men's Christian Association (YMCA) official. Among those supporting Balch's nomination for the prize was Wellesley president Mildred McAfee Horton. Balch donated her $17,000 share of the prize money to the WILPF.

In poor health and living on a limited income during her later years, Balch nevertheless continued her activism.

She was honorary chairwoman of the Women's International League, and in 1959 served on a commission that organized a 100th anniversary celebration in honor of Jane Addam's birth held the following year.

Balch entered Mr. Vernon Nursing Home in Cambridge, Massachusetts, in 1956 and died there of pneumonia at age 94 on January 10, 1961.

### Further Reading

Both John Herman Randall, Jr.'s *Emily Greene Balch of New England, Citizen of the World* (1946) and *Improper Bostonian: Emily Greene Balch* (1964) by Mercedes M. Randall, are biographies of note. Further insight into Balch's activism can be found in *Beyond Nationalism: The Social Thought of Emily Greene Balch* (1972) by Mercedes M. Randall. □

# Lucille Ball

**The face of comedienne Lucille Ball (Lucille Desiree Hunt; 1911-1989), immortalized as Lucy Ricardo on *I Love Lucy,* is said to have been seen by more people worldwide than any other. "Lucy" to generations of television viewers who delighted at her rubber-faced antics and zany impersonations (among them Charlie Chaplin's Little Tramp), she was a shrewd businesswoman, serious actress, and Broadway star as well.**

Born Lucille Desiree Hunt on August 6, 1911, she and her mother, DeDe, made their home with her grandparents in Celoron, outside Jamestown, New York, after her father's death in 1915.

Lucy's mother encouraged her daughter's penchant for the theater. The two were close, and DeDe Ball's laugh can be heard on almost every *I Love Lucy* sound track. But from Lucy's first unsuccessful foray to New York, where she won—and lost—a chorus part in the Shubert musical *Stepping Stones,* through her days in Hollywood as "Queen of the B's" (grade B movies), the road to *I Love Lucy* was not an easy one.

In 1926 she enrolled at the John Murray Anderson/Robert Milton School of Theater and Dance in New York. Her participation there, unlike that of star student Bette Davis, was a dismal failure. The proprietor even wrote to tell Lucy's mother that she was wasting her money. It was back to Celoron for the future star.

After a brief respite, the indomitable Lucy returned to New York with the stage name Diane Belmont. She was chosen to appear in Earl Carroll's *Vanities,* for the third road company of Ziegfeld's *Rio Rita,* and for *Step Lively,* but none of these performances materialized. She found employment at a Rexall drugstore on Broadway; then she worked in Hattie Carnegie's elegant dress salon, moonlighting as a model. Lucille Ball's striking beauty always differentiated her from other comediennes.

At the age of 17, Lucy was stricken with rheumatoid arthritis and returned to Celoron yet again, where her mother nursed her through an almost three-year bout with the illness.

Determined, she found more success in New York the next time when she became the Chesterfield Cigarette Girl. In 1933 she was cast as a last-minute replacement for one of the twelve Goldwyn girls in the Eddie Canter movie *Roman Scandals,* directed by Busby Berkeley. (Ball's first on-screen appearance was actually a walk-on in the 1933 *Broadway Thru a Keyhole.*) During the filming, when Lucy volunteered to take a pie in the face, the legendary Berkeley is said to have commented, "Get that girl's name. That's the one who will make it."

Favorable press from her first speaking role in 1935 and the second lead in *That Girl from Paris* (1936) helped win her a major part in the Broadway musical *Hey Diddle Diddle,* but the project was aborted by the premature death of the male lead. It would take roughly another 15 years for Lucy to attain stardom.

She worked with many comic "greats," including the Three Stooges, the Marx Brothers, Laurel and Hardy, and Buster Keaton, with whom she honed her extraordinary skill in the handling of props. She gave a creditable performance as an aspiring actress in *Stage Door* (1937) and earned praise from critic James Agee for her portrayal of a bitter, handicapped nightclub singer in *The Big Street* (1942).

Lucy first acquired her flaming red hair in 1943 when, after *The Big Street,* MGM officials signed her to appear opposite Red Skelton in Cole Porter's *DuBarry Was a Lady*. (Throughout the years, rumors flew as to the color's origin, including one that Lucy decided upon the dye job in an effort to somehow rival Betty Grable.)

It was on the set of an innocuous film, *Dance, Girl, Dance,* that Lucille Ball first met her future husband, Cuban bandleader Desi Arnaz. Married in 1940, they were separated by Desi's travels for much of the first decade of their marriage. The union, plagued by Arnaz's alcoholism, workaholism, and philandering, dissolved in 1960.

The decade prior to Lucy's television debut was filled with intermittent parts in films and the more satisfying role of Liz Cooper, the scatterbrained wife on the radio program *My Favorite Husband* (July 1947 to March 1951).

Determined to work together and to save their marriage, the couple conceived a television pilot. Studio executives were dubious. The duo was forced to take their "act" on the road to prove its viability and to borrow $5,000 to found Desilu Productions. (After buying out Arnaz's share and changing the corporation's name, Lucy eventually sold it to Gulf Western for $18 million.) They persevered, and *I Love Lucy* premiered on October 15, 1951.

Within six months the show as rated number one. It ran six seasons in its original format and then evolved into hour-long specials, accumulating over 20 awards, among them five Emmys. *I Love Lucy* is one of television's four "all-time hits."

The characters Lucy and Ricky Ricardo became household words, with William Frawley and Vivian Vance superbly cast as long-suffering neighbors Fred and Ethel Mertz. More viewers tuned in for the television birth of "Little Ricky" Ricardo than for President Eisenhower's inauguration. The show was the first in television history to claim viewing in more than ten million homes. It was filmed before a studio audience, in sequence, and helped to revolutionize television production by utilizing three cameras.

*I Love Lucy* begat *Lucy in Connecticut* (1960); in turn, *The Lucy-Desi Comedy Hour* (1962-1967); then *The Lucy Show* (1962, with Vivian Vance, later called *The Lucille Ball Show,* running until 1974); and, finally, in 1986, the ill-fated *Life with Lucy,* with Gale Gordon.

The Lucy Ricardo character may be viewed as a downtrodden housewife, but compared to other situation comedy wives of television's "golden years' she was liberated. The show's premise was her desire to share the show-biz limelight with her performer husband and to leave the pots and pans behind. Later series featured Lucy as a single mother and as a working woman "up against" her boss.

Following her initial retirement from prime time in 1974 Lucy continued to make guest appearances on television, too numerous to mention. Broadway saw her starring in *Mame* (1974), a role with which she identified. (Her other Broadway appearance after her career had "taken off" was in *Wildcat* in 1960.) Her last serious role was that of a bag lady in the 1983 made-for-television movie *Stone Pillow*.

Lucy was married to comic Gary Morton from 1961 until the time of her death on April 26, 1989, eight days after open-heart surgery. She was survived by her husband, her two children by Arnaz, Luci and Desi Junior, and millions of fans who continue to watch her in re-runs of *I Love Lucy*, which is now also available on video cassette.

### Further Reading

Chapters devoted to Lucille Ball can be found in *Women in Comedy* (1986) by Linda Martin and Kerry Segrave and in *Funny Women* (1987) by Mary Unterbrink. Biographies include *The Lucille Ball Story* (1974) by James Gregory, *Lucy* (1986) by Charles Higham, and *Forever Lucy* (1986) by Joe Morella and Edward Z. Epstein. Desi Arnaz's 1976 autobiography, *A Book,* chronicles their years together from his perspective, and Bart Andrews' *Lucy and Ricky and Fred and Ethel: The Story of "I Love Lucy"* (1976) features a complete plot summary for each of the show's episodes. *People* magazine paid special tribute to Lucy in its August 14, 1989, issue. □

# Toni Cade Bambara

**Toni Cade Bambara (1939-1995), who initially gained recognition as a short story writer, has branched out into other genres and media in the course of her career, yet she continues to focus on issues of racial awareness and feminism in her work.**

Born Toni Cade on March 25, 1939, in New York City, she later acquired the name "Bambara" after discovering it as part of a signature on a sketchbook in her great-grandmother's trunk. Bambara was generally silent about her childhood, but she revealed a few details from her youth. In an interview with Beverly Guy-Sheftall in *Sturdy Black Bridges: Visions of Black Women in Literature,* Bambara discussed some women who influenced her work: "For example, in every neighborhood I lived in there were always two types of women that somehow pulled me and sort of got their wagons in a circle around me. I call them Miss Naomi and Miss Gladys, although I'm sure they came under various names. The Miss Naomi types . . . would give me advice like, 'When you meet a man, have a birthday, demand a present that's hockable, and be careful.' . . . The Miss Gladyses were usually the type that hung out the window in Apartment 1-A leaning on the pillow giving single-action advice on numbers or giving you advice about how to get your homework done or telling you to stay away from those cruising cars that moved through the neighborhood patrolling little girls." After attending Queens College in New York City and several European institutions, Bambara worked as a free-lance writer and lecturer, social investigator for the New York State Department of Welfare, and director of recreation in the psychiatry department at Metropolitan Hospital in New York City. As she told Guy-Sheftall, writing at that time seemed to her "rather frivolous . . . something you did because you didn't feel like doing any work. But . . . I've come to appreciate that it is a perfectly legitimate way to participate in a struggle."

Bambara's interest in black liberation and women's movements led her to edit and publish an anthology entitled *The Black Woman* in 1970. The work is a collection of poetry, short stories, and essays by such celebrated writers as Nikki Giovanni, Audre Lorde, Alice Walker, and Paule Marshall. *The Black Woman* also contains short stories by Bambara, who was at that time still writing under the name of Cade. According to Deck, Bambara saw the work as "a response to all the male 'experts' both black and white who had been publishing articles and conducting sociological studies on black women." Another anthology, *Tales and Stories for Black Folks,* followed in 1971. Bambara explained in the introduction to this short story collection that the work's aim is to instruct young blacks about "Our Great Kitchen Tradition," Bambara's term for the black tradition of storytelling. In the first part of *Tales and Stories,* Bambara included works by writers like Langston Hughes, Alice Walker, and Ernest Gaines—stories she wished she had read while growing up. The second part of the collection contains stories by students in a first year composition class Bambara was teaching at Livingston College, Rutgers University. Deck wrote that Bambara's inclusion of professional writers and students in a single work "shows her desire to give young writers a chance to make their talents known to a large audience." Additionally, such a mixture "would have helped her inspire young adults to read, to think critically, and to write."

Most of Bambara's early writings—short stories written between 1959 and 1970 under the name Toni Cade—were collected in her next work, *Gorilla, My Love* (1972). Bambara told Claudia Tate in an interview published in *Black Women Writers at Work* that when her agent suggested she assemble some old stories for a book, she thought, "Aha, I'll get the old kid stuff out and see if I can't clear some space to get into something else." Nevertheless, *Gorilla, My Love* remains her most widely read collection. Deck noted that after the publication of her first collection, "major events took place in Toni Cade Bambara's life which were to have an effect on her writing." Bambara traveled to Cuba in 1973 and Vietnam in 1975, meeting with both the Federation of Cuban Women and the Women's Union in Vietnam. She was impressed with both groups, particularly with the ability of the Cuban women to surpass class and color conflicts and with the Vietnamese women's resistance to their traditional place in society. Furthermore, upon returning to the United States, Bambara moved to the South, where she became a founding member of the Southern Collective of African-American Writers. Her travels and her involvement with community groups like the collective influenced the themes and settings of *The Sea Birds Are Still Alive* (1977), her second collection of short stories. These stories take place in diverse geographical areas, and they center chiefly around communities instead of individuals. With both collections, critics noted Bambara's skill in the genre, and many praised the musical nature of language and dialogue in her stories, which she herself likens to "riffs" and "be-bop."

Although Bambara admittedly favored the short story genre, her next work, *The Salt Eaters* (1980), is a novel. She explained in *Black Women Writers:* "Of all the writing forms, I've always been partial to the short story. . . . But the major publishing industry, the academic establishment, reviewers, and critics favor the novel . . . Murder for the gene-deep loyalist who readily admits in interviews that the move to the novel was not occasioned by a recognition of having reached the limits of the genre or the practitioner's disillusion with it, but rather Career. Economics. Critical Attention. A major motive behind the production of *Salt.*" The novel, which focuses on the recovery of community organizer Velma Henry from an attempted suicide, consists of a "fugue-like interweaving of voices," Bambara's speciality. *The Salt Eaters* succeeded in gaining more critical attention for Bambara, but many reviewers found the work to be confusing, particularly because of breaks in the story line and the use of various alternating narrators. Others appreciated her "complex vision," however, and further praised her ability to write dialogue.

Since the publication of *The Salt Eaters* in 1980, Bambara devoted herself to another medium, film. She told Tate in *Black Women Writers at Work:* "Quite frankly, I've always considered myself a film person. . . . There's not too much more I want to experiment with in terms of writing. It gives me pleasure, insight, keeps me centered, sane. But, oh, to get my hands on some movie equipment." Bambara nevertheless remained committed to working within black communities, continuing to address issues of black awareness and feminism in her art.

On December 9, 1995, Bambara died of colon cancer in Philadelphia.

## Further Reading

Beizer, Janet L., *Black Women Writers (1950-1980): A Critical Evaluation,* edited by Mari Evans, Anchor Books, 1979.

*Contemporary Literary Criticism,* Volume 19, Gale, 1984.

*Dictionary of Literary Biography, Volume 38: Afro-American Writers after 1955: Dramatists and Prose Writers,* Gale, 1985.

Parker, Bell and Beverly Guy-Sheftall, *Sturdy Black Bridges: Visions of Black Women in Literature,* Doubleday, 1979.

Pearlman, Mickey, editor, *American Women Writing Fiction: Memory, Identity, Family, Space,* Universty Press of Kentucky, 1989.

Prenshaw, Peggy Whitman, editor, *Women Writers of the Contemporary South,* University Press of Mississippi, 1984.

Tate, Claudia, editor, *Black Women Writers at Work,* Continuum, 1983. □

# Djuna Barnes

**Djuna Barnes (1892–1982) was a major literary figure in Paris of the 1920s and 1930s, who retired into reclusiveness and produced only a small body of work.**

A major figure on the Paris literary scene of the 1920s and 1930s, Djuna Barnes was best known for her experimental novel *Nightwood,* one of the most influential works of modernist fiction. Described by Elizabeth

Hardwick of the *Times Literary Supplement* as "a writer of wild and original gifts," Barnes was acclaimed by such writers as "Graham Greene, Samuel Beckett, Janet Flanner, Laurence Durrell, Kenneth Burke, Sir Herbert Read, and Dylan Thomas," Andrew Field pointed out in the *New York Times Book Review*. Field noted, too, that "a list just as long could be made of important writers who borrowed heavily from her." Barnes was at various times a poet, journalist, playwright, theatrical columnist, and novelist. But her prolific career was brought to a voluntary end in the 1930s when Barnes virtually gave up writing and retreated into nearly half a century of silence. She lived like a recluse, "a form of Trappist," Louis F. Kannenstine quoted her as saying in the *Dictionary of Literary Biography*, refusing to grant interviews or to approve the reprinting of most of her early writings. Because of this silence, Barnes's work is still not as widely celebrated as is that of many of her contemporaries.

Born in 1892 in Cornwall-on-Hudson, New York, Barnes began writing at an early age to support her mother and three brothers. She contributed frequently to New York City newspapers and to such magazines as *Smart Set* and *Vanity Fair*. In 1915, her first collection, *The Book of Repulsive Women: 8 Rhythms and 5 Drawings*, appeared as a chapbook. With the production in 1919 of three one-act plays by Eugene O'Neill's Provincetown Players, Barnes first gained serious recognition for her work. Her contributions to modernist publications of the day established her reputation among the avant-garde community. In 1920, Barnes left New York for Paris, where she was to live for the next twenty years and write the "relatively small body of work" upon which her "literary reputation must ultimately rest," as Kannenstine stated. This small body of work consists of four volumes: *A Book*, *Ladies Almanack*, *Ryder*, and *Nightwood*.

*A Book*, a collection of Barnes's plays, short stories, poems, and drawings, appeared in 1923. The plays produced by the Provincetown Players are collected here, as well as early stories set in Paris and inspired by the people Barnes knew there. The poet Raymond Radiguet, who died at the age of twenty, is the inspiration for one story. Two Dutch sisters, friends of Barnes and fixtures of Paris cafe society, inspire two other stories. All of these characters "are restless, estranged from society and themselves," Kannenstine wrote. Later editions of *A Book* were published as *A Night among the Horses* and *Spillway*. *Horses* adds several short stories to the original collection, while *Spillway* consists only of the short stories from the original collection.

In *Ladies Almanack*, published in 1928, Barnes based her characters on prominent lesbian writers of 1920s Paris, particularly those in author Natalie Barney's circle of friends. Written in Elizabethan prose, the book depicts a lesbian society in which one woman is sainted. Barnes described the book as "a slight satiric wigging," as Hardwick quoted her. The satire, however, is gentle and amiable. "The primary intention of *Ladies Almanack*," Kannenstine believed, "is to confront the anomaly of sexual identity." The book was privately printed and distributed in Paris.

Barnes's first novel, *Ryder*, was also published in 1928. As in *Ladies Almanack*, there is an element of satire in the book. Barnes parodies "biblical language, Chaucer, heroic couplets, mystical literature, the epistolary novel, mock-epic tales, and other forms," Donald J. Greiner explained in the *Dictionary of Literary Biography*. *Ryder* is ostensibly a family chronicle revolving around Wendell Ryder, his wife, mother, and mistress. Ryder brings misery to all the women in his life because of his conviction that he has a mission to love women. Told in nonchronological chapters, many of which could stand on their own, *Ryder* is a "kaleidoscope of moods and styles," Joseph Frank wrote in *Sewanee Review*. Many of the qualities for which Barnes is known are first displayed in *Ryder*. "Of the fantastical quality of her imagination; of the gift for imagery, . . .; of the epigrammatic incisiveness of her phrasing and her penchant, akin to the Elizabethans, for dealing with the more scabrous manifestations of human fallibility—of all these there is evidence in *Ryder*," Frank stated. Greiner believed that the publication of *Ryder* moved Barnes into the ranks of important literary innovators. "With *Ryder*," he noted, "she joined [James] Joyce, [T. S.] Eliot, and [Ezra] Pound in breaking through the conservative restrictions on poetry and fiction by looking over her shoulder at past literary models while stepping toward the future with experiments in technique and structure that would influence writing for the next fifty years."

Although *Ryder* was considered a bold experiment, it is *Nightwood*, Barnes's second novel, that most critics believed to be her most successful and important work. It is, Stephen Koch wrote in the *Washington Post Book World*, "a recognized masterpiece of modernism." *Nightwood* combines comedy and horror in a fiction without narrative structure or conventionally developed characters. "It would be more appropriate," Kannenstine believed, "to speak of *Nightwood*'s situation than its plot." *Nightwood*, Frank explained, "lacks a narrative structure in the ordinary sense." It is, however, organized according to nonliterary models. Various critics have demonstrated that *Nightwood* borrows its structure from poetry, music, drama, psychology, or the visual arts, but Kannenstine maintained that no one explanation of its structure was correct. Instead, "all are correct: all of these function simultaneously," he declared. "The novel is essentially transgeneric." It also incorporates a broad spectrum of literary styles, including that of the Elizabethans and Jacobeans, the writers of the Old Testament, and the Surrealists, while "parodying the venerable traditions of plot, character, setting, and theme, and maintaining extreme authorial detachment," as Greiner wrote in the *Dictionary of Literary Biography*.

The book traces the love affairs of the young woman Robin Vote in 1920s Paris. She first marries Felix Volkbien, but leaves him for the journalist Nora Flood. She then leaves Nora for Jenny Petherbridge. Brokenhearted, Nora turns to Dr. Matthew O'Connor, but he is unable to relieve her suffering and eventually breaks down. "The plot relates little more than the theft of one person's lover by another," Sharon Spencer observed in *Space, Time and Structure in the Modern Novel*. "Yet, through the heightened intensity of its language, and through the adroit structuring of its disjunct elements, *Nightwood* leaves the reader with a coherent and powerful impression of spiritual agony." This agony is commented on by Stanley Edgar Hyman in *Standards: A Chronicle of Books for Our Time.* Hyman compared *Nightwood* to Nathanael West's *Miss Lonelyhearts,* another tragic novel of the 1930s. "In the years since the 30s," Hyman wrote, "we have had nothing to equal those two great cries of pain, in their combination of emotional power and formal artistry." "For all its power," Koch said of *Nightwood,* "this is the bleakest modernism of all, a modernism like a wailing wall."

Although *Nightwood* has a tragic and even nightmarish side, it is also a humorous novel. Elizabeth Pochoda, commenting in *Twentieth Century Literature,* called *Nightwood* "a tremendously funny book in a desperately surgical sort of way." The novel's humor lies in its wit and its use of paradox and hoax, Pochoda argued, and all actions in the novel "are reduced to their initial hoax. Only then is sympathy allowable. The apparently touching love story of Robin and Nora is also a kind of hoaxing, and we are not permitted to weep with Nora over her loss. Once the bloodthirsty nature of such love is uncovered we are allowed the sympathy appropriate to such an inevitable delusion." Greiner, writing in *Critique: Studies in Modern Fiction,* saw the paradoxical combination of humor and sadness as fundamental to all black humor. Barnes's "sense of humor is evident from the beginning," Greiner wrote, "and her use of funny elements with a depressing theme reflects the perplexing mixture so vital to black humor." *Nightwood,* Greiner concluded, "remains the most successful early example of the American black humor novel."

While interweaving humor and horror, *Nightwood* explores the theme of "man's separation from his primitive, yet more fundamental animal nature," Greiner observed in the *Dictionary of Literary Biography.* This separation between human and animal is expressed by Dr. O'Connor who, at one point in the novel, states that man "was born damned and innocent from the start, and wretchedly—as he must—on these two themes—whistles his tune." As Pochoda saw it, the reduction of all actions in *Nightwood* to "their initial hoax" eventually reveals the futility of language to communicate truth. Beginning with a historical allusion, the novel "turns its back on history, on faith in coherent expression, and finally on words themselves," Pochoda stated. "The novel bows down before its own impotence to express truths." In the last scene of the novel, Robin is transformed into a dog. This scene of devolution into beast is written, in contrast to the exuberance of the rest of the book, in a plain and unenergetic style to show the ultimate failure of language to overcome the animal within man. "The novel," Pochoda noted, "ends in wordlessness and failure, with the impasse of life intact and its contradictions nicely exposed."

Writing in the *International Fiction Review,* Robert L. Nadeau had a Freudian explanation for the devolution in *Nightwood.* He argued that the novel "does not depict human interaction on the level of conscious, waking existence. It is rather a dream world in which the embattled forces of the human personality take the form of characters representing aspects of that personality at different levels of

its functioning." The transformation of Robin into an animal takes place, Nadeau wrote, "after she divests herself of the demands of the superego, or that whole complex of forms and values known as "civilization,'.... She is an animal—pure and simple."

In his biography *Djuna: The Life and Times of Djuna Barnes,* Field showed that much of *Nightwood* is autobiographical. He identified the main characters as friends of Barnes in Paris and found that Barnes herself was the character Nora. Robin was identified as Thelma Wood, a woman with whom Barnes had a love affair. But how much of the novel is taken from life is unclear. Field's account, Koch maintained, "is sometimes impossibly evasive, especially on matters sexual." Hardwick saw the biography as being "under considerable strain" because Barnes "was noted for her silence."

Shortly after publishing *Nightwood,* Barnes ceased writing and, in 1940, she returned to New York City. For the rest of her life she lived in a small apartment in Greenwich Village and published only one play and two poems. Her withdrawal from the literary world caused her reputation to pale. And Barnes's refusal to allow much of her earlier work for magazines to be reprinted kept the scope of her achievement unknown. In her book *Shakespeare and Company,* Sylvia Beach admitted that Barnes "was not one to cry her wares."

Despite her reserve, Barnes maintained a secure place in American letters because of *Nightwood,* which has been in print since it first appeared in 1936. *Nightwood,* Greiner wrote in the *Dictionary of Literary Biography,* "stands high in the list of significant twentieth-century American novels." Nadeau described it as "a truly great piece of American fiction," while Dylan Thomas, according to Field in the *New York Times Book Review,* called *Nightwood* "one of the three great prose books ever written by a woman." Hardwick believed that to Barnes's name "there is always to be attached the splendor of *Nightwood,* a lasting achievement of her great gifts and eccentricities." Barnes was, Koch maintained, a "strange and impossible genius." Since the 1970s, some of Barnes's earlier writings have been found and reprinted in book form and a bibliography of her work has been assembled by Douglas Messerli. Greiner believed that "Djuna Barnes's work will eventually receive the attention it deserves."

## Further Reading

Baldwin, Kenneth H. and David K. Kirby, editors, *Individual and Community: Variations on a Theme in American Fiction,* Duke University Press, 1975.
Beach, Sylvia, *Shakespeare and Company,* Harcourt, 1959.
Broe, Mary Lynn, editor, *Silence and Power: A Re-evaluation of Barnes,* Southern Illinois University Press, 1986.
Cohn, Ruby, *Dialogue in American Drama,* Indiana University Press, 1971.
*Contemporary Literary Criticism,* Gale, Volume 3, 1975, Volume 4, 1975, Volume 8, 1978, Volume 9, 1979, Volume 29, 1984.
Cook, Albert, *The Meaning of Fiction,* Wayne State University Press, 1960.
*Dictionary of Literary Biography,* Gale, Volume 4: *American Writers in Paris, 1920-1939,* 1980, volume 9: *American Novelists, 1910-1945,* 1981.

Field, Andrew, *Djuna: The Life and Times of Djuna Barnes,* Putnam, 1983 (published in England as *The Formidable Miss Barnes: The Life of Djuna Barnes,* Secker & Warburg, 1983).

Fowlie, Wallace, *Love in Literature: Studies in Symbolic Expression,* Indiana University Press, 1965.

Frank, Joseph, *The Widening Gyre: Crisis and Mastery in Modern Literature,* Rutgers University Press, 1963.

Friedman, Melvin, *Stream of Consciousness: A Study in Literary Method,* Yale University Press, 1955.

Gildzen, Alex, editor, *A Festschrift for Djuna Barnes on Her 80th Birthday,* Kent State University Libraries, 1972.

Hyman, Stanley Edgar, *Standards: A Chronicle of Books for Our Time,* Horizon Press, 1966.

Kannenstine, Louis F., *The Art of Djuna Barnes: Duality and Damnation,* New York University Press, 1977.

Messerli, Douglas, *Djuna Barnes: A Bibliography,* David Lewis, 1975.

Muir, Edwin, *The Present Age from 1914,* Cresset Press, 1939.

Nemerov, Howard, *Reflexions on Poetry & Poetics,* Rutgers University Press, 1972.

Nin, Anais, *The Novel of the Future,* Macmillan, 1968.

Scott, James B., *Djuna Barnes,* Twayne, 1976.

Spencer, Sharon, *Space, Time and Structure in the Modern Novel,* New York University Press, 1971.

Taylor, William E., editor, *Modern American Drama: Essays in Criticism,* Everett/Edwards, 1968.

*Atlantic,* May, 1962.

*Berkeley Daily Gazette,* March 31, 1961.

*Chapel Hill Weekly,* September 9, 1962.

*Chicago Sunday Tribune,* April 8, 1962.

*Critique: Studies in Modern Fiction,* spring, 1964, August, 1975.

*Hollins Critic,* June, 1981.

*International Fiction Review,* July, 1975.

*Journal of Aesthetics,* September, 1957.

*Massachusetts Review,* summer, 1962.

*Modern Fiction Studies,* winter, 1973-74.

*Nation,* January 2, 1924, April 3, 1937.

*New Statesman,* October 17, 1936, February 8, 1958.

*New York Herald Tribune Book Review,* October 14, 1923, March 7, 1937, April 29, 1962.

*New York Times,* April 20, 1958, June 28, 1980.

*New York Times Book Review,* April 29, 1962, January 9, 1983, December 1, 1985.

*Northwest Review,* summer, 1958.

*Renascence,* fall, 1962.

*San Francisco Chronicle,* April 13, 1958.

*Saturday Review,* November 17, 1928.

*Sewanee Review,* summer, 1945, summer, 1968.

*Southern Review,* Number 2, 1966-67, January, 1969.

*Time,* April 20, 1962.

*Times Literary Supplement,* April 4, 1958, September 12, 1980, January 21, 1983, October 7, 1983, March 20, 1987.

*Twentieth Century Literature,* May, 1976 *Virginia Quarterly Review,* autumn, 1958.

*Washington Post Book World,* February 1, 1981, June 12, 1983.

*Chicago Tribune,* June 21, 1982.

*Newsweek,* July 5, 1982.

*New York Times,* June 20, 1982.

*Publishers Weekly,* July 2, 1982.

*Times* (London), June 21, 1982.

*Washington Post,* June 21, 1982. □

# Clara Barton

**The American humanitarian Clara Barton (1821-1912) was the founder of the American Red Cross. Her work made her a symbol of humanitarianism.**

Clara Barton was born on Dec. 25, 1821, in North Oxford, Mass. She was the youngest child of Stephen Barton, a farmer and state legislator who had served in the Revolution under Gen. Anthony Wayne; she later recalled that his tales made war early familiar to her.

Well-spoken and well-read, at the age of 15 Clara Barton began teaching at nearby schools. In 1850 she went to teach at Bordentown, N.J., where state tradition required paid schooling and thus served few children. Barton offered to teach without salary if payment were waived. She later took pride in having established the first free school in New Jersey and having raised enrollment in Bordentown from 6 to 600. When town officials decided to appoint a male administrator over her, she resigned. At this time she suffered her first crisis of nervous illness, associated in part with uncertainty about her future.

In 1853 she obtained an appointment as copyist in the Patent Office in Washington, D.C., becoming the first woman in America to hold such a government post. She continued this work till April 1861, when the Civil War began and she determined to serve the Federal troops.

## Civil War Activities

Although the U.S. Sanitary Commission was formed in June 1861 to aid soldiers, Barton had little association with it. (Casual reports later misnamed her as one of its founders.) Her own enterprise involved appeals for provisions to be carried into the war zones; she collected and stored them in Washington for personal distribution. In 1862 the U.S. surgeon general permitted her to travel to the front, and she implemented this order with directives from generals John Pope and James S. Wadsworth, who welcomed her work. Barton was present with Federal forces during the siege of Charleston, S.C., and also at engagements in the Wilderness and at Fredericksburg, Va., and elsewhere.

Barton's mission was not primarily that of a nurse. She became increasingly adept at obtaining and passing out provisions, though her courage and humanity made her a vital presence everywhere. In 1864 she made her most influential connection, joining Gen. Benjamin F. Butler with the Army of the James. She later visited the notorious prison camp at Andersonville, Ga., to identify and mark Union graves.

In 1865 she conceived the project of locating missing soldiers and obtained a note of endorsement from President Lincoln. She set up the Bureau of Records in Washington and traced perhaps 20,000 names. She also lectured on her experiences until her voice failed in 1868.

## Franco-Prussian War

Barton's health continued to trouble her; in 1869 she went to Geneva, Switzerland, for rest and a change. There, officials of the International Red Cross, organized in 1864, urged her to seek United States agreement to the Geneva Convention recognizing the work of the Red Cross; the powerful U.S. Sanitary Commission had been unable to obtain it. But before Barton could turn to the task, the Franco-Prussian War began.

She offered her services to the Grand Duchess of Baden in administering military hospitals. Her most original idea (developed further in later situations) was to put needy Strasbourg women to work sewing garments for pay. Later, with the French defeated and Paris held by the Commune, she entered the starving city to distribute food and clothing. She served elsewhere in France—in Lyons again instituting her work system. She was awarded the Iron Cross of Merit by the German emperor, William I, in 1873; this was one of many such honors.

## American Red Cross

Clara Barton settled in Danville, N.Y., where for several years she was a semi-invalid. In 1877 she wrote a founder of the International Red Cross, offering to lead an American branch of the organization. Thus, at 56 she began a new career.

In 1881 Barton incorporated the American Red Cross, with herself as president. A year later her extraordinary efforts brought about United States ratification of the Geneva Convention. She herself attended conferences of the International Red Cross as the American representative. She was, however, far from bureaucratic in interests. Although wholly individualistic and unlike reformers who worked on programs for social change, she did a great social service as activist and propagandist.

In 1883 Barton served as superintendent of the Women's Reformatory Prison, Sherborn, Mass., thus deviating from a career marked by single-minded commitment to her major cause. As a Red Cross worker, she went to Michigan, which had been ravaged by fires in 1882, and to Charleston, S.C., which had suffered an earthquake. In 1884 she traveled the Ohio River, supplying flood victims. Five years later she went to Johnstown, Pa., to help it recover from a disastrous flood. In 1891 Barton traveled to Russia, which was enduring famine, and in 1896 to Turkey, following the Armenian massacres. Barton was in her late 70s when the Cuban insurrection required relief measures. She prepared to sail in aid of Cubans, but the outbreak of the Spanish-American War turned her ship into a welfare station for Americans as well. As late as 1900 she visited Galveston, Tex., personally to supervise relief for victims of a tidal wave. In 1900 Congress reincorporated the Red Cross, demanding an accounting of funds. By 1904 public pressures and dissension within the Red Cross itself had become too much for Barton, and on June 16 she resigned from the organization. (She even entertained unrealistic thoughts of beginning another one.) A figure of international renown, she retired instead to Glen Echo, Md., where she died on April 12, 1912.

## Further Reading

Clara Barton was the subject of innumerable sketches and books, many merely eulogistic and even fanciful. She herself wrote *The Story of My Childhood* (1907), as well as enlightening accounts of her work, such as *The Red Cross in Peace and War* (1899). Most useful for general purposes is Ishbel Ross, *Angel of the Battlefield: The Life of Clara Barton* (1956). William E. Barton, *Life of Clara Barton, Founder of the American Red Cross* (2 vols., 1922), is adulatory but reproduces revealing letters. Percy H. Epler, *The Life of Clara Barton* (1915), details her life as it appeared to her contemporaries. □

# Katharine Lee Bates

**American poet and educator Katharine Lee Bates (1859-1929) was a leading force in the early development of Wellesley College in Massachusetts and a noted literary scholar. She captured her place in American history, however, when she penned the patriotic poem "America the Beautiful," which was first published in 1895. A musical setting of Bates's vision of the natural beauty and noble ideals of America later became a popular song that was unsuccessfully nominated to become the country's national anthem.**

Katharine Lee Bates was an educator and writer who is best known for her poem, "America the Beautiful." After its publication in the *Boston Evening Transcript* in 1904, the poem gained nationwide popularity for its celebration of the spirit and natural beauty of the country. The musical setting of "America the Beautiful," created in the 1920s, was an unsuccessful contender to become the national anthem, but has remained one of the United States' most recognized and beloved songs.

Bates, the youngest of four children, was born August 12, 1859, in Falmouth, Massachusetts. Her father, William Bates, was a minister who had attended Middlebury College in Vermont and Andover Theological Seminary. Her mother, Cornelia Frances Lee Bates, was a schoolteacher who had been educated at Mount Holyoke College. The Bates had moved to the whaling town of Falmouth on Cape Cod in 1858, when William was offered the position of minister of the Congregational church there. Only a month after his youngest daughter was born, however, William Bates died of a spinal tumor. His death placed the family in economic straits. The pension provided to the Bates family was not sufficient to live on, so they all helped bring in extra money where they could. Bates's mother raised and sold vegetables and poultry and also worked as a seamstress. Her two brothers earned cash by picking cranberries, catching and selling herring and muskrat skins, and herding cows. Everyone in the household also did piece work taken in from a local tag manufacturer. Despite their impoverished situation and the necessity of long hours of work, Cornelia Bates strived to provide her children with an education.

## Studied at Wellesley College

The family's fortune improved when they moved to Grantville, a town near Wellesley, Massachusetts, so that Cornelia could attend to an ailing sister. There, friends of the family secured a house for them and Bates was able to complete her schooling at Needham High School in the early 1870s. During her high school years, Bates discovered that a new college for women was being built in the nearby town of Wellesley. She set her sights on attending the new institution; after her family moved to Newtonville in 1874, she prepared for Wellesley by teaching and attending advanced courses at Newton High School. She was accepted to the college in 1876 and enrolled in Wellesley's second graduating class.

Bates thrived in the atmosphere of learning at Wellesley. In addition to the regular course work in her chosen fields of English and Greek, the college curriculum there included daily exercise such as boating and calisthenics as well as an hour of housework chores a day. Her favorite spot on the campus was the Browning Room, a quiet, comfortable room where she could peruse the papers of the poet Elizabeth Barrett Browning. She also enjoyed roaming the picturesque New England landscape around the college. Her solitary pursuits, however, did not keep her from being an active and admired part of the student body. She was elected by her fellow students to serve on the committee that drafted the class constitution and she was voted class president. During her student days at Wellesley, she decided to become an educator, an ambition she would fulfill in that very school. She also began to demonstrate her poetic abilities during this time, reading one of her poems at her graduation in her role as Class Day poet.

After her graduation in 1880, Bates began teaching at Natick High School. Only three years later, she became a member of the English department at Wellesley, where she would remain for the rest of her career. She left a permanent stamp on the style and quality of education at the college, earning the respect and affection of both fellow teachers and students for her innovative ideas. In 1890, her duties increased when she was named chair of the English department. Despite her teaching and administrative duties, Bates found time to compile an impressive number of publications during her career. Her more than forty books included not only volumes of her own poetry (some of which was published under the pseudonym James Lincoln), but also translations of Spanish and Icelandic works of literature, children's literature, critical versions of literary works, anthologies, and literary histories. Her work earned her a reputation as a noted scholar in literature.

## Poem Inspired by Travels

Bates occasionally traveled throughout the country and to Europe to continue her studies and to give lectures. Her journeys to the western states in the year 1893 provided the inspiration for the poem that made Bates famous. It was during that summer that she visited the World's Columbian Exposition in Chicago and marveled at the impressive architecture of the exhibition halls celebrating the wonders of the age. Continuing on to a lecture engagement in Denver,

Colorado, Bates was further moved by the beauty of the landscape she viewed on a trek to the top of Pike's Peak. In her journal, Bates recorded the feelings of awe and pride that these events had created in her in a poem now known as "America the Beautiful." The poem first appeared in a publication called *The Congregationalist* on July 4, 1895. The response to the work was very positive; after receiving a number of suggestions from readers, Bates wrote a revised version which was published in the *Boston Evening Transcript* in November of 1904. This new poem gained an even wider acclaim and soon was known throughout the country. As years passed, the patriotic poem continued to grow in popularity. In the 1920s, a contest to create a musical score for the poem was sponsored by the National Federation of Music Clubs. The resulting song captured the heart of Americans, and some felt that it should become the national anthem—an honor it did not receive. But the poem and its author had succeeded in becoming an established part of American cultural history.

Bates did not let her fame as the author of "America the Beautiful" distract her from her duties at Wellesley. She continued an active career as a scholar, teacher, and administrator until her retirement in 1925. Her family was an important part of her professional and personal life throughout these years: her sister Jane assisted with Bates' household chores and typing her manuscripts and her mother helped to translate Spanish literature and folktales for her books. Bates often entertained at her home, hosting gatherings for students and colleagues as well as noted literary guests such as the poets Robert Frost, Carl Sandburg and William Butler Yeats. She continued her own writing after her retirement, producing a number of articles and book reviews as well as a collection of poetry, *The Pilgrim Ship,* which was published in 1926. After a series of illnesses in her final years, Bates died of pneumonia on March 28, 1929, in Wellesley. While her literary studies and translations remain a respected body of work, it is her poem "America the Beautiful" that has become her most memorable contribution to American literature. The praises for the natural and spiritual resources of the United States contained in her verses captured a sense of national identity and pride that continues to resonate in the American imagination.

## Further Reading

For more information see Burgess, Dorothy Whittemore Bates, *Dream and Deed: The Story of Katharine Lee Bates,* University of Oklahoma Press, 1952; Drury, Michael, "Why She Wrote America's Favorite Song," *Reader's Digest,* July 1993, pp. 90-93. □

# Kathleen Battle

**American soprano Kathleen Battle (born 1948) divided her career between the opera and concert singing. Her light, sweet voice and charming stage presence were especially suited to operatic ingénue roles.**

Lyric coloratura soprano Kathleen Battle was born on August 13, 1948, in Portsmouth, Ohio. The youngest of seven children whose father was a steel worker, she attended public schools in a segregated school system. She remained relatively unexposed to opera until her teens and, no doubt aware of the limited opportunities afforded to African Americans, steered a practical course for herself, studying typing and shorthand in high school. Although she took the advice of a high school music teacher to study music at the University of Cincinnati College Conservatory, she opted not for the performance curriculum but for an education degree, which would enable her to teach. Her voice teacher during her college years was Franklin Bens.

Having received a bachelor's degree in 1970 and a master's in 1971, Battle taught grades four through six for the next two years in the Cincinnati public school system. Meanwhile, she continued to take voice lessons and also to study German and acting while taking singing jobs in and around Cincinnati.

In 1972 she auditioned successfully for Thomas Shippers, then the director of both the Cincinnati Symphony Orchestra and the Spoleto Festival. He arranged for her professional debut that year in a performance of the Brahms *Requiem* in Spoleto. Her American debut followed as a

repeat performance of the piece with the Cincinnati Orchestra later that year.

The following year Battle came to the attention of James Levine while singing at the Cincinnati May Festival. He immediately engaged her in his guest-conducting tour around the United States. Included in this tour was the Ravinia Festival, to which she returned for several summers as an artist in residence. She moved to New York in 1975 after an engagement in a Broadway production of Scott Joplin's *Treemonisha*.

She made her professional operatic debut as Rosina in Rossini's *Barber of Seville* with the Michigan Opera Theater, and her New York debut followed in 1976 with the City Opera as Susanna in Mozart's *The Marriage of Figaro*. But it was again Levine who brought her rapidly to stardom. In 1977 he offered her the role of the shepherdess in Wagner's *Tannhauser* at the Metropolitan Opera, where her debut took place on December 22, 1977. Battle's physical beauty, captivating stage presence, and a seemingly effortless virtuosity quickly made her a favorite there; and the following years secured her reputation.

Possessing a light, sweet voice of extreme agility, Battle wisely avoided the heavier operatic roles. Among composers she favored Mozart for his precision and clarity of line, his rhythmic vitality, and the appropriateness of the color and weight of his music to her voice. Mozart roles included Pamina in *The Magic Flute,* Susanna in *The Marriage of Figaro,* Despina in *Cosi fan tutte,* and Blonde in *The Abduction* from the *Seraglio.* Other important parts were Zerbinetta in *Ariadne auf Naxos* and Zdenka in *Arabella,* both by Richard Strauss, another favorite composer; Oskar in Verdi's *Un ballo in maschera;* and Norina in Donizetti's *Don Pasquale.*

Battle did not limit her career to the opera, but divided appearances rather equally between opera, song recitals, and performances of vocal works involving larger ensembles. She achieved much commercial success for recordings of her song recitals, which were additionally attractive in that they frequently offered music other than the standard fare. Among her most popular song recordings are those with the guitarist Christopher Parkening (*The Pleasure of Their Company*), the violinist Itzhak Perlman (*The Bach Album*), and the trumpeter Winton Marsalis (*Baroque Duet*). In 1990 she presented a concert of spirituals, also recorded, with Jessye Norman (*Spirituals in Concert*). Although the concert received some criticism for its "pseudo-Gershwin" arrangements, both singers triumphed over what could have been an inappropriate artificiality. Battle often closed song recitals with a group of spirituals.

Other popular recordings are *Kathleen Battle Sings Mozart, Salzburg Recital,* and *At Carnegie Hall.* In June 1986 she gave a command performance, nationally televised, for President Reagan at the White House. She was awarded an honorary Doctorate from the University of Cincinnati in 1983.

Battle's reputation as a temperamental singer was well-known and was documented along with her rise to fame. In February 1994 she was dismissed from the Met's production of Donizetti's *Fille du Régiment* for what officials cited as her "unprofessional actions during rehearsals." At the same time the company withdrew all other offers for future engagements.

Battle has been pursuing other avenues through a variety of professional performances. In 1995, Battle's voice was heard on four albums, and she appeared on the television special *An Evening with Kathleen Battle and Thomas Hampson.* She opened Lincoln Center's 1995-96 jazz season with a concert, and has appeared on tour throughout the United States. With Christopher Parkening she released *Angels Glory,* a compilation of Christmas songs for the 1996 season. *A Christmas Celebration* was released in 1997, and also includes music for the holidays.

### Further Reading

One of the few opera singers to achieve commercial success, Kathleen Battle continued to be charted by all of the music magazines and journals, including *Billboard, Stereo Review,* and *Opera News.* Among the most substantial articles on Battle's career are "Fortune's Favorite: A Conversation with Kathleen Battle" in *Opera News* (March 13, 1982) and "The Sweet Song of Kathleen Battle" in *Fanfare* (1986). The circumstances surrounding her dismissal from the Met are detailed in *The New York Times* (February 8, 1994). □

# Mary Ritter Beard

**Mary Ritter Beard (1876-1958) was active in the struggles for women's suffrage and for trade union reform. With her husband Charles Austin Beard she wrote several books, including the multivolume *The Rise of American Civilization*. On her own she wrote several books about women, the most important of which was *Woman as Force in History: A Study of Traditions and Realities*.**

Mary Ritter Beard was born into a secure, Republican, middleclass world in Indianapolis, Indiana, on August 5, 1876. Her father, Eli Foster Ritter, was an attorney by occupation and a zealous temperance advocate and stalwart of the local Methodist church. Her mother, Narcissa Lockwood, a former school-teacher active in local community and church activities, was primarily caught up in rearing her family of six, of which Beard was the elder daughter. At the age of 16 she attended DePauw University, not far from home, as had her father and as did all her siblings. In college she met and in 1900 married Charles Austin Beard (1874-1948).

The young couple spent two years in England, partly in Manchester, then the center of labor and feminist ferment, and both movements absorbed their energies. At Oxford, where her husband studied history and helped to found Ruskin Hall, a college designed for workingclass men, she discovered the militant women's movement and met and worked with leading English radical suffragists.

The Beards returned to the United States in 1902 and both began graduate study at Columbia University, but she soon left her academic studies in sociology. By then the mother of two children, she chose to devote her time to the struggles for women's suffrage and for trade union reform. For example, she helped the National Women's Trade Union League organize the New York shirt-waistmaker's strike in 1909 and protest the Triangle factory fire in which more than 100 young girls and women were killed.

She became an activist in the women's suffrage movement as organizer, publicist, and fundraiser. Her particular interest in workingclass women, a legacy from her years in England, led her to active participation in the Wage Earner's League, the Woman Suffrage Party's organization for working women. When a militant faction of the National Woman Suffrage Association began to form under the leadership of Alice Paul, Beard went with this group, originally known as the Congressional Union, later splitting away to form the Woman's Party.

Although Beard stayed with the women's suffrage movement for years, she slowly detached herself from the role of activist and moved toward the role of analyst and social critic. A break did finally come when, after the suffrage amendment was won in 1920, the Woman's Party centered its activities on the passage of the Equal Rights Amendment. Beard left the organization, choosing instead to support the idea of protective legislation for working women. She was one of many feminists, especially those concerned with working women, who initially opposed the Equal Rights Amendment (ERA).

## Writing with a Partner

The Beards were partners for almost 50 years, raised two children, established an exciting and loving home together, and shared a political commitment that carried them often into the public arena on controversial issues. They are most well-known today for their collaboration on major works. The Beards' first joint venture, *American Citizenship,* appeared in 1914. In 1920 they issued *The History of the United States* . The first two volumes of their monumental history of the nation appeared in 1927. The total work is titled *The Rise of American Civilization.* In 1939 another two volumes of The Rise appeared, and in 1942 the concluding volume was issued. *The Rise of American Civilization* shaped the thinking of generations of Americans. *A Basic History of the United States,* their "last will and testament of the American people," said her husband, was published in 1944.

Beard published two books alone while she was involved in activist politics. The first, *Woman's Work in Municipalities,* appearing in 1915, was a lengthy essay in the tradition of muckraking literature, demonstrating the varied and essential work of women in cities. In 1920 she published *A Short History of the American Labor Movement,* designed for readers with little knowledge of the struggle of working people in the United States. Her only other book written alone that did not deal with women was a long essay, *The Making of Charles A. Beard,* which was published in 1955, seven years after her husband's death.

The rest of her long and active intellectual life was devoted to writing books and articles and speaking endlessly on what became the major theme of her public life— that women are and have always been a central force in history and culture, that women have been active, assertive, competent contributors to their societies, but that history books do not reflect their role. Women are left out of history, are made to seem invisible, she said, and she saw as her mission a reconstruction in order to end that invisibility.

Women had succeeded, after 80 years of active struggle, in acquiring the vote, but with that victory came the belief that women's history began with the suffrage struggle. To Beard, such a belief was a denial of all the histories of women, and, therefore, a denial of self in the women who were living in the present. The core of everything she wrote and everything she did was shaped by her conviction that women were undeniably a force in civilization, and that history and politics were incomplete without that recognition. She devoted her energies to trying to persuade all people, but women particularly, of their own historic past and of the power that was within their reach to change the present. She began a crusade for women's minds that took many forms.

## Writing Alone

Most important, she wrote *On Understanding Women,* published in 1931, which ushered in the decade of her most creative work. In 1933 she edited a collection of writing by women called *America Through Women's Eyes.* In 1934 she edited, with Martha Bensley Bruère, *Laughing Their Way: Women's Humor in America* . In 1946 her most famous work appeared: *Woman as Force in History: A Study of Traditions and Realities.* Reprinted in 1962 and again in 1971, it had its third printing in 1973. In 1953 she published *The Force of Women in Japanese History.*

*Woman as Force in History* represents the culmination of her years of study and writing on the subject and stands as the mature statement of her thesis on the historic role of women. Many of the ideas and themes she developed in earlier years were pulled together and deepened in this major work. Her analysis of the ideas of the legal theories of William Blackstone and their impact on American feminists occupies a significant portion of what is new and of immense significance in this volume.

In pre-industrial times, she asserted, women were often discriminated against and were seen by theologians and moralists as evil and inferior, but in reality women so often defied law and custom that it is not possible to use any single formula to describe woman's role. Women of the ruling class often wielded great power, and women of the lower classes suffered as much or more from their class position as from their gender. It was not until the rise of democratic government and the expansion of political power to ordinary men that women as a group were excluded from positions of power. It was with the development of capitalism, she argued, that discrimination on account of sex, regardless of class, became pervasive, and it was during this time that women were driven out of the professions, out of politics, and out of power. The feminist movement, born during this period of diminished rights, assumed that such restrictions always existed and thus passed on a view of history that was invalid and incomplete.

Even in her role as intellectual and social critic, Mary Ritter Beard retained her activist impulse. In 1934 she wrote an extraordinary 50-page pamphlet entitled "A Changing Political Economy as it Affects Women," which was a detailed syllabus for a women's studies course—the first of its kind—and she tried desparately to persuade many colleges and universities to establish such a course. Later in the 1930s, in an effort to create some tangible demonstration of women's lives and women's pasts, she developed the idea of establishing a women's archive. For five years she tried to establish, finance, organize, structure, house, and publicize what became the World Center for Women's Archives. The object of the center was to assemble and preserve all source material dealing with women's lives, a clearinghouse of information on the history of women.

In the spring of 1941 she was involved in a new project, a feminist critique of the *Encyclopaedia Britannica,* financed by the *Encyclopaedia* itself and carried out by a staff of three women that Beard selected. The final report, submitted after 18 months, is an intriguing 40-page document which is filled with provocative ideas for further research.

Mary Ritter Beard died in August 1958 at the age of 84, but the echo of her voice and the impact of her ideas remain.

## Further Reading

The best way to become familiar with the ideas of Mary Ritter Beard is to read her books, especially *Woman as Force in*

*History,* although this is not an easy work to understand. The only extensive appraisal of her life and work is Ann J. Lane's *Mary Ritter Beard: A Sourcebook -*(1978), which also contains significant selections from her writings and a thorough bibliography. Other valuable assessments are Berenice A. Carroll, "Mary Beard's *Woman as Force in History:* A Critique," Massachusetts Review (Winter-Spring 1972) and reprinted in *Liberating Women's History: Theoretical and Critical Essays ,* edited by Berenice A. Carroll (1976); Carl N. Degler, "*Woman as Force in History by Mary Beard,*" Daedalus (Winter 1974); and Ann J. Lane, "Mary Ritter Beard: Women as Force," in *Feminist Theorists: Three Centuries of Women's Intellectual Traditions,* edited by Dale Spender (1983).

## Additional Sources

Turoff, Barbara K., *Mary Beard as force in history,* Dayton, Ohio: Wright State University, 1979. □

# Catharine Beecher

**American author and educator Catharine Beecher (1800-1878) was responsible for creating a new social attitude that placed greater value on women's work in the home and their role as educators and moral guides for the young. Her book *Treatise on Domestic Economy* (1841) was a best-selling work that provided practical household advice while extolling the virtues of domestic life. She also was an active proponent for the creation of schools for women, arguing that for their special role as instructors of children, women required a thorough education.**

Catharine Beecher was a nineteenth century proponent of women's rights and education for women. While she did not advocate a radical change in women's roles, she did fight for increased recognition of the importance of the work women did in managing homes and raising families. She also believed that women should expand their place in society by becoming teachers, allowing them to use their nurturing skills and moral conscience in a professional sphere. To encourage the spread of these ideas, Beecher published a number of books providing guidance and praise for domestic life, such as her extremely popular *Treatise on Domestic Economy* (1843). She also founded schools and organizations devoted to training women to become teachers. Beecher held the view that the woman, as educator and spiritual guide for families, was the basis of a well-ordered and moral society. This theme contributed to a growing feminist attitude that women did not have to be weak, passive creatures, but could be strong, contributing members of their communities.

Beecher was born September 6, 1800, in the town of East Hampton on Long Island, New York. She was the oldest child of Lyman and Roxanna Ward Beecher. Each of her parents had a strong influence on the values she touted as an

adult. Her father was a Presbyterian minister who came from a family of Calvinist colonists. He was a prominent figure in the evangelical religious movement of the early 1800s known as the Second Great Awakening. His strong personality and religious convictions were apparent not only in the religious revivals that he held, but in his dominant presence in the Beecher home as well. Beecher's mother, also from a respected family, played a traditional role in the home and attempted to pass along her domestic skills to her children. Beecher was ambivalent about both the religious and domestic aspects of her life as a young woman. She initially disliked domestic duties, preferring to spend her time outside or studying. Later in life, however, she came to view domestic responsibilities as a valuable and sacred contribution to home and community. Similarly, her religious instincts fluctuated throughout her life, and she never was able to come to terms with her faith.

The Beechers moved to Litchfield, Connecticut, in 1809. The following year, Beecher entered Miss Pierce's school, a well-respected institution for young women. Her education there stressed not only the acquisition of social skills, but also the growth of a moral consciousness and leadership abilities. Beecher thrived at the school, but was forced to leave at the age of 16 after the death of her mother. She returned home to tend to the domestic duties of the household, including raising her younger brothers and sisters and doing the cooking and sewing for the family. After her father remarried in 1817, she remained for another year at home before taking a teaching job in New London, Connecticut, in 1818.

## Focused on Education of Women

At the age of 22, Beecher was engaged to a Yale University professor of natural history named Alexander Fisher. Her choice was not a whole-hearted one, however. While her father was quite pleased with Fisher, Beecher herself was concerned that his unaffectionate nature would not make him an ideal husband. The marriage never occurred—Fisher was killed in a shipwreck off the coast of Ireland in the spring of 1822. Beecher never again entertained thoughts of marriage. Instead, she turned her energies to what would become her life's main passion, the education of women.

In 1823, Beecher opened the Hartford Female Seminary in Hartford, Connecticut. At her school, she combined a solid core of courses in algebra, chemistry, history, Latin, philosophy, and rhetoric with an emphasis on developing the moral and religious character of her students. The institution was very successful, and as its principal, Beecher became a popular and respected figure in Hartfield. Her accomplishments and her growing reputation as a talented teacher inspired Beecher to write about her educational philosophy. In her 1829 essay, "Suggestions Respecting Improvements in Education," she declared that the primary goal of education should be to provide a basis for the development of the student's conscience and moral makeup. To facilitate this kind of instruction in her school, Beecher unsuccessfully sought to hire an associate principal to manage the teaching of religion. Failing to secure an assistant, Beecher suffered from a nervous breakdown and left the school in the hands of her sister Harriet for several months while she recovered. Upon her return, she took on the task of religious and moral instruction herself.

With the beginning of the 1830s, Beecher became more interested in the roles her female students would take on in society. While she believed that running a home and raising a family was an important and influential contribution by women, she also felt that women should be given more responsibility and respect outside the home. She saw the field of teaching as the perfect professional arena for women—it allowed them an independent and consequential role in their community, but at the same time it was an acceptably "feminine" role. In addition, the growing populations of the western areas of the country were creating an increased demand for teachers. Beecher was appalled that in states like Ohio, perhaps one third of children did not have access to schools.

## Founded School for Teacher Training

To encourage more women to become teachers, Beecher realized there needed to be more opportunities for women to be educated and trained for the profession. She made it her mission to provide such training. In 1831, she left the East Coast to join her father in Cincinnati, Ohio, where he had been name president of the Lane Theological Seminary. There she opened the Western Female Institute, a school devoted to instructing young women so that they, in turn, could instruct others. Beecher hoped that her school could serve as a model for a nationwide system of teacher colleges. She presented her ideas on the subject in an 1835 lecture that was published under the title "An Essay on the Education of Female Teachers." In Cincinnati, she began a fundraising effort to support her school and the creation of similar schools. But Beecher was not well-liked in the city; many people felt that she was a cultural elitist. Her abolitionist views were also suspect in an area divided on the issue of slavery. Unable to win the financial or philosophical support of residents, enrollment in Beecher's school steadily declined until it was finally forced to close in 1837.

The townspeople's opinions apparently had little effect on Beecher's own values, however. That same year, she published a tract that called on women to unite against the system of slavery, titled "Slavery and Abolition with Reference to the Duty of American Females." In this essay, Beecher began to formulate her idea that women could have a powerful influence on the character of the nation by creating a virtuous and harmonious domestic realm, in this way providing a stable, moral basis for society. Writing became the new channel through which Beecher attempted to spread her philosophy and make a living. She began to turn out a large amount of material, but it was not until the publication of her *Treatise on Domestic Economy* in 1841 that she finally reached the wider audience that she sought. The book was an incredible success, going through almost 15 printings in as many years and earning her fame across the nation.

## Celebrates Domesticity in Best-seller

The *Treatise* provided women with a practical and moral guide to domestic life. It presented information on such topics as cooking, child care, and general health care. In this way, it presented a handy single source of household knowledge that had not existed before. But even more important was the philosophy in which Beecher couched her advice. She saw such domestic concerns not as mundane drudgery but as "the greatest work," a devotion to the welfare of others that provided the basis of a healthy society. The mission of women, according to Beecher, was to form the moral and intellectual character of children, and in order to fulfill this duty successfully, women required a quality education. Through their examples of skilled nurturing and intelligent teaching, women could use their home life as a secure base from which to reach out and create change in the rest of society. Beecher's ideas did not radically attack traditional gender roles, rather it justified and glorified them. This support of the family and social hierarchy struck a chord of comfort and stability in the public, making Beecher a celebrity.

With the success of her book, Beecher was able to found the Women's Education Association in New York in 1852. The organization was devoted to raising funds for the establishment of women's schools. Beecher was never satisfied with the amount of money raised by the organization (it eventually dissolved in 1862), so she undertook a number of public appearances across the country in which she solicited donations, promoted women's education, and discussed her books. She also sought donations from friends and relatives for her education ventures. She further supported educational causes by attending teacher's confer-

ences and sustaining a correspondence with a wide range of people.

In the last years of her life, Beecher returned to the East, where she lived with various relatives. She had a particularly close relationship with her sister Harriet Beecher Stowe, best-known as the author of the novel *Uncle Tom's Cabin*. The sisters worked together to write an 1869 sequel to the *Treatise on Domestic Economy* entitled *The American Woman's Home*. Beecher was active in fighting for women's education for the rest of her years. She died in Elmira, New York, on May 12, 1878. Through her writings, public appearances, and the schools she helped to found, Beecher had helped to gain recognition for the value of women's work in society. Although she did not challenge the traditionally subordinate place of females, she did present a new vision of women as a strong and influential force that helped to determine the direction and conscience of the nation. Her emphasis on bringing women into the teaching profession also changed notions about women's education and careers, providing a basis for the continued growth of feminist thought in the nineteenth century.

## Further Reading

See also Barker-Benfield, Graham J., and Catherine Clinton, *Portraits of American Women*, St. Martin's Press, 1991; Kerber, Linda K., and Jane S. DeHart, *Women's America*, 3rd ed., Oxford University Press, 1991; and Sklar, Kathryn Kish, *Catharine Beecher: A Study in Domesticity*, W. W. Norton, 1976. □

# Ruth Fulton Benedict

**The American cultural anthropologist Ruth Fulton Benedict (1887-1948) originated the configurational approach to culture. Her work has provided a bridge between the humanities and anthropology, as well as background for all later culture-personality studies.**

Ruth Fulton was born in New York City, the daughter of a surgeon. She entered Vassar College in 1905 and specialized in English literature. After graduation she taught English in a girls' secondary school.

In 1914 she married the biochemist Stanley Benedict, and the next 5 years were spent waiting for the children who never came and experimenting with a variety of creative tasks, such as writing poetry (her pen name as a poet was Anne Singleton), studying dance, and exploring the lives of famous women of the past. In 1919 she began to study anthropology and received her doctorate from Columbia University in 1923.

## Configurational Theory

Her first anthropological work was a study of the way in which the same themes, such as the "Vision Quest," were organized differently in different Native American cultures. During the next 9 years she was editor of the *Journal of*

*American Folk-Lore* and did a substantial amount of fieldwork among the Native Americans of the South-west. In all of this early work she was impressed with the extraordinary diversity of human cultures, but she did not yet have any way of integrating this diversity.

In the summer of 1927, while doing fieldwork among the Pima, she developed her configurational theory of culture: each culture could be seen as "personality writ large"—a set of emphases derived from some of the innumerable potentialities of the human personality. *Patterns of Culture* (1934), her best-known book, develops this theme. This book contrasts the Native American cultures of the Southwest as Dionysian and Appolonian, borrowing terminology from Nietzsche; and Kwakiutl and Dobuan cultures as megalomaniac and paranoid, borrowing terms from psychiatry. This eclectic choice illustrated her open-ended approach to history and her lesser concern with universals. She is sometimes associated with a theory of cultural relativity which treats all values as relative; actually she was deeply committed to the relevance of anthropology to man's control of his own evolution.

## Cross-Cultural Studies

During the 1940s she devoted her energies to dispelling myths about race (*Race: Science and Politics,* 1940) and to a discussion of how warfare, now outmoded, could be superseded. During World War II she worked on studies of countries to which the United States had no access: Romania, the Netherlands, Thailand, and Japan. After the war she published *The Chrysanthemum and the Sword: Patterns of Japanese Culture* (1946), which was the best received of all the anthropological studies of national character. In 1947 she was elected president of the American Anthropological Association, and in 1948, belatedly, she was designated full professor of anthropology at Columbia University.

In 1947 Benedict inaugurated a great cross-cultural study, the Columbia University Research in Contemporary Cultures (France, Syria, China, Russia, Eastern European Jews, Czechoslovakia), in which 120 scholars from 14 disciplines and of 16 nationalities worked harmoniously together. In the summer of 1948 she visited Europe for the first time since 1926 and saw again at firsthand some of the cultures she had analyzed at a distance. She had gone to Europe against the advice of physicians, and she died a week after her return in September 1948, leaving a devoted group of younger collaborators to finish the work.

## Further Reading

Margaret Mead, *An Anthropologist at Work: Writings of Ruth Benedict* (1959), is a study of Mrs. Benedict's life that includes many of her shorter papers and a selection of her poems. Erik H. Erikson wrote *Ruth Fulton Benedict: A Memorial* in 1949. Her life and career are recounted in Hoffman R. Hays, *From Ape to Angel: An Informal History of Social Anthropology* (1958), and Abram Kardiner and Edward Preble, *They Studied Man* (1961). Marvin Harris, *The Rise of Anthropological Theory: A History of Theories of Culture* (1968), discusses the importance of her work.

## Additional Sources

Benedict, Ruth, *An anthropologist at work: writings of Ruth Benedict,* Westport, Conn.: Greenwood Press, 1977.
Caffrey, Margaret M. (Margaret Mary), *Ruth Benedict: stranger in this land,* Austin: University of Texas Press, 1989.
Dimitroff, Gail., *Guiding spirits: an inquiry into the nature of the bond between Ruth Benedict and Margaret Mead,* San Diego: G. Dimitroff, 1983.
Mead, Margaret, *Ruth Benedict,* New York, Columbia University Press, 1974.
Modell, Judith Schachter, *Ruth Benedict, patterns of a life,* Philadelphia: University of Pennsylvania Press, 1983. □

# Dorothy Lewis Bernstein

**Dorothy Lewis Bernstein (born 1914) conducted research focused on the Laplace transform, a mathematical function used in the solution of partial differential equations that has been widely applied in the twentieth century in conjunction with operational calculus.**

Dorothy Lewis Bernstein is a distinguished mathematician and educator in the fields of applied mathematics, statistics, and computer programming. Her research focused on the Laplace transform, a mathematical function named after the French mathematician Pierre-Simon Laplace. The Laplace transform is used in the solution of partial differential equations (equations that contain the partial derivatives of functions of two or more variables) and has been widely applied in the twentieth century in conjunction with operational calculus. Bernstein was a pioneer in incorporating applied mathematics and computer science into the undergraduate mathematics curriculum. In 1979, she became the first woman president of the Mathematical Association of America, a national association concerned with college mathematics.

Bernstein was born in Chicago on April 11, 1914, to Jacob and Tillie Bernstein, who were Russian immigrants. The family lived in Milwaukee during Bernstein's youth. In 1930, Bernstein began her studies at the University of Wisconsin at Madison. During her junior and senior years, she studied mathematics under an independent curriculum. In 1934, based on an oral examination and her thesis on the complex roots of polynomials (mathematical expressions containing certain algebraic terms), she received both a bachelor's (summa cum laude) and a master's degree in mathematics.

After another year at Madison as a teaching fellow, Bernstein received a scholarship to the doctoral program in mathematics at Brown University in Rhode Island. As Ann Moskol indicates in *Women of Mathematics,* Bernstein's experiences at Brown reflect various forms of discrimination. Bernstein's graduate teaching was restricted to only three female students. When she sought advice on finding a teaching position, the graduate school dean advised her not to apply in the South because she was Jewish or in the West because of her gender. Bernstein underwent an unusually arduous doctoral examination, which her advisor later acknowledged was due to her gender and to her midwestern university credentials.

Nonetheless, Bernstein independently secured a teaching position at Mount Holyoke College in Massachusetts. Bernstein taught at Mount Holyoke from 1937 to 1940, completing her doctorate from Brown in 1939 with a thesis related to the Laplace transform. In 1941, Bernstein returned to Madison as an instructor. In the summer of 1942, she was a research associate at the University of California at Berkeley under the Polish mathematician and statistician Jerzy Neyman. In 1943, Bernstein took an instructorship at the University of Rochester in New York, where she became an assistant professor in 1946.

At Rochester, Bernstein's research was directed toward exploiting the computational potential of digital computers (their ability to perform complex mathematical operations on large amounts of data at high speeds) in solving partial differential equations. This research, intended for military application and conducted in affiliation with the Office of Naval Research, led to the publication of Bernstein's *Existence Theorems in Partial Differential Equations* in 1950. In 1951, Bernstein was a member of the Institute for Advanced Study in Princeton, New Jersey. Bernstein became an associate professor at Rochester in 1951, and a full professor in 1957. From 1957 to 1958, she was a visiting professor at the University of California in Los Angeles.

In 1959, Bernstein assumed a professorship at Goucher College in Baltimore, Maryland, where she chaired the mathematics department from 1960 to 1970 and directed the computer center from 1961 to 1967. She served on the board of governors of the Mathematical Association of America, the professional association with which she was most closely involved, from 1965 to 1968. As a department administrator at Goucher, Bernstein brought applied mathematics and the emerging field of computer sciene into the undergraduate mathematics curriculum, and integrated computer programming into her own courses in statistics. Moskol notes that Bernstein "believed that applied mathematics not only made material more relevant to students, but it also motivated them to understand the axioms and theorems of pure mathematics, which could then be used in applied problems." Bernstein's practial vein was further indicated by the internship program she established for Goucher's math majors.

During her tenure at Goucher, Bernstein was also involved through the National Science Foundation in promoting computer programming instruction and the use of computers in advanced mathematics courses at area high schools. She helped establish the Maryland Association for Educational Use of Computers in 1972 and served on its governing board from 1972 to 1975. Bernstein was vice-president of the Mathematical Association of America from 1972 to 1974 and president from 1979 to 1981. She also served on the Joint Projects Committee and the Joint Committee on Women of the Mathematical Association of America, the American Mathematical Society, and the Society of Industrial and Applied Mathematics, and on the editorial board of the *Two Year College Mathematics Journal*. Bernstein retired from Goucher College in 1979.

## Further Reading

Moskol, Ann, "Dorothy Lewis Bernstein," in *Women of Mathematics,* edited by Louise S. Grinstein and Paul J. Campbell, Greenwood, 1987, pp. 17-20.
Coon, Geraldine A., "Coon on Bernstein," *Goucher Quarterly,* fall, 1979, pp. 16-17. □

# Mary Frances Berry

**Mary Frances Berry (born 1938) is a groundbreaking African American woman. She was the first black woman to head a major research university, was appointed Assistant Secretary of Education by President Jimmy Carter in 1977, and became commissioner and vice chairman of the United States Commission on Civil Rights in 1980. She is a professor at the University of Pennslvania and remains active in a variety of social and political issues.**

Born on February 17, 1938, in Nashville, Tennessee, Mary Frances Berry is the second of the three children of George and Frances Berry. Because of economic hardship and extenuating family circumstances, Mary Frances and her older brother were placed in an orphanage for a time. Throughout her early life, Berry was subjected to poverty and to the cruelty that accompanies racial prejudice. However, she proved to be a determined and resilient child with an innate intellectual ability and curiosity.

Berry persevered in her studies in the segregated schools of Nashville and eventually found a mentor, Minerva Hawkins, one of the black teachers at her high school. At the time, Berry was in the tenth grade, bored with school, and experiencing the usual uncertainties that come with adolescence. Hawkins challenged her to keep learning and growing so that she could one day reach her full potential. While Berry had someone with whom she could discuss academic subjects and her plans for the future, she also had the encouragement and support of her mother, who was determined to provide better opportunities for her children. Berry recalled in *Ms.* that her mother would say, "You, Mary Frances! You're smart. . . . You can think, you can do all the things I would have done if it had been possible for me. . . . You have a responsibility to use your mind, and to go as far as it will take you." In 1956 Berry succeeded in making herself, her mother, and her mentor proud by graduating with honors from Pearl High School.

Philosophy, history, and chemistry were Berry's main areas of interest as she began college at Fisk University in Nashville. She later transferred to Howard University in Washington, D.C. After earning her bachelor of arts degree in 1961, Berry began graduate studies in the department of history at Howard. As a grad student, she sharpened her

skills in historical methodology and applied them in researching the black experience and U.S. history. In addition to attending classes and studying, she worked nights in various hospital laboratories to help defray college expenses.

Berry then decided to leave Howard University and continue her graduate studies in history at the University of Michigan. Her chosen area of study was U.S. history with a concentration in constitutional history. Because of her outstanding academic record, Berry was awarded the Civil War Roundtable Fellowship Award in 1965. The next year, with a Ph.D. to her credit, Berry accepted a position as an assistant professor of history at Central Michigan University. That same year, she also began studies for a law degree at the University of Michigan Law School. Berry reminisced in *Ms.* that her mother had always told her, "Be overeducated. If somebody else has a master's degree, you get a Ph.D. If somebody has that, then you get a law degree too."

In 1970 she was awarded her J.D. degree and accepted a full-time position as the acting director of the Department of Afro-American Studies at the University of Maryland. Educational administration suited Berry, and she was eventually named director of Afro-American Studies at the university. This promotion was followed by an appointment to the post of interim chairperson of the Division of Behavioral and Social Sciences. From 1974 to 1976 she served as provost for this division, thus becoming the highest-ranking black woman on the University of Maryland's College Park campus.

When the Board of Regents at the University of Colorado offered Berry the chancellorship of the university's Boulder campus in 1976, she accepted and became the first black woman to head a major research university. A year later, she took a leave of absence from her duties at Boulder to accept newly elected U.S. president Jimmy Carter's invitation to serve in the Department of Health, Education and Welfare (HEW). As the assistant secretary for Education from 1977 to 1980, Berry again broke new ground: she was the first African American woman to serve as the chief educational officer in the United States.

## Appointed to U.S. Commission on Civil Rights

In 1980 President Carter appointed Berry to the U.S. Commission on Civil Rights, a bipartisan agency that monitors the enforcement of civil rights laws. Along with Berry, he appointed Blandina Cardenas Ramirez and commissioned a massive affirmative action study. In doing so, Carter planted "many seeds ... that would later grow to entangle the commission in turmoil under [President Ronald] Reagan" theorized James Reston, Jr., in *Rolling Stone.* When the affirmative action study was published, it supported setting goals and timetables for correcting historic discrimination of blacks and women, particularly in the workplace.

In his 1980 presidential campaign, Reagan had spoken against affirmative action, and the newly published study put him in an uncomfortable position. According to Reston, the Commission on Civil Rights was viewed by Reagan and his staff as "a pocket of renegades that needed to be cleaned out." Reston continued: "Reagan wanted his own people everywhere, and no agency—regardless of ... its historic independence and bipartisanship—escaped attention." In 1984, Reagan attempted to fire Berry, a registered Independent, along with Democrat Ramirez and another Democratic commissioner.

In the *Washington Post,* Berry expressed her frustration over Reagan's attempt to remove members of the commission who disagreed with his viewpoints. She felt that his actions reduced the U.S. Civil Rights Commission from "watchdog of civil rights" to "a lapdog for the administration." Berry and Ramirez successfully sued Reagan in a federal court and retained their seats on the commission. Berry became known as "the woman the president could not fire." Joan Barthel wrote in *Ms.* that Berry's "convictions [kept] her clinging stubbornly to her outcast's seat on the commission." Berry responded: "I tell [my friends] the happiest day of my life was when Reagan fired me. . . . I was fired because I did what I was supposed to do. His firing me was like giving me an A and saying 'Go to the head of the class.'"

## Scholarly Pursuits

Berry returned to Howard University as a professor of history and law in 1980. By 1987, she had accepted the post of Geraldine R. Segal Professor of American Social Thought at the University of Pennsylvania. Throughout the 1980s, she increased her involvement in social activism and published two books, *Long Memory: The Black Experience in America* and *Why ERA Failed: Politics, Women's Rights, and the Amending Process of the Constitution. Long Memory,* co-authored by John Wesley Blassingame, a professor of southern and African American history at Yale, uses autobiographies, poetry, and newspaper stories to document the responses of people of color to oppression and racism in the United States. The text is designed to be used in survey courses on the African American experience.

*Why ERA Failed,* published in 1986, suggests that the controversial Equal Rights Amendment failed because it lacked the broad consensus it needed at both the national and the local levels. Berry contends that ERA supporters made a mistake by not building state-to-state coalitions of support for the amendment. In addition, she maintains that certain U.S. Supreme Court actions—actions aimed at removing common forms of discrimination throughout the nation—actually worked against the amendment's passage; according to Berry, the American public became less inclined to support the idea of a sweeping constitutional amendment because judicial measures, no matter how small, were already being taken to curtail discriminatory practices.

## Stepped Up Role in Global Activism

Academic analyses comprised only one part of Berry's professional life. In 1984 she wanted to raise the collective American consciousness on apartheid in South Africa. The issue of South Africa's government-imposed policy of racial segregation was being discussed by groups throughout the United States, but little was actually being done to end it. Berry felt that it was time to take action. On Thanksgiving Eve of 1984, Berry, TransAfrica head Randall Robinson, and Congressman Walter Fauntroy visited the South African embassy in Washington, D.C., and presented a list of demands: they wanted longtime political prisoner Nelson Mandela of the African National Congress—as well as other anti-apartheid leaders—set free, and they wanted a new South African constitutional conference planned. The three activists vowed that they would wait while the ambassador called Pretoria, the seat of the country's government, with their demands.

Their actions had been carefully planned for what is traditionally a slow news day. As Berry told *Ms.,* "If you're going to help people in their struggle, you should be smart for them. . . . If your demonstration doesn't get media coverage, you might as well not have it." The media was indeed there to record Berry, Robinson, and Fauntroy being handcuffed and led away in a paddy wagon. The effect was just what the trio had hoped for. Barthel recounted in *Ms.:* "Here was not just another campus radical; here was Dr. Mary Frances Berry, a member of the Commission on Civil Rights, a professor of history and law, a member of the bar, a scholar with published books to her credit, with more citations and honorary degrees than her wall could hold. Here was a former Assistant Secretary of Health, Education, and Welfare, once a provost at the University of Maryland, and chancellor at the University of Colorado at Boulder."

## Spearheaded Free South Africa Movement

Berry, Robinson, and Fauntroy were arraigned on Thanksgiving Day and released on their own recognizance. At a press conference the day after Thanksgiving, the trio introduced their Free South Africa Movement (FSAM). At 4:15 p.m. each day thereafter for a full year, a picket line formed at the South African embassy and ended with a press conference that invariably appeared on the evening news. Celebrities and activists such as Paul Newman, Tony Randall, Gloria Steinem, some of the Kennedys, and members of Congress came by to lend support. Altogether Berry was arrested five times, but she never gave up hope. "Progressive politics is not passé," she told *Ms.,* "and there are things we can do to make change, and to lay the groundwork for change later on."

Over the next year, the Free South Africa Movement spread throughout the country. Colleges, universities, and cities were divesting themselves of holdings in companies that operated in South Africa. Eventually Nelson Mandela was released from prison in South Africa and economic sanctions were imposed against the country. Early in 1992, Berry, Robinson, and Fauntroy had reason to rejoice when a referendum approved the dismantlement of apartheid. "Now, we want to see a day when the black violence will end, and one man, one vote will come," stated Berry in the *Washington Post.* That day came in the spring of 1994, when Mandela—once a powerless prisoner of apartheid—became the new president in his country's first free and fair multiracial elections.

## Tackled Child Care Issues

Having made an impact on the international front, Berry returned in the 1990s to domestic issues—like employment, pay equity, and the state of the American family. Family issues and women's rights were the topics of her 1993 book *The Politics of Parenthood.* Historically, notes Berry, child care was not the sole province of mothers. By the mid-nineteenth century, however, the tradition of the man as the breadwinner and the woman as the homemaker was firmly entrenched in American society. When women joined the work force in droves during the 1970s, the notion of women as primary care takers held on. "Even among activists for parental leave," wrote Berry, "the argument is that the *mother* needs more help because now women are out in the world. But the evidence from psychologists is that children can be cared for by anyone, so long as it's good, consistent care."

Berry told Kenneth Walker in *Emerge* that the central civil rights message of her book is that until mothers are freed from the primary responsibility of child rearing, they cannot pursue their economic or other destinies. In response to Walker's statement that many people believe that the high crime rate and increasing number of troubled children is a result of the absence of a good mother, Berry replied, "If my child is bad, it's because our whole extended family network is not working. To say my child is bad because he doesn't have a good mother, I mean, it's like an alien notion, because the mother [alone] is just not responsible."

Reviewing Berry's book in the *Christian Science Monitor*, Laura Van Tuyl stated, "Berry presents a dispassionate history of the women's movement, day care, and home life, showing the persistent obstacles to economic and political power that have confronted women as a result of society's definition of them as 'mothers.' [She] . . . attributes the failure of the Equal Rights Amendment, the languishing of the women's movement in the '80s, and years of bickering over federal parental-leave and child care bills to an unwillingness to rethink gender roles."

Berry continues in her determined struggle for racial, economic, and gender-based justice. "Basically, I'm an optimist," she remarked in *Ms.* "I honestly believe—and I'm sorry, I know this sounds boring—that in the end, truth and justice will prevail. . . . My mother used to tell me, 'Remember, sometimes when it seems like you're losing, you're winning. It all comes out in the wash.'"

### Further Reading

Berry, Mary Frances, *The Politics of Parenthood: Child Care, Women's Rights, and the Myth of the Good Mother*, Viking, 1993.
*Christian Science Monitor*, May 13, 1993, p. 13.
*Ebony*, January 1979, p. 80.
*Emerge*, June 1993, p. 58; September 1993, p. 6.
*Essence*, October 1984, p. 12.
*Jet*, March 20, 1989, p. 10; October 11, 1993, p. 14.
*Los Angeles Times*, April 19, 1993, p. E-2.
*Ms.*, January 1987, p. 68; November/December 1990, p. 88.
*Nation*, May 23, 1987, p. 692.
*New Republic*, August 16, 1993, p. 30.
*New York Times*, February 10, 1993, p. A-19.
*New York Times Book Review*, October 19, 1986, p. 7.
*New York Times Magazine*, September 13, 1987, p. 93.
*Publishers Weekly*, January 11, 1993, p. 46.
*Rolling Stone*, March 13, 1986, p. 41.
*Society*, May/June 1988, p. 94.
*USA Today*, January 28, 1992, p. A-11; April 12, 1993, p. A-12.
*Washington Monthly*, December 1986, p. 58; October 1987, p. 46.
*Washington Post*, January 18, 1984; March 19, 1992, p. 19. □

# Mary McLeod Bethune

**Mary McLeod Bethune (1875-1955), an African American teacher, was one of the great educators of the United States. She was a leader of women, a distinguished adviser to several American presidents, and a powerful champion of racial equality.**

Mary McLeod was born in Mayesville, S.C. Her parents, Samuel and Patsy McLeod, were former slaves; Mary was the fifteenth of 17 children. She helped her parents on the family farm and first entered a Presbyterian mission school when she was 11 years old. Later she attended Scotia Seminary, a school for African American girls in Concord, N.C., on a scholarship. She graduated in 1893; there she had met some of the people with whom she would work closely.

Though she had a serious turn of mind, it did not prevent her from being a lively dancer and developing a lasting fondness for music. Dynamic and alert, she was very popular and the acknowledged leader of her classmates. After graduating from Scotia Seminary, she attended the Moody Bible Institute.

### Career as an Educator

After graduation from Moody Institute, she wished to become a missionary in Africa; however, she was unable to pursue this end. She was an instructor at the Presbyterian Mission School in Mayesville in 1896 and later an instructor at Haines Institute in Augusta, Ga., in 1896-1897. While she was an instructor at Kindell Institute in Sumpter, S.C., in 1897-1898, she met Albertus Bethune, whom she later married.

Bethune began her career as an educator in earnest when she rented a two-story frame building in Daytona Beach, Fla., and began the difficult task of establishing a school for African American girls. Her school opened in October 1904, with six pupils, five girls and her own son; there was no equipment; crates were used for desks and charcoal took the place of pencils; and ink came from crushed elderberries. Thus began the Daytona Literary and Industrial School for Training Negro Girls, in an era when most African American children received little or no education.

At first Bethune was teacher, administrator, comptroller, and custodian. Later she was able to secure a staff, many of whom worked loyally for many years. To finance and expand the school, Bethune and her pupils baked pies and made ice cream to sell to nearby construction gangs. In addition to her regular classes, Bethune organized classes for the children of turpentine workers. In these ways she satisfied her desire to serve as a missionary.

As the school at Daytona progressed, it became necessary to secure an adequate financial base. Bethune began to seek financial aid in earnest. In 1912 she interested James M. Gamble of the Proctor and Gamble Company of Cincinnati, Ohio, who contributed financially to the school and served as chairman of its board of trustees until his death.

In 1923 Bethune's school for girls merged with Cookman Institute of Jacksonville, Fla., a school for boys, and the new coeducational school became known as Bethune-Cookman Collegiate Institute, soon renamed Bethune-Cookman College. Bethune served as president of the college until her retirement as president emeritus in 1942. She remained a trustee of the college to the end of her life. By 1955 the college had a faculty of 100 and a student enrollment of over 1,000.

## Other Activities

Bethune's business activities were confined to the Central Life Insurance Company of Tampa, Fla., of which she was president for several years; the Afro-American Life Insurance Company of Jacksonville, which she served as director; and the Bethune—Volusia Beach Corporation, a recreation area and housing development she founded in 1940. In addition, she wrote numerous magazine and newspaper articles and contributed chapters to several books. In 1932 she founded and organized the National Council of Negro Women and became its president; by 1955 this organization had a membership of 800,000.

Bethune gained national recognition in 1936, when President Franklin D. Roosevelt appointed her director of African American affairs in the National Youth Administration and a special adviser on minority affairs. She served for 8 years and supervised the expansion of employment opportunities and recreational facilities for African American youth throughout the United States. She also served as special assistant to the secretary of war during World War II. In the course of her government assignments she became a close friend of Eleanor Roosevelt. During her long career Bethune received many honorary degrees and awards, including the Haitian Medal of Honor and Merit (1949), the highest award of the Haitian government.

Bethune died in Daytona Beach on May 18, 1955, of a heart attack. She was buried on the campus of Bethune-Cookman College.

## Further Reading

The best biography of Mrs. Bethune is Rackham Holt, *Mary McLeod Bethune* (1964). See also Catherine Owens Peare, *Mary McLeod Bethune* (1951), and Emma Gelders Sterne, *Mary McLeod Bethune* (1957). Edwin R. Embree, *13 Against the Odds* (1944), includes a chapter on Mrs. Bethune. Shorter

accounts of her are in Russell L. Adams, *Great Negroes: Past and Present* (1963; 3d ed. 1969), and in Walter Christmas, ed., *Negroes in Public Affairs and Government*, vol. 1 (1966). Background studies include John Hope Franklin, *From Slavery to Freedom: A History of Negro Americans* (1947; 3d rev. ed. 1967), and Bernard Sternsher, ed., *The Negro in Depression and War: Prelude to Revolution, 1930-1945* (1969), which contains a selection by Bethune. □

# Bridget Bishop

**Bridget Bishop (died 1692) was a tavern keeper whose wild temperament and flamboyant dress eventually caused her to be tried and hanged for witchcraft.**

The seventeenth century was a time of great religious excitement both in Europe and America. The turmoil over religious beliefs may have led to the search for witches, which reached a high point in the colony of Salem, in present-day Massachusetts, in the late seventeenth century. It had been widely believed even before the Puritans left England that witchcraft was a well-practiced profession in Europe. (A witch, it was thought, made a pact with the devil in exchange for supernatural powers.) In the fifteenth and sixteenth centuries, thousands of people, mostly women and children, were tried and sentenced to death for this crime in Germany.

## Witchcraft in history

Witchcraft had been a crime long before the trials in Massachusetts Bay Colony. The ancient Hebrews and Romans were convinced that some people had the power to enchant others or take the shapes of animals, and they believed that these people obtained their powers by making an agreement with the devil. In Europe during the sixteenth century, especially during the period of intense religious upheaval known as the Reformation, there was a renewed interest in witches. Tests for witchery, including a test to "swim" the suspected witches, or to dunk them in water until they were ready to confess their evil ways, became popular.

In England, King James II was an ardent believer in the evil of witchery. He had written a description of the antics of witches, which he spread throughout England, and offered a reward for exposing one of those who followed the devil. In the colonies, the brilliant preacher Cotton Mather had been caught up in the study of witches and had written about them in *Memorable Providences Relating to Witchcraft and Possessions*. Suspected witches were being brought to trial as early as the 1630s, and over the years many had been banished or put to death. Each colony came to hold witchery as a crime punishable by death.

By the 1690s, it seemed no one was safe from the devil. Even upstanding citizens in Salem and the surrounding communities were being accused of witchery. So who better to suspect of being a witch than Bridget Bishop?

## Early life

Little is known of Bishop's early life, though she was noted for her unusual ways. She dressed gaudily for her day, outfitting herself in red bodices for daily wear and in laces, often brightly dyed, for evening. (Samuel Shattuck, who dyed many of Bishop's laces, would later testify against her at her trial.) She made quite a picture, dressed in her famous black cap, black hat, and red bodice looped with laces of different colors.

Bishop owned two taverns, one in Salem Village and one in Salem Town. She got along well with the men—especially the young ones—who patronized these taverns. Much to the dismay of her neighbors, she allowed them to play "shovel board" (shuffle board) at all hours. One neighbor had even found it necessary to storm the tavern late one night and throw the playing pieces in the fire to quiet the merriment. Later, the incident was used against Bishop when her accusers remembered that the very next day that neighbor had become "distracted," or suffered a breakdown.

## Known for temper

Bishop's temper alone was enough to make her suspect. All the community knew that often when her second husband bounced his wagon across the stream to their house, a loud and bitter argument followed. Before that, she had become the Widow Wasselbe when her first husband died under mysterious circumstances. Some, even then, had suspected her of causing Wasselbe's death. Later she married Thomas Oliver, but that marriage had not lasted. She finally married a successful lawyer, Edward Bishop, but sometimes she still called herself Bridget Oliver.

In 1679 Bishop had been accused of practicing witchcraft, but was rescued by the testimony of her minister, John Hale. Later, in 1687, she was again accused, and again acquitted. These charges stemmed from several claims against Bishop. She had been accused at least once of contributing to the death of a neighbor, and more than once of causing someone she had argued with to become ill. She had also been charged with taking part in the devil's sacraments on the Witches' Sabbath. On this day, it was believed, those faithful to the devil gathered together in the woods to worship him. The devil, in turn, would leave his mark on the body of each witch, a sign that he and the witch had made an agreement.

## Origin of witch trials

Throughout the colonies the signs of a witch were well known: administering sacraments in the devil's name on the Witches' Sabbath, and dancing wildly and nude at the celebration in the forest. As in Europe, different colonies resorted to torture to extract the truth from suspected witches. Even before the Salem Witch Trials of 1692 to 1695, there had been more than 100 accusations of witchery in the colonies.

In 1692 a group of young Salem girls, for no apparent reason, began falling into wild fits and imagining that people's spirits—preparing to do evil—were separating from their bodies. Often they saw these people carrying the devil's book (in order to enlist others in their evil causes) and, just as often, they saw these people in the company of a dark man (presumably the devil in human form). These girls kept company with a female slave from the West Indies named Tituba, who was reported to have practiced some forms of magic. Spurred on by an overzealous witch-hunter, the minister Samuel Parris, the girls made accusation after accusation against Bishop and other suspected witches.

## Examination

On April 19, 1692, Bishop was summoned to be examined by a preliminary court headed by John Hathorne (ancestor of the writer Nathaniel Hawthorne). Also summoned that day were Giles Corey, the elderly husband of Martha Corey who once seemed ready to name his wife a witch but now stubbornly defended her; Abigail Hobbes, accused of falsely baptizing her own mother in the name of Satan; and Mary Warren, a servant girl whose imprisonment while waiting for this examination drove her insane.

The first part of the examination had the accusers confront the accused. The young girls had been instructed, perhaps by Parris, in what to do. When Bishop raised her arm, they did too. When she was asked whether she was a witch and she answered "I do not know what a witch is" and rolled her eyes, the girls rolled their eyes too. They acted as though Bishop controlled them. Although the girls' actions did not seem to trouble Bishop, it influenced the opinions of the authorities. Bishop was sent to Salem Prison to await trial.

## Trial

The Court of Oyer and Terminer met at Salem in June 1692. Acting as chief magistrate, or judge, was Deputy Governor Stoughton. Bartholomew Gidney, Samuel Sewell, John Richards, William Sergeant, Wait Winthrop, and Nathaniel Saltonstall served as additional judges.

Since much of the testimony against her had been brought out in the examination, Bishop was already convicted in the minds of many in the town. There was little real evidence against Bishop, but the colonists believed their certainty alone could determine her guilt. Cotton Mather, the most powerful minister in the area, described the trial and the colonists' attitudes: "There was little occasion to prove the witchcraft, this being evident and notorious to all beholders" (Starkey, p. 153).

Nevertheless, the judges listened to the parade of accusers. Bishop's earlier history was repeated: the noisy shovel board games late at night at her tavern, her bad temper, her first husband's mysterious death. Also, witnesses reported that as she was led to court, Bishop's sideward glance at the church had caused a board to detach from a wall and fly across the room.

Some women of the community searched Bishop's body for the always-evident sign that she had made a commitment to the devil. After sticking pins in her, they found an unusual spot, which they testified about in court.

### Damaging testimony

Samuel Shattuck testified that Bishop was a flamboyant dresser who often came to him to have various pieces of lace dyed. Some of these pieces seemed too small for a woman to wear, he noted. (It was well known that witches often used dolls to represent their victims when casting spells; Shattuck implied that this was how Bishop used the lace pieces.)

William Stacy recalled that at age twenty-two he had been stricken with smallpox and that it was Bishop who nursed him back to health. (Bishop was said to have had power over men, which grew as she became older.) Later, however, Stacy had begun to doubt Bishop, and had talked with others about her. For this, he said, Bishop had plagued him. Once, he testified, the wheel of his wagon had stuck in a hole in the road. When he stepped out to look at it, however, the hole had disappeared. Now, although he was a decent father and husband, Stacy said, the shade of Bishop plagued him in his sleep.

Samuel Gray, Richard Corman, and Jack Louder were also pestered by the image of Bishop as they slept. Sometimes her image turned into a black pig, a monkey, the feet of a cock, or the face of a man. Gray suspected that because the men had declined her friendship she had punished their families. Bishop, Gray testified, had been the cause of the deaths of his and Shattuck's sons (she had first driven Shattuck's son insane) and of the daughter of another.

The most damaging testimony was given by John Bly. Bishop had employed him to tear down a cellar wall in her former house. Inside the wall, he claimed, he had found dolls ("poppets") made of rags and hogs' bristles with pins stuck through them.

Bishop's own testimony worked against her too. She was found guilty of telling lies, since some of the details she gave conflicted with what others said. Also, according to the court, early questioning had supposedly shown knowledge of witchcraft, yet Bishop claimed to have no knowledge of it.

### No defense

Any evidence in Bishop's favor was not allowed. While they were in jail, Bishop had asked Mary Warren, one of the other accused witches, about the claims made against Bishop. Warren told Bishop that the girls had manufactured the evidence against her. Bishop attempted to use Warren's statements in court, but the authorities would not permit the remarks of a person they considered insane to go on the record.

Bishop's son would have testified on her behalf, too, but he had been arrested after beating the truth about the false accusations out of an Indian servant and then accusing the girls who were the prime witnesses in all the trials of game-playing. He had even suggested that beatings might return the girls to their senses, too.

In the end, there were no witnesses to defend Bishop. Even John Hale, the minister who had defended her in 1687, was now convinced of her guilt. Meanwhile, the young girls continued to be bothered by the evil cast upon them, they were convinced, by Bishop.

### Sentencing

Bishop was found guilty of witchery and sentenced to be hanged, but hanging was forbidden by an old Massachusetts law. Conveniently, an old colonial law that made witchcraft a life-or-death offense was "discovered" and, on June 8, 1692, again passed into law. On June 10, High Sheriff George Cowan reported that he had hanged Bridget Bishop on Gallow Hill from the branch of a large oak tree.

### Further Reading

Boyer, Paul, and Stephen Nissenbaum, eds., *Salem Village Witchcraft,* Belmont: Wadsworth Publishing Company, 1972.

Hall, David D., *Witch-hunting in Seventeenth-Century New England,* Boston: Northeastern University Press, 1991.

Starkey, Marion L., *The Devil in Massachusetts,* Garden City, New York: Doubleday, 1969. □

# Elizabeth Bishop

**Elizabeth Bishop (1911-1979) was a poet whose vivid sense of geography won her many honors.**

Elizabeth Bishop barely knew her parents. Her father died of Bright's disease eight months after she was born in Worcester, Massachusetts, February 8, 1911. Her mother, Gertrude, never got over the death of her husband William and suffered a nervous collapse, eventually going insane. She was removed to a sanatorium when her young daughter was five.

One of her earliest and most vivid memories of her mother was of a ride in a swan boat in the Boston Public Garden. Bishop was dressed in black, as had been her wont since her husband's death. "One of the live swans paddling around us bit my mother's finger when she offered it a peanut," Bishop wrote. "I remember the hole in the black glove and a drop of blood on it." Thus was the beginning of a lifelong habit of observing minute, yet significant, details.

Most of her early years were spent with relatives, whom Bishop later described as taking care of her because they felt sorry for her. She did not stay in one place too long, not always by choice. Her sudden removal from her carefree childhood home with her maternal grandparents in the coastal town of Great Village, Nova Scotia, was a traumatic experience. She loved Canada and was unhappy at the wealthy Bishop residence in Worcester, where her father had been born. She wrote in "The Country Mouse," which was published posthumously:

I had been brought back unconsulted and against my wishes . . . to be saved from a life of poverty and provincialism, bare feet, suet puddings, unsanitary school slates, perhaps even from the inverted *r*'s of my mother's family. With this surprising extra set of

grandparents, until a few weeks ago no more than names, a new life was about to begin.

In "The Country Mouse," a humorous account of the nine months spent as a reluctant guest at the home of Sarah and John Wilson Bishop, a successful contractor who had erected buildings at Harvard and Princeton, Bishop presents some of the scenes which found their way into her poems. One of the most poignant was the waiting room of a dentist office to which she had accompanied her Aunt Jenny (Consuelo in the poem). Although she was not yet seven, she was able to read and was browsing through the pages of a 1918 *National Geographic* while her aunt was being ministered to.

"Suddenly, from inside, came an *oh* of pain—Aunt Consuelo's voice—"

This did not surprise her, because she thought of her aunt as "a foolish, timid woman." What caught her off guard was the realization that she was *her* "foolish aunt . . . falling, falling . . . into cold, blue-black space."

" . . . I felt: you are an *I*, you are an *Elizabeth*, you are one of *them* ."

It was the first time she had ever referred to herself in her poetry.

Bishop was more the observer with a vivid sense of place. She visited the Nova Scotia of her childhood, spent two years in Europe shortly after she graduated from Vassar, and travelled to North Africa, Mexico, Key West, and Brazil.

She had stopped off in Rio de Janeiro en route to sailing the Strait of Magellan, but suffered a violent reaction after eating a cashew fruit. When she recovered she stayed on in Brazil for 15 years.

Bishop wrote sparingly, publishing only five slim volumes of poetry in 35 years, but what she wrote received high acclaim. In 1945 her work was selected from among over 800 entries in the Houghton Mifflin Poetry Competition, and the 30 poems submitted were published the following year as *North & South*. This collection, together with her second volume, *A Cold Spring,* earned her the Pulitzer Prize for 1956. She received the National Book Award for *The Complete Poems* in 1970, was the first American to receive the *Books Abroad/Neustadt International Prize for Literature*—she was chosen by an international jury of writers—and the National Book Critics Circle Award for *Geography III,* her last book of poems, in 1977.

As one can tell from her titles, her lifelong passion for travelling influenced her poetry. "I think geography comes first in my work," she told an interviewer, "and then animals. But I like people, too. I've written a few poems about people."

Appropriately, one of her earliest poems, "The Map," describes "Labrador's yellow, where the moony Eskimo has oiled it" and points out that because of cramped space the names of seashore towns run out to the sea and cities cross neighboring mountains. Yet maps are not merely guides to geographical places, nor are they aesthetic objects only. As with most of her poems, "The Map" one sees is not just the colors of the rainbow confined to irregular shapes. One sees Bishop's poem as a guide to the way she views and senses the patterns of life.

"Man-Moth," inspired by a typographical error in the *New York Times*—the intended word was *mammoth*—describes the nocturnal New Yorker whose home is "the pale subways of cement" where

Each night he must be carried through artificial tunnels and dream recurrent dreams. Just as the ties recur beneath his train, these underlie his rushing brain. . . . He has to keep his hands in his pockets, as others must wear mufflers.

The fantasy of the man-moth travelling through New York's underground and, when occasionally emerging to the street, seeing the moon "as a small hole at the top of the sky" has a Kafkaesque quality. When asked to contribute her favorite poem to an anthology called *Poet's Choice,* Bishop submitted "Man-Moth," commenting on the misprint that gave her the idea: "An oracle spoke from the page of the *New York Times,* kindly explaining New York City to me, at least for the moment."

Other of her poems that have been highly praised included "The Burglar of Babylon," a ballad set in Rio; "A Miracle for Breakfast," about hunger; "Jeronimo's House," one of her Key West poems; "The Moose," about a bus trip; and "The Fish," her most popular poem.

So frequently has this poem been anthologized that shortly before her death Bishop declared that she would rather have any of her poems but "The Fish" included in a collection, and, if publishers insisted, she asked that they print three of her other poems with it. In the poem the fish, wearing five old pieces of broken lines "like medals," gets a reprieve and is returned to the sea.

One of the reasons for the popularity of this poem was the strong praise it received from Randall Jarrell. Bishop, who was uncommitted to any school of poetry, was also admired by poets as disparate as John Ashbery, Octavio Paz, Robert Lowell, and Marianne Moore. She also knew Ezra Pound, W.H. Auden, Pablo Neruda, and Carlos Drummond, one of Brazil's most popular poets, whose work she translated from the Portuguese.

But it was Marianne Moore who had the greatest influence of all of these. While still at Vassar, Bishop met Moore through the college librarian, Fanny Borden, niece of the accused ax-murderer Lizzie Borden. After an initial interview in the New York Public Library, the two poets began a long friendship, launched when Bishop helped Moore pilfer a few hairs from a baby elephant at a circus to replace strands of the rare hair on her bracelet. Bishop kept the adult elephants and the guard busy while Moore snipped away.

Moore helped to convince Bishop to abandon her plans to study medicine and to work at her poetry instead. Critics have said that the two poets shared the same gift of acute observation and understated wit. And each of them was fond of animals. Besides Moore, Bishop credited George Herbert and Wallace Stevens as being important influences on her.

Bishop died suddenly of a ruptured cerebral aneurism in her Boston apartment on October 6, 1979. She was 68 years old.

## Further Reading

A critical study of Bishop's work is Anne Stevenson's *Elizabeth Bishop* (1966). *Elizabeth Bishop and Her Art* was edited by Lloyd Schwartz and Sybil P. Estess (1983). *The Complete Poems: 1927-1979* supersedes the earlier *Complete Poems* (1969). *Elizabeth Bishop: The Collected Prose,* edited by Robert Giroux in 1984, contains essays and accounts of her life not published when she was alive. □

# Shirley Temple Black

**Shirley Temple Black (born 1928) was an American who devoted her career first to films and then to public service. The United States ambassador to Czechoslovakia from 1989 till 1992, she was still remembered by millions of fans for her success as a child movie star in the 1930s.**

Shirley Temple was born in Santa Monica, California, on April 23, 1928. She was the youngest of three children. Her father was a bank teller. As a child Shirley Temple began to take dance steps almost as soon as she began to walk, and her mother took her to dancing

school when she was about three and a half years old. She also took her daughter on endless rounds of visits to agents, hoping to secure a show business career. Persistence paid off. Little Shirley obtained a contract at a small film studio and one of the great careers in film history began.

Her first contract was with Educational Pictures Inc., for whom she worked in 1932 and 1933. She appeared in a serial entitled *Baby Burlesks,* followed by a two-reeler, *Frolics of Youth,* that would lead to her being contracted by the Fox Film Corporation at a salary of $150 per week. The first full-length feature that she appeared in for Fox was 1934's *Carolina.* It was another Fox release of that year that made her a star: *Stand Up and Cheer.* Although she only appeared in a subsidiary role, she made a big hit in this picture by singing and dancing "Baby Take a Bow." She appeared in eight other full-length films (not to mention her ongoing work in serials and short subjects) that year, including *Little Miss Marker* and *Bright Eyes.* The first of these is especially notable because it was her first starring role. The culmination of 1934 was the Academy of Motion Pictures Arts and Sciences award of a special miniature Oscar to her "in grateful recognition of her outstanding contribution to screen entertainment during the year, 1934." One cannot help but assume that the industry-dominated academy was most impressed by her status as the number one box office draw of the year, but her special Oscar was unique in that it represented the first and only time that an Oscar has been awarded on the basis of a poll of the film-going public.

## Film Star of the 1930s

Through the rest of the decade Shirley Temple's star soared. And it was not only her delectable dimples and 56 corkscrew curls that would keep her at the top of the box office listings. She was a spectacularly talented child, able to sing and dance with style and genuine feeling. Gifted with perfect pitch, she was a legendary quick study who learned her lines and dance routines much faster than her older and more experienced co-stars. She would make 15 films in the next six years, becoming one of the most popular stars of the Great Depression years and making over $30 million for the newly organized Twentieth Century-Fox Film Corporation. The company's chief executive, Darryl Zanuck, arranged for a staff of 19 writers to exclusively develop film projects for her. Studio wags described her character, which evolved through such films as *The Little Colonel* (1935), *Captain January* (1936), *Wee Willie Winkie* (1937), *Heidi* (1937), and *Rebecca of Sunnybrook Farm* (1938), as "Little Miss Fix-It" whose cuteness and precocious presence of mind helped grown-ups through real-life difficulties. And as her popularity rose, so did her salary—to $10,000 per week.

But unfortunately little of the built-up popularity would be hers to claim by the time she was an adult. As she reports in her autobiography, her father's questionable management of her funds, coupled with both of her parents' healthy regard for their own interests, enabled only a fraction of the immense fortune that she earned to accrue to Shirley herself. By 1940 she had appeared in 43 feature films and shorts and an entire industry had sprung up whose products celebrated the glories of Shirley Temple: dolls, dresses, coloring books, and other sundry merchandise. She also earned enormous sums by commercially endorsing all sorts of products. These endeavors brought in an even larger amount of money than her studio salary. She got more fan mail than Greta Garbo and her picture was taken more frequently than President Franklin D. Roosevelt's. Shirley Temple will always be a symbol of the nation's longing for good times and good cheer during the severe economic woes of the Great Depression.

By the decade's end she was no longer quite a child, and when *The Blue Bird* (1940) proved unpopular at the box office and the next film that she starred in fared poorly as well, Twentieth Century-Fox devised a means of getting rid of the "property" that had saved the fledgling studio from bankruptcy. She would try to maintain her acting career through the 1940s but never again would she come even close to the stardom of her childhood. Film audiences would simply not allow the adorable girl who had sung "On the Good Ship Lolly Pop" and "Animal Crackers (in My Soup)" to grow up.

There had never been a child star so talented as she. Actress, singer, and dancer—Shirley Temple was a unique performer. The "industry" that rose up to promote her did not exist to support her stardom so much as it was a reflection of it. Moreover, Shirley Temple's true greatness as a screen idol has survived to the present day as her films are revived on television and re-released on videocassettes. New generations of fans have grown up marveling at her talent wholly apart from any studio hype or pressurized product tie-ins marketed to bedazzle them. Her matchless and enduring talent has proven to be enchantment enough.

It is arguable that nothing could have been done to preserve the lustre of her magic. Yet her ongoing struggles as an adult would prove her to be as heroic in her own life as she had ever been on the screen. A difficult first marriage to actor John Agar caused her to mature quickly. Almost immediately thereafter came the realization that her parents had been looking out for their own best interests rather than hers.

As she had done in so many of her films, she rallied. After marrying the successful California businessman Charles Black in 1950, with whom she raised her children (Linda from her first marriage and Charles and Lori from her second), she embarked on a career in television. The success of her two children's series enabled her to pursue her commitment to children's issues with vigor. In 1961 she co-founded the National Federation of Multiple Sclerosis Societies.

Her concern over domestic social ills caused her to realize that life as a private citizen could not satisfy her desire to make the world a better place. She ran for Congress in 1967 and was defeated. This was only the beginning of her involvement in public service. In 1969 she was appointed to serve as a representative to the United Nations. Her exemplary work at the UN led to a second career for Shirley Temple Black. In 1972 she was appointed representative to the UN Conference on the Human Environment and also served as a delegate on the Joint Committee for the USSR-USA Environmental Treaty. The next year she served as a US commissioner for the United Nations Educational, Scientific, and Cultural Organization (UNESCO).

Black overcame a great challenge in 1972 when she successfully battled breast cancer. When she publicly disclosed that she had a mastectomy, she gave courage to millions of women. Two years later she was appointed ambassador to Ghana, where she was warmly received by the people of that nation. Upon completion of her tour of duty in Africa, President Ford made her the US chief of protocol. In all of her various diplomatic functions, Black's intelligence, spirit, and zeal contributed greatly to her country's prestige and furthered its world position. Democratic President Carter paid tribute to her tact and flawless taste when he chose her (Black had been a lifelong Republican) to make the arrangements for his inauguration and inaugural ball in 1977.

But the triumphs of her adult life no more ruffled her poise and grace than her earlier tribulations. Her marriage and family life with Charles Black was as rewarding to her as her career as a diplomat was distinguished. Indeed, by 1981 she was such an established pillar of the public service community that she became one of the founding members of the American Academy of Diplomacy. In 1988 she was appointed Honorary Foreign Service Officer of the United States, the only person with that rank. She went on to serve as the US ambassador to Czechoslovakia from 1989 until 1992. Such honors are ultimately the true measure of her career's meaning. Latter-day film industry recognition such as the Life Achievement Award of the American Center of Films for Children or the full-sized Oscar that she was given in 1985 were echoes of a past that, while still resonant for "Shirley Temple," were not quite relevant for Shirley Temple Black. According to Black, her more than 25 years of social service have been just as enjoyable as her years in Hollywood.

Black is working on a book about her diplomatic career, which, she told Susan Bandrapalli in a 1996 *Christian Science Monitor* interview, she expects to take quite some time to complete. Her first book, *A Child's Story* took eight years to write. Black also stated that she was concerned about the lack of civility in the world today and said, "People should show more kindness and understanding."

The title of a recent biography (*American Princess*) does not do her justice. Through her lifetime of service in the arts and public life, Black has exemplified the spirit of self-sacrifice and persistent striving that Americans have aspired to for generations. She is truly an American heroine.

## Further Reading

Shirley Temple Black wrote a candid and tasteful autobiography, *Child Star* (1988), detailing her years in Hollywood. Anne Edward's *American Princess*, published the same year, is an adequately researched, if slightly sensationalized, treatment of her life. Jeanine Basinger has written a study of her films, *Shirley Temple* (1975), which comments briefly on her life but is mostly concerned with sketching her film career. Another satisfactory examination of her movies is *The Films of Shirley Temple* by Robert Windeler. Black's career as a diplomat and as an environmental and children's rights activist keeps her in the headlines of magazines and newspapers, and nostalgia for her days of childhood stardom will no doubt keep her name in the columns of other journals as well. See *Christian Science Monitor* (April 25, 1996), *People Weekly* (November 28, 1988). □

# Elizabeth Helen Blackburn

**American molecular biologist Dr. Elizabeth H. Blackburn (born 1948) is credited with the discovery of telomerase, an enzyme critical to the reproductive process of gene cells.**

D r. Elizabeth H. Blackburn is renowned for her discovery of the genetic enzyme "telomerase." Blackburn isolated and precisely described telomeres in 1978, thus enhancing the understanding of deoxyribonucleic acid (DNA) on the part of molecular biologists around the world. The subsequent discovery of telomerase in 1985 brought new insight into the complex functions of gene cells and the mysteries of their replication. Importantly, the discovery has given new hope to cancer researchers and opened new vistas for the science of gerontology.

## Tasmanian Roots

Blackburn was born in Hobart, on the island of Tasmania (in Australia), on November 26, 1948. Her parents, Drs. Harold and Marcia (Jack) Blackburn, were physicians, and their only child quickly developed a love of science.

## Higher Education

Blackburn started college at the University of Melbourne on the Australian mainland. There she completed her undergraduate studies, earning a bachelor of science degree in 1970. She continued at Melbourne and received her master of science degree in 1971. She went on to Cambridge University in England, where she earned a Ph.D. in molecular biology in 1975. She developed her doctoral thesis on sequencing of nuclear acids.

From England she moved to the United States, to Yale University in New Haven, Connecticut. At Yale, from 1975 until 1977, she studied chromosomes—their structures and replication—on a research fellowship. It was during those years that she first began to explore the phenomenon of telomeres, the tiny structures that cap the ends of chromosomes and which contribute to the stability of the gene cells.

In 1977 Blackburn moved to California, to the San Francisco Bay Area, to continue her research into the nature of the telomere projections of chromosomes. She worked, once again as a research fellow, at the University of California in San Francisco (UCSF). By that time she had traveled halfway around the world in pursuit of her educational goals. In 1978 she accepted her first position, as an assistant professor at the University of California in Berkeley.

## The Discovery of Telomerase

As an assistant professor at Berkeley, Blackburn continued her research on the behavior of telomeres. Eventually she noticed a relationship between telomere size and the ability of a chromosome to divide and duplicate.

In 1985, she and her graduate assistant, Carol W. Greider, successfully isolated "telomerase." Telomerase is the enzyme that synthesizes new telomeres in DNA and controls the length of the telomeres. The discovery was a breakthrough for biologists everywhere. It enabled researchers to create artificial telomeres to control the duplication of gene cells. The discovery was a great stimulant to genetic research.

The historical discovery, isolation of the telomerase enzyme, brought international acclaim to Blackburn. In 1988, in recognition of her scientific accomplishment, she received the Eli Lilly Award for Microbiology. She was also elected a foreign associate of the National Academy of Science in 1993, having in 1990 received that academy's Molecular Biology Award. Yale University, home of her first postdoctoral research and her early studies of telomeres, bestowed her with an Honorary Doctor of Science degree in 1991. She was elected a Fellow of the Royal Society of London in 1992.

## A Professor and a Writer

Blackburn was promoted to a full professorship at Berkeley in 1986, where she taught and managed a laboratory until 1990. She then transferred to the San Francisco campus of the University of California as a professor in the Department of Microbiology and Immunology and of Biochemistry and Biophysics.

In 1992, Blackburn was a contributing writer to the *Harvey Lectures: 1990-91,* an annual reference publication by prominent scientists. *Harvey Lectures* features information on biomedical research. The 1990-91 edition spotlights Elizabeth Blackburn, together with David Beach, and Francis S. Collins.

One year later, in 1993, Blackburn was named Chairwoman of the Department of Microbiology and Immunology at UCSF. That assignment further distinguished Blackburn: she was the first woman in the history of the university to hold the post.

In 1995 she published *Telomeres (Monograph 29),* a collection of essays on telomeres, which she edited along with Carol W. Greider. The book was well received, and, according to *Science* editor Carolyn Price, the publication, "is both timely and much needed. The literature [on telomeres] has become increasingly diverse and voluminous, making it difficult for the newcomer to the field.... *Telomeres* provides an excellent, easy-to-read introduction for such readers.... A major strength of the book lies in the breadth of its coverage and the way it links diverse topics...."

In 1990, with her students Guo-Liang Yu, John Bradley, and Laura Attardo, Blackburn published an article wherein they described the detrimental effect on genetic reproduction of the inability to make proper telomeric sequences.

They found that telomeres cannot function properly when telomerase is defective. The telomeres eventually shrink, so that the genes cannot reproduce themselves properly, and the genes eventually die. This effect is significant to cancer research, because cancer cells are known to have excessive telomere length. Gerontologists (scientists who study the aging process) are also studying the effect of telomerase on telomeres, because the telomeres in human cells are known to shrink in connection with the aging process.

In addition to her research duties and her professorship at the University of California, Blackburn gives lectures and seminars on telomeres and cancer. She was among the presenters of the Dean's Research Seminar Series on Telomeres and Cancer in January of 1997. The Conference was transmitted via video relay to major San Francisco Hospitals.

Blackburn's scientific research is supported in part by the National Institute of General Medical Sciences (NIGMS). This work overall falls under the category of "basic biomedical research," or undirected research. This means that she is exploring to learn whatever can be known about cells. She is not looking for something in particular. The American Cancer Society also supports her work by providing postdoctoral fellowship assistance for her activities, and the National Science Foundation (NFS) supports predoctoral fellowship assistance for research by her students.

## Personal Highlights

In all, Elizabeth Blackburn is a scientist, a teacher, a wife, and a mother. She met her husband, John Sedat, in England. Their mutual interest in molecular biology brought them together as students at Cambridge. They were married in 1975, after Blackburn moved to the United States. Sedat is a scientist in his own right, and is a professor of biochemistry and biophysics at UCSF. The couple has one son, Benjamin, born in 1986. Blackburn takes motherhood very seriously, and publicly attests to the importance of time spent with her family. In her on-line article, "Balancing Family and Career: One Way That Worked," she spoke out on several topics, including the importance of devoting the appropriate time to parenting.

In the article she upheld the right of every woman to choose a career without fear of discrimination for embracing motherhood. Blackburn commented, "It makes no sense that career avenues be closed to a woman because of a temporary situation [the responsibilities of mothering young children]. . . . [The woman who chooses to be a mother] has been educated and trained for years in her . . . work . . . a huge investment of her life. . . . [T]he culture . . . needs to change so that when a woman says she has family needs, she won't feel this forever damns her as a serious scientist."

Blackburn further discussed (in her article) the most memorable week of her life, which occurred at age 37 when she received her full professorship at UCSF and discovered in the same week that she was about to become a mother.

## Professional Memberships

Blackburn was elected to the American Association for the Advancement of Science (AAAS) in 1991. She has been a foreign associate of the National Academy of Science since 1993, and a Fellow of the Royal Society of London since 1992. She served as president of the American Society for Cell Biology (ASCB) in 1998, and represented the ASCB to the Joint Steering Committee for Public Policy and Bioethical Research Advocacy.

Blackburn's discovery of telomerase brings new promise of the eradication of fungal infections such as those in "immunocompromised" patients, and hopes that new cures will be found for many cancers. Further research on telomerase one day might even provide a means to significantly slow the aging process that afflicts every human being.

## Further Reading

Beach, David, Elizabeth H. Blackburn, and Francis S. Collins, *The Harvey Lectures: 1990-1991* (Harvey Lecture Series, 86), Wiley-Liss, 1992.

Blackburn, Elizabeth H., and Carol W. Greider, *Telomeres (Monograph 29),* Cold Spring Harbor Laboratory Press, 1995.

Kipling, David, *The Telomere,* Oxford University Press, 1995.

*Science,* July 21, 1995, p. 396(5); January 26, 1996, p. 455(2).

"Balancing Family and Career: One Way That Worked," *Next Wave,* http://www.nextwave.org/pastfor/blackbur.htm (March 18, 1998). □

# Elizabeth Blackwell

**The first woman in America to receive a medical degree, Elizabeth Blackwell (1821-1910) crusaded for the admission of women to medical schools in the United States and Europe.**

Elizabeth Blackwell was born on Feb. 3, 1821, in Bristol, England. Her parents emigrated with their nine children to New York City when Elizabeth was 12. Mr. Blackwell soon became an ardent abolitionist. In 1838 the Blackwells moved to Cincinnati, Ohio; within a few months Mr. Blackwell died and left his family unprovided for. The three oldest girls supported the family for several years by operating a boarding school for young women.

In 1842 Blackwell accepted a teaching position in Henderson, Ky., but local racial attitudes offended her strong abolitionist convictions, and she resigned at the end of the year. On her return to Cincinnati a friend who had undergone treatment for a gynecological disorder told Blackwell that if she could have been treated by a woman doctor she would have been spared an embarrassing ordeal, and she urged Elizabeth to study medicine. The following year Blackwell moved to Asheville, N.C., where she taught school and studied medicine in her spare time. Her next move, in 1846, was to a girls' school in Charleston, S.C., where she had more time to devote to her medical studies.

When her attempts to enroll in the medical schools of Philadelphia and New York City were rejected, she wrote to a number of small northern colleges and in 1847 was admitted to the Geneva, N.Y., Medical College. All eyes were upon the young woman whom many regarded as immoral or simply mad, but she soon proved herself an outstanding student. Her graduation in 1849 was highly publicized on both sides of the Atlantic. She then entered La Maternité Hospital for further study and practical experience. While working with the children, she contracted purulent conjunctivitis, which left her blind in one eye.

Handicapped by partial blindness, Dr. Blackwell gave up her ambition to become a surgeon and began practice at St. Bartholomew's Hospital in London. In 1851 she returned to New York, where she applied for several positions as a physician, but was rejected because of her sex. She established private practice in a rented room, where her sister Emily, who had also pursued a medical career, soon joined her. Their modest dispensary later became the New York Infirmary and College for Women, operated by and for women. Dr. Blackwell also continued to fight for the admission of women to medical schools. During the Civil War she organized a unit of women nurses for field service.

In 1869 Dr. Blackwell set up practice in London and continued her efforts to open the medical profession to women. Her articles and her autobiography (1895) attracted widespread attention. From 1875 to 1907 she was professor of gynecology at the London School of Medicine for Women. She died at her home in Hastings.

### Further Reading

Biographies of Elizabeth Blackwell include Rachel Baker, *The First Woman Doctor: The Story of Elizabeth Blackwell, M. D.* (1944); Ishbel Ross, *Child of Destiny: The Life Story of the First Woman Doctor* (1949); and Peggy Chambers, *A Doctor Alone: A Biography of Elizabeth Blackwell, the First Woman Doctor, 1821-1910* (1956). Elizabeth Blackwell's career is studied at length in Ruth Fox Hume, *Great Women of Medicine* (1964). There is a brief biographical sketch in Victor Robinson, *Pathfinders in Medicine* (1912; 2d ed. 1929). See also Elizabeth Blackwell, *Pioneer Work in Opening the Medical Profession to Women: Autobiographical Sketches* (1895), and Richard H. Shryock, *The Development of Modern Medicine: An Interpretation of the Social and Scientific Factors Involved* (1936; rev. ed. 1947). □

# Sarah Gibson Blanding

**Sarah Gibson Blanding (1898-1985) enjoyed the distinction of becoming one of the first women to serve in important U.S. government administrative posts during World War II.**

Sarah Gibson Blanding began her career as an assistant professor of political science at the University of Kentucky in 1937. Her credentials included a year of study at the London School of Economics (1928-1929). She remained at the University of Kentucky, later becoming the dean of women, until 1941, when she became director of the New York State College of Home Economics at Cornell University. During her tenure there wartime demands for home-economics services quadrupled. She expedited requests for help by promoting food and nutrition education, child-care techniques, conservation and preservation of war materials in short supply, mass feeding, and maintenance of equipment.

### Dewey Calls

Blanding's efforts at Cornell did not go unnoticed. During the last years of World War II Gov. Thomas Dewey of New York appointed Blanding to several state government posts, including director of the Human Nutrition Division of the State Emergency Food Commission and consultant to the State Defense Council's Division of Volunteer Participation. But her work was not limited to the local or state levels. As the war progressed, she was selected as the only female member of several national committees, which enhanced her reputation as an administrator.

### The Presidency of Vassar

In February 1946 Blanding sought and obtained the post of president of Vassar College, succeeding Henry MacCracken, who had been president since 1915. She was selected because she was "the best possible person, man or woman." *The New York Herald Tribune* noted that Blanding "was a fresh, vigorous, and resourceful person with a mind of proved capacity, and, most of all, balanced judg-

**Further Reading**
Jean Nowell, "New President Greets 1,440 at Vassar Opening," *New York Herald Tribune*, 8 September 1946, p. 33. □

# Amelia Jenks Bloomer

**An American advocate of woman's rights in the early days of the feminist movement, Amelia Jenks Bloomer (1818-1894) spent most of her life working for the cause. She was also a reformer of women's clothing and helped promote "bloomers."**

Amelia Jenks was born into a family of modest means in Homer, N.Y., on May 27, 1818. Her formal education was negligible, consisting of only a few years in grammar school. At the age of 22 she married Dexter Bloomer, a lawyer and part owner of the *Seneca Falls County Courier*. A man of Quaker background and progressive social principles, he encouraged his wife to write articles on temperance and other social issues for his newspaper and for other periodicals.

In 1848, at the age of 30, Bloomer attended the first public Woman's Rights Convention at Seneca Falls, N.Y., but she took no part in the proceedings. A few months later she began to publish her own temperance newspaper, *The Lily*, which was immensely successful, gaining a circulation of 4,000 within a few years. At this time in her career Amelia Bloomer was a small, slight, dark-haired woman with good features and a pleasant expression. Timid and retiring by nature, she was a sternly serious person, seemingly lacking in any sense of humor.

Prodded by Elizabeth Cady Stanton, who also lived in Seneca Falls, Bloomer devoted increasing space in *The Lily* to questions concerning woman's rights, such as unequal educational opportunities, discriminatory marriage and property laws, and suffrage. In 1851 *The Lily* supported the reform in women's dress which came to bear Bloomer's name. Female fashion in the 1850s consisted of unhealthy, tightly laced corsets, layers of petticoats that could weigh well over 10 pounds, and floor-length dresses that dragged in the filth of the era's unpaved and unswept streets. The bloomer costume dispensed with corsets in favor of loose bodices, substituted baggy ankle-length pantaloons for petticoats, and cut the gowns to above the knee. Such a costume had been worn at the utopian New Harmony colony in Indiana in the 1820s and as resort wear during the 1830s, and Mrs. Bloomer was by no means the originator of the revival in 1851. But her promotion of it attached her name to the sensation. Woman's-rights advocates, such as Elizabeth Cady Stanton and Susan B. Anthony, wore the reform dress for a year or so but abandoned it when they concluded that the ridicule it frequently elicited was preventing a fair hearing of their views. Mrs. Bloomer continued to wear the dress until the late 1850s, but, conservative by nature (she never shared the liberal religious views or abolitionist senti-

ment." She believed that her main mission was to maintain Vassar's high quality of education for women; ironically, this came at a time when the college, to help alleviate the overcrowding of men's colleges, began accepting male war veterans on the GI Bill as students working toward Vassar degrees.

## National Honors

Blanding received national recognition for her efforts on behalf of women's education at Vassar. She toured often, lecturing that the balance of good and evil was so precarious that the scales could be tipped in either direction, so democracy was in a perilous position. In the process she received honorary doctorates from several colleges, including the University of Kentucky. She was appointed by President Harry S Truman to the National Commission on Higher Education, whose aim was to reexamine the system of education in the United States; later Governor Dewey appointed her to a committee to study the need for a state university system in New York. At her inauguration to the National Commission on Higher Education in October 1946, Blanding was given the War Department's Civilian Service Award for her service to the secretary of war. Cited during the ceremony were her exceptional efforts in developing activities for the Women's Army Corps and her leadership as a member of the army and navy committees on welfare and recreation. She was then appointed to the War Department Civilian Advisory Council and to the Chief of Staff 's Advisory Committee for the Women's Army Corps.

ments of her sisters in the movement), even she eventually opposed bloomers as inexpedient.

Bloomer moved to Council Bluffs, Iowa, in 1855, where she abandoned *The Lily* but continued to work actively in the woman's-suffrage movement of that state. She lectured and wrote widely, served as president of the state Woman Suffrage Association between 1871 and 1873, and corresponded with and arranged lectures for Lucy Stone, Susan B. Anthony, and Elizabeth Cady Stanton in Iowa. She retired increasingly into private life in the 1870s, troubled by poor health. She died at Council Bluffs on the last day of 1894.

Amelia Bloomer's work never matched the incessant and selfless activity of some of her contemporaries, but she contributed to the suffrage movement far more profoundly than the generally facetious use of her name would indicate.

## Further Reading

Bloomer's husband, Dexter C. Bloomer, published the *Life and Writings of Amelia Bloomer* (1895) shortly after her death. Most of the general works on the 19th century woman's-suffrage movement take note of her. The most valuable work treating her career in some detail is Louise R. Noun, *Strong-Minded Women: The Emergence of the Woman-Suffrage Movement in Iowa* (1970). See also Eleanor Flexner, *Century of Struggle: The Woman's Rights Movement in The United States* (1959); Robert W. Smuts, *Women and Work in America* (1959); Aileen S. Kraditor, *The Ideas of the Woman Suffrage Movement, 1890-1920* (1965); Andrew Sinclair, *The Better Half: The Emancipation of American Women* (1965); and William L. O'Neill, *Everyone Was Brave* (1969). □

# Ella Reeve Bloor

**Ella Reeve "Mother" Bloor (1862-1951) was an American leader in fighting for the rights of those she characterized as "the world's unfortunates," and worked tirelessly as a labor organizer, Communist leader, and social activist.**

Mother Bloor is one of the most tireless and accomplished crusaders and agitators the United States has ever seen. Over more than 60 years she worked for woman's suffrage, the Women's Christian Temperance Union, organized and raised funds for such causes as the Sacco-Vanzetti case and the American League against War and Fascism, and also served as an accomplished labor organizer. A radical activist, Ella Bloor had little patience with ideological debate. Her single goal was "to make life happier for the world's unfortunates."

## Early Life

Reeve was born July 8, 1862 near Mariner's Harbor on Staten Island and grew up there and in New Jersey, the self-described daughter of "a rich old Republican over on Staten Island." Her ancestors had fought in the Revolutionary and Civil wars. She attended public schools, briefly went to the Ivy Hall Seminary, and then was taught by her mother at home. When Reeve was 17, her mother died in childbirth, and Ella was responsible for caring for her nine younger siblings.

## Early Political Interests and First Marriage

Reeve's father leaned toward political and religious conservatism, so that when she became interested in social and political reform as a teenager, she turned to her great uncle, Dan Ware, who was an abolitionist, Unitarian, and freethinker. Ware had a strong influence on her intellectual growth. When she was 19 Reeve married Dan Ware's son, Lucien Ware, an aspiring lawyer. She gave birth to six children over eleven years, Grace, Harold, Helen, Buzz, and two who died in infancy. During those years Ella Ware was introduced to the woman's suffrage movement and became active in the Women's Christian Temperance Union and the Ethical Culture Society of Philadelphia. She also became interested in the labor movement and organized the Philadelphia streetcar workers in the early 1890s.

Her political activism caused tension in her marriage, and the couple separated and were divorced in 1896. However, Lucien Ware was not apolitical himself. He would go on to receive the Order of Lenin for helping the Soviet Union with the mechanization and collectivization of its agriculture, led the charge for the U.S. Communist Party's agrarian reform program, and introduced Alger Hiss to Whittaker Chambers in 1934 before dying in an automobile accident in 1935.

## Second Divorce and Radical Exploration

After her divorce Reeve was active and independent, exploring possible occupations. She took courses at the University of Pennsylvania and wrote two children's books. She and her children then moved to the utopian community of Arden, Delaware, which was established by socialists. In 1897 she married socialist Louis Cohen, and the couple had two children, Richard and Carl, but were separated in 1902 and later divorced.

## Political Activism

Reeve then became a political activist. She was always committed to improving the status of women but devoted her energies to left-wing politics and the labor movement. Ella Cohen met Eugene Debs in 1895, and he convinced her of the necessity of socialism. She joined the Socialist Labor Party in 1901. In 1905 she moved to Connecticut and became the state organizer for the party.

In 1906 her friend, writer Upton Sinclair, urged Ella Cohen to investigate conditions in the Chicago meatpacking industry. Sinclair wanted her to gather evidence for a government investigation documenting the charges he made against the industry in *The Jungle.* Richard Bloor, a fellow socialist and young pottery worker, went along to protect her. Sinclair feared it would be scandalous to have an unmarried team of investigators and convinced Ella Cohen to publish the reports under the name Ella Bloor. Although the couple quickly split up, she continued to use the name Ella Bloor for the rest of her life.

I would be too conspicuous going about unescorted to saloons and other places where men gather and talk," the *New York Times* quoted her as explaining. "In explaining the investigation to the public, Upton Sinclair thought it best to refer to us as Mr. and Mrs. Bloor, and the name has clung to me ever since. Richard Bloor was a Welsh immigrant, about half my age, and there was no romance associated with our association."

## Socialism

Bloor spent the next twelve years organizing for the Socialist Party and for the United Cloth Hat and Cap Makers Union. Her work on behalf of coal miners won her an honorary membership in the United Mine Workers of America. Bloor opposed World War I as imperialist and was arrested for antiwar activities. In 1918 she was Socialist Party candidate for lieutenant governor of New York. Disillusioned by the support of many Socialist Party leaders for the war, in 1919 Bloor helped form the Communist party and the Communist Labor party, which soon merged. Bloor worked devotedly for the party for the rest of her life, recruiting members from among miners, farmers, machinists, steelworkers, and needle workers.

In 1925, at the age of 63, Ella Bloor hitchhiked from New York to San Francisco on a cross-country tour for the *Daily Worker.* She held meetings in cities along the way, recruiting party members and selling subscriptions. In the 1920s she was active in the unsuccessful defense of Nicola Sacco and Bartolomeo Vanzetti. She also continued her labor organizing work, traveling to the coal mines to support strikers.

## The 1930s

When the Depression hit, Mother Bloor, as she was then called, went to Washington to join the hunger marches of the unemployed. By the 1930s, when she was in her seventies, Mother Bloor was a sought-after speaker for the Communist Party, traveled extensively, and served as middlewestern regional secretary of the Farmers National Conference. While traveling to North Dakota to rally support for the United Farmers' League, she met Andrew Omholt, a farmer, party organizer and Communist Party candidate for Congress in North Dakota who soon became her third husband. She continued her party campaigning and labor organizing through the 1930s. In 1937 she made her second visit to the Soviet Union as an honored guest at the celebration of the 20th anniversary of the October Revolution. She visited that country several times, twice as a delegate to the Red International of Trade Unions, and once extolled the Soviets for their "democratic success."

At the age of 72 in 1936 she served a 30-day jail sentence in Nebraska after a mass farmers protest meeting. Her final campaign was during World War II, when she spoke at public rallies and on the radio on the theme "Win the War Against Fascism." In her lifelong fight for the "world's unfortunates," Mother Bloor suffered more than 30 arrests (although she claimed it was over 100), countless threats of violence, and frequent harassment by police.

On March 2, 1951 Bloor suffered a spinal injury from a fall near her home at Coopersburg, Pennsylvania, about 40 miles north of Philadelphia. During her several-month stay at Quakertown Hospital she received visitors from across the country, most of whom she was unable to recognize. Hospital attendants said she sang often during her stay, especially "The Star-Spangled Banner," singing all four verses. She spent a short time in a convalescent home before her death on August 10, 1951 from a stroke.

### Further Reading

Thomas L. Edwards and Richard C. Edwards, "Ella Reeve Bloor," in *Notable American Women: The Modern Period,* edited by Barbara Sicherman, Carol Hurd Green, Ilene Kantrov, and Harriette Walker (Cambridge, Mass.: Harvard University Press, 1980), pp. 85-87. □

# Judy Blume

**Perhaps the most popular contemporary author of works for upper elementary to junior high school readers, Judy Blume (born 1938) is the creator of frank, often humorous stories which focus on the emotional and social concerns of suburban adolescents.**

Although Blume is best known for her fiction for adolescents, she began her career by writing books for younger children, an audience she still continues to address; *Tales of a Fourth-Grade Nothing* (1972) and *Superfudge* (1980), two entertaining tales about ten-year-old Peter and his incorrigible baby brother, Fudge, are especially popular with readers. *Are You There, God? It's Me, Margaret* (1970) depicts eleven-year-old Margaret's apprehensions about starting her period and choosing her own religion. At the time of the book's publication, Blume was praised for her warm and funny recreation of childhood feelings and conversation, but was criticized for her forthright references to the human body and its processes. *Margaret* is now considered a groundbreaking work due to the candor with which Blume presents previously taboo subjects. *Forever* (1975), in which Blume relates the particulars of her eighteen-year-old heroine's initial sexual experience, created an even greater furor. Despite the fact that it was published as an adult book, protestors pointed out that Blume's name and characteristically uncomplicated prose style attracted a vulnerable preteen audience who could be influenced by the intimate details of the novel. In *Tiger Eyes* (1981), Blume relates the story of how fifteen-year-old Davey adjusts to her father's murder. Hailed by many critics as Blume's finest work for her successful handling of a complex plot, *Tiger Eyes* includes such issues as alcoholism, suicide, anti-intellectualism, and violence. *Letters to Judy* (1986) was a promoted as a response to the voluminous amount of mail that Blume receives from her readers. Selecting a number of representatives letters to reprint anonymously with accompanying comments, she created the book for a dual purpose: to enable children to see that they are not alone and to make parents more aware of their children's needs.

Reviewers commend Blume for her honesty, warmth, compassion, and wit, praising her lack of condescension, superior observation of childhood, and strong appeal to children. Critics are strongly divided as to the success of Blume's plots, characterization, writing style, and non-judgmental approach; they object to her uninhibited language and permissive attitude toward sexuality, and complain that her cavalier treatment of love, death, pain, and religion trivializes young people and the literature written for them. However, most commentators agree that Blume accurately captures the speech, emotions, and private thoughts of children, for whom she has made reading both easy and enjoyable.

### Further Reading

*Children's Literature Review,* Gale, Volume 2, 1976, Volume 15, 1988.
*Contemporary Literary Criticism,* Gale, Volume 12, 1980, Volume 30, 1984.
*Dictionary of Literary Biography,* Volume 52: *American Writers for Children since 1960: Fiction,* Gale, 1986.
Fisher, Emma and Justin Wintle, *The Pied Pipers,* Paddington Press, 1975.
Gleasner, Diana, *Breakthrough: Women in Writing,* Walker, 1980.
Lee, Betsey, *Judy Blume's Story,* Dillon Press, 1981.
Weidt, Maryann, *Presenting Judy Blume,* Twayne, 1989. □

# Nellie Bly

**Journalist and reformer Elizabeth Cochrane Seaman, better known as Nellie Bly (1864-1922), gained fame at the end of the nineteenth century for her investigative reports of abusive conditions in the cities of Pittsburgh and New York. Her writing style was marked by first-hand tales of the lives of the underclass, which she obtained by venturing into their world in a series of undercover adventures. She riveted the attention of the nation with a more light-hearted assignment in the winter of 1889-90 when she successfully imitated Jules Verne's fictional journey *Around the World in Eighty Days* in only 72 days.**

Elizabeth Cochrane Seaman, who wrote under the pen name Nellie Bly, was a journalist who gained nationwide fame for her investigative reports on abuses in various companies and public institutions. Her stories were not only reform-minded, but filled with first-hand adventure; she undertook such stunts as having herself admitted to an insane asylum, working in a factory sweatshop, and getting herself arrested in order to get a glimpse of the experiences of some of the most downtrodden of urban America. In her greatest escapade, Bly set out to imitate Jules Verne's imaginary trip around the world in less than 75 days while Americans anxiously awaited tales of her travel. Bly distinguished herself as a reporter at a time when the field was dominated by men, and her accomplishments won a greater measure of acceptance for other women journalists.

Bly was born Elizabeth Cochran on May 5, 1864, in Cochran Mills, Pennsylvania. She was the youngest of three children of Michael and Mary Jane Cochran. The Cochrans had both been married previously. Mary Jane, who came from a wealthy Pittsburgh family, was a widow with no children from her first marriage. Michael Cochran was a self-made industrialist who had begun his career as a laborer and eventually became a mill owner, property owner, and associate judge. He had seven children from his earlier marriage, including five boys. As a child, Bly was determined to keep up with her older brothers. She would join in even the roughest activities, including races and climbing trees, to prove herself their equal.

Bly was educated at home by her father in her early years, but he died in 1870 when she was only six years old. Her mother married a third time, but it was an unhappy relationship that ended in divorce. She and her mother lived for a while on the money her father had saved and Bly was sent to school near their home to prepare for a teaching career. While her performance at school was not impressive, she proved to be a creative and talented writer. At the age of 16, the family funds were depleted and Bly and her mother moved to stay near relatives in Pittsburgh. Around this time, she added the 'e' to her last name, feeling that "Cochrane" had a more elegant air.

## Became Reporter in Pittsburgh

Once in Pittsburgh, Bly looked for a way to make a living so her relatives would not have to support her. At that time, a single woman had few professional options. Basically, she could become a teacher or a companion for a wealthy woman. Bly, however, wanted to become a writer. While the odds were not with her, Bly was able to make a profession out of writing due to her extraordinary personality and determination. She got her break in 1885, after a letter she had written to the *Pittsburgh Dispatch* caught the eye of the paper's editor, George A. Madden. In response to an editorial maintaining that women should remain at home rather than entering the professional or political sphere, Bly had written a spirited letter that argued women were perfectly capable of independent thought and meaningful careers. Impressed with the words of the piece, which was signed only "Lonely Orphan Girl," Madden published an ad requesting to speak with the writer of the letter. Bly responded, and at a meeting between the two, Madden asked what kind of stories she might write if she could be a journalist. She indicated that she wanted to tell the stories of ordinary people, and so Madden gave Bly her first journalistic assignment—a piece on the lives of women. Upon receiving her submission, Madden was pleased with the results and published it under the "Lonely Orphan Girl" pseudonym.

For her next article, Bly suggested the topic of divorce. Her editor was unsure that a single young woman could write a convincing article on the subject, but Bly produced a well-researched piece that included some of her father's legal notes on divorce as well as interviews with women who lived near her. Madden agreed to publish the article, but insisted that she find a different pen name—it would seem inappropriate for a story on divorce to be signed by "Little Orphan Girl." The story appeared under the name Nellie Bly—inspired, according to some stories, by the popular Stephen Foster song "Nelly Bly"—and this became the moniker that she would work under for the rest of her career.

## Uncovered Factory Hazards and Abuses

Bly was hired as a full-time reporter for the *Dispatch*, earning a salary of five dollars a week. Her initial stories concerned the welfare of Pittsburgh's working class and poor, and the depressed and dangerous conditions she uncovered led to a number of reforms. She developed a reputation for bringing her readers a first-hand look at these topics. To investigate an unsafe factory, she took a job there herself and reported how the establishment was a firetrap that paid low wages to women who were required to work long and difficult shifts. She also traveled to the slums of the city to present a picture of children forced to work all day in order to provide for their families. While Bly's stories raised the indignation of Pittsburgh's citizens and inspired changes, the institutions she attacked were displeased and threatened to remove their advertisements from the newspaper. To appease their customers, the editors of the *Dispatch* changed the focus of Bly's writing, giving her cultural and social events to cover. While the caliber of her writing remained high, Bly yearned to continue her investigative work. She decided to go to Mexico and write about the conditions of the poor there. For several months, she contributed stories about disparities in Mexican society to the *Dispatch*. She then returned to Pittsburgh in 1886.

### Reported on Asylum Conditions

Seeking a job as a serious journalist, not just a society columnist, Bly moved to New York City in 1887. There she sold some of her stories about Mexico to newspapers, but found that no one wanted to hire a female as a reporter. Resourceful as ever, Bly managed to turn this experience itself into a story that she sold to her former employers in Pittsburgh. Finally, she managed to arrange an interview with the managing editor of the *New York World*, John Cockerill. Cockerill and the paper's owner, Joseph Pulitzer, liked Bly's stories, but were seeking something more dramatic and attention-getting. Bly was ready for the challenge. With Cockerill, she devised the idea of getting herself admitted to New York's insane asylum for the poor, Blackwell's Island, in order to discover the truth behind reports of abuses there. After being placed in the institution, Bly dropped her act of insanity, but found that doctors and nurses refused to listen to her when she stated she was rational. Other disturbing practices there included feeding the patients vermin-infested food, physical and mental abuse by the staff, and the admission of people who were not psychologically disturbed but simply physically ill or maliciously placed there by family members—as in the case of one woman who was declared insane by her husband after he caught her being unfaithful. After ten days in the asylum, Bly was removed by a lawyer from the newspaper, as had been previously arranged. The resulting stories by Bly caused a sensation across the country, effected reforms at Blackwell's Island, and earned her a permanent post at the *World.*

New York was ripe with possibilities for Bly's style of reporting, and she gained a national reputation for her daredevil methods of getting a story. To get an inside view of the justice system, she pretended to commit a robbery and found that women prisoners were searched by male officers because no women were employed by the jail. She also exposed a fraudulent employment agency that was taking money from unsuspecting immigrants, a health clinic where unqualified doctors experimented on patients, and a lobbyist who had successfully bribed a number of state politicians. Her work also included interviews with some of the most famous figures of the day, including Buffalo Bill and the wives of presidents Ulysses S. Grant, James Garfield, and James K. Polk.

### Raced around the World

Bly's most notorious stunt, however, was her trek across the globe in the spirit of the 1873 book *Around the World in Eighty Days* by French author Jules Verne. Bly's plan was to accomplish the feat in only 75 days. Traveling alone, Bly began her journey on November 14, 1889, on an ocean liner heading from New Jersey to London. As she made her way from Europe to the Middle East, Ceylon, Singapore, Hong Kong, and Japan, Americans kept up on her progress through her stories sent in by cable. The *World* made the most of the adventure, turning Bly into a celebrity who inspired songs, fashion, and even a game. She returned to New York in triumph on January 25, 1890, after only 72 days. The town welcomed her arrival with a huge celebration and parade.

Bly was married in 1895 to Robert Livingston Seaman, a millionaire who owned the Iron Clad Manufacturing Company and the American Steel Barrel Company. She retired from writing to assist her husband in his businesses and became president of his companies after Seaman's death in 1904. Her business instincts were poor, however, and in 1911 she declared bankruptcy and returned to journalism. During this period of her career she covered World War I from the Eastern Front and then took a job with the New York *Evening Journal.* But her days as a household name were long past. Upon her death from pneumonia on January 27, 1922, in New York, few people remarked on her passing. Only the *Evening Journal* published a piece on her significance, calling her the country's best reporter. Despite her relative obscurity at the end of her life, Bly's impact was a lasting one. Her unique and energetic approach to reporting launched new trends in journalism, and her insistence on covering difficult topics—despite her gender—set a precedent for journalistic careers for women.

### Further Reading

For more information see Belford, Barbara, *Brilliant Bylines: A Biographical Anthology of Notable Newspaperwomen in America,* Columbia University Press, 1986; Kroeger, Brooke, *Nellie Bly: Daredevil, Reporter, Feminist,* Times Books, 1994; and Rittenhouse, Mignon, *The Amazing Nellie Bly,* E. P. Dutton, 1956. □

# Sissela Ann Bok

**Although she was born in Sweden and educated at the Sorbonne University in Paris, Sissela Ann Bok (born 1934) may be considered one of the premier American women moral philosophers of the latter part of the 20th century. Respected by fellow scholars, she was also highly regarded by the media, which often sought her views on ethics and philosophy.**

Sissela Bok was born in Stockholm, Sweden, on December 2, 1934, the daughter of Gunnar and Alva (Reimer) Myrdal. After studying in Europe she came to the United States, where she received her BA and MA degrees from George Washington University, concentrating in clinical psychology. She went on to earn her Ph.D. from

Harvard University (1970) in philosophy. Meanwhile in 1955 she married Derek Bok, who later was named president of Harvard University. They had three children.

Bok taught at Harvard University, Radcliffe Institute, Simmons College, Tufts University, the John F. Kennedy School of Government, and Brandeis University. She published, in Sweden, *Alva: Ett Kvinnoliv*, a biography of her mother, Alva Myrdal, who shared the 1982 Nobel Peace Prize with Alfonso Garcia Robies. She wrote extensively for more than a dozen philosophical and ethical journals. However, Bok was probably best known for her books in the field of applied ethics, including *The Dilemma of Euthanasia* (1975), *Lying: Moral Choice in Public and Private Life* (1979), *Ethics Teaching in Higher Education* (1980), *Secrets: On the Ethics of Concealment and Revelation* (1984), and *A Strategy for Peace: Human Values and the Threat of War* (1989).

## Medical Problems and Moral Questions

*The Dilemmas of Euthanasia*, edited with John A. Behnke (the editor of the journal *BioScience*), was a groundbreaking book that discussed the moral dilemmas created by a new medical success, that of the ability to keep terminally ill patients alive beyond the normal expectations. Bok and Behnke gathered together leading analysts in this new field of applied ethics to explore ways to resolve the obvious moral problems resulting from the possibility of the use of euthanasia to end the life of a terminally ill patient. Bok's contribution to the collection of essays was the article "Euthanasia and the Care of the Dying," the introductory article in the collection and the one most influential in further discussions of the morality of euthanasia. In the preface of the book Bok asked what were the appropriate moral questions as euthanasia became more and more medically feasible:

"How far should physicians go in delaying death? Which of the many techniques for prolonging life can they, in good conscience, omit in caring for a terminally ill patient? What can patients ask doctors to do and forbear in those cases where there is a conflict between prolonging life and easing suffering? Is there anything a person can do before becoming a patient to decrease the chances of being reduced to intolerable levels of suffering, loneliness, and dehumanization?"

*Lying: Moral Choice in Public and Private Life* is one of the most significant books in philosophy written in the 20th century, and it alone established Bok's reputation as a moral philosopher of international renown. It is a book which intellectually lies at the heart of the debate over private and public morality, and it has had enormous influence upon the change of the moral mood in the United States. It is clear that the new direction of the medical profession to tell the truth about a patient's condition and prognosis was based in large measure upon Bok's book, in which she stated:

"But if someone contemplates lying to a patient or concealing the truth, the burden of proof must shift. It must rest, here, as with all deception, on those who advocate it in any one instance. They must show why

they fear a patient may be harmed or how they know that another cannot cope with the truthful knowledge." The book concludes with a powerful paean to openness and honesty in speech and action:

"Individuals, without a doubt, have the power to influence the amount of duplicity in their lives and to shape their speech and action. They can decide to rule out deception wherever honest alternatives exist, and become much more adept at thinking up honest ways to deal with problems. They can learn to look with much greater care at the remaining choices where deception seems the only way out. They can make use of the test of publicity to help them set standards to govern their participation in deceptive practices. Finally, they can learn to beware of efforts to dupe them, and make clear their preference for honesty even in small things."

## Teaching and Studying Ethics

*Teaching Ethics in Higher Education,* edited with Daniel Callahan of the Hastings Center, was a timely and important book that gathered together (with the support of the Rockefeller Brothers Fund and the Carnegie Corporation for Education) important ethicists to ponder the question of how to teach ethics, both on the college campus and generally within American culture. The concern of the book is to focus "on the extent and quality of that (ethical) teaching, and on the possibilities and problems posed by widespread efforts to find a more central and significant place for ethics in the curriculum." Bok's particular contribution to the book was the essay "Whistleblowing and Professional Responsibilities," which analyzed the moral conflicts which exist within government, particularly when one wants to stick one's neck out and report malfeasance and immorality within governmental operations. She clearly saw the differences that exist between dissent, breach of loyalty, and accusation, all putative forms of "whistleblowing." Effective "whistleblowing," according to Bok, requires an audience, some larger forum, where a rational appeal to justice can be made. And, of course, it also requires the political possibility of a concerted public response—a democratic and open society is necessary if "whistleblowing" is going to have any moral consequence at all.

*Secrets: On the Ethics of Concealment and Revelation* continues the exploration of moral issues begun in *Lying*. In this book Bok discussed the choices of how to act and how to shape one's moral conduct in private and public life. It is a comprehensive study of the phenomenon of keeping secrets in our society. In her analysis of secrets she includes the police and the journalistic, scientific, political, academic, and business communities. But secrecy, of course, is also an expression of personal choice, and therefore Bok analyzed the following topics: secrecy and morality, secrecy and openness, secrecy and self-deception, confessions, gossip, and secrecy and accountability. Secrecy is defined by Bok as "intentional concealment," which she argued was a neutral definition so that no moral judgment may be made from the beginning that secrets are on the one hand determined as guilty or threatening, or on the other as awesome and worthy of respect.

A later book, *A Strategy for Peace: Human Values and the Threat of War,* was a major work, as substantial and important a book as had been written in the 1980s. (The topic was what Erik Erikson called the "species-wide nuclear crisis.") Based on lectures that Bok gave at Harvard University, the objective of the book is to propose a framework of moral principles to serve as a strategy for peace. She rejected the calls for a "new ethics" or, as she put it, "some worldwide religious or psychological or political conversion after which peace will arrive, as it were, by itself." She also rejected utopian schemes of international harmony, such as world government and programs which propose the miraculous transformation of society. She was also fearful to entrust the survival of humanity to the uncertainties of a world balance of power. Bok remembered well Voltaire's dictum: "Those who can make you believe absurdities, can make you commit atrocities."

## Belief in the Laws of Humanity

Bok relied for her concepts of peace and of strategy on Immanuel Kant's essay "Perpetual Peace" and the book *On War* by Carl von Clausewitz. These works have always been considered antithetical in their perspectives. Bok demonstrated instead that the perspectives of one can enrich the other and that together they can serve to provide the insights by which a strategy of peace can be generated to meet the current threat to universal human life. Precisely because the danger to future human life is so great, all of us have an unprecedented incentive, as Bok argued, "to seek joint ways of breaking out of the impasse"; we are all "under equal necessity" to find a way out—or we all die.

She believed that the most basic "laws of humanity," the most basic human drive for survival, now gives us a reason to confront our traditional enemies from the larger perspectives that survival requires. And those larger perspectives speak first the language of religion and morality, stressing character and principled conduct, found in thinkers of the Christian pacifist tradition represented by Tolstoy, Gandhi, and Martin Luther King, the medieval "just war" theorists, and the proponents of a "perpetual peace"; the second voice emphasizes the need for competence, insight, and good planning and is represented by the political realism of such thinkers as Thucydides, Machiavelli, Clausewitz, Churchill, and Kissinger, who argued that the value of one's own survival must override all other values. Bok wanted to bring together the two traditions of thought: "The language of morality and that of strategy are both indispensable in the face of the present crisis."

Bok's global perspective informed by moral characteristics took seriously Kant's moral law to "act only according to that maxim whereby you can at the same time will that it should become a moral law," which means practically that individuals, communities or nations, and a future federation of states would act only in a way which respected all human beings in their own right, rather than treating them merely as means to other ends. Moral constraints are thereby presented which can bring about a climate in which the threat of war can be reduced. They are constraints on violence, deceit, and breaches of trust—all of which predate debates about the complex problems of equality, liberty, justice, human rights, and all of which are "common even in primitive human groups long before one can talk about states, much less an international community."

Bok identified in Clausewitz's *On War* the argument that the objective of a war is survival and national self-preservation. The political goal of survival ought to be common to all wars, Clausewitz insisted, and for that reason he argued that defense is superior to attack as a form of fighting. Its object, preservation, is less costly and can more likely be achieved. But whatever the nature of the war, what matters most is survival. Consequently, Bok maintained, following Clausewitz, that nuclear wars have no place today in sound political strategy; the massive piling up of nuclear weapons cannot any longer assure the survival of any nation.

Bok, a distinguished fellow at the Harvard Center for Population and Development Studies, published *Common Values* in 1996. Angered by "the disgraceful accommodations with evil around the world that moral relativists have reached," Bok promotes pluralistic yet diverse social practices based upon a universally shared understanding and knowledge of "certain minimal moral principles." Bok's concern with moral relativists is confusing. She believes that all, and not merely some, cultures recognize her "certain minimal moral principles," although they may not live up to them. These values really are minimal, and include: "duties of support and loyalty, injunctions against harm and deceit, and procedural justice". Bok puts forth a call to arms in the defense of a universal morality and believes that the minimal moral values she attributes to every culture allow for an objective criteria by which to assess all social practices and cultures. Bok is at her best in *Common Values*. She explores far more questions than she offers answers for, but plants them in the reader's consciousness just the same.

Sissela Bok demonstrated that an academic philosopher can feel deeply for the moral anguish of a people in the face of changes in the fabric of our society. Her moderate and rational perspectives on these issues have already changed the way we, as a society, make moral decisions. Her philosophical influence has been noteworthy.

## Further Reading

There is little published material on Sissela Bok. For further information see her contributions to the *Encyclopedia of Bioethics* (1978) and the bimonthly *Hastings Center Report* from the Hastings Center, Hastings-on-Hudson, New York 10706. See also the *Christian Century* (November, 1989); *American Health* (September 1989); and *JAMA, The Journal of the American Medical Association* (February 1989). The biography of her mother, *Alva Myrdal: A Daughter's Memoir,* was published in English in 1991. □

# Gertrude Simmons Bonnin

**Native American activist and writer of the Sioux tribe Gertrude Simmons Bonnin (1876-1938) was**

**prominent in the Pan-Indian movement of the 1920s and 1930s. She devoted her life to lobbying for the rights of Native Americans.**

One of the most outspoken voices raised on behalf of Native Americans during the early twentieth century was that of Gertrude Simmons Bonnin, a granddaughter of the famous Sioux chief Sitting Bull. As a writer, she produced a number of essays and short stories that established her as a significant figure in Native American literature. Her enduring legacy, however, is that of a reformer and activist devoted to improving the lives of Native Americans both on and off the reservation. Calling upon her skills as an orator, Bonnin made numerous appearances before government officials in Washington and ordinary citizens throughout the nation to draw attention to the plight of Native Americans trapped in poverty and despair.

Bonnin was born to a Native American mother and a white father at the Yankton Sioux Agency in South Dakota on February 22, 1876. She spent her early childhood on the reservation, immersed in traditional Sioux ways. But when she was about eight, she left to attend a Quaker missionary school for Indians located in Wabash, Indiana. After a difficult and unhappy adjustment period, young Gertrude finally settled in and completed a three-year term, then returned home for four years before going back for another three-year course of study. Following her graduation in 1895, she went on to Earlham College in Richmond, Indiana, earning recognition as the winner of a state-wide oratory contest.

After leaving college in 1897, Gertrude Simmons, as she was then known, secured a teaching position at Pennsylvania's Carlisle Indian School. While the time she spent there was not pleasant, she did manage to make some contacts in the eastern literary establishment that enabled her to begin publishing some of her work (under her Sioux name, Zitkala-Sa, or Red Bird) in such well-known magazines as *Harper's* and *Atlantic Monthly.* In 1899, she resigned from the Carlisle faculty and enrolled at the New England Conservatory of Music in Boston to study violin. Free to pursue her writing and her music in a cultural milieu she enjoyed, she was happier than she had been in many years. In 1901, she published her first full-length book, *Old Indian Legends,* a collection of Native American stories. But she still felt somewhat torn between two worlds, and she very much wanted to do something for those she had left behind on the reservation.

Returning to South Dakota around 1902, she met and married a fellow Yankton Sioux, Raymond Talesfase Bonnin, who worked for the Indian Service. They soon moved to the Uintah and Ouray Reservation in Utah, where Gertrude Simmons Bonnin worked as a clerk and a teacher. During this same period, she also became involved with the Society of American Indians, a Native American reform organization founded in 1911 at Ohio State University. The first group of its kind to be established and managed solely by Native Americans, it operated on the principle that assimilation was ultimately the best course for the country's Native American population. To that end, the Society focused its efforts not only on government reforms but on activities such as increasing Native American employment in the Indian Service (the federal agency charged with managing Indian affairs), codifying laws pertaining to Native Americans, achieving Native American citizenship, opening the courts to all just claims regarding land settlements between Native Americans and the government, and preserving Native American history.

In 1916, Bonnin was elected secretary of the Society of American Indians, and not long after, she and her husband moved to Washington, D.C. From her new base in the nation's capital, which she would call home for the rest of her life, she continued to serve as secretary of the Society (until 1919) and editor of its major publication, *American Indian Magazine.* She also joined forces with a number of other organizations spearheading Native American rights and reform, including the American Indian Defense Association and the Indian Rights Association. In addition, she began lecturing extensively from coast to coast, speaking to women's clubs and other groups on Indian affairs and lobbying for Indian citizenship. Her work on behalf of the latter met with success in 1924 with the passage of the Indian Citizenship Bill.

Both Bonnin and her husband devoted a great deal of their time to meeting with officials of the federal government on behalf of individual Native Americans and tribes. They also testified before various congressional committees on a wide variety of issues. Many of their findings were the result of their own investigations and travels throughout the country visiting reservations and noting the need for improvements in areas such as health care, education, conservation of natural resources, and preserving Native American cultural traditions.

In 1926, following the disbanding of the Society of American Indians, the Bonnins formed the National Council of American Indians (NCAI). Like the Society, the NCAI was made up exclusively of Native Americans; Gertrude Bonnin served as its president. Its focus was also on reform, and to that end, Bonnin directed her energies toward lobbying for Native American legislation in Congress and calling attention to the deficiencies of the Indian Service.

The spirit that motivated these efforts finally prompted some government officials to take a closer look at the Indian Service. In 1928, U.S. Secretary of the Interior Hubert Work commissioned a group of scholars to study living conditions among Native Americans, focusing in particular on economic activity, education, health, and the federal government's administrative policies and practices. Under the direction of Dr. Lewis Meriam, the Institute for Government Research conducted an exhaustive survey and published the results in a landmark report entitled *The Problem of Indian Administration,* more commonly known as the Meriam Report. Its description of the "deplorable" state of life on the reservations—the high death rate among all age groups, the failure of the educational system, the widespread poverty and malnutrition—focused national attention on the plight of Native Americans and increased pressure on the government to take immediate action.

In mid-December of 1928, Bonnin voiced her thoughts on the findings of the Meriam Report at a meeting of the Indian Rights Association in Atlantic City, New Jersey. According to the text of the speech, as furnished by the Harold B. Lee Library at Brigham Young University, which houses the Gertrude Simmons Bonnin Collection, Bonnin declared: "As an Indian, speaking earnestly for the very life of my race, I must say that this report by the Institute for Government Research, *The Problem of Indian Administration*, is all too true, although I do not always concur in their conclusions, which tend to minimize the responsibility of the Bureau [of Indian Affairs]." Bonnin described the conditions on most reservations as below poverty level, with food being scarce and very few educational and employment opportunities. In the speech, Bonnin detailed provisions available in reservation schools: "The subcommittee of the Senate Indian Affairs Committee is holding hearings right now, and sworn testimony reveals horrible conditions—rotten meat, full of maggots, and spoiled flour which mice and cats had defiled, are fed to children in government schools. Sworn statements amply show that the report of the Institute for Government Research could all be transformed into the superlative degree and not begin to tell the whole story of Indian exploitation."

Bonnin also commented on the quality of education available to young Native Americans in her address: "The Indian race is starving—not only physically, but mentally and morally. It is a dire tragedy. The government Indian schools are not on a par with the American schools of today. The so-called 'Indian Graduates from Government Schools' cannot show any credentials that would be accepted by any business house. They are unable to pass the Civil Service examinations. The proviso in Indian treaties that educated Indians, wherever qualified, be given preference in Indian Service employment is rendered meaningless. Indians are kept ignorant and 'incompetent' to cope with the world's trained workers, because they are not sufficiently educated in the government schools."

While it did not bring about major improvements, the Meriam Report did exert some influence on government policies regarding Native Americans during the administrations of Herbert Hoover (1928-33) and his successor, Franklin D. Roosevelt (1933-45). Hoover, for example, appointed two leading members of the Indian Rights Association as commissioner and assistant commissioner of the Bureau of Indian Affairs. As part of his Depression-era reforms, Roosevelt pushed for the Indian Reorganization Act of 1934 and its promised "Indian New Deal," which granted Indians more self-government and the right to keep observing their own cultural ceremonies and other events.

As for Bonnin, she remained active in the reform movement throughout the 1930s. She continued lobbying Congress, particularly on behalf of the Sioux and the Utes, and frequently lectured across the United States, often appearing in native dress to dramatize her message. While she devoted less time to her writing, she renewed her interest in music and even composed an Indian opera entitled *Sun Dance*. After her death in 1938 at the age of only sixty-one, Bonnin was buried in Arlington National Cemetery.

## Further Reading

Bonnin, Gertrude Simmons, *Old Indian Legends* (reprint of original 1901 edition), University of Nebraska Press, 1985.

Bonnin, Gertrude Simmons, *American Indian Stories* (reprint of original 1921 edition), University of Nebraska Press, 1985.

Gridley, Marion E., *American Indian Women*, Hawthorn Books, 1974.

Jones, Louis Thomas, *Aboriginal American Oratory: The Tradition of Eloquence Among the Indians of the United States*, Southwest Museum (Los Angeles), 1965.

*American Indian Quarterly*, winter, 1988, pp. 27-40.

*Journal of the West*, July, 1984, pp. 3-6.

*New York Times*, January 27, 1938, p. 21.

Gertrude Simmons Bonnin Collection, Harold B. Lee Library, Brigham Young University. □

# Evangeline Cory Booth

**British-born humanitarian Evangeline Cory Booth (1865-1950) was one of the early commanders of the Salvation Army in the United States. Her work to help the nation's poor and her efforts to provide aid to U.S. soldiers in Europe during World War I won her the admiration of the American public. In 1934 she was elected general—the Salvation Army's highest post—culminating a lifetime of service to the religious charity.**

Evangeline Cory Booth was a member of the founding family of the Salvation Army, a religious organization formed by her father with the aim of aiding the needy. In her role as commander of the Salvation Army in the United States, she gained acceptance for the group's work and ideals throughout American society, particularly after organizing assistance to soldiers during World War I. Her success in expanding the Salvation Army in the United States was apparent in the increased number of centers and followers during her tenure as well as her personal popularity among the public. In 1929 her work was recognized when she was elected to the post of General of the Salvation Army, making her the head of the entire organization.

## Born into Salvation Army Family

Booth was born with the name Evelyne on December 25, 1865, in London, England, and was known to her family as Eva. She was one of the five children of William Booth, who in the year of Booth's birth, founded the East London Revival Society. The Society later took the name the Christian Mission before taking its final shape as the religious and charitable organization known as the Salvation Army. Like her siblings, Booth devoted her life to the work of the Army—to assist the poor and spread Christian values. She did not receive any formal education, but spent her adolescent years among the poor of London. Becoming a sergeant in the Army at the age of 15, she sold the organization's publication, *War Cry*, in the streets. When she was a bit older, her assignment included selling matches in the im-

mated 75,000 people came to pay respects to her open casket and a New York newspaper compared the size of her funeral procession to that of president Ulysses S. Grant. Evangeline was selected to serve as the new U.S. commander, but she was intimidated at the prospect of trying to live up to her sister's greatness. Her father encouraged her, however, telling her that he believed she was destined to a career of great accomplishment. His daughter ultimately fulfilled his predictions. From the time of her induction as American commander in 1904, until her retirement from the post in 1934, the organization more than doubled the number of stations, its property holdings grew to a value of 48 million dollars, and its bank accounts increased to 35 million dollars.

Once arriving in New York, Booth immediately began to address the extreme poverty she found among immigrants there. One of the main problems was hunger; she attacked this by establishing bread lines and programs to feed school children. The public was incredibly responsive to her calls for help and surprised her by exceeding her expectations when she held donation drives. Other public service projects she took on were providing emergency relief during disasters, providing aid to hospitals, and helping the elderly. By focusing on such activities, Booth won over support from people who had initially been wary of the Salvation Army's religious overtones. She also used her oratorical talent to speak out on other topics that crossed religious boundaries, including women's rights and the prohibition of alcohol.

poverished area of Marylebone while dressed in rags like the poor around her. Although all the Booth children went on to hold high posts in the Army, it was Evelyne Booth who would serve for the longest period of time and bring the Army to a new level of influence and popularity. As an adult, she changed her name to Evangeline to emphasize the spiritual solace she hoped to bring to the poor while at the same time alleviating their physical suffering.

In 1895, at the age of 30, Booth arrived in Canada to replace her brother Herbert as field commissioner of the Salvation Army in that country. Having worked in some very rough environments in England, Booth found conditions around the city of Toronto to be relatively placid, and she worried that there would not be much for her to do in Canada. But she soon found her calling in the frontier areas of the north such as the Yukon and Alaska, where gold prospectors had formed unruly boom towns. For nine years she traveled and preached among the settlers and the native people of the area in what she later called "one of the most arduous toils in my experience."

## Expanded Army in United States

But not even her challenging work in Canada could prepare her for the scope of her next task. In 1903, her sister Emma, the commander of the United States Salvation Army, died in New York City. Emma had created a solid foundation for the Army in the United States; at the time of her death its assets were worth 1.5 million dollars and almost 700 stations had been founded across the country. She was mourned as one of the country's greatest citizens—an esti-

## Won Appreciation for Wartime Service

It was her efforts to use the Salvation Army to assist soldiers in World War I, however, that won Booth and her organization the lasting respect and appreciation of the American public. Under the leadership of Booth, the Salvation Army sent members to the front lines of the war in Europe, where they cared for the wounded, established canteens, and loaned money to soldiers. This wartime aid was considered so important by the U.S. government that it excused Salvation Army members from military duty so they could be free to continue their charitable work. The country showed its appreciation for the Salvation Army after the war by donating 15 million dollars during a special nationwide project to assist the organization. In addition, the group and its leader were praised by some of the leading political and military figures of the war, including presidents Theodore Roosevelt and Woodrow Wilson, British prime minister Lloyd George, and U.S. generals John Joseph Pershing and Leonard Wood. Booth herself was recognized with a Distinguished Service Medal in October of 1919.

## Elected General of Salvation Army

In the 1920s, the Salvation Army suffered a period of internal turmoil. After William Booth's death in 1912, his son Bramwell had become the second general, or head official, of the Salvation Army. While Evangeline was recovering from a throat operation in 1922, Bramwell Booth attempted to undermine her position by dividing the United States command into three separate groups, each with its own commander. Americans, however, were extremely supportive of the beloved U.S. commander and were quick to voice their disapproval of her brother's move. The general was forced to back off his position, but his reputation had been weakened. In 1929, the Salvation Army held its first election for the post of general and Bramwell Booth was replaced with Edward J. Higgins. When the next elections were held in 1934, Salvation Army members turned to the woman who had done so much to raise the image of the organization, electing Evangeline Booth to the position of general. She completed only one five-year term before retiring from the organization in 1939 at the age of 74. Having served the Salvation Army in three different nations during her long career, it seemed fitting that her last years were spent overseeing an organization that had grown to an international success with volunteers in more than 50 countries. Booth died in her adopted country of the United States at Hartsdale, New York, on July 17, 1950.

## Further Reading

For more information see Wilson, P. W., *General Evangeline Booth of the Salvation Army,* Scribners, 1948. □

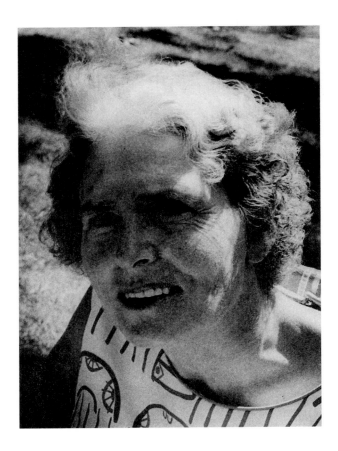

# Margaret Bourke-White

**American photographer Margaret Bourke-White (1904-1971) was a leader in the new field of photo-journalism. As a staff photographer for *FORTUNE* and *LIFE* magazines, she covered the major political and social issues of the 1930s and 1940s.**

Born in New York City on June 14, 1904, Margaret Bourke-White was the daughter of Joseph and Minnie White. (She added "Bourke," her mother's name, after her first marriage ended). One of the original staff photographers for *LIFE* magazine, she was a pioneer in the field of photo-journalism. She photographed the leading political figures of her time: Franklin Roosevelt, Winston Churchill, Joseph Stalin, and Mahatma Gandhi. She also called attention to the suffering of unknown people, from the poor sharecroppers in America to the oppressed Black coalminers in South Africa. An adventuresome lady who loved to fly, Bourke-White was the first accredited woman war correspondent during World War II and the first woman to accompany a bombing mission.

Bourke-White first revealed her talent for photography while a student at Cornell University. Using a secondhand Ica Reflex camera with a broken lens, she sold pictures of the scenic campus to other students. After graduation she opened a studio in Cleveland, where she found the industrial landscape "a photographic paradise." Initially specializing in architectural photography, her prints of the Otis Steel factory came to the attention of *TIME* magazine publisher Henry Luce, who was planning a new publication devoted to the glamour of business.

In the spring of 1929 Bourke-White accepted Luce's offer to become the first staff photographer for *FORTUNE*

magazine, which made its debut in February 1930. Her subjects included the Swift meatpacking company, shoemaking, watches, glass, papermills, orchids, and banks. Excited by the drama of the machine, she made several trips to the Soviet Union and was the first photographer to seriously document its rapid industrial development. She published her work in the book *Eyes on Russia* (1931).

Bourke-White, working out of a New York City studio in the new Chrysler Building, also handled lucrative advertising accounts. In 1934, in the midst of the Depression, she earned over $35,000. But a *FORTUNE* assignment to cover the drought in the Plains states opened her eyes to human suffering and steered her away from advertising work. She began to view photography less as a purely artistic medium and increasingly as a powerful tool for informing the public. In 1936 she collaborated with Erskine Caldwell, author of *Tobacco Road,* on a photo-essay revealing social conditions in the South. The results of their efforts became her best-known book, *You Have Seen Their Faces* (1937).

In the fall of 1936 Bourke-White joined the staff of *LIFE* magazine, which popularized the photo-essay. Her picture of the Fort Peck dam in Montana adorned the cover of *LIFE's* first issue, November 11, 1936. On one of her first assignments she flew to the Arctic circle. While covering the Louisville flood in 1937 she composed her most famous single photograph, contrasting a line of Black people waiting for emergency relief with an untroubled white family in its car pictured on a billboard with a caption celebrating the American way of life.

In early 1940 Bourke-White worked briefly for the new pictorial newspaper *PM,* but by October she returned to *LIFE* as a free lance photographer. With Erskine Caldwell (to whom she was married from 1939 to 1942) she travelled across the United States and produced the book *Say Is This the U.S.A.?* In the spring of 1941 they were the only foreign journalists in the Soviet Union when the Germans invaded Russia.

During World War II Bourke-White served as an accredited war correspondent affiliated with both *LIFE* and the Air Force. She survived a torpedo attack on a ship she was taking to North Africa and accompanied the bombing mission which destroyed the German airfield of El Aouina near Tunis. She later covered the Italian campaign (recorded in the book *They Called It "Purple Heart Valley"*) and was with General George Patton in spring 1945 when his troops opened the gates of the concentration camp at Buchenwald. Her photos revealed the horrors to the world.

In 1946 *LIFE* sent Bourke-White to India to cover the story of its independence. Before she was allowed to meet Mahatma Gandhi she was required to learn how to use the spinning wheel. Frustrated at the moment because of a deadline, she later reflected, "Nonviolence was Gandhi's creed, and the spinning wheel was the perfect weapon."

On a second trip to India to witness the creation of Pakistan, Bourke-White was the last journalist to see Gandhi, only a couple of hours before his assassination.

In December of 1949 she went to South Africa for five months where she recorded the cruelty of apartheid. In 1952 she went to Korea, where her pictures focused on family sorrows arising from the war. Shortly after her return from Korea she first noticed signs of Parkinson's disease, the nerve disorder which she battled for the remaining years of her life. Her autobiography, *Portrait of Myself,* was started in 1955 and completed in 1963. On August 27, 1971, Margaret Bourke-White died at her home in Darien, Connecticut. She left behind a legacy as a determined woman, an innovative visual artist, and a compassionate human observer.

## Further Reading

Margaret Bourke-White wrote or co-authored 11 books. Her most famous is *You Have Seen Their Faces* (1937), with Erskine Caldwell, on social conditions in the South during the Depression. Also see her informative autobiography, *Portrait of Myself* (1963). There are two good collections of her photographs which also contain biographical information, *For the World to See: The Life of Margaret Bourke-White* by Jonathon Silverman (1983) and *The Photographs of Margaret Bourke-White,* edited by Sean Callahan (1972). □

# Barbara Boxer

**Barbara Boxer (born 1940) is a Democratic Senator from California.**

Barbara Boxer was one of six women elected to the U.S. Senate in 1992. Representing California as a Democrat, she was part of a larger movement that swept an increased number of women into positions of power within the government. A 10-year veteran of Congress, Boxer rose through her energetic and combative style, and her fealty to the liberal causes which had first inspired her entrance into politics—feminism and environmentalism chief among them. The product of a conventional background and upbringing, Boxer was inspired by the social upheavals of the 1960s to look beyond her home and family to make her mark on the world at large.

Boxer's origins and early years gave little hint of the career she would eventually pursue. She was born in Brooklyn, New York, the child of immigrants, in 1940. Boxer later recalled a conventional and happy middle-class childhood, which included education in the local public schools. As a "child of the '50s," Boxer wrote in her memoir, *Strangers in the Senate,* she wore cinch belts and layers of crinolines, as well as hoop skirts, to conform to the dictates of fashion. Nonetheless, in high school, she and a friend took on the job of coaching the boys' baseball team, an unconventional choice.

Boxer made another unconventional choice when she entered Brooklyn College in 1958 and became one of the few women at the institution to chose a major of economics, instead of education. For her minor, Boxer chose political science. She also served as a cheerleader for the Brooklyn College basketball team.

In her final year of college, at age 21, Barbara Levy married Stewart Boxer, another student, who was then 23. The two moved into a one-room efficiency apartment at the back of a building on Ocean Boulevard, paying $90 a month in rent. When the building's owner failed to provide promised amenities, such as a carpeted and painted lobby, the energetic Boxer circulated a petition in the building to pressure the landlord into fixing things up.

After graduating from college Boxer sought a job in the New York financial world to support her husband while he completed his law degree at Fordham University. She tried to enter one of the stockbroker training programs run by the big Wall Street firms, but was turned down on the basis of her sex. Boxer then took a job as a secretary, and studied for the stockbroker's exam independently. Even after she passed, Boxer was not allowed to sell securities and earn commissions, so she left her job and took a position with a firm that would allow her to do so.

Boxer was working as a stockbroker when the event that she later identified as the birth of her political consciousness took place: the assassination of President John F. Kennedy in 1963. With this event, and the later political assassinations of the 1960s, Boxer began to look beyond her own private life and aspirations to address larger social issues and concerns.

In 1965 Boxer moved with her husband to northern California. The couple had been determined to own a house and raise a family, and they felt that real estate was more affordable there than in the New York metropolitan area. While her husband was completing his exams at Fordham, Boxer quit her job and relocated to San Francisco to find a house. She was seven months pregnant with her first child at the time, and gave birth to her son—two months prematurely—the day after she arrived.

Boxer and her husband soon settled in San Francisco, and their second child, a daughter, came into the family in 1967. Although Boxer later recalled that she was primarily concerned with her family life during that time, she and her husband opposed the war in Vietnam, and felt strongly enough about their position to take part in a peace march, which wound through the city to Golden Gate Park.

Also in 1967, Boxer and her husband moved to the city suburbs, buying a $40,000 house in Marin County, north of the city. This area would later become the basis of her political constituency. The year after they had moved to Marin, Boxer witnessed the assassination of Robert Kennedy live on television, and this violent act, she later recalled, shocked her forever from her routine private life.

Joining with other women from her community, who were young, college-educated mothers like her, Boxer and her friends in the town of Greenbrae embarked on a number of social initiatives. Among their first efforts was a program called Education Corps of Marin, designed to train high school drop-outs for jobs. This program was eventually taken over by the local school system.

In addition, Boxer became involved in the environmental movement as well as in anti-war activities. In 1970 she oversaw publicity for a campaign to put a peace initiative on the ballot, which, surprisingly, carried the day. She worked for other local ballot initiatives and for progressive candidates. Marin Community Video and the Marin Alternative, a progressive, grassroots, political network, also earned her attention. At the same time Boxer devoted her energy to a number of women's and children's groups, helping to found the Kentfield After School Child Care Center, and taking part in Woman's Way, a women's support group.

## Declares Candidacy

On the strength of these activities, Boxer declared her candidacy for elective office for the first time in 1971. Although her husband was equally well qualified to represent the progressive environmental constituency with which the couple had become involved, he could not afford to sacrifice his lucrative law practice for the $11,000 annual salary paid to members of the Marin County Board of Supervisors, so Barbara ran, becoming the first serious female candidate in two decades. Although Boxer won a three-way primary race, she ran into serious obstacles in her main campaign, many of which were related to her gender. Even women who worked told her of their doubts that she could care for her young children properly while holding down such a responsible position. In the final election, in November of 1972, Boxer lost by a narrow margin.

Following this defeat, Boxer re-entered the workforce. She took a position as a reporter for the *Pacific Sun*, becoming an associate editor of the publication from 1972 to 1974. At that time, she returned to the world of politics, as a congressional aide working for the representative from the Fifth Congressional District of California. Boxer held this post until 1976, when she ran again for the Marin County Board of Supervisors. This time, she was elected.

As a Marin County Supervisor, Boxer maintained her strong commitment to the environmental movement. She urged the closure of all nuclear power plants in the state of California, and worked for other liberal causes during her six years in the post. From 1977 to 1982, she served on the Bay Area Air Quality Management Board, of which she was the president from 1979 to 1981. Boxer was also the president of the Marin County Board of Supervisors from 1980 to 1981.

## Elected to House

In the early 1980s Boxer's local congressional district, the Sixth District of California, was redrawn in a manner that helped to insure the re-election of incumbent John L. Burton, a Democrat. When Burton, a longtime friend and mentor of Boxer, chose instead to retire, Boxer ran for the seat he was vacating in the U.S. House of Representatives. She won the 1982 election as a Democrat.

Boxer took office in Washington as a freshman representative at the start of 1983, and became president of the Democratic New Members Caucus of the House of Representatives. The district Boxer went on to represent for five terms, covering ten years, included parts of the city of San Francisco, as well as Marin County, her home base. In Congress, Boxer continued to champion the liberal causes that had brought her popularity with the constituents of this area in the past. Boxer was assigned to sit on the Armed Service Committee, where she was one of the few committed liberal members, and became co-chair of the Military Reform Caucus. Boxer was also appointed to the Select Committee on Children, Youth, and Families. In addition, she chaired the subcommittee on government activities.

In Congress Boxer made a name for herself as a staunch opponent of defense spending. She opposed the costs of stealth aircraft and the Patriot missile, pushing repeated floor amendments in the house to cut government spending for these projects. Boxer also voted against funding for the Nicaraguan contras. In addition, she lent support to the Congressional Black Caucus in its recommendation that the defense budget be cut in half.

Boxer became best known as a representative for publicizing particularly egregious cases of wasteful military spending. Posing for photographers with a $7,622 coffee pot for a cargo plane, and a $600 toilet seat cover, she dramatized the issue of government excess, bringing public pressure to bear on efforts to reform government procurement. As a result of these efforts, Boxer was able to take partial credit for a series of military procurement reform amendments, which included a 1988 measure to protect whistle-blowers, and a measure to allow competitive bidding for contracts to provide spare parts to the military. Despite her best efforts, however, Boxer was unable to keep the Presidio, a historical military base in San Francisco, off the list of military bases to eventually be closed.

Boxer opposed the entry of the United States into the Persian Gulf war in 1991, and she sponsored an effort that would have required prior Congressional approval of covert American actions in foreign countries. This resolution, which was seen a threat to the secrecy of war plans and anti-terrorist operations, was unanimously defeated on the floor of the House, as even Boxer withdrew her support for the amendment.

As a representative Boxer also maintained her commitment to women's issues. She was an original co-sponsor of the Family and Medical Leave Act benefitting workers with children or other family responsibilities, and she put up a strong opposition to the gag rule forbidding abortion counseling at federally funded health clinics. As a supporter of the Freedom of Choice Act, Boxer sponsored an amendment to provide federal funding for abortions in cases of rape or incest, which was passed, but vetoed by President George Bush. Boxer won the respect of the powerful former chairman of the House Ways and Means Committee, Dan Rostenkowski, in her fight to pass this bill, with her forthright appeal for his support of the abortion amendment.

Boxer also pursued a campaign to open up the men's club of Congress to greater participation by women. As part of this effort, she tried to win more extensive locker room facilities for female representatives, inspiring an apocryphal story about her presence in the men's locker room at an inopportune moment. The most important moment in her struggle to instill greater equality for women in the U.S. Congress, however, came during hearings to consider Clarence Thomas for a seat on the U.S. Supreme Court, when Boxer joined with other female representatives to bring their concerns about the treatment of Anita Hill to the attention of members of the Senate Judiciary Committee. The group of women was refused entrance to a meeting of this committee, after being told that "strangers" were not permitted in the room. Boxer was so incensed by the idea that she and the other female representatives were considered "strangers" in the Senate that she later wrote a book using this phrase as its title, describing the progress of women in politics in her lifetime.

## Runs for Senate

The treatment of Hill at the Senate hearings proved to be a political watershed, and when California Senator Alan Cranston announced that he would relinquish his seat after being tainted in a savings and loan scandal, Boxer decided to give up her secure Congressional berth and run for the Senate as a long-shot candidate in 1992. She made the lack of female representation in the U.S. Senate a cornerstone of her campaign.

Boxer's first obstacle in her campaign for the Senate was a tough primary, with two strong male contenders who also had solid records on women's rights. With a strong fund-raising operation in place, as well as the support of groups such as EMILY's List, and the Hollywood Women's Political Committee, Boxer raised more than $2 million by the start of 1992, which allowed her to triumph in the June primary.

Boxer then went on to face Bruce Herschensohn, a conservative television commentator, in the general election. Despite her ten-year Congressional career, she cast herself as a Washington outsider, whose gender made her a gadfly to the establishment. This picture was somewhat damaged by the revelation during the campaign that she had bounced 143 checks at the U.S. House of Representatives bank. Despite this setback, Boxer relied on her ability to identify issues that voters cared about, and get her position across in a punchy and appealing manner. In a year in which more women than ever before were elected to the Senate, Boxer won her race in November of 1992, becoming, along with Dianne Feinstein, one of two women to make up the California delegation.

As a senator Boxer has continued to push the liberal agenda she supported as a representative, and she has remained sensitive to issues of importance to women. She joined the effort to pressure Senator Bob Packwood, under fire for sexual harassment, to fully disclose his actions, and she mounted a campaign, with the other five women in the Senate, to punish a Navy admiral for the Tailhook sex scandal. Boxer has worked for increased funding for breast cancer research and domestic violence programs. She also staunchly supported an openly gay San Francisco woman for a job at the Department of Health and Human Services, and she fought to end restrictions on gays in the military.

In addition, Boxer has remained true to her roots in the environmental movement. She is on the Committee on Environment and Public Works and belongs to three of its subcommittees. She battled a plan to place a radioactive dump in the California desert and pushed for the restoration of ten wetlands areas in California. Boxer has also worked hard to restore the ailing economy of her home state. In the name of California jobs, she endorsed a controversial proposal to deploy National Guard troops along the Mexican border to cut down on illegal immigration. She also supported a move to give members of the agricultural industry more time to renegotiate federal water contracts.

As the ranking member of the Subcommittee on International Finance, Boxer promotes America's competitiveness in today's global economy by lowering trade barriers and expanding exports.

In support of her pro-choice stance, Boxer cosponsored the Freedom of Choice Act and pushed for passage of both the Freedom of Access to Clinic Entrances Act and the Family Medical Leave Act.

In an effort to keep in touch with the constituents of her vast state, Boxer began inviting voters to write to her, and she was soon receiving more mail than any other senator. This outpouring suggests that Boxer has done an effective job of reaching out to the voters of California. Boxer appears to be laying the groundwork for a long career in the Senate, capping her evolution into an effective feminist and liberal politician.

## Further Reading

*California Journal,* April 1, 1992; June 1, 1994.
*Ms.,* March/April 1992, p. 86.
*National Review,* October 19, 1992, p. 21.
*New York Times,* October 25, 1993, p. A15.
Additional information was obtained from Senator Boxer's Home Page on the Internet. □

# Marion Zimmer Bradley

**Popular fantasy writer Marion Zimmer Bradley (born 1930) is considered a pioneer in the field of woman-based science fiction, creating strong, independent female protagonists in her many popular novels and short stories.**

Beginning her career in the 1950s, author Marion Zimmer Bradley has built almost a cult following on the heels of her popular "Darkover" books. While largely ignored by mainstream reviewers, Bradley's fiction has been embraced by her fans as what *Feminist Writers* essayist Nancy Jesser calls "one of the early manifestations of proto-feminist science fiction." In her writing, the prolific Bradley has worked in several genres, including Gothic novels, teleplays, children's books, lesbian novels, and bibliographies of gay and lesbian fiction. She addresses such issues as gender, technology, alienation, the evolution of society, culture, and human relationships by placing her characters in highly imaginary worlds, many with a Celtic flavor.

## Began Professional Writing Career at Age 17

Bradley, who was born in Albany, New York, on June 3, 1930, knew from an early age that she wanted to be a writer. Fascinated by the science-fiction writing of the era, she started her own amateur science-fiction magazine before she was even out of high school. However, Bradley was too practical to think that a young woman could make writing her life's work; after graduating from high school she enrolled at New York State College with the intention of becoming a teacher. But her marriage to Robert Alden Bradley in 1949 would put a halt to these career plans, and the birth of a son would occupy much of her time during the 1950s. It was not until 1964 that the industrious Bradley completed her education, graduating from Abilene, Texas's Hardin-Simmons University with a triple bachelor's degree in English, Spanish, and psychology. She then attended graduate school at the University of California, Berkeley for another three years. Meanwhile, she continued to write, composing short stories and experimenting with longer works containing science-fiction and fantasy elements.

In 1949, the same year she got married, Bradley sold her first story to a sci-fi publication. Three years later she began what she considers her "professional" writing career, with the sale of yet another story to the magazine *Vortex Science Fiction.* Throughout the remainder of the 1950s she managed to juggle the demands of motherhood—at the time moms were expected to stay at home—with her desire to write. Bradley would not publish her first full-length book until 1961, when the sci-fi novel *The Door through Space* was released. This novel seemed to open a floodgate for Bradley; in 1962 alone her byline would appear on five different volumes: three novels under her own name and two other works under various pseudonyms. While readers might marvel at how Bradley could be so prolific, at least one of the novels published in 1962—*The Planet Savers*—had actually made its first appearance serialized in the pages of *Amazing Science Fiction Stories* three years earlier. Now in book form, *The Planet Savers* would become the first of Bradley's "Darkover" novels.

## The World of Darkover

The 20 novels that comprise the bulk of the "Darkover" series are among Bradley's most popular works of fiction. The series is named after a lost colony wherein social habits and technology develop independently of the earthlings who established it because it was overlooked for many generations. In addition to developing psychic abilities, Darkoverians have divided along gender lines: a patriarchal society exists apart from a woman-centered society of "Free Amazons." In Bradley's futuristic world, nothing is gained without sacrifice. According to Susan M. Shwartz in *The Feminine Eye: Science Fiction and the Women Who Write It,* "For every gain, there is a risk; choice involves a testing of will and courage . . . on Darkover any attempt at change of progress carries with it the need for pain-filled choice." Clearly, to survive within such a world Bradley's protagonists—particularly the female characters her readers most closely identify with—must be strong, intelligent, and determined.

Among the most popular Darkover novels are 1965's *Star of Danger*, 1976's *The Shattered Chain*, and *Heirs of Hammerfell*, a more recent work published in 1989. *The Shattered Chain* is agreed upon by most critics as among the best of the series. It is the story of a quest, a traditional story form in which the main character must surmount a series of obstacles on her way to achieving her goals. In Bradley's version, Lady Rohana, a member of the privileged ruling class, attempts to free a friend from a tribe of men who chain women up to demonstrate their power over them. To accomplish her task, Rohana gains the help of the Free Amazons, but only at the cost of reassessing her own life and values.

The Darkover novels occupied much of Bradley's time during the 1960s and 1970s, although she also managed to find the time to publish a collection of short fiction, *The Dark Intruder and Other Stories*, as well as several volumes of literary criticism. Bradley's personal life was undergoing transition during this period as well; she divorced her first husband in 1964, and married for a second time shortly thereafter. She and her second husband, Walter Henry Breen, would raise three children (Bradley's son from her first marriage, plus a son and daughter of their own) before divorcing in 1990. The demands of parenthood on her limited time may have multiplied, but they did little to staunch Bradley's enthusiasm for writing—or her published output. Perhaps these demands are at the root of her efforts to find, through the dilemmas of her fictional female protagonists, that ideal balance between a woman's duty to self and her obligations to others. She published over 30 books between 1965 and 1980, and in 1984 undertook a long-term project: editing a series of short-story collections for New York-based DAW publishers under the *Sword and Sorceress* title.

## A Sci-Fi Writer in King Arthur's Court

Hailed by several critics as Bradley's most notable novel, *The Mists of Avalon* was published in 1983 and remained on the *New York Times* best-seller list for 16 weeks. Taking place in Arthurian Britain, called Britannia, the novel features such well-known female characters as Morgan Le Fay and the Lady of the Lake, given heightened strength of will under Bradley's pen as they perform their parts in the tragic legend of King Arthur. Although published afterward, the novels *The Forest House* and *Lady of Avalon* serve as precursors to *The Mists of Avalon*, detailing the chain of events leading up to the events surrounding Bradley's version of the King Arthur legend. *The Forest House* tells of the relationship between the priestess Eilan and Gaius Marcellius, an officer in the Roman occupation army with whom she conceives a son, Gawan. *Lady of Avalon* finds Britannia now firmly ruled by the Romans, with Christian priests working to gain strides with the population against the ancient Druidic religions. In *The Mists of Avalon*—a lengthy volume of over 850 pages—the Arthurian legends are retold from the perspective of the enchantress Morgaine, a follower of the ways of wicca and a priestess of the ancient Goddess religion. Despite her powers, Morgaine is unable to defend the ancient goddesses against the inexorable crush of Christianity, and her failure embitters her. She must watch as womankind reverts from a respected sex to a berated one, condemned as the source of original sin by the patriarchal Christian teachings.

## Fantasy as a Means to Discover a Different Truth

Women of another quasi-mythic period of history fall under Bradley's scrutiny in *The Firebrand*, which she published in 1987. Taking the written history surrounding the Trojan War as her starting point, Bradley weaves a tale of heroism as Kassandra, daughter of the King of Troy and an Amazon, attempts to save her kingdom from patriarchal Dorian invaders. In this novel, as in much of her work, Bradley constructs an alternative to the male-dominated "reality" passed down through traditional written histories. She admitted in an interview with Lisa See of *Publishers Weekly* that the transition from the bronze to the iron age did indeed cause the destruction of such Cretan cities as Mycenae, the home of the legendary ruler Agamemnon. But Bradley believes that in viewing this period of history objectively—"as though no one had ever written about [it] before"—another history is revealed. "Here were two cultures that should have been ruled by female twins—Helen and Klytemnestra," she stated to See. "And what do you know? When they married Menelaus and Agamemnon, the men took over their cities." This interest in viewing the past through a different perspective—a perspective that might ultimately reveal hidden truths—is at the heart of Bradley's intent as a writer.

In response to her many fans, Bradley began the *Marion Zimmer Bradley's Fantasy Magazine* in 1988. While she has remained active as an editor, working on her magazine as well as editing the annual *Sword and Sorcery* anthology for DAW, her output as a novelist has decreased in recent years due to health issues. Still, imaginative fictions such as 1995's *Ghostlight* and its sequel, *Witchlight*, continue to issue from Bradley's pen on occasion, to the pleasure of her many fans. Interestingly, from her home in Berkeley, California, Bradley has also managed to extend the Darkover saga beyond her own novels by inviting others to create their own vision of her mythic world. Under her editorship, anthologies such as *Domains of Darkover* and *Towers of Darkover* allow other writers to navigate Bradley's fantastic worlds, taking new paths, creating characters with fresh viewpoints, and entertaining readers with alternative renditions of Bradley's sci-fi saga.

## Further Reading

Arbur, Rosemarie, *Leigh Brackett, Marion Zimmer Bradley, Anne McCaffrey: A Primary and Secondary Bibliography*, Hall, 1982.

*Feminist Writers*, St. James Press, 1996, pp. 60-63.

Spivak, Charlotte, *Merlin's Daughters: Contemporary Women Writers of Fantasy*, Greenwood Press, 1987.

Staicar, Tom, editor, *The Feminine Eye: Science Fiction and the Women Who Write It*, F. Ungar, 1982.

Wise, S., *The Darkover Dilemma: Problems of the Darkover Series*, T-K Graphics, 1976.
*Extrapolation*, summer 1993.
*Journal of Popular Culture*, summer 1993, pp. 67- 80.
*Los Angeles Times Book Review*, February 3, 1983.
*Publishers Weekly*, October 30, 1987.
*Science Fiction Review*, summer, 1983.
*New York Times Book Review*, January 30, 1983.
*West Coast Review of Books*, number 5, 1986.
Marion Zimmer Bradley Homepage, http://www.mzb.fm.com (March 15, 1998). □

# Anne Dudley Bradstreet

**Anne Dudley Bradstreet (ca. 1612-1672) was a Puritan poet whose work portrays a deeply felt experience of American colonial life. She was the daughter and wife of Massachusetts governors.**

Anne Dudley, born about 1612 probably in Northampton, England, grew up in the cultivated household of the Earl of Lincoln, where her father, Thomas Dudley, was steward. Tutored by her father and availing herself of the extensive library, she was highly educated. Her later work reveals familiarity with Plutarch, Du Bartas, Sir Walter Raleigh, Quarles, Sidney, Spenser, perhaps Shakespeare, and, of course, the Bible. At 16, she writes, she experienced conversion.

Shortly thereafter she married Simon Bradstreet, then 20 years old; orphaned at 14, he had been her father's protégé. He graduated from Emmanuel College and, like the Dudleys, had strong Nonconformist convictions. In 1630 the Bradstreets sailed to America aboard the *Arbella* with Dudley and the Winthrop company. The Bradstreets lived in Salem, Boston, Cambridge, and Ipswich, and settled finally on a farm in North Andover, Mass.

Bradstreet was a devoted wife and the mother of eight children. Her husband became a judge and legislator, later royal councilor and governor. His duties required that he be away from home frequently. Their wilderness life was hard; Indian attack was a constant threat, and Bradstreet suffered poor health. Yet, she managed to use her experience and religious belief in creating a small but distinguished body of poetry.

In 1647 Bradstreet's brother-in-law, the Reverend John Woodbridge, took some of her poetry to England, where, without her knowledge, he had it published in 1650 under the title *The Tenth Muse Lately Sprung Up in America. . . .* For the most part the book consists of four long poems, which may actually be considered one long poem, traditional in subject matter and set, rather mechanically, in heroic couplets. "The Four Elements," "The Four Humours in Man's Constitution," "The Four Ages of Man," and "The Four Seasons of the Year" are allegorical pieces, heavily influenced by Joshua Sylvester's translation of Du Bartas's *Divine Weeks and Works.*

Bradstreet herself added to and corrected her next volume, *Several Poems . . . ,* published posthumously in Boston in 1678. In this volume she deals more with her New England life, her family and natural surroundings. It includes "Contemplations," the fine, long reflective poem on death and resurrection in nature, as well as the dramatic poem "The Flesh and the Spirit," the lively words of "The Author to Her Book," and moving verses addressed to her husband and children. Her prose "Meditations" and some of her more confessional pieces remained in manuscript until 1867, when John H. Ellis published her complete works.

Most critics consider Bradstreet America's first authentic poet, especially strong in her later work. In her own day she was praised by Cotton Mather in his *Magnalia,* by Nathaniel Ward, and others.

## Further Reading

*The Works of Anne Bradstreet* was edited by Jeannine Hensley, with an interesting foreword by poet Adrienne Rich (1967). John Berryman, *Homage to Mistress Bradstreet* (1956), is a moving biographical tribute. Samuel Eliot Morison's chapter on Anne Bradstreet in *Builders of the Bay Colony* (1930; rev. ed. 1958) is a colorful introduction to her life and work. A readable study of Mrs. Bradstreet's writings is Josephine K. Piercy, *Anne Bradstreet* (1965). □

# Fanny Brice

**Fanny Brice (1891-1951) was a vaudeville, Broadway, film, and radio singer and comedienne.**

Fanny Brice was born on October 29, 1891, on New York's Lower East Side. She was the daughter of Charles Borach, a saloonkeeper, and Rose Stern, a real estate agent. As a child she sang and danced in her father's saloon, and at the age of 13, after winning an amateur contest, she sang and played piano in a movie theater. Brice's acute sense of humor made its way into her act early on. She began to work parody into her songs and toured in burlesque. In 1910 she was asked by Max Spiegel to be in *The College Girls* at a major New York theater and also to do a benefit he was producing. Since this was an important job for her she asked Irving Berlin to write her some songs, one of which—"Sadie Salome, Go Home"—became a Brice trademark. The song told the story of a Jewish dancer who shocked her family by going on the stage. It required a Jewish accent for its comic effect. The audiences loved this character, and from then on Brice's most successful characters would be drawn from her own Jewish background.

Aside from discovering her forte, Brice was rewarded for this performance with a job on Broadway in Florenz Ziegfeld's *Follies* of 1910. This was the beginning of an association between the famous impresario and the talented comedienne that would last for 14 years. In 1911 she left New York and toured the vaudeville circuit, during which

time she created two more characters which became her hallmarks: the "vamp" and the pretentious "dancer."

Following the tour she appeared as the major attraction at two important theaters: the Victoria in Times Square and the Victoria Palace in London. She also played a Yiddish soubrette, a part specifically written for her, in Shubert's *The Whirl of Society*, which also starred Al Jolson. She played the same part in another Shubert hit, *Honeymoon Express*, and she played the female lead in Jerome Kern's *Nobody Home*.

In 1916 Brice returned to the *Ziegfeld Follies* with her popular skit "The Blushing Bride." She remained with Ziegfeld until 1924, in all appearing in seven editions of the *Follies* and four revues.

Brice was considered to be one of the greatest comediennes on Broadway. Although she was an attractive, graceful woman offstage, she elicited the audience's sympathy and laughter by bringing out the imperfections of her characters. She could be ugly, lack grace, and be mischievous—all for a laugh. She could bring out pathos and at the same time mock sentimentality. In her vaudeville number "You Made Me Love You" the first half was a heart rending song, followed by Brice laughing at her own sentiment by kicking her heels, winking her eyes, swinging on the curtain, and then lifting her skirt to show off her knock knees Not only did she make fun of herself but she parodied standard theatrical styles and actors of the period, such as the Barrymores. Brice also appeared several times with W. C. Fields in a popular family sketch.

In 1921 Brice introduced "My Man" to American audiences. She stood on an empty stage against a lamppost and sang the painful song about a woman whose total devotion to her "man" had brought nothing but unhappiness. Perhaps the pathos she brought to that character was from her personal experience—her husband, Nickie Arnstein, had just been jailed for embezzlement and she had to stand by him. This was one of her few totally straight performances, and it is one for which she will be remembered.

In 1924 Brice, displeased with the material Ziegfeld was giving her, returned to vaudeville for a time. She played the lead role in the film "My Man" and then appeared in Billy Rose's (her third husband) *Sweet and Low* (1930) in which she introduced "Babykins," a three year old in a high chair. This character was the starting point for another Brice trademark, "Baby Snooks."

In the Shubert's 1936 *Follies* she did a spoof of "My Man" in which she said that she had been singing about "that bum" for more than 15 years. This satire on the sentiment in the song was much more her style than the straight emotionality of the earlier delivery. In the same show she did a parody of Shirley Temple in an act with Bob Hope in which she played a child star who couldn't remember her lines.

Due to ill health Brice left Broadway for Los Angeles, where she made a few film appearance, including MGM's *Ziegfeld Follies* (1946) (she was the only Ziegfeld star who appeared in this film). She also immortalized "Baby Snooks" during her ten year radio series.

Despite her work in film Brice was a daughter of the stage. She knew exactly how to reach an audience and she gave her whole self with no reserves. During each performance she would get bigger and bigger until she seemed to envelop the audience with her whole being.

In 1938 *Rose of Washington Square,* a film suggesting the life of Brice, was made and Brice sued the producer. Yet it was through another film and Broadway show, *Funny Girl,* in which Brice was played by Barbra Streisand, that Brice's unique contributions to the theater became known to later generations. A fantasized version of her life focussing on her Ziegfeld days and her marriage to Nickie Arnstein, the play brings back to life her favorite characters and songs. Through this play her life has become inextricably linked with that of her characters, Sadie and "Second Hand Rose"—the poor but spunky Jewish city girls.

Aside from her theater career, Brice was a dress designer, painter, and interior decorator. She had two children, William and Frances. She died May 19, 1951, of cerebral hemorrhage, at the age of 59.

## Further Reading

A concise biography and analysis of Fanny Brice's work is included in *The Great Clowns of Broadway* (1984) by Stanley Green. Reviews, an interview, and a short biography can be found in *Famous Actors and Actresses on the American Stage,* Vol. 1 (1975) by William C. Young. Daniel Blum's *Great Stars of the American Stage* (1952) includes a short biography and photographs. For background information on the *Ziegfeld*

*Follies* and Brice's role in their creation, see Randolph Carter's *The World of Flo Ziegfeld* (1974).

### Additional Sources

Goldman, Herbert G., *Fanny Brice: the original funny girl,* New York: Oxford University Press, 1992.
Grossman, Barbara Wallace, *Funny woman: the life and times of Fanny Brice,* Bloomington: Indiana University Press, 1991. □

# Gwendolyn Brooks

**Gwendolyn Brooks (born 1917) was the first African American to receive a Pulitzer Prize for Poetry and is best known for her intense poetic portraits of urban African Americans.**

Gwendolyn Brooks was born on June 7, 1917, in Topeka, Kansas. The eldest child of Keziah (Wims) Brooks, a schoolteacher, and David Anderson Brooks, a janitor who, because he lacked the funds to finish school, did not achieve his dream of becoming a doctor. Brooks grew up in Chicago and, according to George Kent, was "spurned by members of her own race because she lacked social or athletic abilities, a light skin, and good grade hair." She was deeply hurt by this rejection and took solace in her writing. She became known to her family and friends as "the female Paul Lawrence Dunbar" and received compliments on her poems and encouragement from James Weldon Johnson and Langston Hughes, prominent writers with whom she initiated correspondence and whose readings she attended in Chicago. By the age of sixteen, she had compiled a substantial portfolio, consisting of over 75 poems.

### Early Career

After graduating from Wilson Junior College in 1936, she worked briefly at "The Mecca," a Chicago tenement building. She participated in poetry readings and workshops at Chicago's South Side Community Art Center, producing verse that would appear in her first published volume, *A Street in Bronzeville* in 1945.

In 1939 she married Henry L. Blakeley, and together they would raise two children: Henry, Jr., and Nora. When she married she became a housewife and mother. But instead of directing her creative energy entirely to domestic chores, Brooks wrote poetry when the children were asleep or later while they were in school. In this way she wrote several collections of poetry, which constitutes her early work: *A Street in Bronzeville, Annie Allen* (1949), *The Bean Eaters* (1960), and *Selected Poems* (1962). During this time she also wrote a novel, *Maud Martha* (1953).

The work of this period is characterized by her portraits of urban African American people involved in their day-to-day activities and by her technical form, lofty diction, and intricate word play. Critics have frequently labeled her early work as intellectual, sophisticated, and academic. Although

these poems sing out against social and sexual oppression, they are frequently complex and, therefore, in need of close textual reading to uncover their protest and Brooks' own social commentary. In many of these works she criticized the color prejudice which African American people inflict on one another by calling attention to their tendency to prefer light-skinned African American people. In *Annie Allen* and *Maud Martha* she examined the conventional gender roles of mother and father, husband and wife, and found that they frequently stifle creativity out of those who try to live up to artificial ideals. But this social criticism tends to be pushed back into the complicated language.

In recognition of these works, in 1950, Brooks was awarded a Pulitzer Prize for Poetry, and became the first African American to be granted this honor.

### New Tone

In 1967, Brooks' work achieved a new tone and vision. She simplified her technique so that her themes, rather than her techniques, stood in the forefront. This change can be traced to her growing political conscienceness, previously hinted at in *Selected Poems,* after witnessing the combative spirit of several young African American authors at the Second Black Writers' Conference held at Fisk University that year. These works include: *In the Mecca* (1968), *Riot* (1969), *Aloneness* (1971), *Family Pictures* (1971), the autobiographical *Report from Part One* (1972), *The Tiger Who Wore White Gloves: Or, What You Are You Are* (1974), *Beckonings* (1975), and *Primer for Blacks* (1980). These works are much more direct, and they are designed to sting the mind into a higher level of racial awareness. Foregoing the traditional poetic forms, she favored free verse and increased the use of her vernacular to make her works more accessible to African Americans and not just academic audiences and poetry magazines.

During the 1970s, Brooks taught poetry at numerous institutions for higher learning, including Northeastern Illinois State College (now Northeastern Illinois University), University of Wisconsin at Madison, and the City College of the City University of New York. She continued to write, and while her concern for the African American nationalist movement and racial solidarity continued to dominate her verse in the early-1970s, the energy and optimism of *Riot* and *Family Pictures* were replaced in the late-1970s with an impression of disenchantment resulting from the divisiveness of the civil rights and "Black Power" movements. This mood was reflected in *Beckonings* (1975) and *To Disembark* (1980), where she urged African Americans to break free from the repression of white American society and advocated violence and anarchy as acceptable means.

Later, Brooks spent her time encouraging others to write by sponsoring writers' workshops in Chicago and poetry contests at correctional facilities. In 1985, she was named as the consultant in poetry for the Library of Congress. In short, she has taken poetry to her people, continuing to test its relevance by reading her poetry and lecturing in taverns, barrooms, lounges, and other public places as well as in academic circles.

In later years Brooks continued to write, with *Children Coming Home* (1992) and *Blacks* (1992). In 1990 Brooks' works were ensured a home when Chicago State University established the Gwendolyn Brooks Center on its campus. She continued to inspire others to write, focusing on young children by speaking and giving poetry readings at schools around the country.

In 1997, on the occasion of her 80th birthday, she was honored with tributes from Chicago to Washington D.C. Although she was honored by many, perhaps the best description of Brooks' life and career came from her publisher, Haki Madhubuti, when he said, "She is undoubtedly one of the top 100 writers in the world. She has been a chronicler of black life, specifically black life on the South Side of Chicago. She has become almost a legend in her own time."

## Honors

In addition to her Pulitzer Prize, Brooks has been awarded an American Academy of Arts and Letters Award (1946), a Guggenheim Fellowship (1946 and 1947), a *Poetry* magazine award (1949), a Friend of Literature Award (1963), a Black Academy of Arts and Letters Award (1971), a Shelley Memorial Award (1976), an *Essence* Award (1988), a Frost Medal from the Poetry Society of America (1989), a Lifetime Achievement Award from the National Endowment for the Arts (1989), a Jefferson Award from the National Endowment for the Humanities (1994), as well as some 49 honorary degrees from universities and colleges, including Columbia College in 1964, Lake Forest College in 1965, and Brown University in 1974. Moreover, she was named poet laureate of Illinois in 1969 and was inducted into the National Women's Hall of Fame in 1988. In 1985 she reached the pinnacle of her career when she became the poetry consultant at the Library of Congress, the second African American and the first African American woman to hold that position.

## Further Reading

The best source of biographical information is Brooks' own autobiography, *Report from Part One* (1972). Critical information on Brooks includes Don L. Lee "The Achievement of Gwendolyn Brooks," in *Black Scholar* (Summer, 1972); Gloria T. Hill "A Note on the Poetic Technique of Gwendolyn Brooks," in *College Languages Association Journal* (December, 1975); Suzanne Juhasz "A Sweet Inspiration . . . of My People: The Poetry of Gwendolyn Brooks and Nikki Giovanni," in *Naked and Fiery Forms* (1976); Hortense J. Spillers "Gwendolyn the Terrible: Propositions on Eleven Poems," in *Shakespeare's Sisters* (1979); George E. Kent "Aesthetic Values in the Poetry of Gwendolyn Brooks," in *Black American Literature and Humanism,* edited by R. Baxter Miller (1981); Mari Evans "Gwendolyn Brooks," in *Black Women Writers, 1950-1980* (1983); and Claudia Tate "Gwendolyn Brooks," in *Black Women Writers at Work* (1983).

Further biographical information on Brooks can found in Shirley Henderson "Our Miss Brooks on Eve of Her 80th Birthday, Poet Offers Some Answers," in the June 6, 1997 issue of the *Chicago Tribune* and in Heather Lalley "Paying Tribute to Illinois' Poet Laureate as Brooks Turns 80, City Finds Words to Describe Her Power to Inspire," in the June 5, 1997 issue of the *Chicago Tribune.* Her life and works are also the subject of George E. Kent *A Life of Gwendolyn Brooks* (1990). □

# Joyce Brothers

**The psychologist Joyce Brothers (born 1927) pioneered the trend to phone-in questions for professional psychological advice. Her rise to prominence in "pop-psych" in electronic media followed her unusual success on a television quiz show in the mid-1950s.**

Joyce Brothers, popular psychologist of a radio, television, and reading audience since 1958, was born about 1927, one of two daughters to Morris K. and Estelle (Rapoport) Bauer. Both her lawyer parents taught their children the importance of academic excellence and the work ethic.

As a bright child, Brothers displayed many of the qualities that would help establish her professional career. She was an honors student in high school, received a B.S. degree with honors in psychology from Cornell University (1947), and obtained her M.A. degree from Columbia University in 1949. She then married a medical student, Milton Brothers, and continued her research and teaching. In 1953 she earned her Ph.D. from Columbia, having completed her dissertation on the topic of anxiety avoidance and escape behavior.

After their daughter was born, Brothers gave up her teaching posts at Columbia and Hunter College (New York City) because she believed it vital in the early development of children to have one parent at home. (In 1974 she said that a father could be that parent, but generally the mother got that responsibility.)

Without her teaching salary the family was soon in financial straits because her husband's resident's income was minimal. To supplement their funds Joyce determined to try for an appearance on the television quiz show *The $64,000 Question* (1955). By laboriously memorizing 20 volumes of a boxing encyclopedia, Joyce Brothers became the only woman and the second person ever to win the top prize. She later remarked that she had good motivation "because we were hungry."

When the *$64,000 CHALLENGE,* which pitted experts in certain fields with the contestant, replaced *The $64,000 Question,* Brothers' boxing knowledge dismayed the seven ex-boxer experts. She answered each question correctly and brought her total earnings to $134,000, making her one of the biggest winners in the history of television quiz shows.

In spite of accusations of quiz show corruption and subsequent investigations which exposed the fact that some contestants were given answers prior to the shows, Brothers emerged unscathed in the quiz-fix scandal. She later revealed that the producers had planned to "knock me out" with impossible questions, but she had memorized her subject so thoroughly that she could provide all the right answers.

Her fame in the quiz shows led to her public psychologist career. In 1956 Brothers cohosted *Sports Showcase,* in which she interviewed prominent sports figures and discussed sports events. Her charm, dignity, and intelligence led to several appearances on television "talk shows."

By 1958 NBC offered her a trial on local afternoon programs in which she advised on the topics of love, marriage, sex, and child-rearing. When she proved an instant success, the same format was telecast nationally. Soon Brothers had several late-night shows (under various titles and formats) which included topics which had been tabooed earlier, such as menopause, frigidity, impotence, and sexual satisfaction. Much of her success was attributed to her sympathetic manner and her ability to discuss issues in laymen's terms rather than professional jargon. Brothers also gave personal advice on a number of phone-in radio programs. Some were taped, while others were "live," which sometimes provided on-the-air drama.

To her colleagues who criticized her for giving advice without knowing her callers well enough, Brothers responded that she did not attempt to treat mental illness, nor did she practice therapy on the air, and that when needed she advised callers to seek professional help. Her supporters also suggested that her public performance approximated group therapy with its many advantages.

Brothers also wrote a syndicated newspaper column for 350 daily newspapers, authored magazine articles, and advised several manufacturers on women's needs. She authored several books, including *Ten Days To A Successful Memory* (1964), *How To Get Whatever You Want Out of Life, What Every Woman Should Know About Men,* and *What Every Woman Ought to Know About Love and Marriage* (1985).

In the 1970s Brothers spoke against sexist bias, citing the need to change textbooks because children quickly pick up sexist attitudes from them. She noted that non-sexist cultures tend to be less war-like because the man does not have to prove that he is big and strong and needs to protect the weaker woman. She called for children to learn that it is fine to be either male or female, thereby developing more positive attitudes about themselves.

Without tremendous organizational ability, Brothers could scarcely have managed her many and varied professional activities. Without her keen interest in learning new things (she taught herself plumbing in college and could do her own electrical wiring), her multi-faceted life would have been less stimulating and her impact on American society less significant. Since she pioneered the psychological phone-in show in the 1960s, the idea proliferated to the extent that by 1985 there was an Association of Media Psychologists to monitor for abuses.

In the 1990s Brothers authored several books, including *Positive Plus: The Practical Plan for Liking Yourself Better* (1995), and *Widowed* (1992). She wrote the latter after losing her husband in 1990, and it is a guide to dealing with grief for women who have lost their spouses. The movie rights to the story were optioned by ABC -TV, and a television movie is scheduled. Brothers also appeared in Garry Marshall's 1996 film, *Dear God.*

Brothers' books have been translated into 26 different languages, and she was a regular columnist for *Good Housekeeping* magazine. In her columns, she addressed family-oriented topics such time together and the secret to a successful marriage. In her June 1994 *Good Housekeeping* article she said, "We are beginning to realize that real solutions to many of the nation's difficult problems may in fact be found in the home." Brothers also regularly wrote on other topical issues such as obsession and the elements of a healthy patient-doctor relationship. Throughout her career, Brothers guest-lectured at colleges and universities.

## Further Reading

Biographical information on Joyce Brothers is limited primarily to interviews given in periodicals, her comments in electronic media, and newspaper accounts of her press conferences. A brief section entitled "The Joyce Brothers Story" in her book *Ten Days To A Successful Memory* (1964) gives insights into that period of her life when she became a successful quiz-show contestant. Additional materials may be gleaned from *Authors In The News*, Vol. 1 (1976); *Coronet* (November 1968), *New York Times* (January 5, 1971), *Newsday* (June 22, 1970), and *Good Housekeeping* (December 1980). A Web site with biographical information can be accessed at www.clark.net/pub/speakers/on-line/spkr1069.html. □

# Charlotte Eugenia Hawkins Brown

**The African American educator and humanitarian Charlotte Eugenia Hawkins Brown (born Lottie Hawkins; 1882-1961) founded the Palmer Memorial Institute in North Carolina as a preparatory school for African Americans in the early 1900s and served as its president for over half a century.**

The rural community of Sedalia, North Carolina, is the site of a memorial to Dr. Charlotte Hawkins Brown, African American educator-humanitarian. Sedalia is 90 miles from Henderson, where Brown was born in 1882. The granddaughter of slaves, Lottie moved to Cambridge, Massachusetts, during her childhood. There she attended the Alston Grammar School, Cambridge English High School, and Salem State Normal School. She changed her name to Charlotte Eugenia in 1900 and acquired the name Brown through her brief marriage to Edward S. Brown whom she met at Cambridge.

Also in 1900, Brown met Alice Freeman Palmer, then president of Wellesley College, who became her friend and mentor. Toward the end of her first year at Salem, in 1901, Brown was introduced to a representative of the American Missionary Association, a philanthropic organization which operated schools for African Americans in the South. The AMA representative offered her a job as teacher of its school in Sedalia, Guilford County, North Carolina. Even as a teenager, Brown was a visionary. Troubled by the lack of educa-

tional opportunities for Blacks in the southern region, she accepted the AMA's offer and returned to her native state in 1901 to teach African American children.

The school was housed in Bethany Congregational Church, but closed only one term after Brown's arrival. Many Sedalia residents wanted the school to continue and appealed to Brown to stay as its principal. She accepted their offer and vowed to justify their faith in her capability. To maintain Palmer's growth and contribute to its further development, Brown continually engaged in fund-raising efforts which were directed primarily toward northern supporters. Her appeals were undergirded with singing and persuasive speeches, and she touched the hearts of people who were responsive to an opportunity to provide an educational facility for southern African Americans.

The renamed Palmer Memorial Institute gained national recognition as a preparatory school for African Americans. In the beginning the school's curriculum emphasized manual training and industrial education for rural living. Later the curriculum was changed to emphasize cultural education. As Palmer and its dynamic founder-president became nationally known, Brown's circle of associates expanded to include Mary McLeod Bethune, Nannie Burroughs, Eleanor Roosevelt, W.E.B. DuBois, and Booker T. Washington.

In 1911 Palmer Memorial Institute was fully accepted by the Southern Association of Colleges and Secondary Schools at a time when few schools for southern African Americans had achieved such recognition. Over one thousand students graduated from Palmer during the presidency of Brown. Each student had been the beneficiary of counsel by a proud and able educator-humanitarian whose career was characterized by a determination to make them "educationally efficient, religiously sincere and culturally secure." After more than half a century as the school's director, she resigned in 1952.

A recipient of honorary doctorates from several colleges, including Wilberforce, Howard, and Lincoln, Brown became the first African American woman to be elected (1928) to the 20th Century Club of Boston, organized to honor leaders in education, art, science, and religion. Brown died in 1961. Palmer Memorial Institute was closed ten years later.

## Further Reading

Published biographical information on Charlotte Hawkins Brown is sketchy and extremely limited in number. Alva Stewart's article on "The Charlotte Hawkins Brown Memorial Historic Site—Remembering the History of Black Education," *Wilson Library Bulletin* (October 1989); Constance Marteena's *The Lengthening Shadow of a Woman* (1977); *The Negro Almanac—A Reference on the African American*, Fifth Edition (1989); and the *Encyclopedia of Black America* (1981) are the best sources available at this time. Additional unpublished information is available through the Department of Cultural Resources, Historic Sites Section, Raleigh, North Carolina. □

# Helen Gurley Brown

**American author and editor Helen Gurley Brown (born 1922) first achieved fame for her book *Sex and the Single Girl*, an immediate best-seller. After Gurley Brown became editor of the faltering *Cosmopolitan*, she transformed it into a sexy, upbeat top-selling magazine for young women in over 27 different countries.**

Helen Gurley Brown was born in Green Forest, Arkansas, on February 18, 1922, and lived in Little Rock, Arkansas until her father, Ira M. Gurley, a schoolteacher, was killed in an elevator accident. Gurley Brown's mother, Cleo (nee Sisco), was left to raise their two daughters. (Helen's sister was partially paralyzed from polio.) "I never liked the looks of the life that was programmed for me—ordinary, hillbilly, and poor," Gurley Brown wrote later, "and I repudiated it from the time I was seven years old." She attended Texas State College for Women (1939-1941), Woodbury College (1942) and received her LL.D from Woodbury University in 1987.

Gurley Brown's first job was with radio station KHJ where she answered fan mail for six dollars per week. From 1942-1945 she worked as an executive secretary at Music Corp. of America, a Beverly Hills talent agency. Once, while reminiscing about her early career days, Gurley Brown recalled how secretaries were required to use the back stairs because the ornate lobby staircase was only for clients and/or male executives.

A major career move for Gurley Brown occurred in 1948 when she became the first woman to hold a copywriter position at Foote, Cone & Belding, a Los Angeles advertising agency. Her ability to produce bright, arresting prose won her two Francis Holmes Advertising Copywriters awards during her tenure at the firm (1948-1958).

She worked for Kenyon & Eckhardt, a Hollywood advertising agency as an account executive and copywriter from 1958-1962.

In 1959, at the age of 37, Helen Gurley married David Brown, then vice president for production at 20th Century Fox. (In later years Brown co-produced *Jaws, Cocoon,* and *The Sting.*) The couple had no children. Gurley Brown once remarked that one secret of their marital success was that her husband never interrupted her on Saturdays and Sundays when she was working upstairs in her office.

Gurley Brown's first book, *Sex and the Single Girl* (1962) revolutionized single women's attitudes towards their own lifestyle. The book became a national best-seller. At a time when *Reader's Digest* and *The Ladies Home Journal* still insisted that a "nice" girl had only two choices, "she can marry him or she can say no," Gurley Brown openly proclaimed that sex was an important part of a single woman's lifestyle. According to Gurley Brown, "The single girl is the new glamour girl." For emphasis, Gurley Brown recounted her own story, the saga of a self-proclaimed "mouseburger," who through persistence, patience, and planning, advanced in her chosen field and then married the man of her dreams.

In 1965, Gurley Brown was hired as editor-in-chief of Hearst Corp.'s faltering general interest magazine *Cosmopolitan*. She revised the magazine's cover image, creating a devil-may-care, sexy *Cosmo* girl. "A million times a year I defend my covers," Gurley Brown admitted. "I like skin, I like pretty. I don't want to photograph the girl next door." The new *Cosmopolitan* often provoked controversy, especially when it published a nude male centerfold of actor Burt Reynolds in 1972.

Relentlessly upbeat, the magazine, like its editor, was filled with advice on how to move ahead in a career, meet men, lose weight, and be an imaginative sexual partner. There was no time for the negative. "I wasn't allowed to write critical reviews," movie critic Liz Smith confessed.

By 1990, *Cosmopolitan* had grown from a circulation of 800,000 in the United States to over 2.5 million. Hearst Corp. claimed that with its 27 international editions *Cosmopolitan* was now one of the most widely read women's magazines in the world and had become the sixth best-selling newsstand magazine in any category.

In the 20 years between publication of *Sex and the Single Girl* and *Having It All* (1982), Gurley Brown's advice changed little. She still refused to print four letter words but graphically described techniques for oral stimulation. "I am still preoccupied with sex," she confessed. "If you want to enchant a man and eventually marry him, you are good to him, easy with him, adorable to be around."

During a *Fortune* magazine interview in Oct. of 1996, Gurley Brown shared several of her rules for being a good executive. "These are my rules, written with some incredulity about being one [an executive] and with probably not enough modesty," she stated. Her guidelines included saying something complimentary before criticizing, saying "no" to time wasters, doing what you dread first, and working harder than anybody else.

In addition to her Francis Holmes Achievement awards (1956-59), Gurley Brown received several awards for journalism, including a Distinguished Achievement Award from the University of Southern California in 1971, an award for editorial leadership from the American Newspaper Woman's Club of Washington, D.C., in 1972, and the Distinguished Achievement Award in Journalism from Stanford University in 1977. In 1985 she received the New York Women in Communications matrix award. She has been dedicated as a "living landmark" by the New York Landmarks Conservancy and the Helen Gurley Brown Research professorship was established in her name at Northwestern University's Medill School of Journalism in 1986. She was inducted into the Publisher's Hall of Fame in 1988.

In January, 1996, Bonnie Fuller, founding editor of Hearst Corp.'s magazine *Marie Claire*, was named Gurley Brown's successor and new editor-in-chief of *Cosmopolitan*. "She [Fuller] thoroughly understands the *Cosmo* girl, and her success . . . certainly prepared her to succeed to the editorship of *Cosmopolitan*," said Gurley Brown. Fuller served an eighteen-month internship under Gurley Brown while Gurley Brown continued as editor-in-chief of *Cosmopolitan's* international publishing program.

## Further Reading

The best glimpse of Helen Gurley Brown is provided through her own books. In addition to *Sex and the Single Girl* (1962), Gurley Brown authored *Sex and the Office* (1965), *Outrageous Opinions* (1967), *Helen Gurley Brown's Single Girl's Cookbook* (1969), *Sex and the New Single Girl* (1970), *Cosmopolitan's Love Book, A Guide to Ecstasy in Bed* (1978), and *Having It All* (1982). See also "What the Women's Movement Means to Me" in *Ms.* (July 1985). ☐

# Rachel Fuller Brown

**With Elizabeth Lee Hazen, Brown (1898-1980) developed the first effective antibiotic against fungal disease in humans—the most important biomedical breakthrough since the discovery of penicillin two decades earlier.**

Rachel Fuller Brown, with her associate Elizabeth Hazen, developed the first effective antibiotic against fungal disease in humans—the most important biomedical breakthrough since the discovery of penicillin two decades earlier. The antibiotic, called nystatin, has cured sufferers of life-threatening fungal infections, vaginal yeast infections, and athlete's foot. Nystatin earned more than $13 million in royalties during Brown's lifetime, which she and Hazen dedicated to scientific research.

Brown was born in Springfield, Massachusetts, on November 23, 1898, to Annie Fuller and George Hamilton Brown. Her father, a real estate and insurance agent, moved the family to Webster Groves, Missouri, where she attended grammar school. In 1912, her father left the family. Brown and her younger brother returned to Springfield with their mother, who worked to support them. When Brown graduated from high school, a wealthy friend of the family financed her attendance at Mount Holyoke College in Massachusetts.

At Mount Holyoke, Brown was initially a history major, but she discovered chemistry when fulfilling a science requirement. She decided to double-major in history and chemistry, earning her A.B. degree in 1920. She subsequently went to the University of Chicago to complete her M.A. in organic chemistry. For three years, she taught chemistry and physics at the Francis Shimer School near Chicago. With her savings, she returned to the University to complete her Ph.D. in organic chemistry, with a minor in bacteriology. She submitted her thesis in 1926, but there was a delay in arranging her oral examinations. As her funds ran low, Brown took a job as an assistant chemist at the Division of Laboratories and Research of the New York State Department of Health in Albany, New York. Seven years later, when she returned to Chicago for a scientific meeting,

Brown arranged to take her oral examinations and was awarded her Ph.D.

Brown's early work at the Department of Health focused on identifying the types of bacteria that caused pneumonia, and in this capacity she helped to develop a pneumonia vaccine still in use today. In 1948, she embarked on the project with Hazen, a leading authority on fungus, that would bring them their greatest acclaim: the discovery of an antibiotic to fight fungal infections. Penicillin had been discovered in 1928, and in the ensuing years antibiotics were increasingly used to fight bacterial illnesses. One side effect, however, was the rapid growth of fungus that could lead to sore mouths or upset stomachs. Other fungal diseases without cures included infections attacking the central nervous system, athlete's foot, and ringworm. Microorganisms called actinomycetes that lived in soil were known to produce antibiotics. Although some killed fungus, they also proved fatal to test mice. Hazen ultimately narrowed the search down to a microorganism taken from soil near a barn on a friend's dairy farm in Virginia, later named streptomyces norsei. Brown's chemical analyses revealed that the microorganism produced two antifungal substances, one of which proved too toxic with test animals to pursue for human medical use. The other, however, seemed to have promise; it wasn't toxic to test animals and attacked both a fungus that invaded the lungs and central nervous system and candidiasis, an infection of the mouth, lungs, and vagina.

Brown purified this second antibiotic into small white crystals, and in 1950 Brown and Hazen announced at a meeting of the National Academy of Sciences that they had found a new antifungal agent. They patented it through the nonprofit Research Corporation, naming it "nystatin" in honor of the New York State Division of Laboratories and Research. The license for the patent was issued to E. R. Squibb and Sons, which developed a safe and effective method of mass production. The product—called Mycostatin—became available in tablet form in 1954 to patients suffering from candidiasis. Nystatin has also proved valuable in agricultural and livestock applications, and has even been used to restore valuable works of art.

In 1951, the Department of Health laboratories promoted Brown to associate biochemist. Brown and Hazen, in continuing their research, discovered two additional antibiotics, phalamycin and capacidin. Brown and Hazen were awarded the 1955 Squibb Award in Chemotherapy. Brown won the Distinguished Service Award of the New York State Department of Health when she retired in 1968, and the Rhoda Benham Award of the Medical Mycological Society of the Americas in 1972. In 1975, Brown and Hazen became the first women to receive the Chemical Pioneer Award from the American Institute of Chemists. In a statement publised in the *Chemist* the month of her death, Brown hoped for a future of "equal opportunities and accomplishments for all scientists regardless of sex."

On retirement, Brown maintained an active community life, and became the first female vestry member of her Episcopalian church. By her death on January 14, 1980, she had paid back the wealthy woman who had made it possible for her to attend college. Using the royalties from nystatin, more importantly, she helped designate new funds for scientific research and scholarships.

### Further Reading

Baldwin, Richard S., *The Fungus Fighters: Two Women Scientists and Their Discovery,* Cornell University Press, 1981.
Vare, Ethlie Ann and Greg Ptacek, *Mothers of Invention,* Morrow, 1988, pp. 124–126.
Yost, Edna, *Women of Modern Science,* Greenwood, 1959, pp. 64–79.
*New York Times,* June 29, 1957, p. 22–26; January 16, 1980, p. D19. □

# Tina Brown

**Jumping onto journalism's fast track in 1974, British-born Tina Brown (Christina Hambly Brown, born 1953) transformed the English magazine *Tatler,* then the U.S. magazines *Vanity Fair* and the *New Yorker,* using controversial topics and challenging images. Her editorial rabbit punches knocked all three magazines into top-seller realm by boosting circulation, ad revenues, and reader interest.**

Assuming the post of editor-in-chief of *Vanity Fair* magazine in 1984, Tina Brown, formerly with Britain's *Tatler,* delighted both skeptics and devotees. *Vanity Fair,* an art and literary magazine popular before World War II, had been reintroduced in 1983 by publisher S.I. Newhouse, Jr., but suffered from weak editorial focus and limp enthusiasm among media critics. As editor, Brown employed a saucy cleverness to both tighten that focus and rouse apathetic critics.

Born in Maidenhead, England, on November 21, 1953, Christina Hambly Brown and her brother, Christopher, were raised by George Hambly Brown and Bettina (Kohr) Brown in Little Marlow, Buckinghamshire. Her film-producer father and her mother (once a press agent for Sir Laurence Olivier) gave Tina not only a loving, comfortable, upper-middle-class home, but the inevitable excitement deriving from close association with the film community. Brown later enjoyed the full range of experience provided by a boarding school education. Attractive, articulate, and intelligent, she was also a known cut-up and quite mischievous on occasion.

While yet in college, Brown won the 1973 drama award given by the (London) *Sunday Times* for her play *Under the Bamboo Tree.* In 1974 she graduated from St. Anne's, Oxford, and soon thereafter landed various assignments with the *Times, Punch,* the *Sunday Telegraph,* and the *New Statesman* on numerous topics focusing on the United States. Brown's sharp, witty prose garnered her the Young Journalist of the Year Award given in 1978 by *Punch,* where she was for several years a columnist. In 1978 Brown became the housemate of *Times* editor Harold Evans, whom she subsequently married on August 20, 1981. They had two children, a son born in 1986 and a daughter born in 1990.

In 1979 Brown took the reins of the *Tatler,* a venerable British publication founded in 1709. Her choice as editor was a gamble on the part of Gary Bogard, the moribund magazine's new owner. Interjecting new life into *Tatler* was a challenge to which Brown was more than equal; as she noted at the time, one of her goals was to achieve "irreverence" in treating certain topics, including the British monarchy, formerly sacred among readers. That this was just the approach needed to expand *Tatler's* readership was only a hunch, but one that paid off handsomely.

Brown's adroit blend of elegant sass, tongue-in-cheek primness, and cutting-edge intelligence saw *Tatler* quadruple its circulation in four years. More important, it ensured the magazine's appeal. Millionaire publisher S.I. Newhouse, Jr., decided to buy the wildly successful *Tatler* in 1982. The following year Brown left as editor, but returned to Newhouse several months later as an editorial adviser to the faltering *Vanity Fair* .

Asked to enhance the flavor of a magazine others had failed to make palatable, Brown served forth a publication that not only bespoke good taste, but whetted the reader's appetite for more. As a result, in January 1984 Brown was named *Vanity Fair's* editor-in-chief, replacing Leo Lerman. It took over a year for her influence to take effect, but money eventually poured in from advertisers and subscribers alike.

In 1986 the magazine was cited as "hottest" by the trade journal *Adweek;* in 1988 Brown was named Editor of the Year by *Advertising Age.*

Thanks to Brown, *Vanity Fair* threw off its stodgy image by covering, courting, and occasionally excoriating celebrities, in much the same way that *Tatler* had done earlier. Some decisions, such as the 1991 cover choice of nude and pregnant actress Demi Moore, were predictably controversial. But it was Brown's use of the unexpected and the titillating that boosted *Vanity Fair's* readership to one million, reversed drooping ad sales, and promoted Brown to virtual celebrity stardom.

Precisely because of their profitability, her strategies were destined to leave *Vanity Fair;* another Newhouse publication, *The New Yorker,* was ailing and needed assistance. Despite the editorial expertise of Robert Gottlieb, whom S.I. Newhouse had put in charge in 1987, *The New Yorker* was in trouble. To salvage a $147 million investment, Newhouse switched editors again. In an outrageous gamble, in July 1992 he announced Gottlieb's resignation and named Tina Brown as *The New Yorker* editor. He later shifted Graydon Carter (founder of *Spy,* another Newhouse publication) into place as head of *Vanity Fair.*

These announcements scandalized and angered *The New Yorker* faithful. Although Brown won admiration for reviving flagging sales of once-healthy magazines, few believed she had the skills to succeed as *The New Yorker* editor, and many felt her previous triumphs were due to lack of discrimination among *Tatler* and *Vanity Fair* readers.

The transition from *Vanity Fair* to *The New Yorker* was not an easy one for Brown, which was evident in her emotional good-bye to *Vanity Fair* staff. Also, some said she worried about being unwelcome at *The New Yorker.* Commenting with scrupulous care about editorial changes, Brown used such terms as "irreverent" and "more timely" to signal her intentions. She denied, though, any desire to promulgate a wholesale transformation of what remained (despite the previously unheard-of use of color on editorial pages) America's most exalted, highly respected literary magazine.

*The New Yorker* continues to draw attention, mainly due to Brown's pannache for drawing it. In 1995 Brown shocked the writing world by inviting Roseanne, the controversial television star, to contribute to the issue on American women.

## Further Reading

Various articles and interviews detail Tina Brown's meteoric rise as magazine editor *par excellence.* These articles can be found in *The American Spectator* (December 1992); *Newsweek* (October 26 and July 13, 1992; September 18, 1995); *TIME* (July 13, 1992); *New York* (July 20, 1992); and *Newsweek* (May 1, 1989). □

# Carol M. Browner

**When President Bill Clinton named Carol Browner (born 1955) as his choice to head up the Environmental Protection Agency (EPA), environmentalists were pleased. Members of the business community, on the other hand, were somewhat skeptical because they feared increased regulations.**

It is no secret that the EPA and the business community have been long-standing adversaries. During her confirmation hearings, however, Browner promised the business community that the regulatory climate would not be hostile toward them. Her experience in Florida had proven that the regulatory burdens on business could be eased without compromising the environment. Browner has been credited by both environmentalists as well as the Florida business community for being fair, knowledgeable, intelligent, and balanced in her approach to the environment and economics.

During her tenure as secretary of the Florida Department of Environmental Regulations, Browner drew both criticism and accolades from environmentalists, agriculturalists, and the business community. Browner's role as a strong negotiator and as an environmental visionary won her much respect in two specific cases in which she was involved while she served as Florida's secretary of Environmental Regulations. Browner was the chief negotiator for

the state of Florida in a suit filed by the Federal Government to restore the Everglades by purifying and restoring the natural water flow to Everglades National Park. This was considered the largest ecological restoration effort ever undertaken in the United States and was projected to cost the state of Florida, the federal government, and sugar cane farmers about $1 billion. While the outcome pleased environmentalists, it infuriated the sugar farmers who would bear the burden of much of the cost. Andy Rackley, vice-president and general manager of the Florida Sugar Cane League, said of Browner in a *New York Times* article, "Having been on the opposite side of the table from her on the Everglades issue, I can tell you she is a formidable opponent."

### Disney Does Wetlands

Browner is also credited with negotiating a successful landmark agreement with the Walt Disney Company that allowed them to develop 400 acres of wetlands on their property in Disney World in exchange for their investment of $40 million to purchase and protect more than 8500 acres of wetlands in central Florida. "[Browner] is a tremendous environmental leader," said Todd W. Mansfield, senior vice-president of Walt Disney Development Company. "She had a vision of protecting an entire ecosystem. She is a very, very long-term thinker." Browner's approach not only responded to the needs of the business community for ongoing development but insured and protected the balance of an ecological system—the wetlands—that would provide a refuge for wildlife spanning thousands of acres in central Florida for decades to come.

Browner is the oldest of three daughters born to Michael Browner and Isabella Harty-Hugues, both academicians whose respect for education undoubtedly had a strong influence on their three daughters. The Browners limited their daughters' television viewing time and encouraged them, instead, to read and pursue their interests.

Browner was born and raised in Florida and her love of the state's natural beauty certainly played into her strong environmentalist attitudes. Growing up in the 1950s and '60s, Browner spent many hours hiking around the Everglades searching out the many species that inhabited the area. It is even said that she once missed school so that she could stay home and finish a watercolor painting of a rare water fowl that landed in a pond near her home.

Browner received both her undergraduate degree in English and her law degree from the University of Florida in Gainesville. Her sister, Michelle, the middle Browner daughter, is a biochemist at the University of California at San Francisco. The third and youngest of the Browner sisters, Stephanie, is completing her doctoral studies at the University of Indiana in American literature. Carol Browner's family feels that her position with the EPA not only allows her to continue to marvel at the natural world she loves but to have a profound and lasting impact on its future.

### Focus on Prevention

Browner is being called one of a new breed of environmentalists because she believes that there can and should be a balance between environmental protection and economic development. She feels that the EPA, in the past, has not brought issues to conclusion quickly enough for businesses to act upon them. "I've found business leaders don't oppose strong environmental programs," said Browner during her confirmation hearings, as stated in the *New York Times.* "What drives them crazy is a lack of certainty." She vowed that the current administration will not hold up federal regulations considered anti-business as the previous administration had done. Her goal is to make the regulatory process more business-friendly. Browner's focus is on preventing pollution rather than on cleanup. Instead of an authoritarian and repressive regulatory environment, Browner looks for economic incentives in pollution prevention. She also works toward greater coordination with the other regulatory agencies within the federal government—energy, interior, transportation, agriculture—to develop a more unified environmental position. Browner also encourages giving individual states the freedom to develop their own environmental protection plans while keeping them under the auspices of the EPA. Browner made her point as stated by Max Gates in *Automotive News* when she said, "No one can tell me that Hawaii and Maine should have the same rules in all cases."

Browner had a formidable task facing her as the new EPA chief, but she also had the support of the Clinton administration. During the presidential campaign, Clinton, along with vice-presidential candidate Al Gore—a noted environmentalist and author of best seller *Earth in the Balance*—promised to make the environment a priority during their administration.

Browner introduced the Common Sense Initiative in 1994. The initiative updates the old method of regulating the environment—dealing with air, water, and land pollution separately—to an industry-by industry approach. Browner, President Clinton, and Vice President Gore announced a package of 25 reforms to streamline environmental regulation in March 1995.

An issue of paramount importance waiting for Browner when she stepped into her new position as EPA chief was that of toxic-waste disposal. Unlike the previous administrations' stances that incineration was the best way to handle the disposal of toxic waste, the new administration announced an 18-month moratorium on the licensing of new incinerators in order to give itself time to study the overall impact of incinerators on the environment. Further, this time enabled the EPA to tighten regulations on 171 unlicensed boilers and industrial furnaces that dispose of nearly five million tons of hazardous waste each year. Browner expanded the Toxic Release Inventory, which ensures the public's awareness of toxic emissions. She also issued the Chemical Manufacturing Rule, which aims to cut smog-producing chemicals by 1 million tons per year.

As Florida's secretary of Environmental Regulations, Browner had a solid foundation from which to approach her new post as chief of the Environmental Protection Agency. While in Florida, Browner managed the country's third-largest state environmental agency with a budget of $650 million and a staff of 1,500 employees. She is credited with revitalizing the department's demoralized workforce and making the agency one of the most active in the state. To date, Browner is the youngest administrator ever to serve with the EPA and only the second woman to hold the top post. As head of the Environmental Protection Agency, Browner oversees 17,000 individuals and is responsible for a budget of $7 billion. It has been said that she listens well, is a strong negotiator, and will compromise when necessary. Similar qualities have been attributed to her boss, Bill Clinton. And like President Clinton, she has opponents and critics on all sides.

Browner is a very organized individual both in her professional career and in her personal life, but she also has a lighter side to her personality, according to her father Michael Browner—a side that the public may never see. He laughingly recalls a time when he and other members of the family were invited to a party at Carol's new house shortly after she and Michael Podhorzer were married. Upon their arrival, and much to their surprise, they were all handed paint brushes. They painted all day and all night according to Mr. Browner.

Carol Browner bikes, skis, and jogs. The jogging is done mostly on a treadmill now because Browner usually arrives home after dark. The family is very active. Five days after her son Zachary was born, the family, including baby, went cross-country skiing. Browner says it was just a short trip and she doesn't want people to get the idea that she's superhuman, but she loves spending time with her family. Family is important to Browner and her husband Michael. Spending time with them continues to be a priority with Browner, even though it requires careful planning, since her position as EPA chief exacts more of her time and energy.

Browner is also very proud of the fact that she and husband Podhorzer, whom she met while both were working for the nonprofit advocacy Citizen Action group and whom she married in 1987, have never employed a housekeeper or a nanny for Zachary. They both share housekeeping chores and they both take equal responsibility for their child. Browner does not want to be branded as "eco-obsessed," but she admits she would consider the availability of curb-side recycling when purchasing a home. She also tries to buy in bulk to lessen packaging waste. Browner believes small things would make a big difference if everyone did them. She also feels that it is crucial to teach our young people how to be good stewards of the land, air and water. When she and Zachary walk to the store she lets him know that it is to save energy. When she gardens, she teaches her young son how to grow things and to respect the environment. When asked by a reporter for *USA Weekend Magazine* what his mom did for a living, Zachary simply said, "she saves things." What Browner wants for her son is not so different from what most parents want for their children. "I want my son to be able to grow up and enjoy the natural wonders of the United States in the same way that I have," stated Browner in the *New York Times*. With everything going on around her, Browner has not lost her idealism. She still wants to leave the world a better place for all of our children.

## Further Reading

*Amicus Journal,* spring 1993.
*Automotive News,* December 14, 1992; February 22, 1993.
*Chemical & Engineering News,* December 21, 1992; March 1, 1993; May 24, 1993.
*Congressional Quarterly Weekly Report,* January 16, 1993.
*Economist,* January 9, 1993.
*Fortune,* March 22, 1993.
*Good Housekeeping,* March 1993.
*Insight,* February 8, 1993.
*National Journal,* February 13, 1993.
*National Parks,* March 1993.
*Nation's Business,* June 1993.
*Nation's Cities Weekly,* January 18, 1993.
*New York Times,* December 12, 1992; December 17, 1992; February 2, 1993; February 7, 1993; February 8, 1993; February 9, 1993; February 12, 1993; May 22, 1993.
*Science,* March 12, 1993.
*Time,* December 21, 1992; February 15, 1993.
*USA Weekend,* May 21-23, 1993.
*Wall Street Journal,* December 11, 1992; January 8, 1993; January 25, 1993; February 8, 1993; February 10, 1993; March 23, 1993; April 5, 1993. □

# Susan Brownmiller

**A career feminist whose work spans the distance from political activism to historical research and novel writing, Susan Brownmiller (born 1935) is most recognized for raising public awareness of violent crimes against women and children.**

Brownmiller was born in Brooklyn on February 15, 1935. She returned to New York City twenty years later, after graduating from Cornell University. She worked for four years as an actress before beginning her journalistic career as assistant to the managing editor of *Coronet.* During the 1960s she worked as a freelance writer with feminist leanings, and also in various capacities for *Newsweek, Village Voice,* NBC, and ABC. Especially relevant to the themes of her later writing, in 1968 Brownmiller cofounded the New York Radical Feminists among whose political actions was a sit-in at the offices of *Ladies Home Journal.* Her first book, *Shirley Chisholm* (1970), a biography of the first African-American Congresswoman, was expanded from a cover story for *The New York Times Magazine* into a book aimed at adolescent audiences. During her work for a 1971 "Speak-Out," Brownmiller so radically revised her own opinions on rape that she began drafting the book which would eventually become *Against Our Will.* Her next book, *Femininity* (1984), was written against the "fear of not being feminine," a fear she feels has been historically imposed upon women. She was inspired to write her first novel, *Waverly Place* (1989), while covering the trial of Joel Steinman for *Ms.* magazine. As she told *Publisher's Weekly* in an interview, "I wrote the novel in a white heat because I was possessed. I had never given myself permission to invent before. It was very liberating." Her most recent work, *Seeing Vietnam: Encounters of the*

came the critical torrent surrounding *Against Our Will*. Although some reviews praised its "informed" and "compelling" "vision," as does Mary Ellen Gates for *The New York Times Book Review*, many more have left Brownmiller's work with more mixed responses. Amanda Heller of *The Atlantic Monthly* declared it to be "intelligent" and "ambitious" but in places given to "a kind of feminist pornography that overwhelms the book's more thoughtful passages." Diane Johnson, writing for *The New York Review of Books*, looked more seriously at the risk of these latter passages, suggesting Brownmiller's rhetoric effectively divides her audience between discouraged women and alienated men. Coming from a radically different perspective, M. J. Sobran, writing for *National Review*, rejected Brownmiller's very premises: "What she is engaged in, really, is not scholarship but henpecking—that conscious process of intimidation by which all women keep all men in terror."

The critical reception of *Femininity* was likewise divided. Anne Collins believed it to be "neither self-deprecating enough to be funny nor winsome enough to evoke rueful empathy." Laura Shapiro agreed, stating, "Brownmiller skips along with a great armful of cliches and truisms and scatters them like rose petals until they're all gone." In stark contrast to such comments, Elizabeth Wheeler announced "Brownmiller has written an important book." Carol Gilligan agreed, writing, "The critical questions are of perspective, power, and judgment."

## Further Reading

*Against Our Will: Men, Women, and Rape,* Brownmiller, Susan, Simon & Schuster, 1975.
*Waverly Place,* Brownmiller, Susan, Grove, 1989.
*Commentary,* February, 1976.
*Commonweal,* December 5, 1975.
*Detroit News,* February 1, 1984.
*Nation,* November 29, 1975.
*National Review,* March 5, 1976. □

*Road and Heart* (1994), also was born from a reporting assignment, this time for *Travel and Leisure*.

*Against Our Will* is perhaps most remarkable for its absolute lack of precedent, for as of 1975 such a comprehensive study of rape's genealogy had yet to be written. Indeed, the book created a clamor against this vast silence. Dredging up facts from the Trojan War to the Vietnam War, Brownmiller uncovered rape as a traditional military strategy. Pouring over centuries of legal history, she described rape as an openly or quietly advocated privilege of husbands over wives, fathers over daughters. The book is broadly and meticulously researched, presenting facts that are indispensable to fields of psychoanalysis, sociology, criminology, and law. Its rhetoric does not shy from its controversial claim that rape "is nothing more or less than a conscious process of intimidation by which *all men* keep *all women* in a state of fear." Behind her commitment to expose rape as a pervasive quality within all cultures stands Brownmiller's interest in empowering an immense society historically paralyzed and atomized by fear. Her third book, *Femininity,* also addresses the societal confinement of women, but the subject matter is considerably more subtle. Femininity, Brownmiller writes, "in essence, is a romantic sentiment, a nostalgic tradition of imposed limitations." According to this book, these limitations have taken the forms of clothing, games, manners, and popular metaphors for the "feminine" body, all of which debilitate women in their efforts to succeed.

Following the calm reception of *Shirley Chisholm,* which *Booklist* reviewed as a "chatty, narrative account,"

# Pearl Sydenstricker Buck

**Pearl Sydenstricker Buck (1892-1973), an American Nobel Prize-winning novelist, dedicated her books and her personal activities to the improvement of relations between Americans and Asians.**

Pearl Sydenstricker was born in Hillsboro, West Virginia, on June 26, 1892. Her parents were Presbyterian missionaries, on furlough at the time of her birth from their activities in Chinkiang, China, although they soon returned there. During the anti-foreign Boxer Rebellion of 1900, the family was forced to flee to Shanghai where, from 1907 to 1909, Buck attended boarding school. She moved to the United States the following year to enter Randolph-Macon Woman's College in Virginia. After receiving a bachelor's degree in 1914, she took a teaching assistantship at the college but almost immediately returned to Chinkiang to care for her ailing mother.

In 1917 she married John Lossing Buck, an American agricultural specialist, with whom she settled in northern China. From 1921 until 1934 they lived chiefly in Nanking, where her husband taught agricultural theory. Buck occasionally taught English literature at several universities in the city, although most of her time was spent caring for her mentally disabled daughter and her infirm parents. In 1925 Buck returned to the United States to pursue graduate studies at Cornell University, where she received a master's degree in English in 1926. Back in Nanking the following year, she barely escaped a revolutionary army attack on the city. Meanwhile, because of her family's financial difficulties, she resolved to begin writing.

## Novels Reflect Love of China

Buck's first novel, *East Wind: West Wind* (1930), a study of the conflict between the old China and the new, was followed by *The Good Earth* (1931), a profoundly affecting novel of Chinese peasant life, which won her a Pulitzer Prize. In 1933 Buck received a second master's degree, this time from Yale University, and in 1934 she took up permanent residence in the United States. In 1935 she divorced John Buck and married Richard J. Walsh, her publisher. Her extensive literary output—*Sons* (1932), *The First Wife and Other Stories* (1933), *The Mother* (1934), *A House Divided* (1935), and biographies of her father and mother, *The Exile* (1936) and *Fighting Angel* (1936) respec-

tively—culminated in a 1938 Nobel Prize for literature, the first ever awarded to a woman.

## Humanitarian Efforts Occupy Later Life

In the next three decades, while continuing to write prolifically, Buck worked to promote racial tolerance and ease the plight of disadvantaged Asians, particularly children. In 1941 she founded the East and West Association to promote greater understanding among the world's peoples, and in 1949 she established Welcome House, an adoption agency for Asian-American children. She always had a special interest in children, and among her many books for them are *The Water-Buffalo Children* (1943), *The Man Who Changed China: The Story of Sun Yat Sen* (1953), *The Beech Tree* (1955), *Christmas Miniature* (1957), and *The Christmas Ghost* (1960). A steadfast supporter of multiracial families, in 1964 she organized the Pearl S. Buck Foundation, which supports Asian-American children and their mothers living abroad.

Although Buck's literary career embraced a variety of genres, almost all of her stories are set in China: the extremely popular novel *Dragon Seed,* its less popular sequel, *The Promise* (1943), and a raft of later novels, including *Peony* (1948), *Letter from Peking* (1957), and *The New Year* (1968). Among her other works, the highly acclaimed *The Living Reed* (1963) details the history of a Korean family during the late 19th and early 20th century. In the late 1940s Buck also authored a trilogy under the pseudonym John Sedges. The novels were later published as *American Triptych* (1958).

## Lauded for Generous Spirit

Buck's play *A Desert Incident* was produced in New York City in 1959. Her ability as an essayist is exemplified by *American Argument* (with Eslanda Goode Robeson, 1949) and *Friend to Friend* (1958), ''a candid exchange'' with Philippine president Carlos P. Rómulo. Buck died of lung cancer in 1973, with more than one hundred written works to her credit. But even more significant, perhaps, were the over three hundred awards she received for her humanitarian efforts on behalf of improved race relations worldwide.

## Further Reading

There has been very little critical attention given to Mrs. Buck's work. Her autobiography is *My Several Worlds* (1954). The best biographical sources are Cornelia Spencer, *The Exile's Daughter: A Biography of Pearl S. Buck* (1944), Paul A. Doyle, *Pearl S. Buck* (1965), and Nora Stirling, *Pearl Buck: A Woman in Conflict* (1983). □

# Selma Burke

**An African American sculptor, Selma Burke (1900–1995) created the relief sculpture rendering of Franklin Delano Roosevelt which appears on the dime.**

Selma Burke is an artist whose career has spanned more than sixty years. She was born in Mooresville, North Carolina, in 1900, and received her training as a sculptor at Columbia University in New York. She also studied with Maillol in Paris and in Vienna with Povoley. World War II interrupted her work in Europe and she returned to the United States to continue her artistic and humanitarian pursuits. She is best known for her relief sculpture rendering of Franklin Delano Roosevelt that was minted on the American dime.

Founder of the Selma Burke Art Center in Pittsburgh, Pennsylvania, she has taught many and supported numerous artists from the period of the Depression through the present day.

The Pearl S. Buck Foundation Woman's Award was given to her in 1987 for her professional distinction and devotion to family and humanity. Notable works include *Falling Angel; Peace;* and *Jim.*

Burke died of cancer August 29, 1995 in New Hope, Pennsylvania.

### Further Reading

*New York Times,* September 2, 1995.
*Washington Post,* September 1, 1995. □

# Frances Hodgson Burnett

**English-born American author Frances Hodgson Burnett (1849-1924) had a long and productive writing career, during which she penned 55 titles, 5 of which became best-sellers and 13 of which were adapted for the stage. Although remembered primarily for her children's books, such as *Little Lord Fauntleroy,* *A Little Princess,* and *The Secret Garden,* Burnett also wrote for adults, including the well-received novel *That Lass o' Lowrie's.***

Burnett was born Frances Eliza Hodgson in Manchester, England, on November 24, 1849, to Edwin and Eliza (Boond) Hodgson. She was the middle of five children. When her father died in 1865, his hardware wholesaling business collapsed, leaving the family with few financial resources. A short while later, Burnett immigrated with her siblings and her mother to rural Tennessee, where they lived with her mother's brother. Burnett was about 16 years old at the time. The only education she had received was in a dame school in England, but she had spent vast amounts of time reading and educating herself on her own. The family had little money, and Burnett's first attempt at earning an income involved running a private school, which was unsuccessful. She then decided to try to sell a story to a magazine. She had been reading stories in ladies' periodicals since she was seven years old and had learned the formula quite well. She was so good, in fact, that the editor of *Godey's Lady's Book,* the magazine to which she submitted the tale, questioned whether it was original. It did not seem likely that a young girl from Tennessee could write such a good story for a British women's magazine. Burnett wrote a second tale to prove her authenticity, and eventually both stories were accepted for publication. "Hearts and Diamonds" appeared in the summer of 1868, and "Miss Carruther's Engagement" was published the following year.

In 1870, Burnett and her family moved to Knoxville, Tennessee, to a house called "Vagabondia." Soon after, Burnett's mother died. At age 20, Burnett found herself in charge of the family, and she continued to write for women's magazines in order to earn an income. She published numerous stories over the next few years, as many as five or six a month. Her first long work, *Vagabondia,* was serialized as *Dolly* in *Peterson's Magazine* in 1873.

### Wife, Mother, and Developing Writer

Burnett married Dr. Swan Moses Burnett, an ear and eye specialist, in 1873. Almost exactly one year later, they had their first son, Lionel. In 1875, the Burnetts moved to Paris, where their second son, Vivian, was born in 1876. During this time, Burnett continued to write and provide financial support for the family. In 1876 she published her first novel, *That Lass o' Lowrie's,* which had first appeared as a serial in *Scribner's Monthly.* The novel, a story of an independent woman in an English mining town, was well received and published in England only a few weeks after its release in America. One reviewer in the *New York Herald* stated that ''there is no living writer (man or woman) who has Mrs. Burnett's dramatic power in telling a story. . . . The publication of *That Lass o' Lowrie's* is a red letter day in the world of literature.'' With the publication of *That Lass o' Lowrie's*, Burnett's popularity as a writer in both the United States and England grew quickly.

In 1877 the Burnetts moved to Washington, D.C., and the next five years became Burnett's most productive time as a writer. During this period she published many works, including *Surly Tim and Other Stories* (1877), which was a collection of early tales; *Haworth's* (1879), about Lancashire industrial life; *Louisiana* (1880), a portrayal of a farmer's daughter; *A Fair Barbarian* (1881), about a young American woman in rural England; and *Through One Administration* (1881), which was based on Burnett's observations while living in Washington. Her novels continued to be received with critical acclaim.

The strains of maintaining a household, raising two children, participating in Washington society, and writing so much during these years took their toll on Burnett. She was often ill and depressed, and referred to herself at this time as a ''pen-driving machine.'' Her marriage was also troubled; she and her husband became estranged. Beginning in 1884, the couple spent more and more time living apart, with the children alternating between their father and mother. Burnett and her husband divorced in 1898.

## *Little Lord Fauntleroy*

Even though Burnett's married life was not without flaw, she found she could still maintain the ideal through her fiction. She often stated, ''The one perfect thing in my life was the childhood of my boys,'' and with the writing of *Little Lord Fauntleroy*, Burnett immortalized her statement. Basing the main character on her son Vivian, Burnett wrote a story about a disinherited American boy who wins back his noble title and fortune without corrupting his own innocence or debasing aristocratic values. The tale was published first as a serial in *St. Nicholas*, a magazine for children, in 1885, then as a book in 1886. The volume was a phenomenal success. *Little Lord Fauntleroy* became a best-seller, was translated into more than a dozen languages, and was produced for the stage in England and France. In addition, a variety of products were created based on the book, including toys, playing cards, writing paper, chocolate, and of course the dark velvet suits with lace collars that characterized Little Lord Fauntleroy in the book's illustrations. Much later, in 1921, Hollywood actress Mary Pickford starred in the first film version.

Because of the success of *Little Lord Fauntleroy*, Burnett and her sons were soon enjoying an expensive, international life-style, including trips to such places as London, Rome, and the French Riviera. The volume also changed the course of Burnett's writing career. From 1886 until 1896, she wrote mainly for children. She also continued to write for the theater, although her plays were not as popular as her novels. One of Burnett's works written during this time was her memoirs, *The One I Knew Best of All: A Memory in the Mind of a Child,* which was written in third person and published in 1893.

## Trouble with the Critics

Phyllis Bixler Koppes noted in *American Women Writers* that Burnett's ''life and writing were characterized by tensions between the serious artist and the popular writer, the independent woman and the self-sacrificing wife and mother.'' As Burnett's career advanced, these tensions were discussed by critics. Some claimed that she had given up serious writing in return for artificial, crowd-pleasing manuscripts that sold well. Other reviewers claimed she had a superficial personality. Details of her life were also critiqued, including her divorce and, later, her unconventional second marriage to her business and stage manager, Stephen Townesend, who was ten years her junior. When Burnett and Townesend separated permanently in 1902, just two years after their nuptials, the reviewers again focused on Burnett's personal life. In more recent times, a contributor to *A Reader's Guide to Twentieth-Century Authors* referred to Burnett as ''the image of the popular Victorian lady novelist,'' who wore wigs, dressed in frilly clothing, and went by the nickname ''Fluffy.''

Not all critics were so harsh, and many praised Burnett's writing, especially her juvenile fiction. A contributor to the *New York Times* commented, ''Many authors can write delightful books for children; a few can write entertaining books about children for adults; but it is only the exceptional author who can write a book about children with sufficient skill, charm, simplicity, and significance to make it acceptable to both young and old. Mrs. Burnett is one of the few thus gifted. . . .'' Another reviewer, *Bookman* contributor Katharine Tynan, had similar sentiments, declaring that ''[i]t is a privilege when such a writer as Mrs. Burnett gives her fresh and living art to writing stories for children.'' In *Children's Literature in Education*, Rosemary Threadgold compared Burnett's adult fiction to her children's tales, noting that Burnett's adult novels tended to follow ''the formula that had brought her so much success.'' In writing for children, however, Threadgold judged Burnett to be ''something of a leader. Her attention to detail, her gifts as a storyteller, and her interest in children all stand her in good stead.''

''The knowledge that she had never lost an appreciative audience for her adult and children's books, however, probably helped Burnett overlook the frequent condescension of the critics,'' declared Phyllis Bixler in the *Dictionary of Literary Biography*. Burnett responded to the critics' demands for more serious writing by publishing *A Lady of Quality* in 1896. The heroine of the novel is a strong-willed girl raised as a boy, who later accidentally kills her former boyfriend, hides his body, and lives happily without punishment or regrets. To many reviewers, this book was a sign that Burnett was no longer interested in being taken seriously. Her popularity with the reading public, however, continued to grow.

Burnett published two more very successful children's books after *Little Lord Fauntleroy*. *A Little Princess*, released in 1905, was adapted for the stage and performed in London and New York. The book was also made into a feature film in 1939 that starred child-actress Shirley Temple. In 1911, *The Secret Garden* was published and has since become a children's classic. The novel tells the tale of an orphan who befriends her sickly cousin (based on Burnett's son Lionel who died of consumption at age 15) and finds an enclosed garden. *The Secret Garden* has been adapted into several films, a number of television programs, and a musical produced in 1993. "*The Secret Garden* will charm every one from the children to the grown-ups," declared a reviewer in a September, 1911, issue of *Literary Digest*.

Burnett also continued to be popular with adults, and several of her novels made the best-seller list. Some of her better known works of this period are tales of fashionable American and British life, such as *The Shuttle* (1907) and its sequel *T. Tembarom* (1913). In 1922, she published *The Head of the House of Coombe*, about social life in London before World War I. During these years, she had moved from her country estate in Kent, England, called Maytham Hall, to a cottage named Plandome on Long Island in New York.

### Remembered as a Children's Author

"Burnett's reputation as a superior children's author remains secure," according to Phyllis Bixler, who further noted that Burnett's best children's books "can entertain a child and often an adult reader almost a century after they were written, an unusual longevity for children's fiction." Fittingly, Burnett's last public appearance was at the opening of the film of *Little Lord Fauntleroy*. She died on October 29, 1924, in Plandome, New York. Burnett once commented to her son Vivian, "With the best that I have in me, I have tried to write more happiness into the world."

### Further Reading

Bixler, Phyllis, *Frances Hodgson Burnett*, Twayne, 1984.

Carpenter, Angelica Shirley, and Jean Shirley, *Frances Hodgson Burnett: Beyond the Secret Garden*, Lerner, 1990.

*Dictionary of Literary Biography*, Volume 42: *American Writers for Children before 1900*, Gale, 1985.

Greene, Carol, *Frances Hodgson Burnett: Author of the Secret Garden*, Children's Press, 1995.

Mainiero, Lina, editor, *American Women Writers*, Frederick Ungar, 1979.

McGillis, Roderick, *A Little Princess: Gender and Empire*, Twayne, 1996.

Thwaite, Ann, *Waiting for the Party: The Life of Frances Hodgson Burnett*, Faber and Faber, 1974.

Ward, Martha, et al., editors, *Authors of Books for Young People*, Scarecrow, 1990.

*Bookman*, December, 1911.

*Children's Literature in Education*, fall, 1988.

*Literary Digest*, September 2, 1911.

*New York Herald*, 1877.

*New York Times*, September 3, 1911. □

# Octavia E. Butler

**Octavia Butler (born 1947) is best known as the author of the Patternist series of science fiction novels in which she explores topics traditionally given only cursory treatment in the genre, including sexual identity and racial conflict. Butler's heroines are black women who are both mentally and physically powerful .**

B utler grew up in a racially mixed neighborhood in Pasadena, California. Her father died while she was very young, and her mother worked as a maid to support the two of them. Butler has written memoirs of her mother's sacrifices: buying her a typewriter of her own when she was ten years old, and to paying a large fee to an unscrupulous agent so Butler's stories could be read. Butler entered student contests as a teenager, and after attending workshops like the Writers Guild of America, West "open door" program during the late 1960s and the Clarion Science Fiction Writer's Workshop in 1970, Butler sold her first science fiction stories.This early training brought her into contact with a range of well-known science fiction writers, including Joanna Russ and Harlan Ellison, who became Butler's mentor.

Four of Butler's six novels revolve around the Patternists, a group of mentally superior beings who are telepathically connected to one another. These beings are the descendants of Doro, a four thousand-year-old Nubian male who has selectively bred with humans throughout time with the intention of establishing a race of superhumans. He prolongs his life by killing others, including his family members, and inhabiting their bodies. The origin of the Patternists is outlined in *Wild Seed*, which begins in seventeenth-century Africa and spans more than two centuries. The Novel recounts Doro's uneasy alliance with Anyanwu, an earth-mother figure whose extraordinary powers he covets. Their relationship progresses from power struggles and tests of will to mutual need and dependency. Doro's tyranny ends when one of his children, the heroine of *Mind of My Mind*, destroys him and united the Patternists with care and compassion. *Patternmaster* and *Survivor* are also part of the Patternist series. The first book set in the future, concerns two brothers vying for their dying father's legacy. However, the pivotal character in the novel is Amber, one of Butler's most heroic women, whose unconventional relationship with one of her brothers is often interpreted in feminist contexts. In *Survivor*, set on an alien planet, Butler examines human attitudes toward racial and ethnic differences and their effects on two alien creatures. Alanna, the human protagonist, triumphs over racial prejudice and enslavement by teaching her alien captors tolerance and respect for individuality. *Kindred* departs from the Patternist series yet shares its focus on male/female relationships and racial matters. The protagonist, Dana, is a contemporary writer who is telepathically transported to a pre-Civil War plantation. She is a victim both of the slave-owning ancestor who summons her when he is in danger and of the slave-holding age in which she is trapped for increasing periods. *Clay's Ark* (1984) reflects Butler's interest in the psychological traits of men and women in a story of a space virus that threatens the earth's population with disease and genetic mutation. In an interview, Butler commented on how Ronald Reagan's vision of a winnable nuclear war encouraged her to write more dystopic material. This shift in focus is most evident in *Parable of the Sower* (1994), a novel which depicts a religious sea-change, set against the backdrop of a strife-ridden inner city in 2025.

Critics have often applauded Butler's lack of sentimentality, and have responded favorably on her direct treatment of subjects not previously addressed in science fiction, such as sexuality, male/female relationships, racial inequity, and contemporary politics. Frances Smith Foster has commented: "Octavia Butler is not just another woman science fiction writer. Her major characters are black women, and through her characters and through the structure of her imagined social order, Butler consciously explores the impact of race and sex upon future society."

## Further Reading

*Contemporary Literary Criticism,* Volume 38, Gale, 1986.
*Dictionary of Literary Biography,* Volume 33: *Afro-American Fiction Writers After 1955,* Gale, 1984.
*Analog: Science Fiction/Science Fact,* January 5, 1981; November, 1984; December 15, 1987; December, 1988.
*Black American Literature Forum,* summer, 1984.
*Black Scholar,* March/April, 1986.
*Equal Opportunity Forum Magazine,* Number 8, 1980.
*Essence,* April, 1979; May, 1989, pp. 74, 79, 132, 134.
*Extrapolation,* spring, 1982.
*Fantasy Review,* July, 1984.
*Janus,* winter, 1978-79.
*Los Angeles Times,* January 30, 1981.
*Magazine of Fantasy and Science Fiction,* February, 1980; August, 1984.
*Ms.,* March, 1986; June, 1987.
*Salaga,* 1981.
*Science Fiction Review,* May, 1984.
*Thrust: Science Fiction in Review,* summer, 1979.
*Washington Post Book World,* September 28, 1980; June 28, 1987; July 31, 1988; June 25, 1989. □

# Jane Byrne

**Jane Byrne (born 1934) won the most astounding political upset in Chicago's history when she unseated incumbent Michael A. Bilandic in the 1979 Democratic primary and went on to become the first woman mayor of Chicago.**

Born in Chicago on May 24, 1934, Jane Margaret (Burke) Byrne showed little interest in politics until the 1960 presidential election. Raised on the north side of Chicago by her father Edward Burke, who was vice president of Inland Steel, and her mother, Katherine Burke, Byrne attended parochial schools. Upon graduation from Saint Scholastic High School, Byrne enrolled in St. Mary-of-the-Woods in Terre Haute, Indiana. On completion of her freshman year she transferred to Barat College in Lake Forest, Illinois. She graduated in 1965 with a bachelor's degree in chemistry and biology. Jane married William P. Byrne, a marine aviator, soon afterward. A little more than one year after the birth of their only child on December 31, 1957, Edward crashed his plane near a naval air station in Chicago and sustained fatal injuries.

Byrne's involvement in politics stemmed partly from that crash. Upon hearing John F. Kennedy talk about the loss of life due to the Cold War, she joined his campaign for president and became secretary-treasurer for the presidential contender's Chicago headquarters. Her efforts impressed the Kennedy organization so much that they offered her a job in Washington, but Byrne decided to remain in Chicago and pursue graduate studies at the University of Illinois, Chicago Circle Campus. Having taught for a while, she planned to pursue a teaching career, but her continued interest in politics and her Kennedy association led to a meeting with Mayor Richard Daley, who urged her to work for his organization. Thus began a political relationship which deeply affected Byrne's future.

After satisfying Daley that she worked hard at the ward level, in 1964 the mayor appointed Byrne to a job in the Head Start program. A year later he promoted her to a job with the Chicago Committee on Urban Opportunity. During this period she studied Chicago politics and became a fiercely loyal Daley supporter. He rewarded her in 1968 by naming her the first woman member of his cabinet. As

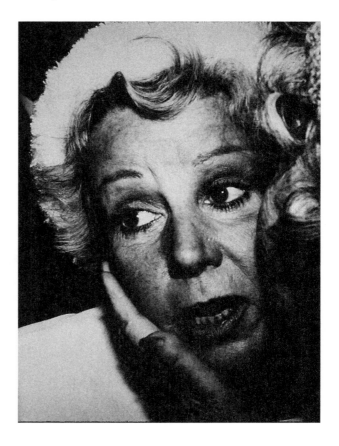

commissioner of sales, weights, and measures, Byrne attempted to uproot corruption and return her office to its original purpose, consumer protection.

Although never accepted by the party regulars, Byrne served as delegate to the 1972 Democratic National Convention and chaired the resolutions committee for the Democratic National Committee the following year. In 1975 Daley named Byrne co-chairperson of the powerful Cook County Democratic Central Committee, much to the distress of many Democratic leaders.

When Daley died of a heart attack in December of 1976, Byrne's political future appeared clouded. Soon after Daley's passing, party regulars stripped Byrne of the Central Committee chair. And the riff between Byrne and the local Democratic Party "machine" widened after Byrne accused the new mayor, Michael A. Bilandic, of not looking out for the public interest and "greasing" a nearly 12 percent cabfare increase for the city. Shortly after hearing those charges, Bilandic fired Byrne from her job as commissioner of sales.

Byrne responded by announcing her decision to run for the Democratic nomination for mayor. Campaigning with funds mostly donated by her new husband, Jay McMullen, and lacking an efficient political organization, Byrne's chances of winning seemed nearly impossible. Even her major campaign issue, the taxicab fare increase, lost its potency when a federal grand jury found no wrongdoing. But snow, which started to fall on New Year's Eve, 1979, gave her an issue to win the mayoralty.

The heavy January and February snow brought Chicago to a near standstill, interrupting public transportation and garbage collection. The inability of the mayor to devise and implement an adequate snow removal plan angered the city's residents. Charging that under Bilandic Chicago was no longer "the city that works," the underdog rode the issue to victory. A break in the bad weather permitted a record turnout to the Democratic primary and secured Byrne the upset victory. In the general election the following April, heavily Democratic Chicago gave Byrne a landslide with 82 percent of the popular vote over Republican Wallace Johnson. Her victory, which included a sweep of all 50 wards, gave her the largest margin of votes in the history of Chicago's mayoral contests.

Byrne's triumph did not mark the end of the powerful Democratic organization, nor did it bring a new era of tranquillity to Chicago politics. Soon after her primary victory Byrne started mending ties with the organization, and after becoming mayor in April she dismissed many reformers who had worked diligently for her election. Furthermore, her acerbity and her politicizing of the mayor's office alienated many former supporters and a large portion of the press. Finally, the very magnitude of problems her administration faced in areas such as fire protection, education, and declining revenues made controversy almost inevitable. Always one for the spotlight, Byrne captured the imagination of many Chicagoans when she moved into the deteriorated Cabrini-Green public housing project in March of 1981. Her stay not only emphasized the horrible conditions many were forced to live with, but helped bring improved services to an area largely neglected by city workers.

Although actions like the Cabrini move increased the mayor's popularity, they were not enough for her to win the Democratic renomination in 1983. In a three-way race, Harold Washington, a Black Congressman, defeated Byrne and the machine's candidate Richard M. Daley, Jr. Unwilling to admit defeat, Byrne initiated a write-in campaign for the general election but called it off for lack of support. Washington won election as mayor, but his political struggles with a hostile city council encouraged Byrne to look forward to the 1987 election.

But in the 1987 Democratic primaries, Byrne lost to Washington again. She then gave the incumbent her support in his ultimately successful bid for reelection. In March 1988, she ran for clerk of the Cook County Circuit Court, but was again defeated in her party's primary, this time by Aurelia M. Pucinski. Once again on November 12, 1990, Byrne announced her candidacy in the 1991 Chicago mayoral elections, and once again she lost in the February 26, 1991 Democratic primary. Richard Daley, Jr., son of the former mayor, won the election. In 1992, Byrne published a mayoral memoir entitled *My Chicago,* which received favorable reviews from both *Publishers Weekly* and *Library Journal.*

## Further Reading

Two biographies which focus on Byrne's pre-mayoral years are Kathleen W. FitzGerald, *Brass: Jane Byrne and the Pursuit of Power* (1981) and Bill and Lori Granger, *Fighting Jane: Mayor Jane and the Chicago Machine* (1980). Byrne told her own story in 1992's *My Chicago.* For more on Byrne's relationship with Daley, see Milton L. Rakove, *We Don't Want Nobody Sent: An Oral History of the Daley Years* (1979). Two books which explore Byrne's role in the 1983 election are Paul Kleppner, *Chicago Divided: The Making of a Black Mayor* (1984) and Melvin G. Holli and Paul M. Green, *The Making of the Mayor of Chicago 1983* (1984.) Other books which refer to Byrne's administration in a larger discussion of Chicago racial politics are *Fire On the Prairie: Chicago's Harold Washington and the Politics of Race* by Gary Rivlin (1992) and *Bitter Fruit: Black Politics and the Chicago Machine* by William J. Grimshaw (1992.) □

# C

## St. Frances Xavier Cabrini

**St. Frances Xavier Cabrini (1850-1917), Italian-born founder of the Roman Catholic Missionary Sisters of the Sacred Heart, became famous as the "the saint of the immigrants" during nearly 3 decades of service in the United States.**

Maria Francesca Cabrini was born on July 15, 1850, at Sant'Angelo Lodigiano. The young girl was drawn toward a life of religious service at an early age, influenced by her older sister, a schoolteacher; her uncle, a priest who captured her imagination with tales of missionary work; and the Daughters of the Sacred Heart, who prepared her for a normal school diploma in 1870. Francesca, who had already vowed herself to virginity at the age of 12, tried to enter the Daughters of the Sacred Heart in 1872 but was denied on grounds of health. She had contracted smallpox while caring for the sick during an epidemic, and though recovered she did not seem physically strong. After brief employment as a teacher in Virdardo, she was persuaded to do charitable work in an orphanage at Codogno, where in 1877 she made her vows. In the same year she was appointed prioress of her new foundation, the Institute of Missionary Sisters of the Sacred Heart, which consisted at the outset of seven orphaned girls whom she had trained. As head of a religious order, she was entitled to be called "Mother."

Mother Cabrini had much to do in Italy, but she soon craved fulfillment of a lifelong wish to do missionary work in China. Pope Leo XIII and Bishop Scalabrini of Piacenza instead urged her to carry her talents to Italian immigrants in the slums of the United States, and dutifully but reluctantly she sailed in 1889 with six sisters. From modest beginnings in the New York City area Mother Cabrini and her followers gradually built a national and international network of some 70 institutions. In 1909 she became an American citizen. Her journeys in behalf of her mission, including 30 crossings of the Atlantic, occupied much of her time and energy, though she remained physically frail throughout her life. When World War I broke out in Europe, she dedicated her hospitals and nuns in Italy to the war effort there. On Dec. 22, 1917, after a brief illness, she died of malaria in her own Columbus Hospital in Chicago.

Cardinal George Mundelein of Chicago and others launched the process of her canonization in 1928. She was pronounced venerable in 1933, beatified in 1938, and canonized in 1946. Her remains, originally at West Park, N.Y., are now enshrined in the chapel of the Blessed Mother Cabrini High School in New York City. St. Frances Xavier Cabrini, though declared to have effected the two miracles necessary for canonization, is best remembered for her energetic labors among immigrants and the poor in the United States and for the establishment and staffing of orphanages, schools, hospitals, convents, and other facilities throughout the world.

### Further Reading

There are many biographies of St. Frances Xavier Cabrini, including Frances Parkinson Keyes's popular account, *Mother Cabrini: Missionary to the World* (1959). More scholarly are the work by a Benedictine of Stanbrook Abbey, *Frances Xavier Cabrini* (1944); Theodore Maynard, *Too Small a World: The Life of Francesca Cabrini* (1945); and Pietro Di Donato, *Immigrant Saint: The Life of Mother Cabrini* (1960). □

# Shirley Caesar

**After hearing the voice of God during a college exam, Shirley Caesar (born 1938) believed it was her duty to spread the Gospel. This "calling" has developed into 150 concerts per year, volunteer work for the poor, numerous Grammy awards, and over 30 record albums.**

With 150 concerts a year, 25 hours a week helping the poor in her Outreach Ministries, several Grammies, and 30 record albums to her credit, Shirley Caesar may seem to be a whole army of gospel singers instead of just one diminutive (5'1, 3/4") cherubic-looking woman. The "Queen of Gospel" packs a lot of wallop in her small frame. Backed by a sixty-person choir, rocking like a tempest, she is a bundle of fireworks on the Fourth of July. The gospel style of song and sermonette, singing that involves both the spoken word and dramatic acting, was developed primarily by Shirley Caesar. She journeys all over the world, sometimes traveling all night to return to her pulpit in Durham, North Carolina, the town where she was born. "It is not easy," said Shirley in her 1995 video *He Will Come* (Word Records), "In fact, sometimes it is downright mind-boggling. But, somehow, even though I'm wearing all of these hats, the Lord helps me to just barrel through it." Shirley has barreled through fifty years of touring and preaching, starting at age ten, and she continues to bring the house down every time she performs.

The tenth of 12 children, Shirley Caesar was born October 13, 1938. Her father James was a tobacco worker who was well-known in the Carolinas as the lead singer in a gospel quartet, the Just Came Four. Shirley began singing with the group at age ten. When she was twelve, her father died, and she began touring with an evangelist named LeRoy Johnson, who also had a television show in Portsmouth, Virginia. In 1951, at thirteen, she recorded her first song "I'd Rather Have Jesus." While still in high school, she toured throughout the Carolinas.

This was a time when Jim Crow laws were still in effect in North Carolina. Shirley remembers restaurants putting up the CLOSED sign when she would arrive. "I went to school in the days when all the white kids got things better," she told *People*, "I remember once when a lady gave cookies to all the kids in the state. The white kids got the fresh ones; we got the stale ones." Despite these obstacles, her beloved mother Hannah taught her to respect herself and to persevere.

Her determination took her to North Carolina Central College where she studied business education. She has said that she got the call to God's work in the middle of a typing test. According to Kim Hubbard of *People*, she heard someone call out her name. Shirley turned to the young woman next to her and asked if she had spoken. When Shirley went home, she lay on the bed, and heard the same voice: "Behold, I have called you from your mother's womb and I have anointed your lips to preach the gospel." Shirley believed that this was a message that foretold special work for her in spreading the Gospel. Around the same time, Shirley heard Chicago's female gospel group, the Caravans, and she saw an opportunity to answer the call. She sought an audition with the group, was immediately hired, and left school for a life of singing and ministry.

The Caravans had several members who became famous in the history of gospel music: Albertina Walker, Inez Andrews, and Sarah McKissick. Each woman had a different style and Shirley's contribution was an energetic and dramatic approach where she would act out the songs and walk among the congregation, engaging the members directly. On the song "I Won't Be Back," she would run through the hall searching for an exit, then leave for a brief period. Her forte was the sermon in the middle of songs that addressed the subject of the song and expounded on its theme. She exhorted the listeners to reach out to God and to take the example of Jesus. On the subject of motherhood, she was particularly effective. Her song "Don't Drive Your Mama Away" tells of a son who is shamed for putting his mother in the rest home.

Along the way, Shirley found a male counterpart in the singer James Cleveland and they made several records together. They became known as the "King and Queen of Gospel." Shirley formed her own group in 1966 called the Caesar Singers, but she would reunite with the Caravans and the Reverend Cleveland occasionally throughout the years. In 1971, she won her first Grammy, for the popular song "Put Your Hand in the Hand of the Man from Galilee." On the night of the awards, she had returned very late from an engagement in Homer, Louisiana. People began banging on her door, and when she eventually answered, her sister Ann, one of her backup singers, shouted "You won!" It was the first Grammy for a black female gospel singer since Mahalia Jackson. Shirley went on to win the award in 1980, 1984, 1985, 1992 and 1994—for an astonishing total of seven Grammys.

Among her numerous honors are eight Dove awards, the Gospel Music Association's highest tribute. She was inducted into the Gospel Hall of Fame in 1982. She was the first female gospel artist to perform at Harvard University. In recent years, Shirley Caesar moved into other media, making several videos: *Live in Memphis, I Remember Mama*, and *He Will Come*. Broadway found that the gospel singer could conquer a big city when Shirley packed them in for the musical *Mama I Want to Sing* (1994). Her second Broadway musical in 1995 was titled *Sing: Mama 2* and her third in 1996 was titled *Born to Sing! Mama 3*. Perhaps her proudest achievement was the creation of a ministry in Durham to provide emergency funds, food and shelter for the needy, the Shirley Caesar Outreach Ministries. When Shirley ran for public office and was elected to the Durham City Council in 1987, she concentrated her efforts on housing and care for the poor and elderly.

Recently, Caesar went into the studio to help recording artist Bishop T.D. Jakes with his upcoming album, "Woman, Thou Art Loosed." The album, recorded live at Jakes' national conference in New Orleans, was released in the summer of 1997.

Her biggest fan, the Rev. Harold I. Williams, whom Shirley has called "my pastor, my best friend, my husband," assessed his wife's character in the 1995 video *He Will Come:* "After twelve years, I'm going to say the same thing I said after the first year I was married to Shirley: exciting! You never know what is coming next. I mean it is *exciting.* It is from one thing to another. She's an exciting person. She's a joy to be around." Most who have seen her perform would agree.

## Further Reading

*American Gospel,* March/April 1992.
*Ebony,* December 1988; March 1994; February 1996.
*Epic Center News:* "http://www.epiccenter.com/EpicCenter/docs/artistbio.qry?artistid=235," July 17, 1997.
*Essence,* October 1990.
*Jet,* Jan. 8, 1990; Aug. 26, 1991; March 9, 1992.
*Journal of American Folklore,* Summer 1991.
*People,* November 9, 1987.
Heilbut, Anthony, *The Gospel Sound* (1985).
Cusic, Don, *The Sound of Light: A History of Gospel Music,* (1993). ☐

# Calamity Jane

**Martha Jane Cannary, known as Calamity Jane (1852-1903), was a notorious American frontier woman in the days of the Wild West. As unconventional and wild as the territory she roamed, she has become a legend.**

The most likely date of Jane Cannary's birth is May 1, 1852, probably at Princeton, Mo. When she was 12 or 13, the family headed west along the Overland Route, reaching Virginia City, Mont., 5 months later. En route Jane learned to be a teamster and to snap 30-foot bullwhackers. Her father died in 1866 and her mother died a year later. Late in 1867 Jane was in Salt Lake City.

Until the early 1870s nothing more is known of Jane. Then she appeared at Rawlins, Wyo., where she dressed and acted like a man and hired out as a mule skinner, bullwhacker, and railroad worker. "Calamity" became part of her name; she was proud of it.

In 1875 Calamity went with Gen. George Crook's expedition against the Sioux, probably as a bullwhacker. While swimming in the nude, her sex was discovered and she was sent back. Excitement and wild adventure lured Calamity, whether it meant joining "her boys" at the bar or fighting with Native Americans. She was adept at using a six-shooter.

In Deadwood, Dakota Territory, in 1876 Calamity found a home. It was an outlaw town, so her escapades and drinking bouts did not seem out of place. One day she accompanied Wild Bill Hickok into town; apparently they had met before. Whether they were ever married, or lovers, may never be known. Jane later did have a daughter, but that she was fathered by Hickok (as the daughter claimed in

1941) is questionable. On August 2 Jack McCall shot and killed Hickok. Calamity took no revenge, as she later claimed, and McCall was legally hanged.

Yet this flamboyant woman was kind, and many remembered only her virtues. During the 1878 Deadwood smallpox epidemic Calamity stayed in the log pesthouse and nursed the patients.

Calamity Jane left Deadwood in 1880 and drifted around the Dakotas and Montana. She next appeared in California and married E. M. Burke in 1885, and her daughter was born sometime before or after this. Alone again in the later 1880s and the 1890s, she wandered through Wyoming and Montana towns, drinking, brawling, and working, even in brothels. Her fame began to grow. In 1896 she joined the Palace Museum and toured Chicago, St. Louis, and Kansas City; she was fired for drunkenness. Calamity came back to Deadwood in 1899, searching for funds for her daughter's education. A successful benefit was held at the Old Opera House. In 1900 Calamity appeared briefly at the Pan-American Exposition in Buffalo, N.Y., as a Western attraction, but she was homesick for the West and soon went back. In poor health, in July 1903 she arrived at the Calloway Hotel in Terry, near Deadwood, where she died on August 1 or 2. She was buried next to Wild Bill Hickok.

## Further Reading

The work with the best scholarly research on Calamity Jane is Nolie Mumey, *Calamity Jane, 1852-1903: A History of Her Life and Adventures in the West* (1950), but the book is difficult to find because it was published in a limited edition.

More readily available and also good is John Leonard Jennewein, *Calamity Jane of the Western Trails* (1953), which separates fact from fiction whenever possible. A short, interesting, debunking account of Calamity Jane is in James D. Horan, *Desperate Women* (1952). □

# Sarah Caldwell

**Sarah Caldwell (born 1928) is the founder of the Boston Opera Group, now known as the Opera Company of Boston. She is also a conductor and artistic director of national renown. She has won international accolades for her use of the dramatic elements of opera and for expanding the operatic repertoire. She has headed several international exchange programs and was named National Medal of Arts recipient in 1996.**

Sarah Caldwell, founder of the Boston Opera Group (1958), now known as the Opera Company of Boston, was born in the small town of Maryville, Missouri in 1924. Soon afterwards her family moved to Kansas City. Caldwell, a child prodigy in both mathematics and music, began violin lessons at the age of four and was holding violin concerts before the age of ten. She attended orchestral performances of the Kansas City Philharmonic as well as stage performances by the Kansas City Repertory Theater. She graduated from Hendrix College, University of Arkansas, then moved to Boston to attend the New England Conservatory of Music, the Boston Symphony's unofficial educational affiliate.

Caldwell was soon studying under Boris Goldovsky, head of the New England Conservatory of Music's Dept. of Opera. She also studied under Richard Burgin, concert master of the Boston Symphony Orchestra. Caldwell's love of music and the theater found its focus in the artistic direction of opera. Goldovsky became her mentor and guide and Caldwell was instructed in all elements of opera, from chorus direction and stagecraft to orchestral conducting and costuming. By the age of 20, Caldwell had staged Vaughan William's *Riders to the Sea.*

As a member of the Conservatory, Caldwell participated in the annual Tanglewood Music Festival. (Tanglewood, Massachusetts has been holding an annual music festival for over sixty years. Musicians from the Boston Symphony traditionally perform in Tanglewood for eight weeks each summer.) She trained the choruses for various concerts.

Serge Koussevitzky, permanent conductor of the Boston Symphony (1924-49) and founder of the Berkshire Music Center (1940), admired Caldwell's work at Tanglewood and recommended that she be placed on the Berkshire Music Center faculty. Caldwell's success at the Berkshire Music Center led to her being named Director of Boston University's Opera Workshop (1953-57). She also created the Dept. of Music Theatre.

As director of the Opera Workshop, Caldwell was able to promote her concept of opera as a dramatic art form as well as search for compositions unfamiliar to American audiences. As one of her first productions, Caldwell staged the American premiere of German composer Paul Hindemith's opera *Mathis der Maler*. Caldwell also invited Igor Stravinsky to conduct his only full-length opera *Rake's Progress*. (Stravinsky's modern opera, composed to a libretto by W. H. Auden and C. Kallman, combines musical elements ranging from Mozart to Italian opera.) Caldwell proved to audiences that Stravinsky's opera could be successfully produced even though an earlier production by the Metropolitan Opera had been given poor reviews.

In 1957, Caldwell, with the help of supporters, founded the Boston Opera Group (renamed the Opera Co. of Boston in 1965). The difficulties of staging full-scale opera productions were considerable but Caldwell's unconventional approach to opera gave her productions an excitement and drama not characteristic of more traditional productions. She insisted upon extensive rehearsals which enabled singers to develop their characters both musically and dramatically. Her commitment to an expanded repertoire led her to stage premieres of several works that were only later put in the repertoire of other opera houses. Through research, she was able to locate and produce previously unperformed editions of familiar pieces. Her goal was to involve the audience by bringing out the inherently dramatic elements of an opera without sacrificing its musical content.

Several of the world's most sought-after opera stars were willing to participate in Caldwell's dramatic production even though they earned less money and had longer rehearsal times. Beverly Sills performed in *Manon* (1962) and Joan Sutherland made her Boston stage debut in *I Puritani*. The Opera Co. of Boston also presented the first east coast performance of *Lulu* (1964), the first American performance of Rameau's *Hippolyte et Aricie* (1966), and staged the American premiere of Schoenberg's *Moses und Aron* (1966).

From 1968-70, the opera company was without a home and was forced to hold performances at a variety of locations including the Kresge Auditorium at the Massachusetts Institute of Technology. In 1971 funding was received from The Ford Foundation and from the National Endowment for the Arts. The Orpheum Theater became the new home for the Opera Co. of Boston; another series of dramatic performances began. Operas produced by the Opera Co. of Boston under Caldwell's artistic direction included Kurt Weill's *Rise and Fall of the City of Mahagonny* (1973), the original French version of Giuseppi Verdi's *Don Carlos* (1973), Sergei Prokofiev's *War and Peace* (1974), and Roger Huntington Sessions' *Montezuma* (1976).

In 1978, after 21 years of rented space, the Opera Co. of Boston moved into its first permanent home in the Savoy Theater, now named The Opera House. Productions included Michael Tippett's English opera *The Ice Break* (1979), Leos Janacek's Czech opera *The Makropulos Affair* (1986), and the first American performances of Zimmermann's *Die Soldaten* (1982), and Puccini's *Madame Butterfly*.

Caldwell's reputation was gaining her both national and international recognition. In addition to conducting orchestras in almost every major concert hall in the United States, from Carnegie Hall to the Dallas Civic Opera House, she was appointed Director of the Wolf Trap Summer Music Festival in Virginia (1980). The first of her cultural exchange programs began as she became involved with special projects in Manila and in Tel Aviv in the early 1980s.

International interest in Caldwell's work took her to China in 1982 for a meeting with the Central Opera Theatre of Peking. Following their meeting, Ming Cho Lee of the Peking opera company produced costumes and sets for an Opera Co. of Boston production of *Turandot*. Caldwell also produced Shchedrin's opera *Dead Souls* as part of a Soviet-American Making Music Together Festival (1988). Despite the daunting logistics of rehearsing and preparing a production with artists who did not speak each other's language, the Festival was a great success.

Reviews of Caldwell productions were as widely diverse as her productions were original. Thor Eckert, Jr., of *Opera News* reviewed the 1984 production of *Turandot* and criticized the "details here and there [that] spoke more of haste than concept." In reviewing *The Makropulos Affair* (1986), Andrew Porter wrote that "the Boston company (was) at full strength presenting an opera that matters, and in a way to bring to life what matters about it most."

Caldwell's achievements with the Opera Company of Boston were astonishing, especially when one considers, as

P. G. Davis said in a review, that it was "put together . . . out of chewing gum, rubber bands and sheer gall." It was Caldwell's ability not to let obstacles distort her vision that won her so many admirers. As she once remarked, "The secret of living is to find people who will pay you money to do what YOU would pay to do if you had the money."

Caldwell was the first recipient of the Kennedy Center Award for excellence. She is also recipient of the Rogers and Hammerstein Award and the 1996 National Medal for Arts.

## Further Reading

There is not as yet a full biography of Sarah Caldwell but her career is outlined in *The New Grove Encyclopedia of Music,* Stanley Sadie, editor (London: 1980) and in *The American Music Handbook,* Christoper Pavlakis, editor (London: 1974). Other sources of interest include *Uncommon Women* by Joan Krufrin (1981), *Opera News, New York Magazine,* and *The New Yorker.* Both magazines have reviewed Caldwell's more unusual productions. An article by Winthrop Sargent *The New Yorker* (Dec. 24, 1973) presents an overall look at Caldwell's life and her work and describes how she created remarkable productions with only a minimal of financial backing and a whole lot of imagination. □

# Maria Callas

**Maria Callas (1923-1977) was one of the great coloratura sopranos of the twentieth century.**

Maria Callas was one of the greatest operatic voices of the 20th century. She revitalized opera and increased its appeal because of her dramatic skill. The extensive range of her singing voice (nearly three octaves) and her ability to emote enabled her to sing many operas that were rarely performed otherwise. Callas biographer Ariana Stassinopoulos said of the singer's dramatic flair, "She brought 'finish' back to the music: each phrase, each word was meticulously weighed . . . she never allowed it to become meaningless embroidery." And Michael Mark of *American Record Guide* noted of the American soprano, "Her strange, haunting, beautiful . . . voice was complemented by an unerring dramatic sense."

## Childhood in America

By most accounts Maria Callas was born Maria Kalogeropoulos in New York City, on December 3, 1923, just four months after her parents, George and Evangelia (Litza) Kalogeropoulos, arrived in New York harbor after emigrating from Greece. Callas was formally baptized Cecilia Sophia Anna Maria. It was around the time of her birth that her father shortened the family name to Callas, and Maria Kalogeropoulos was known as Maria Callas by the time she started school.

Callas and her sister, Jackie, grew up enmeshed in bitter sibling rivalries. Jackie, the elder by five years, was tall and slim—everyone's favorite. Maria was not short, but she was not as tall as Jackie, and so appeared more plump in

comparison. When Callas was only five years old, she suffered a concussion and was hospitalized for over three weeks, after being dragged unconscious by an automobile. She quickly learned to appreciate the attention she received from concerned family and friends during her recuperation.

At age seven Callas began her musical studies by taking piano lessons. She loved opera music even as a youngster, and she had a beautiful voice. She especially loved to sing *La Paloma*. She took great comfort in listening to the many opera records in her family's collection. Young Callas soon discovered that she had a natural talent and a flair for the dramatic. She won several amateur talent contests while she was in elementary school, and was a popular performer on children's radio shows.

### Adolescence in Greece

When Callas graduated from the eighth grade in 1937, her mother decided to return to Greece in order for Callas to receive voice training in the classical tradition. Once in Greece, Callas never resumed her academic studies. Instead she studied with popular voice coaches. First with Maria Trivella at the National Conservatory in Athens, and then with Elvira de Hidalgo at the Odeon Athenos. Callas also studied French and drama. She was a dedicated pupil, driven by a spirit of excellence. At times she observed even David, her pet canary, and attempted to learn from his warble. Her other bird, Elmina, was known to faint and fall off her perch from the intensity and pitch of Callas's high notes. It was all fun to Callas, who seemed happy only when she was singing. Callas's teachers, and later her directors

and producers, were continually amazed at her exceptional memory. She easily learned music and lyrics in a matter of days, where others would require weeks or months.

As Callas matured, she developed a close relationship with her music coach, Elvira de Hidalgo, and it was de Hidalgo who arranged for Callas's first professional performance at the National Lyric Theater in Athens in November of 1940. While her performance would be a success, life in Athens soon changed; the outbreak of World War II and the Nazi occupation of Greece had a profound effect on everyone in the country, including the young soprano. Stories are told that during the occupation Callas sometimes performed for enemy soldiers in return for food and security for herself, her mother, and her sister. Her career, meanwhile, was stifled.

### Finds Success in Italy

After the occupation, de Hidalgo encouraged Callas to move to Italy to establish her career. However, against all advice, Callas returned to the United States in 1945, determined that she could make a name for herself on her own terms. Although she remained in America for the next two years, it was at the Arena in Verona, Italy where she finally got her start.

After rejection and failure in the United States she finally went to Verona, on a contract. Her Italian debut, held on August 3, 1947, was a performance of *La Gioconda* at the Verona Arena. She went on to perform *Tristan and Isolde* and *Turandot* in Venice in 1948. She sang the title role in Bellini's *Norma,* her most popular role, for the first time in Florence in 1948.

Initially Callas received minimal acclaim, although audiences in Italy were receptive to her talent. It was a quirk of fate in 1949 that finally brought her to prominence. When another diva fell ill during a run of *I Puritani,* Callas agreed to sing the part of Elvira on one week's notice. Callas, who was performing as Brunhilde in *Die Walkure* at the time, managed to perform both operas, alternating between the two works from one night to the next. The public was duly impressed at her versatility. Critics took note, and her career began to soar.

### Marriage and International Acclaim

Almost immediately upon her arrival in Verona in 1947 she met Giovanni Battista Meneghini, a wealthy Veronian industrialist. He was 30 years her senior, and his family did not approve of Callas or her profession, yet the two fell in love. They married on April 21, 1949. The couple lived mostly in Verona. Meneghini withdrew from his business interests to manage Callas's promising career and generally devoted his life to fulfilling her every need.

During the late 1940s and 1950s, Callas toured Argentina, Mexico, and Brazil. She worked with famed Maestro Tullio Serafin, and noted directors Franco Zefferelli, Francesco Siciliani, and Luchino Visconti.

Highly professional, Callas performed 47 roles during her brief career. Her greatest role was that of Norma, which she performed 90 times. Callas developed a strong identity with the Druid priestess of the operatic tale, and once confided to Serafin, "It, *Norma,* will never be as good as it is now in my mind unsung." Whenever Callas performed in *Norma,* she reportedly became exhausted and drained from the physical intensity of her emotion.

Callas's first performance at La Scala in Milan was in *Aida,* in April of 1950, as a stand-in, a replacement for famed soprano Renata Tibaldi. On December 7, 1951, she made her official debut at the noted Italian opera house as Elena in *I Vespri Siciliani.* She went on to perform there for ten years, a total of nearly 200 performances. She interpreted nearly two dozen roles, including her most famous, Norma.

## Finds Fame in America

Callas's U.S. debut was at the Lyric Opera of Chicago in 1954. On October 19, 1956 she debuted at the New York Metropolitan Opera where she performed in *Norma.* Coinciding with her Metropolitan Opera debut, Callas was featured on the cover of *Time,* on the issue dated October 27, 1956.

During the peak of her career Callas easily fit the stereotype of a portly and highly emotional diva, but in 1952 she experienced a dramatic weight loss. By 1954 she was 65 pounds lighter. She continued to perform, and her career exploded into greatness. She added new operas to her repertoire, including *Madame Butterfly,* which she had previously avoided because she felt awkward and ungraceful.

## New Image Expands Opportunities

After the mid-1950s Callas successfully resurrected the macabre operas, including Cherubini's *Medea,* Verdi's *Macbeth,* and Donizetti's *Anna Bolena,* each of which required exceptional vocal range and acting talent. Will Crutchfield commented of her unique ability in *New Yorker,* "Callas presented to the . . . public a phenomenon of sheer capacity, . . . she revived a repertory based on capacity. High notes and low, power in full cry and delicacy in pianissimo, fast passagework and sustained legato had not been completely present in one soprano in generations."

The list of Callas's performances is lengthy: *Tosca, La Traviata, Abduction from the Seraglio, Parsifal, Aida, Nabucco, Il Trovatore,* and many more. In 1951 she performed the world premiere of Hayden's *Orfeo ed Euridice.* Surviving tapes and recordings of Callas include her 1952 *La Gioconda,* the complete opera, with Fedora Barbieri. Miscellaneous tapes also remain from a series of master classes she gave at the Juilliard School of Music in New York, where Callas taught briefly before her death.

## The Years of Decline

During the late 1950s the vocalist's personal life began to deteriorate, and this tragically affected her career. She became increasingly linked socially with the "international jet set," those people of wealth and power known as the "idle rich." Through her new-found friends she became acquainted with shipping magnate Aristotle Onassis, and the couple's friendship soon developed into an extramarital affair. This was not the first time that Callas's name was associated with illicit liaisons, and she and her husband separated in 1959, divorcing finally in 1971. Onassis eventually divorced his wife, Tina, and married Jacqueline Kennedy, widow of the late President John F. Kennedy, but he also remained involved with Callas.

The intrigues of Callas's personal life soon overshadowed her professional life. The stresses of jet set living, as well as the strain she had put on her voice throughout her career began to take their toll. Callas cancelled a performance at the Edinburgh Festival in 1957. In 1958 she answered to breach of contract charges from the American Guild of Musical Artists. A downward spiral was in motion. Her former manager, Richard Bagarozy, sued her for back commissions. She cancelled a performance in Rome after the first act. She was dismissed from the Metropolitan Opera. Although she returned briefly to perform at the Met between 1964 and 1965, she never resurfaced as the great talent of her youth.

## The Callas Persona

As an actress, Callas was known for her timing and spontaneity, as well as for her incredible vocal range. She attributed her extraordinary stage presence to myopia: She was rarely nervous, she claimed, because she could not see the audience. In fact, Callas insisted she could barely see the conductor, and was free therefore to lose herself in the composer's work to the exclusion of all else.

Callas's timing and spontaneity even extended to curtain calls. After one memorable performance, she was showered with flowers. She took one and handed it to famed conductor Arturo Toscanini who had attended the performance. The audience was ecstatic. Even during the years of her decline, when some of the audience threw vegetables instead of flowers, to express their annoyance, Callas retained her composure. She kept the flowers for herself and tossed the vegetables down to the orchestra.

Callas died unexpectedly in Paris on September 16, 1977, shortly before her 55th birthday. Just as no record exists of Callas's birth, her death also remains shrouded in mystery, the cause of her death never fully explained. (Her body was cremated without an autopsy.) Such facts serve to intensify the mystique of the soprano's life. Duncan Scott of *Knight-Ridder/Tribune News Service* said of Callas: "As in the case of . . . other icons, Callas's real accomplishments were swallowed up by the power of her own myth."

## Further Reading

Meneghini, Giovanni Battista, *My Wife Maria Callas,* translated by Henry Wisneski, Farrar Straus, 1982.
Stassinopoulos, Arianna, *Maria Callas, The Woman behind the Legend,* Simon & Schuster, New York, 1981.
*American Record Guide,* November-December 1993, p. 272.
*Atlantic Monthly,* October 1997, p. 102.
*Knight-Ridder/Tribune News Service,* September 15, 1997, p. 915K0226.
*New Yorker,* November 13, 1995, pp. 94-102.
*Opera News,* April 16, 1994, p. 12.
*Time,* October 27, 1956. □

# Annie Jump Cannon

**The American astronomer Annie Jump Cannon (1863-1941) made her most outstanding contribution to modern astronomy in the field of stellar spectral classification.**

Annie Jump Cannon was born in Dover, Delaware, on December 11, 1863, the daughter of Wilson Lee Cannon and Mary Elizabeth Jump Cannon. One of the first Delaware women to enroll in college, she attended Wellesley College (class of 1884). Back at Wellesley in 1894 after a decade at home, she did graduate studies in mathematics, physics, and astronomy. In 1895, Cannon registered as a special student in astronomy at Radcliffe College, staying there two years.

The newly elected director of the Harvard College Observatory, Edward C. Pickering, had put Williamina P. Fleming in charge of hiring a staff of women assistants. Between 1885 and 1900, Fleming selected 20 assistants—including Cannon, who joined the staff in 1896—to sort photographs of stellar spectra.

Cannon's early work dealt mostly with variable stars. Her greatest contributions remain in the field of stellar spectral classification. She discovered more than 300 variable stars on the photographic plates. A large number were detected from spectral characteristics. At Harvard the spectra of stars had been sorted into various groups, following the alphabetical order (A, B, C, and so on). Cannon created the definitive Harvard system of spectral classification. She rearranged groups, omitted some letters, added a few, and made new subdivisions. She proved that the vast majority of stars are representatives of only a few species. These few spectral types, with rare exceptions, can be arranged in a continuous series. Following five years of research (1896-1901), Cannon published in 1901 a description of 1,122 of the brighter stars.

Cannon's paramount contribution to astronomy was *The Henry Draper Catalogue,* named after the first man to photograph stellar spectra. In the Draper catalogue can be found spectral classifications of virtually all stars brighter than ninth or tenth magnitude, "a colossal enterprise embracing 225,300 stars" (Owen Gingerich).

She had described her classification in 1900 and, slightly modified, again in 1912. Most of the work of classifying the spectra was performed between 1911 and 1915. The first volume of the catalogue appeared in 1918, the ninth and final volume in 1924. She published about 47,000 additional classifications in the *Henry Draper Extension* (1925-1936) and several thousand more in the *Yale Zone Catalogue* and *Cape Zone Catalogue.* Moreover, 86,000 were printed posthumously in 1949. In 1922 Cannon's system of classification was adopted by the International Astronomical Union as the official system for the classification of stellar spectra. That same year she spent half a year at Arequipa, Peru, photographing the spectra of the southern stars.

Throughout her career, in the absence of a hearing aid, Cannon suffered from complete deafness. In discussions about the election of a woman to the National Academy of Sciences, Raymond Pearl of Johns Hopkins declared he could not vote for Cannon on the grounds she was deaf. Incidentally, the first woman astronomer was not elected to the academy until 1978.

Cannon was curator of astronomical photographs in charge of the collection of Harvard plates starting in 1911. In 1914 she was elected an honorary member of the Royal Astronomical Society. At that time women could not become regular members.

Honors bestowed upon Cannon after 1920 resulted from initiatives taken by her director, Harlow Shapley (and also by Henry Norris Russel, professor of astronomy at Princeton University), due to the lack of recognition at Harvard itself. She received four American and two foreign honorary degrees: from the University of Delaware; Wellesley, her *Alma Mater;* Oglethorpe University; and Mount Holyoke College and from the University of Groningen (Holland) and Oxford University (the first woman ever to be granted such distinction).

In 1931 she was awarded the Draper Medal of the National Academy of Sciences. In 1932 she was the laureate of the Ellen Richards Prize. She turned it over to the American Astronomical Society for a triennal award for distinguished contributions to astronomy by a woman of any nationality. Margaret Rossiter wrote: "Perhaps because she had never won an award from the AAS or been elected its president (she was treasurer from 1912 to 1919), she wanted more recognition for younger women." In 1938 President James Bryant Conant of Harvard University made her the William Cranch Bond Astronomer, a nonfaculty appointment. In the summer of 1940 she retired officially but continued to work actively until a few weeks before her death, on April 13, 1941, in Cambridge, Massachusetts.

Her life and work inspired other women to follow in her footsteps, to dedicate their abilities to science, and, for many, to choose a career in the field of astronomy.

## Further Reading

On Annie Jump Cannon as a woman scientist, see the classic work by Margaret W. Rossiter, *Women Scientists in America Struggles and Strategies to 1940* (1982). A biography of Cannon was written by Owen Gingerich: "Cannon, Annie Jump," in: *Dictionary of Scientific Biography* (1971). At the death of Cannon, two important obituaries were published, one by the first laureate of the Annie Jump Cannon Prize in 1934, Cecilia Payne Gaposchkin, in *Science* (May 9, 1941), and the other by R. L. Waterfield, in *Nature* (June 14, 1941). Apart from recalling the scientific career of Cannon, they paid homage to her personality. □

# Jennifer Capriati

**In March of 1990, Jennifer Capriati (born 1976) turned pro on the cutthroat women's professional tennis circuit.**

"Even though I'm going to be playing older ladies, when I'm out there playing, I'm as old as they are," she told the *New York Times*. "I have no fear. I guess I was just born with that kind of mind." And that kind of talent.

Capriati, the youngest tennis player ever to turn pro, was met with overwhelming expectations from both the tennis world, the public, and the media upon her debut at the Virginia Slims tournament in Boca Raton, Florida. The pressure was not just for her potential in tennis, but for her potential as the best charismatic draw for the U.S. women's circuit since Chris Evert.

The question is whether or not Jennifer Capriati is capable of living through this. She seems more likely to stumble down the path of former tennis pros like Jimmy Arias, Andrea Jaeger, and Tracy Austin. There is a reason why that path is becoming somewhat of a cliché. Capriati's short life in this pressure cooker is one explanation.

Headlines trumpeted Capriati as the "Teen Queen of Tennis," "Eighth Grade Wonder," and "The Next Chris Evert." Her own coach, Tom Gullikson of the U.S. Tennis Association, said flatly to a *Los Angeles Times* reporter, "It's our viewpoint that [Capriati] is without question the most talented young pro in the world, man or woman." Interviewers scrounged for details of her life—she was five-foot-seven, 130 pounds, shoe size 8 1/2. Her favorite rap song: "Bust A Move." Favorite foods: hamburgers, chips, hot fudge sundaes. Favorite movie star: Johnny Depp. Favorite color: pink. Favorite pet: the family Shih Tzu, Bianca.

Meanwhile, Capriati just hoped she wouldn't look "dorky" on television, and she told the *Los Angeles Times* she'd like to be remembered this way: "I'd like, you know, when I retire, like, you know, when I go down the street, people would say, 'There's Jennifer Capriati, the greatest tennis player who ever lived.'" The concept of a young, pretty teenager who could sigh over Twizzlers licorice, white leather mini skirts, and the baby on the TV show, *The Simpsons*, while also blasting her way to the top of the tennis circuit, ignited thousands of new Capriati fans. One magazine writer wondered whether people wanted to see history in the making or really just had a weird fascination with seeing a player who might be a flash in the pan, used up, and burnt out by age 21. But those apprehensions were at first blotted out by the sheer talent and exuberance of Capriati's early play. In her first match she knocked off four seeded players and advanced to the finals before being beaten by Argentina's Gabriela Sabatini on March 11. With every later tournament, she showed her raw, powerful talent with booming ground strokes, a 94 m.p.h. overhead serve, and cool nerves that belied her young age.

In April, she reached the finals of the Family Circle Magazine Hilton Head Cup, finally losing to Martina Navratilova. Capriati was delighted, still, just to be there; she called Navratilova "a lege, you know, like, a legend." In June, seeded No. 17, she reached the quarterfinals of the French Open before she was beaten by No. 1 Monica Seles of Yugoslavia. In July she made it to the quarterfinals of Wimbledon, ranked No. 12, before losing to Germany's Steffi Graff. On July 16, she won her first professional title, at the Mount Cranmore International tournament in New Hampshire. In August, she was defeated in the early rounds at the U.S. Open, where she was ranked 16th. In September, as sixth seed, she made it to the quarterfinals of the Nichirei International Tennis Championship in Tokyo.

Though she didn't win any big matches, many believed Capriati had set the stage for her advancement to the pinnacle of women's tennis. It was a climb she was groomed for from infancy. Jennifer Capriati was born in 1976 on Long Island, New York, to Stefano and Denise Capriati. Her Bronx-born mother, who is a Pan Am flight attendant, met her father in Spain in 1972. Stefano Capriati, a native of Milan, Italy, was a resident of Spain, where he was a movie stuntman and a self-taught tennis pro. They married and settled in Spain. Stefano Capriati knew Jennifer would be a tennis player when she was still in the womb, says Denise Capriati, who played recreational tennis until the day she went into labor with Jennifer. "Stefano knew she would be a tennis player . . . just by the way I carried her," she told *Sports Illustrated*. They moved to New York so Jennifer could be born in the United States, then moved back to Spain. Another child, Steven, was born three years later.

When Jennifer was a baby, her father did cribside calisthenics, propping her backside with a pillow and helping her do situps. When she was four years old, the family moved to Fort Lauderdale, Florida, to further Jennifer's tennis. By then, she could hold her own with a ball machine. "Already she could rally a hundred times on the court," her father said. He took her to see Jimmy Evert, tennis star Chris Evert's father. Evert did not even want to meet her since she was only four, but when he saw her skill he agreed to take her as a student. He coached her from age four to age nine. Along the way, Jennifer became friends with Chris Evert. In 1987, the tennis star gave Jennifer a Christmas bracelet that reads, "Jennifer, Love Chris" that Jennifer wears in all her matches.

From age ten to 13, Jennifer was coached by Rick Macci in Haines City, Florida, then went to the Hopman Tennis Academy at Saddlebrook resort in Wesley Chapel, where she got a third coach, Tom Gullickson. But the driving force in her budding career was her father, whom she called her main coach and whom the other members of her entourage called "the main boss." Stefano Capriati considers himself a tennis father, in the best sense of the term, noting that there is a difference between pushing and aiding. "You try to direct her in the right way, and you see she has the potential," he told the *Los Angeles Times*. "I see she enjoys it. After 9-10 years old, you cannot direct them anymore. They must want it."

As a junior tennis player, Jennifer wanted it. She relished the competition. In 1988 at age 12, she won the U.S. 18-and-under championships on both hard and clay courts. In 1989 she won the 18-and-under French Open, made the quarterfinals at Wimbledon, and won the junior title at the U.S. Open. The rules said girls under 14 could not turn pro, but in 1989, her father, coaches, and tennis boosters thought she was ready. "People say she's only 13, but they miss the point. She's already put in 10 years," said tennis legend Billie Jean King, Jennifer's periodic doubles partner. "I'm telling you," said her former coach, Rick Macci, in *Sports Illustrated*. "She's scary."

However, the United States Tennis Federation was stubborn. It would not allow Jennifer to play until the month of her 14th birthday. Her father thought about challenging the rule in court, then changed his mind. Already, Jennifer Capriati was getting lucrative endorsement contracts. The Italian sportswear maker Diadora of Caerano Di San Marco gave her $3 million to endorse their line and Prince gave her $1 million to endorse their tennis rackets. Later in the year, she made a commercial for Oil of Olay face cream. "First, immortality, then the SATs," joked *Newsweek*. But it was no joke: before even turning pro, Capriati was the third highest endorsed tennis player behind Chris Evert and Martina Navratilova. John Evert, Chris Evert's brother, became Capriati's business manager.

## Turns Pro

In between the relentless pace of tennis, Jennifer Capriati went through eighth grade at Palmer Academy in Wesley Chapel. When she couldn't go to school, she'd take her homework with her or have it sent to her on the road by fax machine. By March when she went pro, she still had to do homework in between matches. In September she started ninth grade at St. Andrew's School in Boca Raton, a 600-student private school. She was prepared to leave the Harry Hopman tennis facility of Saddlebrook and was offered a contract as touring pro at the Broken Sound Club in Boca

Raton. But later that month, her parents changed their minds.

Uncomfortable in a temporary home in Boca Raton, the Capriatis went back to Saddlebrook and Jennifer returned to the Palmer Academy, where she had attended eighth grade. The family intended to move to Broken Sound in January, then realized it would be better to remain at Saddlebrook. "There is life besides tennis," said Denise Capriati. "Jennifer was so happy to see her friends again. Jennifer's emotional happiness is the bottom line."

Also in September of 1990, ranked 12th in the world, Jennifer traveled to Tokyo for the Nichirei tennis championship. The remainder of the year she planned to do an exhibition match for former first lady Nancy Reagan, one for Chris Evert, and then hoped to make the Virginia Slims Championships in New York in November. The pace was grueling, but her spirits were high. "I feel like a kid, kidwise. But tenniswise, I feel I guess I have talent, I guess," she told the *Los Angeles Times*. "When I'm on the court, I just block out everything I'm thinking about and bring out my tennis stuff. When I'm off, I'm just a kid."

Her tennis stuff continued to wow observers. One coach praised her aggressive style, unpredictability, and power: "She was strong before, but her movement wasn't very good. Now she covers the court as well as any of the men I can think of," said Tommy Thompson, head tennis pro at Saddlebrook, to the *New York Times*. "She's going to be different than most women, who tend to play very defensively, because she's very confident at net. She has no fear when she's going in there to volley. Thompson said later in the *Washington Post*, "She's a kid off the court but a killer on it."

Whether the kid can continue life as a killer on the court without becoming overwhelmed is the question many had as her first six months on the circuit ended. While Capriati appeared to have a solid head on her shoulders, there were the inevitable comparisons with Andrea Jaeger and Tracy Austin, both of whom started tennis as young sensations but burned out from injuries and pressure. Jaeger won her first pro tournament at 14 but left the tour at 19 because of shoulder injuries. Austin, at 16, was the youngest player ever to win the U.S. Open, in 1979, but foot and back injuries sidelined her permanently at age 19. When asked about this by interviewers, Capriati sighs and replies wearily. "It's like, you know, it's not my fault," she says of Jaeger's and Austin's short-lived careers in the *Los Angeles Times*. "Why does everybody think it's going to happen to me? How do they know what my limit is?"

As time went on, she started to learn her limit. In 1991, Capriati peaked. She ranked in the Top 10 (No. 6) after reaching the finals of the U.S. Open and Wimbledon. In 1992, she won the gold medal in the Olympics at Barcelona, but no other tournaments. In September, after losing in the first round of the U.S. Open, Capriati returned to Florida from the tour to recover from bone chips and tendinitis in her elbow. In November, she moved out of her parents' home to an apartment. She later announced in January of 1993 that she was taking a leave from the tour to complete high school. In March, she dropped out of high school and moved to Boca Raton.

## Enters Rehab

In May of 1994, Capriati was arrested in Coral Gables, Florida for possession of marijuana. According to *People* magazine, the arrest followed a weekend of serious partying with other teenagers. One of the teens, Thomas Wineland, was booked for possession of suspected crack cocaine and drug paraphernalia. He later claimed that he and Capriati smoked crack for a couple of hours, then smoked reefers, took painkillers, and drank. Two days after the arrest, Capriati started a drug rehabilitation program at Mount Sinai Medical Center in Miami Beach.

A flurry of criticism and "I told you so" articles followed from the media. Mike Lupica of *The Sporting News* wrote an article reflecting the thoughts of those who know Capriati. He had plenty of negative things to say about Stefano Capriati and the Capriati entourage. He wrote, "The short-term marketing was brilliant. The short-term thinking was stupid and greedy." *Tennis* magazine commented, " . . . the women's tour kept changing its rules to make sure Capriati played as often as possible. They were called by many 'The Capriati Rules.' Four years later, suddenly very concerned about little girls playing tennis for a living, the same group passed rules limiting play for teenagers. They also should have been called 'The Capriati Rules.'"

Capriati did come back and play one match in November 1994—losing to Anke Huber in Philadelphia. She then remained absent from tennis until February 1996. She won two matches in the Faber Grand Prix in Germany, finally losing in the quarterfinals. Anne Person Worcester, The Corel WTA Tour's chief executive officer, told *Tennis* magazine, "The hardest part about coming back for her is not the tennis, not the other players, not the fans; it's the media." Worcester believes that only Capriati's drug arrest, not her accomplishments will be highlighted in everything written about her. *Tennis* magazine suggested that Capriati will have to find the right support group to accompany her on the tour to keep the pressure at bay. Stefano Capriati, now divorced from Jennifer's mother, Denise, traveled with Jennifer to Germany, but insisted that he was not pushing her. He told *Tennis*, "She will decide what it is she wants. Whatever she will decide, I will give. Whatever she needs, I give."

Capriati lost in the first round of the French Open in May 1996. *The Sporting News* reported that five days later, she had another brush with the law. Capriati was at a nightclub in Miami with her boyfriend. Police said she got into an argument with him and tried to punch him. Her boyfriend ducked, and Capriati accidentally hit a waitress. Club security turned her over to the police. The state attorney will determine if charges will be filed.

In late June, Capriati decided not to play Wimbledon—one of the biggest tournaments of the year. She withdrew due to lack of preparation, according to her spokesperson. Also, Capriati will not be able to defend her Barcelona Olympic gold medal in Atlanta because her current ranking of 104 is too low. The women's coach, Billie Jean King,

commented to *The Sporting News,* "I've told Jennifer all along, 'You've got no chance.'"

At 20 years old, Jennifer Capriati had won more tournaments and made more money in two years than most professional tennis players do in an entire career. Her success has also provided her with many options: she could take her money and pay for college and forget tennis; she could half-heartedly play a few tournaments a year, eventually leaving tennis; or she could come back and play tennis with everything she can muster because *she* wants it. Her true fans can only hope that she finds the courage and support she needs to live a normal life.

## Further Reading

*Detroit Free Press,* June 6, 1990; June 8, 1990; June 30, 1990; July 3, 1990; July 16, 1990; August 31, 1990; September 4, 1990; September 14, 1990.
*Fort Lauderdale News and Sun-Sentinel,* September 16, 1990; September 25, 1990.
*Los Angeles Times,* May 27, 1990.
*Newsweek,* May 14, 1990.
*New York Times,* March 5, 1990; May 20, 1990.
*People,* May 30, 1994.
*Sports Illustrated,* February 26, 1990; March 19, 1990; April 16, 1990.
*Tennis,* January, 1996; May, 1996.
*The Sporting News,* February 7, 1994; June 5, 1996; June 19, 1996.
*Time,* March 26, 1990. □

# Hattie Wyatt Caraway

**Elected to the U.S. Senate in early 1931 to complete her late husband's term, Hattie Wyatt Caraway (1878-1950) won election to a full six-year term in 1932 (and again in 1938) to become the first woman elected to the U.S. Senate in her own right.**

Hattie Wyatt Caraway was born on February 1, 1878, near Bakersville, Tennessee. When she was four years old, in 1882, her family moved to nearby Hustburg, Tennessee, where Hattie grew up working on the family farm and waiting on customers in her father's general store. A bright girl, she had already learned the alphabet before attending a nearby one-room school-house and entered Dickson (Tennessee) Normal College at the age of 14.

At Dickson she met Thaddeus Horatio Caraway, a fellow student several years older than she. She earned a B.A. degree in 1896. After graduation, Hattie, by now engaged to Thaddeus, set out to teach school. The couple married in 1902, after Thaddeus earned his law degree. They settled in Jonesboro, Arkansas, where Hattie gave birth to two sons, Paul Wyatt and Forrest, and managed the house while her husband established a legal and political career.

Thaddeus Caraway was elected to the United States Congress in 1912. While in Washington, D.C., Hattie gave birth to their third son, Robert Easley. She maintained their home in Washington, raising their children, seldom socializing outside the family, and leaving the business of politics to her husband. A Democrat, Thaddeus was elected to the Senate in 1920. A staunch supporter of his poor-white farm constituency, Thaddeus was reelected in 1926 but suffered a blood clot after kidney stone surgery and died unexpectedly in 1931, not completing his term.

Arkansas law required a special election to elect a senator to complete Caraway's term. In the interim Governor Harvey Parnell appointed Hattie to the post out of respect for her husband. Hattie Caraway entered the 72nd Congress in December 1931 with a commission from the governor to occupy her husband's Senate seat until the special election, called for January 1932.

The Arkansas Democratic Committee, unable to agree on a candidate for the special election, ended up nominating Hattie as a compromise. In Arkansas, part of the Democratic "Solid South," the Democratic nomination assured Hattie's election. Governor Parnell supported her with the understanding that she would step aside and make way for his candidacy in the election of 1932. In these strange circumstances Hattie Caraway became the first woman elected to the Senate. As an historic "first," this shy, quiet, at times awkward, 54-year-old housewife became the subject of enormous publicity. One journalist called her "one of the most visible women in America."

In sharp contrast to her voluble husband, Caraway would sit in the Senate chamber knitting or reading while

she listened politely to the endless speeches. Despite her apparent diffidence, she was determined to continue her husband's work, to vote, as he would have, in unswerving support of the interests of the poor farm people now suffering through the deepening Great Depression.

As the deadline approached in Arkansas to announce candidacy for the regular senatorial election in 1932, seven men, including Governor Parnell, prepared to run for "Fighting Thad" Caraway's Senate seat. They were dumbstruck when, at the very last moment, Hattie's application to run for the Senate arrived in Little Rock by special delivery. One opponent was quoted as saying that out of the estimated 300,000 votes, "she might receive 3,000" from feminists and personal friends.

Hattie found a powerful friend and champion in her neighbor in the Senate, the junior senator from Louisiana, Huey P. Long. Caraway supported Long's proposals for tax reform and redistribution of wealth to the farm poor. She launched her campaign with much fanfare but little success until Long arrived in Arkansas and in one week stumped with her across the state. Caraway visited 31 counties, giving 39 speeches and personally addressing more than 200,000 people. She won the Democratic primary, receiving 44.7 percent of the vote. In November 1932 Hattie Caraway became the first woman elected to a full six-year term in the United States Senate.

With a Democratic president in the White House, Senator Caraway worked devotedly if quietly in support of most of Franklin Roosevelt's New Deal programs. As a member of the Agriculture and Forestry Committee she was well positioned to help her people in Arkansas. "These are matters I know something about," she said. "You can tell by looking at me that I'm a farm woman."

In 1938 she edged out her opponent, whose slogan blatantly proclaimed, "Arkansas needs another man in the Senate," winning her second full term, this time without the aid of Huey Long, who had been assassinated in 1935. Caraway opposed Lend Lease for fear it would lead to war and defended local control against the president's policy to end the poll tax, which had disqualified many African-Americans in Arkansas from voting. But once World War II was declared she did much to help the grieving relatives of war victims and continued as one of Roosevelt's faithful backers.

Caraway lost the Democratic primary in her bid for a third term in 1944, but did not retire from politics. President Roosevelt named her to the Employees Compensation Commission and later to the Employees Compensation Appeals Board. Known forever as the first woman senator, if not for her forceful leadership, Senator Caraway's assessment of women in politics was characteristically simple and to the point. In 1943 she endorsed the Equal Rights Amendment (first introduced two decades earlier) by declaring, "There is no sound reason why women, if they have the time and ability, shouldn't sit with men on city councils, in state legislatures, and on Capitol Hill. Particularly if they have ability!" On December 22, 1950, Hattie Caraway suffered a stroke and died at the age of 72.

## Further Reading

For additional information on Hattie Caraway see Hope Chamberlin, *A Minority of Members: Women in the U.S. Congress* (1973); Diane D. Kincaid, ed., *Silent Hattie Speaks, the Personal Journal of Senator Hattie Caraway* (1979); George Creel, "The Woman Who Holds Her Tongue," *Colliers* (September 18, 1937); and Hermann B. Deutsch, "Hattie and Huey," *Saturday Evening Post* (October 15, 1932).

## Additional Sources

Caraway, Hattie Wyatt, *Silent Hattie speaks: the personal journal of Senator Hattie Caraway,* Westport, Conn.: Greenwood Press, 1979. ☐

# Martha Carey Thomas

**The American educator Martha Carey Thomas (1857-1935) was a proponent of woman's rights and president of Bryn Mawr.**

Carey Thomas was born in Baltimore, Md., on Jan. 2, 1857, the oldest of 10 children of Dr. James Carey Thomas and Mary Whitall Thomas. Both parents were active members of the Society of Friends. Her intellectual development was strongly influenced by the militant feminism of her mother and her aunt Hannah Whitall Smith, a renowned preacher and reformer.

After attending private schools, Carey Thomas entered Cornell, then the only eastern university admitting women, as a junior, graduating in 1877 as a member of Phi Beta Kappa. Although admitted to graduate study at Johns Hopkins University by special vote of the trustees, she was dissatisfied with the policy that prevented her from attending seminars. In 1879 she went to Germany to continue her philological studies. She spent 3 years at Leipzig, which refused to grant degrees to women, as did Göttingen, where she also tried. Finally Zurich accepted her dissertation, and her brilliant defense won her a doctorate *summa cum laude* in 1882.

In 1884 Carey Thomas accepted the post of dean and professor of English literature at Bryn Mawr, then about to open as a college for women. She desired to build it into an institution that would encourage women to follow careers without having to face the difficulties with which she had struggled. Convinced that women deserved exactly the same education as men and needed even higher standards than men to succeed, she molded a curriculum that offered more advanced work than that given in many men's colleges and upheld the highest academic standards. She helped recruit an outstanding faculty which permitted offering graduate work modeled after that at Johns Hopkins. In 1894 she became president of Bryn Mawr, a post she held until her retirement in 1922. Her addresses to the student body were vividly remembered by many alumnae, inspiring them to strive for success in the professional careers that she had done so much to open to them.

Carey Thomas also helped open the Johns Hopkins Medical School to women by raising substantial sums on condition that no sexual discrimination be followed. She was active in the fight for woman's suffrage, helped organize the Summer School for Women Workers in Industry, and was the first woman trustee of Cornell. She played a major role in the League to Enforce Peace.

Carey Thomas never married. She died in Philadelphia on Dec. 2, 1935.

## Further Reading

Barbara M. Cross, ed., *The Educated Woman in America* (1965), contains informative selections from Carey Thomas's addresses along with a perceptive introduction. An excellent biography, clearly presenting Carey Thomas's ideas and activities, is Edith Finch, *Carey Thomas of Bryn Mawr* (1947).

## Additional Sources

Horowitz, Helen Lefkowitz., *The power and passion of M. Carey Thomas,* New York: Alfred A. Knopf, 1994. ☐

# Hattie Carnegie

**Hattie Carnegie (1889-1956) was a prominent fashion dress designer in the United States during the 1930s.**

Hattie Carnegie, born Henrietta Kanengeiser in Vienna in 1889, was one of the premier dress designers of the 1930s. Not only did she make her mark through her elegant designs, she also trained a generation of fashion designers that shaped American style for decades. Carnegie started her career as a milliner. Her father, an artist and designer, introduced her to the world of fashion and design, and by age fifteen she had found work trimming hats. Five years later she opened a shop on East Tenth Street in New York called Carnegie—Ladies Hatter. The shop was successful, and within a few years she moved to the tony Upper West Side, where she took up dress design. However, she never learned to sew. A friend explained that "Hattie couldn't sew a fine seam, but she had a feeling about clothes and a personality to convey her ideas to the people who were to work them out." She changed the name of her business in 1914 to Hattie Carnegie, Inc., and by the 1920s was the toast of the fashion world from her new location in the Upper East Side.

### "Simple, Beautiful Clothes"

Carnegie's belief in simplicity fit perfectly with the streamlining of 1930s design. She believed that "simple, beautiful clothes . . . enhance the charm of the woman who wears them. If you have a dress that is too often admired, be suspicious of it." The dress, she insisted, must fit and not overpower the woman who wears it. She was unabashedly devoted to Paris fashion and made regular buying trips throughout the 1920s and 1930s. Yet while she was a self-declared Francophile, she adapted French style to American

tastes by offering a blend of style and comfort that suited many fashion-conscious Americans who still wanted their clothes to have a French flair.

## Designing for the Middle Class

Carnegie's expensive original designer clothes were out of reach for many Americans, but this did not limit her influence on American design. Hers were among some of the most widely copied designs by popularly priced designers. As the decade wore on, Carnegie added a modestly priced, ready-to-wear line of clothing that proved to be the most lucrative of her enterprises. She made her modestly priced clothes more available to the average consumer by permitting some department stores to carry the new line, breaking from her usual practice of selling her clothes at her own shop. This practice secured her influence over both haute couture and popular wear.

## Training a New Generation

Throughout the 1930s Carnegie's booming business attracted several young designers who trained under her. Norman Norell, Claire McCardell, Paula Trigére, Pauline De Rothschild, and Jean Louis, among others, spent years working under her tutelage. As her business grew, so did her interests. She added accessories, perfumes, chiffon handkerchiefs, silk hose, and cosmetics. By the 1940s Carnegie was well established as one of America's top designers.

### Further Reading

L. H., "Profiles: Luxury, Inc.," *New Yorker,* 10 (31 March 1934): 23-27.
Caroline Rennolds Milbank, *New York Fashion: The Evolution of American Style* (New York: Abrams, 1989). □

# Anna Ella Carroll

**Anna Ella Carroll (1815–1893) was a political writer and aid to Presidents Lincoln and Grant during the civil war and reconstruction. Her patriotism and diligence helped secure a victory for the north.**

On August 29, 1815, Anna Ella Carroll was born in a lavish, twenty-two-room manor called Kingston Hall, which rested on a large Maryland plantation stocked with cotton, wheat, and tobacco. Anna was a bright, blue-eyed baby with dark red curls and a fair complexion. She had in girlhood a fierce temper and an independent spirit, balanced with an equally strong tendency to shower her family with love. Her sense of independence would remain with her, carrying her through the adventures that lay ahead.

For generations, the Carrolls had been an influential family in America. Thomas King Carroll and Juliana Stevenson Carroll, Anna's parents, were extremely wealthy and well-respected people of the South. As a teenager, Juliana had been an accomplished organist for the Episcopal church. Thomas Carroll was a powerful lawyer whose partners included Francis Scott Key, the composer of America's national anthem. Anna Carroll's paternal grandfather, Charles Carroll, signed the Declaration of Independence. Her maternal grandfather, Doctor Henry Stevenson, served as an officer and a surgeon in the British navy during the Revolutionary War. He operated on Tory soldiers and American prisoners of war alike, earning the respect of men on both sides.

## Life at Kingston Hall

Anna Carroll was the first of eight children, only two of whom were boys. She soon became Anne to her family and friends, rarely using her real birthname, even in adulthood. Anne led a privileged life as a child, with a slave caretaker, Milly, to care for her every need from the time she was born. She also had a personal servant, a beautiful slave girl her own age named Leah, who tended her for many years. Anne and Leah became friends, yet they always observed the boundaries of their positions as mistress and servant.

From a very early age, Anne was the favorite of her well-educated father. In his eldest daughter, Thomas Carroll recognized the thirst for learning he had had as a boy. Proving that he did not subscribe to the popular notion that girls should not be educated, Thomas spent many hours reading Shakespeare's plays to his daughter. His readings continued as she grew older so that by the age of eleven she was reading with her father essays by the Scottish historian

Alison. By the age of twelve, Anne had learned to assist her father in his work by finding legal passages from his law books for use in his debates with Southern legislators.

## Father's secretary

In the spring of 1829, when Anne was thirteen, democrat Andrew Jackson was elected president, and Thomas ran for and was elected governor of Maryland by a Jackson-supporting legislature. His new position took him to Annapolis, Maryland, away from his family. Back at Kingston Hall, Anne took on new responsibilities as her father's secretary, screening visitors and answering letters on his behalf. She even started a book of newspaper clippings for him, selecting articles dealing with the ever-increasing tension between the Southern planters and the people in the North, whose views and life styles were very different. In the spring of 1831, Anne and her family traveled to Annapolis to visit Thomas. She was excited by this opportunity to observe firsthand the workings of the government.

Several years later, in 1837, after Thomas had returned home from his governorship, the nation fell into a terrible depression, and the Carrolls lost much of their fortune. The plantation and Kingston Hall were becoming too much to afford financially. Though they had at least 200 slaves to account for, they were not willing to sell them to slave traders who would separate the families that had been kept together. Luckily, a distant relative returning to the States from South America had enough money to buy the house and well over half the slaves. The remaining slaves went with the family to a smaller plantation, up the Choptank River, called Warwick Fort Manor.

## Off to Baltimore

After her family was settled in their new environment, Carroll decided it was time to leave home and try to make her own way in the world. Now twenty-two, she announced to her parents that she and Leah would head for Baltimore, Maryland, the second-largest city in the United States at the time. She hoped they could not only support themselves but have enough money left over to send back home.

Leah, a skilled seamstress, found employment almost immediately working for wealthy families in Baltimore. As she worked in their homes, she would listen carefully to their gossip about new businesses and bring the word directly to Anne. Anne learned to act quickly on Leah's leads, tracking down new business owners and using her writing ability to compose letters for mailing lists, generate publicity, and create advertising. Her public relations work soon earned her enough to send home a few extra dollars to her brothers and sisters. She worked steadily for seven years in Baltimore, making a name for herself as a skilled publicity writer.

## From railroads to politics

At the age of twenty-nine, Carroll began writing press releases for railroad companies in Baltimore. Her work for the railroads, as well as her family's strong political background, allowed her to easily slip into the world of politics that was so familiar to her. She became affiliated with the Whig party, meeting such people as the army chief of staff Winfield Scott. With Carroll, Scott discussed his war strategies in the invasion of Mexico, which resulted in the acquisition of California, New Mexico, and parts of Utah, Arizona, and Colorado.

Because of her acquaintance with Scott, Carroll began sitting in regularly at the visitors' gallery in the Senate, where she met many powerful men and future presidents, such as James Buchanan, whom she briefly dated. She also became close friends with Millard Fillmore in the early 1850s, shortly after he was sworn in as president following Zachary Taylor's death.

## Frees slaves

In the midst of her budding political career, Carroll had many discussions with Northern abolitionists about slavery. To satisfy her personal belief that slavery was wrong, Carroll freed all twenty of her slaves, whom she had inherited from her father. This was a dangerous move in 1853, a year in which any freed slaves were considered fair game for recapture. So Carroll used her political influence to persuade abolitionists to accompany her former slaves to safety in Canada.

## Confidante

In 1854 Fillmore began seeking Carroll out as a confidante and, because his first wife had died, as a possible second wife. But Carroll had a personal agenda to fulfill. She wanted to make an impact in the political world but not as the president's wife. Although she refused Fillmore's proposal, she continued to help him in his campaign for the presidency in 1856, which he lost to James Buchanan.

Also in 1856, Carroll met railroad mogul Cornelius Garrison. Her knowledge of railroads, which she had gained from writing press releases for various railroad companies, impressed Garrison so much that he hired her as an assistant planner for new railroad lines. Railroads, in fact, prompted Carroll to write her first major political essay, "The Star of the West," in which she discussed the importance of building railroad lines in order to keep the Union together and improve the economy.

"The Star of the West" was quite successful among Union supporters when it was published in 1856. Carroll's writing caught the interest of Republicans, many of them former Whigs, who shared her earnest desire for the Union to stay together. She met with Republican senators, wrote other pro-Union essays, and, in 1860, optimistically watched Abraham Lincoln sworn in as president of a nation divided by the argument over secession and slavery.

## Politics over marriage

When she was forty-five, Carroll became romantically involved with Lemuel Evans, a member of the secret service assigned to protect President Lincoln. Evans offered Carroll her second marriage proposal, which she refused. She was concentrating on her political writing at the time. Carroll began working on a new document, *Reply to Breckenridge*, in which she spoke out against the anti-Lincoln Southerners, headed by such people as Senator Samuel Breckenridge, who wanted the nation divided. She even touched on strategies for keeping the nation united. In one part of the *Reply*, Carroll stated, "There can be no equivocal position in this crisis; and he who is not with the Government is against it, and an enemy to his country" (Wise, p. 110). Her powerful writing caught Lincoln's eye and, in the summer of 1861, he not only demanded government funding to publish 50,000 copies of the manuscript and distribute them throughout the states, but he also sent Carroll a telegram inviting her to the White House for a confidential interview.

## A woman advises the president

Upon meeting Lincoln, Carroll was impressed by his loyalty to the Union, a sentiment which she fully shared. Although they had met in social situations before, this was the first time they were able to talk in depth about the state of the nation. Lincoln spoke frankly with Carroll about his need for her expert strategical mind and extensive political background. He had a war on his hands and he needed all the help Carroll could offer. Lincoln asked her to become an unofficial member of the Cabinet, acting as a top adviser to him, with access to the White House at any time of the day or night. She enthusiastically accepted the offer.

Carroll was immediately assigned to work directly with the Assistant Secretary of War Thomas Scott. Her first assignment was to travel by train to St. Louis, Missouri, to observe and report the general sentiment of the soldiers stationed along the Mississippi River. As a woman, she probably would not be suspected of being an informer to the president, for women in government were unheard of at the time. The trip proved to be a strenuous one for Carroll, with hours of traveling in hot, overcrowded railroad cars. The farther along the river she traveled, the more she discovered that hopes in the Union army were not high. Many of the soldiers confessed to her that the current plan of attack, to move down the Mississippi and take the Southern army head-on was simply too obvious. The Confederate army was ready and waiting at the mouth of the river. In the event that a Northern gunboat became disabled, it would float, with the southerly flowing current, right into the hands of the enemy. The soldiers feared that too many lives would be lost with this unimaginative battle plan.

By the time she arrived at her hotel in St. Louis, Carroll felt an impending sense of doom for the Union army. She knew that too much blood had been shed already and sought to hasten the end of the war. Under the light of an oil lamp, she studied the crude maps of the land for a better route, one that would take the South by surprise. After many hours, a brilliant alternative dawned on Carroll: the Tennessee River!

## The Tennessee River Plan

Carroll worked all night on her discovery, devising a plan that would cut the Southern forces in half by intercepting the very railroad lines she had helped design years earlier. The South was now using these lines to transport supplies to their troops. If troops could not get food and ammunition from the Charleston and Memphis railroads, they would be forced to surrender immediately. The Union army could use the Tennessee River to surprise the Confederate army from an angle they were not expecting. Moreover, the Tennessee River flowed north, so any troubled gunboats would float with the current back to the safety of the Northern army bases.

Carroll had masterminded an amazing plan, but she still had some crucial questions to answer: Was the Tennessee deep enough to hold gunboats? What were the water current speeds? Where were the points of landing? She wasted no time in seeking out a river pilot loyal to the North. Charles Scott knew the Tennessee River well and he gave Carroll the information she needed to ensure that her plan would succeed. He even pointed out that the Tombigbee River, which flowed directly to Mobile, Alabama, was a short distance from the middle of the Tennessee. With this information, Carroll added to her outline the taking of Mobile via the Tombigbee. Wasting no more time, she drew up a comprehensive version of the Tennessee River Plan, and sent one copy to the secretary of war and one to the president in mid-November 1861.

## "Relief, joy and hope"

According to Secretary of War Scott, when Lincoln received Carroll's proposed battle plan, he expressed "overwhelming relief, joy and hope" (Greenbie and Greenbie, p. 295). The president ordered the plan to go into effect as a military strategy in February 1862, keeping very silent about whose idea it was. Many gunboats under the command of Ulysses S. Grant were ordered up the Tennessee River and, within two weeks, two Confederate forts, 13,000 prisoners, and sixty-five guns were captured. The enormous success of the mission made people across the nation want to know who could have come up with such a successful scheme. There were rumors of a woman working in Washington, but Carroll's name was not leaked to the public. Meanwhile, Kentucky had been defeated, Tennessee was struggling, and, in accordance with Carroll's plans, Northern troops were heading for Vicksburg, Mississippi.

The war was far from over, however. As it raged on, Carroll continued to work side by side with Lincoln and Grant until the war's end in 1865. During the final months of war, Lincoln began planning the reconstruction of the country, with Carroll at his side offering advice.

On March 1, 1865, while Carroll and the president looked for ways to pick up the pieces of the shattered country, she received an anonymous letter from Fort Delaware. It read: "Madame: It is rumored in the Southern army that you furnished the plan or information that caused the United States Government to abandon the expedition designed to descend the Mississippi River, and transferred the armies up the Tennessee River in 1862. We wish to know if this is true. If it is, you are the veriest of traitors to your section, and we warn you that you stand upon a volcano. Confederates" (Greenbie and Greenbie, p. 415).

The warning worried Carroll, but everyone, it seemed, was receiving threats from bitter Confederates. She was never harmed in any way, unlike Lincoln. His plans for reconstruction were cut short with his assassination in April

1865. Exhausted from work and grief, Carroll was now fifty. Yet she by no means intended to quit the business of government simply because of the war's ending.

## Carroll advises Grant

Grant, with whom Carroll had communicated by telegraph from Washington many times when he was in the battlefield, was being backed by an overwhelming number of people for the office of the presidency. Grant asked Carroll to do what she did best—advise him from his post as general of the Union army to his job as president of the United States.

## The quest for recognition

Carroll needed Grant as much as he needed her. Feeling that the time had come for her to be officially recognized for her invaluable duties to the United States government, Carroll sought Grant's support. Also, she still had unpaid bills to printing companies, who printed copies of her speeches and pamphlets, equaling over $6,000. The Carroll family fortune had been used up, and Carroll had lived very modestly throughout her period of service to several presidents.

Carroll prepared a statement for Congress, "A Memorial," and published it on June 8, 1872. In it were quotes from some of the most influential men in government, who argued that she be given the recognition and monetary compensation she was rightly due. She quoted such statements as this one from Benjamin Wade, president of the Senate in 1869: "I know that some of the most successful expeditions of the war were suggested by you, among which I might instance the expedition up the Tennessee River. . . . I also know in what high estimation your services were held by President Lincoln . . . I [hope] that the Government may yet confer on you some token of acknowledgement for all these services and sacrifices" (Greenbie and Greenbie, pp. 436-37).

## Secret remains a secret

Carroll also had the backing of Thomas Scott and Lemuel Evans, who was now chief justice of the supreme court of Texas. To their testimonies, she added her own: "I cannot . . . detract from our brave and heroic commanders to whom the country owes so much; and . . . I believe that . . . they would be gratified to see me or anyone properly rewarded" (Wise, pp. 189-90). This may have been true, but unfortunately there were too many men in the government who wanted this secret of a woman military adviser to remain just that. They would not recognize her role in any official sense.

Although Grant knew the truth about Carroll's responsibility in the war, other top advisers chose to bury the truth and promote Grant as the real war hero. Grant did not argue with this decision, causing Carroll to lose her faith in her former friend. Her "Memorial" and other claims for recognition disappeared from government files several times over, drawing the process out for years. In fact, Carroll did not receive any promise of payment from the government until James A. Garfield was elected in 1880 and Congress

considered a bill demanding that Carroll receive back-pay as a major general in quarterly installments from November 1861 to the end of her life. However, this bill disappeared at the same time that Garfield was shot, and it was replaced with another in 1881, offering fifty dollars a month from the passage of this new bill until the end of Carroll's lifetime. This offer was financially incomparable to the salary of a major general, and an insult to such an important political figure. Nevertheless, Carroll had no choice but to accept it, for during her nine-year fight for recognition, she had grown ill and needed the money to take care of herself.

## Final days

Carroll and her younger sister, Mary, lived together in Washington, D.C., on Carroll's meager government pension. Under Mary's devoted care, Carroll continued her writing well after she was bedridden. In a room piled high with books and letters, next to a vase of fresh flowers Mary brought almost daily, Carroll enjoyed the last years of her life by a window that gave her a view of the West. She accepted visitors until her last days, including her long-time love, Lemuel Evans.

On the morning of February 19, 1893, Anna Ella Carroll died, surrounded by family and friends. In accordance with her wishes, she was buried in the churchyard of the Old Trinity Church in Cambridge, Massachusetts, next to her father, mother, and other members of the Carroll family. She remains revered by those who recognize her selfless devotion and vital contributions to her country.

## Further Reading

Greenbie, Sydney, and Marjorie Barstow Greenbie, *Anna Ella Carroll and Abraham Lincoln,* Tampa: University of Tampa Press, 1952.

Wise, Winifred E., *Lincoln's Secret Weapon,* New York: Chilton Company, 1961.

Young, Agatha, *The Women and the Crisis: Women of the North in the Civil War,* New York: McDowell, Obolensky, 1959. □

# Rachel Louise Carson

**Rachel Louise Carson (1907-1964) was an American biologist and writer whose book *Silent Spring* aroused an apathetic public to the dangers of chemical pesticides.**

Rachel Carson was born May 27, 1907, in Springdale, Pa. A solitary child, she spent long hours learning of field, pond, and forest from her mother. At college she studied creative writing and in 1932 obtained a master's degree in biology from the Johns Hopkins University. She did postgraduate studies at the Woods Hole Marine Biological Laboratory.

In 1936, Carson served as an aquatic biologist with the U.S. Bureau of Fisheries. After her first book, *Under the Sea Wind* (1941), she soon became editor in chief of the Fish and Wildlife Service, U.S. Department of the Interior. In 1951 *The Sea around Us* brought its author instant fame. At the top of the best-seller list for 39 weeks, it was translated into 30 languages. For it, the shy, soft-spoken Carson received the National Book Award, the Gold Medal of the New York Zoological Society, and the John Burroughs Medal.

The following year Carson left the government to undertake full-time writing and research. As a scientist and as an observant human being, she was increasingly disturbed by the overwhelming effects of technology upon the natural world. She wrote at the time: "I suppose my thinking began to be affected soon after atomic science was firmly established . . . It was pleasant to believe that much of Nature was forever beyond the tampering reach of man: I have now opened my eyes and my mind. I may not like what I see, but it does no good to ignore it."

When *Silent Spring* appeared in 1962, the lyric pen and analytical mind of Carson produced an impact equaled by few scientists; she aroused an entire nation. More than a billion dollars worth of chemical sprays was being sold and used in America each year. But when Carson traced the course of chlorinated hydrocarbons through energy cycles and food chains, she found that highly toxic materials, contaminating the environment and persisting for many years in waters and soils, also tended to accumulate in the human body. While target insect species were developing immunities to pesticides, because of these poisons birds were not reproducing. She proposed strict limitations on spraying

programs and an accelerated research effort to develop natural, biological controls for harmful insects.

The pesticide industry reacted with a massive campaign to discredit Carson and her findings. Firmly and gently, she spent the next 2 years educating the public at large: "I think we are challenged as mankind has never been challenged before to prove our maturity and our mastery, not of nature, but of ourselves." She died on April, 14, 1964, at Silver Spring, Md.

### Further Reading

The most authoritative book on Rachel Carson and the pesticide issue is Frank Graham, *Since Silent Spring* (1970). The references in the back of the book are recommended for up-to-date information on pesticides, their use, and control. ☐

# Mary Cassatt

**Mary Cassatt (1845-1926), an American painter, is considered a member of the French impressionist group. Best known for her series of paintings of a mother and child, she also portrayed fashionable society.**

Mary Cassatt was born in Pittsburgh, Pa., on May 23, 1845. As a child, she lived for a time in France. She studied at the Pennsylvania Academy of Fine Arts in Philadelphia. In 1866 she began her travels in Italy, Spain, and Holland, finally settling in Paris. There she exhibited at the Salon and met Edgar Degas, who was her real teacher, as she was his only pupil.

Despite her success at the Salon, Cassatt's sympathies lay with the impressionists, and in 1877 at Degas's suggestion she joined the group and exhibited with them in 1879. Her work sold well, particularly in Philadelphia, and she in turn bought paintings by the French impressionists. She also helped American friends, such as the Havemeyers, form their collections of impressionist paintings. Cassatt remained strongly American in her sentiments, as many expatriates do, and she wrote the American painter J. Alden Weir that "at some future time I shall see New York the artists' ground."

Cassatt's brother, Alexander, brought his family to Paris in 1880, the first of many trips. Although she never married, she was enchanted by her nieces and nephews and excelled in painting children, who dominate her subject matter. Her early work, done with the impressionists, is probably her best, but she remains known as the painter and poet of the nursery.

The paintings of Mary Cassatt, filled with light and joy, give a false impression of this strong-minded and somewhat difficult woman. She was at her best in her relations with other artists, for only in this environment did she consider herself among her intellectual equals. In later life she suffered from ill health and failing eyesight and was totally

general background see John Rewald, *The History of Impressionism* (1946; rev. ed. 1961). ☐

# Carrie Chapman Catt

**The American reformer Carrie Chapman Catt (1859-1947) designed the strategy for the final victory of the woman's-suffrage movement in 1920 and founded the League of Women Voters.**

Carrie Lane was born in Ripon, Wis., on Jan. 9, 1859. She was raised in Iowa and graduated from the state college. Her first husband died soon after their marriage, and 4 years later, in 1890, she married George Catt, a prosperous engineer. In 1895 she became chairman of the Organization Committee of the National American Woman Suffrage Association (NAWSA), and in 1900 she succeeded Susan B. Anthony as president of NAWSA. Her husband's ill health forced Catt to resign in 1904, but after his death the next year she returned to active service as president of the International Woman Suffrage Alliance. Later she assumed command of the New York woman's-suffrage movement, then struggling to win a statewide referendum authorizing the vote for women. Although the New York campaign was not completed until 1917, Catt's brilliant management of it made her the obvious choice to become president of NAWSA in 1915, when discontent with Dr. Anna Howard Shaw's faltering leadership forced her to step down.

Catt reorganized NAWSA, installed her own people in key positions, and in 1916 worked out a 6-year plan to secure a constitutional amendment that would enfranchise women. America's entry into World War I forced the issue. No doubt women would have gained the ballot some day, but they got it in 1920 mainly because of Catt. Under her direction the amendment was lobbied torturously through Congress and then, in the face of substantial opposition, through the state legislatures. The issue was in doubt until Tennessee, at the last minute, became the thirty-sixth state to ratify the 19th Amendment on Aug. 26, 1920.

Catt was notable for her intelligence, strength of character, and self-discipline. An effective speaker, a superb organizer, a diplomat and a politician, she converted NAWSA from a loose coalition of societies into a tightly knit political machine. She had pacifist inclinations and helped launch the Woman's Peace party, but she broke with it when American entry into World War I was imminent. By the same token, although she served on the Woman's Committee of the Council of National Defense during that war, she did only enough work to establish her credentials as a patriotic American. In both cases her first loyalty and best energies went to the suffrage movement.

In 1919 Catt founded the League of Women Voters as a vehicle for nonpartisan suffragists and as an instrument to advance those reforms for which women had sought the ballot. Later she fulfilled her early pacifist ambitions by

blind at her death. She died in her château at Mesnil-Beaufresne on June 14, 1926.

## Painting Style

Midway in her career Cassatt ceased to be an impressionist painter. Her early works have the delicacy, the atmospheric effects, the play of light and shadow associated with the style, but she never used broken color and her use of complementary colors was slight. Paintings like *La Lo* are indeed impressionist pictures and have the characteristic instantaneous effect of being caught out of the corner of the eye. But her paintings of mothers and children are fully realized and three-dimensional; the drawing is classical and complete; and the color, far from being light and separated into its component parts, is flat and sometimes rather acid, like the Japanese prints which influenced her so much. These careful figure studies, completely rendered, in no way reflect the infinite variety of nature or the passing world, as the paintings of the impressionists did; they exist entirely in the hothouse atmosphere of the nursery, with no sound except the little cries.

## Further Reading

The only thorough treatment of Mary Cassatt's life is Frederick A. Sweet's excellent *Miss Mary Cassatt, Impressionist from Pennsylvania* (1966). Sweet had access to family letters and papers that provide the basis for a new understanding of her character. Other biographies include Forbes Watson, *Mary Cassatt* (1932), and Julia M. H. Carson, *Mary Cassatt* (1966). For

establishing a Committee on the Cause and Cure of War, which was the largest of the women's peace groups during the 1920s. A lifelong internationalist, she supported both the League of Nations and the United Nations. Unlike many feminists, Catt was not discouraged by the modest gains women made after receiving the vote. She never thought that enfranchising women would revolutionize the human condition, and as long as her strength held out she continued to work for social justice and social welfare in a variety of fields. She died on March 9, 1947.

### Further Reading

The only biography of Catt is Mary G. Peck, *Carrie Chapman Catt* (1944). The fact that the author was a friend and colleague of Catt for 40 years gives the book a special authority, but a full study of this important woman based on the extensive documentary material now available is needed. Carrie C. Catt and Nettie R. Shuler, *Woman Suffrage and Politics* (1923), is informative since it draws on some of Mrs. Catt's own experiences. Volumes 4 (1903), 5 (1922), and 6 (1922) of the *History of Woman Suffrage*, edited by Ida H. Harper, contain much useful material. □

# Linda Chavez

**Hispanic American civil rights activist Linda Chavez (born 1947) gained political attention for her conservative view that government policies such as affir-**mative action do a disservice to Hispanics and other minorities by perpetuating racial stereotypes. Originally a Democratic supporter, her ideas about civil rights and education reform were embraced by the Republican administration of president Ronald Reagan in the 1980s. After an unsuccessful bid for public office herself, Chavez became a prominent political commentator with writings such as her 1991 book, *Out of the Barrio: Toward a New Politics of Hispanic Assimilation.*

Driven by a desire to destroy negative stereotypes of Hispanic minorities in America as helpless, illiterate, and impoverished, activist Linda Chavez has fought to do away with government attitudes and programs that treat Hispanics as a homogenous unit. However, the conservative remedies she has supported, including the elimination of affirmative action and racial quota systems in various areas of society, have met with hostility from liberal politicians and civil rights activists in the Hispanic community. Originally a Democrat, Chavez switched her affiliation after finding more support for her ideas in the administration of Republican President Ronald Reagan, where she served as an advisor and White House staff member in the 1980s. Although her own attempt to win elected office was unsuccessful, as a political commentator and writer she has remained a prominent figure in the national debate on racial policy.

Chavez was born into a middle-class family in Albuquerque, New Mexico, on June 17, 1947. Her parents, both devout Catholics, came from different racial backgrounds; her mother was Anglo-American and her father was Hispanic. Racial prejudice was not a concern of her early years. The city of Albuquerque was predominately Hispanic, and so she did not encounter difficulties because of her race there. Her father was proud of his heritage as a descendant of seventeenth-century Spanish settlers and also took pride in his country, which he served as a soldier during World War II. But these were qualities that were considered part of private life, not subjects for the public sphere. Her father's quiet approach to his racial identity was influential in Chavez's own ideas later in her life.

## Saw Reform Possibilities in Education

Chavez first came into contact with racial prejudice when her family moved to Denver, Colorado, when she was nine. The negative attitudes about minorities that she witnessed there inspired her to join in civil rights movements supporting the causes of Hispanics, African Americans, and women when she was a teenager. She also became to determined to excel in her schoolwork in order to overcome the low expectations of her as a Hispanic. After graduating from high school, she attended the University of Colorado, where she decided to pursue a career in teaching. Having tutored some Mexican American students through the college, she knew that teaching was a sometimes difficult job, but one that could play an important role in social reform. During her undergraduate studies, she was married to Christopher Gersten in 1967, but kept her maiden name. In 1970, she graduated from the University of Colorado with a bachelor's degree.

Chavez went on to the University of California at Los Angeles (UCLA), where she began a graduate program in English literature. She soon became frustrated, however, with the way she was treated by faculty and students because she was Hispanic. In one particularly negative experience, Chavez was given the task of teaching a course on Chicano literature, even though she initially resisted because of the lack of published material in the area. When the department insisted she go through with the course, she put together an appropriate reading list, but found many students in her class were unwilling to read the books or pay attention during her lectures. This disheartening situation reached a peak when some students she had failed in the course vandalized her home in an act of vengeance. Chavez left the university in 1972 and moved to Washington, D.C., with her husband.

## Active in Education Issues

In the nation's capital, Chavez did not return to teaching but did remain active in educational issues. She worked with the National Education Association (NEA), the largest teachers' union in the country, and served as a consultant on education to the federal government's Department of Health, Education, and Welfare. In addition, she became an active member of the Democratic National Committee, participating in the promotion of a number of liberal causes.

She eventually landed a position with the nation's second-largest teachers' union, the American Federation of Teachers (AFT), which was known as an influential force in education policy. Chavez became a well-known voice on the topic of education reform in her role as editor of the AFT's publication, *American Educator.* She began to attract notice among conservative politicians in Washington with her editorials calling for a renewed emphasis on traditional educational standards. Throughout the 1970s, Chavez also became increasingly dissatisfied with liberal views on the position of minorities in America. In her personal experience, she felt that liberals sought her out simply because of her symbolism as a Hispanic, not for her own ideas. Similarly, she felt that national programs that did not allow minorities to advance based on their own merits, but gave them financial assistance or employment preference solely because of their race, was demeaning. Hispanics should not be stereotyped as helpless minorities who could not get ahead without government aid, but should be encouraged to succeed through individual effort, she maintained.

With the election of Ronald Reagan to the presidency in 1980, Chavez found growing sympathy for her ideas among conservatives. She became a consultant for the Reagan administration in 1981, and in 1983 she was appointed by the president to serve as director of the U.S. Commission on Civil Rights. The commission was a nonpartisan body responsible for evaluating the government's success in implementing and upholding civil rights laws. Chavez criticized certain aspects of the country's civil rights laws, however, and strongly denounced the affirmative action programs that had been designed to ensure that minorities were represented in certain fields of employment. While she argued that her goal was to foster an unprejudiced environment that evaluated individuals solely by their ability, regardless of race, liberal activists accused her of supporting Republican efforts to dismantle the government's role in ensuring civil rights to minorities.

## Views Supported by Republicans

Finding herself lacking support from most Hispanic activists and Democrats, Chavez officially joined the Republican Party after being hired onto Reagan's White House staff in 1985. As director of the Office of the White House Public Liaison, she was the most powerful woman on the staff. Her position gave her an increased level of influence with the president, and she also worked to lobby Congress and a variety of public groups to accept administration policies. She left this post after less than a year's time in order to run a campaign in Maryland for a U.S. Senate seat. Republican Party officials were enthusiastic about her run for senator, hoping that her image as a Hispanic, woman, and married mother of three children would win votes away from the single, white Democratic contender, Barbara Mikulski.

But Republican hopes that Maryland's primarily Democratic voters would abandon their party preference for a more conservative candidate were unrealized. The state's citizens were distrustful of Chavez's short residence in Maryland and her shift in political philosophy. Behind in the polls, the Republicans began a negative campaign, during which Chavez further alienated voters when she criticized Mikulski's unmarried status and her staff insinuated that the Democrat had ties to lesbian groups. After a major defeat on election day, Chavez decided to remove herself from the political arena.

## Book Fuels Debate on Race

She returned to social and educational issues by becoming president of the organization U.S. English. The nonprofit group's aim was to gain the official recognition of English as the national language. After discovering the prejudices against Catholics and Hispanics of the founder of U.S. English, however, she resigned in 1988. Over the coming years, Chavez established herself as policy expert and political commentator. The Manhattan Institute for Policy Research, a conservative think-tank, made her a fellow, and she became a regular contributor of editorials on politics to periodicals. She also published a book on her ideas, *Out of the Barrio: Toward a New Politics of Hispanic Assimilation* in 1991, bringing her renewed attention from politicians and the press. The work reaffirmed her belief that affirmative action and other programs that focused on the lower socio-economic levels of Hispanic society created an unrealistic and unflattering picture of Hispanics as a group. As had been the case throughout her career, Chavez's words were controversial with many, but nonetheless had the effect of bringing about serious discussions about the state of the nation's attitude toward minorities. She was the focus of a number of book reviews and also gained the national spotlight when she appeared on television programs such as *The McNeil/Lehrer News Hour.*

Despite the criticism she has received from many liberal and Hispanic American groups for her conservative views, Chavez has emerged as one of the most visible and influential figures fighting for civil rights and educational reforms. Her thought and example as a successful political personality has made her a role model for some in the Hispanic community, inspiring a growing number of politicians in the minority group to join the Republican Party in the 1990s. Chavez's insistence that racial equity cannot be accomplished by government policies based on stereotypes has given the American public and its leaders additional considerations in the debate on government's role in the welfare of minorities.

## Further Reading

See also Arias, Maria, "Making People Mad," *Hispanic,* August 1992, pp. 11-16; Brimelow, Peter, "The Fracturing of America," *Forbes,* March 30, 1992, pp. 74-75; Chavez, Linda, *Out of the Barrio: Toward a New Politics of Hispanic Assimilation,* Basic Books, 1991; Grenier, Jeannin, "The Women Versus Woman Race," *Ms.,* November 1986, p. 27; and Telgen, Diane, and Jim Kamp, editors, *Notable Hispanic American Women,* Gale Research, 1993. □

# Judy Chicago

**Judy Chicago (born 1939) was an American artist and activist best known for large-scale collaborative installation artworks—*The Dinner Party* and *The Birth Project*—both based on feminist themes and *The Holocaust Project*—based on the atrocities committed by the Nazi Party during World War II.**

Judy Chicago was born Judith Cohen in Chicago, July 20, 1939. She assumed the surname of her hometown in 1969 to assert her independence from the patrilineal convention which gives a woman the surname of a father or husband. The daughter of political activists, her father was a union organizer, and her mother was a professional in a time when women working outside of the home were rare. Chicago studied at the Art Institute of California and later at the University of California at Los Angeles. Married three times, the artist lived and worked in Benicia, California.

Judy Chicago first gained recognition in the 1960s as Judith Gerowitz and did large, highly crafted sculptures of simple geometric forms that could be termed "minimalist." Eschewing the more traditional sculptural media of bronze and stone, Chicago worked in a variety of materials: painting on porcelain, airbrush painting on automobile hoods, and using fireworks to make drawings in the air. From the early 1970s her work focused on feminist themes, often using the motif of a flower or butterfly to symbolize a woman's sexuality and incorporating conversational language written directly on the artwork. Her work was always noted for its high level of technical finish. In addition to her artwork, Chicago taught college art classes, established the first feminist art programs and galleries, and very notably started *Womenspace,* an all-female art collective.

## Controversy at the Dinner Party

Chicago is best known for three ambitious projects— *The Dinner Party,* completed in 1979, *The Birth Project,* completed in 1985, and *The Holocaust Project,* completed in 1993. The first two works summarized her stance as a feminist artist and her conviction that women have been left out of the telling of history. These projects were collaborations in which Chicago worked with teams of women artists and craftspeople in materials traditionally associated with women: quilting, needlework, china painting, and tapestry.

The *Dinner Party* took two years of work with a crew of 400 people. It was a three-sided table forming a triangle along which were 39 place settings with plate, goblet, and embroidered cloth. Each setting symbolized an illustrious woman from history or mythology ranging from a primordial goddess to the American painter Georgia O'Keefe. On the floor inside the triangular table were the names of 999 more women. Each place setting contained symbols of the woman, often derived from a flower-motif suggesting a vagina. The artwork opened at the San Francisco Museum of Art in 1979 and toured the United States, also being shown at the Brooklyn Museum. *The Dinner Party* met controversy and mixed critical response wherever it went, being variously described as visionary and Utopian or as obscene and overly didactic. Several museums withdrew offers to show the work in spite of record attendance rates, and Chicago drew criticism for perceived careerism and exploitation of her numerous volunteers.

## Explorations into Birth and Death

Chicago's next major work was *The Birth Project.* Intended to celebrate the act of giving birth, which she observed is rarely treated in Western art while being common in the art of other cultures, it also drew controversy from male-based mainstream culture. Unlike *The Dinner Party,* this project was two-dimensional and consisted of approximately 100 needlework designs that summarized the birthing process as culled from interviews she conducted with women from around the country regarding their experiences giving birth. Chicago made this artwork, like *The Dinner Party,* a collaboration that challenged the idea of the artist as an isolated, individual creator. Begun in 1982, the needlework designs were executed by women from the United States, Canada, and New Zealand.

Chicago has also produced, with her third husband, Donald Woodman, a project confronting the horror of Nazi inflicted genocide during World War II. *The Holocaust Project* is described by Chicago as being her personal record of trying to understand this awful epoch of recent history. A multimedia piece consisting of painting, photography, needlework, silk-screen, tapestry, and stained glass, Chicago and Woodman spent over two years re-

searching and visiting key sites of the Holocaust in Europe. 1993 saw the completion of this ambitious and rather uncomfortable project.

## Late Nineties, Continued Shock

Into the nineties Chicago still incited controversy and outrage with her works. A 1990 attempt to find a permanent home for *The Dinner Party* at the University of the District of Columbia, was thwarted when she encountered much of the same opposition as before. A later exhibition in 1996 of *The Dinner Party* at the Armand Hammer Museum of Art at UCLA drew further criticism. As David Joselit wrote in *Art in America,* "ongoing theoretical and artistic disputes, not to mention the hostility of mainstream critics to an openly feminist project, conspired to engulf (the exhibition) in an often mean-spirited buzz of disapproval."

Despite the controversy surrounding them, these projects were immensely popular, but usually with audiences that do not regularly follow the arts. This populist appeal coincided with a general resurgence of feminist activity in the 1970s. Chicago's work was part of the movement within art circles to open up opportunities for women artists and to reinstate prominent artists such as Angelica Kauffman (1741-1807) and Artemesia Gentileschi (1590-1642) who had been written out of art history. In addition, museums organized retrospective exhibitions for contemporary artists Alice Neel and Louise Bourgeois.

Beyond the feminist aspects of Chicago's work, it also ran parallel with several aesthetic tendencies of the visual art of the 1960s. Artists in general were experimenting with all kinds of materials, challenging the conventional expectations of a work of art. Artists such as Claes Oldenburg and Robert Morris began to work with fabric and cloth. Sculpture could be soft, amorphous, and impermanent. Chicago's projects were collaborative and involved hundreds of people, like the wrapping projects of artist Christo, and went against the prevailing myth of the artist as an alienated loner. Judy Chicago's work called into question distinctions between high art (painting and sculpture) and crafts, between art made for its own sake and engaged activist art in the service of political ideas. It generated a great deal of critical discussion, and she had both ardent admirers and strident detractors.

## Further Reading

Chicago wrote an autobiography, *Through the Flower, My Struggles as a Woman Artist* (1982), which chronicled her emergence as an artist and her involvement with the women's movement in the early 1970s. A sequel, *Beyond the Flower* was later written (1996). She had a retrospective exhibition in 1984 at the ACA galleries in New York accompanied by a catalog, *Judy Chicago, the Second Decade* (1984), which is the most complete record of her work up to that point. Chicago has also published books detailing her more recent works including *The Birth Project* (1985) and *The Holocaust Project: From Darkness into Light* (1993). Her joint exhibition with other female artists such as Yoko Ono and Mary Kelly is documented in *Sexual Politics: Judy Chicago's Dinner Party in Feminist Art History* (1996). Articles about *The Dinner Party* appeared in *Newsweek Magazine* (April 2, 1979), *Ms.* (June 1, 1979), and *Art in America* (April 1980). *Newsweek* also carried an article about *The Birth Project* (October 31, 1983), as did *Art in America* (November 1984). Later articles include pieces in *The New Statesman and Society* (March 25, 1994), *New York Times Book Review* (March 24, 1996), and *Art in America* (January 1997). A profile of Chicago is included in Eleanor Munro's *Originals: American Women Artists* (1979). For more information about women artists in history, see Anne Sutherland Harris' *Women Artists 1550-1950* (1976). ☐

## Julia McWilliams Child

**Chef, author, and television personality, Julia McWilliams Child (born 1912) probably did more for French-style food preparation than any other gourmet in history.**

Julia Child was born to a well-to-do family in Pasadena, California, on August 15, 1912. Her parents, John and Julia McWilliams, raised Julia, her sister, and her brother in comfort; the family had servants, including a cook, and the children were sent to private schools. The children, all of whom were unusually tall, loved outdoor sports. In 1930 Julia went to Smith College in Massachusetts, where she majored in history. After graduation she took a job as a copywriter for a furniture company in New York City and enjoyed an active social life.

At the outbreak of World War II she joined the Office of Strategic Services, predecessor to the Central Intelligence Agency, seeking adventure in exotic locales. After a stint in Washington she was sent abroad as she had wished, but she worked as a file clerk, not as a spy, and her experience was distinctly unglamorous—she traveled on troop ships, slept on cots, and wore army fatigues. While in Ceylon (now Sri Lanka) in 1943 she met Paul Cushing Child, a member of a distinguished Boston family. Although his particular branch of the family was not rich, he had traveled widely, pursued several careers, and, at 41, was a sophisticated artist working as a cartographer and as the designer of Lord Mountbatten's headquarters. Although she was ten years younger and several inches taller, the two were immediately attracted to each other. He admired her unaffected manner, and she found his affectionate nature and cosmopolitan outlook irresistible. The romance bloomed when both were assigned to China, and it was while there that Child, a noted gourmet, introduced her to cooking.

Although they were in love, Julia and Paul were reluctant to commit to a permanent relationship during wartime. After the war she returned to California, where her conservative Republican father was unenthusiastic about her new beau, who was artistic and a Democrat. She was undeterred, however, and she began to study cooking at a school in Beverly Hills. On September 1, 1946, Julia and Paul were married, and the couple moved to Washington, D.C., where he had taken a position with the Foreign Service.

In 1948 her husband was posted to Paris. Child quickly came to appreciate the French way of life, especially French food. She decided she wanted to learn the intricacies of French cooking and, after studying French at the Berlitz School, enrolled at the famous Cordon Bleu. She made many friends who also were interested in French cuisine, and with two of these, Simone Beck and Louisette Bertholle, she formed a cooking school called L'Ecole des Trois Gourmandes (School of the Three Gourmets).

With Simone Beck, Child began working on a cookbook based on their cooking school experiences, and she continued her writing while she followed her husband on several postings throughout Europe. He retired in 1961, and the Childs settled in a large house with a well-equipped kitchen in Cambridge, Massachusetts.

The year 1961 was a landmark year for the Childs. In addition to her husband's retirement and a major move, Child's book, *Mastering the Art of French Cooking*, was published. The book, noted for the clarity and completeness of its instructions, its attention to detail and explanation, and its many useful photographs, was an immediate critical and popular success. Child was hailed as an expert and her views and advice were much sought after. She began writing articles on cooking for *House and Garden* and *House Beautiful* and also had a regular cooking column in the *Boston Globe*.

In 1963, after an enjoyable appearance on a television panel show in Boston, Child expanded her efforts in television with a weekly 30-minute cooking program, "The French Chef." This proved even more successful than her book: with her admittedly eccentric style, good humor, knowledge, and teaching flair, she became a popular cult figure. Her work was recognized with a Peabody Award in 1965 and an Emmy Award in 1966.

*The French Chef Cookbook,* a cookbook based on the television series, was published in 1968. Additional television shows, notably "Julia Child and Company" (1978-1979), "Julia Child and More Company" (1980), and "Dinner at Julia's" (1983), were accompanied by well-received cookbooks, and in the 1970s and 1980s Child wrote regular columns for *McCalls* and *Parade* magazines and made frequent appearances on "Good Morning America" on ABC. In addition, she was a founder of the American Institute of Wine and Food, an association of restaurants dedicated to the advancement of knowledge about food and wine. In 1989 *The Way to Cook,* a lengthy cookbook dealing with both basic and advanced subjects, was published, and at age 77 Child happily undertook an extended tour to promote it. She recognized the need for advertisement and frankly enjoyed the attention: "You've got to go out and sell it," she declared. "No sense spending all that time—five years on this one—and hiding your light under a bushel. . . . Besides, I'm a ham."

Late in 1989 her husband suffered a stroke and had to be moved to a nursing home near Cambridge. She visited daily and called frequently, but found life without her constant companion lonely. Accordingly, she kept busy with a regular exercise routine, lecturing, writing, and working on television programs. She even provided a cartoon voice for a children's video. In 1992 her television show, "Cooking with the Master Chefs," was produced and in 1993 the accompanying cookbook was published. In August 1992, 170 guests paid $100 or more to attend her 80th birthday party (proceeds to the American Institute of Food and Wine). And her place as a gastronomic icon was assured when she became the first woman to be inducted into the Culinary Institute Hall of Fame in October 1993.

Child lost her lifelong friend and career partner when her husband died in 1994. Not long after that she was quoted as saying that she had nothing left to write. Nonetheless the years 1995 and 1996 each brought a new book and TV series combination from the indefatigable Child: *In Julia's Kitchen with Master Chefs* (1995), and *Baking with Julia* (1996). In 1997 she celebrated her 85th birthday, once again with a fund raiser for the American Institute of Food and Wine. This one-woman dynamo continues to host an annual luxury tour to Italy for food buffs

Although a staunch advocate of classic French cuisine, Child in the course of her career modified her approach to cookery to reflect contemporary needs and trends, such as developing a repertoire requiring less fat, red meat, and time. Above all, she supported a sensible approach to eating characterized by moderation and including all types of food. She rejected what she called "food fads," which she held responsible for widespread unhealthy attitudes toward eating in the United States. In her work she endeavored consistently and successfully to enhance the public's awareness and appreciation of, and need for, wholesome, skillfully prepared food.

## Further Reading

The best single source of biographical information on Julia Child is contained in Mary Ellen Snodgrass' *Late Achievers: Famous People Who Succeeded Late in Life* (1992). Snodgrass' chapter on Julia Child is well-balanced and well-researched. A brief, breezily-written and appreciative sketch of Julia Child and her career is contained in Gregory Jaynes' "A Holiday Bird and a Free-Range Chat with Julia" (*LIFE,* December 1989). For a glimpse of the Childs at home, see Charles Grandee, "Grandee at Large: Julia Child—Still Cooking at 76," in *House and Garden* (June 1989). Julia's relationship with Paul Child is explored in Roberta Wallace Coffey's "Julia and Paul Child" (*McCalls,* October 1988), which also contains interesting information on Paul's background and career. In an interview, "Eat, Drink, and Be Sensible" (*Newsweek,* May 27, 1991), Julia Child explains her views on food and the goals of her career.

## Additional Sources

*Entertainment Weekly,* December 10, 1993.
*Town & Country Monthly ,* December 1994.
*The Wine Spectator* June 30, 1997.
*Forbes,* May 5, 1997. ☐

# Lydia Maria Francis Child

**The popularity and moral force of the American author Lydia Maria Francis Child (1802-1880) contributed to the impact radical abolitionists exerted on the antislavery debate that preceded the Civil War.**

Lydia Maria Francis was born in Medford, Mass., of an old New England family, on Feb. 11, 1802, and revealed early her sensibilities and intelligence. Her novels of pioneer life, *Hobomok* (1824) and *The Rebels* (1825), opened a literary career for her. *Juvenile Miscellany,* an annual that she instituted in 1826, pioneered in its field, and her later publications appealed to girls and wives. In 1828 she married David Lee Child, a Harvard College graduate who had capped an idealistic, adventurous youth by becoming a lawyer. As a state legislator and editor of the *Massachusetts Journal,* he seemed on a successful path.

Both were converted to abolitionism by William Lloyd Garrison, but it was Lydia who most startled conventional circles with her *Appeal in Favor of That Class of Americans Called Africans* (1833). This tract made abolitionists of such noteworthy persons as the Reverend William Ellery Channing and Charles Sumner. It also, however, closed various social circles to her and caused her book sales to fall. Her *Juvenile Miscellany* suspended, she pressed on as author and abolitionist. She published several abolitionist compilations, as well as biographies of notable women and the groundbreaking *History of the Condition of Women in Various Ages and Nations* (1835). Her husband introduced beet sugar manufacture in the United States and penned important abolitionist pamphlets. However, he was impractically dedicated to agricultural experiments, and his wife was required to manage their often-constricted finances.

In 1840 Child assumed the editorship of the *National Anti-Slavery Standard,* representing Garrison in New York. While there she wrote *Letters from New York* (1843, 1845), which contained much of contemporary interest. Her husband joined her in the work in 1843. The next year, embittered by factional differences between abolitionists, she returned to private life, settling in Wayland, Mass. Among her later books was *Progress of Religious Ideas through Successive Ages* (1855), which once more broke ground in its religious liberalism.

When John Brown was wounded in the raid on Harpers Ferry, Va., in 1859, Child asked permission to nurse him; this resulted in an exchange of letters which were read nationwide. *Correspondence between Lydia Maria Child and Gov. Wise and Mrs. Mason of Virginia* (1860) exhibited her abolitionist prose at its strongest.

Child's later writings struck a summary note, as in *Looking toward Sunset* (1864). Many of her works were outmoded, but her own character evoked admiration. She survived her husband 6 years, dying on July 7, 1880. A memorial volume, *Letters* (1883), was introduced by John Greenleaf Whittier and included Wendell Phillips's funeral address.

### Further Reading

Two biographies of Child are Helene G. Baer, *The Heart Is like Heaven: The Life of Lydia Maria Child* (1965), and Milton Meltzer, *Tongue of Flame: The Life of Lydia Maria Child* (1965). She is discussed in numerous works, including Thomas Wentworth Higginson, *Contemporaries* (1899), and

Margaret Farrand Thorp, *Female Persuasion: Six Strong-minded Women* (1949). Her works are described in volume 2 of Jacob Blanck, *Bibliography of American Literature* (1957).

### Additional Sources

Clifford, Deborah Pickman, *Crusader for freedom: a life of Lydia Maria Child,* Boston: Beacon Press, 1992.
Karcher, Carolyn L., *The first woman in the republic: a cultural biography of Lydia Maria Child,* Durham: Duke University Press, 1994. □

# Alice Childress

**Alice Childress (1920–1994) is an author whose writing is characterized by its frank treatment of racial issues. Because her books and plays often deal with such subjects as miscegenation and teenage drug addiction, her work can be controversial.**

Alice Childress's work is noted for its frank treatment of racial issues, its compassionate yet discerning characterizations, and its universal appeal. Because her books and plays often deal with such controversial subjects as miscegenation and teenage drug addiction, her work has been banned in certain locations. She recalls that some affiliate stations refused to carry the nationally televised broadcasts of *Wedding Band* and *Wine in the Wilderness,* and in the case of the latter play, the entire state of Alabama banned the telecast.

Childress notes in addition that as late as 1973 her young adult novel *A Hero Ain't Nothin' but a Sandwich* "was the first book banned in a Savannah, Georgia school library since *Catcher in the Rye,* which the same school banned in the fifties." Along with other contemporary and classical works, *A Hero Ain't Nothin' but a Sandwich* has been at the center of legal battles and court decisions over attempts to define obscenity and its alleged impact on readers. Among the most famous cases was *Board of Education, Island Trees Union Free School District v. Pico* (102 S. Ct. 2799) in which a Stephen Pico, then a high school student, and others sued the Board on the grounds that their First Amendment Rights had been denied. The case became the first ever of this type to be heard in the U.S Supreme Court. Justice Brennan found for the plaintiffs, having determined that a school board's rights were limited to supervising curriculum, but not the general content of a library. Despite special-interest groups' growing resistance to controversial subjects in books, Childress's writing continues to win praise and respect for being, as a *Variety* reviewer terms, "powerful and poetic."

A talented writer and performer in several media, Childress has commented about the variety of genres in which she writes: "Books, plays, tele-plays, motion picture scenarios, etc., I seem caught up in a fragmentation of writing skills. But an idea comes to me in a certain form and, if it stays with me, must be written out or put in outline form before I can move on to the next event. I sometimes wonder about writing in different forms; could it be that women are used to dealing with the bits and pieces of life and do not feel as [compelled to specialize]? The play form is the one most familiar to me and so influences all of my writing—I think in scenes.''

In an autobiographical sketch for Donald R. Gallo's *Speaking for Ourselves,* Childress shares how theater has influenced her fiction writing: ''When I'm writing, characters seem to come alive; they move my pen to action, pushing, pulling, shoving, and intruding. I visualize each scene as if it were part of a living play. . . . I am pleased when readers say that my novels feel like plays, because it means they are very visual.''

Alice Childress began her career in the theater, initially as an actress and later as a director and playwright. Although ''theater histories make only passing mention of her, . . . she was in the forefront of important developments in that medium,'' writes *Dictionary of Literary Biography* contributor Trudier Harris. Rosemary Curb points out in another *Dictionary of Literary Biography* article that Childress's 1952 drama *Gold through the Trees* was ''the first play by a black woman professionally produced on the American stage.'' Moreover, Curb adds, ''As a result of successful performances of [her 1950s plays *Just a Little Simple* and *Gold through the Trees*], Childress initiated Harlem's first all-union Off-Broadway contracts recognizing the Actors Equity Association and the Harlem Stage Hand Local.''

Partly because of her pioneering efforts, Childress is considered a crusader by many. But she is also known as ''a writer who resists compromise,'' says Doris E. Abramson in *Negro Playwrights in the American Theatre: 1925-1959.* ''She tries to write about [black] problems as honestly as she can.'' The problems Childress addresses most often are racism and its effects. Her *Trouble in Mind,* for example, is a play within a play that focuses on the anger and frustration experienced by a troupe of black actors as they try to perform stereotyped roles in a play that has been written, produced, and directed by whites. As Sally R. Sommer explains in the *Village Voice,* ''The plot is about an emerging rebellion begun as the heroine, Wiletta, refuses to enact a namby-Mammy, either in the play or for her director.'' In the *New York Times,* Arthur Gelb states that Childress ''has some witty and penetrating things to say about the dearth of roles for [black] actors in the contemporary theatre, the cutthroat competition for these parts and the fact that [black] actors often find themselves playing stereotyped roles in which they cannot bring themselves to believe.'' And of *Wedding Band,* a play about an interracial relationship that takes place in South Carolina during World War I, Clive Barnes writes in the *New York Times,* ''Childress very carefully suggests the stirrings of black consciousness, as well as the strength of white bigotry.''

Critics Sommer and the *New York Times*'s Richard Eder find that Childress's treatment of the themes and issues in *Trouble in Mind* and *Wedding Band* gives these plays a timeless quality. ''Writing in 1955, . . . Alice Childress used the concentric circles of the play-within-the-play to examine the multiple roles blacks enact in order to survive,'' Sommer remarks. She finds that viewing *Trouble in Mind*

years later enables one to see ''its double cutting edge: It predicts not only the course of social history but the course of black playwriting.'' Eder states: ''The question [in *Wedding Band*] is whether race is a category of humanity or a division of it. The question is old by now, and was in 1965, [when the play was written,] but it takes the freshness of new life in the marvelous characters that Miss Childress has created to ask it.''

The strength and insight of Childress's characterizations have been widely acknowledged; critics contend that the characters who populate her plays and novels are believable and memorable. Eder praises the ''rich and lively characterization'' of *Wedding Band.* Similarly impressed, Harold Clurman writes in the *Nation* that ''there is an honest pathos in the telling of this simple story, and some humorous and touching thumbnail sketches reveal knowledge and understanding of the people dealt with.'' In the novel *A Short Walk,* Childress chronicles the life of a fictitious black woman, Cora James, from her birth in 1900 to her death in the middle of the century, illustrating, as *Washington Post* critic Joseph McLellan describes it, ''a transitional generation in black American society.'' McLellan notes that the story ''wanders considerably'' and that ''the reader is left with no firm conclusion that can be put into a neat sentence or two.'' What is more important, he asserts, is that ''the wandering has been through some interesting scenery, and instead of a conclusion the reader has come to know a human being complex, struggling valiantly and totally believable.'' And of Childress's novel about teenage heroin addiction, *A Hero Ain't Nothin' but a Sandwich,* the *Lion and the Unicorn*'s Miguel Ortiz states, ''The portrait of whites is more realistic in this book, more compassionate, and at the same time, because it is believable, more scathing.''

Some criticism has been leveled at what such reviewers as Abramson and Edith Oliver believe to be Childress's tendency to speechify, especially in her plays. ''A reader of the script is very much aware of the author pulling strings, putting her own words into a number of mouths,'' Abramson says of *Trouble in Mind.* According to Oliver in the *New Yorker,* ''The first act [of *Wedding Band*] is splendid, but after that we hit a few jarring notes, when the characters seem to be speaking as much for the benefit of us eavesdroppers out front . . . as for the benefit of one another.''

For the most part, however, Childress's work, particularly her novels for young adults, has been acclaimed for its honesty, insight, and compassion. When one such novel, *Those Other People,* was published in 1989, it was acknowledged by very few of the traditional children's reviewing sources. The novel deals with a teenage boy's fears about admitting to his homosexuality. Childress has created characters who confront homophobia, racism, and social taboos honestly and with dignity. In her review for *School Library Journal,* Kathryn Havris notes that *Those Other People,* skillfully and realistically addresses young people's responses to these problems. This author, says Havris, ''has presented the problems and reactions with a competence that deserves reading.''

In *Crisis,* Loften Mitchell notes: "Childress writes with a sharp, satiric touch. Character seems to interest her more than plot. Her characterizations are piercing, her observations devastating." In his review of *A Hero Ain't Nothin' but a Sandwich,* Ortiz writes: "The book conveys very strongly the message that we are all human, even when we are acting in ways that we are somewhat ashamed of. The structure of the book grows out of the personalities of the characters, and the author makes us aware of how much the economic and social circumstances dictate a character's actions."

In discussing how she came to write books for teenagers, Childress remarks in *Speaking for Ourselves* that she wanted to "deal with characters who feel rejected and have to painfully learn how to deal with other people, because I believe all human beings can be magnificent once they realize their full importance." "My young years were very old in feeling," she comments elsewhere. "I was shut out of so much for so long. [I] soon began to embrace the low-profile as a way of life, which helped me to develop as a writer. Quiet living is restful when one's writing is labeled 'controversial.'

"Happily, I managed to save a bit of my youth for spending in these later years. Oh yes, there are other things to be saved [besides] money. If we hang on to that part within that was once childhood, I believe we enter into a new time dimension and every day becomes another life-time in itself. This gift of understanding is often given to those wh constantly battle against the negatives of life with determination."

Childress died on August 14, 1994 in New York City. At the time of her death she had been at work on a novel about her African great-grandmother, who'd been a slave in her childhood, and her Scotch-Irish great-grandmother.

## Further Reading

Abramson, Doris E., *Negro Playwrights in the American Theatre, 1925-1959,* Columbia University Press, 1969.

Betsko, Kathleen, and Rachel Koenig, *Interviews with Contemporary Women Playwrights,* Beech Tree Books, 1987.

*Children's Literature Review,* Volume 14, Gale, 1988.

*Contemporary Literary Criticism,* Gale, Volume 12, 1980, Volume 15, 1980.

*Dictionary of Literary Biography,* Gale, Volume 7: *Twentieth-Century American Dramatists,* 1981, Volume 38: *Afro-American Writers after 1955: Dramatists and Prose Writers,* 1985.

Donelson, Kenneth L., and Alleen Pace Nilson, *Literature for Today's Young Adults,* Scott, Foresman, 1980, third edition, HarperCollins, 1989.

Evans, Mari, editor, *Black Women Writers (1950-1980): A Critical Evaluation,* Doubleday-Anchor, 1984.

Gallo, Donald R., editor, *Speaking for Ourselves: Autobiographical Sketches by Notable Authors of Books for Young Adults,* National Council Teachers of English, 1990.

Hatch, James V., *Black Theater, U.S.A.: Forty-five Plays by Black Americans,* Free Press, 1974.

Mitchell, Loften, editor, *Voices of the Black Theatre,* James White, 1975.

Street, Douglas, editor, *Children's Novels and the Movies,* Ungar, 1983.

*Crisis,* April, 1965.

*Freedomways,* Volume 14, number 1, 1974.

*Horn Book,* May-June, 1989, p. 372.

*Interracial Books for Children Bulletin,* Volume 12, numbers 7-8, 1981.

*Jet,* September 5, 1995.

*Lion and the Unicorn,* fall, 1978.

*Los Angeles Times,* November 13, 1978; February 25, 1983.

*Los Angeles Times Book Review,* July 25, 1982.

*Ms.,* December, 1979.

*Nation,* November 13, 1972.

*Negro Digest,* April, 1967; January, 1968.

*Newsweek,* August 31, 1987.

*New Yorker,* November 4, 1972; November 19, 1979.

*New York Times,* November 5, 1955; February 2, 1969; April 2, 1969; October 27, 1972; November 5, 1972; February 3, 1978; January 11, 1979; January 23, 1987; February 10, 1987; March 6, 1987; August 18, 1987; October 22, 1987.

*New York Times Book Review,* November 4, 1973; November 11, 1979; April 25, 1981.

*School Library Journal,* February, 1989, p. 99.

*Show Business,* April 12, 1969.

*Variety,* December 20, 1972.

*Village Voice,* January 15, 1979.

*Washington Post,* May 18, 1971; December 28, 1979.

*Wilson Library Bulletin,* September, 1989, pp. 14-15. ☐

# May Edward Chinn

**May Edward Chinn (1896–1890) is best remembered for the racial barriers she confronted as one of the first black women physicians in New York City.**

May Edward Chinn is best remembered for the racial barriers she confronted as one of the first black women physicians in New York City. Denied hospital privileges and research opportunities at New York City hospitals early in her career, she became a family doctor in Harlem, where she was the only practicing African American woman physician for several years. For her determination to provide medical care to the disadvantaged and for her work in cancer detection, she received honorary doctor of science degrees from New York University and Columbia University, and a distinguished alumnus award from Columbia Teachers College.

May Edward Chinn was born on April 15, 1896, in Great Barrington, Massachusetts. Her mother, Lulu Ann, was the daughter of a Chickahominy Native American and a slave. Her father, William Lafayette, was the son of a slave and a plantation owner. Chinn went to the Bordentown Manual and Training Industrial School, a boarding school in New Jersey, and spent one year of her childhood on the estate of Charles Tiffany, the jewelry magnate, where her mother was a live-in cook. The Tiffanys treated Chinn like family and took her to classical music concerts in New York City. She later learned to play the piano and became an accompanist to popular singer Paul Robeson in the early 1920s. Chinn played classical music and church music throughout her life and performed for African American soldiers during World War I. Although she never completed high school, she was admitted to Columbia Teachers Col-

lege on the basis of her entrance examination. Originally intending to pursue a degree in music, Chinn quickly abandoned music for science because a music professor who believed that African Americans were unsuited for classical music ridiculed her, but another professor praised her for a paper she had written on sewage disposal. In 1921 she received a bachelor's degree in science from Columbia Teachers College, and in 1926 she became the first African American woman to graduate from Bellevue Hospital Medical College.

Upon graduation Chinn found that no hospital would allow her practicing privileges. The Rockefeller Institute had seriously considered her for a research fellowship until they discovered that she was African American. With her fair skin and last name, many assumed that she was white or Chinese. She later told Muriel Petioni, former president of the Society of Black Women Physicians, that African American workers often snubbed her because they assumed she was passing as white, and they did not want to jeopardize her position.

Though she was the first black woman intern at Harlem Hospital, racial and gender discrimination kept her from obtaining hospital privileges there. Chinn described her early practice in Harlem as akin to an old-fashioned family practice in the rural South a century earlier. She performed major medical procedures in patient's homes, while minor procedures were done in her office. She told George Davis of the *New York Times Magazine* "that conditions were so bad that it seemed that you were not making any headway."

To get at the roots of poverty, she earned a master's degree in public health from Columbia University in 1933.

In the 1940s Chinn became very interested in cancer but was still prohibited from establishing formal affiliations with New York hospitals. Instead, she had her patients' biopsies read secretly for her at Memorial Hospital. In 1944 she was invited to join the staff of the Strang Clinic, a premier cancer detection facility affiliated with Memorial and New York Infirmary hospitals. She worked there for twenty-nine years and became a member of the Society of Surgical Oncology.

In her autobiographical paper written in 1977, Chinn noted that the committees established by Mayor LaGuardia after the Harlem riots of 1935 were pivotal in integrating blacks into medicine in New York City. As committee findings were reported in the newspapers, conditions began to change. Chinn saw this firsthand when she became the first African American woman granted admitting privileges at Harlem Hospital in 1940.

African American male doctors were another source of discrimination. In a *New York Times* interview with Charlayne Hunter-Gault in 1977, she described three types: "those who acted as if I wasn't there; another who took the attitude 'what does she think that she can do that I can't do?' and the group that called themselves support[ive] by sending me their night calls after midnight." Like other African American women physicians of her era, Chinn worked long hours but never got rich from her practice. By 1978 Chinn had given up her practice and begun examining African American students as a consultant to the Phelps-Stokes Fund. In late 1980 she died at age eighty-four at a Columbia University reception honoring a friend.

## Further Reading

Brozan, Nadine, "For a Doctor at 84, A Day to Remember," in *New York Times,* May 17, 1980, p. 12.

Davis, George, "A Healing Hand in Harlem," in *New York Times Magazine,* Apr. 22, 1979, pp. 40 + .

Ennis, Thomas W., "Obituary: Dr. May Edward Chinn, 84, Long a Harlem Physician," in *New York Times,* Sect. II, Dec. 3, 1980, p. 11.

Hunter-Gault, Charlayne, "Black Women M.D.'s: Spirit and Endurance," in *New York Times,* Nov. 16, 1977, pp. C1 + .

Petioni, Muriel, *Interview with Laura Newman,* conducted on March 11, 1994. □

# Shirley Anita St. Hill Chisholm

**Shirley Anita St. Hill Chisholm (born 1924) was the first Black woman to serve in the United States Congress. She served as the representative for the 12th district of New York from 1969 until 1982. In 1972, when she became the first black woman to actively run for the presidency of the United States, she won**

**ten percent of the votes at the Democratic National Convention.**

Born in Brooklyn, New York, to Barbadian parents, Chisholm was raised in an atmosphere that was both political and religious. Her father was a staunch follower of the West Indian political activist Marcus Garvey, who advocated black pride and unity among blacks to achieve economic and political power. Chisholm received much of her primary education in her parents homeland, Barbados, under the strict eye of her maternal grandmother. Chisholm, who returned to New York when she was ten years old, credits her educational successes to the well-rounded early training she received in Barbados.

Attending New York public schools, Chisholm was able to compete well in the predominantly white classrooms. She attended Girls' High School in Bedford-Stuyvesant, a section of the city with a growing poor black and immigrant population. She won tuition scholarships to both Oberlin and Vassar, but at the urging of her parents decided to live at home and attend Brooklyn College. While training to be a teacher she became active in several campus and community groups. Developing a keen interest in politics, she began to learn the arts of organizing and fund raising. She deeply resented the role of women in local politics, which consisted mostly of staying in the background, sponsoring fund raising events, and turning the money over to male party leaders who would then decide how to use it. During her school years, she became interes-

ted in the Delta Sigma Theta Sorority and the National Association for the Advancement of Colored People and eventually joined both groups.

## From Classroom to Congress

After graduating *cum laude* from Brooklyn College in 1946 Chisholm began to work as a nursery school teacher and later as a director of schools for early childhood education. In 1949 she married Conrad Chisholm. She continued to teach but her political interest never waned. After a successful career as a teacher, Chisholm decided to run for the New York State Assembly in 1964. She won the election.

During the time that she served in the assembly, Chisholm sponsored 50 bills, but only eight of them passed. The bills she sponsored reflected her interest in the cause of blacks and the poor, women's rights, and educational opportunities. One of the successful bills provided assistance for poor students to go on for higher education. Another provided employment insurance coverage for personal and domestic employees. Still another reversed a law that caused female teachers in New York to lose their tenure while they were out on maternity leave.

Chisholm served in the State Assembly until 1968 and then decided to run for the U.S. Congress. Her opponent was the noted civil rights leader James Farmer. Possibly because Chisholm was a well-known resident of Bedford-Stuyvesant and Farmer was not, she won easily. Thus began her tenure in the U.S. House of Representatives from the 91st through the 97th Congress (1969-1982). Always considering herself a political maverick, Chisholm attempted to focus as much of her attention as possible on the needs of her constituents. She served on several House committees: Agriculture, Veterans' Affairs, Rules and Education, and Labor. During the 91st Congress when she was assigned to the Forestry Committee, she protested saying that she wanted to work on committees that could deal with the "critical problems of racism, deprivation and urban decay." (There are no forests in Bedford-Stuyvesant.)

Chisholm began to protest the amount of money being expended for the defense budget while social programs suffered. She argued that she would not agree that money should be spent for war while Americans were hungry, illhoused, and poorly educated. Early in her career as a congresswoman she began to support legislation allowing abortions for women who chose to have them. Chisholm protested the traditional roles for women professionals—secretaries, teachers, and librarians. She argued that women were capable of entering many other professions and that they should be encouraged to do so. Black women, too, she felt, had been shunted into stereotypical maid and nanny roles from which they needed to escape both by legislation and by self-effort. Her antiwar and women's liberation views made her a popular figure among college students, and she was beseiged with invitations to speak at college campuses.

## Presidential Contender

In 1972 Chisholm made the decision that she would run for the highest office in the land—the presidency. In addition to her interest in civil rights for blacks, women, and the poor, she spoke out about the judicial system in the United States, police brutality, prison reform, gun control, politician dissent, drug abuse, and numerous other topics. She appeared on the television show "Face the Nation" with three other democratic presidential candidates: George McGovern, Henry Jackson, and Edmund Muskie. George McGovern won the presidential nomination at the Democratic National Convention, but Chisholm captured ten percent of the delegates' votes. As a result of her candidacy, Chisholm was voted one of the ten most admired women in the world.

After her unsuccessful presidential campaign, Chisholm continued to serve in the U.S. House of Representatives for another decade. As a member of the Black Caucus she was able to watch black representation in the Congress grow and to welcome other black female congresswomen. Finally, in 1982, she announced her retirement from the Congress.

## Final Years

From 1983 to 1987 Chisholm served as Purington Professor at Massachusetts' Mt. Holyoke College where she taught politics and women's studies. In 1985 she was the visiting scholar at Spelman College, and in 1987 retired from teaching altogether. Chisholm continued to be involved in politics by cofounding the National Political Congress of Black Women in 1984. She also worked vigorously for the presidential campaign of Jesse Jackson in 1984 and 1988. "Jackson is the voice of the poor, the disenchanted, the disillusioned," Chisholm was quoted as saying in *Newsweek*, "and that is exactly what I was."

In 1993 President Bill Clinton nominated Chisolm as Ambassador to Jamaica, but due to declining health, she withdrew her name from further consideration.

## Further Reading

Chisholm has written two autobiographical accounts, *Unbought and Unbossed* (1970) and *The Good Fight* (1973). There are several other books about her political career which are especially geared to young readers. A few of them are: Lenore K. Itzkowitz, *Shirley Chisholm for President* (1974); James Haskins, *Fighting Shirley Chisholm* (1975); and Nancy Hicks, *The Honorable Shirley Chisholm, Congresswoman from Brooklyn* (1971). The *Congressional Record* for the 91st through 97th Congress can be used to find the texts of Chisholm's speeches. □

# Katherine Chopin

**A popular local colorist during her lifetime, Katherine Chopin (1851-1904) is best known today for her psychological novel *The Awakening* (1899) and for such often-anthologized short stories as "Desiree's Baby" and "The Story of an Hour."**

Chopin was born to a prominent St. Louis family. Her father died in a train accident when Chopin was four years old, and her childhood was most profoundly influenced by her mother and great-grandmother, who descended from French-Creole pioneers. Chopin also spent much time with her family's Creole and mulatto slaves, becoming familiar with their unique dialects. She read widely as a child, but was an undistinguished student at the convent school she attended. She graduated at age seventeen and spent two years as a belle of fashionable St. Louis society. In 1870 she married Oscar Chopin, a wealthy Creole cotton factor, and moved with him to New Orleans. For the next decade, Chopin pursued the demanding social and domestic schedule of a Southern aristocrat, her recollections of which would later serve as material for her short stories. In 1880, financial difficulties forced Chopin's growing family to move to her father-in-law's home in Cloutierville, a small town in Natchitoches Parish located in Louisiana's Red River bayou region. There, Chopin's husband oversaw and subsequently inherited his father's plantations. Upon his death in 1883, Chopin insisted upon assuming his managerial responsibilities, which brought her into contact with almost every segment of the community, including the French-Acadian, Creole, and mu-

latto sharecroppers who worked the plantations. The impressions she gathered of these people and Natchitoches Parish life later influenced her fiction.

In the mid-1880s Chopin sold most of her property and left Louisiana to live with her mother in St. Louis. Family friends who found her letters entertaining encouraged Chopin to write professionally, and she began composing short stories. These early works evidence the influence of her favorite authors: the French writers Guy de Maupassant, Alphonse Daudet, and Moliere. At this time Chopin also read the works of Charles Darwin, Thomas Huxley, and Herbert Spenser in order to keep abreast of trends in scientific thinking, and she began questioning her Roman Catholic faith as well as socially imposed mores and ethical restraints. After an apprenticeship marked by routine rejections, Chopin began having her stories published in the most popular American periodicals, including *America*, *Vogue*, and the *Atlantic*. The success of the collections *Bayou Folk* (1894) and *A Night in Acadie* (1897) solidified her growing reputation as an important local colorist. Financially independent and encouraged by success, Chopin turned to longer works. Although she had published the novel *At Fault* in 1890, that work displays many of the shortcomings of an apprentice novel and failed to interest readers or critics. Publishers later rejected a novel and a short story collection on moral grounds, citing their promotion of female self-assertion and sexual liberation. Undaunted, Chopin completed *The Awakening*, the story of a conventional wife and mother who, after gaining spiritual freedom through an extramarital affair, commits suicide when she realizes that she cannot reconcile her new self to society's moral restrictions. The hostile critical and public reaction to the novel largely halted Chopin's career; she had difficulty finding publishers for later works and was ousted from local literary groups. Demoralized, she wrote little during her last years.

The stories in *Bayou Folk*, Chopin's first collection, largely reflect her skills as a local colorist and often center on the passionate loves of the Creoles and Acadians in her native Natchitoches Parish. For example, "A Lady of Bayou St. John" portrays a young widow who escapes the sexual demands of a suitor by immersing herself in memories of her dead husband, while "La Belle Zoraide" chronicles a mulatto slave's descent into madness after her mistress sells her lover and deprives her of their child. Recent critics occasionally detect in *Bayou Folk* the melodramatic conventions of popular magazine fiction. Nevertheless, they laud Chopin's meticulous description of setting, precise rendering of dialects, and objective point of view. In addition, commentators perceived in several stories universal themes that transcend the restrictions of regional fiction. One such story, the often-anthologized "Desiree's Baby," examines prejudice and miscegenation in its portrayal of Armand Aubigny, a proud aristocratic planter, and his wife Desiree. When she gives birth to a son possessing African characteristics, Aubigny assumes that Desiree is of mixed racial heritage and turns his wife and child out of his house. However, while burning his wife's possessions, Armand discovers a letter written by his mother, which reveals that she and

therefore Armand belong to the race "cursed by the brand of slavery."

In *A Night in Acadie* Chopin continued to utilize the Louisiana settings that figured in *Bayou Folk*. However, the romanticism of the earlier collection is replaced by a greater moral ambivalence concerning such issues as female sexuality, personal freedom, and social propriety. Bert Bender observed that Chopin's "characters transcend their socially limited selves by awakening to and affirming impulses that are unacceptable by convention. Unburdened of restricting social conventions, her characters come to experience the suffering and loneliness, as well as the joy, of their freedom; for the impulses that they heed are a mere part of a world in which change and natural selection are first principles." For example, in "A Respectable Woman" a happily married woman becomes sexually attracted to Gouvernail, a family friend invited by her husband to visit their home for a week. Disturbed by her feelings, she is relieved when Gouvernail leaves, but as the following summer approaches, she encourages her husband to contact him again, ambiguously promising that "this time I shall be very nice to him." Chopin later expanded upon this essentially amoral perception of adultery in "The Storm," a story written near the end of her career, which portrays a woman's extra-marital affair as a natural impulse devoid of moral significance.

Chopin also explored the connection between selfhood and marriage in *A Night in Acadie*. Several stories reflect her contention that security and love cannot compensate for a lack of control over one's destiny. In "Athenaise," for instance, the title character, a naive young bride, leaves Cazeau, her devoted yet insensitive husband, twice; first returning home to her parents, then traveling to New Orleans. Although Cazeau retrieves her from her parents, he refuses to follow her to the city after drawing an unsettling parallel between his actions toward her and his father's treatment of a runaway slave. A month after arriving in New Orleans, however, Athenaise learns that she is pregnant, and, thinking of her husband, experiences "the first purely sensuous tremor of her life." Now accepting her role as wife and mother, she reconciles with Cazeau. While some critics contend that Chopin likely formulated this conclusion, like other happy endings to her stories, to appease the moral sensibilities of her editors and publishers, most regard it as an appropriate ending to an incisive portrait of the limitations and rewards of marriage.

Early reviewers of *A Night in Acadie* objected to the volume's sensuous themes. Similar concerns were later raised by publishers who rejected Chopin's next volume, *A Vocation and a Voice*. Although Chopin continuously pursued its publication until her death, the volume did not appear as a single work until 1991. In these stories Chopin largely abandons local setting to focus upon the psychological complexity of her characters. Tales such as "Two Portraits," "Lilacs," and "A Vocation and a Voice," examine contrary states of innocence and experience and ways that society divides rather than unites the two. In "The Story of an Hour," the best known work in the collection, Chopin returns to the issue of marriage and selfhood in her portrayal of Mrs. Mallard, a woman who learns that her husband has died in a train accident. Initially overcome by grief, she gradually realizes that his "powerful will" no longer restricts her and that she may live as she wishes. While she joyfully anticipates her newfound freedom, however, her husband returns, the report of his death a mistake, and Mrs. Mallard collapses upon seeing him. Doctors then ironically conclude that she died of "heart failure—of the joy that kills." In evaluating *A Vocation and a Voice*, Barbara C. Ewell observed: "[The] collection, which includes some of Chopin's most experimental stories, reveals how intently she had come to focus her fiction on human interiority, on the interplay of consciousness and circumstance, of unconscious motive and reflexive action. Such psychological elements, combined with technical control, indicate a writer not only in command of her craft but fully in tune with the intellectual currents of her time. In many ways, *A Vocation and a Voice* represents the culmination of Chopin's talents as a writer of the short story."

*The Awakening* is considered Chopin's best work as well as a remarkable novel to have been written during the morally uncompromising America of the 1890s. Psychologically realistic, *The Awakening* is the story of Edna Pontellier, a conventional wife and mother who experiences a spiritual epiphany and an awakened sense of independence that change her life. The theme of sexual freedom and the consequences one must face to attain it is supported by sensual imagery that acquires symbolic meanings as the story progresses. This symbolism emphasizes the conflict within Pontellier, who realizes that she can neither exercise her new-found sense of independence nor return to life as it was before her spiritual awakening: the candor of the Creole community on Grand Isle, for example, is contrasted with the conventional mores of New Orleans; birds in gilded cages and strong, free-flying birds are juxtaposed; and the protagonist selects for her confidants both the domesticated, devoted Adele Ratignolle and the passionate Madame Reisz, a lonely, unattractive pianist. The central symbol of the novel, the sea, also provides the frame for the main action. As a symbol, the sea embodies multiple pairs of polarities, the most prominent being that it is the site of both Edna Pontellier's awakening and suicide.

After the initial furor over morality and sexuality in *The Awakening* had passed, the novel was largely ignored until the 1930s, when Daniel S. Rankin published a study of Chopin's works that included a sober assessment of *The Awakening*'s high literary quality and artistic aims. During the succeeding decades, critical debate surrounding *The Awakening* has focused on Chopin's view of women's roles in society, the significance of Pontellier's awakening, her subsequent suicide, and the possibility of parallels between the lives of Chopin and her protagonist. George Arms, for example, has contended that Chopin was a happily married woman and devoted mother whose emotional life bore no resemblance to Pontellier's, while Per Seyersted has noted her compelling secretive, individualistic nature and her evident enjoyment of living alone as an independent writer. Priscilla Allen has posited that male critics allow their preconceptions about "good" and "bad" women to influence their interpretations of Chopin's novel, arguing that they too often assume that Edna's first priority should have been to her family and not to herself. Like Allen, Seyersted brings a feminist interpretation to *The Awakening,* and points out that the increasing depiction of passionate, independent women in Chopin's other fiction supports the theory that she was in fact concerned about the incompatibility of motherhood and a career for women living during the late nineteenth century. These questions about Chopin's depictions of women's roles in society have led to a debate about the significance of Pontellier's suicide. The ambivalence of the character as she wrestles with the new choices that confront her has left the suicide open to many interpretations. Carol P. Christ, like Seyersted, interprets the death as a moral victory and a social defeat—the act of a brave woman who cannot sacrifice her life to her family, but will not cause her children disgrace by pursuing a scandalous course. In a contrasting assessment of Pontellier's choice to die, James H. Justus likens the protagonist's gradual withdrawal from society and responsibility to a regression into childhood selfishness because she refuses to compromise and cannot control her urge for self-assertion. Often compared to the protagonist of Gustave Flaubert's *Madame Bovary*, Pontellier differs primarily in her desire for selfhood, even at the risk of loneliness, while Madame Bovary seeks romantic fulfillment.

Once considered merely an author of local-color fiction, Chopin is today recognized for her pioneering examination of sexuality, individual freedom, and the consequences of action—themes and concerns important to many later twentieth-century writers. While their psychological examinations of female protagonists have made Chopin's short stories formative works in the historical development of feminist literature, they also provide a broad discussion of a society that denied the value of sensuality and female independence. Per Seyersted asserted that Chopin "was the first woman writer in America to accept sex with its profound repercussions as a legitimate subject of serious fiction. In her attitude towards passion, she represented a healthy, matter-of-fact acceptance of the whole of man. She was familiar with the newest developments in science and in world literature, and her aim was to describe—unhampered by tradition and authority—man's immutable impulses. Because she was vigorous, intelligent, and eminently sane, and because her background had made her morally tolerant, and socially secure, she could write with a balance and maturity, a warmth and humor not often found in her contemporaries."

## Further Reading

Cather, Willa, *The World and the Parish*, Volume II: *Willa Cather's Articles and Reviews, 1893-1902*, edited by William M.Curtin, University of Nebraska Press, 1970.

Chopin, Kate, *The Complete Works of Kate Chopin* (two volumes), edited by Per Seyersted, Louisiana State University Press, 1969.

Chopin, Kate, *The Storm and Other Stories, with The Awakening* edited by Seyersted, Feminist Press, 1974.

*Concise Dictionary of American Literary Biography: Realism, Naturalism, and Local Color, 1865-1917*, Gale, 1988.

Diamond, Arlyn and Lee R. Edwards, *The Authority of Experience: Essays in Feminist Criticism*, University of Massachusetts Press, 1977.

*Dictionary of Literary Biography*, Gale, Volume 12: *American Realists and Naturalists*, 1982, Volume 78: *American Short-Story Writers, 1880-1910*, 1988. □

# Connie Chung

**In 1993 when Connie Chung (born 1941) became the co-anchor of the "CBS Evening News," she was the first Asian American and the second woman ever to be named to the coveted post of nightly news anchor at a major network.**

Constance Yu-hwa Chung was born on August 20, 1946, in suburban Washington, D.C., to Margaret Ma and William Ling Ching Chung. Her father had been an intelligence officer in China's Nationalist Army who fled his war-torn homeland for the United States in 1944.

Chung earned a degree in journalism from the University of Maryland in 1969. Her first job was with WTTG-TV, an independent television station in the nation's capital. Later she secured a job at CBS' Washington bureau, aided in part by the Federal Communications Commission's timely mandate for stations to hire more minorities. In her early years with CBS, Chung covered stories such as the 1972 presidential campaign of George McGovern, anti-Vietnam War protests, and the presidency of Richard M. Nixon.

In 1976, Chung moved to Los Angeles to becom an anchor at the local CBS affiliate, KNXT (now KCBS). She began hosting three news broadcasts a day, and the station went from third to second place in ratings. In 1983, she took a drastic pay cut and moved to NBC where she worked as a correspondent and anchored several shows and prime-time news specials. She also served as political analysis correspondent for the network. In 1989, Chung announced that she would leave NBC for CBS when her current contract expired. Her contract with CBS was reported to be worth $1.5 million annually. Her initial duties at CBS included hosting "West 57th," "The CBS Sunday Night News," and serving as the principal replacement for Dan Rather on "The CBS Evening News."

On June 1, 1993, Connie Chung became the co-anchor of the "CBS Evening News." She became the first Asian American and only the second woman ever to named to the coveted post of nightly news anchor at a major network, traditionally thought of as the pinnacle of broadcast journalism. In addition to her role as co-anchor, Chung began hosting "Eye to Eye with Connie Chung," a popular prime-time television news magazine that highlighted interviews with controversial newsmakers, a specialty of Chung's. Her time in the limelight was limited. Her desire for higher level interviews caused a stir with the network and Chung's credibility suffered as she continued to cover the tabloid stories assigned to her. Her 1995 firing from the co-anchor position and subsequent loss of "Eye to Eye with Connie Chung" disturbed many who were pleased to see a woman reaching new heights in journalism. Dan Rather's seeming indifference to Chung's firing fueled the rumor that he pulled strings to have her let go.

Chung received numerous accolades for her work, including three National Emmy Awards, a Peabody, a 1991 Ohio State Award, a 1991 National Headliner Award, two American Women in Radio and Television National Commendations, a 1991 Clarion Award, and in 1990 she was chosen as favorite interviewer by *U.S. News and World Report* in their annual "Best of America" survey.

On December 2, 1984, Chung married television journalist Maury Povich, host of "The Maury Povich Show," a syndicated day-time television talk show. Their adoption of a son, Matthew Jay Povich, came shortly after Chung's firing from CBS. She has been a full-time mother since her departure from the network, but talks have surfaced suggesting she and Povich will collaborate on a news show, to be produced by Dreamworks Televison, once his contract with "The Maury Povich Show" runs out in 1997. □

# Sandra Cisneros

**Drawing heavily upon her childhood experiences and ethnic heritage Sandra Cisneros (born 1954) creates characters who are distinctly Hispanic and often isolated from mainstream American culture by**

**emphasizing dialogue and sensory imagery over traditional narrative structures.**

Born in Chicago, Cisneros was the only daughter among seven children. Concerning her childhood, Cisneros recalled that because her brothers attempted to control her and expected her to assume a traditional female role, she often felt like she had "seven fathers." The family frequently moved between the United States and Mexico because of her father's homesickness for his native country and his devotion to his mother who lived there. Consequently, Cisneros often felt homeless and displaced: "Because we moved so much, and always in neighborhoods that appeared like France after World War II— empty lots and burned-out buildings—I retreated inside myself." She began to read extensively, finding comfort in such works as Virginia Lee Burton's *The Little House* and Lewis Carroll's *Alice's Adventures in Wonderland.* Cisneros periodically wrote poems and stories throughout her childhood and adolescence, but she did not find her literary voice until attending the University of Iowa's Writers Workshop in the late 1970s. A breakthrough occurred for Cisneros during a discussion of French philosopher Gaston Bachelard's *The Poetics of Space* and his metaphor of a house; she realized that her experiences as a Hispanic woman were unique and outside the realm of dominant American culture. She observed: "Everyone seemed to have some communal knowledge which I did not have—and then I realized that the metaphor of *house* was totally wrong

for me. . . . I had no such house in my memories. . . . This caused me to question myself, to become defensive. What did I, Sandra Cisneros, know? What *could* I know? My classmates were from the best schools in the country. They had been bred as fine hothouse flowers. I was a yellow weed among the city's cracks."

Shortly after participating in the Iowa Workshop, Cisneros decided to write about conflicts directly related to her upbringing, including divided cultural loyalties, feelings of alienation, and degradation associated with poverty. Incorporating these concerns into *The House on Mango Street,* a work that took nearly five years to complete, Cisneros created the character Esperanza, a poor, Hispanic adolescent who longs for a room of her own and a house of which she can be proud. Esperanza ponders the disadvantages of choosing marriage over education, the importance of writing as an emotional release, and the sense of confusion associated with growing up. In the story "Hips," for example, Esperanza agonizes over the repercussions of her body's physical changes: "One day you wake up and there they are. Ready and waiting like a new Buick with the key in the ignition. Ready to take you where?" Written in what Penelope Mesic called "a loose and deliberately simple style, halfway between a prose poem and the awkwardness of semiliteracy," the pieces in *The House on Mango Street* won praise for their lyrical narratives, vivid dialogue, and powerful descriptions.

*Woman Hollering Creek and Other Stories* is a collection of twenty-two narratives revolving around numerous Mexican-American characters living near San Antonio, Texas. Ranging from a few paragraphs to several pages, the stories in this volume contain the interior monologues of individuals who have been assimilated into American culture despite their sense of loyalty to Mexico. In "Never Marry a Mexican," for example, a young Hispanic woman begins to feel contempt for her white lover because of her emerging feelings of inadequacy and cultural guilt resulting from her inability to speak Spanish. Although Cisneros addresses important contemporary issues associated with minority status throughout *Woman Hollering Creek and Other Stories,* critics have described her characters as idiosyncratic, accessible individuals capable of generating compassion on a universal level. One reviewer observed: "In this sensitively structured suite of sketches, [Cisneros's] irony defers to her powers of observation so that feminism and cultural imperialism, while important issues here, do not overwhelm the narrative."

Although Cisneros is noted primarily for her fiction, her poetry has also garnered attention. In *My Wicked Wicked Ways,* her third volume of verse, Cisneros writes about her native Chicago, her travels in Europe, and, as reflected in the title, sexual guilt resulting from her strict Catholic upbringing. A collection of sixty poems, each of which resemble a short story, this work further evidences Cisneros's penchant for merging various genres. Gary Soto explained: "Cisneros's poems are intrinsically narrative, but not large, meandering paragraphs. She writes deftly with skill and idea, in the 'show-me-don't-tell-me' vein, and her points leave valuable impressions." In her poetry, as in all her works, Cisneros incorporates Hispanic dialect, impressionistic metaphors, and social commentary in ways that reveal the fears and doubts unique to Hispanic women. She stated: "If I were asked what it is I write about, I would have to say I write about those ghosts inside that haunt me, that will not let me sleep, of that which even memory does not like to mention. . . . Perhaps later there will be a time to write by inspiration. In the meantime, in my writing as well as in that of other Chicanas and other women, there is the necessary phase of dealing with those ghosts and voices most urgently haunting us, day by day."

### Further Reading

*Americas Review,* Spring, 1987, pp. 69-76.
*Bloomsbury Review,* July-August, 1988, p. 21.
*Chicano-Riquena,* Fall-Winter, 1985, pp. 109-19.
*Glamour,* November, 1990, pp. 256-57.
*Los Angeles Times,* May 7, 1991, p. F1.
*Los Angeles Times Book Review,* April 28, 1991, p. 3.
*Mirabella,* April, 1991, p. 46. □

# Liz Claiborne

**Founder of one of the world's most successful women's apparel manufacturing companies, Liz Claiborne (born 1929) was a pioneer in designing reasonably priced, good quality clothing for modern working women.**

Liz Claiborne (Elisabeth Claiborne Ortenberg) was born March 31, 1929, in Brussels, Belgium, where her father, Omer V. Claiborne, was a banker for the Morgan Guaranty Trust Company. In the 1930s Omer, his wife Louise Fenner Claiborne, and their young daughter returned to their home in New Orleans, where Liz received a strict Roman Catholic upbringing. Her father did not consider formal education important, and before Claiborne graduated from high school he sent her to Europe to study art in Belgium and France. Although her parents expected her to become an artist, Claiborne, whose mother had taught her to sew, wanted to study fashion and pursued a career as a clothing designer.

When she was 21 years old her sketch for a woman's coat won a Jacques Heim design competition sponsored by *Harper's Bazaar* magazine. With this award and her sketching ability, Claiborne began working on Seventh Avenue in New York City's garment district as a design assistant and a model. From 1950 to 1955 she held several positions designing sportswear, tailored clothing, and high fashion. From 1955 to 1960 she was a dress designer for the Dan Keller company. From 1960 to December 1975 she was the principal designer for Youth Guild, the junior dress division of Jonathan Logan, a major women's apparel manufacturer. During this time Claiborne also raised her son from her first marriage to Ben Schultz and two step-children from her second marriage to Arthur Ortenberg, a textile manufacturer and consultant.

Claiborne saw a need in the marketplace for more comfortable but professional apparel for working women. Claiborne's fashion sense told her women could use clothing that was easier to wear and softer than the tailored business suits, blouses, and bow ties then sold in department stores. Unable to convince her employer to enter the mix-and-match coordinated sportswear market for working women, Claiborne started her own company.

Liz Claiborne, Inc. was founded on January 19, 1976, with approximately $250,000, including $50,000 of Claiborne's and her husband's savings. Ortenberg was the company's secretary and treasurer; industry executive and friend Leonard Boxer was in charge of production; and the fourth key executive, Jerome Chazen, joined the company in 1977 to direct marketing operations. Sales for the first year were over $2 million, as Claiborne's collection of pants, skirts, shirts, sweaters, and jackets was instantly popular.

Priced in a moderate range, from about $40 to $100, and sold in department stores, the Liz Claiborne label became known for its good quality materials, comfortable fit, good construction, color selection, and clean silhouettes. Not a couture designer but more of a stylist, Claiborne produced a collection of fashionably appropriate clothing that perfectly matched late-20th-century working women's clothing needs.

As sales increased from $2.6 million in 1976 to $117 million in 1981, production, delivery, and marketing demands increased in proportion. Credit for a well managed company belonged to the original management team of

Ortenberg, Boxer, and Chazen. The company was regarded as one of the best managed in the highly competitive and volatile women's fashion apparel business.

Liz Claiborne, Inc. became a public company in 1981. Within a few years their stock holdings made Claiborne and Ortenberg millionaires. The company's market share continued to expand and the profits were high. To continue increasing its market share as well as to diversify its product, Claiborne expanded her fashion lines to include petites, dresses, shoes, accessories, menswear, and perfume between 1981 and 1986. Six years later there were 19 divisions. Computer analysis of sales and traveling consultants provided the company with constant feedback, making it possible to quickly fill or reduce merchandise orders. The majority of merchandise was manufactured in the Far East with an overseas staff to monitor quality control.

The company's success was partly due to what Ortenberg described as an "exploding market" of millions of baby-boomer women who during the 1980s were graduating from college and graduate schools to enter the professions. Encouraged by Claiborne's merchandise selection, women were becoming more confident about dressing for work and selected clothing that was appropriate for work and reflected their personalities.

In 1986, when company sales reached $1.2 billion, it joined the list of *Fortune* magazine's 500 largest industrial companies in the United States; it was one of only two companies started by a woman included on the list. Also in 1986 Claiborne, who was company president, became chairman of the board and chief executive officer. Until she retired in 1989, Claiborne remained the creative force behind the company's success and advised its design teams. She always emphasized fit, color, comfort, and good value as the company's goals.

In spring 1988 the company opened its first retail stores, and by spring 1992 it had approximately 45 stores. Sales were $2.1 billion for 1992. However, by early 1993 the company began to feel the effects of a growing popularity of discount stores compared to department stores in their decreasing sales.

Claiborne and her husband retired from active management of the company in 1989 to pursue their environmental and philanthropic interests. The Liz Claiborne and Art Ortenberg Foundation was established in 1989 with assets of $10 million; it provides substantial support for wilderness preservation. They spent six months of each year at a ranch house in Swan Valley, Montana; they also had a home on Fire Island, New York, and one on the Caribbean Island of St. Barts.

In 1990 Claiborne and her husband were elected to the National Business Hall of Fame, sponsored by Junior Achievement. A few of the many honors awarded Claiborne were induction into the National Sales Hall of Fame in 1991 and an honorary Doctorate degree from the Rhode Island School of Design the same year.

Liz Claiborne Inc. remains a fashion mainstay in mid-1997. Sales for 1996 reached $2.2 billion and the company now employs over 7000. Liz Claiborne herself remains active through a variety of charities. She and her husband still travel between their homes and avoid the public eye as much as possible.

## Further Reading

There are several sources for additional information on Liz Claiborne's business and fashion sense. Elsa Klensch's interview article in *Vogue* (August 1986) gives Claiborne's views on how fashion had changed since 1976. "Can Ms. Fashion Bounce Back?" *Business Week* (January 16, 1989) discusses the company's growth, market share, and history. Valerie Steele, *Women of Fashion, Twentieth Century Designers* (1991) provides a brief perspective on the Liz Claiborne label, emphasizing its practicality and clothing for ordinary working women. *Liz Claiborne, Inc. 1992 Annual Report* describes each division and indicates its relative success. □

# Margaret Antoinette Clapp

**The winner of the 1948 Pulitzer Prize for biography, Margaret Antoinette Clapp (1910-1974) was a distinguished American educator who served as president of Wellesley College from 1949 to 1966.**

Margaret Clapp was born April 10, 1910, in East Orange, New Jersey, the daughter of Anna Roth and Alfred Chapin Clapp, an insurance agent. She graduated from East Orange High School in 1926 and from Wellesley College in 1930. She received an A.B. from the latter with a focus on history and economics. While in college she was named a Wellesley College Scholar, an award given for academic excellence.

Following graduation she taught English literature at the Todhunter School for Girls in New York City. She stayed in this position for 12 years, during which time she also worked at Columbia University for her master's degree in history, which she received in 1937. During World War II and shortly thereafter she taught in the history departments of various universities in the New York City area, including the City College of New York (1942-1944), Douglass (1945-1946), and Columbia (1946-1947). At the same time Clapp continued her graduate studies at Columbia in American history.

Her doctoral dissertation was on John Bigelow (1817-1911), an intriguing 19th-century political figure who was an active supporter of the Free Soil movement in the pre-Civil War period (the attempt to ensure that all subsequent territories admitted to the union be free and not slave states). Known also for other progressive ideas such as prison reform, Bigelow served as editor of the New York *Evening Post,* as New York secretary of state, and as American ambassador to France. Philosophically, he was attracted to Swedenborgianism, a 19th-century mystical doctrine derived from the writings of Emmanuel Swedenborg (1688-1772).

In the biography which grew from her thesis Clapp stressed the influence of Swedenborg's theories upon Bige-

low. She wrote the dissertation under the direction of Allan Nevins. *Forgotten First Citizen: John Bigelow* was published in 1947 and won the Pulitzer Prize for biography in 1948.

Following a brief term at Brooklyn College, Clapp assumed the presidency of Wellesley College in 1949. At the time there were only four other women in the country serving as presidents of major colleges. An effective administrator, Clapp expanded Wellesley's facilities and resources considerably. The endowment multiplied threefold during her tenure, and three new dormitories, a faculty club, and a new library wing were added to the campus. In addition, Clapp instituted a generous leave policy for junior faculty and increased faculty salaries by 150 percent. In 1950 Clapp edited a collection of articles, *The Modern University*, to which she contributed a chapter on the national postsecondary education scene following World War II.

A feminist during the 1950s when conventional notions of feminine identity were at a peak, Clapp maintained that women's sole purpose in life was neither motherhood nor wifedom. Against the then popular Freudian "mystique" (that women violated their natural destiny by becoming educated professionals), Clapp urged that women pursue careers and that social programs such as day care centers and domestic services be provided to allow women to combine work with domestic commitments.

In 1966 Clapp retired from Wellesley and the following year served briefly as chief administrator of a women's college (Lady Doak) in Mandurai, India. In 1968 she accepted a position as United States cultural attaché to India.

Later she served as minister-councilor of public affairs in the United States Information Agency (USIA), an office she held from 1970 to 1971.

Clapp retired from public life in the early 1970s and returned to Tyringham, Massachusetts, where she died of cancer in 1974. The library at Wellesley is named in her honor, a fitting tribute to a woman who furthered the cause of women's education during a period when national interest in it was at a low ebb.

## Further Reading

No biography of Clapp yet exists. Short summaries may be found in *Notable American Women* and *American Women Writers*. She was the subject of a cover story in *Time* on October 10, 1949. Clapp's papers are at Wellesley College. Several issues of the *Wellesley Alumnae Magazine* (notably those of March 1958, November 1961, and July 6, 1966) include articles by or about her. □

# Patsy Cline

**Vocalist Patsy Cline (1932-1963) was one of the first women to break into the country and western music scene, which was, until then, dominated by men.**

Up until Patsy Cline's recordings in the late 1950s and early 1960s there were only a handful of country and western female singers; and the title of queen belonged solely to Kitty Wells. It was Cline who dethroned Wells with classic performances on cuts like "Walkin' After Midnight" and the Willie Nelson composition "Crazy," which combined the pop characteristics of Patti Page and Kay Starr with the hillbilly traits of Hank Williams. All three singers were major influences on Cline's style.

## Career Began at Age Four

Cline's entertainment career began at the tender age of four, when she won a local amateur contest for tap dancing in her hometown of Winchester, Virginia. By age eight she was playing the piano and singing in her church's choir. In 1948 the drugstore counter girl began singing in nightclubs with Bill Peer and his Melody Boys. Wally Fowler of the Grand Ole Opry convinced the 16-year-old to go to Nashville for an appearance on Roy Acuff's "WSM Dinner Bell" radio program. Cline hung around Nashville trying to break into the industry but ended up working as a club dancer.

Cline headed back home shortly thereafter and continued singing with Peer's band until 1954, when she returned to Nashville and signed a contract with William McCall's 4 Star Sales Co. out of Pasadena, California. Cline's first recording session was on June 1, 1955, and her first three songs were leased to Coral Records, a subsidiary of Decca. Part of her deal with 4 Star, which included one-time session fees with no royalties, stipulated that she could only record material that belonged to McCall's company. This may have been part of the reason that the majority of her

performing the song but was finally convinced by one of the regulars on Godfrey's show, Janette Davis. The television audience went wild and gave Cline a standing ovation.

4 Star rushed to release the single on February 11 and it shot all the way to number three on *Billboard'* s country chart. More importantly, however, "Walkin'" also rose to number 17 on the pop charts. Donn Hecht had originally written the tune for Kay Starr, who turned it down, but Cline and Bradley managed to use it as a vehicle to bridge the gap between hillbilly and pop. McCall, whose company was eventually shut down as a result of questionable business dealings, was unfortunately too slow in following up on the hit. He did convince Cline to renew her contract, but it took another six months before she recorded another session, "Fingerprints"/"A Stranger in My Arms." Her remaining work with 4 Star was unspectacular and in 1959 she jumped to Decca Records, insisting upon a $1,000 advance.

## Vocals Soared to New Heights

It wasn't until 1961, one year after she became a regular cast member of the Grand Ole Opry, that Cline had her second hit, "I Fall to Pieces." The song went to number one on the country charts and was joined by "Crazy," another Top 10 hit of 1961. Cline's vocals began to soar to new heights on material that was less restrictive than 4 Star's catalog. For the next two years she recorded major hits with "She's Got You" (a number-one hit), "When I Get Through With You, You'll Love Me," "Faded Love," and "Leavin' On Your Mind" (all Top 10's).

Cline was just coming into her own when tragedy struck on March 5, 1963. On the way home from a Kansas City benefit for disc jockey Cactus Jack Callat, Cline, Randy Hughes, Cowboy Copas, and Hawkshaw Hawkins were killed when the airplane they were flying in crashed near Camden, Tennessee. At the age of 31 she had been performing for over twenty years, yet recording for less than eight.

## A Legend

Ironically, perhaps her most identifiable tune, "Sweet Dreams," was released posthumously and also broke the Top 10. Even with her relatively small collection of songs, Cline managed to break new ground and influence hundreds of female, and some male, country singers since. Loretta Lynn, undoubtedly Cline's most successful pupil, recorded a tribute LP, *I Remember Patsy,* featuring nine of Cline's songs.

"Patsy Cline knew how to cry on both sides of the microphone," wrote Donn Hecht in *The Country Music Encyclopedia.* "And the why of it all, explained by many, understood by few, is slowly becoming a legend unparalleled by any other country entertainer since Hank Williams."

early work did not sell very well. She was also tackling a wide variety of styles that made it hard to categorize her.

## Radical Image

Producer Owen Bradley was trying to create a new genre with Cline by bathing her voice in full, jazzy orchestrations at his Quonset Studios in an effort to counter the rising popularity of rock and roll. According to *The Listener's Guide to Country Music,* "Patsy Cline was his ultimate country success. For him, she played down her country characteristics. For her, he played down his popular music background. The results were records full of tension and dynamics."

It would, however, take some time before the formula caught on, as the country scene was changing from hillbilly to country and western and was still mainly dominated by male artists. Cline's radical image as a two-fisted, hard-drinking woman definitely made her stand out from the rest of the Nashville crowd, but any chance of success would rely on her voice and songs. Her talents shined on both slow torchers and up-tempo cuts but her 4 Star sessions never did fully realize her potential, with the exception of "Walkin' After Midnight."

## "Walkin' After Midnight" a Hit

Cline recorded the tune on November 8, 1956, but it was the rendition of the song she performed on *Arthur Godfrey's Talent Scouts* television program on January 28, 1957, that got the industry's attention. She had debated

## Further Reading

Lazarus, Lois, *Country Is My Music!,* Messner, 1980.
Malone, Bill, *Country Music U.S.A.—A Fifty-Year History,* American Folk Society, 1968.
Oermann, Robert K., with Douglas B. Green, *The Listener's Guide to Country Music,* Facts on File, 1983.

Stambler, Irwin, and Grellun Landon, *The Encyclopedia of Folk, Country & Western Music,* St. Martin's Press, 1983.

*Stars of Country Music—Uncle Dave Macon to Johnny Rodriguez,* edited by Bill C. Malone and Judith McCulloh, University of Illinois Press, 1975.

Shestack, Melvin, *The Country Music Encyclopedia,* KBO, 1974.

□

# Hillary Rodham Clinton

**Described as the first major U.S. female political figure since Eleanor Roosevelt, Hillary Rodham Clinton (born 1947) was considered a force to be reckoned with in American politics. Married to Bill Clinton, the 42nd president of the United States, she figured prominently in the Clinton administration with substantial influence on domestic policy-making.**

A First Lady with an independent professional identity, Hillary Rodham Clinton had experience as a corporate lawyer, a tenacious fighter for educational reform, a nationally recognized expert on children's legal rights, and a director of both corporate and nonprofit boards. Hillary Diane Rodham was born on October 26, 1947, in Chicago, Illinois. She grew up with two younger male siblings in Park Ridge, a conservative, upper-class suburb north of the city. Her parents, Hugh and Dorothy Howell Rodham, reared their three children with traditional mid-American values that stressed family, church, school, and social obligations that evolved from the adage that "to whom much is given, much is expected."

As a youth Rodham was influenced by her religious training in Methodism, with its emphasis on personal salvation and active applied Christianity. A seminal influence in her teen years was a youth minister, the Reverend Don Jones, who introduced Rodham and her peers to some of the issues, causes, and movements of the time and who encouraged involvement in direct social action. It was under Jones's guidance that she read religious philosophers such as Soren Kierkegaard and Dietrich Bonhoeffer; babysat the children of migrant farm workers; and met the Reverend Dr. Martin Luther King, Jr., when he came to Chicago on a speaking tour.

Rodham attended the public schools of Park Ridge and in 1965 enrolled in Wellesley College, where she majored in political science and took a minor in psychology. Her undergraduate years were important to her developing world view and growing sense of personal empowerment. An exceptional communicator, she was a catalyst for many of the movements for change occurring on the Wellesley campus and was involved also in a number of off-campus activities. She spent her final undergraduate summer in Washington, D.C., working for the House Republican Conference and returned to campus to spend her senior year as president of the student government. Graduating with highest distinction in 1969, Rodham gave the first student address delivered during commencement in the history of the college. In the fall she enrolled in Yale University Law School, where she was among 30 women in the class of 1972.

## Experience in Washington, D.C.

Rodham's experiences at Yale helped to focus her areas of interest and commitment toward issues related to children, particularly poor and disadvantaged ones. She became acquainted with Marian Wright Edelman, a civil rights attorney who headed up the Washington Research Project, a non-profit group based in Washington, D.C., later to be known as the Children's Defense Fund. Spending a summer internship in Washington, D.C., Rodham was assigned by Edelman to Walter Mondale's Senate subcommittee, which was studying the plight of migrant families. In subsequent years at Yale she volunteered to work in the Yale Child Studies Center and the Yale-New Haven Hospital, assisted the New Haven Legal Assistance Association, and engaged in several other projects aimed at improving understanding of, and effecting improvements in, the legal system where children were concerned. An extra year of study at Yale prior to her graduation in 1973 further refined her expertise in child law issues.

After graduation Rodham moved to Washington and took a full-time position with the Children's Defense Fund. As staff attorney, she worked on juvenile justice problems, traveling the country comparing census data with school populations and becoming involved in litigations related to juvenile issues. In January 1974 she was chosen as one of 43 lawyers handpicked to work on the legal staff of the House Judiciary Committee, which was charged with preparing impeachment proceedings against President Richard Nixon resulting from the Watergate scandal. When Nixon resigned on August 9, 1974, and the legal staff disbanded, she accepted a teaching position at the University of Arkansas Law School. It was in Arkansas in 1975 that she married Bill Clinton, whom she had met while attending Yale.

## A Life in Little Rock

Two years after their marriage Bill Clinton became attorney general of Arkansas, and the couple moved to Little Rock. In 1977 Hillary Clinton joined the prestigious Rose Law Firm, said to be one of the oldest law firms west of the Mississippi River, and became involved in an area of law known as "intellectual property." Her primary focus, however, remained in the area of children's rights, and she helped found Arkansas Advocates for Children and Families. She continued to write on the rights of children, revising an earlier article published in the *Harvard Educational Review.* The revised essay, "Children's Rights: A Legal Perspective," appearing in *Children Rights: Contemporary Perspectives,* developed and refined her arguments for the implementation of children's legal rights. She also was appointed by President Jimmy Carter to the board of the Legal Services Corporation in Washington (1978 to 1981), a federally-funded program that provided legal assistance to the poor. In January 1978, following her husband's successful bid for the governorship, Clinton became Arkansas' first lady. Later that year she also became the first woman ever to become a partner in the Rose Law Firm. In February 1980 she gave birth to a daughter, Chelsea Victoria.

In her 11 years as first lady of Arkansas, Clinton continued to pursue activities aimed at public service and policy reforms in the state. In her husband's second term she served as chair of the Arkansas Education Standards Committee, established to study the state's educational system and to recommend changes in the standards for public schools. Released to the public in September 1983, the standards report was controversial in several aspects, although it would eventually become state law. In 1985 Hillary Clinton also gave leadership to the establishment in Arkansas of the Home Instruction Program for Pre-School Youngsters (HIPPY). The program, which brought instruction and tutorials into impoverished homes to teach four- and five-year-olds, became one of the largest programs in the country, with over 2,400 mothers participating.

In 1987 she was elected chairperson of the board of the Children's Defense Fund and of the New World Foundation, a philanthropic organization headquartered in New York that had helped launch the Children's Defense Fund. In that year, too, Hillary and Bill Clinton were awarded the National Humanitarian Award by the National Conference of Christians and Jews. Enjoying a national prominence, Hillary Clinton held directorships on the boards of directors of several corporations, including Wal-Mart, TCBY Enterprises (yogurt), and Lafarge (cement). She would also be cited by the *National Law Journal* in 1988, and again in 1991, as one of the "One Hundred Most Influential Lawyers in America."

Analyses of Clinton were varied; however, they generally pointed to her "spiritual center" and her "continuous textured development." *People* magazine, as one example, noted that "her social concern and her political thought rest on a spiritual foundation" (January 25, 1993). The "politics of virtue" according to the *The New York Times Magazine,* informed the actions of the newest First Lady (May 23, 1993).

## In the White House

As the wife of the president of the United States Clinton remained an advocate for many of the programs and issues to which she earlier devoted her time and professional expertise. Her stated goal of "making a difference" in the world led her to press for reforms in many aspects of the American system, including health care and child welfare. Hers is said to be "the most purely voiced expression of the collective spirit of the Clinton administration, a spirit that is notable . . . for the long reach of its reformist ambitions . . . ." (*The New York Times,* May 23, 1993). She provided leadership in a number of areas, with the most notable appointment in the first year of the Clinton administration being head of the Task Force on National Health Care, with responsibility for preparing legislation, lobbying proposals before Congress, and marshaling strategy for passage of a comprehensive reform package.

Her White House agenda beyond health care reform included promoting diversity in personnel appointments—an effort she began with her role in the transition group—and pushing for children's issues. With an office in the White House's west wing, close to the center of power, Clinton was expected to remold the role of First Lady for the 21st century.

Clinton has remained an active and vital figure in the White House throughout her husband's presidency. In August of 1995, Hillary Clinton was invited to deliver the keynote address at the United Nations International Conference on Women near Beijing, China. Early in 1996 Clinton and her daughter Chelsea made a goodwill trip to South Asia, addressing women's issues in Pakistan and India.

In November 1996 Bill Clinton was re-elected president of the United States. In that same year Hillary Clinton published her first book entitled *It Takes a Village: And Other Lessons Children Teach Us.*

## Further Reading

Several biographies provide coverage of Hillary Rodham Clinton's personal and professional life as well as her philosophical development and early tenure in the White House. These include the following: Norman King, *Hillary: Her True Story* (1993); Donnie Radcliffe, *Hillary Rodham Clinton: A First Lady for Our Time* (1993); and Judith Warner, *Hillary Clinton: The Inside Story* (1993). Short biographical articles and political analyses are found in a variety of magazines and newspapers. Recommended among these are Patricia O'Brien, "The First Lady with a Career?" *Working Woman* (August 1992); Margaret Carlson, "All Eyes on Hillary," *TIME* (September 14,

1992); Michael Kelly, "Saint Hillary," *The New York Times Magazine* (May 23, 1993); and "The Clintons: Taking Their Measure," *U.S. News and World Report* (January 31, 1994). Additional information may be obtained from the White House web site at http://www.whitehouse.com. □

# Jacqueline Cochran

**Jacqueline Cochran (1910-1980) rose from childhood poverty to become an aviation pioneer. She was the first woman to fly in the Bendix Trophy Transcontinental Race in 1935, winning it in 1938, and was the first woman to ferry a bomber across the Atlantic Ocean in support of the war effort in 1941. By 1961, she had become the first woman to break the sound barrier and held more speed records than any other pilot in the world.**

The achievements of Jacqueline Cochran would be remarkable for anyone but are even more spectacular considering her humble beginnings and the fact she chose to compete in an arena not readily open to women of her time. An orphan, Cochran's exact birth date is uncertain. While she was raised with the name of her foster family, Cochran later picked from a phone book the name she would make famous. Early years offered little comfort. Cochran recounted in her autobiography *Jackie Cochran: An Autobiography* how she didn't have shoes until buying her own when she was eight. "Food at best consisted of the barest essentials—sometimes nothing except what I foraged for myself in the woods of the Northern Florida sawmill towns my foster family called home. . . . I've often heard that if you want someone to really enjoy the pleasures of heaven, then just pitch her into hell for a spell. Perhaps that's why I enjoyed my life to the brimful."

## Childhood in Poverty

Cochran attempted to leave the squalor of her childhood by running away with the circus. The circus left without her, but it wasn't long before she found another way out. In her early teens she moved in with a Jewish family that owned hair salons. Underage, Cochran worked mixing dyes when she secured a promotion by threatening her employer with disclosure to child labor authorities. A year later, Cochran moved to Montgomery, Alabama, to work in another salon. There, a prominent client secured her admission to nursing school. She recalled that "the formal academic requirements for entry had been waived for me, as promised," Cochran wrote in her autobiography. "I'm certain that hospital had never admitted a second-grade dropout to the program before." Following training, Cochran abandoned hope of passing the state board exam. "My handwriting alone, not to mention my rudimentary arithmetic, would never have allowed me to pass." She went to work for a Florida country doctor where a license wasn't a necessity. Fearful the quality of treatment she and the doctor were

providing was worse than none at all, Cochran left medicine and moved to Pensacola, Florida, where she became part owner of a beauty shop. There she picked "Cochran" out of the phone book.

In 1929 she moved to New York City and blustered Charles of the Ritz into offering her a salon job she ended up turning down. "I was so stubborn." Cochran went to work in a Saks Fifth Avenue salon. In 1932 on a trip to Miami, she met Floyd Odlum, the successful businessman whom she would marry in 1936. "Every orphan dreams of marrying a millionaire, but I had no idea at first that Floyd Odlum was worth so much money." Cochran confided her idea of becoming a traveling cosmetics saleswoman. His mind on the Depression, Odlum said success could only come from covering a large territory. "Get your pilot's license," he told her. In the year they met, the two made a wager: if Cochran could get her license in three weeks, Odlum would pay the $495 course fee. Cochran won the bet.

## Took to the Skies Immediately

Emboldened by her success, Cochran set out on a solo flight to Canada, learning compass navigation from a helpful fellow aviator along the way. A commercial pilot's license followed, as did Cochran's entry in her first race in 1934, the MacRobertson London-to-Australia race. With a great deal of effort by Cochran and others working on her behalf, she secured a plane with which to enter the race, one manufactured by the Granville Brothers called a Gee Bee. "There were few pilots who flew Gee Bees and then lived to talk about it. Jimmy Doolittle was one. I was another." Cochran flew the race with copilot Wesley Smith. Malfunctioning flaps put the pair down in Bucharest, Rumania, and out of the race.

One year later, in 1935, Cochran entered her first Bendix Trophy Cross-Country Air Race, a race that is "to aviators what the Kentucky Derby still is to horse breeders," Cochran wrote. The year before she had managed to get the race open to women but didn't make it to the starting line herself. Cochran finished third in the 1937 Bendix and won the famous race in 1938; the same year First Lady Eleanor Roosevelt awarded her the first of 15 Harmon Trophies she would win. That first trophy was her recognition for setting three speed records. After winning the 1938 Bendix race from Burbank, California, to Cleveland, Ohio in 8 hours, 10 minutes and 31 seconds in a Seversky Pursuit, Cochran set a new women's west-to-east transcontinental record of 10 hours, 7 minutes, 10 seconds.

## Always A Lady

Women could compete with and often surpass men, but being ladylike also was a Cochran priority. Before stepping from the cockpit, she usually paused to apply lipstick. No longer a teen-ager mixing hair dye in someone else's beauty parlor, Cochran set about building her own cosmetics empire. "I told Floyd that I wanted my own beauty business so I could end up at the top. I had started at the bottom and supervising shampoos and permanents was not for me anymore." In 1935, the same year she entered her first Bendix race, Jacqueline Cochran Cosmetics began manufacturing operations. A popular product was Cochran's "Perk-Up" cylinder, a container holding enough makeup for any woman traveling light. "I would take one on all my trips, all my races."

There were many more races, victories and records. In 1939, Cochran established a women's national altitude record and broke the international open-class speed record for men and women. The following year she broke the 2,000 km international speed record and the 100 km national record. During this time one of Cochran's dearest friends was fellow aviator Amelia Earhart, who Cochran met in 1935.

## Lost Famous Friend to Skies

Cochran assured readers of her autobiography she and Earhart were not competitors. Earhart flew for distance; Cochran was after speed, but she later did pursue distance and altitude. Earhart shared in Cochran's interest in parapsychology, first sparked by Odlum. Cochran and Earhart used what they considered extra-sensory powers to locate the crash sites of downed aircraft. Earhart's husband, George Putnam, was skeptical and someone Cochran considered less than a friend. "I didn't like that man at all." But Putnam called on Cochran for help when Earhart failed to arrive at a planned stop on her 1937 quest to encircle the globe. Cochran wrote she "saw" Earhart after her plane went down over the South Pacific. "'Circling—cannot see island—gas running low' were the last words anyone heard from Amelia, including me. That still hurts," Cochran wrote.

In spite of the achievements of Cochran and others, women aviators had to fight for the right to serve their country during World War II. Cochran was in the forefront of the battle. In June 1941, Cochran became the first woman to pilot a bomber across the Atlantic Ocean. However, because she had some difficulty operating the plane's hand brake during practice flights, she was forced to turn the controls over to a male pilot on take-off and landing. The flight was a milestone male pilots fought all the way. Cochran was accused of wanting to make the flight for publicity reasons. Male pilots also charged that allowing women to fly bombers would take work away from themselves. Someone tried to prevent Cochran's flight by holding up a required visa. "In a contest of power and friends, I knew I could win, so I contacted the American consul in Montreal, who called the Passport Department in D.C. and, voilà the visa arrived sooner than someone else ever predicted."

## Organized Women for War

Seeing British women ferrying planes for their country's war effort gave Cochran the idea to start a similar program in the United States. She told President Franklin D. Roosevelt her plan over lunch. Cochran was against integrating women aviators into the U.S. war effort on a piecemeal basis. "I felt that a few good women pilots amidst all the men would simply go down as a flash in the historical pan. I wanted to make a point with my planned program." Perhaps she did have extra-sensory powers; it would be many years after the war before women aviators would receive recognition for their contributions.

In preparation for a larger effort in the United States, Cochran organized a group of 25 female American aviators to ferry planes for Great Britain's Air Transport Auxiliary. "More than a month before Pearl Harbor brought World War II to America, I was off on my own wartime project—a project that would take me away from Floyd and home for nearly three years." The British program was a success, and the United States decided a similar program also would work. In 1942, Cochran was assigned the task of training 500 women pilots. The number would eventually grow to more than 1,000. A bill had been introduced in Congress to militarize Cochran's pilots and incorporate them into the Army Air Corps, giving them military benefits. This is what Cochran wanted as she saw plans for a separate Air Force. She fought attempts to make her pilots part of the Women's Army Corps. In 1943, the Women's Airforce Service Pilots (WASPs) was formed, and Cochran was named director of women pilots.

"The Women's Airforce Service Pilots program really proved something," WASP member Margaret Boylan is quoted saying in Cochran's autobiography. "It was a marvelous period of history, made possible by Jackie Cochran. When you consider how competitive this woman was with other women equal to her, it's amazing that she worked so hard for our benefit." Among the obstacles the women pilots and Cochran overcame was the belief women's flying ability was affected by their menstrual cycles. More than 25,000 women applied for WASP training; 1,800 were accepted and 1,074 graduated. The women aviators flew about 60 million miles for the Army Air Forces with only 38 fatalities, about one to every 16,000 hours of flying.

Cochran lost the battle to have the WASPs militarized in 1944, denying the women pilots military benefits including the GI bill. The WASP program was deactivated at the end of 1944. In 1977, Congress passed a bill giving the WASPs honorable discharges and declaring them veterans. It took two more years to make it official.

### Broke Her Own Records

Cochran's aviation career continued well after the war, as did other activities. She was the first woman to enter Japan after the World War II, and she traveled to the Far East as a correspondent for *Liberty* magazine. In 1956 she ran, unsuccessfully, for a California congressional seat, campaigning by flying her plane around her own district.

In 1953, Cochran was the first woman to break the sound barrier and received a Gold Medal from the Fèdèration Aèronautique Internationale. She was president of the organization, holding two terms, from 1958 to 1961. In 1962 she established 69 inter-city and straight-line distance records for aircraft manufacturer Lockheed and was the first woman to fly a jet across the Atlantic. The same year Cochran set nine international speed, distance and altitude records in a Northrop T-38 military jet. In 1963, Cochran set the 15-25 km course record in a Lockheed F-104 Starfighter, going 1,273.109 mph, and broke the 100 km course record with a speed of 1,203.686 mph. The following year she began resetting her own records in the Lockheed F-104G Starfighter. In the 15-25 km course she set a record of 1,429.297 mph; for the 100 km course her record was 1,302 mph; and for the 500 km course she set a record of 1,135 mph.

Not only was Cochran competitive with herself; she was competitive with others. When she was a child, Cochran was forced to give a cherished doll, her only doll, to a younger sister in her foster family. When they were adults, the younger sister sought Cochran's aid in New York City. Cochran gave it but demanded her childhood doll as payment. At Cochran's insistence, she was buried with that doll following her death in 1980 at her Indio, California home.

### Further Reading

Cochran, Jacqueline, *The Stars at Noon,* Ayer, 1979.
Cochran, Jacqueline, and Maryann Bucknum Brinley, *Jackie Cochran: An Autobiography,* Bantam Books, 1987.
Fisher, Marquita O., *Jacqueline Cochran: First Lady of Flight,* Garrard, 1973.
McGuire, Nina, Sammons, Sandra Wallus and Sandra Sammons,*Jacqueline Cochran: America's Fearless Aviator,* Tailored Tours, 1997.
Smith, Elizabeth Simpson, *Coming Out Right: The Story of Jacqueline Cochran, the First Woman Aviator to Break the Sound Barrier,* Walker & Co., 1991.
Wayne, Bennett, *Four Women of Courage,* Garrard, 1975.
*Los Angeles Times* (Orange County Edition) October 2, 1996.
*Stamps,* February 24, 1996; March 30, 1996.
*USA Today,* October 14, 1994.
*U.S. News & World Report,* November 17, 1997.
''Jacqueline Cochran,'' *Allstar Network,* http://www.allstar.fiu.edu/aero/cochran1.htm (March 6, 1998).
''Jacqueline Cochran,'' *First Flight,* http://www.firstlfight.org/shrine/jacqueline_cochran.html (March 6, 1998).
''Jacqueline Cochran,'' *Motor Sports Hall of Fame,* http://www.mshf.com/hof/cochran.htm (March 6, 1998). ☐

# Bessie Coleman

**Bessie Coleman (1892-1926) was the first African American to earn the coveted international pilot's license, issued in Paris (June 15, 1921) by the Fédération Aéronautique Internationale.**

Bessie Coleman was born on January 26, 1892, in a one-room, dirt-floored cabin in Atlanta, Texas, to George and Susan Coleman, the illiterate children of slaves. When Bessie was two years old, her father, a day laborer, moved his family to Waxahachie, Texas, where he bought a quarter-acre of land and built a three-room house in which two more daughters were born.

When George Coleman's hopes for a better living in Waxahachie remained unfulfilled, and with five of his nine living children still at home, he proposed moving again, this time to Indian territory in Oklahoma. There, on a reservation, his heritage of three Native American grandparents would give him the civil rights denied to both African Americans and Native Americans in Texas. In 1901, after Susan refused to go with him, he went to Oklahoma on his own, leaving his family behind in Waxahachie. Susan found work as a domestic, her two sons became day laborers, and Bessie was left to be the caretaker of her two younger sisters.

Education for Coleman was limited to eight grades in a one-room schoolhouse that closed whenever the students were needed in the fields to help their families harvest cotton. Already responsible for her sisters and the household chores while her mother worked, Coleman was a reluctant cotton picker but an intelligent and expert accountant. The only member of the family who could accurately add the total weight of the cotton they picked, she increased the total whenever she could by putting her foot on the scale when the foreman wasn't looking.

Coleman easily established her position as family leader, reading aloud to her siblings and mother at night, winning the prize for selling the most tickets for a church benefit, and assuring her ambitious church-going mother that she intended to ''amount to something.'' After completing school she worked as a laundress and saved her wages until 1910 when she left for Oklahoma to attend Langston University. She left after one year when her funds were exhausted.

Back in Waxahachie Coleman again worked as a laundress until 1915 when she moved to Chicago to live with her older brother, Walter, a Pullman porter. Within months she became a manicurist and moved to a place of her own while she continued to seek—and finally, in 1920, to find—a goal for her life: aviation.

Cultivating the friendship of leaders in South Side Chicago's African American community, Coleman found a sponsor in Robert Abbott, publisher of the nation's largest African American weekly, the *Chicago Defender*. There were no African American aviators in the area and, when no white pilot was willing to teach her to fly, Coleman appealed to Abbott, who suggested that she go to France. The French, he said, were not racists and were the world's leaders in aviation.

Coleman took French language lessons while managing a chili parlor and, with backing from Abbott and a wealthy real estate dealer, Jessie Binga, she left for France late in 1920. There she completed flight training at the best school in France and was awarded her F.A.I. (Fédération Aéronautique Internationale) license on June 15, 1921. She returned to the United States in September 1921 but soon realized that she needed to expand her repertoire and learn aerobatics if she were to make a living giving exhibition flights. She went back to Europe the following February and for the next six months gained further flying experience in Holland, France, and Germany.

Back in New York in August 1922, Coleman outlined to reporters the objectives she intended to pursue for the remainder of her life. She would be a leader, she said, in introducing aviation to her race. She would found a school for aviators of any race, and she would appear before audiences in churches, schools, and theaters to arouse the interest of African Americans in the new, expanding technology of flight.

Intelligent, beautiful, and eloquent, Coleman often exaggerated her remarkable-enough accomplishments in the interest of better publicity and bigger audiences. She even achieved occasional brief notice from the press of the time, which ordinarily confined its coverage of African Americans to actors, athletes and entertainers or those involved in sex, crime, or violence. But the African American press of the country, primarily weekly newspapers, quickly proclaimed her "Queen Bell."

In December 1922, after a number of successful air shows on the East Coast and in Chicago, Coleman walked out on the starring role of a New York movie in production, publicly denouncing the script as "Uncle Tom stuff" demeaning to her race. The abrupt move alienated a number of influential African American critics and producers and threatened to end her career. But Coleman bounced back by going to California and air-dropping advertising leaflets for a tire company in exchange for money to buy a JN4, or "Jenny"—a surplus U.S. Army training plane from World War I.

On February 4, 1923, however, within only days of getting her plane, Coleman crashed shortly after takeoff from Santa Monica en route to her first scheduled West Coast air show. The Jenny was destroyed and Coleman suffered injuries that hospitalized her for three months. Returning to Chicago to recuperate, it took her another 18 months to find backers for a series of shows in Texas. Her flights and theater appearances there during the summer of 1925 were highly successful, earning her enough to make a down payment on another surplus Jenny she found at Love Field, Dallas.

To raise the rest of the money, in January 1926 she returned to the East Coast, where she had signed up for a number of speaking engagements and exhibition flights in borrowed planes in Georgia and Florida. In Florida she met the Rev. Hezekiah Keith Hill and his wife, Viola Tillinghast, community activists from Orlando who invited her to stay with them. She also met Edwin M. Beeman, heir to the Beeman Chewing Gum fortune, whose interest in flying led him to give her the payment due on her airplane in Dallas. At last, she wrote to one of her sisters, she was going to be able to earn enough money to open her school for fliers.

Coleman left Orlando by train to give a benefit exhibition for the Jacksonville Negro Welfare League, scheduled for May 1, 1926. William D. Wills, the young white mechanic-pilot who flew her plane to her from Love Field, made three forced landings en route. Two local pilots who witnessed his touchdown at Jacksonville's Paxon Field said later that the Jenny was so worn and so poorly maintained they couldn't understand how it made it all the way from Dallas. On April 30 Wills piloted the plane on a trial flight while Coleman sat in the other cockpit to survey the area over which she was to fly and parachute jump the next day. Her seat belt was unattached because she had to be able to lean out over the edge of the plane while picking the best sites for her program. At an altitude of 1,000 feet, the plane dived, then flipped over, throwing Coleman out. Moments later Wills crashed. Both were killed.

Coleman had three memorial services—in Jacksonville, Orlando, and Chicago, the last attended by thousands. She was buried at Chicago's Lincoln Cemetery and gradually, over the years following her death, achieved recognition at last as a hero of early aviation and of her race.

## Further Reading

The best source of information on Bessie Coleman is *Queen Bess—The Life of Bessie Coleman* (1993), written by Doris Rich in large part to correct the many misstatements in contemporary sources. Two reliable places where information can be found are the DuSable Museum of African American History in Chicago and the National Air and Space Museum, Smithsonian Institution, Washington, D.C.

## Additional Sources

Fisher, Lillian M., *Brave Bessie: flying free*, Dallas, Tex.: Hendrick-Long Publishing Co., 1995.

Freydberg, Elizabeth Hadley, *Bessie Coleman, the brownskin lady bird*, New York: Garland Pub., 1994.

Rich, Doris L., *Queen Bess: daredevil aviator*, Washington: Smithsonian Institution Press, 1993. □

# Eileen Collins

**On February 4, 1995, at 12:22 a.m. in Cape Canaveral, Florida, thousands of people held their breath as Lieutenant Colonel Eileen Collins (born 1956)**

**launched the U.S. Space Shuttle Discovery into the heavens on her first mission as pilot.**

Flames burst from the shuttle's engines as smoke enveloped the launch pad. During the shuttle's violent ascent, acceleration is so forceful that the astronauts are pinned against their seats and breathe with difficulty as G-forces pound against their chests. The shuttle approaches an escape velocity of 3,000 miles per hour and later accelerates to 17,500 miles per hour. From her position inside the craft, U.S. Air Force Lieutenant Colonel Eileen Collins handled the takeoff with extraordinary confidence.

Perhaps piloting the shuttle seemed to be all in a day's work for Collins because she had rehearsed the takeoff hundreds of times in a simulator. She spent the previous month practicing takeoffs and landings for up to 14 hours per day and, during the previous six months, spent an average of three hours per day in the simulator. But the morning of February 4 was the real thing, and there was no room for error. Fear and excitement undoubtedly swelled in Collins as the price of failure was contemplated.

### First Woman to Pilot Shuttle

Although Collins's trip was the Discovery's twentieth flight and the sixty-seventh for the shuttle program, the voyage was a special one for a few reasons. First, the Discovery made a history-making rendezvous with the Russian Mir space station. Second, Collins was the first female pilot

ever to fly the shuttle. Nineteen other women have been astronauts, beginning with Sally Ride in 1983, and have performed research and made space walks and repairs, but Collins was the first to actually pilot the craft.

Collins's responsibility for the flight included steering the space ship by firing small rockets, monitoring flight instruments, and handling the function of radar and navigation systems. Although the space shuttle was like no other aircraft she had ever been in, she mentioned in an interview with *Ad Astra* magazine before the launch, "I would say that every aircraft I have ever flown will have some transfer to flying the space shuttle." And Colonel Collins has flown many planes, logging over 4,000 hours in 30 different types of aircraft.

With all the flying experience Collins has under her belt, it would seem that she has been flying all of her life, but in fact, she had never stepped into a plane until she was 19 years old. Since Collins's parents could not afford the flying lessons she longed to take, she took part-time jobs to save up the $1,000 she would need. Alan Davis, the retired air force pilot who trained her, told the *New York Times*, "She was very quick to pick it up. She was very quiet and very reserved, but also very determined and very methodical."

### Dreams of Flight

Collins's flying lessons were a long awaited gift to herself. Since her childhood, she loved going to the airport with her parents and sitting on the hood of their car to watch planes take off as she drank root beer. They would also go to Harris Hill and watch gliders sail off cliffs while she told herself that one day she would be in the cockpit when one of those planes took off. As a teen, she read military books on flying, but she recalled even earlier memories of a love for flight. In fifth grade, she read an article on the pros and cons of the space program. "Even then, I couldn't understand why we shouldn't spend money on the space program," she told *Ad Astra*.

Those were big dreams for a little girl born in the small town of Elmira, New York. Collins is the second of four children of James and Rose Marie Collins, who separated when she was nine years old. Part of Collins's childhood was subsequently spent in public housing, living on food stamps. Apparently, in school, she made a favorable impression on her teachers. Her high school chemistry instructor still remembers exactly where she sat in his class. He told the *New York Times*, "Second seat, second row," pointing to a picture of a shy, long-haired girl in a yearbook.

Collins graduated from Elmira Free Academy in 1974 and registered at Corning Community College. She received her associate's degree in math two years later and had intentions of being a math teacher. She also went on to receive a bachelor of arts in math and economics from Syracuse University. Some interesting things, however, were happening elsewhere in the world. In the same year she graduated from high school, the U.S. Navy accepted its first female pilots. Two years later, the U.S. Air Force accepted their first female pilots. And in 1978, they chose four female applicants from the 120 who applied for Air Force

Undergraduate Pilot Training. One of the accepted applicants was Collins.

Also in 1978, the National Aeronautics and Space Administration (NASA) began accepting women into the space program. Ironically, the first female astronauts did their parachute training at Vance Air Force Base in Oklahoma at the same time Collins was there for air force training. Although always intrigued with space, it was the first time Collins realized that being an astronaut was possible. She later credited the other female astronauts who have gone before her. She told *Ad Astra,* "The fact that women have been in the NASA program since 1978 has helped me assimilate to the program. The first female astronauts were so excellent that it really paved the way for the future of women." Nevertheless, Collins felt there was tremendous pressure on her and commented in the *New York Times,* "I realize I can't afford to fail because I would be hurting other women's chances of being a pilot."

After graduating from pilot training in 1979 at the age of 23, Collins became the first female flight instructor. From 1979 to 1990, she taught in Oklahoma, California, and Colorado. In addition to giving soldiers flying lessons, she was also a math instructor at the U.S. Air Force Academy in Colorado Springs. A student as well as a teacher, she took pilot training classes at the Air Force Institute of Technology and, at age 32, was the second woman ever to attend Air Force Test Pilot School. Collins also received a master of science degree in operations research from Stanford University in 1986 and a master of arts degree in space systems management from Webster University in 1989.

## Chosen by NASA

Then, in January of 1990, NASA selected Collins to become an astronaut. According to NASA biographical data, she was initially assigned to Orbiter systems support. She also served on the astronaut support team responsible for Orbiter prelaunch checkout, final launch configuration, crew ingress/egress, and landing/recovery, and as a spacecraft communicator (CAPCOM). She was later, of course, made space shuttle pilot for the Mir space station rendezvous flight in February of 1995.

The Mir space station is an artificial Russian satellite designed to revolve in a fixed orbit and serve as a base for scientific observation and experimentation. Eventually, the Mir will be permanently occupied, and space shuttles will transport astronauts to and from the station. This mission of February 4, 1995, was a dry run to lay the groundwork for an actual landing scheduled for the summer of that year. Collins explained the mission to a reporter in *Ad Astra:* "The best comparison to what we are going to do is the Apollo 10 mission that descended to within 15 kilometers of the lunar surface, and the Apollo 11 mission that landed on the Moon." The rendezvous continued a trend of international cooperation between Russia and the United States. Space exploration has also strengthened relationships between other nations, including Canada, Japan, and European countries.

A change in the Spacehab module that the shuttle would be carrying into orbit caused a postponing of the launch, which was originally scheduled for May of 1994. Although the nine-month delay was frustrating, Collins took the extra time to learn the Russian language and familiarize herself with the Mir. Then, just before the next scheduled flight, there was a failure in one of the three navigation units required to control the shuttle's steering. Engineers worked around the clock, and NASA delayed the trip another 24 hours. When the launch finally took place, the astronauts discovered a minor propellant leak on one of the jet thrusters. Though the leak would be manageable, the Russian astronauts became worried about the Mir's exposure to damage by such a close encounter and rearranged the rendezvous for a safer 1,000 feet, instead of the scheduled 38 feet. NASA scientists negotiated with the Russians, reassuring them that their space station was in no danger. The Russians were eventually convinced and agreed to the original 38 foot close encounter. Throughout the obstacles and delays, Collins handled the pressure with amazing calmness.

Collins credits her rugged astronaut training for preparing her for adversity. Although her pilot experience helped, NASA stretched her far beyond anything she thought possible. She recounted in *Ad Astra,* "20% of our basic astronaut training takes us through land and water survival, parachute training, field trips to all the NASA centers, and geology field trips. . . . About 70% of our basic course concerns learning the space shuttle [and] another part is called enrichment training where we learn a little bit about everything—oceanography, the history of the space program, astronomy, orbital mechanics, weather, medicine—all taught at various intervals to give us a feel for the big picture."

Collins later noted that the simulator was one of the hardest parts of her training. During an eight-minute artificial launch, trainers input up to 20 different malfunctions. She remarked in *Ad Astra,* "You have to prioritize and organize quickly: What's wrong? How to fix it? Find the procedure, then do the procedure. Then you get interrupted with another malfunction. Then you have to decide which one will 'kill me' now, in ten seconds, or in minutes."

As hard as training is in the 1990s, it was much more barbaric 30 years before. Concerning the training of the 1960s, the *Irish Times* wrote, "[The astronauts later claimed] the physical and psychological tests were devised by a sadist. . . . [They] rode exercise bikes to exhaustion, swallowed a meter-long rubber hose, drank radioactive water and were prodded, tilted, and spun until they couldn't stand." Such tests were given to the women who were almost the first female astronauts and who share a special relationship with Collins. Known as FLATS (fellow lady astronaut trainees), the 26 women were tested in 1961 along with male astronauts. Thirteen of them passed, becoming known as the Mercury 13. NASA, however, canceled the project before the women ever soared into the galaxy. Sarah Ratley, one of the Mercury 13, told the *Kansas City Star* after Collins's takeoff, "We all knew Eileen and just kind of felt like we were there going up with her saying, 'Go, go, go.' It was a feeling as if we had finally made it."

In April of 1994, the FLATS had an official gathering, to which they had invited Collins. She returned the favor by offering the 11 surviving women special seats for the Mir launch. Collins told a Cable News Network (CNN) correspondent, "I feel like so many of them have become friends of mine now, and I'm sort of carrying on their dream." She offered to carry with her on the shuttle such mementos as a scarf worn by aviator Amelia Earhart, known for various female "firsts," and a pilot's license signed by Orville Wright for the famed flier Evelyn (Bobbi) Trout in 1924. Everyone gave something except Jerri Truhill, who explained on National Public Radio (NPR), "I told [Collins] she was carrying my dreams, that was all that was necessary."

When the space shuttle thundered into the horizon early in the morning on February 4, 1995, some of the onlookers cried. Women have come a long way in the field of aviation and astronautics, and Collins took them one step further.

## Further Reading

*Ad Astra,* July/August 1994, p. 30; January/February 1995, pp. 32-36.
*Detroit Free Press,* January 30, 1995, p. 5A.
*Gannet News Service,* February 11, 1995.
*Houston Chronicle,* February 11, 1995, p. 16.
*Irish Times,* February 11, 1995, p. 8.
*Kansas City Star,* February 16, 1995, p. C1.
*New York Times,* February 1, 1995, p. A7; February 5, 1995, p. 15;
*Pittsburgh Post-Gazette,* February 4, 1995, p. A6; February 9, 1995, p. A1.
*U.S. News & World Report,* February 13, 1995, p. 22.
*Washington Post,* February 3, 1995, p. A8; February 4, 1995, p. A3.
*Washington Times,* March 12, 1995, p. A2.
*Working Woman,* February 1995, p. 14.
Additional information for this profile was obtained from *The Week in Review,* CNN, February 12, 1995; *Weekend Edition,* NPR, February 11, 1995; and NASA biographical data, January 1994. ☐

# Marva Collins

**Schoolteacher Marva Collins's (born 1936) dedication to Chicago's Westside Preparatory School, which she opened in 1975, moved the producers of television's *60 Minutes* to do a feature on her and inspired a made-for-TV film.**

Teachers need nothing more than "books, a blackboard, and a pair of legs that will last the day," Marva Collins told Dan Hurley in *50 Plus* magazine. These three things were essentially all that Collins had when she opened the Westside Preparatory School in Chicago, Illinois, in 1975 with the $5,000 she had contributed to her pension fund. Disillusioned after teaching in the public school system for 16 years, Collins decided to leave and open a school that would welcome students who had been rejected by other schools and labeled disruptive and "unteachable." She had seen too many children pass through an ineffective school system in which they were given impersonal teachers, some of whom came to school chemically impaired.

A firm believer in the value of a teacher's time spent with a student, Collins rejected the notion that the way to solve the problems faced by U.S. schools was to spend more money. Collins also shunned the audiovisual aids so common in other classrooms because she believed that they created an unnecessary distance between the teacher and the student. By offering a plethora of individual attention tempered with strict discipline and a focus on reading skills, Collins was able to raise the test scores of many students, who in turn went on to college and excelled. "It takes an investment of time to help your children mature and develop successfully," declared Collins in *Ebony*.

## Indelible Impression Left by Father

Collins was born Marva Delores Nettles on August 31, 1936, in Monroeville, Alabama. Collins has described her childhood as "wonderful" and filled with material comforts that included riding in luxury cars and having her own horse. Her father, Alex Nettles, was a successful merchant, cattle buyer, and undertaker. He lavished attention and praise on his daughter and her younger sister, Cynthia. By challenging Collins to use her mind, he instilled in her a strong sense of pride and self-esteem.

"[My father] never presumed that any task was too challenging for me to try nor any concept too difficult for me to grasp," noted Collins in *Ebony*. "He gave me assignments that helped build my confidence and gave me a sense of responsibility." As a child, Collins managed the store's inventory, kept track of invoices, and deposited the store's money in the bank. From these early experiences, she developed the philosophy she would use later in life to teach children, one that entailed providing encouragement and positive reinforcement.

Collins attended Clark College in Atlanta, Georgia. After graduating in 1957 with a bachelor's degree in secretarial sciences, she returned to Alabama to teach typing, shorthand, bookkeeping, and business law at Monroe County Training School. Having never intended to be a teacher, she left the profession in 1959 to take a position as a medical secretary at Mount Sinai Hospital in Chicago. While in the city she met Clarence Collins, a draftsman, whom she married on September 2, 1960.

## Left Teaching to Start Her Own School

In 1961 Collins returned to teaching as a full-time substitute in Chicago's inner-city schools because she missed helping youngsters discover the joy of learning. Working against a tide of indifferent teachers who, in Collins' words, were creating "more welfare recipients" soon left her weary and angry. With her pension money and the support of her husband, Collins opened the Westside Preparatory School in the basement of Daniel Hale Williams University.

Collins made a point of not accepting federal funds because she did not want to abide by all the regulations that such backing required. Craving more independence than she had in the university setting, Collins soon moved the school into the second floor of her home, which she and her husband had renovated to accommodate approximately twenty children ranging from four to fourteen years old. Located in one of Chicago's poorest neighborhoods, the school was eventually moved to its own building near Collins's home. Shortly after this move, enrollment increased to over two hundred students.

## The Media Focus on Collins

Collins started attracting media attention in 1977 after an article on her and the Westside Preparatory School appeared in the *Chicago Sun-Times*. Several national publications printed her story, and she was featured on the popular television program *60 Minutes* in an interview with Morley Safer. In 1981 CBS presented a Hallmark Hall of Fame special entitled *The Marva Collins Story*, starring Cicely Tyson.

Late in 1980 Collins was considered for the post of secretary of education by U.S. President Ronald Reagan. Preferring to continue teaching and running her school, Collins announced that she would not accept the position if it were offered to her. She believed that she could make a bigger difference by working with the children in Chicago than she could by immersing herself in the paperwork the job in Washington, D.C., would surely bring. The Chicago school board and the Los Angeles County school system also offered her positions. Again, she declined.

Collins's method of teaching, spelled out in her 1982 book *Marva Collins' Way*, provides students with a nurturing atmosphere in which they learn the basics—reading, math, and language skills. Gym class and recess are considered superfluous. When writing about Collins and her school, many journalists comment on the familiar sight of young children reading such classics as *Aesop's Fables* and works by William Shakespeare and Geoffrey Chaucer. Each day students write papers and memorize a quotation of their choice. In addition, they are expected to read a new book every two weeks and to report on it.

Collins guides all of this activity with a strong dose of love and personal concern for each student. Any child who has to be disciplined understands that it is the behavior, not the child himself, that is objectionable. In an interview in the *Instructor*, Collins pointed out that "teacher attitude is very important" and that she believed that the "children should be given a lot of my time."

## Collins and School Criticized

In 1982, however, Collins was assailed by criticism from several fronts. Charges against her ranged from accepting federal funds—she had always adamantly claimed that she would not—to reports that she had exaggerated her students' test scores. An independent investigation revealed that Collins received $69,000 through the Comprehensive Employment and Training Act (CETA). Collins refuted these charges early in 1982 as a guest on the *Phil Donahue Show*, during which she claimed that the CETA money had come to her through a social services agency and that she had no idea the money had originated in Washington, D.C.

A majority of the parents of Westside's students rallied behind her, declaring that they were pleased with the work Collins was doing with their children. Support also came from Morley Safer who had stayed in contact with Collins after her appearance on *60 Minutes*. In the March 8, 1982, issue of *Newsweek*, Safer was quoted as saying: "I'm convinced that Marva Collins is one hell of a teacher."

Kevin Ross, a former Creighton University basketball star, would no doubt agree with Safer. Ross came to the Westside Preparatory School in the fall of 1982 because he had not acquired basic education skills after four years of college. Working with Collins, Ross was able to double his reading and math scores and triple his language score within one school year.

Collins chose Ross to deliver the commencement address at Westside's eighth grade graduation. He was quoted in *Newsweek* as telling the graduating class to "learn, learn, and learn some more" so that the debate on the potential of inner-city school children would become "as obsolete as covered wagons on the expressway." Others also support Collins's work. She received donations from many individuals, most notably rock star Prince, who became cofounder and honorary chairman of Collins's National Teacher Training Institute, created so Collins could retrain teachers using her methodology.

Shortly before her 50th birthday, Collins was interviewed by *50 Plus* magazine and was asked if she felt, after all the media hype, that she had passed her peak. She responded: "All of that means nothing, except what I get for the children. Those were fleeting moments. . . . Being a celebrity isn't important. It's what the children learn that's important." Material possessions are not what matters to Collins; what does matter is that she be remembered for her contribution to society. She expressed the fundamental purpose of her work when she told an *Instructor* correspondent, "I take the children no one else wants."

## Further Reading

*American Spectator,* April 1983.
*Black Enterprise,* June 1982.
*California Review,* April 1983.
*Chicago Tribune Book World,* October 31, 1982.
*Christian Science Monitor,* November 20, 1981; September 9, 1982.
*Ebony,* February 1985; August 1986; May 1990.
*Essence,* October 1981; November 1985.
*50 Plus,* June 1986.
*Good Housekeeping,* September 1978.
*Harper's Bazaar,* December 1981.
*Instructor,* January 1982.
*Jet,* November 6, 1980; October 4, 1982; February 7, 1983; July 29, 1985; August 10, 1987; August 1, 1988.
*Life,* spring 1990.
*Los Angeles Times Book Review,* December 12, 1982.
*Newsweek,* March 8, 1982; June 27, 1983.
*New York Times,* December 19, 1980; December 21, 1980; March 7, 1982; November 4, 1990.
*People,* December 11, 1978; February 21, 1983.
*Saturday Review,* April 14, 1979.
*Time,* December 26, 1977.
*TV Guide,* November 28, 1981.
*Variety,* June 18, 1986.
*Wall Street Journal,* March 15, 1981.
*Washington Monthly,* February 1980.
*Washington Post Book World,* November 14, 1982. □

# Rita R. Colwell

**As a scientist and professor, Rita R. Colwell (born 1934) has investigated the ecology, physiology, and evolutionary relationships of marine bacteria.**

Rita R. Colwell is a leader in marine biotechnology, the application of molecular techniques to marine biology for the harvesting of medical, industrial and aquaculture products from the sea. As a scientist and professor, Colwell has investigated the ecology, physiology, and evolutionary relationships of marine bacteria. As a founder and president of the University of Maryland Biotechnology Institute, she has nurtured a vision to improve the environment and human health by linking molecular biology and genetics to basic knowledge scientists had gleaned from life and chemistry in the oceans.

Rita Rossi was born in Beverly, Massachusetts, November 23, 1934, the seventh of eight children to parents Louis and Louise Di Palma Rossi. Her father was an Italian immigrant who established his own construction company, and her mother was an artistic woman who worked to help ensure her children would have a good education. She died when her daughter was just thirteen years old, but she had been proud of her success in school. In the sixth grade, after Rossi had scored higher on the IQ exam than anyone in her school's history, the principal asked sternly whether she understood that she had the responsibility to go to college. Rossi had answered, "Yes, ma'am," and eventually received a full scholarship from Purdue University. She earned her bachelor of science degree with distinction in bacteriology in 1956. Although she had been accepted to medical school, Rossi chose instead to earn a master's degree so that she could remain at the same institution as graduate student Jack Colwell, whom she married on May 31, 1956. Colwell would have continued her studies in bacteriology, but the department chairman at Purdue informed her that giving fellowship money to women would have been a waste. She instead earned her master's degree in the department of genetics. The University of Washington, Seattle, granted her a Ph.D. in 1961 for work on bacteria commensal to marine animals, which is the practivce of an organism obtaining food or other benefits from another without either harming or helping it. Colwell's contributions included establishing the basis for the systematics of marine bacteria.

In 1964, Georgetown University hired Colwell as an assistant professor, and gave her tenure in 1966. Colwell and her research team were the first to recognize that the bacterium that caused cholera occurred naturally in estuaries. They isolated the bacterium from Chesapeake Bay and in ensuing years sought to explain how outbreaks in human populations might be tied to the seasonal abundance of the host organisms in the sea, particularly plankton. In 1972, Colwell took a tenured professorship at the University of Maryland. Her studies expanded to include investigations on the impact of marine pollution at the microbial level. Among her findings was that the presence of oil in estuarine and open ocean water was associated with the numbers of bacteria able to break down oil. She studied whether some types of bacteria might be used to treat oil spills. Colwell and her colleagues also made a discovery that held promise for improving oyster yields in aquaculture—a bacterial film formed on surfaces under water attracted oyster larvae to settle and grow.

In the spirit of using knowledge gained from the sea to benefit humans and the environment, Colwell prepared a seminal paper on marine biotechnology published in the journal *Science* in 1983. It brought attention to the rich resources of the ocean that might be tapped for food, disease-curing drugs, and environmental clean-up by the applications of genetic engineering and cloning. In order to realize the potential of marine biotechnology as originally outlined in her 1983 paper, Colwell helped foster the concept and growth of the University of Maryland Biotechnology Institute, established in 1987. As president of the U.M.B.I., she has formed alliances between researchers and industry and has succeeded in raising funds to develop the center as a prestigious biotech research complex.

In addition, Colwell has held numerous professional and academic leadership positions throughout her career and is a widely published researcher. At the University of Maryland, Colwell was director of the Sea Grant College from 1977 to 1983. She served as president of Sigma Xi, the American Society for Microbiology, and the International Congress of Systematic and Evolutionary Biology, and was president-elect of the American Association for the Advancement of Science. Colwell has written and edited more than sixteen books and over four hundred papers and articles; she also produced an award-winning film, *Invisible Seas.* Her honors included the 1985 Fisher Award of the American Society for Microbiology, the 1990 Gold Medal Award of the International Institute of Biotechnology, and the 1993 Phi Kappa Phi National Scholar Award.

Colwell is the mother of two daughters who pursued careers in science. She is an advocate for equal rights for women, and one of her long-standing aspirations is to write a novel about a woman scientist. Her hobbies include jogging and competitive sailing.

## Further Reading

Andrews, Joan Kostick, "Lady With A Mission," in *Natural Science,* May, 1991, pp. 304–310.
Henderson, Randi, "Scientist Plays Many Roles," in *The Baltimore Sun,* October 13, 1991.
Sherman, Scott L., "The Long Road From the Laboratory," in *Warfield's,* August, 1990. □

# Jill Kathryn Ker Conway

**Jill Kathryn Ker Conway (born 1934) was a historian interested in the role of women in American history. She became the first woman president of Smith College in 1975.**

Jill Kathryn Ker was born in Hillston, New South Wales, Australia, a small town 75 miles from her parents' sheep station, on October 9, 1934. She earned her B.A. and a university medal at the University of Sydney in 1958 and received her Ph.D. from Harvard University in 1969. Her unpublished but widely-cited dissertation, "The First Generation of American Women Graduates," an intellectual history of Jane Addams and other progressive women reformers, almost single-handedly rekindled scholarly interest in women's contributions to Progressive Era America.

While attending Harvard University Jill Ker met and married John Conway, a history professor in whose course she was a teaching assistant. She followed him to Toronto, where he became one of the founders of York University and she joined the faculty of the University of Toronto. There she lectured on American history while completing her dissertation. Jill Conway rose to the rank of associate professor in 1972. From 1973 to 1975 she served as the first woman vice president for internal affairs at the University of Toronto.

In the mid-1970s, Toronto, like other major universities, was struck with student rebellions, giving Conway an opportunity to demonstrate her cool and unflappable administrative style. In 1975 she was appointed the first woman president of Smith College, the largest privately-endowed college for women in the United States. For this achievement, *Time* magazine named her one of its 12 "Women of the Year." Conway's appointment heralded a change in leadership of the so-called Seven Sisters Colleges, and as a result of this breakthrough all of them became headed by women by the early 1980s.

Initially, Conway found herself at the helm of a prestigious but flagging educational institution. In the early 1970s, Smith, like the other Seven Sisters, suffered a decline in status as bright women flocked to the newly coeducational Ivy League universities. Conway helped to restore Smith's luster as the premier women's college in the United States. A superb fund-raiser, she increased the endowment from $82 million to $220 million. To accomplish this, Conway became a peripatetic president, criss-crossing the country to solicit alumnae, foundation, and corporate support. Her executive abilities were well recognized, as she served as director of IBM World Trade Americas/Far East Corporation, Merrill Lynch, and on the board of overseers of Harvard University. Despite a hectic administrative schedule Conway maintained her commitment to teaching and scholarship. She taught a course on the "Social and Intellectual Context of Feminist Ideologies in Nineteenth and Twentieth Century America." In 1982 she published *The Female Experience in 18th and 19th Century America.*

In the first portion of her presidency, Conway changed the college from a genteel institution which eschewed feminist ideals into a women's college that respected and reflected feminist values. Through a strong financial aid program, Smith for the first time admitted older, working women and welfare recipients as Ada Comstock scholars. Conway expanded the career development office and took pride in promoting the "old girl" network among alumnae. She endorsed the expansion of athletic facilities, enabling Smith to become the first women's college to join the National Collegiate Athletic Association. Conway articulated a concern that Smith tenure more women faculty, and she frequently publicized the plight of women scholars and the value of women's institutions in educational journals. While not in favor of a women's studies program at Smith per se, Conway did encourage the development of the Smith College Project on Women and Social Change funded by the Andrew W. Mellon Foundation. Out of her presidential budget she helped launch The Society of Scholars Studying Women's Higher Educational History, a group of researchers studying women's intellectual history.

Some highly publicized conflicts erupted in the closing years of Conway's presidency. In 1983, following student and faculty protests, Conway had to inform the U.S. ambassador to the United Nations, Jeane J. Kirkpatrick, that she could not guarantee that Kirkpatrick would receive her honorary degree and be heard as the commencement speaker without incident. The ambassador declined the offer to speak and was given her degree by the Smith trustees in a private ceremony. When newly unionized food-service workers tried to organize Smith's Davis Student Center acrimony developed between the workers and the administration. The unionized workers claimed they were being unfairly treated by a "paternalistic and male dominated" management. The dispute was quietly settled.

While funding for privately endowed, small, liberal arts colleges diminished throughout the early 1980s, Conway's capable leadership allowed Smith College to survive and grow. In an era that some term "post-feminist," Conway's contributions to women's higher education and her sponsorship of separate women's institutions made her an important spokeswoman for contemporary feminism. By the end of her presidency Conway was perturbed by a new generation of women students, less overtly feminist but strongly career-oriented. According to her, this change in the attitudes of the Smith student body was "the only disappointment in a decade." She called for women students to retain an interest in service to society and not to embrace unthinkingly high-earning professions. In this she remained faithful to the ideals of the social feminists of the Progressive generation whose careers she so well illuminated in her pioneering research. Conway also served as a visiting scholar at Massachusetts Institute of Technology. In March of 1996, she succeeded to vice-chairman of the John S. and James L. Knight Foundation, and in February of 1997, Conway was made a member on the Board of Trustees at Adelphi University in New York.

## Further Reading

Jill Conway is listed in *Canadian Who's Who* (1984) and in *Who's Who of American Women,* 14th edition (1985-1986). Conway is discussed in "Women of the Year: Great Changes, New Chances, Touch Choices," *Time* (January 5, 1976); Elizabeth Stone, "What Can an All Women's College Do for Women," *Ms* (1979); and Hal Langur, "Jill Conway," *Daily Hampshire Gazette* (June 27, 1985).
Two fascinating autobiographies recount Conway's life—from her childhood in Australia, and her decision to come to the United States (*The Road From Coorain,* 1990), to her life in the United States up until she was about to assume the presidency at Smith College (*True North,* 1994). □

# Elizabeth Cotten

**Versatile folk/blues singer, songwriter, and guitarist Elizabeth Cotten (1892-1987)—creator of the classic song "Freight Train"—performed in concert for the first time at age 67 and won a Grammy Award in 1985 at age 93.**

American folk and blues musician Elizabeth Cotten, composer of the folk song classic "Freight Train" and recipient of a 1985 Grammy Award at age 93,

began her career in music at an age when most people prepare for retirement. At 67 years of age Cotten, known as "Libba" by the folksinging Seeger family who discovered her talent, performed live in concert for the first time. A former maid, this versatile musician was also a songwriter and guitarist. Legendary for strumming left-handed on a guitar designed for right-handers, rather than reverse the strings she would play the guitar backwards, "pick[ing] with her left hand and chord[ing] with her right," wrote Martin F. Kohn of the *Detroit Free Press.* Playing the guitar and banjo, using "two-finger" and "three-finger" stylings, became her musical signature. This "Cotten style" of playing the guitar has made her one of the "finest fingerpickers on record," noted a contributor for *Guitar Player* magazine.

## Child's Play

Though "Libba" Cotten had not become a professional musician until she was 67 years old, she had composed folk songs and played the guitar and banjo as a child. By approximately eight years of age Cotten, then Elizabeth Nevills, taught herself how to play the banjo. Practicing on her brother's banjo, she created a style of guitar playing that, half a century later, was imitated by many guitarists across America. As Kristin Baggelaar and Donald Milton remarked in *Folk Music: More Than a Song,* "Libba Cotten's bass runs are used frequently by other guitarists, and her basic picking styles have become standard patterns for folk guitar." At age 11 she composed the classic folk song "Freight Train." Copyrights to the song, however, were not secured to her until 1957, some 50 years after its original composition. By age 14 she had collected a generous array of rag and dance tunes, some of which she had composed herself.

From approximately the ages of 12 to 15, Elizabeth worked as a housekeeper for neighbors in her hometown of Chapel Hill, North Carolina, a position she would hold on and off for most of her life. She earned 75 cents a month. When she had enough money saved, she bought her first guitar, a Sears & Roebuck Stella demonstrator guitar for $3.75, and kept her family up nights as she practiced religiously. Urged by the Baptist Church, however, to give up music and attend to more serious and appropriate activities for a young African American woman of her time, Elizabeth abandoned her guitar and took a walk down the aisle.

## The Domestic Life

Elizabeth Nevills married Frank Cotten in February of 1910 when she was 15 years old and had one child, a daughter, Lillie, by the time she was 16. She, Frank, and Lillie frequently moved between Chapel Hill, Washington, D.C., and New York City for Frank's business. They finally settled in New York City as a family where Frank eventually owned his own business. During this time Elizabeth held a string of odd jobs, mainly housekeeping and some work in a furniture store. The marriage was not a lasting one, however. As soon as their daughter married, Elizabeth and Frank Cotten divorced, and Elizabeth moved to Washington, D.C., to live with her daughter, and eventually grandchildren and great-grandchildren.

In Washington, D.C., in late 1940s, Elizabeth Cotten worked in a popular downtown department store called Lansburgh's before the holidays. Elizabeth worked on the fifth floor where dolls were sold. One day a woman came to the store with her two daughters and bought some dolls from Elizabeth. The woman was Ruth Crawford Seeger, a noted music teacher and composer of folk songs and her husband, Charles Seeger, was a musicologist. As the dolls were being packaged, one of the little girls, Peggy Seeger, wandered away from her mother and sister. Elizabeth found the little lost girl and returned her to her mother. Ever grateful to her, Mrs. Seeger offered Elizabeth a job as her family's Saturday housekeeper. Shortly after her encounter with Ruth Seeger, Elizabeth quit her sales position at Lansburgh's and accepted Mrs. Seeger's offer. Elizabeth worked for the Seegers and remained friends with them for many years.

## A Musical Maid

The Seeger household provided fertile ground for Elizabeth's musical talent to take root and grow. It was in the Seeger home that Elizabeth Cotten, besides ironing and baking bread, developed her craft as a musician. Ruth Seeger was in the process of compiling a selection of folksongs for children and teaching her own children, Mike, Peggy, and Penny, about folk music when Elizabeth joined the family. "Libba," Peggy's childhood nickname for Elizabeth, learned along with the kids. Elizabeth practiced on Peggy's guitar, fooled around with the chords every chance she got, and sang out a few tunes to accompany the music, often in the kitchen with the door closed. One Saturday, while the Seegers were practicing their music and singing together, "Libba" casually announced that she used to play the guitar. The Seegers, thus, first heard "Freight Train" in their own home.

The significance and subsequent popularity of "Freight Train" can be traced to its beginnings. The railroad train, explained Ed Badeaux in *Sing Out,* "[from] its very first beginnings . . . , became a symbol of freedom and adventure to America's common folk." As a small child, Elizabeth and her brothers, not unlike the Seegers, would gather together, play the guitar and/or banjo, and compose their own songs. "Freight Train" was one song Elizabeth composed entirely by herself and, as Badeaux quoted Mike Seeger, "'was largely inspired by the train running near her [childhood] home.'" The popular 1960s and 1970s folksinging group, Peter, Paul, and Mary, performed and recorded their own version of "Freight Train" which became an American hit in 1963.

## A Second Career

After approximately ten years with the Seegers, in 1959, at age 67, Elizabeth Cotten performed professionally for the first time. She and Mike Seeger conducted a joint concert together, the first for both of them. "Libba" and Mike would perform together in coffee houses and at folk festivals throughout their careers as musicians. She would accompany him and his band the "New Lost City Ram-

blers." In turn, he would open shows for her, tune her instruments; they performed as a team.

Peggy Seeger also figured prominently in Elizabeth's development as a recognized musician. In 1957 Peggy took "Freight Train" to Europe as the popularity of folk music returned and made the song a hit abroad. Much to her regret, though, Peggy allowed some English gentlemen to tape her performance of the song, and they unfortunately later took full credit for composition of the song. As Ed Badeaux noted, "the rights to a song are oftentimes unfortunately a matter of public domain versus individual ownership. Vocalists perform and record other people's songs all of the time. Without proper documentation, it is almost impossible for a composer to protect his/her work from theft. Fortunately for Elizabeth Cotten, though, due to growing enforcement of copyright laws in the late 1950s, she was eventually rightfully credited with composition of the classic song."

From 1957, at 65 years of age, until her death in 1987 at age 95, Elizabeth Cotten recorded approximately six albums, performed live, and toured widely. She recorded her first solo album, *Negro Folk Songs and Tunes,* in 1957 for Folkways Records. Three other of her more well known albums are *Elizabeth Cotten, Volume II: Shake Sugaree,* 1967, *Elizabeth Cotten Volume III: When I'm Gone,* 1975, and *Elizabeth Cotten Live!,* 1983, for which she won a 1985 Grammy award. She was well into her seventies when she toured America with the popular blues singer, Taj Mahal. In the last 20 years of her life she performed at universities, music halls, and folk festivals across America, by which time she was a great-grandmother. She also performed on television and visited school children nationwide as involvement for projects sponsored by the National Endowment For The Arts. In 1978 she performed at Carnegie Hall in New York City, the most prestigious concert hall for musicians in the world. At 90 years of age she started a National Tour in 1983 called Folk City. The tour began in New York City where she opened with Mike Seeger.

## A Legendary Musician

Though born poor and black in the late 1800s, at a time when racial prejudice was very much alive in America and with only a fourth grade education, Elizabeth Cotten nonetheless became a highly respected musician. "There's no one like her . . . that was ever recorded," Mike Seeger had told Jon Pareles of the *New York Times* in 1983 at the opening of his and Elizabeth's National Folk City tour. Her distinctive "Cotten-Style" of playing the guitar, coupled with her simple, sincere love for guitar and song, made her a beloved personality in folk music.

A Burl Ives Awardee in 1972 for her vital role in folk music, a Grammy Award in 1985 for her album *Elizabeth Cotten Live!,* deemed best ethnic or traditional folk recording that year, and a National Heritage Fellowship from the National Endowment For The Arts, 1984, have secured her a place in American folk music history. "Libba had," said Ed Badeaux "what most of us can only strive for—a rich musical heritage and the ability to express that heritage beautifully through her playing." Her turn-of-the-century parlor music, a mixture of gospel, ragtime, and blues, was truly music composed, played, and sung from the heart.

## Further Reading

Baggelaar, Kristin, and Donald Milton, *Folk Music: More Than a Song,* Crowell, 1976.

"For These 'Youngsters' Life Begins at 80," in *Ebony,* February 1981, p. 62.

Harris, Sheldon, *Blues Who's Who,* Da Capo Press, 1979.

Lanker, Brian, *I Dream A World,* Stewart, Tabori, and Chang, 1989, pp. 156-57.

Hitchcock, H. Wiley, and Stanley Sudie, *The New Grove Dictionary of American Music,* Macmillan Press, 1986, p. 515.

"Ordinary Women of Grace: Subjects of the I Dream a World Photography Exhibit," in *U.S. News & World Report,* February 13, 1989, p. 55.

Southern, Eileen, *Biographical Dictionary of Afro-American and African Musicians,* Greenwood Press, 1982, pp. 85-86.

Lawless, Ray M., *Folksingers and Folksongs in America,* 2nd edition, 1965, pp. 504, 682-683.

Silber, Irwin, and Fred Silber, *Folksingers' Wordbook,* Oak Publications, p. 63.

"Blues With A Feeling," in *Guitar Player,* November 1994, p. 152.

"Elizabeth Cotten at 90, Bigger Than The Tradition," in *New York Times,* January 7, 1983, January 9, 1983, June 30, 1987.

"Elizabeth Cotten, 95, Noted Folk Singer, Dies," in *Jet,* August 17, 1987, p. 18.

Badeaux, Ed, "Please Don't Tell What Train I'm On," in *Sing Out,* September 1964, pp. 7-11.

"Life Begins at 71 For N.Y. Domestic," in *Detroit Courier,* December 25, 1967.

Kohn, Martin F., "The Freight Train lady brings her songs to town," in *Detroit Free Press,* March 21, 1977.

Gerrard, Alice, "Libba Cotten," in *Frets 2,* January 1980, pp. 26-29.

Reisner, Mel, "Maid Finally Wins Grammy," in *The Indianapolis Star,* September 1, 1985.

Lane, Bill, "Past 80 and Still Singing: Octogenarians Sippie Wallace, Elizabeth Cotten, & Alberta Hunter Don't Let Age Hold Them Back," in *SEPIA,* December 1980. □

# Prudence Crandall

**American educator Prudence Crandall (1803-1890) made one of the early experiments in providing educational facilities for African American girls.**

Prudence Crandall was born on Sept. 3, 1803, in Hopkinton, R.I., to a Quaker family. Her father moved to a farm at Canterbury, Conn., in 1813. She attended the Friends' Boarding School at Providence, R.I., and later taught in a school for girls at Plainfield, Conn. In 1831 she returned to Canterbury to run the newly established Canterbury Female Boarding School. When Sarah Harris, daughter of a free African American farmer in the vicinity, asked to be admitted to the school in order to prepare for teaching other African Americans, she was accepted. Immediately, the townspeople objected and pressured to have Harris dismissed.

Crandall was familiar with the abolitionist movement and had read William Lloyd Garrison's *Liberator*. Faced with the town's resolutions of disapproval, she met with abolitionists in Boston, Providence, and New York to enlist support for the transformation of the Canterbury school into a school for African American girls. The *Liberator* advertised for new pupils. In February 1833 the white pupils were dismissed, and by April, 20 African American girls took up studies. A trade boycott and other harassments of the school ensued. Warnings, threats, and acts of violence against the school replaced disapproving town-meeting resolutions.

Abolitionists came to Crandall's defense, using the issue as a stand against opposition to furthering the education of freed African Americans. Despite attacks the school continued operation. On May 24, 1833, the Connecticut Legislature passed a law prohibiting such a school with African Americans from outside the state unless it had the town's permission, and under this law Crandall was arrested in July. She was placed in the county jail for one night and then released under bond.

A prominent abolitionist, Arthur Tappan of New York, provided money to hire the ablest lawyers to defend the Quaker school teacher at her trial, which opened at the Windham County Court on Aug. 23, 1833. The case centered on the constitutionality of the Connecticut law regarding the education of African Americans. The defense held that African Americans were citizens in other states, were so therefore in Connecticut, and could not be deprived of their rights under the Federal Constitution. The prosecution denied that freed African Americans were citizens. The county

court jury failed to reach a decision. Although a new trial in Superior Court decided against the school, when the decision reached the Supreme Court of Errors on appeal, the case was dismissed for lack of evidence.

The judicial process had not stopped the operation of the Canterbury school, but the townspeople's violence against it increased and finally closed it on Sept. 10, 1834. Crandall had married a Baptist preacher, Calvin Philleo, on Sept. 4, 1834. He took her to Ithaca, N.Y., and from there they went to Illinois and finally to Elk Falls, Kans., where she lived until her death on Jan. 28, 1890. In 1886 the Connecticut Legislature had voted her an annual pension of $400.

## Further Reading

Wendell P. and Francis J. Garrison, *William Lloyd Garrison, 1805-1879: The Story of His Life Told by His Children* (4 vols., 1885-1889), and John C. Kimball, *Connecticut's Canterbury Tale: Its Heroine Prudence Crandall and Its Moral for Today* (1886), are informative accounts of Prudence Crandall's work. See also Thomas E. Drake, *Quakers and Slavery in America* (1950), and Dwight L. Dumond, *Antislavery: The Crusade for Freedom in America* (1961).

## Additional Sources

Strane, Susan, *A whole-souled woman: Prudence Crandall and the education of Black women,* New York: W.W. Norton, 1990.

Welch, Marvis Olive, *Prudence Crandall: a biography,* Manchester, Conn.: Jason Publishers, 1983. ☐

until she met Mr. Macready and learned his method." By 1845 she was hailed in London as an actress with the "godlike gift" of genius. Three years later she played a command performance before Queen Victoria as Katherine in *Henry VIII.*

When Cushman returned to the United States in 1849, she found herself not only a celebrated actress but a symbol of the achievement of American culture. She sustained her reputation as the greatest American tragedienne until her retirement in 1875.

Her talent lay in portraying women of great passion and pathos; in such roles her muscular frame and powerful yet controlled voice could overwhelm and sometimes frighten the audience. The mysterious old gypsy Meg Merrilies in *Guy Mannering* was her most famous role, followed by Lady Macbeth, Queen Katherine, and Nancy in the dramatization of *Oliver Twist.* So strong was her presence that she won praise in men's roles, playing Romeo, Cardinal Wolsey, and Hamlet.

As early as 1852 Cushman made the first of many farewell appearances. She knew that she was suffering from cancer; the disease plagued her for the next 24 years and was finally the indirect cause of her death from pneumonia in Boston in 1876. Yet until the end she continued to act, and when her strength failed, she gave dramatic readings. Both on and off the stage she was a lady of dignity, passion, and majesty.

# Charlotte Cushman

**The actress Charlotte Cushman (1816-1876) was the first great American-born tragedienne, in a career spanning 4 decades.**

Charlotte Cushman, who was descended from one of the original Pilgrim families, was born in Boston in 1816. Faced with poverty in her late teens, she determined to become an opera singer, a career for which her remarkable voice—a full contralto and almost full soprano—well suited her. But while performing in New Orleans, she strained her voice by reaching too high, and at the age of 19 her singing career ended.

Undaunted, Cushman decided to become an actress. Her debut as Lady Macbeth in New Orleans in 1835 began a career that lasted for 40 years and encompassed almost 200 roles. After her first success Cushman joined New York theater companies, where at least two plays were performed each evening and the bill was changed each day. Here she served a diligent apprenticeship; yet, after 8 years, she was still in "miserable, frightful uncertainty" about her career.

Then in 1843, William Macready, the great English actor, played Macbeth to her Lady Macbeth. He was so impressed by Cushman's undisciplined talent that he urged her to go to London for training. In appreciation for this fortuitous advice, she later said she had "groped in darkness

### Further Reading

The most intimate portrait of Charlotte Cushman was done by her friend Emma Stebbins, *Charlotte Cushman, Her Letters and Memories of Her Life* (1878). It is extremely sympathetic and somewhat sentimental but provides evidence of Cushman's strength and sensitivity in private and public life. William Winters includes private recollections and accounts of her performances in *Other Days* (1908) and *The Wallet of Time,* vol. 1 (1913). Two excellent if brief analyses of Cushman's talent and place appear in Lloyd Morris, *Curtain Time* (1953), and Garff Wilson, *A History of American Acting* (1966). □

# D

## Mary Daly

**Mary Daly (born 1928) was considered the foremost feminist theoretician and philosopher in the United States.**

Mary Daly was born in Schenectady, New York, on October 16, 1928. Educated in Catholic schools, she received her first Ph.D. from St. Mary's College/Notre Dame University in 1954. Between 1959 and 1966 she taught philosophy in Junior Year Abroad programs in Fribourg, Switzerland. She also received doctorates in theology and philosophy from the University of Fribourg in 1963 and 1965. After 1966 she was a member of the theology department of Boston College.

Daly was in the forefront of American feminist thinking, both in terms of her early appearance as a feminist writer and in terms of the depth, originality, and power of her work. Her first feminist book, *The Church and the Second Sex* (1968), was published at the very beginning of the women's liberation movement that emerged in the late 1960s. In that work Daly both documented the history of misogynism in the Catholic Church from the time of the early Fathers through the reign of Pope Pius XII and explored the limitations placed on women's development by the Church's perpetuation of the myth of the "Eternal Feminine." This was the belief that the true nature of women is to be self-sacrificing, passive, and docile, and that women are fulfilled only in physical or spiritual motherhood. Daly called for creative and independent women to exorcise the stifling image of the Eternal Feminine by "raising up their own image" and fulfilling their potential. She also urged the Church to contribute to the exorcism of antifeminism by ending discrimination against women in the ministry, eliminating the barriers that isolate nuns from the world, and examining the conceptual inadequacies that underlie and perpetuate androcentric theology. For example, the attribution of male gender to a transcendent God and the identification of women with sexuality, matter, and evil.

### Book Threatens Job

Considerable furor followed the publication of *The Church and the Second Sex*. Daly was threatened with the loss of her job at Boston College and was finally granted tenure only after some months of student protests and widespread media publicity. The experience radicalized her view of the oppressiveness of patriarchal structures and was the catalyst of her transformation from a reformist Catholic to a post-Christian radical feminist.

In her next book, *Beyond God the Father* (1973), Daly challenged the whole edifice of patriarchal religion. She argued that its myths and theological constructs, by legitimating male superiority and displacing evil onto the female as the prototypical Other, not only oppress half the human race but foster social structures and ways of thinking that produce racism, genocide, and war. She rejected not only the gender identification of God but the concept of God as a static noun (supreme being) rather than active verb (Be-ing). To "'hypostatize transcendence,' to objectify God as a 'being,'" she wrote, is to "envisage transcendent reality as finite. 'God' then functions to legitimate the existing . . . status quo."

She saw in the women's movement an authentic challenge to patriarchal religion, a challenge that confronted the fathers' "demonic distortion of Be-ing" with an "ontological, spiritual revolution . . . pointing beyond the idolatries of sexist society and sparking creative action in

**161**

and toward transcendence.'' She attempted to salvage some traditional Christian images by radically transforming their content; she argued that redemption from the evils of the sexist order can be brought about only by women, that the New Being (theologian Paul Tillich's term for Christ) will be manifested in women, and that the prophecy of the Second Coming points to the re-emergence of a strong female presence capable of altering ''the seemingly doomed course of human evolution.''

## Departs Christian Symbolism

In the years following the publication of *Beyond God the Father* Daly left behind all Christian symbolism and rooted her theology completely in women's experience. *Gyn/Ecology* (1978) was concerned with the process of women's ''becoming'' (which Daly described in mythic terms as a journey to the Otherworld) and with the demonic obstacles to that process, the deceptive myths and sadistic practices of patriarchal culture. Subtitled *The Metaethics of Radical Feminism, Gyn/Ecology* was an attempt to see through the deceptive and confusing maze of patriarchal thinking about good and evil and to go beyond it into what Daly called the deep background of language and myth.

Daly explored the deadly ''foreground'' myths that shackle women's minds and recounted the psychological and physical destruction of women by such practices as Indian suttee, Chinese footbinding, African genital mutilation, European witchburning, and American gynecology.

Having named and described the male-created demons that block the passage to female Selfhood in the last section of the book, Daly then charted the deeper passages through which women spin and spiral into women-identified and woman-honoring consciousness. In the process of making this journey Daly reclaimed language—the ''power of naming''—and forged it into an instrument for the liberation of women's minds from oppressive patriarchal myths and for the expression of deeper levels of women's psychological and spiritual experience. Though not always easy reading, this transformed language—incandescent, metaphoric, alliterative, playful, inventive, punning, charged with sheer energy, anger, and humor—is a brilliant manifestation of the emergence of a ''metapatriarchal'' women's consciousness.

## Language Key to Self

*Pure Lust* (1984), subtitled *Elemental Feminist Philosophy,* was concerned with First Philosophy, traditionally defined as ontology or the philosophy of being. Daly reiterated her earlier rejection of the objectified noun *being* as an inadequate expression of the constantly creating and unfolding Powers of Be-ing, and she defined the ultimate concern of feminist philosophy as ''biophilic participation in Be-ing.'' Be-ing was not separated from nature in Daly's thinking; it was to be found in the elemental nature of the Self, the earth, and the cosmos; Daly saw matter and spirit as unified and the cosmos as enspirited and ensouled.

In *Pure Lust,* as in *Gyn/Ecology,* her method of discovering and connecting with the sources of Be-ing was through language: she explored the etymological roots of words and their multiple, double-edged, obscure, and obsolete meanings in order to discover and open up the deep meanings of words and make them suitable for women's journey toward fuller participation in Elemental Be-ing. Though that journey is both outward and inward—outward with the evolutionary unfolding of the cosmos—in *Pure Lust,* as in *Gyn/Ecology,* Daly focused primarily on the journey inward and back, through the mazes of patriarchal barriers, to women's Archaic origins and original Selves, to the rediscovery of their primordial life-affirming power, connectedness, and creativity.

Daly's *Websters' First New Intergalactic Wickedary of the English Language Conjured in Cahoots with Jane Caputi* was published in 1987. The book is an indictment of patriarchy and male dominated institutions in which Daly harnesses the power of naming to make her point. In the book, she defines ''positively revolting hag,'' a term she uses to describe herself. For Daly it means, ''a stunning, beauteous Crone; one who inspires positive revulsion from phallic institutions and morality. . . .'' In Daly's lexicon, cockalorum means ''a self-important little cock. Examples: Napoleon, Andy Warhol, Fiorello La Guardia, Mickey Mouse,'' and a crone is ''a Great Hag of History, long-lasting one; Survivor of the perpetual witchcraze or patriarchy.'' Daly's dictionary was followed by *Outercourse: The Be-Dazzling Voyage,* based on her unpublished *Logbook of a Radical Feminist Philosopher.* This effort was followed by work for Daly's next book, to be called *Quintessence.* ''This work is in some respects a successor to my philosophical autobiography, *Outercourse,* and in other ways it is a logical/ontological successor to my earlier works, *Beyond God the Father, Gyn/Ecology,* and *Pure Lust,*'' wrote Daly.

During the 1980s and 1990s, Daly continued to lecture to audiences around the world. She was an outspoken critic of popular phenomena such as the Christian men's movement as personified by an organization called the Promise Keepers. Answering a reporter who asked, ''who has hurt women?'' Daly responded, ''These creeps, the Promise Keepers, rightwing Christians. It's not just the ancient fathers of the church and it's not just the church. It's all the major religions.''

Writing in *The New Yorker* in 1996, Daly articulated her thoughts on the empowerment of women. ''Women who are Pirates in a phallocratic society are involved in a complex operation. First, it is necessary to Plunder—that is, righteously rip off—gems of knowledge that the patriarchs have stolen from us. Second, we must Smuggle back to other women our Plundered treasures. In order to invent strategies that will be big and bold enough for the next millennium, it is crucial that women share our experiences: the chances we have taken and the choices that have kept us alive. They are my Pirate's battle cry and wake-up call for women who I want to hear.''

## Further Reading

There is no biography of Mary Daly. For biographical information, see *Contemporary Authors* (1st revision) and the autobiographical preface to the Harper Colophon edition of *The Church and the Second Sex* (1975).

**Additional Sources**

Ratcliffe, Krista, *Anglo-American Feminist Challenges to the Rhetorical Traditions: Virginia Woolf, Mary Daly, Adrienne Rich,* Southern Illinois University Press, 1996. □

]] —Rich,

# Dorothy Dandridge

**Dorothy Dandridge (1922-1965) was the first African American woman to receive an Academy Award nomination for best actress for her performance in the 1954 film *Carmen Jones*. Her glamorous image and turbulent life have inspired many to compare her to another equally tragic Hollywood figure, Marilyn Monroe.**

One of the most strikingly beautiful and charismatic stars ever to grace Hollywood, Dorothy Dandridge blazed a number of significant trails during her short but noteworthy career as the first African American actress to achieve leading-role status. Yet hers was also a deeply troubled life, marked by the scars of a miserable childhood, a string of failed personal relationships, numerous career setbacks, and ongoing struggles with drug and alcohol abuse. Racism was also one of the demons with which she had to contend, for Dandridge came of age in an era when the entertainment world was rife with demeaning racial stereotypes.

A native of Cleveland, Ohio, Dorothy Jean Dandridge was born in 1922 to Ruby Dandridge and her estranged husband, Cyril. As children, Dorothy and her older sister, Vivian, traveled to schools and churches around the country performing in song-and-dance skits scripted by their mother, who longed for a career in show business. By 1930, Ruby Dandridge had left Cleveland with her daughters to seek her fortune in Hollywood. There the family survived on what Ruby could earn playing bit parts in the movies or on radio, usually as a domestic servant—the kind of character role typically offered to black actors and actresses at that time. Meanwhile, Dorothy was subjected to years of physical, sexual, and emotional abuse at the hands of her mother's female lover.

## Achieved Early Fame in Nightclubs

Around 1934, Dorothy and Vivian teamed up with another singer named Etta Jones and, billed as the Dandridge Sisters, began touring with a popular band. Their talents eventually landed them a regular spot at the famous Cotton Club in Harlem, New York where white audiences flocked to see a wide variety of black performers. Dorothy went on to make her Hollywood debut in 1937 with a bit part in the classic Marx Brothers film *A Day at the Races,* followed a couple of years later by an appearance of the Dandridge Sisters with jazz trumpeter Louis Armstrong in *Going Places.* By 1940, however, the trio had disbanded, and Dorothy set out on her own.

In 1941 and 1942, Dandridge worked in several musical film shorts and Hollywood features before marrying Harold Nicholas of the celebrated Nicholas Brothers dance duo. While he pursued a film career, she temporarily set aside her ambitions to await the arrival of their first child in 1943. However the marriage was an unhappy one almost from the start, due to Nicholas's philandering. The couple's difficulties were compounded when their daughter, Harolyn (known as Lynn), was diagnosed as being severely mentally retarded due to brain damage suffered at birth. She was eventually institutionalized. For the rest of her life, Dandridge blamed herself for Lynn's condition.

Dandridge and her husband finally divorced in 1949. Deeply depressed over what she perceived as her failure as a wife and as a mother, she decided that the best way to cope with her sad situation was to keep busy. She took singing, acting, and dance lessons to regain her confidence and soon hit the road with a nightclub act that eventually took her all over the world. In 1951, she became the first African American to perform in the Empire Room of the Waldorf-Astoria Hotel in New York City. That same year, she also broke attendance records at the Mocambo in Hollywood. Despite her success, Dandridge constantly battled insecurities about her looks and her talent and such anxiety often left her feeling physically ill before, during, or after a performance. Additionaly, she absolutely detested the cigarette smoke, the drinking, and the often obnoxious male patrons she had to endure on the nightclub circuit.

## Launched Film Career

Before long, however, Dandridge's film career began to blossom. In addition to some bit parts, she played an African princess in the 1951 movie *Tarzan's Peril* and a teacher in 1953's *Bright Road.* In 1954, she won the lead role in the movie that would make her a star—*Carmen Jones,* a lavish musical based on the nineteenth-century French opera *Carmen* by Georges Bizet that tells the story of a beautiful but fickle gypsy girl whose seductive ways lead to tragedy. In director Otto Preminger's updated version, set in Florida during World War II, Bizet's gypsy girl is transformed into a sultry black factory worker who corrupts a young black soldier, betrays him, and then pays the ultimate price for her actions. Featuring an all-black cast that, in addition to Dandridge, included Harry Belafonte, Pearl Bailey, and Diahann Carroll, *Carmen Jones* proved to be a critical and commercial success. It not only established Dandridge as a bona fide sex symbol, it also earned her the honor of being the first African American to receive a best actor or actress Academy Award nomination.

Dandridge almost did not get to play Carmen Jones. When she first auditioned for Preminger, she struck him as being far too elegant and ladylike for the part. She, however, was determined to become a movie star, so she acquired an authentic-sounding southern accent, put on a tight skirt and low-cut blouse, applied heavy eye makeup and tousled her hair, and headed off for a second audition. This time, Dandridge electrified Preminger with her grasp of the character and won the part on the spot. She also captivated the director personally, but their liaison was an unfortunate one that caused Dandridge a great deal of sorrow.

Although Dandridge did not win the Oscar for *Carmen Jones,* which went to Grace Kelly for her role in *The Country Girl,* she still became the toast of Hollywood. Reporters and photographers trailed in her wake. Articles about her appeared in black as well as white publications, including a cover story in *Life* magazine that described her as one of the most beautiful women in America. Even the foreign press lavished her with attention. For a while, it looked as if Dandridge would be the one to force the movie industry to acknowledge the reality of racial integration.

## Challenged Racial Stereotypes

Despite receiving such acclaim, Dandridge waited in vain for more demanding film roles to come her way. Instead, she was usually offered parts that were little more than variations on the Carmen Jones character—that is, lusty young women of dubious morality who meet with tragic ends. It was a frustrating turn of events for Dandridge, who took pride in working hard at her craft only to see herself locked into a racial stereotype. Sadly, studio bosses believed that white moviegoers would not accept African American actresses in roles other than that of the domestic servant or the trampy seductress.

As a result, three years passed before Dandridge starred in another film. This one, too, generated headlines, but not just for her performance. *Island in the Sun* (1957) was a daring foray into interracial romance that paired Dandridge with a white leading man. It was the first time a major

American film had depicted such a relationship, and some audiences reacted with shock despite its extremely cautious approach to the subject matter. In the wake of the controversy, a number of theaters (mostly in the South) refused to show *Island in the Sun.* Nevertheless, it was a hit at the box office, and Dandridge went on to make several other movies dealing with the same theme, including *The Decks Ran Red* in 1958, *Tamango* in 1960 (a French production that could not obtain distribution in the United States), and *Malaga* in 1961.

Dandridge's final film triumph came in 1959 in the all-black musical *Porgy and Bess,* which many consider her finest performance. For her skillful portrayal of Bess (opposite Sidney Poitier as Porgy), Dandridge received a Golden Globe Award nomination for best actress in a musical.

## Struggled against Depression

With the dramatic roles she wanted to play in short supply, Dandridge resumed her singing career after *Porgy and Bess* was released. It was while she was on tour in Las Vegas that she met white restaurateur Jack Denison, who, in 1959 became her second husband. Much like her first marriage, this one was a failure almost from the very beginning. Always fearful of poverty, Dandridge had saved much of the money she had earned as an actress, but soon lost everything after making a series of bad investments in her husband's business. Denison then took off, leaving her alone, broke, and depressed; she divorced him in 1962 and was forced to declare bankruptcy the following year. An attempt to revive her acting career went nowhere, and before long Dandridge had turned to pills and alcohol to ease her despair, which took a heavy toll on both her mental and physical well-being.

For a brief period in early 1965, it seemed that Dandridge might succeed in getting her life back in order. She left Hollywood for Mexico, where she checked into a health spa and worked at getting in shape. Several deals were in the works, including starring roles in a couple of new movies. However, on September 8, 1965, just a few days after returning to Hollywood, the forty-two-year-old Dandridge was found dead in her apartment of an overdose of antidepressant medication. Authorities could not determine whether it was an accident or suicide.

In January 1984, Dandridge finally received the recognition she had long deserved when her gold star was unveiled on Hollywood Boulevard's Walk of Fame. A crowd of fans of all ages attended the ceremony, joined by a number of prominent black actors and actresses, including her former co-stars Belafonte and Poitier. As her biographer, Donald Bogle, noted in *Essence,* they had gathered there to honor "a pioneer" who "cleared a path for so many to follow" with her determination to make something more of herself than society was ready to accept. "After all these years," concludes Bogle, "there still has never been another woman in American motion pictures quite like Dorothy Dandridge."

## Further Reading

Bogle, Donald, *Dorothy Dandridge: A Biography,* Amistad Press, 1997.

Mills, Earl, *Dorothy Dandridge: A Portrait in Black,* Holloway House, 1970.

*Notable Black American Women,* Gale, 1992.

*Ebony,* September 1986, pp. 136-146; August 1997.

*Essence,* October 1984; May 1997, p. 114.

*Jet,* February 6, 1984, p. 55.

*New Yorker,* August 18, 1997, pp. 68-72.

*People,* July 28, 1997.

*Premiere* (special issue on women in Hollywood), winter 1993, pp. 85-89.

*Time,* September 1, 1997, p. 73.

John-Hall, Annette, "Brief Flame," *Philadelphia Online,* http://www3.phillynews.com/packages/history/notable/dot26.asp (April 1, 1998).

Wayne, Renee Lucas, "Rediscovering the Black Bombshell: Maybe Dorothy Dandridge Will Finally Get Her Due," *Philadelphia Online,* http://www.phillynews.com/daily_news/97/Sep/18/features/DAND18.htm (April 1, 1998). □

# Angela Davis

**A scholar, activist, and professed Communist, Angela Davis (born 1944) became a leading advocate of civil rights for blacks in the United States.**

In August 1970 Angela Yvonne Davis was catapulted into the national spotlight when she was put on the list of the ten most wanted criminals in the United States. An armed black man, Jonathan Jackson, entered the Marin County, California, Civic Center on August 7, 1970, with a weapon owned by Davis and attempted, along with three San Quentin prisoners, to take hostages. Jackson's intention was to hold the hostages until several inmates of Soledad Prison, including Jackson's brother, George, were released. During the attempt three of the assailants and the presiding judge were killed and three others wounded. A warrant was issued for Davis's arrest. She fled, eluding the police until October 1970. After a total of 16 months in prison in New York—where she was apprehended—and in California, Davis's trial began.

The prosecutor alleged that Davis engineered the plan to kidnap the judge and jurors because of her love for George Jackson. The prosecution presented witnesses who testified that they had seen Davis with Jonathan Jackson in the days preceding the August 7 incident. Davis and her defense attorneys argued that Davis was a political activist concerned with prison reforms and the oppression of the poor in general and was not moved to a crime of passion because of her feeling for Jackson. The all-white jury, composed of eight women and four men, acquitted Davis on all counts in June 1972.

Davis, a self-avowed Communist, was born in Birmingham, Alabama, in 1944. Both her parents were college educated. Her mother was a teacher and her father, after teaching for a short time, went into business for himself. The

Davises moved into an all-white neighborhood when Angela was very young. Racial antipathy was fomenting in the city and the Davises knew that they were not welcome in the neighborhood. The homes of several black families who moved in after the Davises were bombed, although the Davises' home was not.

Angela Davis encountered segregation in almost every area of her life. In housing, school, stores, church, and social life, the ubiquitous "white only" or "colored only" signs, both visible and invisible, were always there. Because Davis had the opportunity to travel to New York during many of her summer vacations her awareness of the difference in racial attitudes and social classes in the South and the North was heightened. Even as a teenager, Davis later wrote, she developed a desire to alleviate the plight of the black and the poor.

Because of superior achievement during her high school years Davis got the opportunity to study at Elizabeth Irwin High School in New York City. There she was regularly exposed to both socialist and communist philosophies and began to develop an interest in these subjects. She was especially interested in mass movements designed to overthrow political domination by elites. Davis's scholastic achievements earned her a scholarship to Brandeis University in Waltham, Massachusetts, where she was one of the few blacks on campus. At the university Davis studied French literature but continued to be interested in philosophy. She studied in France during her junior year. While there, she learned of the September 1963 bombing of a church in her hometown, Birmingham, that resulted in the death of four black girls. She knew three of them.

During her senior year at Brandeis, Davis studied philosophy with Herbert Marcuse, who later became her graduate adviser. After graduating magna cum laude and Phi Beta Kappa from Brandeis in 1965, Davis applied for a scholarship to study philosophy at the Goethe University in Frankfurt. After two years she returned to the United States to study for her doctorate with Marcuse, who was then teaching at the University of California at San Diego. While in graduate school she became politically active with groups such as the Black Panthers, the Student Non-Violent Coordinating Committee (SNCC), and Ron Karenga's US-Organization. In 1968 she became a member of the Communist Party and joined one of its local organs, the Che-Lumumba Club.

As a requirement for her doctorate Davis had to teach for one year and was appointed to the faculty at the University of California, Los Angeles. Her appointment was challenged because she had indicated on her application that she was a Communist. There was a regulation that Communists were not allowed to teach in California state universities. Consequently, the governing body of the university, the Board of Regents, and the governor, Ronald Reagan, attempted to fire Davis. She waged a court battle against her dismissal and won. Later, however, in June 1970, she was fired for her political activity.

After she was acquitted of the charges stemming from the August 7, 1970 incident, she taught black philosophy and women's studies at San Francisco State College. In

1980 and 1984 she ran on the Communist Party ticket for vice president of the United States. By 1983 she was working with the National Alliance against Racist and Political Repression and had been awarded an honorary doctorate from Lenin University.

Throughout the 1980s and 1990s Davis taught courses at several universities, and in 1997 continued to teach at the University of California at Santa Cruz. At the university she acted as presidential chair of a minority women's studies department. She has stated that she hopes young people will continue to seek new solutions. In *Essence* she said, "History is important, but it also can stifle young people's ability to think in new ways and to present ideas that may sound implausible now but that really may help us develop radical strategies for moving into the next century."

### Further Reading

Much has been written about Angela Davis. She is coauthor of a volume entitled *If They Come in the Morning* (1971) and the author of *Angela Davis, An Autobiography* (1974), *Women, Race and Class* (1983), and *Women, Culture & Politics* (1989). The transcript of the Marin County court case (#52613) is available on microfilm. Several other books discuss the same case. Some of these are Charles R. Ashman, *The People* vs. *Angela Davis* (1972); Regina Nadelson, *Who is Angela Davis?* (1972); J. A. Parker, *Angela Davis, the Making of a Revolutionary* (1973); and Bettina Aptheker, *The Morning Breaks* (1975). □

# Bette Davis

**Considered by some to be unappealing in her first screen tests, Bette Davis (1908-1989) went on to become one of Hollywood's greatest actresses. She won two Best Actress Academy Awards and was nominated eight other times.**

Bette Davis's career, which spanned some 60 years, included 86 films and 15 television movies. In addition to the countless honors and awards, she earned the respect and admiration of audiences and colleagues alike. She was best known for playing strong and often scheming characters. Her large, expressive eyes, exaggerated mannerisms, distinctive voice and diction, and ubiquitous cigarettes became her trademarks. She is often credited with broadening the range of roles available to actresses as well. Her fans can still recite her most memorable lines, such as when Davis, portraying an aging stage legend in *All About Eve*, (1950) tells her guests to "fasten your seatbelts, it's going to be a bumpy night!"

The elder daughter of Harlow Morrell, a lawyer, and Ruth (Favor) Davis, she was christened Ruth Elizabeth, but was called Bette as a child and kept the name throughout her career. Davis was born in Lowell, Massachusetts, on April 5, 1908. After her parents divorced in 1916, she and her sister Barbara moved frequently throughout New England while their mother pursued a photography career.

Both girls attended boarding school in the Berkshires and high school in Newton, Massachusetts. Davis graduated from a finishing school, Cushing Academy, in Ashburnham, Massachusetts, with an idea that she might try acting. Not the so-called conventional beauty of the day, she received little encouragement, but in what would become typical Davis style, she made up her own mind and headed for New York City.

Her experience in New York City was not encouraging either. In fact, Davis was rejected when she tried to enroll in the famed acting school of Eva Le Gallienne, noted actress, director, and producer. Le Gallienne told her to study some other field. Undaunted, Davis was admitted to the John Murray Anderson's drama school instead. She got a role with George Cukor's stock company in Rochester, New York.

For the next four years, she hung around New York City and the Cape Playhouse in Dennis, Massachusetts, where she worked as an usherette in between playing bit parts. Her first major role was in an off-Broadway production of *The Earth Between* (1928). After a brief tour in *The Wild Duck*, Davis reached Broadway. The comedy *Broken Dishes* opened in November of 1929 and ran for six months. That led to a 1930 production of *Solid South*, which led to a screen test in Hollywood. She failed the screen test.

Critics who viewed Davis's 1930 screen test at Goldwyn studios said she had no audience appeal. So, she tested at Universal and was hired, even though it was said that studio boss Carl Laemmle also didn't think she had appeal.

However, she was cast in two films in 1931, *Bad Sister* and *Seed.* The critics ignored her in both.

With her strong resolve about to cave in and force her to leave Hollywood, Davis got a break when George Arliss offered her the part opposite him in *The Man Who Played God* from Warner Brothers. She won good reviews and a long-term contract. Thus began a succession of films with Warner, most mediocre and unmemorable. But poor as the films were, the talent and unique quality of Davis began to emerge so that critics started to praise her while panning her movies.

Fighting the studio for better roles became a way of life for Davis as she clawed her way to the top of the film world. She fought for and won the right to be loaned out to RKO in 1934 to play Mildred, the selfish waitress who manipulates an infatuated medical student, in John Cromwell's *Of Human Bondage.* Suddenly, the world was introduced to a brilliant new actress.

One might have thought that Davis's career was on the upswing, but Warner continued to cast her in poor quality films. There were two exceptions. In *Dangerous,* Davis played a failed actress who tries to murder her husband. For this role, she won her first Best Actress Academy Award in 1935. She also appeared with Humphrey Bogart and Leslie Howard (her co-star in *Of Human Bondage*) in *The Petrified Forest* in 1936. Growing disgusted with the studio's offerings, Davis refused any more roles and was suspended without pay. She sued. Warner Brothers and the movie world were astounded; this was not expected behavior of the time. Although Davis lost her battle in court, Warner Brothers apparently got the message for they paid her legal fees and began offering her more suitable roles.

The stature of Davis, the actress, continued to grow. Ty Burr of *Entertainment Weekly* noted that "Davis was a top box office draw throughout the '30s and '40s, and in 1948 she was the highest paid star in Hollywood." Among her memorable roles in the 1930s and 1940s were: *Jezebel,* 1938, for which she won her second Academy Award for her portrayal of "a witchy Southern belle" according to Burr; *Dark Victory,* 1939, which she once told Harry Bowman of the *Dallas News* was her favorite film; *The Private Lives of Elizabeth and Essex* and *Juarez,* also 1939; *All This and Heaven Too* and *The Letter,* both 1940; *The Little Foxes,* 1941; *Now Voyager,* 1942; *Watch on the Rhine,* 1943; *The Corn Is Green,* 1945; *Deception* and *A Stolen Life,* both 1946; and the delightful *June Bride,* (1948) which showed her comic touch.

Despite the praise and awards, by the end of the 1940s, Davis's career seemed to be slowing down, mainly for lack of good material. But in true Davis style, she came through with perhaps the greatest performance of her career as the troubled, aging star, Margo Channing, whose life and career are being taken over by a cunning newcomer, Eve, played by Anne Baxter in *All About Eve* (1950). It was a biting satire on the world of the theater. Davis won the New York Film Critics best actress of the year award.

After a number of films in the 1950s, Davis's career seemed to slow down again. But she was back on top in the early 1960s, with two shockers. In 1962, Davis appeared in the smash *Whatever Happened to Baby Jane?,* playing opposite Joan Crawford. Crawford played the physically handicapped sister at the mercy of her demented sister, Baby Jane Hudson (Davis), a former child star. It was ghoulish and audiences loved it. This was followed by *Hush, Hush, Sweet Charlotte,* (1965) with Davis (co-starring Olivia de Havilland and Joseph Cotton) playing a recluse who is haunted by the unsolved murder of her lover many years earlier.

During the 1970s and 1980s, Davis continued to appear in films, mainly on television. As she marched cantankerously into old age, she appeared on many talk shows, delighting her audiences with her feisty, undaunted in the face-of-aging spirit. She was the fifth recipient of the American Film Institute's Life Achievement Award in 1977, the first woman to be so honored. In 1979, she won an Emmy Award for *Strangers: The Story of a Mother and Daughter.* One her best features became the inspiration for a number one pop song, "Bette Davis Eyes," in 1982.

Davis wrote two autobiographies, *The Lonely Life* (1962) and *This 'N That* (1987), the latter to refute her daughter's (Barbara Davis [B.D.] Hyman) 1985 tell-all book *My Mother's Keeper,* which portrayed Davis as an abusive alcoholic. She was also married four times. In 1932, she married Harmon Oscar Nelson, Jr.; they divorced in 1938. Her second marriage was to Arthur Farnsworth, a businessman from Boston who died in 1943. She married and divorced artist William Grant Sherry in 1945; they had a daughter named Barbara. In 1950, she married actor Gary Merrill, whom she met while making *All About Eve.* They adopted two children, Michael and Margot, and were divorced in 1960.

In the last five years of her life, Davis had a mastectomy, suffered with cancer and had several strokes. She probably was not kidding when she, according to an on-line biography commented, "Old age is not for sissies." Davis died on October 6, 1989, in Neuilly-sur-Seine, France, outside of Paris. She had just attended the San Sebastian Film Festival in Spain where she had been honored for a lifetime of film achievement. In the late 1990s, her son Michael created the Bette Davis Foundation and awarded American actress Meryl Streep the first ever Bette Davis Lifetime Achievement Award.

## Further Reading

Davis, Bette, and Michael Herskowitz, *This 'N That,* Putnam, 1987.
Hadleigh, Boze,*Bette Davis Speaks,* Barricade Books, 1996.
*Chicago Tribune,* October 9, 1989.
*Dallas News,* March 20, 1974.
*Entertainment Weekly,* August 13, 1993; Fall 1996.
*Los Angeles Times,* October 7, 1989.
*Modern Maturity,* July/August 1994.
*New York Times,* October 8, 1989.
"Bette Davis,"*All-Movie Guide,* http://205.186.189.2/cgi-win/AVG.exe?sql = 2P_IDP 17295 (May 14, 1998).
"Bette Davis," *Database—Katz Biography,* http://www.tvgen.com/movies/katz/1789.sml (May 14, 1998).
"Bette Davis," *Internet Movie Database,* http://us.imdb.com (May 14, 1998).

"Bette Davis," *Welcome to the Golden Years—the Superstars,* http://www.geocities.com/Hollywood/9766/davis.html (May 14, 1998).

"Connery, Streep, Davis Honored," (April 17, 1998), http://www.mrshowbiz.com/ (May 14, 1998). □

# Dorothy Day

**Dorothy Day (1897-1980) was a founder of the Catholic Worker Movement which joined radical social reform with the Roman Catholic faith in a movement for social justice and peace.**

Dorothy Day was born on November 8, 1897, in Brooklyn, New York, the daughter of John J. and Grace (Satterlee) Day. Her father was a newspaper sports writer whose search for a steady job caused the family to travel widely during her pre-adolescent years. She spent part of her youth (1904-1906) in California where her father worked until the San Francisco earthquake compelled him to find another job. In 1906 the family moved to Chicago where the elder Day was employed by a local newspaper. She felt extremely isolated from family and friends during those pre-adolescent years, which she remembered in one of her many books as *The Long Loneliness* (1952).

Even as a youngster Day developed a taste for literature and writing and did much of both. She also had several religious experiences which would affect her later in life. In 1914 she finally escaped from her restrictive family milieu by matriculating as a student at the University of Illinois in Urbana. There she promptly fell in with a small crowd of radical students, many of whom were Jewish-Americans discriminated against by the general university community. Her closest friend at the university, a wealthy young Jewish woman from Chicago who shared Day's literary and political tastes, radicalized Dorothy politically (the friend later become a prominent Communist). Even before she left the university after only two years, during which academic studies grew sterile and failed to stimulate her, Day had become a part of the pre-World War I American youth rebellion against the conventions of their parents. She and her radical friends wanted to create a new and freer society—in the language of the day, "to transvalue all values."

Bored by academic life, excited by new social, cultural, and political ideas, it was natural for Day to seek to develop herself in what was then (1916) the center of an American bohemian culture. She moved to New York where she immediately joined in the lively life of the Greenwich Village and Lower East Side rebels and radicals. Day almost immediately found a job as a feature writer on the *New York Call*, the nation's largest and most influential socialist daily. Soon she was involved fulltime in the city's radical political and cultural scene, meeting and becoming close to many of the era's most famous personalities. In the winter of 1917-1918 she became a close friend of the playwright Eugene O'Neill, whom she saw through many bouts with alcohol. Day also developed friendships with Floyd Dell and Max Eastman, who made her an assistant editor of their new magazine, *Masses*—one of the most famous radical cultural publications in American history.

But American participation in World War I led to government suppression of left-wing organizations and publications and left Day and her radical friends adrift. Troubled by her aimless life among Greenwich Village bohemians, in 1918 she took a position as a probationary nurse at Kings County Hospital in Brooklyn. Nursing, however, failed to satisfy Day's search for meaning in life, although it did involve her in her first serious and tumultuous love affair. In 1919 she left the hospital to work for a time as a writer on the successor journal to *Masses, The Liberator*. This, too, brought her little satisfaction, and in 1920, for reasons still unclear, she married Barkeley Tober, an oft-wed literary promoter. Only a year later Day dissolved this, her only formal marriage.

For the next several years she seemed to drift aimlessly, working as a reporter for the New Orleans *Item* in 1922-1923 and also as an occasional writer for the Catholic journal *Commonweal*. While in New Orleans she wrote and published a commercially successful, partly autobiographical novel, *The Eleventh Virgin* (1924). With the money from her novel, Day moved back to the New York area, buying a beach cottage on Staten Island. She resumed contact with the city's intellectuals and wrote occasional pieces for *The New Masses*. In 1925 she began living with a biologist and anarchist (one Foster Batterham), with whom she had a daughter, Tamar Teresa, born on March 3, 1927. After the daughter's birth Batterham left and Day began to immerse herself in religious literature and theology. Unknown to many of her old and close friends, Day on December 28, 1927, had herself and her daughter baptized in a small Staten Island Roman Catholic Church. For the remainder of her life she would remain a dedicated daughter of the Church. She had made a strange personal journey from a diluted childhood Protestantism through years as a rebellious bohemian, ultimately to find solace in the Catholic faith, a journey which she described poignantly in one of her autobiographical fragments, *From Union Square to Rome* (1938).

At first, however, even her new religious faith brought Day no clear purpose in life. In 1929 she toyed with scriptwriting in Hollywood but without satisfaction. A year later she moved with her small daughter to Mexico City, where they lived on the edge of poverty. That same summer she returned to the United States where the onset of the Great Depression swept her back into the movement for social reform. In December 1932 she went to Washington to report on a Communist-led hunger march. On her return to New York City she met Peter Maurin, a former French peasant and social agitator, who convinced her that radical social reform and the Roman Catholic faith could be united. Day now found a purpose in life that would remain with her for the remainder of her days. Together with Maurin she founded a movement which would carry Jesus's original message to the most dispossessed of workers. They would prove that Catholicism served the poor as well as the rich, the weak better than the mighty. Through their newspaper, *Catholic Worker,* and hospitality houses which they established as havens for homeless workers, Day and Maurin promoted their singular version of Catholicism as a social reform movement.

For the next 50 years Day and the Catholic Worker Movement were at the forefront of all Catholic reform efforts. Young American Roman Catholics, eager to improve secular society while remaining faithful to their church, flocked to hear Day's message. The Berrigan brothers (Daniel and Philip), Michael Harrington, and many others fell under her spell, which turned them into radical social reformers. Other Catholics influenced by Day served as activists in the industrial union movement led by the Congress of Industrial Organizations, in the civil rights movement beginning in the 1950s, and increasingly in the peace movement which assumed growing importance in the nuclear age. Echoes of Day's approach to religion and reform could also be found in the "liberation theology" movement which emerged in Latin America in the 1960s.

By the time she died on November 29, 1980, Day had had an enormous impact on both American Catholicism and reform. It was an impact which lived on as revealed in the pastoral letters issued by the American Roman Catholic bishops in 1983 and 1984 on the issues of nuclear weapons and the economy.

## Further Reading

William D. Miller, *Dorothy Day, a Biography* (1982) is a full and excellent account of the subject's life and career. Two equally excellent books describe and analyze the history of the Catholic Worker Movement: William D. Miller, *A Harsh and Dreadful Love: Dorothy Day and the Catholic Worker Movement* (1972) and Mel Piehl, *Breaking Bread: The Catholic Worker and the Origin of Catholic Radicalism in America* (1982). Several of Day's own books, aside from the ones cited in the article, might also be profitably consulted, especially *House of Hospitality* (1939) and *On Pilgrimage: The Sixties* (1973). □

# Ruby Dee

**Ruby Dee's acting career has spanned more than 50 years and has included theater, radio, television, and movies. She has also been active in such organizations as the National Association for the Advancement of Colored People (NAACP), the Southern Christian Leadership Conference (SCLC), and the Congress of Racial Equality (CORE).**

## Early roles

Ruby Dee was born in Cleveland, Ohio, on October 27, 1924, but grew up in Harlem, attending Hunter College in New York. In 1942, she appeared in *South Pacific* with Canada Lee. Five years later, she met Ossie Davis while they were both playing in *Jeb.* They were married two years later.

Ruby Dee's movies roles from this period include parts in *No Way Out* (1950), *Edge of the City* (1957), *Raisin in the Sun* (1961), Genet's *The Balcony* (1963), and *Purlie Victorious* (1963), written by Davis. Since 1960, she has appeared often on network television.

In 1965, Ruby Dee became the first black actress to appear in major roles at the American Shakespeare Festival in Stratford, Connecticut. Appearances in movies including *The Incident* (1967), *Uptight* (1968), *Buck and the Preacher* (1972), *Black Girl* (directed by Davis) (1972), and *Countdown at Kusini* (1976) followed. Her musical satire *Take It from the Top,* in which she appeared with her husband in a showcase run at the Henry Street Settlement Theatre in New York premiered in 1979.

As a team, Ruby Dee and Ossie Davis have recorded several talking story albums for Caedmon. In 1974, they produced "The Ruby Dee/ Ossie Davis Story Hour," which was sponsored by Kraft Foods and carried by more than 60 stations of the National Black Network. Together they founded the Institute of New Cinema Artists to train young people for jobs in films and television, and then the Recording Industry Training Program to develop jobs in the music industry for disadvantaged youths. In 1981, Alcoa funded a television series on the Public Broadcasting System titled "With Ossie and Ruby," which used guests to provide an anthology of the arts. Recent film credits include *Cat People* (1982) and, with Ossie Davis, Spike Lee's *Do the Right Thing* (1989).

## "A neat piece of juggling"

Actress and social activist Ruby Dee expressed her philosophy in *I Dream a World: Portraits of Black Women Who Changed America:* "You just try to do everything that comes up. Get up an hour earlier, stay up an hour later, make the time. Then you look back and say, 'Well, that was a neat piece of juggling there—school, marriage, babies, career.' The enthusiasms took me through the action, not the measuring of it or the reasonableness."

Dee's acting career has spanned more than 50 years and has included theater, radio, television, and movies. She and her husband, actor Ossie Davis, have raised three children and been active in such organizations as the National Association for the Advancement of Colored People (NAACP), the Southern Christian Leadership Conference (SCLC), and the Congress of Racial Equality (CORE), as well as supporters of civil rights leaders such as Dr. Martin Luther King and Malcolm X.

Ruby Ann Wallace was born on October 27, 1924, in Cleveland, Ohio. Her parents, Marshall and Emma Wallace, in search of better job opportunities, moved the family to New York City, ultimately settling in Harlem. Emma Wallace was determined not to let her children become victims of the ghetto that the area was quickly becoming. Dee and her siblings studied music and literature. In the evening, under the guidance of their school-teacher mother, they read aloud to each other from the poetry of Longfellow, Wordsworth, and Paul Laurence Dunbar. The influence of this education became apparent early in Dee's life when as a teenager she began submitting poetry to the *New York Amsterdam News,* a black weekly newspaper.

## Pursued Education

Her love of English and poetry motivated Dee to study the arts, especially the spoken arts. Her mother had been an elocutionist who, as a young girl, wanted to be in the theater. Fully realizing the value of a good education, Dee decided that the public schools of Harlem, where so many of the black girls were being "educated" to become domestics, were not for her. She underwent the rigorous academic testing required for admittance to Hunter High School, one of New York's first-rate schools that drew the brightest girls. The self-confidence and poise that Dee's mother had instilled in her helped Ruby adjust to her new environment populated with white girls from more privileged backgrounds. A black music teacher, Miss Peace, provided encouragement to the young Ruby, telling her to go as far and as quickly as she could.

While in high school, Dee decided to pursue acting. In an interview with the *New York Times,* she related that this decision was made "one beautiful afternoon in high school when I read aloud from a play and my classmates applauded." After graduation she entered Hunter College. There Dee joined the American Negro Theater (ANT) and adopted the on-stage name Ruby Dee. The struggling theater had little money, so in addition to rehearsing their parts the troupe sold tickets door-to-door in Harlem and performed all the maintenance duties in the theater, located in a basement auditorium of the 135th Street Library. Dee found the work she did with the ANT to be a memorable part of her training. Other young actors who started at the ANT and eventually became famous include Harry Belafonte, Earle Hyman, and Sidney Poitier.

While still at Hunter College, Dee took a class in radio training offered through the American Theater Wing. This training led to a part in the radio serial *Nora Drake.* When she graduated from Hunter College in 1945, Dee took a job at an export house as a French and Spanish translator. To earn extra income, she worked in a factory painting designs on buttons. Dee knew, however, that the theater was to be her destiny.

## Landed First Broadway Role

In 1946 Dee got her first Broadway role in *Jeb,* a drama about a returning black war hero. Ossie Davis, the actor in the title role, caught Dee's attention. After watching him do a scene in which he was tying a necktie, Dee experienced an awareness that she and Davis would share some type of connection. Critical reviews of the play were good, but the play ran for only nine performances. Dee's intuition, however, proved to be true. She and Davis became close friends and worked together in the road company production of *Anna Lucasta.* Later they played Evelyn and Stewart in Garson Kanin's *Smile of the World* and were married on December 9, 1948, during a break in rehearsals for that play.

Dee's first movie was *Love in Syncopation,* which was released in 1946. In 1950 she appeared in *The Jackie Robin-*

son Story as the legendary baseball player's wife. Also in that year she appeared in *No Way Out*, the story of a black doctor—played by Sidney Poitier—who is accused of causing the death of his white patient. The film was revolutionary for its time because it was the first American film in which blacks and whites confronted each other in a realistic way.

Over the next decade, Dee appeared in several plays and movies in which she was cast as the consummate wife or girlfriend—patient, always understanding, all-forgiving. Such roles spurred at least one publication to refer to her as "the Negro June Allyson." A few parts helped Dee break free from this stereotyping. Of note is the role of the ebullient Lutiebelle Gussie Mae Jenkins in Davis's 1961 play *Purlie Victorious*. In this satire on black/white relationships, Davis plays the preacher Purlie who, with Lutiebelle's assistance, helps to outwit a white plantation owner. In 1963 this highly successful play was made into a movie titled *Gone Are the Days* and was later musicalized as *Purlie*.

Dee again was typecast as a long-suffering wife and daughter-in-law in the Broadway production of Lorraine Hansberry's *A Raisin in the Sun*. She recreated her role as Ruth Younger in 1963 film version of the play. Donald Bogle, in his book *Toms, Coons, Mulattoes, Mammies, and Bucks*, noted that prior to *A Raisin in the Sun*, Dee's roles made her appear to be "the typical woman born to be hurt" instead of a complete person. Bogle continued, "But in *A Raisin in the Sun*, Ruby Dee forged her inhibitions, her anemia, and her repressed and taut ache to convey beautifully the most searing kind of black torment."

## Broke Free From Typecasting

The one role Dee feels put an end to her stereotyped image was that of Lena in the 1970 production of Athol Fugard's *Boesman and Lena*. Fugard, a white South African dramatist, portrays the dilemma of South Africa's mixed race people who are rejected by both blacks and whites. Lena wanders the South African wilderness and ekes out a living with her brutish husband Boesman, played by James Earl Jones. Dee told interviewer Patricia Bosworth in the *New York Times* that "Lena is the greatest role I've ever had." It was also her first theater role since 1966, and she was not sure she could do it. Her husband encouraged her, saying that the part could have been written for her even though Fugard had originally written the role of Lena with a white actress in mind.

Dee immediately felt a bond with Lena. "I relate to her particular reality," she told Bosworth, "because it is mine and every black woman's. I can understand the extent of her poverty and her filth and absolute subjugation. . . . On one level [Boesman and Lena] represent the universal struggle of black against white, man against woman. But they are also victims of something that is permeating an entire culture."

Dee finally realized that she was being offered a great part at a time when few, if any, good parts were written for black actresses. In the *New York Times* interview she revealed, "I have always been reticent about expressing myself totally in a role. But with Lena I am suddenly, gloriously free. I can't explain how this frail, tattered little character

took me over and burrowed so deep inside me that my voice changed and I began to move differently. . . . [I am as] alive with her as I've never been on stage." Critics took note of Dee's performance. Clive Barnes wrote in his *New York Times* review of the play: "Ruby Dee as Lena is giving the finest performance I have ever seen. . . . Never for a moment do you think she is acting. . . . You have no sense of someone portraying a role. . . . her manner, her entire being have a quality of wholeness that is rarely encountered in the theater."

Beginning in the early 1960s, Dee made numerous appearances on television including roles in the *Play of the Week* and in such television series as *The Fugitive, The Defenders, The Great Adventure,* and *The Nurses*. In 1968 she played Alma Miles, the wife of a neurosurgeon, on *Peyton Place,* the first black actresses to be featured in this widely-watched nighttime serial. Her performance in an episode of the series *East Side, West Side* earned her an Emmy nomination. In 1991 Dee's performance in *Decoration Day* won her an Emmy.

Dee and Davis collaborated on several projects designed to promote black heritage in general and other black artists in particular. In 1974 they produced *The Ruby Dee/ Ossie Davis Story Hour* which appeared on over 60 stations on the National Black Network. In conjunction with the Public Broadcasting System (PBS), they produced the series *With Ossie and Ruby* in 1981. It was work that Dee found particularly satisfying because she got to travel the country talking to authors and others who could put the black experience in perspective. She believes that the series made black people look at themselves outside of the problems of racism.

## Took Up Civil Rights Causes

Issues of equality and civil rights have long been a concern of Dee's. Her activism can be traced back to when she was 11 years old and her music teacher lost her job when funds for the Federal Music Program were cut. The teacher, terrified that she could not find another job in the Depression-ridden country, committed suicide. At a mass meeting following the teacher's death, Adam Clayton Powell was the principal speaker and Dee was chosen to speak in favor of restoring the music program. Several years would pass before Dee became actively involved in civil rights.

The year was 1953, and the cause was Julius and Ethel Rosenberg. The Rosenbergs had been convicted of wartime sabotage and were scheduled to be executed. Dee's vocal protest of the planned executions were expressed in several interviews with the press. Some accused her of being exploited by the Communists; others were convinced she was a card-carrying member of the party.

Dee's notoriety for denouncing the U.S. Government's decision to execute the Jewish Rosenbergs eventually parlayed itself into her first non-black part in a play. In *The World of Sholem Aleichem*, Dee played the Defending Angel. This experience helped Dee realize that racism and discrimination were not the exclusive provinces of black people—other races and cultures experienced it also. Dee began to understand how art and life blended together and how all human cultures are interrelated. She was inspired by these events to make a firm commitment to social activism.

Future events solidified this commitment. In September 1963, a hate bomb was thrown into a Birmingham, Alabama, church. The bomb killed four young black girls as they sat in their Sunday school class. People throughout the country were outraged by this senseless murder. Dee and Davis, along with other artists, formed the Association of Artists for Freedom. The group launched a successful boycott against extravagant Christmas spending and urged people to donate the money to various civil rights groups. Dee and Davis were involved in and supported several other civil rights protests and causes including Martin Luther King's March on Washington. In 1970 the National Urban League honored them with the Frederick Douglass Award, a medallion presented each year for distinguished leadership toward equal opportunity.

### Established Dramatic Art Scholarship

By establishing the Ruby Dee Scholarship in Dramatic Art, Dee put into action her commitment to help others. The scholarship is awarded to talented young black women who want to become established in the acting profession. Both she and Davis have donated money and countless hours of time to causes in which they believe. They founded the Institute of New Cinema Artists as a way to train chosen young people for film and television jobs. Their Recording Industry Training Program helps develop jobs for disadvantaged youths interested in the music industry.

Dee has also used her talent to make recordings for the blind and to narrate videocassettes that address issues of race relations. She has reinterpreted West African folktales for children and published them as *Two Ways to Count to Ten* and *Tower to Heaven*. Dee returned to poetry, her early love, to edit *Glowchild and Other Poems* and to collect her poems and short stories in a volume titled *My One Good Nerve*.

Dee's remarkable acting talent has endured over the years. She continued to appear in theater, movies and television throughout the 1970s and '80s. In 1990 Dee appeared in the television movie *The Court Martial of Jackie Robinson*, playing Jackie Robinson's mother Mallie. John Leonard writing in *New York* laments that the movie gives Dee too little to do but commends Dee for "deliver[ing] one fine line" as she reprimands her son who is about to sabotage his courtship with Rachel. With fervor Dee, in the role of Mallie, states: "I didn't raise my boys to have sharecropper minds!" Leonard attributes the conviction with which Dee played her part to the fact that she played the role of Rachel herself over 40 years ago.

Director Spike Lee cast Dee in the role of Mother Sister—and Davis in the role of "Da Mayor"—for his controversial 1989 film *Do the Right Thing*. As Mother Sister, Dee plays a widow who lives in a brownstone and spends her time watching the neighborhood through a ground-floor window. In *New Republic* Stanley Kauffmann described Dee as "that fine actress with an unfulfilled career

in white America" and described her role in Lee's movie "as a sort of neighborhood Delphic oracle." Davis plays a beer-drinking street philosopher who is in love with Mother Sister.

As racial tension rises in the neighborhood, Mother Sister and Da Mayor are unable to do anything to diffuse it. According to Terrence Rafferty in the *New Yorker,* these two characters "stand for the older generation, whose cynical, 'realistic' attitude toward living in a white society may have kept them from finding ways out of their poverty but may also have helped keep them alive." Lee also cast the pair as the parents of the main character in *Jungle Fever*.

In 1988 *Ebony* featured Dee and Davis as one of "Three Great Love Stories." Explaining the success of their long marriage, Dee told *Ebony:* "The ratio of the good times to the bad times is better than 50-50 and that helps a lot. . . . We shared a great deal in common; we didn't have any distractions as to where we stood in society. We were Black activists. We had a common understanding." Davis added, "We believe in honesty. We believe in simplicity. . . . We believe in love. We believe in the family. We believe in Black history, and we believe heavily in *involvement*."

### Further Reading

*Black Women in America,* Carlson, 1993.
Bogle, Donald, *Blacks in American Film and Television,* Garland, 1988.
Bogle, Donald, *Toms, Coons, Mulattoes, Mammies, and Bucks,* Viking, 1973.
*Directory of Blacks in the Performing Arts,* Scarecrow Press, 1990.
Fax, Elton C., *Contemporary Black Leaders,* Dodd, 1970.
Lanker, Brian, *I Dream a World: Portraits of Black Women Who Changed America,* Stewart, Tabori, Chang, 1989.
Salley, Columbus, editor, *The Black 100,* Citadel Press, 1993.
*Commonweal,* January 13, 1989, p. 21; July 14, 1989, p. 403.
*Cosmopolitan,* August 1991, p. 28.
*Ebony,* February 1988, p. 152.
*Essence,* May 1987, p. 28.
*Jet,* December 5, 1988, p. 55.
*Library Journal,* October 1, 1991, p. 153; January 1992, p. 198.
*Nation,* July 17, 1989, p. 98.
*National Review,* August 4, 1989, p. 45.
*New Republic,* July 3, 1989, p. 24.
*Newsweek,* July 3, 1989, p. 64.
*New York,* August 22, 1988, p. 142; October 22, 1990, p. 136; November 26, 1990, p. 165.
*New Yorker,* July 24, 1989, p. 78.
*New York Times,* June 23, 1970; July 12, 1970.
*People,* July 3, 1989, p. 13.
*Publishers Weekly,* June 10, 1988, p. 80; May 17, 1991, p. 63.
*School Library Journal,* October 1990, p. 76; July 1991, p. 67; March 1992, p. 196. □

# Ada E. Deer

**Ada E. Deer (born 1935) was the first woman to head the U.S. Bureau of Indian Affairs (BIA).**

Life-long advocate for social justice, Ada E. Deer was the first woman to head the U.S. Bureau of Indian Affairs (BIA). As Assistant Secretary for Indian Affairs in the Interior Department, she was "turning the BIA upside down and shaking it," as she told hundreds of Navajos in Arizona a month after taking office in late July of 1993. For Deer, an activist for the rights of American Indians, youth, and women, turning things upside down was nothing new. Her career as a social worker, leader in numerous community and political organizations, and her successful fight to restore federal recognition to the Menominee Tribe all attest to her actions on behalf of human rights and her belief in coalition building. She told members of the Alaska Federation of Natives in August of 1993, as quoted in the *Tundra Times,* "I want to emphasize (that) my administration will be based on the Indian values of caring, sharing, and respect. . . . These values have been missing too long in the halls of government."

Deer was born in Keshena on the Menominee Indian Reservation in northeastern Wisconsin on August 7, 1935. She is the eldest of five children (her siblings are Joseph Deer, Jr., Robert Deer, Ferial Skye, and Connie Deer); four other children died in infancy. Her mother, Constance Stockton (Wood) Deer, is an Anglo-American from Philadelphia and a former BIA nurse. Her father was Joseph Deer, a nearly full-blood Menominee Indian who was a former employee of the Menominee Indian Mills; he died at the age of 85 on January 10, 1994. For the first 18 years of Deer's life, her family lived in a log cabin near the Wolf River with no running water or electricity. Deer told the Senate Committee on Indian Affairs at the hearing to confirm her as head of the BIA that "while all the statistics said we were poor, I never felt poor in spirit. My mother . . . was the single greatest influence on my life. She instilled in me rich values which have shaped my lifetime commitment to service."

This service began with a solid education in the Shawano and Milwaukee public schools. An outstanding student, Deer graduated in the top ten of her high school class before attending the University of Wisconsin-Madison on a tribal scholarship. She was one of two Native Americans out of 19,000 students, and became the first Menominee to graduate from the university. She received her B.A. in social work in 1957; and in 1961, she went on to become the first Native American to receive a M.S.W. from Columbia University.

From the time she was a graduate student and over the next ten years, Deer held several professional positions. She was employed as a social worker in New York City and Minneapolis Public Schools. She also worked with the Peace Corps in Puerto Rico. It was between the years of 1964 and 1967 that Deer had her first job with the BIA in Minnesota as Community Service Coordinator. From 1967 to 1968, she served as Coordinator of Indian Affairs in the University of Minnesota's Training Center for Community Programs. During the same time, Deer served on the Joint Commission on Mental Health of Children, Inc., and in 1969 she became a member of the national board of Girl Scouts of the U.S.A., a post she held until 1975. During the summer of 1971, Deer studied at the American Indian Law Program at the University of New Mexico and then briefly attended the University of Wisconsin-Madison Law School. She left after one semester to work on an urgent tribal matter that was to become her major focus over the next several years.

## Fights to Regain Menominee Tribe Recognition

As part of the U.S. government's 1950s termination policy—an attempt to assimilate Indians forcibly—the U.S. Congress passed in 1954 the Menominee Termination Act. Fully implemented by 1961, it meant the loss of federal recognition of the Menominee Tribe and along with it, the closing of membership rolls, a loss of benefits such as health and educational services, and an imposition of state jurisdiction. The Menominees were taxed and had to sell off ancestral lands to pay the bills. As Deer testified in her confirmation hearing, the Menominees "literally went from being prosperous to being Wisconsin's newest, smallest and poorest county."

Deer left law school and returned to what was now Menominee County to help gather together tribal leaders to regain control of tribal interests from a group of Menominee elites, and to attempt to reverse termination. There, in 1970, Deer and many others created a new political organization known as Determination of Rights and Unity for Menominee Shareholders (DRUMS). With assistance from the Native American Rights Fund and local legal aid organizations, Deer and other leaders of DRUMS fought to regain federal recognition for the Menominees. Their tactics included a

220-mile "march for justice" from Menominee County to the capital in Madison. As a vital part of the restoration effort, in 1972 and 1973 Deer served as vice president and lobbyist in Washington, D.C., for the National Committee to Save the Menominee People and Forest, Inc.

Author Nicholas C. Peroff stated in *Menominee Drums* that Deer's positive attitude concerning restoration was evident in her comment to a *Washington Post* reporter in 1973: "Mainly I want to show people who say nothing can be done in this society that it just isn't so. You don't have to collapse just because there's federal law in your way. Change it!" The efforts of Deer and the members of DRUMS resulted in national publicity for the issue of termination and finally the introduction of a bill in Congress to reverse this policy for the Menominees. On December 22, 1973, President Nixon signed the Menominee Restoration Act into law.

From 1974 to 1976, Deer chaired the Menominee Tribe and headed the Menominee Restoration Committee. After its work was completed, she resigned. In 1977, she became a Senior Lecturer in the School of Social Work and in the American Indian Studies Program at the University of Wisconsin-Madison, where she taught until 1993. Deer also moved into the democratic political arena more fully at this time, serving as legislative liaison to the Native American Rights Fund from 1979 to 1981. In 1982, Deer was a candidate for Wisconsin secretary of state. In 1984, she was delegate-at-large at the Democratic National Convention and vice-chair of the National Mondale-Ferraro Presidential Campaign. In 1992, Deer almost became the first Native American woman in Congress; after a strong showing in the Second Congressional District of Wisconsin, she lost in the general election to Republican Scot Klug. May of 1993, however, brought a nomination by President Clinton from a field of four candidates (including Navajo tribal chairman Peterson Zah) to head the BIA. Congress, with overwhelming support from its members and from tribal leaders, confirmed her nomination in July of 1993.

## Turning the BIA Around

With the BIA, Deer inherited an agency that is infamous for its bureaucracy and historically poor relations with tribes. Deer has had to contend with, among many issues, budget reductions for her agency; conflicts between tribes and localities over land management, water resources, and mineral rights; tribal recognition; education; and religious freedom. Deer is a strong proponent of Indian self-determination; this coincides with the BIA's planned reorganization which will shift more power to tribes. Her approach since being in office has been to visit individual Indian tribes, bringing them together with businesses, organizations, and government entities to find ways to work cooperatively, with the ultimate goal of helping tribes gain economic self-sufficiency. Deer, in her confirmation hearing, maintained: "I want to help the BIA be a full partner in the effort to fulfill the Indian agenda developed in Indian country. The best way we can do this is for the tribes to decide what needs to be done and for the tribes to do it on their own terms, with our enthusiastic support."

Deer's motto in life is "one person can make a difference." For the difference she has made in her many spheres of activity, she has received numerous awards over her lifetime. Deer was one of the Outstanding Young Women of America in 1966. In 1974, she received the White Buffalo Council Achievement Award, along with honorary doctorates from the University of Wisconsin-Madison and Northland College. Other honors include the Woman of the Year Award from Girl Scouts of America (1982), the Wonder Woman Award (1982), the Indian Council Fire Achievement Award (1984), and the National Distinguished Achievement Award from the American Indian Resources Institute (1991).

There have been many achievements during Deer's tenure as Assistant Secretary. Some examples are: the recognition of over 220 Alaska Native villages, the increasing number of self-governance tribes and tribres who contract for programs previously administered by the federal government, and the reorganization of the Bureau. Deer is also active in many initiatives undertaken by the Clinton administration. She is a member of the President's Inter-Agency Council on Women which is charged with the implemention of the Platform for Action agreed upon at the UN's Fourth Conference on Women. In addition, she has testified before the UN Human Rights Committee and is the lead for the domestic activities in conjuction with the Decade of the World's Indigenous Peoples working closely with the State Department.

## Further Reading

*Biographical Dictionary of Indians of the Americas,* Volume 1, Newport Beach, California, American Indian Publishers, 1991; 181-182.

Deer, Ada, and R. E. Simon, Jr., *Speaking Out,* Chicago, Children's Press Open Door Books, 1970.

Deer, Ada, "The Power Came from the People," in *I Am the Fire of Time: The Voices of Native American Women,* edited by Jane B. Katz, New York, Dutton, 1977.

*Department of the Interior:* "http://www.doi.gov/bia/adabio.html," July 18, 1997.

Hardy, Gayle J., *American Women Civil Rights Activists: Biobibliographies of 68 Leaders, 1825-1992,* Jefferson, North Carolina, McFarland, 1993; 128-134.

*Native American Women,* edited by Gretchen M. Bataille, New York, Garland Publishing, 1993; 76-78.

*Native North American Almanac,* edited by Duane Champagne, Detroit, Gale Research, 1994; 1041.

Peroff, Nicholas C., *Menominee Drums: Tribal Termination and Restoration, 1954-1974,* Norman, University of Oklahoma Press, 1982.

*Reference Encyclopedia of the American Indian,* sixth edition, edited by Barry T. Klein, West Nyack, New York, Todd Publications, 1993; 504-505.

Cohen, Karen J., "Ada Deer Tries to Start Fire Under Bureaucracy," *Wisconsin State Journal,* March 20, 1994; B1.

"Female BIA Chief 'Shaking Agency Up,'" *Denver Post,* September 2, 1993; B2.

Richardson, Jeff, "Ada Deer: Native Values for BIA Management," *Tundra Times,* September 8, 1993; 1.

Worthington, Rogers, "Woman Picked to Lead Indian Bureau," *Chicago Tribune,* May 20, 1993; A1.

*Nomination of Ada Deer: Hearing before the Committee on Indian Affairs, United States Senate, One Hundred Third Con-*

gress, First Session, on the Nomination of Ada Deer to be Assistant Secretary for Indian Affairs, July 15, 1993, Washington, D.C., Washington, D.C., U.S. Government Printing Office, 1993. □

# Agnes de Mille

**An American dancer and author, Agnes de Mille's (1905-1993) creative contribution to 20th-century ballet was as remarkable as her choreography for Broadway musical theater. She inspired awe for her personal courage and determination in the face of declining health in later years.**

Agnes de Mille was born on September 18, 1905, in New York City into a theatrical family. Her father, William Churchill de Mille, wrote plays for David Belasco on Broadway and later became a Hollywood film producer. His brother, Cecil Blount de Mille, was a famous Hollywood film director. De Mille's maternal grandfather was Henry George, a social reformer and political economist who was famous for proposing the single tax.

When she was a child the family moved to Hollywood. The family's values were shaped by prevailing emphases on success and glamour as well as respect for intellectual life. During her teens her parents divorced and de Mille was torn between becoming a dancer and actress or pleasing her father, who was unsympathetic to a stage career. Having seen performances of Anna Pavlova and the Ballets Russes with Vaslav Nijinsky, as well as American dance pioneers Isadora Duncan and Ruth St. Denis, de Mille enrolled in ballet classes in Hollywood with Theodore Kosloff. While continuing ballet lessons, she agreed to attend college at the University of California, Los Angeles (UCLA), and graduated as an English major, cum laude. Later her mother gave support to her dance career, taking her to live in New York while her younger sister, Margaret, attended Barnard College and later helping to finance her trips abroad.

In New York she performed with the Grand Street Follies, choreographed a solo program (1928), and studied modern dance with Martha Graham, who opened her New York studio in 1927. In 1931 she appeared with Graham, Doris Humphrey, Charles Weidman, and Helen Tamiris in Dance Repertory Theater, a short-lived attempt at collaboration among the early pioneers of American modern dance.

De Mille left for Europe in 1932, performing recitals of her work in London, Paris, and Copenhagen. In London she staged dances for Cole Porter's Nymph Errant starring Gertrude Lawrence. Marie Rambert, with whom she studied ballet, invited her to join the Ballet Club where she worked with Frederic Ashton and Anthony Tudor, then young and emerging choreographers associated with Rambert. She created a role in the premiere of Tudor's Dark Elegies (1937).

On occasional return visits to the United States she appeared in Leslie Howard's Broadway production of Ham-

let (1936) and the MGM film of Romeo and Juliet (1937). With the outbreak of World War II in Europe in 1939 she returned to New York permanently.

For the first season of Ballet Theatre (now American Ballet Theatre) in 1940 de Mille choreographed Black Ritual to Darius Milhaud's Creation du Monde with an African American cast. She earned the credit for convincing the company's managing director, Richard Pleasant, to invite Tudor to leave England and join Ballet Theatre, an important turn for American ballet history.

De Mille's big breakthrough as a choreographer came in 1942 with her ballet Rodeo for Ballets Russe de Monte Carlo. The original score was by Aaron Copland; the set design by Oliver Smith. She originally danced the Cowgirl, the female lead. This ballet remains in the repertories of many companies and is among her best known ballets, along with Fall River Legend (1948), a psychological study of Lizzie Borden based on her murder trial. Rodeo, a down-home story about cowboys and ranch life out West, provided de Mille with the invitation to choreograph Rodgers and Hammerstein's musical Oklahoma in 1943. This collaboration led to a life-long career with the Broadway musical, perhaps most significant of her choreographic achievements. Oklahoma was a landmark in that de Mille introduced the dream ballet to further the story through dance. This changed the course of the Broadway musical, making dance an integral part of the theatrical experience.

De Mille always saw dance as theatrical, expressive. She used body movement and motivated gesture as a kind of speech and drew from the technical vocabularies of classical ballet, modern dance, and folk and social dance. Although inspired by many subjects, her ballets were essentially American and favored themes dealing with its social history.

Known also as the author of many books, which she claimed she wrote in her "spare time," de Mille was a tireless and outspoken advocate for dance and for federal support for the arts. Drawing from her own experience as a choreographer, she was concerned that dances be copyrighted and that choreographers receive royalties. She served as first chairman of the dance panel of the National Endowment for the Arts in 1965. She was also first president of the Society of Stage Directors and Choreographers in 1965.

De Mille founded two dance companies during her career: the Agnes de Mille Dance Theater (1953-1954) and the Heritage Dance Theater, a folk-oriented company formed in 1973, which used a lecture-demonstration format to present audiences with American dance history. The company toured widely until 1975, when de Mille suffered a cerebral hemorrhage just prior to a benefit performance at the Hunter College Playhouse in New York.

With extraordinary determination and courage, de Mille underwent extensive rehabilitation and learned to write with her left hand. She recovered sufficiently to resume her activities as a writer and choreographer, as well as spokesperson for dance.

De Mille was married to Walter Prude, a manager of concert artists, from 1943 until his death in 1988. (Her courtship and marriage are described in her autobiographical work, *And Promenade Home*, and in *Martha.*) She died of a stroke on October 7, 1993, in New York City at the age of 88. She was survived by a son, Jonathan Prude, and grandsons David Robert Prude and Michael James Prude.

De Mille received more than a dozen honorary degrees. She was elected to the Theater Hall of Fame in 1973. She received the Handel Medallion, New York City's highest achievement in the arts, in 1976; the Kennedy Center Award in 1980; and the National Medal of the Arts in 1986. Other awards include: Donaldson Award, Antoinette Perry (Tony) Award, Dance Magazine Award, Capezio Award, and De la Torre Bueno Award for writings on dance.

### Further Reading

The following are de Mille's ballets (listed chronologically): *Black Ritual* (1940); *Three Virgins and a Devil* (1941); *Rodeo* (1942); *Tally-Ho* (1944); *Fall River Legend* (1948), based on the Lizzie Borden murder trial; *The Harvest According* (1952), inspired by a Walt Whitman poem with material from the Civil War ballet in *Bloomer Girl; Rib of Eve* (1956); *The Bitter Weird* (1961); *The Four Marys* (1965), about Civil War slaves; *The Wind in the Mountains* (1965); *A Rose for Miss Emily* (1971), based on the William Faulkner story; *Texas Fourth* (1976); *The Informer* (1988), about the struggles between the English and Irish in 1917 and 1921; and *The Other* (1992), a symbolic depiction of the encounter between a young woman and death.

She choreographed the following Broadway musicals: *Oklahoma* (1943); *Bloomer Girl* (1944), a Civil War ballet; *Carou-*

*sel* (1945); *Brigadoon* (1947); *Allegro* (1947), which she also directed; *Gentlemen Prefer Blondes* (1949); *Paint Your Wagon* (1951); *Goldilocks* (1958); *Kwamina* (1961); and *110 in the Shade* (1963).

De Mille's major article on Martha Graham, first published in *Atlantic Monthly* (1950), was later a chapter in *Dance to the Piper* (1952). Her last book, *Martha: The Life and Work of Martha Graham* (1991), a lively biography of the famous American dance pioneer, also contains much about the author and her long friendship with Graham. Other personal memoirs include: *And Promenade Home* (1958); *Speak to Me, Dance with Me* (1973) about the years spent in London with Marie Rambert and the Ballet Club; *Where the Wings Grow* (1978), a recollection of her girlhood at the family's summer colony in Sullivan County, New York; and *Reprieve* (1981), written in collaboration with her doctor, dealing with her first stroke in 1975 and her courageous recovery. Other works by de Mille include *To a Young Dancer* (1962), an advice book; *The Book of the Dance* (1963), an illustrated history of dance; *Lizzie Borden: A Dance of Death* (1968), about her choreography for *Fall River Legend; Portrait Gallery* (1990); "Russian Journals" in *Dance Perspectives* (1970); *The Dance in America* (1971); and *America Dances* (1980). □

# Mary Williams Dewson

**Mary Williams Dewson (1874-1962), widely known as Molly Dewson, was a reformer, government official, and organizer of women for the Democratic Party.**

Molly Dewson was born in Quincy, Massachusetts, on February 18, 1874. In her youth a number of influences awakened in her an interest in public affairs. Her father gave her an appetite for reading books on politics and government. Many of her neighbors and female relatives—such as her aunt Elizabeth Putnam, a pioneer in reforming delinquent girls—were active in public causes.

After attending private schools in the Boston area, she entered Wellesley College, where she was an excellent student. She was also president of her class in her junior and senior years, organized the Wellesley Athletic Association, introduced the Australian ballot for class elections, and began the Wellesley alumnae fund by raising money for the first class gift.

Upon graduating in 1897, she quickly established herself as one of the ablest of the generation of younger women who seconded the initiatives of such older women reformers of the progressive era as Jane Addams and Florence Kelley. Dewson got her first job when the Women's Educational and Industrial Union, the most important women's club in Boston, hired her to investigate and improve the living and working conditions of female domestics in the Boston area. Then, as the organizer and first superintendent of the Massachusetts Parole Department for delinquent girls between 1900 and 1912, she became a national authority on the rehabilitation of juvenile offenders.

As executive secretary of an investigating commission set up by the Massachusetts legislature she produced a report on the living conditions of women and children in industry. The report became the basis of the 1912 Massachusetts minimum wage act, the first such act passed in modern industrial America. Dewson went on to become a leader in the Massachusetts campaign of 1915 for the passage of a referendum favoring woman suffrage and then assumed the leadership of the state Suffrage Association.

After World War I Florence Kelley chose Dewson to take charge of the National Consumers League's national campaign for state minimum wage laws for women and children. Then switching to the New York Consumers League in 1924, she became the president. Dewson soon emerged as the leader of the Women's Joint Legislative Conference, most notably in lobbying for the passage through the New York legislature of a 1930 act limiting the hours of women and children in industry to 48 hours a week.

Starting in 1928 Eleanor Roosevelt, who was active in the Consumers League and in the Women's Division of the Democratic Party, persuaded Dewson to accept various positions of leadership within the Democratic Party in New York and on the national level in order to make women more effective in politics. As director of the Women's Division of the Democratic Party in Franklin D. Roosevelt's presidential campaigns of 1932 and 1936, Dewson led in trying to make women voters an important part of the voting coalition behind President Roosevelt. She believed that his New Deal program was the best hope for enacting national legislation to protect working men and women in industry.

Through the Women's Division Dewson developed many techniques to stimulate women who were timid about becoming politicians to be campaigners, party officials, and even candidates for office. She thus created the first effective nationwide vote-getting organization of women ever sponsored by a political party. This organization marked the decisive entrance of women into party politics on both the national and state levels.

Dewson found some time in the 1930s to promote industrial and welfare programs in such capacities as official adviser to Frances Perkins (secretary of labor) and as presidential appointee to the Social Security Board in 1937. But, due to chronic heart trouble, she resigned from the board in 1938 and, except for occasional participation in party affairs, retired to her home in Castine, Maine, where she died in 1962.

## Further Reading

A short biography of Dewson by Paul C. Taylor is in *Notable American Women: The Modern Period* (1980). She figures prominently in Susan Ware, *Beyond Suffrage: Women in the New Deal* (1981). Dewson's importance to Eleanor Roosevelt is illustrated in Joseph P. Lash, *Eleanor and Franklin* (1971) and to Frances Perkins in George Martin, *Madam Secretary: Frances Perkins* (1976).

## Additional Sources

Ware, Susan, *Partner and I: Molly Dewson, feminism, and New Deal politics*, New Haven: Yale University Press, 1987. ☐

# Emily Dickinson

**One of the finest lyric poets in the English language, the American poet Emily Dickinson (1830-1886) was a keen observer of nature and a wise interpreter of human passion. Her family and friends published most of her work posthumously.**

American poetry in the 19th century was rich and varied, ranging from the symbolic fantasies of Edgar Allan Poe through the moralistic quatrains of Henry Wadsworth Longfellow to the revolutionary free verse of Walt Whitman. In the privacy of her study Emily Dickinson developed her own forms and pursued her own visions, oblivious of literary fashions and unconcerned with the changing national literature. If she was influenced at all by other writers, they were John Keats, Ralph Waldo Emerson, Robert and Elizabeth Barrett Browning, Isaac Watts (his hymns), and the biblical prophets.

Dickinson was born on Dec. 10, 1830, in Amherst, Mass., the eldest daughter of Edward Dickinson, a successful lawyer, member of Congress, and for many years treasurer of Amherst College, and of Emily Norcross Dickinson, a submissive, timid woman. The Dickinsons' only son, William Austin, also a lawyer, succeeded his father as treasurer of the college. Their youngest child, Lavinia, was the chief housekeeper and, like her sister Emily, remained at home, unmarried, all her life. The sixth member of this tightly knit group was Susan Gilbert, an ambitious and witty schoolmate of Emily's, who married Austin in 1856 and moved into the house next door to the Dickinsons. At first she was Emily's confidante and a valued critic of her poetry, but by 1879 Emily was speaking of her "pseudo-sister" and had long since ceased exchanging notes and poems.

## Early Education

Amherst in the 1840s was a sleepy village in the lush Connecticut Valley, dominated by the Church and the college. Dickinson was reared in Trinitarian Congregationalism, but she never joined the Church and probably chafed at the austerity of the town. Concerts were rare; card games, dancing, and theater were unheard of. For relaxation she walked the hills with her dog, visited friends, and read. But it is also obvious that Puritan New England bred in her a sharp eye for local color, a love of introspection and self-analysis, and a fortitude that sustained her through years of intense loneliness.

Dickinson graduated from Amherst Academy in 1847. The following year (the longest time she was ever to spend away from home) she attended Mount Holyoke Female Seminary at South Hadley, but because of her fragile health she did not return. At the age of 17 she settled into the

Dickinson home and turned herself into a competent house-keeper and a more than ordinary observer of Amherst life.

## Early Work

It is not known when Dickinson began to write poetry or what happened to the poems of her early youth. Only five poems can be dated prior to 1858, the year in which she began gathering her work into hand-written fair copies bound loosely with looped thread to make small packets. She sent these five early poems to friends in letters or as valentines, and one of them was published anonymously without her permission in the *Springfield Republican* (Feb. 20, 1852). After 1858 she apparently convinced herself she had a genuine talent, for now the packets were carefully stored in an ebony box, awaiting inspection by future readers or even by a publisher.

Publication, however, was not easily arranged. After Dickinson besieged her friend Samuel Bowles, editor of the *Republican,* with poems and letters for 4 years, he published two poems, both anonymously: "I taste a liquor never brewed" (May 4, 1861) and "Safe in their Alabaster Chambers" (March 1, 1862). And the first of these was edited, probably by Bowles, to regularize (and thus, flatten) the rhymes and the punctuation. Dickinson began the poem: "I taste a liquor never brewed—/ From Tankards scooped in Pearl—/ Not all the Frankfort Berries/ Yield such an Alcohol." But Bowles printed: "I taste a liquor never brewed,/ From tankards scooped in pearl;/ Not Frankfort berries yield the sense/ Such a delicious whirl." She used no title; Bowles titled it "The May-Wine." (Only seven poems were pub-lished during her lifetime, and all had been altered by editors.)

## Friendship with T. W. Higginson

In 1862 Dickinson turned to the literary critic Thomas Wentworth Higginson for advice about her poems. She had known him only through his essays in the *Atlantic Monthly,* but in time he became, in her words, her "preceptor" and eventually her "safest friend." She began her first letter to him by asking, "Are you too deeply occupied to say if my verse is alive?" Six years later she was bold enough to say, "You were not aware that you saved my life." They did not meet until 1870, at her urging, surprisingly, and only once more after that. Higginson told his wife, after the first meet-ing, "I was never with anyone who drained my nerve power so much. Without touching her she drew from me. I am glad not to live near her."

What Dickinson was seeking was assurance as well as advice, and Higginson apparently gave it without knowing it, through a correspondence that lasted the rest of her life. He advised against publishing, but he also kept her abreast of the literary world (indeed, of the outside world, since as early as 1868, she was writing him, "I do not cross my father's ground to any house or town"). He helped her not at all with what mattered most to her—establishing her own private poetic method—but he was a friendly ear and a congenial mentor during the most troubled years of her life. Out of her inner turmoil came rare lyrics in a form that Higginson never really understood—if he had, he would not have tried to "edit" them, either in the 1860s or after her death. Dickinson could not take his "surgery," as she called it, but she took his friendship willingly.

## Years of Emotional Crisis

Between 1858 and 1866 Dickinson wrote more than 1100 poems, full of aphorisms, paradoxes, off rhymes, and eccentric grammar. Few are more than 16 lines long, com-posed in meters based on English hymnology. The major subjects are love and separation, death, nature, and God—but especially love. When she writes "My life closed twice before its close," one can only guess who her real or fancied lovers might have been. Higginson was not one of them. It is more than likely that her first "dear friend" was Benjamin Newton, a young man too poor to marry, who had worked for a few years in her father's law office. He left Amherst for Worcester and died there in 1853.

During a visit to Philadelphia a year later Dickinson met the Reverend Charles Wadsworth. Sixteen years her senior, a brilliant preacher, already married, he was hardly more than a mental image of a lover. There is no doubt she made him this, but nothing more. He visited her once in 1860. When he moved to San Francisco in May 1862, she was in despair. Only a month before, Samuel Bowles had sailed for Europe to recover his health. Little wonder that in her first letter to Higginson she said, "I had a terror . . . — and so I sing as the Boy does by the Burying Ground—because I am afraid." She needed love, but she had to indulge this need through her poems, perhaps because she felt she could cope with it no other way.

When Bowles returned to Amherst in November, Dickinson was so overwhelmed she remained in her bedroom and sent a note down, "... That you return to us alive is better than a summer, and more to hear your voice below than news of any bird." By the time Wadsworth returned from California in 1870 and resettled in Philadelphia, the crisis was over. His second visit, in 1880, was anticlimax. Higginson had not saved her life; her life was never in danger. What had been in danger was her emotional equilibrium and her control over a talent that was so intense it longed for the eruptions that might have destroyed it.

## Last Years

In the last 2 decades of her life Dickinson wrote fewer than 50 poems a year, perhaps because of continuing eye trouble, more probably because she had to take increasing responsibility in running the household. Her father died in 1874, and a year later her mother suffered a paralyzing stroke that left her an invalid until her death. There was little time for poetry, not even for serious consideration of marriage (if it was actually proffered) with a widower and old family friend, Judge Otis Lord. Their love was genuine, but once again the timing was wrong. It was too late to recast her life completely. Her mother died in 1882, Judge Lord 2 years later. Dickinson's health failed noticeably after a nervous collapse in 1884, and on May 15, 1886, she died of nephritis.

## Posthumous Publication

How the complete poems of Dickinson were finally gathered is a publishing saga almost too complicated for brief summary. Lavinia Dickinson inherited the ebony box; she asked Mabel Loomis Todd, the wife of an Amherst astronomy professor, to join Higginson in editing the manuscripts. Unfortunately, they felt even then that they had to alter the syntax, smooth the rhymes, cut some lines, and create titles for each poem. Three volumes appeared in quick succession: 1890, 1891, and 1896. In 1914 Dickinson's niece, Martha Dickinson Bianchi, published some of the poems her mother, Susan, had saved. In the next 3 decades four more volumes appeared, the most important being *Bolts of Melody* (1945), edited by Mrs. Todd and her daughter, Millicent Todd Bingham, from the manuscripts the Todds had never returned to Lavinia Dickinson. In 1955 Thomas H. Johnson prepared for Harvard University Press a three-volume edition, chronologically arranged, of "variant readings critically compared with all known manuscripts." Here, for the first time, the reader saw the poems as Dickinson had left them. The Johnson text of the 1,775 extant poems is now the standard one.

It is clear that Dickinson could not have written to please publishers, who were not ready to risk her striking aphoristic style and original metaphors. She had the right to educate the public, as Poe and Whitman eventually did, but she never had the invitation. Had she published during her lifetime, adverse public criticism might have driven her into deeper solitude, even silence. "If fame belonged to me," she told Higginson, "I could not escape her; if she did not, the longest day would pass me on the chase ... My barefoot

rank is better." The 20th century has lifted her without doubt to the first rank among poets.

## Further Reading

Thomas H. Johnson edited *The Letters of Emily Dickinson* (3 vols., 1958). His three-volume variorum edition of her poems (1955) was followed by a one-volume *The Complete Poems of Emily Dickinson* (1960) and a selection of 575 poems, *Final Harvest* (1961).

The best of the early biographies of Emily Dickinson is George Whicher, *This Was a Poet: A Critical Biography of Emily Dickinson* (1938). It has been superseded by Richard Chase, *Emily Dickinson* (1951); Thomas H. Johnson, *Emily Dickinson: An Interpretive Biography* (1955); and David Higgins, *Portrait of Emily Dickinson: The Poet and Her Prose* (1967). Jay Leyda, *The Years and Hours of Emily Dickinson* (2 vols., 1960), is a valuable source book.

There are numerous critical studies. The best general appreciation is Charles R. Anderson, *Emily Dickinson's Poetry: Stairway of Surprise* (1960). More recent studies are Clark Griffith, *The Long Shadow: Emily Dickinson's Tragic Poetry* (1964); Albert J. Gelpi, *Emily Dickinson: The Mind of the Poet* (1965); Ruth Miller, *The Poetry of Emily Dickinson* (1968); and William R. Sherwood, *Circumference and Circumstance: Stages in the Mind and Art of Emily Dickinson* (1968). Richard B. Sewall edited *Emily Dickinson: A Collection of Critical Essays* (1963). Equally useful is Cesar R. Blake and Carlton F. Wells, eds., *The Recognition of Emily Dickinson: Selected Criticism since 1890* (1964).

Emily Dickinson's place in the history of American poetry is well established in Roy Harvey Pearce, *The Continuity of American Poetry* (1961), and Hyatt H. Waggoner, *American Poets from the Puritans to the Present* (1968). □

# Dorothea Lynde Dix

**Dorothea Lynde Dix (1802-1887) was an American reformer whose pioneer efforts to improve treatment of mental patients stimulated broad reforms in hospitals, jails, and asylums in the United States and abroad.**

On April 4, 1802, Dorothea Dix, the daughter of Joseph and Mary Dix, was born in Hampden, Maine. When Joseph failed at farming, he became an itinerant preacher and wrote, printed, and sold tracts, which his wife and daughter laboriously sewed together. Dorothea remembered her childhood in that bleak, poverty-stricken household as a time of loneliness and despair. At the age of 12 she ran away from home and made her way to Boston, where she persuaded her grandmother to take her in. Two years later Dorothea went to Worcester to live with a great aunt and opened a school, which she maintained for 3 years. She returned to Boston in 1819 to attend public school and to study with private tutors.

## Teaching Career

In 1821 Dix opened an academy for wealthy young ladies in her grandmother's house. She also conducted a free school for poor children. As a teacher, she was a strict disciplinarian, a rigorous moralist, and a passionate explorer of many fields of knowledge, including the natural sciences. Her contagious joy in teaching made her schools highly successful. During convalescent periods from attacks of chronic lung disease, she wrote children's books.

In 1835 ill health forced Dix to abandon teaching; she went abroad for 2 years. When she returned to America, she was in better health but irresolute about her future. Four years of indecision ended when she volunteered to teach a Sunday school class for young women in the East Cambridge, Mass., jail. She discovered that the quarters for the insane had no heat, even in the coldest weather. When the jailer explained that insane people did not feel the cold, and ignored her pleas for heat, she boldly took the case to court and won.

### Mental Institution Reforms

For 2 years Dix traveled throughout Massachusetts, visiting jails, workhouses, almshouses, and hospitals, taking notes on the deplorable conditions she observed. In 1845 Dr. Samuel Gridley Howe presented her "Memorial to the Massachusetts Legislature." The address began, "I proceed, gentlemen, briefly to call your attention to the *present* state of insane persons confined within the Commonwealth, in *cages, closets, cellars, pens; chained, naked, beaten with rods,* and *lashed* into obedience." This dramatic presentation caused a public controversy which won the support of Charles Sumner and other public figures in the resulting newspaper debate. Despite bitter opposition, the reform bill passed by a large majority.

Dix went on to other northeastern states and then throughout the country, state by state, visiting jails, almshouses, and hospitals, studying their needs, and eliciting help from philanthropists, charitable organizations, and state legislatures for building and renovating facilities and for improving treatment. During these years she founded new hospitals or additions in Massachusetts, Rhode Island, New York, New Jersey, Pennsylvania, and Canada and received approval to found state hospitals by the legislatures of Indiana, Illinois, Kentucky, Tennessee, Missouri, Maryland, Louisiana, Alabama, South Carolina, and North Carolina.

### European Crusade

In 1848 Dix took her fight to Congress in an attempt to win appropriation of 12,500,000 acres of land, which would provide tax revenue for asylums. The bill finally passed both houses only to be vetoed by President Franklin Pierce. The discouraged reformer then traveled through England, Ireland, and Scotland, inspecting mental hospitals. English and Irish institutions were not bad, but Scottish facilities were appalling, and Miss Dix set about to improve them, taking her case finally to the lord advocate of Scotland.

Perhaps Dix's most significant European accomplishment was in Rome, where she discovered that "6,000 priests, 300 monks, 3,000 nuns, and a spiritual sovereignty, joined with the temporal powers, had not assured for the miserable insane a decent, much less an intelligent care." She negotiated an audience with Pius IX, who was moved by her appeal and personally verified her reports. He ordered construction of a new hospital and a thorough revision of the rules for the care of mental patients. Before her return to the United States, Dix evaluated hospitals and prisons in Turkey, Greece, Italy, France, Austria, Russia, Scandinavia, Holland, Belgium, and Germany and recommended reforms.

### Civil War Nurse

In 1861 Dix volunteered her services for wartime duty in the Civil War. Appointed "superintendent of women nurses," she set up emergency training programs, established temporary hospitals, distributed supplies, and processed and deployed nurses. Despite wartime hardships she never relaxed her standards of efficient service, proper procedure, and immaculate hospital conditions. Her inspections of army hospitals did not make her popular with authorities, and her stringent ideas of duty and discipline were not shared by the relatively untrained nurses and jealous officials, who resented her autocratic manner. Although she was often discouraged by petty political opposition and the ever present problems of inadequate facilities, supplies, and staff, she carried out her duties until the end of the war.

Dix resumed her reform efforts until age forced her to retire. Until her death in 1887 she made her home in the Trenton, N.J., hospital, which she had often referred to affectionately as her "first child."

### Further Reading

The most commonly cited biographies of Dorothea Dix are early ones. Francis Tiffany, *The Life of Dorothea Lynde Dix* (1890), is a standard work which contains copious quotations from letters and reports. More recent is Helen E. Marshall, *Dorothea Dix: Forgotten Samaritan* (1937). Additional details are provided in Gladys Brooks's concise and popular *Three Wise Virgins* (1957). See also Albert Deutsch, *The Mentally Ill in America: A History of Their Care and Treatment from Colonial Times* (1937; 2d ed. 1949), and Norman Dain's brief but scholarly *Concepts of Insanity in the United States, 1789-1865* (1964). □

# Grace Hoadley Dodge

**Grace Hoadley Dodge (1856–1914) was one of the early feminists devoting her time and energy to improve the education and social status of women in the early 1900s.**

A tireless supporter of women's issues, Grace Hoadley Dodge devoted her life to improvements in women's education, esteem, and safety at a time when women were just beginning to gain greater access to social privileges. Her vision of the possibilities for women came to fruition through her work with many associations and clubs, including the Young Women's Christian Association, the New York Travelers' Aid Society, and the Teachers College of Columbia University, which she founded. She contributed her time and talent generously to these associations, and worked actively in money-raising campaigns for them until her death in 1914.

In a letter to Mrs. Dave Hennen Morris, Dodge expounded on her efforts regarding the Teachers College: "I realized that the country needed trained teachers, and it was needed to make teaching a profession like that of law and medicine. I realized that expert professors, buildings, grounds, endowment, and so forth, were needed; in other words, money. I knew that the president, or professors could not go out and ask for money, and felt that I must. It was hard to know how to ask or whom to ask. Certain friends gave what they could, but much more was needed. I felt the spiritual force of this need. . . . I used to give months for several years to secure friends for the college. . . . God blesses the persistent effort."

Born the eldest of six children to William Earl and Sarah (Hoadley) Dodge in 1856, Grace Hoadley Dodge benefitted from the wealth and business savvy of her family. Her grandfather, William Earl Dodge, had founded the prominent New York firm of Phelps, Dodge & Co., of which her father was a partner. Her mother's father, David Hoadley, was a high ranking executive of large financial concerns. And her grandmother, Melissa Phelps Dodge, imparted the business know-how of her father, the successful Anson G. Phelps. Surrounded by such successful people, Grace Dodge developed strong business and management skills. Since she was a woman, however, she could not apply her talents as her forefathers had to ventures in copper, silk, or railroads.

Dodge's formal education came from private tutors and, starting in 1872, two years at Miss Porter's school for young ladies at Farmington, Connecticut. At Miss Porter's school, Dodge determined that her interests lay not in the program offerings, but in helping other people in need. At age eighteen, Dodge dropped out of Miss Porter's school. Unable to enter society as a desirable debutante like many of her more dainty and beautiful peers, Dodge became intrigued by the charitable activities of evangelist Dwight L. Moody.

Wishing to use her wealth and ambition to help others, Dodge began her distinguished career as a social worker and philanthropist, teaching Sunday School at Madison Square Chapel in 1874 and adding sewing classes one year later. Sympathetic to Grace's philanthropic desires, William E. Dodge put his daughter in contact with Louisa Lee Schuyler, organizer of the State Charities Aid Association; during their first interview Miss Schuyler made Grace Dodge a member of the association's Committee on the Elevation of the Poor in Their Homes. In 1876, Dodge began a five-year teaching career in the industrial school at the Children's Aid Society. Her work at the Children's Aid Society made her realize the need to instruct many working girls about fundamental aspects of household chores and health care. Dodge began holding discussion groups for silk factory girls, which developed into a fellowship program

and a club with cooking and sewing classes. A resident doctor was added as well, and the club eventually grew into the Working Girls' Society. Dodge attended many Society discussion groups during this period, educating herself about the many and varied predicaments facing working-class women at this time. Armed with this information, she initiated tenement reform in 1879 from her position as chairperson of the Committee on the Elevation of the Poor.

In addition to her work at the Children's Aid Society and the State Charities Aid Association, Dodge taught "kitchen garden classes," which used kindergarten play methods to teach household arts to working-class girls. The success of the Kitchen Garden classes prompted organizers to enlist Dodge's help in forming the Kitchen Garden Association in 1880. The group was later reorganized into the Industrial Education Association in 1884, when it began to provide manual training for boys and promote the teaching of domestic and industrial classes in public schools. Dodge ran the association as its vice-president. Her efforts gained her additional recognition, and in 1886 she was given one of the first two seats given to women on New York City's board of education. During her three years of service on the board, she advocated manual training, secured evening classes for working girls, and became spokesperson for 3,500 New York women teachers.

The Industrial Education Association evolved into the Teachers College in 1889 under the guidance, vision, and dogged determination of Grace Dodge; following her suggestion, the college became a part of Columbia University in 1889. A decade after Grace Dodge's death, Mrs. Leonard Elmhurst wrote in *Founding Teachers College* of Dodge's vision and commitment to the school: "Being a trustee of Teachers College, I always feel in that institution a vivid sense of what her vision of education meant, not only to her generation but to the thousands of men and women who throng those halls today. She is still referred to in our trustee meetings and Dean Russell carries her spirit to us as if he only consulted with her yesterday."

Grace Dodge was still very active in her philanthropy until her death in 1914. She helped establish the Girls' Public School Athletic League in 1905, acted as president of the Young Women's Christian Association of the United States in 1906, and was influential in the consolidation of church groups into the New York Travelers Aid Society in 1907 and the organization of the American Social Hygiene Association in 1912. □

# Elizabeth Hanford Dole

**Elizabeth Hanford Dole (born 1936), has worked as a lawyer, White House aide, cabinet officer, and president of the American Red Cross.**

Elizabeth Hanford was born and grew up in Salisbury, North Carolina, the daughter of wholesale flower dealers. She was a political science major at Duke University, received a master's degree in education from Harvard in 1960, and graduated from Harvard Law School in 1965 as one of 25 female graduates in a class of 500. Dole was often described as friendly, gracious, and "brainy," attributes which led to her election as college May Queen and student body president as well as to Phi Beta Kappa, and the national honor society.

After law school Hanford went to Washington, where she earned a reputation as a consumer advocate in (what was then) the Department of Health, Education and Welfare; as executive director of the Presidential Committee for Consumer Interests; and as deputy director of the U.S. Office of Consumer Affairs. Although briefly employed in private law practice, her primary professional commitment soon became public service.

In 1973 Hanford was nominated to be one of five commissioners on the Federal Trade Commission (FTC). Once appointed she became known for her enforcement of the Equal Credit Opportunity Act of 1975 and for an FTC investigation of nursing home abuses. A colleague at the FTC remembered her priorities as ". . .the poor, the handicapped, minorities, and women. She really cared about them."

## Married Republican Senator Robert Dole of Kansas

Hanford married Robert Dole, the senior senator from Kansas, in 1975 and they quickly became known as Washington's premier "Power Couple" because of their prominent roles in national politics. However glamourous that designation may seem, it referred strictly to their jobs and not their social life. According to the New York Times, the Doles often "return to their two bedroom apartment at the Watergate complex after a 12-hour day and either heat up a . . . frozen meal or go to a nearby Chinese restaurant." Their lives revolve almost totally around their work. And according to Dole, the work experiences shared in her "dual career" marriage, often provided a source of satisfaction and enjoyment. "It's a great way of sharing even if you can't share all the information, and you don't have as much time together . . . you share a sense of pride in each other's accomplishments." Marrying late in life, she was nearly 40 and the Senator was 53, the Doles had no children and lived in Washington's famous Watergate Apartments.

Religion also played an important role in Dole's personal life. Although raised a devout Methodist she, for the most part, kept her religious views private. With little fanfare or publicity she regularly attended church and often performed charitable services for nursing home residents. A turning point came in 1987 when, in evangelical fashion, she provided her Christian "testimony" at the National Prayer Breakfast in Washington, D.C. Afterwards Dole became a favorite of Christian conservatives and began to speak regularly to religious groups around the country.

## Achieved Prominence as a Republican

Previously a Democrat, Dole became a registered Independent during her early years in Washington. Following her marriage, she became a Republican and campaigned vigorously when her husband ran for vice-president on the unsuccessful Ford-Dole ticket in 1976. With her husband's own campaign for the presidency in 1979, she resigned as FTC commissioner to campaign for him full-time. Although that campaign, too, was unsuccessful, by 1980, "Liddy" Dole was becoming well-known as one of the Republican Party's most outstanding female leaders and recognized, just as much as her more famous husband, as a contender for high political office.

## Served in Reagan and Bush Administrations

In 1983 President Ronald Reagan appointed Dole as Secretary of Transportation, the first woman in American history to hold that cabinet position. As "Madame Secretary" she headed an organization of 102,000 employees and administered a budget of $28 billion. Problems facing the new administrator included highways, bridges, mass transit, air traffic control, shipping, Conrail, and the Washington, D.C. public transportation system. Since the Secretary of Transportation is also the director of the U.S. Coast Guard, she was the first woman to command an armed service in the United States. At that time, Transportation was rapidly becoming an important cabinet post since it involved 20 percent of the gross national product and touched the lives of most Americans.

During her first month as Transportation Secretary, Dole "moved a mountain" and agreed to provide $70 million in existing Department of Transportation (DOT) and Amtrak funds to start making Union Station, the antiquated train station in Washington, D.C., "alive and vibrant with people . . . a center of activity for our city of Washington and for this nation."

Safety became Dole's "first issue" at the Department of Transportation. She endorsed the concept of a third brake light on cars and air bags to protect passengers in case of collision. In an effort to promote the use of airbags, DOT provided 5,000 new government cars and 500 state police cars with air bags. Her early victories at Transportation included winning government funds for new passenger railway lines and the passage of a maritime reform bill. *Washington Monthly* also credited her with adding more Federal Aviation Administration inspectors, fighting deceptive airline scheduling, and campaigning for higher drinking ages and for single-licensing of truck drivers to prevent "outlaw drivers from getting relicensed in other states."

Dole abandoned her earlier support for the Equal Rights Amendment after joining the anti-ERA Reagan administration. But she made it a point to increase the number of women at DOT as well as benefits, such as work place day care centers, designed to keep them there. Despite her identification with liberal consumer issues and former support for ERA, Dole received strong backing from the conservative Reagan administration. Critics, however, viewed her commitment to important issues as secondary to her ambition. The *Chicago Tribune* questioned the logic that transformed her from a "Democrat who had worked for President Lyndon Johnson's Great Society to a Republican who pampered big business, from a federal trade commisssioner who decried big-business mergers to a Secretary of Transportation who sanctioned almost every airline merger that came her way. The *Washington Monthly* summarized this feeling when it observed that, instead of an ideologue, Dole was "the consummate role player, her positions defined by her job description rather than deeply felt beliefs."

Dole resigned as Secretary of Transportation in 1987 to campaign for her husband's second attempt at the presidency. Although the campaign itself was unsuccessful, Dole again received high marks as a campaigner. Because of her previous cabinet-level experience under Reagan, and her immense popularity within the Republican Party, Dole was tabbed as the new Secretary of Labor by President George Bush in 1989. As Secretary of Labor, Dole negotiated a raise in the minimum wage, oversaw efforts to break "glass ceiling" restrictions that prevented movement of women and minorities into high executive positions, and was widely credited with the settlement of the United Mine Workers strike against the Pittson Coal Company.

## Headed the American Red Cross

In 1990 Dole resigned as Secretary of Labor to become the president of the American Red Cross. As head of the Red Cross she oversaw a $1.8 billion annual budget, 32,000 employees, and 1.4 million volunteers. Priorities during her first tenure included issues such as improving the safety of the nation's blood supply against AIDS, responding to world emergencies caused by famine, war, and natural disasters, and improving the charitable giving by Americans to humanitarian organizations. In 1996 Dole took a one-year leave of absence to assist her husband's final campaign for the presidency.

## Played Prominent Role in 1996 Campaign

According to the *New York Times*, Dole's leave of absence from the Red Cross was illustrative of her belief in and committment to her husband. It was the fourth time that she had "either quit or taken leave from powerful jobs to help along her husband's White House ambitions. Her intense loyalty was again displayed at the 1996 Republican National Convention with her talk-show style "Why I Love Bob" speech where she descended from the podium and spoke in personal terms about her husband to the nation. Saying that she would tell stories that her husband would not mention himself, Dole proceeded to deliver, in near flawless performance, a condensed biography of the Senator from his childhood days in Kansas to his current run for the White House.

So successful was Dole's speech that, after the convention, she acquired her own staff of 30, a travel budget of $1.5 million, and a leased 14-seat jet to campaign separately for her husband. Depite her efforts, though, the Senator was unable to overcome a slow campaign start and was subsequently defeated by incumbent President Bill Clinton.

Dole returned to her position as President of the American Red Cross in 1997. Her priorities for her second tenure included the reeingeering of national headquarters to ensure greater responsiveness for service delivery and the strengthening of the disaster relief fund.

Dole continued her popularity as a guest speaker by delivering the 1997 commencement address to her alma mater, Duke University. Although she remained silent on future political aspirations of her own, Dole still remained a Republican Party favorite and may yet again return to high political office.

## Further Reading

For more information see Elizabeth and Robert Dole, *The Doles: Unlimited Partners* (1988).

There is no book length biography of Elizabeth Hanford Dole, but she is listed in *Who's Who in America* (1984-1985, 43rd edition). Articles about Dole are in *Vogue* (October 1984) and *Working Woman* (April 1983), and a profile of her appeared in the *Washington Post* on January 8, 1983. Additional profiles appeared in *The New York Times* on July 19 and October 13, 1996. □

# Hilda Doolittle

**The American poet, translator, and novelist Hilda Doolittle (1886-1961), generally called H. D., was an imagist whose lyric art conveys intense feelings through sharp images and "free" forms.**

Hilda Doolittle was born on Sept. 10, 1886, in Bethlehem, Pa.; her father was a professor. She entered Bryn Mawr College in 1904. She had met Ezra Pound in 1901, and in 1905, while he was studying at the University of Pennsylvania, he introduced her to William Carlos Williams, then a medical school student at the university. She quit school in 1906 because of ill health. During the next 5 years she studied Greek and Latin literature, tried Latin translation, and wrote a few poems. By 1911 the apprenticeship of this tall young woman, attractive in a long-faced, large-eyed way, was nearly over.

Doolittle toured Europe and stayed on in London, where Pound took her under his wing. She and Richard Aldington found a common interest in carrying over into English the spare beauty of Greek art and literature. Pound called them *Imagistes,* thus creating a new literary movement based on common speech, the exact word, new rhythms, absolute freedom in choosing subjects, clarity, and concentration. Pound helped both poets get published, persuading Doolittle in 1913 to sign herself "H. D., Imagiste." (H. D. remained perhaps the only faithful imagist, less out of

decision than because her natural way of writing simply coincided with Pound's program.)

H. D. married Aldington in 1913. In 1916 he left for World War I front lines, and she issued her first volume, *Sea Garden,* also succeeding him as literary editor of the *Egoist.* A year later she resigned because of poor health and was replaced by T. S. Eliot. The anxieties of the war, a miscarriage, and her husband's infidelity overwhelmed her. In 1919, pregnant, ill with pneumonia, and saddened by the death of her father, she separated from Aldington and later had a daughter, Perdita.

Winifred Ellerman, a wealthy novelist-to-be known as "Bryher," became H. D.'s friend and benefactor. They settled in neighboring houses in a Swiss village in 1923. Thereafter H. D. lived either in Switzerland or in London. Meanwhile she issued *Hymen* (1921) and *Heliodora* (1924). *Collected Poems* (1925) established her place in modern poetry. "Helen" and the more sustained lament "Islands" are representative selections.

H. D.'s first novel, *Palimpsest* (1926), deals with the trials of sensitive women and artists in a harsh world. Her second novel was *Hedylus* (1928). In 1927 she published a verse play, *Hippolytus Temporizes.* A new volume of poems, *Red Roses from Bronze* (1931), and *The Hedgehog* (1936), prose fiction, like her early volumes contained choruses translated from Greek plays. Her most ambitious translation was *Euripides' Ion* (1937). The following year she divorced Aldington.

H. D. was in London during World War II. *By Avon River* (1949) deals with Shakespeare and Elizabethan and Jacobean writers. *Tribute to Freud* (1956) records her gratitude for her psychoanalysis. Her novel *Bid Me to Live* (1960) is an account of a situation that approximates her marital breakup. Her most ambitious work, *Helen in Egypt* (1961), concludes that perfect love can be found only in death. She died that year in Switzerland.

In all of H. D.'s poetry, discrete colors and forms, frugal rhythms, focused emotions, and clarity of thought suggest a Greek miniaturist or, in longer works, a Japanese scroll painter.

## Further Reading

There are two full-length studies of Hilda Doolittle: Thomas B. Swann, *The Classical World of H. D.* (1962), and Vincent Quinn, *H. D.* (1968). Biographical material is also available in the autobiographies of Richard Aldington, *Life for Life's Sake* (1941), and Bryher (pseudonym of Winifred Ellerman), *The Heart to Artemis: A Writer's Memoirs* (1962). Stanley K. Coffman, *Imagism: A Chapter for the History of Modern Poetry* (1951), discusses the movement of which H. D. seems the best representative. □

# Rheta Childe Dorr

**Rheta Childe Dorr (1868–1948) was a member of the National Woman Suffrage Association. Her work as a journalist was not widely accepted as proper**

woman's work. She fought hard for women's suffrage.

As a child in Nebraska, Rheta Childe routinely disobeyed her parents. At age twelve she sneaked out of the house to attend a women's rights rally led by Elizabeth Cady Stanton and Susan B. Anthony. Her parents found out when the newspaper printed the names of those who had joined the National Woman Suffrage Association. She began working at the age of fifteen, over the objections of her parents, so that she could become independent and prove her industry. She was conservative by nature but became a rebel upon viewing a tombstone inscribed "Also Harriet, wife of the above."

## Self-Expression

In 1890 Childe went to New York City to study at the Art Students' League and decided that she would become a writer. When John Pixley Dorr, a man twenty years older than she, visited from Lincoln, they fell in love and were soon married. She was swept away by his good looks and love of books. They lived in Seattle for two years, where their son Julian was born. Rheta wrote articles for the New York newspapers, which her husband found to be an unacceptable activity. They soon parted by mutual consent, and Rhea returned to New York with their young son, determined to make a living as a journalist.

## Cads and Editors

Dorr was shocked at how she was treated in New York City. Editors would not put her on the staff simply because she was a woman, and when she complained that the rates they paid for freelance articles could not support a family, they said they could find other women to work for those rates. She finally got a break by persuading Theodore Roosevelt to be photographed (something he hated) and was rewarded with an ill-paying job on the *New York Evening Post*, which she left within a year. Her first overseas assignment was to cover the coronation of a new king in Norway, and on the way back she attended the International Woman Suffrage Alliance meeting in Copenhagen, where she met prominent British suffragists.

## "The Woman's Invasion"

Returning to New York almost penniless, Dorr resolved to be done with the society pages that passed for women's journalism. She proposed to the editor of *Everybody's* that she go underground as a worker and write about her experiences. She spent a year working in a laundry, a department store, on an assembly line, and as a seamstress but was often too exhausted to do more than make notes about her experiences. A cowriter named William Hard was assigned to help her, but Dorr resisted giving her notes over to him. She was shocked to see the magazine begin a series with her title, ideas, and experiences but with the byline of William Hard. She hired a lawyer and at least prevented the publication of a book by Hard exploiting her work.

## International Suffrage

In 1910, with the assistance of *Hampton's Magazine*, Dorr published *What Eight Million Women Want,* an account of suffrage clubs, trade unions, and consumer leagues that had sprung up all over Europe and the United States. In 1912 she went to Sweden, Germany, and England to interview leaders in the women's movement, and she spent the winter of 1912-1913 in Paris assisting British suffragist Emmeline Pankhurst in writing Pankhurst's autobiography, *My Own Story.* When she returned to the United States, she went to work for the *New York Evening Mail* and wrote a daily column, "As a Woman Sees It." Not everyone was moved by her arguments: interviewing Woodrow Wilson in 1914, she asked him about woman's suffrage. He replied, "I think that it is not proper for me to stand here and be cross-examined by you."

## The Russian Revolution

Having twice been to Russia, Dorr was anxious to observe the 1917 revolution. One night she lay in her hotel bed listening to the murder of a general in the next room. When she tried to leave the country after five months, all of her notes were confiscated by the authorities so she wrote *Inside the Russian Revolution* (1917) entirely from memory. In her opinion, Russia had become "a barbarous and half-insane land. . . . Oratory held the stupid populace spellbound while the Germans invaded the country, boosted Lenin into power and paved the way for the treaty of Brest-Litovsk. . . . Russia was done."

### War Correspondence

Since her son Julian was serving in the army in France, she asked editors to send her back to Europe. When the French government refused to grant her press credentials because she was a woman, she signed on as a lecturer with the YMCA. She walked into a mess tent where her son was eating. Astonished, he cried, "Mother!" and no soldier would sit down until she found a chair. Mothers were unquestioningly better received than female war correspondents. Later Dorr covered the Women's Death Battalion in Russia and described an incident in which fellow soldiers broke into their barracks in order to rape them but were held off by the women at gunpoint. In addition to her many wartime articles, she also wrote *A Soldier's Mother in France* (1918) for women on the home front. Dorr, along with Louise Bryant, Mary Roberts Rinehart, and Bessie Beattie, pioneered the way for women to become war correspondents. After spending many more years in Europe, and writing more books, including her autobiography, *A Woman of Fifty,* Dorr died in Bucks County, Pennsylvania, in 1948 at age eighty. □

# Rita Frances Dove

**Rita Frances Dove (born 1952) is a poet, writer, and educator. In 1993, she became the youngest to hold the title of poet laureate of the United States Library of Congress.**

In announcing Rita Frances Dove's appointment, Librarian of Congress James H. Billington said, "I take much pleasure in announcing the selection of a younger poet of distinction and versatility. Having had a number of poet laureates who have accumulated multiple distinctions from lengthy and distinguished careers, we will be pleased to have an outstanding representative of a new and richly variegated generation of American poets. Rita Dove is an accomplished and already widely recognized poet in mid-career whose work gives special promise to explore and enrich contemporary American poetry."

Rita Frances Dove was born in Akron, Ohio, on August 28,1952. She was the second of four children born to Ray Dove and Elvira Elizabeth (Hord) Dove. Her father was one of ten children and was the first in his family to go to college, earning a master's degree in chemistry. At the time of her birth however, her father was working as an elevator operator for the Goodyear Tire and Rubber Company because he could not get hired as a research scientist. Eventually, her father broke the color barrier and became the first African American chemist to work for Goodyear.

From a young age, she wrote plays and stories which her classmates performed. In high school she wrote a comic book along with her older brother which featured characters named Jet Boy and Jet Girl who could fly and communicate telepathically. "One of the things that fascinated me when I was growing up was the way language was put together,

and how words could lead you into a new place," she told Mohammed B. Taleb-Khyar in a 1991 interview for *Callaloo.* "I think one reason I became primarily a poet rather than a fiction writer is that though I am interested in stories, I am profoundly fascinated by the ways in which language can change your perceptions."

She was named a presidential scholar in 1970, when she was designated one of the hundred best high school graduates in the nation. A few months later, she enrolled at Miami University, in Oxford, Ohio, as an English major. A writers' conference she attended with one of her high school English teachers had shown her that writing could be a career. She also took many German language courses and practiced the cello consistently. She decided to become a professional poet while in college and told her parents while on a Thanksgiving break. "[My father] swallowed once," she said, recalling that day, "and said 'Well, I've never understood poetry, so don't be upset if I don't read it.'" Faculty members at Miami University were more surprised than her family with her career decision. She said that, "declaring one's intention to be a poet was analogous to putting on a dunce cap," and that many at the school treated her as if she was "throwing away [her] education."

She graduated *summa cum laude* from Miami University in 1973 and was a Fulbright fellow at the University of Tubingen, Germany from 1974 to 1975. In Germany, she studied expressionist drama and the works of twentieth-century German lyric poets Ranier Maria Rilke and Paul Celan. Her political awareness "increased dramatically" while she was in Germany because she found herself "on display in a strange environment where some people pointed with fingers at [her] and others pitied [her] as a symbol for centuries of brutality and injustice against blacks." It was also in Germany that she met her future husband, Fred Viebahn, a novelist. They married in 1979 and have a daughter, Aviva Chantal, who was born in 1983.

## Early Career

After returning from Europe, she enrolled at the University of Iowa, where she was a teaching/writing fellow in the Writer's Workshop. She received her Master of Fine Arts at the University of Iowa in 1977, the year *Ten Poems,* her first chapbook of verse was published. In 1980, her second chapbook, *The Only Dark Spot in the Sky,* was published. Her first book-length poetry collection, based on her master's thesis, *The Yellow House on the Corner,* was published in 1980.

Dove's second poetry collection, *Museum,* was published in 1983 and based on her travels abroad from 1979 to 1981. In 1981, Dove joined the faculty of Arizona State University at Tempe as an assistant professor. She was the only African American out of a staff of over seventy members in the English Department. After being promoted to a full professor for the last two years of her stay at Arizona State University, she accepted a position as a professor of English at the University of Virginia at Charlottesville in 1989. In 1992, the university named her Commonwealth Professor of English.

## Poet Laureate

The United States Congress created the position of poet laureate in 1985, when it upgraded the half-century-old office of poetry consultant at the Library of Congress. The official title for the position is "Library of Congress Poet Laureate Consultant in Poetry" and offers a $35,000 stipend for the one year term.

On October 1, 1993, Dove became the nation's seventh poet laureate by succeeding Mona Van Duyn. In 1993, she gave the first official poetry reading at the White House in more than a dozen years. In her role of poet laureate, she aimed to keep poetry in the public eye and to expose the mass of American society to a form of language that it might not see otherwise. She tried to be "a force" for poetry and revitalize "serious literature." She said that otherwise the country would "drown in the brutalization of a truncated, dehumanized language." Displaying her entrepreneurial energies, she said that she hoped to raise funds for readings of poetry linked with jazz; a conference among scientists, artists, and writers; and "town meetings" focused on poetry. "I'm hoping that by the end [of my tenure], people will think of a poet laureate as someone who's out there with her sleeves rolled up, not sitting in an ivory tower looking out at the Potomac." She succeeded in this aim, and James H. Billington said that she had come up with "more ideas for elevating poetry in the nation's conscienceness than there is time to carry out in one year." To this aim, he offered, and she accepted his February 1994 invitation to serve another one-year term until late-1994.

After her term finished, she went back to teaching at the University of Virginia and keeps a tireless schedule of public appearances around the country to promote poetry and literature. For the occasion of the Olympiad in Atlanta, Georgia over the summer of 1996, Dove's works were scored for Andrew Young and read at the games.

## Honors

She has held fellowships from the National Endowment for the Arts, the Guggenheim and Mellon Foundations, the National Humanities Center, and the Center for Advanced Studies at the University of Virginia. With the support of the National Endowment for the Humanities, she served as writer-in-residence at Tuskegee Institute as a Portia Pittman fellow. Robert Penn Warren, while poet laureate himself, the first to hold that designation, selected Dove for the Lavan Younger Poet Award bestowed by the Academy of American Poets. She was president of the Associated Writing Programs, made up of persons teaching creative writing in colleges and universities. She holds honorary doctorates from Miami University and Knox College and was inducted into the Ohio Women's Hall of Fame in 1991.

Dove's activities ranged widely outside the world of academia. She served on the Advisory Board for Literature of the National Endowment for the Arts, was a judge for the Walt Whitman Award, the Pulitzer Prize, the National Book Award, and the $75,000 Ruth Lilly Prize, described as "the largest poetry prize in the United States." She held the Ohio Governor's Award in the Arts and the General Electric Foundation Award. She was also an editor of *Callaloo.* She was the Phi Beta Kappa poet at a Harvard University commencement an the New York Public Library selected her as a "Literary Lion."

Dove's poems have appeared in a wide range of journals, including *Black Scholar* and the *Yale Review,* and have been reprinted in such anthologies as *Early Ripening: American Women's Poetry Now,* edited by Marge Piercy (1987). She also published five books of poetry, *The Yellow House on the Corner* (1980), *Museum* (1983), *Thomas and Beulah,* which won a Pulitzer Prize (1986), and *Grace Notes* (1989), and *Mother Love* (1995); as well as a book of short stories, *Fifth Sunday* (1985), and a novel, *Through the Ivory Gate* (1992).

Dove's sometimes intensely personal poetry displays her deeply informed grasp of literary technique. Helen Vendler, a leading critic and student of poetry, wrote in the *New York Review of Books* that "Dove has planed away unnecessary matters: pure shape, her poems exhibit the thrift that Yeats called the sign of a perfected manner."

Arnold Rampersad, director of African American Studies at Princeton University and a specialist in writing by African Americans, wrote that "Dove is perhaps the most disciplined and technically accomplished black poet to arrive since Gwendolyn Brooks began her remarkable career in the nineteen forties. . . ." He spoke also of "the absence of strain in her voice, and the almost uncanny sense of peace and grace that infuses this wide-ranging poetry. . . ."

Typical of her impressive grasp of classical prosody applied to a modern idiom is her spare free-verse sonnet

"Flash Cards" from *Grace Notes,* which evokes childhood memories of studying with her father:

> In math I was the whiz kid, keeper
> of oranges and apples. What you don't understand,
> master, my father said; the faster
> I answered, the faster they came.
> I could see one bud on the teacher's geranium
> one clear bee sputtering at the wet pane.
> The tulip trees always dragged after heavy rain
> so I tucked my head as my boots slapped home.
> My father put up his feet after work
> and relaxed with a highball and The Life of
>     Lincoln.
> After supper we drilled and I climbed the dark
> before sleep, before a thin voice hissed
> numbers as I spun on a wheel. I had to guess.
> Ten, I kept saying, I'm only ten.

"Horse and Tree," also from *Grace Notes,* catches a child's excitement about nature and carousels; "Stitches," from the same volume, tersely records the frightening tension during a moment of surgery.

## Further Reading

For further biographical material on Dove, see the introductions to her books reported in the text. Articles relevant to her efforts to resuscitate poetry today are Louis Simpson's remarks in the *New York Times Book Review* (March 1, 1992), and essayist Joseph Epstein's essay "Who Killed Poetry?" in *Commentary* (August 1988).

Information on Dove's post-poet laureate career can be found in the *Atlanta Constitution* (July 22, 1996); the *Christian Science Monitor* (September 7, 1995); the *Detroit News* (April 18, 1996); and the *New York Times* (November 5, 1995). ☐

# Katherine Drexel

**Dedicating her life and her fortune to philanthropy, Katherine Drexel (1858-1955) founded a Catholic order of sisters, the Sisters of the Blessed Sacrament, to work for Native Americans and African Americans.**

Katherine Drexel was born in Philadelphia on November 26, 1858, the second daughter of Francis Drexel, a highly prosperous banker, and Hannah Langstroth, a Quaker. Hannah died five weeks later; her father married Emma Bouvier in 1860. They were devout Catholics, and both gave a great deal of their time and money to philanthropic activities. The children were educated privately and were encouraged to conduct a Sunday school for children of the employees at their family's summer home. The family travelled extensively in Europe and took a 6,000 mile trip through the American West in the private railroad car lent her father by James J. Hill, head of the Great Northern Railroad.

Drexel's full social and philanthropic life was jarred by the protracted illness, and then death in 1883, of her stepmother, to whom she was very devoted; two years later, her father died. She thought seriously of entering a convent where she could be totally absorbed in contemplation and prayer, but was persuaded by her religious counsellor not to make a hasty decision. Meanwhile, the Drexel young women were begged by a stream of churchmen to use their great wealth to help, as their parents had, in meeting the many crying needs of the Church—especially for missions in the West and the South. In 1889 Drexel began a novitiate with the Sisters of Mercy in Pittsburgh, with the understanding that in two years she would found her own order, the Sisters of the Blessed Sacrament, committed to the service of Native and African Americans; she would, she vowed, "be the mother and servant of these races."

Having taken a vow of poverty, she lived the rest of her life with extreme frugality. At the same time, her income from her father's trust (which increased substantially when her older sister died in childbirth) amounted to more than a $1,000 a day; she probably was, as the newspapers regularly declared, "the richest nun in the world." Receiving innumerable requests for aid, she concentrated her gifts on works which she could inspect and where—if possible—her Sisters could serve.

In the late 19th century Americans, especially in the East, were increasingly distressed by the abuse or neglect of the American Indians. The Catholic Church, hampered by poverty and the importunate needs of Catholic immigrants in the eastern cities, had been able to do less than many religious groups; and, the Church felt, with considerable reason, that the federal government discriminated against Catholic efforts both to minister to professedly Catholic Native Americans and to proselytize among non-Christian Native Americans. In the same years, most African Americans lived in the South; the Church was weak there, and hardly needed the additional stigma that would likely attend efforts that might seem in any way to jeopardize white supremacy.

In her 60 years of service, Drexel, more than any other person, spearheaded the effort of the Church to respond more compassionately and more efficiently to the needs of Native and African Americans. She gave more than $12 million of her own money, and at her death 501 members of her order supported 49 houses in 21 states. She was in a very real sense a one-woman foundation. She reviewed personally every request, often indicating her decision with a note on the letter of inquiry. She travelled tirelessly. She gave strong priority to the creation of church buildings and schools. No believer in segregation, she recognized that in her time a segregated church or school was often the most that could be hoped for. A strong advocate of liberal education (she helped establish what came to be Xavier University in New Orleans—the first Catholic college for African Americans), she readily acquiesced in the belief that for many African Americans "vocational" education was the most pressing need. She generally confined her response to pleas for aid to inspecting, buying land, erecting buildings, and—occasionally—paying salaries. She had neither the time nor the inclination to supervise. One result of her practice was that she almost completely avoided conflict with the priests and bishops in charge of the missions.

By the terms of her father's will, she enjoyed only the income from the trust he had established. She was urged, from time to time, to use that income to create an endowment that would sustain, after her death, the institutions she had helped create. She did not do so. Perhaps she wanted to continue to make the spending decisions herself. Probably she wanted the Catholic laity, if not the whole American people, eventually to assume the responsibility of maintaining the institutions she had help start. Certainly she wholeheartedly endorsed the traditional notion that religious institutions should ultimately put their reliance on God's grace.

She received many awards in her lifetime, including the first honorary degree given by The Catholic University to a woman. She suffered a heart attack in 1935, and though she partly recovered, she was obliged to give up her leadership of the order. She lived in retirement with the sisters until her death in 1955, in her 97th year. In 1964 the Church began the long process of determining whether Mother Katherine should be beatified.

## Further Reading

Brief, informative biographies of Mother Drexel are Nancy A. Hewitt, *Notable American Women: The Modern Period* (1980) and Katherine Burton, *New Catholic Encyclopedia* (1967). Burton's *The Golden Door* (1957) is a sentimental biography of Drexel. Sister Consuela Maria Duffy, a member of the order Mother Drexel founded, has written a more balanced study, *Katherine Drexel* (1966). □

# Barbara Dudley

**A leading activist on behalf of global environmental protectionism, Barbara Dudley (born 1947) became executive director of Greenpeace in the United States in 1993.**

Greenpeace is an organization that has garnered world attention (and new members) through its rather unorthodox approach and techniques meant to call attention to the degradation of the earth's ecosystem. Barbara Dudley served as executive director during the mid-1990s, and her exceptionally qualified background worked well within the group's emphasis upon collective efforts and its downplay of the role of individual leadership. A committed activist on issues ranging from civil and women's rights to the environment and the peace movement for 25 years, Dudley brought to Greenpeace a diverse background of activism and managerial skills precisely at a time when, at the start of the 1990s, the organization as a whole underwent restructuring and issues prioritization.

The Greenpeace movement made its first dramatic appearance in 1971. A small group of environmentalists and

peace activists in Vancouver, British Columbia, calling themselves the "Don't Make a Wave Committee," sent two small boats to Amchitka in the Aleutian Islands to protest American weapons experiments in Alaska, thereby dramatizing the issue of human safety versus nuclear testing. In later years Greenpeace moved to the forefront of the struggle aimed at safeguarding the planet and its human inhabitants, animal life, vegetation, and natural resources; it came to symbolize the increasingly significant role of voluntary, nonpartisan, nongovernmental associations in international life.

## Lifetime of Activism

Born in 1947, Dudley received her undergraduate degree from Stanford University and a law degree from the University of California, Berkeley. Fluent in Spanish, she worked from 1979 to 1983 for California's Agricultural Labor Relations Board in a number of positions, including senior counsel and counsel to the board. Her assignments there involved overseeing litigation as well as training staff in cases of unfair labor practice. Throughout the 1980s Dudley provided legal counsel on migrant worker issues, senior citizens' rights, and tenants' rights at the Legal Services Corporation, the California Rural Legal Assistance Program, and the National Lawyers Guild Military Law Project. From 1983 to 1987 she was president and executive director of the National Lawyers Guild in New York, overseeing some 8,000 attorneys, law students, and legal workers in the organization's 175 chapters nationwide.

Dudley also taught law and politics courses at the University of California at Berkeley. Prior to joining Greenpeace she was first a program officer and then executive director of the Veatch Program. One of the most progressive grant foundations in the United States, this program distributed some $9 million to organizations around the country to promote such causes as environmental protection and environmental justice issues, community organizing, and rural and urban development.

## New Challenges

In September 1992 Dudley, then age of 46, was selected executive director of Greenpeace USA, and officially took up the post on January 1, 1993. At that point Greenpeace had branches in 30 countries, over four million registered supporters and countless enthusiasts worldwide, a staff of 400 full-time members plus part-timers and volunteers in the thousands, and a reported budget of about $150 million. Its funds came exclusively from voluntary contributions, but its finances were said to be in disarray.

Over the years Greenpeace activists served on a number of fronts, often mobilizing spontaneously, indiscriminately, and without much planning in order to stop whaling, prevent dumping of toxic and nuclear wastes, or campaign against nuclear development and weapons. In the course of doing so Greenpeace militants acquired—indeed, oftentimes consciously encouraged and sought—a confrontational image. Dudley's successful nomination as executive director of one of the main branches, Greenpeace USA, ushered in a more media-savvy approach, though she conceded in one speech before the Stanford Graduate School of Business that "we supply the media with the sound bites they need. That's what brings us the support of the public." By the late 1990s, Greenpeace press releases offered a contact person "on site"—that is, at the demonstration— who could be reached via a cellular phone number.

### The "Make a Wave" Committee

Dudley's priorities involved first coordinating the efforts of nearly two million supporters across the United States; integrating activities and consulting with Stephen Sawyer, her predecessor and beginning in 1992 executive director of Greenpeace International, headquartered in Amsterdam; and finally, redefining the group's principal objectives. Accordingly, under Dudley's influence Greenpeace outlined for itself four major campaign areas: atmosphere and energy, ocean ecology and forests, toxins, and disarmament. It also recognized a need to broaden its support base, attempting to connect with minorities and the disadvantaged, while also pointing up the greater impact of environmental degradation upon the world's poor.

Equally significant, Greenpeace appeared to be shifting away from attention-grabbing stunts. Instead of being daredevils for the environment—scrambling up smokestacks in Michigan to protest sulfur dioxide emissions and acid rain, or putting themselves in inflatable boats between whales and Russian whaling vessels—Greenpeace lobbyists worked harder at strengthening legislation that protects the atmosphere, conserves dwindling natural resources, and encourages alternative energy sources. As mirrored in Dudley's own career, Greenpeace was in the process of giving up its flair for the outrageous; becoming savvy in the use of computers, the media, and a global communications network; and stimulating the world community to see "mutual security" in the larger, environmental sense by practicing the arts of lobbying and compromise. Her tenure at Greenpeace USA ended in the summer of 1997, when she resigned to pursue other interests.

### Further Reading

There is little published material on Barbara Dudley. Some of her writings, speeches, and activities can be accessed on the Internet by doing a search for "Barbara Dudley" of "Greenpeace" on the World Wide Web (August 5, 1997). □

# Isadora Duncan

**The American dancer and teacher Isadora Duncan (1878-1927) is considered one of the founders of modern dance.**

I sadora Duncan was born Dora Angela Duncan on May 27, 1878, in San Francisco. By the age of 6 Isadora was teaching neighborhood children to wave their arms, and by 10 she had developed a new "system" of dance with her sister Elizabeth, based on improvisation and interpretation. With her mother as accompanist and her sister as partner,

Isadora taught dance and performed for the San Francisco aristocracy.

The Duncans went to Chicago and New York to advance their dancing careers. Disheartened by their reception in eastern drawing rooms, they departed for London. In Europe, Duncan won recognition. She shocked, surprised, and excited her audience and became a member of the European intellectual avantgarde, returning triumphantly to America in 1908.

Duncan attacked the system of classical ballet, which was based on movement through convention, and rejected popular theatrical dance for its superficiality. She encouraged all movement that was natural, expressive, and spontaneous. Conventional dance costumes were discarded in favor of Greek tunics and no shoes to allow the greatest possible freedom of movement.

Experimenting with body movements, she concluded that all movements were derived from running, skipping, jumping, and standing. Dance was the "movement of the human body in harmony with the movements of the earth." Inspired by Greek art, the paintings of Sandro Botticelli, Walt Whitman's poems, the instinctual movements of children and animals, and great classical music, she did not dance *to* the music as much as she danced *the* music. For her, the body expressed thoughts and feelings; each dance was unique, each movement created out of the dancer's innermost feelings. Her dances were exclusively female, celebrating the beauty and holiness of the female body and

reflecting the emergence of the "new woman" of this period.

After World War I Duncan traveled throughout Europe. Her first school (in Berlin, before the war) had collapsed for lack of funds. In 1921 she accepted the Soviet government's offer to establish a school in Moscow. But financial problems continued. Meanwhile, she married the poet Sergei Yesenin. When the couple came to America in 1924 at the height of the "Red scare," Duncan was criticized for her "Bolshevik" dances. Returning to Russia, her husband committed suicide.

By 1925 Duncan's life had been filled with tragedy. In 1913 her two illegitimate children had been accidently drowned; she had had a stillbirth; and she became disillusioned with the Soviet Union. She was famous but penniless. In 1927, while riding in an open sports car, her scarf caught in a wheel and she was strangled.

Isadora Duncan's death was mourned by many. She left no work that could be performed again, no school or teaching method, and few pupils, but with her new view of movement she had revolutionized dance.

## Further Reading

There is no balanced assessment of Isadora Duncan's life. The best introduction is her own passionate and sensitive autobiography, *My Life* (1927). She has been eulogized by friends— see Mary Desti, *The Untold Story: The Life of Isadora Duncan, 1921-1927* (1929)—exposed by enemies, and sometimes appreciated by scholars. A scholarly but badly written biography is Ilya Schneider, *Isadora Duncan: The Russian Years* (1969). Recent, more dispassionate accounts are Allan Ross Macdougall, *Isadora: A Revolutionary in Art and Love* (1960), and Walter Terry, *Isadora Duncan: Her Life, Her Art, Her Legacy* (1964). □

# Katherine Dunham

**As a dancer and choreographer, Katherine Dunham (born 1910) wowed audiences in the 1930s and 1940s when she combined classical ballet with African rhythms to create an exciting new dance style.**

Dancer, choreographer, and anthropologist Katherine Dunham was born on June 22, 1910, in Glen Ellyn, Illinois, a small suburb of Chicago, to Fanny June (Guillaume) and Albert Millard Dunham. She was their second and last child together. Her brother, Albert Dunham Jr., was almost four years old when she was born. She adored him and thought of him as her protector. Their mother, who was French Canadian and Indian, was 20 years older than their African-American father.

Fanny Dunham had been married once before, to a man whose last name was Taylor. Their marriage ended in divorce and they had three children together: Louise and Fanny June (Taylor) Weir, who had families of their own by the time Dunham was born, and a son, Henry, who was mentally disabled. All of Fanny Dunham's children and grandchildren lived with her and her second husband under one roof in Glen Ellyn, making their house very crowded.

## Mother Died

When Dunham was three years old, her mother died after a lengthy illness. She had owned property in Chicago, but it was sold to pay off her grown children's debts and her doctor bills. Albert Dunham, who had been working as a tailor, could no longer afford to keep his house in the mostly-white suburb of Glen Ellyn and was forced to sell it. This created a rift between him and his wife's grown children that would last for years.

Dunham and her brother, Albert Jr., went to live with their father's sister, Lulu Dunham, in a tenement slum in Chicago, while their father tried to make a better living as a traveling salesman. Lulu Dunham worked as a beautician and sometimes her relatives would baby-sit Katherine while Albert Jr. was in school.

## Introduced to Theater

One of those baby-sitters, Clara Dunham, had come to Chicago with her daughter, Irene, hoping to break into show business. They and other amateur performers began rehearsing a musical/theatrical program in the basement of their apartment building, and Dunham would watch. Although the program wasn't a success, it provided Dunham with her first taste of show business.

Dunham and her brother were very fond of their Aunt Lulu. However, because she was experiencing financial

difficulties, a judge granted temporary custody of the children to their half-sister Fanny June Weir, and ordered that the children be returned to their father as soon as he could prove that he could take care of them.

## Home Was Dismal

When Dunham was about five years old, her father married an Iowa schoolteacher named Annette Poindexter. They moved to Chicago and were granted custody of the children, and Dunham grew to love her step-mother. Her father bought a dry cleaning business in Chicago and all four members of the family worked there, as they lived in a few rooms in back of the business.

Family problems emerged when Albert Sr. began to physically abuse his wife and children and became increasingly violent. Consequently, Dunham longed to get away from him.

In high school, Dunham excelled in athletics. She also took dancing lessons and joined an after-school club that put on dance recitals. However, her father began demanding that she spend more time working at the dry cleaners, leaving her very little time for her extra-curricular activities.

Albert Jr., who was valedictorian of his senior class, received a scholarship and went away to college, against the wishes of his father. A short time later, Annette Dunham left her abusive husband and went to live in another part of the city. Dunham, who was still in high school, went with her. However, she was forced to continue working for her father's business, in order to help support her step-mother.

## Became Scholar

Dunham began attending junior college at the age of 17. During her second and final year there, her brother convinced her to take a Civil Service exam. If she passed, he said, she could become a librarian for the city. She passed the exam, graduated from junior college and began working at the Hamilton Park Branch Library, which was in a white, middle-class, suburban district of the city. The other librarians refused to eat lunch with her because she was black. However, she was not aware of the discrimination at first, because she was just glad to be free of her father.

Following in her brother's footsteps, Dunham enrolled in the University of Chicago, where she earned a master's degree and Ph.D. in anthropology. She also took dance lessons and participated in theater productions there. To help pay for her education, she opened a dance school in 1930.

## Researched Dances

In 1935, Dunham received a fellowship to conduct anthropological field research. She used the grant to study African-based dances in the Caribbean. She knew that each Caribbean island had its own unique form of dance. However, all of the dances had a common denominator: They all had been influenced in some way by the African slaves who had been brought there by various colonial overseers.

Dunham wanted to discover exactly what that common denominator was and which dance moves had come

from Africa. She spent 18 months in the Caribbean, documenting its various dances.

## Found Answer

She found that of all the Caribbean islands, the purest forms of African dance were in Haiti. She theorized that this was because Haiti had won its independence as a nation long before any other country had freed its African slaves. "Haitians ground their hips, circled their haunches, executed mesmerizing pelvic movements, and shrugged a ritual called 'zepaules, accenting their shoulders. It was all fundamental African technique, identical to what is done in, say, Dakar, and on which variations persist in African-American communities everywhere," wrote Paula Durbin in an article about Dunham that appeared in the January/February 1996 issue of *Americas* magazine.

Dunham fell in love with Haiti and its people, and later bought a home and opened a dance school and medical clinic on the island. She chronicled her work in the Caribbean in her book, *Journey to Accompong,* and wrote about her experiences in Haiti in her book, *Island Possessed.*

## Created New Style

When Dunham returned to the United States, she combined the ethnic dances she had learned in the Caribbean with classical ballet and theatrical effects. The result was an entirely new art form, called the "Dunham technique." It has also been referred to as "Afro-Caribbean dance."

In 1940, she formed The Dunham Dance Company, an all-black dance troupe, to perform her technique. The company gave its first show in New York City and performed a revue called "Tropics and le Jazz Hot." Audiences in the United States had never seen anything like it. As Durbin wrote in the *Americas* article, "Everything moved—shoulders twitched, torsos arched, hips popped—and Martha Graham proclaimed Dunham 'the high priestess of the pelvic girdle.'" Graham is considered to be the founder of modern dance.

## Fought Segregation

Dunham and her company toured North and South America in the 1940s and 1950s, fighting segregation along the way. In 1952, the management of a hotel in Brazil refused to let Dunham join her husband, John Pratt, in his hotel suite because she was black and he was white. Dunham, who had been married to Pratt since 1940, filed a lawsuit against the hotel, and as a result, the Brazilian legislature quickly passed a bill outlawing discrimination in public places. In addition to touring with her company, which disbanded in 1957, Dunham operated a dance school in New York from 1944 through 1954. She also choreographed many ballets, stage shows and films, including the movies, "Stormy Weather" and "Pardon My Sarong." During this same period, she and her husband adopted their daughter, Marie Christine.

## Opened Illinois School

In the 1960s, Dunham visited East St. Louis, Illinois, a very poor African-American community in the southern part of the state. She wanted to do something to help the children there and decided to open a school. In 1967 she opened the Katherine Dunham Centers for the Arts and Humanities. At the school, disadvantaged children can learn classical ballet, martial arts, the Dunham technique, foreign languages and, most importantly, self-discipline. The campus also includes the Dunham Museum, which houses costumes and other artifacts, and the Institute for Intercultural Communication.

## Held Hunger Strike

In 1992 Dunham went on a 47-day hunger strike to protest the exclusionary U.S. policy toward Haitian refugees. Due to political unrest in their homeland, thousands of Haitians fled their country for the United States in the early 1990s. In 1991 and 1992, the U.S. Coast Guard intercepted some 35,000 Haitian refugees as they tried to enter the United States. Most of them were returned to Haiti.

Dunham has diabetes and arthritis and uses a wheelchair. She still lives and teaches in East St. Louis, Illinois, and has begun work on another autobiography.

## Further Reading

Ben-Itzak, Paul, "Dunham Legacy Stands At Risk," in *Dance Magazine,* January 1995, pp. 42, 44.
Durbin, Paula, "The First Lady of Caribbean Cadences," in *Americas,* 1996, pp. 36-41.
Greene, Carol, *Katherine Dunham: Black Dancer,* Childrens Press, Inc., 1992. □

# E

## Amelia Mary Earhart

**The American aviator Amelia Mary Earhart Putnam (1897-1937) remains the world's best-known woman pilot long after her mysterious disappearance during a round-the-world flight in 1937.**

Amelia Mary Earhart was born on July 24, 1897, the daughter of Edwin and Amy Otis Earhart. Until she was 12 she lived with her wealthy maternal grandparents, Alfred and Amelia Harres Otis, in Atcheson, Kansas, where she attended a private day school. Her summers were spent in Kansas City, Missouri, where her lawyer-father worked for the Rock Island Railroad.

In 1909 Amelia and her younger sister, Muriel, went to live with their parents in Des Moines, Iowa, where the railroad had transferred her father. Before completing high school she also attended schools in St. Paul, Minnesota, and Springfield, Illinois, while her father fought a losing battle against alcoholism. His failure and its consequent humiliation for her were the root of Amelia's lifelong dislike of alcohol and desire for financial security.

Amy Earhart left Edwin in Springfield in 1914, taking her daughters with her to live with friends in Chicago, where Amelia was graduated from Hyde Park School in 1915. The yearbook described her as "A.E.—the girl in brown (her favorite color) who walks alone."

A year later, after Amy Earhart received an inheritance from the estate of her mother, she sent Amelia to Ogontz School in Philadelphia, an exclusive high school and junior college. During Christmas vacation of her second year there Amelia went to Toronto, Canada, where Muriel was attending a private school. In Toronto Amelia saw her first amputees, returning wounded from World War I. She immediately refused to return to Ogontz and became a volunteer nurse in a hospital for veterans where she worked until after the armistice of 1918. The experience made her an ardent, life-long pacifist.

From Toronto Earhart went to live with her mother and sister in Northampton, Massachusetts, where her sister was attending Smith College. In the fall of 1919 she entered Columbia University, but left after one year to join her parents, who had reconciled and were living in Los Angeles.

In the winter of 1920 Earhart saw her first air show and took her first airplane ride. "As soon as we left the ground," she said, "I knew I had to fly." She took lessons at Bert Kinner's airfield on Long Beach Boulevard in Los Angeles from a woman—Neta Snooks—and on December 15, 1921, received her license from the National Aeronautics Association (NAA). By working part-time as a file clerk, office assistant, photographer, and truck driver, and with some help from her mother, Earhart eventually was able to buy her own plane. However, she was unable to earn enough to continue what was an expensive hobby.

In 1924, when her parents separated again, she sold her plane and bought a car in which she drove her mother to Boston where her sister was teaching school. Soon after that Earhart re-enrolled at Columbia but lacked the money to continue for more than one year. She returned to Boston where she became a social worker in a settlement house, joined the NAA, and continued to fly in her spare time.

In 1928 Earhart accepted an offer to join the crew of a flight across the Atlantic. The flight was the scheme of George Palmer Putnam, editor of *WE,* Charles Lindbergh's book about how he became, in 1927, the first person to fly across the Atlantic alone. The enterprising Putnam chose

**195**

1933: Breaks her own transcontinental speed record

1935: First person to fly solo across the Pacific from Hawaii to California

First person to fly solo from Los Angeles to Mexico

Breaks speed record for non-stop flight from Los Angeles to Mexico City to Newark, New Jersey

1937: Sets speed record for east-west crossing from Oakland to Honolulu

Honors and awards she received included the Distinguished Flying Cross; Cross of the Knight of the Legion of Honor, from the French Government; Gold Medal of the National Geographic Society; and the Harmon Trophy as America's outstanding airwoman in 1932, 1933, 1934, and 1935.

On July 2, 1937, 22 days before her 40th birthday and having already completed 22,000 miles of an attempt to circumnavigate the earth, Earhart and her navigator, Fred Noonan, disappeared over the Pacific somewhere between Lae, New Guinea, and Howland Island. The most extensive search ever conducted by the U.S. Navy for a single missing plane sighted neither plane nor crew. Subsequent searches since that time have been equally unsuccessful. In 1992, an expedition found certain objects (a shoe and a metal plate) on the small atoll of Nikumaroro south of Howland, which could have been left by Earhart and Noonan. In 1997 another female pilot, Linda Finch, recreated Earhart's final flight in an around the world tribute entitled "World Flight 97." The event took place on what would have been Earhart's 100th birthday. Finch successfully completed her voyage, the identical route that Earhart would have flown, around the world.

### Further Reading

The first biography to tell a life story rather than a mystery tale of disappearance was Doris L. Rich, *Amelia Earhart: A Biography* (1989). Mary S. Lovell's *The Sound of Wings* (1989) is an interesting study of Putnam as well as Earhart, concluding with his death in 1950. Earhart's sister, Muriel Morrissey, in *Courage Is the Price* (1963) and Jean Backus in *Letters from Amelia* (1982) focus on family relationships. Dick Strippel's *Amelia Earhart: The Myth and the Reality* (1972) debunks the numerous theories based on Earhart's supposed capture and/or execution by the Japanese as well as claims she was acting as a spy for the U.S. Government. Brief, accurate biographies are in the Smithsonian Institution studies *United States Women in Aviation (1919-1929)* by Kathleen Brooks-Pazmany (1983) and *United States Women in Aviation (1929-1940)* by Claudia M. Oakes (1978). See also Susan Ware, *Still Missing: Amelia Earhart and the Search for Feminism* (1994). Information on Linda Finch can be obtained from http://www.worldflight.com. (July 1997). □

her for his "Lady Lindy" because of her flying experience, her education, and her lady-like appearance. Along with pilot Wilmer Stultz and mechanic Louis Gordon, she crossed the Atlantic (from Newfoundland to Wales) on June 18-19, 1928. Although she never once touched the controls (she described herself afterward as little more than a "sack of potatoes"), Earhart became world-renowned as "the first woman to fly the Atlantic."

From that time Putnam became Earhart's manager and, in 1931, her husband. He arranged all her flying engagements, many followed by often strenuous cross-country lecture tours (at one point, 29 tours in 31 days) for maximum publicity. However Earhart did initiate one flight of her own. Resenting reports that she was largely a puppet figure created by her publicist husband and something less than a competent aviator, she piloted a tiny, single-engine Lockheed Electra from Newfoundland to Ireland to become—on May 20-21, 1932, and five years after Lindbergh—the first woman to fly solo across the Atlantic.

During the scarcely more than five years remaining in her life, Earhart acted as a tireless advocate for commercial aviation and for women's rights. The numerous flying records she amassed included:

1931: Altitude record in an autogiro

First person to fly an autogiro across the United States and back

1932: Fastest non-stop transcontinental flight by a woman

# Sylvia A. Earle

**Sylvia A. Earle (born 1935) is a leading American oceanographer and former chief scientist. Earle is a devout advocate of public education regarding the**

**importance of the oceans as an essential environmental habitat.**

Sylvia A. Earle is a former chief scientist of the National Oceanic and Atmospheric Administration (NOAA) and a leading American oceanographer. She was among the first underwater explorers to make use of modern self-contained underwater breathing apparatus (SCUBA) gear, and identified many new species of marine life. With her former husband, Graham Hawkes, Earle designed and built a submersible craft that could dive to unprecedented depths of 3,000 feet.

Sylvia Alice (Reade) Earle was born in Gibbstown, New Jersey on August 30, 1935, the daughter of Lewis Reade and Alice Freas (Richie) Earle. Both parents had an affinity for the outdoors and encouraged her love of nature after the family moved to the west coast of Florida. As Earle explained to *Scientific American,* "I wasn't shown frogs with the attitude 'yuk,' but rather my mother would show my brothers and me how beautiful they are and how fascinating it was to look at their gorgeous golden eyes." However, Earle pointed out, while her parents totally supported her interest in biology, they also wanted her to get her teaching credentials and learn to type, "just in case."

She enrolled at Florida State University and received her Bachelor of Science degree in the spring of 1955. That fall she entered the graduate program at Duke University and obtained her master's degree in botany the following

year. The Gulf of Mexico became a natural laboratory for Earle's work. Her master's dissertation, a detailed study of algae in the Gulf, is a project she still follows. She has collected more than 20,000 samples. "When I began making collections in the Gulf, it was a very different body of water than it is now—the habitats have changed. So I have a very interesting baseline," she noted in *Scientific American.*

In 1966, Earle received her Ph.D. from Duke University and immediately accepted a position as resident director of the Cape Haze Marine Laboratories in Sarasota, Florida. The following year, she moved to Massachusetts to accept dual roles as research scholar at the Radcliffe Institute and research fellow at the Farlow Herbarium, Harvard University, where she was named researcher in 1975. Earle moved to San Francisco in 1976 to become a research biologist at and curator of the California Academy of Sciences. That same year, she also was named a fellow in botany at the Natural History Museum, University of California, Berkeley.

Although her academic career could have kept her totally involved, her first love was the sea and the life within it. In 1970, Earle and four other oceanographers lived in an underwater chamber for fourteen days as part of the government-funded Tektite II Project, designed to study undersea habitats. Fortunately, technology played a major role in Earle's future. A self-contained underwater breathing apparatus had been developed in part by Jacques Cousteau as recently as 1943, and refined during the time Earle was involved in her scholarly research. SCUBA equipment was not only a boon to recreational divers, but it also dramatically changed the study of marine biology. Earle was one of the first researchers to don a mask and oxygen tank and observe the various forms of plant and animal habitats beneath the sea, identifying many new species of each. She called her discovery of undersea dunes off the Bahama Islands "a simple Lewis and Clark kind of observation." But, she said in *Scientific American,* "the presence of dunes was a significant insight into the formation of the area."

Though Earle set the unbelievable record of freely diving to a depth of 1,250 feet, there were serious depth limitations to SCUBA diving. To study deep-sea marine life would require the assistance of a submersible craft that could dive far deeper. Earle and her former husband, British-born engineer Graham Hawkes, founded Deep Ocean Technology, Inc., and Deep Ocean Engineering, Inc., in 1981, to design and build submersibles. Using a paper napkin, Earle and Hawkes rough-sketched the design for a submersible they called *Deep Rover,* which would serve as a viable tool for biologists. "In those days we were dreaming of going to thirty-five thousand feet," she told *Discover* magazine. "The idea has always been that scientists couldn't be trusted to drive a submersible by themselves because they'd get so involved in their work they'd run into things." *Deep Rover* was built and continues to operate as a mid-water machine in ocean depths ranging 3,000 feet.

In 1990, Earle was named the first woman to serve as chief scientist at the National Oceanic and Atmospheric Administration (NOAA), the agency that conducts underwater research, manages fisheries, and monitors marine spills. She left the position after eighteen months because she felt that she could accomplish more working independently of the government.

Earle, who has logged more than 6,000 hours under water, is the first to decry America's lack of research money being spent on deep-sea studies, noting that of the world's five deep-sea manned submersibles (those capable of diving to 20,000 feet or more), the U.S. has only one, the *Sea Cliff*. "That's like having one jeep for all of North America," she said in *Scientific American*. In 1993, Earle worked with a team of Japanese scientists to develop the equipment to send first a remote, then a manned submersible to 36,000 feet. "They have money from their government," she told *Scientific American*. "They do what we do not: they really make a substantial commitment to ocean technology and science." Earle also plans to lead the $10 million deep ocean engineering project, Ocean Everest, that would take her to a similar depth.

In addition to publishing numerous scientific papers on marine life, Earle is a devout advocate of public education regarding the importance of the oceans as an essential environmental habitat. She is currently the president and chief executive officer of Deep Ocean Technology and Deep Ocean Engineering in Oakland, California, as well as the coauthor of *Exploring the Deep Frontier: The Adventure of Man in the Sea* and sole author of *Sea Change: A Message of the Ocean*, published in 1995.

## Further Reading

Brownlee, Shannon, "Explorers of the Dark Frontiers," in *Discover*, February, 1986, pp. 60–67.
Holloway, Marguerite, "Fire in Water," in *Scientific American*, April, 1992, pp. 37–40. □

# Mary Baker Eddy

**The American founder of the Christian Science Church, Mary Baker Eddy (1821-1910) showed a unique understanding of the relationship between religion and health, which resulted in one of the era's most influential religious books, "Science and Health."**

Mary Baker was born July 16, 1821, at Bow, N.H. A delicate and nervous temperament led to long periods of sickness in her early years, and chronic ill health made her weak and infirm during much of her adult life. In 1843 she married George Washington Glover, but he soon died and she returned home, where she had her only child. She married Daniel Patterson, a traveling dentist, in 1853; however, his frequent trips and her invalidism led to a separation by 1866 and a divorce several years later. In 1877 she married Asa Gilbert Eddy.

In her quest for health, she had visited Dr. Phineas P. Quimby of Portland, Maine, in 1862, and found that his nonmedical principles cured her. She absorbed his system and became a disciple. In 1866 she claimed to have been completely cured of injuries suffered in a fall by what she called "Christian science." By 1870 she was teaching her new-found science in collaboration with practitioners who did the healing. Her key ideas were published in *Science and Health with Key to the Scriptures* (1875).

This book and Mary Baker Eddy's forceful personality attracted numerous followers, and on Aug. 23, 1879, the Church of Christ, Scientist, was chartered. Asa Eddy helped organize the movement. Mrs. Eddy chartered the Massachusetts Metaphysical College in 1881, where she taught her beliefs. Asa Eddy died in 1882, and the next year Mrs. Eddy began to publish the *Journal of Christian Science*.

Her fame spread, support grew, and Mrs. Eddy became wealthy. But dissensions divided the Church, and in 1889 "Mother Eddy" moved to Concord, N.H., apparently withdrawing from leadership. In seclusion, however, she restructured the Church organization: the First Church of Christ, Scientist, in Boston was established on Sept. 23, 1892, as the mother church. Mrs. Eddy was its head, and all other churches were subject to its jurisdiction. Though internal quarrels diminished, they continued to the end of her life. Partly to guarantee a trustworthy newspaper for the movement, Mrs. Eddy began publishing the *Christian Science Monitor* in 1908. That year she moved to Chestnut Hill near Boston, where she died on Dec. 3, 1910.

## Further Reading

*Science and Health with Key to the Scriptures* (1875 and later editions) is the most important of Mrs. Eddy's writings. Sibyl Wilbur, *The Life of Mary Baker Eddy* (1908), is the laudatory official biography. A friendly but more scholarly study is Robert Peel, *Mary Baker Eddy* (2 vols., 1966-1971). Critical accounts are Edwin F. Dakin, *Mrs. Eddy: The Biography of a Virginal Mind* (1929), and Ernest S. Bates and John V. Dittemore, *Mary Baker Eddy: The Truth and the Tradition* (1932). □

# Marian Wright Edelman

**Marian Wright Edelman (born 1939) was a lobbyist, lawyer, civil rights activist who founded the Children's Defense Fund in 1973 to advocate children's rights.**

Marian Wright Edelman was born in Bennetsville, South Carolina, on June 6, 1939 and was named for the singer Marian Anderson. She was the youngest of five children born to Arthur Jerome Wright and Maggie Leola (Bowen) Wright. She spent her early years in Bennettsville. It was, as she described it, a small-town, socially segregated childhood. She went to racially segregated public schools, but excelled academically. She took piano and voice lessons and became a drum majorette in her high school band.

## Beginnings of Her Advocacy

Edelman's quest for political, economic, and social rights and justice has its beginnings in her childhood. The elder Wrights instilled in their children a strong sense of service to others by their words and deeds. Indeed, as Edelman wrote, "Service is the rent we pay to be living. It is the very purpose of life and not something you do in your spare time." She was expected to help out with chores at the nearby Wright Home For the Aged, the first such institution for African-Americans in South Carolina, which her father founded and her mother ran. "The only time my father wouldn't give me a chore was when I was reading, so I read a lot," she said of those years.

When she was 14-years-old, her father died after suffering a heart attack. "The last thing he said to me before he died was, 'Don't let anything get between you and your education,'" she said. Driven by these words, she went to Spelman College, an historic African-American institution for women in Atlanta, Georgia. While at college, she won a Merrill scholarship to study abroad. Her search for a broad international perspective took her to classes at the Sorbonne in Paris, the University of Geneva in Switzerland, and with the help of a Lisle Fellowship, to Moscow just prior to starting her senior year.

She had planned on a career in the foreign service, but changed her plans as the events of the 1960s' civil rights movement occurred. Caught up in the African-American social consciousness of the times, she participated at sit-ins in Atlanta's City hall and was arrested. "Segregation was

wrong, something to be fought against," she said. The experiences stimulated her to believe that she could contribute to social progress through the study of law. She entered Yale Law School on a scholarship after receiving her undergraduate degree in 1960. She did not love law but explained that she decided to study law "to be able to help black people, and the law seemed like a tool [I] needed."

## Early Advocacy

Edelman began her career as a lawyer hired by the NAACP (National Association for the Advancement of Colored People) in New York after receiving her law degree in 1963. After one year she moved to Jackson, Mississippi, to continue her work with the association. She became the first African-American woman admitted to the Mississippi State Bar Association. Her career changed direction after she became a lawyer for the Child Development Group in Mississippi and successfully lobbied for the restoration of Federal funds for the Mississippi Head Start programs. This started her subsequent life-long effort to lobby for children's interests.

She met Peter Benjamin Edelman, a staff assistant to Democratic Senator Robert F. Kennedy, while he was conducting research in Mississippi. They were married on July 14, 1968, and have three sons: Joshua Robert, Jonah Martin, and Ezra Benjamin. They moved to Washington, D.C., where he continued to work and she began to expand her work on the problem's of Mississippi's poor to the national political arena.

Edelman started the Washington Research Project of the Southern Center for Policy Research. It was created to lobby and research programs to assist children in poverty. In 1971 the Edelmans moved to Boston, where Peter served two years as vice-president of the University of Massachusetts. She directed the Center for Law and Education at Harvard University. That year *Time* magazine named her one of the top 200 young leaders in America.

## Founds CDF

Under Edelman's guidance the Children's Defense Fund (CDF) was founded in 1973. It was to become a major advocate, research, and lobbying organization designed to seek aid for children. She campaigned for a number of programs. Among these were programs to help children remain healthy, stay in school, and avoid teenage pregnancy; to prevent child abuse; and to stop drug abuse. In her words, the CDF "works with individuals and groups to change policies and practices resulting in neglect or mistreatment of millions of children."

Again the Edelmans moved as their career paths evolved. Her husband joined the faculty of Georgetown University Law Center in Washington, D.C., in 1979. She relocated with her family to join him. There she continued to be president of the Children's Defense Fund, working long hours to convince government officials of the need for her children's aid programs.

When Bill Clinton was elected U.S. president in 1992, it was expected that Edelman, a friend and intellectual soul mate to First Lady Hillary Clinton, who had served as chairman of the CDF, would command a level of attention within the new administration that had been absent during the tenures of Presidents Bush and Reagan. There were even rumors that she would join the cabinet, bet she was quick to discount such rumors. "I need to work outside government, on my own," she said.

In 1992, Edelman and the CDF began its "Leave No Child Behind" campaign. She estimated that it would cost as much as $47 billion to fulfill all the goals of a fully-funded Head Start, proper medical insurance for all children and their pregnant mothers, vaccinations for every child, and an expanded children's tax credit for children. She tirelessly lobbies for these goals because she believes that "Investing in [children] is not a national luxury or a national choice. It's a national necessity. If the foundation of your house is crumbling, you don't say you can't afford to fix it while you're building astronomically expensive fences to protect it from outside enemies. The issue is not are we going to pay—it's are we going to pay now, upfront, or are we going to pay a whole lot more later on."

On June 1, 1996, Edelman and the CDF held their "Stand For Children" in Washington, D.C. An estimated 200,000 supporters showed up to march in support of children and the CDF's goals. Many of Edelman's critics had previously criticized Edelman and her ideas as outdated. But with the large support she received during "Stand For Children," she demonstrated that she and the CDF are still a force to contend with in American politics.

In 1997, Edelman criticized President Clinton for his welfare reform package by warning it could lead to record numbers of uninsured children, increased child abuse, and rising firearms deaths. The CDF's "The State of America's Children Yearbook 1997" criticized the package and warned that "if America does not stand up now for its children, it will not stand strong in the new millennium."

Edelman has been widely recognized for her spirited activity as a lobbyist for her causes. She lectures, writes, and travels to convince others of the many needs facing young people. She is the author of the books, *Families In Peril: An Agenda For Social Change* (1987); *Portrait of Inequality: Black and White Children in America* (1990); *The Measure of Our Success: A Letter to My Children and Yours* (1992); and *Guide My Feet: Meditations and Prayers on Loving and Working for Children* (1995). She is also the author of several reports, and many articles in support of children and her causes. All the while, she stressed that she is a doer rather than a scholar. She believed that problems must be broken down and a range of strategies must be considered to achieve goals. She was less interested in forming theories than "in feeding, clothing, housing, and educating as many American children as soon as possible." She was also able to balance her hectic, social-oriented work with the demands of a family.

## Further Reading

Marian Wright Edelman has written about her spiritual, family, and community values and thoughts in *The Measure of Our Success: A Letter to My Children and Yours* (1992). She described her programs and research findings and the work of the Children's Defense Fund in *Families in Peril: An Agenda for Social Change* (1987). Her biographies appear in *Who's Who in America, Who's Who Among Black Americans, Notable Black American Women, Black Women in America,* and *African American Biographies*.

Biographical information on Edelman can be found in the May 10, 1992 issue of the *Washington Post* and the March 15, 1997 issue of *Afro-American*. ☐

# Mamie Doud Eisenhower

**The wife of President Dwight D. "Ike" Eisenhower, Mamie Eisenhower (1896-1979) represented what was to 1950s America the ideal American wife: exuding quiet strength, finding satisfaction in domestic duties, supporting her husband unhesitatingly.**

Mamie Eisenhower was the first lady of the United States at a time when home and family were considered to be of paramount importance. As first ladies often are, she was expected to serve as a role model for the American wife. Mamie Doud and Dwight D. "Ike" Eisenhower met in 1915 in San Antonio, Texas, where Eisenhower was a young army officer and high-school football coach and Mamie was wintering with her parents. They were married the next year. For Mamie, life as a military wife was initially harsh: the Douds were a close and socially prominent family, and life with Ike was relatively lean and lonely. Over the next several decades she dutifully followed her husband when she could, and raised the family herself when she could not. Her husband, meanwhile, became increasingly prominent as a military leader.

## New Pressures

At the end of World War II Eisenhower was a national hero, and for his wife this meant a measure of celebrity to which she was unaccustomed as well as the opportunity to meet important world leaders. The general became president of Columbia University in 1948; throughout Ike's tenure at Columbia Mrs. Eisenhower was a gracious hostess to scores of famous visitors. When her husband decided to enter the presidential campaign in 1952, Mamie—a self-professed homebody—found that she would have to shed her aversion to public life: "there would be nothing he would ask during the campaign that I would not do," she recalled. As a campaign wife she subjected herself to daily appearances and interviews and answered thousands of letters.

## Life in the White House

After Eisenhower won the presidency, Mrs. Eisenhower was able to return to a degree of domestic stability in the White House. By this time she was used to overseeing a staff, and she saw that the executive mansion was run efficiently. She also lent her services to charitable causes, and she made the White House more historic by leading a drive to recover authentic presidential antiques. She and her hus-

band observed a division of labor ("Ike took care of the office—I ran the house") although the president valued his wife's insights into political personalities of the time.

## Public Ideal

For the eight years of the Eisenhower presidency Mamie Eisenhower represented the public ideal of the American wife: exuding quiet strength, finding satisfaction in domestic duties, supporting her husband unhesitatingly. Eisenhower observed of her: "I personally think that Mamie's biggest contribution was to make the White House livable, comfortable, and meaningful for the people who came in. She was always helpful and ready to do anything. She exuded hospitality. She saw that as one of her functions and performed it, no matter how tired she was." When Eisenhower left office in 1961, he and Mrs. Eisenhower were at last allowed something like a peaceful retirement, although Eisenhower kept busy in the role of elder statesman until his death in 1969. Mamie Eisenhower lived quietly after her husband's death until her own death in 1979.

## Further Reading

Dorothy Brandon, *Mamie Doud Eisenhower* (New York: Scribners, 1954).
Steve Neal, *The Eisenhowers: Reluctant Dynasty* (Garden City, N.Y.: Doubleday, 1978). □

# Joycelyn Elders

**Confirmed as the 16th Surgeon General of the United States on September 7, 1993, Joycelyn Elders (born 1933) was the first African American and only the second female to head up the U.S. Public Health Service. In her brief 15-month tenure, Elders added tobacco use, national health care, and drug and alcohol abuse to her platform.**

Jocelyn Elders was born Minnie Jones on August 13, 1933, in the southwestern farming community of Schaal, Arkansas. She took the name Jocelyn in college. She was the first of Haller and Curtis Jones's eight children. Living in a poor, segregated pocket of the country, she and her siblings struck a balance between laboring in the cotton fields and attending an all-black school 13 miles from home. One of her earliest childhood memories was being taught to read by her mother, Haller, who had an eighth grade education which was quite remarkable for an African American woman at that time. By the time she neared graduation from high school, Elders earned a scholarship to the all-black, liberal arts Philander Smith College in Little Rock, the state's capital. Initially, higher education looked doubtful for Elders as her father did not want to let her go. He felt that her contribution to the family was much more important. He did not see the long-term value of education. With all her pleading, Haller Jones could not get her husband to budge. Elders had resigned herself to staying home and continuing to pick cotton. She hadn't counted on her paternal grandmother, for whom she was named, to come to her aid, but whatever grandma Minnie said, she was allowed to go to college in September. Her family picked extra cotton to earn the $3.43 for her bus fare. She was the first in her family to take the road to higher education.

## Found Inspiration in African American Woman Doctor

At school, Elders was particularly drawn to the study of biology and chemistry and concluded that being a lab technician was her highest calling, the professional mountaintop. But her ambitions rose a notch when she heard Edith Irby Jones (no relation), the first African American to study at the University of Arkansas School of Medicine, speak at a college sorority. Jocelyn Jones, who had not even met a doctor until she was 16 years old, imagined herself as a healer.

After graduation from college, Elders married briefly and then joined the U. S. Army's Women's Medical Specialist Corps. In 1956, she entered the Arkansas Medical School on the G.I. Bill two years after the Supreme Court, in its Brown v. Board of Education decision, ruled that separate but equal education was unconstitutional. But while segregation in some areas had been declared illegal by judicial order, an underlying discriminatory mindset in American society could not be so easily erased. As the lone black student and only one of three students of color in her class,

she was required to use a separate university dining room, where the cleaning staff ate. But she accepted this arrangement without argument, as this was the only social world to which she was accustomed. She met her second husband, Oliver Elders, when, in order to make additional money, she performed the physicals for high school students on the basketball team he managed. They were married in 1960.

After an internship in pediatrics at the University of Minnesota, Jocelyn Elders returned to Little Rock in 1961 for her residency and was quickly appointed chief pediatric resident, in charge of the all-white and all-male battery of residents and interns. Over the next 20 years, Elders combined a successful clinical practice with research in pediatric endocrinology (the study of glands), publishing well over 100 papers, most dealing with growth problems and juvenile diabetes. Her pioneering work captured the attention of the state's medical community, and physicians routinely referred to her their cases of juveniles with insulin-dependent diabetes.

It was this branch of science that led her to the study of sexual behavior and planted the seeds for her public sector advocacy. Recognizing that diabetic females face a health risk if they become pregnant at too young an age—the hazards include spontaneous abortion and possible congenital abnormalities in the infant—Elders saw the urgent need to talk about the dangers of pregnancy with her patients and to distribute contraceptives in order to limit those dangers. "If I wanted to keep those kids healthy, I decided I had no choice but to take command of their sexuality at the first sign of puberty," Elders told the *New York Times*. "I'd

tell them, you're gonna have two good babies, and I'm gonna decide when you're gonna have them." The results were clear: of the 520 juvenile diabetics Elders treated, approximately half were female, and only one became pregnant.

## Taking Action Against Societal Health Crises

But for every young adult in her care, there were thousands throughout the state whose sexual behavior went unmonitored and whose irresponsible, uneducated actions were contributing to America's dubious distinction of having the highest rate of teenage pregnancy in the industrialized world. Elders could not turn her back on this situation. She had done that once before, when she was a pediatric resident. A young girl with a thyroid condition, upon being told that she could go home from the hospital, had confided to Elders that she didn't want to leave the safety of her room—that her father, uncles and brothers sexually abused her every Saturday night. Elders was reluctant to believe her. This was also a time before doctors could report suspected child abuse with immunity. So Elders did nothing, and sent the child home. Inaction, she vowed, would be a sin of which she would never again be guilty.

In 1986, the year before Clinton named Elders director of the Arkansas Department of Health, 20 percent of the state's total births were to teenage mothers, compared to approximately 13 percent on a national level. The costs of the birthrate profile were, in Elder's view, enormous. Taxpayers in Arkansas dished out more than $82 million in fiscal 1987 for Arkansas adolescents and their children. Equally, if not more important, was the unquantifiable price paid by a society in which a frighteningly large number of emotionally immature young adults became parents to unwanted children. The *Boston Globe* quoted Elders as describing a poor teenager with a baby as "captive to a slavery the 13th Amendment [the Emancipation Proclamation abolishing slavery] did not anticipate." With the incidences of sexually transmitted diseases on the rise, and the specter of AIDS hanging over the heads of all sexually active people, Elders recognized the urgent need for bolder government involvement and an intense public education campaign.

## Fought with Conservatives and Religious Groups

Elders glimpsed one of the approaches she would champion in office when she visited the state's first school-based health clinic in the Ozark mountain community of Lincoln, where contraceptives were given to students on request and where senior class pregnancies had subsequently fallen from 13 to one. Under Elders, 18 other school clinics opened, though only four of them were authorized by their local boards of education to distribute condoms. As Elders campaigned for the clinics and expanded sex education throughout the state, she became engaged in a heated battle with both political conservatives—who criticized her effort to increase the government's role in the lives of U.S. citizens, particularly in an area as private as sexual behavior—and members of some religious groups—who feared that the distribution of condoms would increase sexual activity, and who rejected the introduction of sex education in schools as a means of institutionally sanctioning abortion.

Elders, who is pro-choice but admits she personally opposes abortion, retaliated with both sober and emotional arguments. She said she would gladly teach abstinence if she felt that approach would work. But in the real world, she maintained, kids will continue to have sex, and it is the job of adults—and the U.S. government—to turn an irresponsible action into a responsible one. She said she considered every abortion her own personal failure, and her role, simply put, was to prevent unwanted pregnancy from ever occurring. She accused anti-abortion activists of having *a love affair with the fetus,* and pointed out in the *Washington Post* that not even abortion foes want to support "any [social] programs that will make [these unwanted children] into productive citizens."

In 1989, in great measure because of Elder's lobbying, the Arkansas State Legislature mandated a kindergarten-through-twelfth-grade course curriculum encompassing not only sex education, but instruction in hygiene, substance-abuse prevention, self-esteem, and the proposition, often overlooked, that sexual responsibility does not belong exclusively to the female. Between 1987 and 1990 though the rate of teenage pregnancy in Arkansas was up, the national rate was considerably higher.

## Stood Ground during Confirmation Process

President Clinton's nomination of Elders for the post of U.S. Surgeon General made her the second African American and fifth woman tapped for a cabinet position—and galvanized on a national level the active critics who had fought her locally in Arkansas. Writing in the *National Review,* Floyd G. Brown, in a rebuttal to her favoring abortion on demand, criticized her for making what in his view is a cavalier judgment that the quality of life—that is, a loving, financially sound environment—"means more than life itself." Still others questioned her support of the abortion-inducing RU-486 pill, the medicinal use of marijuana, and her urging of television networks to lift their ban on airing condom ads. "I find it rather strange that we can advertise cigarettes and beer to the young but then get nervous when there is talk of something [condoms] that can save lives but not about some things that kill," she remarked in *Advertising Age.*

Some of the most persistent attacks against her nomination concerned her involvement with the National Bank of Arkansas. She and others serving on the bank's board of directors were sued by the bank for allegedly violating the National Banking Act by authorizing $1.5 million in bad loans. The suit was settled, but the terms were not disclosed. Elders resigned from her position as director of the Arkansas Health Department in July 1993 after questions were raised about her drawing a full-time salary there while also working two days a week as a paid consultant to U.S. Health and Human Services secretary Donna Shalala.

Although some Republicans succeeded in delaying the confirmation vote, Elders gained the backing of the American Medical Association and former U.S. Surgeon General C. Everett Koop. On September 7, 1993, the Senate gave Elders the nod 65-34. Democratic senator Edward Kennedy, citing the lashing doled out by several of his coleagues, was quoted in the *Boston Globe* as saying, "She has come through this unfair gauntlet of excessive criticism with flying colors."

Elders platform as U.S. Surgeon General was to continue with her work regarding teen pregnancy, she was also concerned with tobacco use, national health care, AIDS, and drug and alcohol abuse. In late 1993 she sparked a great debate regarding the legalization of street drugs such as heroin and cocaine which was misrepresented in the media and by her opponents. What Elders, in fact, proposed was that the issue be studied. She did not back away from this stance even after the arrest and conviction of her son, Kevin, who was appealing a ten-year sentence for selling an eighth of an ounce of cocaine to a police informant in July of 1993. Claiming entrapment, Kevin Elders, nevertheless, openly acknowledged a decade-long drug problem.

Gun control was a major issue for Elders. Every day 135,000 youngsters take guns to school, more than 100 are shot, and 30 are killed, she told the *Journal of the American Medical Association (JAMA)*. She sees this issue as being intrinsic to the health of the nation.

## The Surgeon General Resigns Amid Controversy

Amidst a sea of controversy over a statement made at World AIDS Day at the United Nations regarding the teaching of masturbation in schools, Dr. Jocelyn Elders was forced to resign her post as U.S. Surgeon General in December 1994. The Surgeon General had just finished a routine speech at the conference on the spread of communicable diseases when, Dr. Rob Clark a New York psychologist, asked her if she would consider promoting masturbation as a means of preventing young people from engaging in riskier forms of sexual activity. Elder, as quoted in *US News & World Report* responded, "With regard to masturbation, I think that it is something that is a part of human sexuality and a part of something that should perhaps be taught." That statement so enraged both conservatives and moderates alike, that it ended in Elder's termination. For Elders the political climate in Washington at that time was less than favorable for even the most minor misstep. The Republicans had just taken over the House of Representatives—for the first time in more than 40 years—and the Clinton administration was reeling. Elders infraction could not be overlooked.

While her departure was stongly applauded by the conservative faction, many were dismayed over the events that transpired and felt that Elders was lassoed and sacrificed to satisfy the chants of conservatives, and the desperation of Democrats to quiet them, as typified in an article by Susan Ager, *Detroit Free Press.* Elders responded not with anger but with grace. She did not buck, nor did she apologize. She stood by her comment, all of her comments, saying "Jocelyn Elders was Jocelyn Elders and I've always tried to speak what I knew to be the truth." Ager went on to say, "[Elders was a] rare public official, she said clearly and fearlessly what we didn't want to hear, but need to think about. I suspect she will be saying the same thing two years from now."

## What Lies Ahead

In January 1995, Jocelyn Elders returned to the University of Arkansas as a faculty researcher, a professor of pediatric endocrinology at Arkansas Children's Hospital. Elders had both strong opponents and supporters as surgeon general. To the conservatives—her strongest opponents—she was "warped, dangerous, and a lunatic." To her supporters she was "noble, heroic, and fearless." Jocelyn Elders saw her mission as Surgeon General to create dialogue on America's health and welfare and the only way to do that, according to Elders, was to get their attention. "I think the Surgeon General's office is the office where it is very important to be able to get people listening to you, thinking about it, and talking about it . . . that is where you get change," she told Dr. Paula Wilson, assistant profession of communication studies Lynchburg College in Virginia.

Elders has no intention of fading into the background now that she is no longer U.S. Surgeon General. She made an impact on the audience she was most concerned about, the youth, and she intends to continue to be their advocate. When asked if there were any hard feelings about being asked to step down, Elders, in an interview with Steve Barnes of the *Progressive Interview,* responded candidly. "No, I don't have any hard feelings. I feel that the President, and the President alone, asked me to be Surgeon General. He gave me an opportunity to serve as Surgeon General, one that I would not have had without him. . . . I would not be the Jocelyn Elders I am today without the things the President did for me."

In February 1997, speaking to a group of 350 physicians at a conference in Long Beach, California, the former Surgeon General spoke "with the same clarity and passion . . . that won her confirmation to the post of U.S. Surgeon General in 1993, that led to her resignation in 1994," according to the *Press-Telegram.* A generation of youth is drowning in an ocean surrounded by the sharks of drugs, homicide and suicide, while many of us are sitting on the moral beach of *Just say no,* she told the opening session. Challenging her audience to become actively involved, Elders said, "There's a great big difference between being concerned and being committed. When you're concerned, its negotiable." On a more personal note she added, "When I went to Washington, I was committed. And what I was about was not negotiable."

When asked what the future holds for Dr. Jocelyn Elders, she told *Progressive* in a March 1995 interview, "I'm going to be the very best doctor I can be. I'm going to try to do some research, looking at problems that impact adolescents. And I'm going to become a real advocate. I'm going to do a lot of public speaking."

## Further Reading

*Detroit Free Press,* December 14, 1994; October 1994; *Jet,* December 26-January 2, 1995; *Lancet,* December 24, 1994; *People,* November 4, 1996; *Playboy,* June 1995; *The Nation,* January 2, 1995; *The Progressive,* March 1995; *The Progressive Interview,* March 1995; *USA Today,* May 1997; *Washington Monthly,* January-February 1997. □

# Gertrude B. Elion

**The American biochemist Gertrude B. Elion (born 1918) won a Nobel Prize for her scientific discovery of drugs to treat leukemia and herpes and to prevent the rejection of kidney transplants.**

Born in New York City in 1918, Gertrude Elion graduated from Hunter College with a B.A. degree in chemistry in 1937. In the midst of the Great Depression it was difficult for a woman to find a job in science. Elion had decided while still in high school to become a cancer researcher but for several years worked as a lab assistant, food analyst, and high school teacher while completing her Masters degree at night. She received an M.S. in chemistry from New York University in 1941.

During World War II, women were needed in scientific laboratories and Elion was hired as a biochemist by the Wellcome Research Laboratories, then in Tuckahoe, New York. There she worked for many years with George Herbert Hitchings, co-recipient with Gertrude Elion of the Nobel Prize in Medicine in 1988. Together, they pioneered pharmaceutical research, discovering and developing drugs to treat previously incurable diseases. Elion was later promoted to senior research chemist and in 1967 became head of the Department of Experimental Therapy.

The theory behind the development of these new drugs suggested by Hitchings was that, since all cells require nucleic acids, one might be able to stop the growth of rapidly dividing cells such as bacteria and tumor cells by substituting false building blocks, or antagonists of nucleic acid bases, in the synthesis of nucleic acids. Thus the replication of the unwanted cells might be prevented. Elion set to work especially on purines, nitrogenous bases that are important constituents of DNA. She was also working part-time on her doctorate at Brooklyn Polytechnic Institute but, given the ultimatum to choose between continuing on her doctorate full-time and keeping her job, she chose the latter. She was later awarded honorary doctorate degrees from George Washington University and several other universities and colleges in recognition of her research.

The early research involved a bacterium, *Lactobacillus casei,* which could synthesize purines given the right chemical substrates. She found her research work fascinating because so little was then known about how nucleic acid was synthesized. James Watson and Francis Crick had not yet determined the structure of DNA, the double helix. The pathways for biosynthesis of purines were not worked out until the mid-1950s by Arthur Kornberg and others.

By 1951 Elion and Hitchings succeeded in developing a number of drugs that interfered with purine utilization

called purine antimetabolites. Two of these were tested at the Sloan-Kettering Institute and were found to be active against leukemia in rodents. One of these, 6-mercaptopurine (6-MP), was then tested on children with acute leukemia at ten American medical centers. At that time there were no effective drugs for these terminally ill children and not even one in three lived as long as one year. The drug 6-MP was found to produce complete, though often temporary, remission. It was approved by the Food and Drug Administration in 1953. The success of this and related purine antimetabolite drugs opened up a whole new area of research in leukemia chemotherapy. Although 6-MP is still widely used, it is now prescribed in combination with several other antileukemic drugs. Almost 80 percent of children with acute leukemia can now be cured.

In the process of studying how 6-MP worked in both animals and humans, Elion developed a closely related compound called azathioprine. It was tested first as an anticancer drug but was later found to have a quite different but important function: it blocked the immune response leading to the rejection of foreign transplants. In 1960 this drug was tried out successfully in a kidney transplant on a collie. By 1962 successful human kidney transplants from unrelated donors became a reality, using azathioprine as an immunosuppressant drug. Cyclosporine made possible successful transplants of livers, hearts, and lungs, but azathioprine is still used in kidney transplants. It is also used to treat other serious diseases such as severe rheumatoid arthritis and systemic lupus.

Another drug that Elion and her coworkers synthesized scientifically—that is, by understanding how it works biochemically—is allopurinol. It can be used for the treatment of gout and other diseases resulting from an excess of uric acid. In gout uric acid crystals accumulate in the joints, causing extreme pain. Allopurinol inhibits the formation of the uric acid.

In 1968 Elion and her group returned to some early work she and Hitchings had done on antiviral drugs. They developed a drug found to be highly active against herpes virus. In 1970 their laboratory moved to North Carolina where they synthesized a new antiviral agent, Acyclovir. This drug is highly effective against several types of herpes virus and is not toxic to normal cells. It has been used in treating herpes since 1981, and also in treating patients with the painful disease known as shingles, caused by the varicella-zoster virus. It has even been a lifesaving drug for patients with herpes encephalitis, a frequently fatal disease. Acyclovir, approved by the Food and Drug Administration 1984, has become one of Burroughs Wellcome's most profitable drugs. Two years later, researchers trained by Elion and Hitchings developed azidothymidine, or AZT, the first drug used to treat AIDS.

Elion retired from Burroughs Wellcome in 1983 but remained there as a scientist emeritus. She served as president of the American Association for Cancer Research in 1983-1984 and on many advisory boards, including chairman of the Steering Committee on the Chemotherapy of Malaria. She also served as research professor of medicine and pharmacology at Duke University, working with advanced medical students who wish to do research on tumor biochemistry and pharmacology sharing her interest and experience.

In 1988, Elion and Hitchings shared the Nobel Prize for physiology or medicine with Sir James Black, a British biochemist. In her Nobel Prize speech, Elion noted that her 40 years of research not only resulted in many therapeutic drugs but that these life-serving agents have been tools to understand nature's mysteries. They led her into whole new areas of medical research, not only in biochemistry and pharmacology but also in immunology and virology.

Elion celebrated a momentous year in 1991 as she became the first woman to be inducted in the National Inventors Hall of Fame. She was also named to the Engineering and Science Hall of Fame and received the National Medal of Science. In 1995, she was named the Higuchi Memorial Award winner and lectured at the University of Kansas.

Elion, who resides in Chapel Hill, North Carolina, continues her work today through the World Health Organization, honorary university lectureships, and assisting students in medical research. Her hobbies include photography, travel and music. Her name appears on 45 patents

## Further Reading

Gertrude Elion described her scientific work in her Nobel Prize speech, quoted in *Science* magazine (April 7, 1989); gave a personal account of her life in *Les Prix Nobel* (1988). Biographical data on Elion appears in the books *Who's Who*

*1997* and the St. Martin's Press' annual biographical dictionary. ☐

# Nora Ephron

**The daughter of successful Hollywood screenwriters, Nora Ephron (born 1941) herself won acclaim during the 1980s for such screenplays as the Academy Award-nominated *Silkwood* and the highly successful comedy *When Harry Met Sally*. In the 1990s Ephron turned to film directing with such works as *This Is My Life* and the romantic comedy *Sleepless in Seattle*.**

Success has marked every phase of Nora Ephron's career as a journalist, novelist, screenwriter, and movie director. Viewing her life and the lives of others, particularly intimates, as material for her works, she is famous for her observations of other people's lives, as well as for her own personal revelations. Ephron was a pioneer of "new journalism" in the 1970s, writing bold essays about social issues of the day, as well as other writers' views. The novel and movie *Heartburn* turned the very public breakup of her second marriage into a best-seller. Such screenplays as *Silkwood* and *When Harry Met Sally* followed and became box office hits. Destined to be in the director's chair, she directed *Sleepless in Seattle,* the 1994 romantic comedy blockbuster.

The daughter of screenwriters Henry and Phoebe Ephron, Ephron and her three sisters grew up in Beverly Hills, amid its glamorous people and surroundings. Her parents had started their careers in New York collaborating on plays, but when Ephron was three, they decided to try parlaying their successes on stage to the screen and moved West. They were among the top screenwriters of the day, and such actors as James Cagney, Marilyn Monroe, Katharine Hepburn, and Spencer Tracy starred in movies they wrote. With such hits as *Carousel, There's No Business Like Show Business,* and *What Price Glory,* the Ephrons set high standards for excellence for their four daughters. Phoebe Ephron, especially, had high expectations and a determined, no-nonsense approach to life—yet, she added to that an infectious sense of humor. In an interview with *Vanity Fair,* Nora Ephron reminisced about her childhood, remembering singing rounds at the dinner table and playing charades afterward. "There was always a great deal of laughter," she said. The atmosphere was electric with creativity and famous people, as well as the daily traumas of raising a family of four.

### A Mind of Her Own

As writers, the Ephrons thoroughly processed the rich material of everyday life and drew upon their experiences, as well as their children's—especially Nora's—for inspiration. Talking, often telling stories around the dinner table became a family ritual. More than her sisters, Ephron en-

joyed and thrived in the nightly competitions to tell the best story. That environment helped her polish a budding humor, which in turn helped her compensate for being a skinny, dark-haired flatchested teen in Beverly Hills High School—a place where appearance was of utmost importance. A classmate recalled in *Vanity Fair,* "Her wit made up for not having the beauty; it was 'Don't mess with me.'" Later, Ephron's letters home from college became the basis for *Take Her, She's Mine.* Family lore has it that Ephron was named for Henrik Ibsen's feminist protagonist in *A Doll's House,* her parents perhaps foreseeing their first born's gift as an outspoken, independent thinker.

Ephron learned how to make the best of what life offered. According to Leslie Bennetts in *Vanity Fair,*" 'No matter what happens,' her mother was fond of saying, 'It's all copy.'" Years later Ephron told a reporter for *New Statesman & Society,* "I think what I learned from my mother was a basic lesson of humor, which is, if you slip on a banana peel, people will laugh at you; but if you tell people you slipped, it's your story—you are in fact the heroine of slipping on the banana peel."

### Comedy or Tragedy

From beneath the laughter, a dark side began to emerge. As Bennetts commented in *Vanity Fair,* it took the girls years to realize that their mother drank too much. Life became increasingly chaotic with their father suffering from manic-depression, and their mother suffering from alcoholism and cirrhosis of the liver, which took her life at 57. The youngest daughter, Amy, added, "Mommy was this sort of closet alcoholic, where her best friends didn't know she drank . . . father was drinking, and it was horrible; my parents used to scream all night. I remember Nora coming home from college one year and she suddenly realized what was going on. We got different parents; she got the upswing, and I got the downswing." Ephron recalled visiting her mother in the hospital near the end and hearing her say, "Take notes, Nora, take notes."

Ephron was determined to leave the West Coast and assert her independence. "I grew up in L.A. knowing that if I didn't get out of there I would die," she later recalled. From Wellesley she headed straight to New York, where she started honing her craft as a reporter at the *New York Post.* Soon she was making the rounds to magazines and getting assignments from *Esquire* and *New York.* On the surface, it appears that she intended to follow the career path of her parents, but the opposite is true. Going into journalism as far away as she could from Hollywood, movies, and screenwriting was her form of rebellion. She became one of the wittiest essayists of the 1970s, challenging the wisdom of luminaries of the day, including Betty Friedan and Brendan Bill. No subject—or person—was off limits; she described male oppression in an article on women in magazine publishing, and took public the stories of famous women betrayed by their husband's infidelity. She gained stature as a respected writer, and notoriety for her no-holds-barred approach. One of her greatest pleasures was criticizing celebrity journalists. During this time her marriage to humorist Dan Greenburg ended acrimoniously after she learned he was having an affair with her best friend.

Then, in an ironic twist of fate, Ephron married the epitome of celebrity journalists, Carl Bernstein, who, along with Bob Woodward, wrote the famous Watergate expose of then President Richard Nixon. The popular "perfect couple" made headlines. It appeared as if they had it all—until the day Ephron learned, after everyone else, that her husband was having an affair with the wife of the British ambassador. To make matters worse, Ephron was pregnant with their second child. In addition to feeling angry, hurt, and humiliated, she felt—and was made to look—stupid. She told *Vanity Fair'* s Bennetts, "I think probably the feeling I like least in the whole world is feeling dumb. I think it was foolish and pathetic of me to have thought it could have worked." The lessons of her youth paid off; she had learned how to take whatever cards life dealt and turn them into a winning hand. She vowed to regain control of her life and not to be a victim.

## A Return to Independence

In the wake of her failed second marriage, Ephron returned to home base, which she considered to be New York, re-established herself, and settled in to exorcise this episode from her life by writing the novel *Heartburn.* An article in *Time* summarized: "The humiliation described in the novel is that she, the witty observer of other people's lives, was unaware of what was going on in her own. The book was her way of ending up knowing more than anyone else. . . ." She evidently hit a nerve because her (by then) ex-husband Bernstein spent years in court trying to prevent her

from making the book into a movie. Eventually a watered-down version was made into a film that had mediocre box office results. In the end, Ephron succeeded—she got the satisfaction of revenge and made money on the book and movie.

As a single mother, financial security became a primary concern, and Ephron turned to screenwriting hoping it would prove to be as lucrative for her as it had been for her parents. She began collaborating with Alice Arlen, with whom she wrote *Silkwood* and *Cookie,* among others, but saved the screenplay of *Heartburn* as a solo venture. *When Harry Met Sally,* another independent project, was a huge success. Vindicated personally and professionally, she decided to risk marriage a third time. In 1981, Ephron married author and screenwriter Nicholas Pileggi.

The more time Ephron spent shepherding her work from paper to film, the more she yearned for full control. She set her sights on directing, and in 1992 broke through Hollywood's gender barrier to direct her first movie, *This Is My Life,* co-written with her sister Delia. Somewhat surprisingly for a woman with two bitter divorces under her belt, the film that solidified her reputation as a director was the 1994 romantic comedy *Sleepless in Seattle.* When asked by a reporter from *Rolling Stone* how she managed to remain a believer in romance, she replied, "If I weren't a romantic, why would I keep doing it? There's no one who's more romantic than a cynic."

## It's All Copy

Directing provides Ephron with long-sought professional fulfillment. She admitted in *Rolling Stone* that some friends even say her sharp tongue is mellowing and attribute the change in disposition to Pileggi. Others partially agree, but add, "She's a very hungry woman. . . . hungry for all the things her parents had—ability, power, the right friends." However, as a commentator in *Time* noted, if Ephron listens to herself, she'll remember that one of the themes in *Heartburn* "is that no one can have it all, that life unravels faster that you can weave it back together." So, make the most of today.

## Further Reading

*New Statesman and Society,* June 30, 1995, p. 32.
*New York,* April 11, 1994, p. 7.
*Rolling Stone,* July 8, 1993, pp. 73-75.
*Time,* January 27, 1992, pp. 62-63.
*Vanity Fair,* February, 1992, pp. 76-90. □

# Myrlie Evers-Williams

**Myrlie Evers-Williams's name may forever evoke the legacy of her first husband, slain civil rights leader Medgar Evers, but Myrlie Evers-Williams (born 1933) has never rested quietly on his laurels. Instead, the first woman elected Board of Directors Chair of the National Association for the Advancement of**

**Colored People (NAACP) has spent a lifetime carving out a formidable civil rights legacy of her own.**

Myrlie Evers-Williams was born in the Mississippi city of Vicksburg in 1933 in her maternal grandmother's frame house to a 16-year-old mother and a 28-year-old father, Evers-Williams was the only child born to the couple, who separated before her first birthday. Because of her mother's age, the family decided that it would be best if Evers-Williams was left in the care of her paternal grandmother, Annie McCain Beasley, a retired school teacher whom she called "Mama."

Though her mother left Vicksburg shortly after her marriage to James Van Dyke Beasley dissolved, Evers-Williams was surrounded by family while growing up. Besides her father and grandmother, with whom she lived, Evers-Williams regularly saw her maternal grandmother, and took piano lessons from her aunt, teacher Myrlie Beasley Polk. It is not surprising, then, that Evers-Williams remembered "only warmth and love and protectiveness from all of the people around me" in *For Us, the Living*, a 1967 memoir she wrote (with William Peters) about her life, and that of Medgar Evers.

Nor is it surprising, in this environment filled with educators, that Evers-Williams would develop a taste and an appetite for learning. A gifted pianist, she hoped to study music in college. However, Evers-Williams was denied the Mississippi state financial aid that would have enabled her

to attend the respected school of music at Fisk University in Nashville and was forced because of segregation to choose a school from Mississippi's two state colleges for African Americans, neither of which offered a major in music. She settled on Alcorn A&M College, where she planned to major in education and minor in music.

It was at Alcorn, during her first day on campus, that Evers-Williams met Medgar Evers, a business student who had started his studies there in the fall term of 1948. Her family initially disapproved of her romance with the older Evers—a World War II veteran roughly eight years her senior—but they continued to see each other steadily. They married on December 24, 1951, in a church in the bride's hometown of Vicksburg.

After roughly two years of study (around the time that Evers graduated from Alcorn), Evers-Williams left college, and the pair eventually settled in Jackson, Mississippi, where Evers (after a stint as an insurance agent) became the state's first NAACP field secretary. Evers-Williams worked alongside him, joining her husband's staff as his secretary. Like her husband, she was incensed by the appalling living conditions endured by sharecroppers.

Evers's efforts in the Mississippi civil rights movement, including attempts to desegregate schools and public buildings and secure voting rights for all citizens, are what led to his murder. He was shot in front of the family house in Jackson on June 12, 1963, as his wife and three children watched helplessly. His killer, white supremacist Byron De La Beckwith, was quickly arrested and charged in the shooting, but all-white juries deadlocked in two trials in 1964, freeing Beckwith. Evers-Williams, who had become active in the NAACP during her marriage, spent the next 30 years trying to bring Beckwith to justice.

Evers-Williams's dogged pursuit of the man who killed Medgar Evers paid off. When the Jackson, Mississippi *Clarion-Ledger* uncovered new information around 1989 suggesting jury tampering and official intervention in the case, Evers-Williams used the fresh evidence to convince reluctant Mississippi officials to conduct a new trial. As she told *People* magazine in 1991, shortly after Beckwith was arrested again, "People have said, 'Let it go, it's been a long time. Why bring up all the pain and anger again?' But I *can't* let it go. It's not finished for me, my children or four grandchildren." On February 5, 1994, a racially diverse Hinds County, Mississippi, jury found Beckwith guilty of the slaying. The victory was especially important for Evers-Williams. "When (the trial) was over, every pore was wide open and the demons left," she told Claudia Dreifus of the *New York Times Magazine* in 1994. "I was reborn when that jury said, 'Guilty!'"

After the murder and the failure of the initial trials to bring a conviction, Evers-Williams moved to the middle class college town of Claremont, California, with her three children. There, she completed work on a bachelor's degree in sociology in 1968 at Pomona College, one of the five Claremont colleges. While in school, Evers-Williams accepted speaking engagements for the NAACP and worked on *For Us, the Living*. In 1983, the book was adapted for a television movie starring Irene Cara and Howard Rollins.

The Claremont Colleges hired Evers-Williams after her graduation as a development director in 1968. Two years later, at the behest of local residents, she made her first foray into the political arena with a run for U.S. Congress as a Democrat in the primarily Republican 24th District. Her bid for office was unsuccessful, but she did capture over 30 percent of the vote in the area.

By the early 1970s, Evers-Williams had moved with her children to New York, where she was a vice president at the advertising firm of Seligman and Latz. In 1975, she joined Atlantic Richfield, a petroleum, chemical, and natural resource firm based in Los Angeles, where she eventually rose to director of community affairs. During this period, she also became a columnist for *Ladies' Home Journal.*

Evers-Williams met the man who would become her second husband at the Claremont Colleges. In 1976 she married longshoreman and civil rights and union activist Walter Williams at Little Bridges Chapel at Claremont College. She did not take Williams's surname at that time out of respect for Medgar Evers. Williams—referred to by Evers-Williams in an article in the July 1991 issue of *Esquire* as "my best friend, my Rock of Gibraltar"—reportedly understood this, and stood by her decision.

Following an unsuccessful run for city council in Los Angeles in 1987, Evers-Williams was appointed one of the five commissioners on the Board of Public Works by Los Angeles Mayor Tom Bradley, where she was in charge of some 5,000 to 6,000 employees and a multi-million dollar budget for basic city services and improvements such as road maintenance. Evers-Williams continued her work with the NAACP along with her other commitments. As vice-chair of the board of the NAACP in 1994, she knew that the group had fallen on difficult times, as it faced mounting debt and scandal. As she acknowledged in the *New York Times Magazine* in 1994, "We need strong leadership, which I hope will include more women at the helm. We need more leaders who guard the monies of the association very carefully—and who do not abuse the privileges that come with leadership."

After considerable deliberation, especially in light of the failing health of her second husband, Evers-Williams announced her decision to run for the position of chair of the NAACP in mid-February of 1995. In a close race for control of the organization's 64-member board of directors later that month, Evers-Williams defeated incumbent William Gibson, a South Carolina dentist who had led the NAACP board since 1985, by 30-to-29.

Following her win, Jack W. White in *Time* magazine quoted Evers-Williams as having told participants at an NAACP meeting in New York, "Duty beckons me. I am strong. Test me and you will see." As White observed, Evers-Williams will need that strength to bolster the organization. As Evers-Williams begins her tenure, she must address the internal troubles and tensions that have shaken the NAACP in recent years. Former executive director Benjamin Chavis was ousted in 1994 after 15 months on the job for sexual harassment and financial mismanagement. Gibson reportedly misspent organization funds as well. The NAACP was about $4 million in debt when Evers-Williams

entered office, and charges of gender discrimination, beyond those levied at Chavis, abounded in the ranks.

Those who know Evers-Williams believed that she was up to the task. Arthur Johnson, president of the Detroit chapter of the NAACP from 1986 to 1993, told the *Detroit Free Press* in February of 1995 that he felt that "Myrlie Evers will raise the sights of NAACP members around the country and will generate a stronger and better feeling of common cause among the members." A February 21, 1995 editorial in the *New York Times* expressed similar confidence in Evers-Williams, arguing that she "seems well suited to the task of reasserting the NAACP's trademark blend of militance and inclusivity," and that she "has given the NAACP a new chance at what looked like the last minute." A writer for the *Nation* was likewise upbeat about her prospects, saying that she brings "a long history of struggle, a large slice of NAACP tradition and great integrity to her new task." Paul Ruffins in the *Nation,* similarly, noted that Evers-Williams offers "a model of life and leadership in the post-civil rights era" as well as significant management experience.

For her part, Evers-Williams has said that she will reach out to younger members of the African American community, that she will work to restore the organization's image and financial state, and that she will focus on present threats to past civil rights achievements, such as affirmative action and fair housing and lending rules. Even this triumph for Evers-Williams was tempered by tragedy, though. Williams, who had urged his wife to seek the top post of the NAACP, lost a lengthy battle with cancer on February 22, 1995, at the couple's Oregon home. Evers-Williams, who had been elected to the post just days earlier, was at his side when he died. "I kept telling him, 'I need to be with you,' and he kept saying, 'This is something you've got to do,'" Evers-Williams related in *Jet.*

Evers-Williams was sworn in as chairperson of the NAACP on Mother's Day, May 14, 1995, at the Metropolitan AME Church in Washington, before over 1,000 supporters. There, according to a report in the *Detroit Free Press,* she renewed her pledge to restore the NAACP in name and deed, telling the assembly, "I will give my all to the NAACP to see that it becomes stronger, to see that we regain our rightful place as the premier civil rights organization in this country." After Evers-Williams' inauguration, Ruffins asserted that the NAACP had "regained its moral center of gravity." Although she faced opposition by some board members, Evers-Williams' involvement seemed to bring a renewal of support for the organization. *Harper's Bazaar* reported a flood of dues from the group's 2200 branches, and noted that much-needed corporate and celebrity donations were coming in again. As Evers-Williams pointed out in *Harper's Bazaar,* the NAACP still has a long way to go. "The perception that we don't have a financial crisis jsut because I was elected is totally erroneous," she noted. However, it appeared that if anyone could get the NAACP back into shape, Evers-Williams could. During her first year of chairmanship, Ever-Williams generated much praise for reducing the organization's deficit, healing wounded souls on the divided board, and hiring Kweisi Mfume as president to guide the NAACP into the next century.

## Further Reading

*Black Enterprise,* May 1995, p. 20.
*Chicago Tribune,* January 14, 1996, Sec. 13, p. 8.
*Detroit Free Press,* February 22, 1995, p. 5A; May 15, 1995, p. 5A.
*Ebony,* June 1988, p. 108.
*Esquire,* July 1991, p. 58.
*Harper's Bazaar,* July 1995, pp. 58-59.
*Jet,* March 6, 1995, p. 32; March 13, 1995, p. 53.
*Nation,* March 13, 1995, p. 332; October 30, 1995, pp. 494-500.
*New York Times,* February 20, 1995, p. A1; February 20, 1995, p. C8; February 21, 1995, p. A14; February 26, 1995, p. A20; February 26, 1995, p. E2.
*New York Times Magazine,* November 27, 1994, p. 68.
*People,* February 11, 1991, p. 45.
*Time,* February 27, 1995, p. 23.
*U.S. News & World Report,* March 6, 1995, p. 32. □

# F

## JoAnn Falletta

**The American conductor JoAnn Falletta (born 1954) served as music director of three orchestras simultaneously while still a young woman. She chose to perform pieces from the non-standard repertoire, trying to select pieces suited to the particular audience.**

JoAnn Falletta was an American conductor whose perseverance and talent helped to place her simultaneously at the helm of three orchestras at a young age. Her success was due to the fresh and electric performances she conducted. This freshness and excitement came from performing pieces that were not in the standard repertoire, but were rather either little-known works by well-known composers or works by unfamiliar composers of the past and present. Falletta aimed to introduce these composers to the regular audiences for classical music and to young listeners who were looking for "something that will put them more in touch with themselves" and who can listen with an open ear and mind to music that is energetic and crisply presented.

The ability to communicate her ideas about particular pieces to orchestra members and to convince and enable them to carry out her conceptions did not come easily or quickly to Falletta, but the desire to do so developed in her as a child. She was born in New York City on February 27, 1954. Raised in the borough of Queens in an Italian-American household, her home was filled with music. As there was no room in the apartment for a piano, JoAnn's father bought her a guitar, which she loved as "it was the perfect instrument, quiet and personal, because I was painfully shy

as a child." Her ability to play the guitar earned her entry into the guitar department at Mannes College of Music, and later she was called by the Metropolitan Opera and the New York Philharmonic whenever music for guitar, mandolin, or lute was required.

### Uncertainty About a Woman Conductor

Her love of the guitar did not diminish her love of conducting. She led the student orchestra at Mannes when she was 18 and requested that she be accepted into the conducting studies program at the college. At first the administration was resistant because of the long period of study necessary combined with the unlikely prospect that a woman would be chosen as musical director of an orchestra. Mannes permitted her transfer, however, and she went on for further study to Queens College (M.A. in orchestral conducting) and the Juilliard School of Music (M.M., D.M.A. in orchestral conducting). Juilliard was no more encouraging to Falletta than Mannes had been, but she persisted and her obvious technical abilities overcame the school's uncertainty about her viability as a conductor.

None of the discouragements she received showed in her attitude toward her training, perhaps because the climate had changed in the years she was studying and, though she was still breaking ground, the concept of a female conductor was no longer considered unthinkable. Jorge Mester helped her to establish a more assertive manner on the podium while still remaining true to her own personality. This meant that she had to discard some of her self-effacing ways of dealing with orchestra players and resulted in a quiet control based on her extraordinary command of the literature. Her talent for communicating a single vision of a work through her baton technique and her

**211**

explanations of musical phrasing to the players produced exciting concerts from coast to coast.

Her career began with the Jamaica (New York) Symphony, which she founded in 1978. It was, in her own words, "absolutely horrible, terrible and an embarrassment to think of now." It consisted of 15 players who rehearsed Monday nights. Gradually the original members were replaced by friends from Juilliard who wanted more orchestral experience and the number of players rose to 80. The name of the orchestra was changed to Queens Symphony and Falletta had her first taste of success in building up an orchestra. At the time she was founding the Queens Symphony, she was also studying at Juilliard and beginning to receive conducting fellowships. She won the Leopold Stokowski Conducting Competition in 1985, the same year she was appointed associate conductor of the Milwaukee Symphony Orchestra where she worked from 1985 to 1988.

Earlier, in 1983, the Denver Chamber Orchestra had appointed her as music director and the growth of that orchestra in popularity and quality matched the transformation of the Queens Symphony. It was just this talent of Falletta's to tap the interest of the community that caused the Bay Area Women's Philharmonic in 1986 and the Long Beach Symphony Orchestra in 1989 to appoint her to be their musical director, bringing the total of orchestras of which she was musical director to three. Each group required a different repertoire, which provided a challenge to JoAnn Falletta. As she admitted, before she accepted the position with the Bay Area Women's Philharmonic, "I didn't know who (the composers) Amy Beach or Louise Farrenc were. It was a whole new world for me." No novice to creative programming, she presented in the spring of 1988 works by Marianne Martines, a student of Haydn's, and a work by Germaine Tailleferre, a 20th-century French composer. In addition, works by Pulitzer prize winner Ellen Taafe Zwilich and Joan Tower expanded her repertoire to include prominent living women composers. She left the Bay Area Women's Philharmonic after 10 years, but remained its artistic director.

Her approach to her audiences was to educate them about and interest them in what was being performed. Frequently she gave talks before performances about the music to be performed. She also presented youth concerts, hoping to create an appreciative audience for classical music in the future, and sought out pieces that reflected the ethnic mix of her constituency. In the case of the Long Beach Symphony, she sought contemporary Asian works to reflect the large Asian population in the area. In 1986, 1987, 1988, and 1989 ASCAP awarded Falletta first and third prizes for creative programming. It was a fitting public recognition of her efforts not to recreate the standard repertoire. To offer this unusual mix of pieces she had learned an extraodinary number of pieces.

## Critical Kudos

Critical acclaim was extremely favorable. *Newsday* referred to her as "one of the finest conductors of her generation. Her baton technique is so utterly communicative that one might as well plug one's ears and simply watch the music take shape through her sensitive, graceful gestures." The *Los Angeles Times* wrote of a performance of Prokofiev's "Symphony No. 5" by the Long Beach Symphony, "Her deliberate tempo in the first movement gave the music an extra-weighty flow, culminating spectacularly in a broad, muscular and percussive climax. This overall measured pace was ever-flexible on a local level, however, pointing up details in the massive architectural design." It was her total command of her score and the clarity of her own conception of it that was transmitted by her baton to the members of the orchestra. The communication from conductor to players to audience depends on strong, forceful leadership, which Falletta was able to provide. *USA Today* wrote: "A cool, precise presence, Falletta is the master of eventful legato. When many conductors try to establish rounded, smooth phrasing, the results are often bland, but Falletta can be suave while maintaining a rich sense of incident. As shown by the famous Nimrod variation, as well as the more introspective moments of Barber's Symphony No. 1, she was best when precipitating an ecstatic moment, inspiring an emotional candidness from the players but never slipping into the sort of self-indulgence that would tax the piece's overall architecture. Her performance of the Barber symphony had a Mahlerian grandeur." The Denver *Rocky Mountain News* wrote that "Falletta is surely destined for classical music stardom."

Stardom in the form of an appointment to a major national orchestra may not come for a time to Falletta, however, although she retained her place with the Long Beach Symphony and had also joined the Virginia Beach Symphony by 1997. Since she maintained a busy schedule of guest conducting around the country and abroad beginning in 1982, she may find herself sought by a major orchestra rather sooner than that. Even while waiting for greater exposure nationally, her ideas about the presentation of music to new audiences will provide guidelines for the future of classical music performance in this country. Falletta favored small, intimate spaces for listening to music, avoiding large, impersonal concert halls. In addition, an exciting repertoire related to the audience's background plus an effort to educate them about music was the formula for her continued success as an orchestral conductor. At the heart of her achievements, however, was the stunning control, the expertise, and the well-thought-out conceptions of the music she conducted.

## Further Reading

Articles about JoAnn Falletta have appeared in newspapers and magazines on both coasts as well as in national magazines. An extensive article appeared in the *San Francisco Magazine* (November 1987) in which her early training and subsequent success are described. On September 9, 1990, the *Los Angeles Times Calendar* published an article by Greta Beigel on Falletta which went into some detail about her development as a conductor. *Musical America* ran a cover story about her (September 1990) and reviewed a concert by the Bay Area Women's Philharmonic (November 1989). The *Los Angeles Times* (September 30, 1990) wrote an article that discussed her musical directorship of the Long Beach Symphony which contained comments by those whom she conducted about her style of leadership. □

# Fannie Merritt Farmer

**Fannie Merritt Farmer (1857-1915) was an American authority in the art of cookery and the author of six books about food preparation.**

Fannie Farmer was born in Boston, Mass., on March 23, 1857. Her parents had hopes of sending her to college. But after high school graduation she suffered a paralytic stroke, and her doctor discouraged all thoughts of further schooling.

While at home as an invalid, Fannie Farmer became interested in cooking. When her physical condition had markedly improved, her parents advised her to seek schooling which would develop and refine her knowledge and abilities in cookery. She liked the idea and enrolled in the Boston Cooking School, where her performance was outstanding. Because of the excellence of her work, upon graduation in 1889 she was invited to serve as assistant director of the school under Carrie M. Dearborn. Farmer's inquiring mind led her into studies, including a summer course at the Harvard Medical School.

After Dearborn's death in 1891, Farmer was appointed director of the school. While there she published her monumental work, *Boston Cooking School Cookbook* (1896), of which 21 editions were printed before her death. It has remained a standard work. She served as director of the school for 11 years. After her resignation in 1902, she established her own school and named it Miss Farmer's School of Cookery. It was decidedly innovative, emphasizing the practice of cooking instead of theory. Its program was designed to educate housewives rather than to prepare teachers. The school also developed cookery for the sick and the invalid. Farmer became an undisputed authority in her field, and she was invited to deliver lectures to nurses, women's clubs, and even the Harvard Medical School.

One of Farmer's major contributions was teaching cooks to follow recipes carefully. She pioneered the use of standard level measurement in cooking. Farmer, her school, and her cook-books were extremely popular. She received favorable newspaper coverage in many American cities, and her influence was widespread. The well-attended weekly lectures at the school were tributes to the value of the work she and her assistants were doing. She also wrote a popular cookery column, which ran for nearly 10 years in the *Woman's Home Companion,* a national magazine.

Farmer was a woman of unusual motivation, intelligence, and courage. Though she suffered another paralytic stroke, she continued lecturing. In fact, 10 days before her death in 1915, she delivered a lecture from a wheelchair.

## Further Reading

For general background on cooking and a brief discussion of Fanny Farmer see Kathleen Ann Smallzried, *The Everlasting Pleasure: Influences on America's Kitchens, Cooks, and Cookery from 1565 to the Year 2000* (1956). □

# Suzanne Farrell

**Suzanne Farrell (neé Roberta Sue Ficker; born 1945) was a versatile classical ballerina who performed with Balanchine and the Ballet of the Twentieth Century. During her almost 30-year career she performed 75 roles in 70 ballets.**

Roberta Sue Ficker, who later selected the name Suzanne Farrell from a phone book, was born on August 16, 1945. She was the third of three daughters of a lower-middle-class family who lived in Mt. Healthy, a quiet town outside Cincinnati, Ohio. Her parents divorced when Farrell was nine. Her main concern was her mother's happiness, and she claims this experience taught her to be adaptable at an early age.

Farrell always dreamed of being a clown but began to dance when she was eight to overcome being an imaginative and spunky tomboy. She and her sisters frequently invited neighbors to attend carnivals held in their garage or back yard. It was not unusual for Suzanne to have choreographed a dance in which her partners were kitchen chairs. By age 10, she had organized the New York City Ballet Juniors, a group of girls from her dance classes. Her first stage experience, at age 12, was with the Cincinnati Summer Opera where she performed in various ballets.

## Succeeding in the Arts

Farrell's mother recognized her daughter's talents and was determined that she succeed in the arts. She studied ballet at the Cincinnati Conservatory of Music after her school day at Ursuline Academy. Her mother supported her interest in performing and in attending concerts. She once wrote an excuse for her to miss school so she could see the New York City Ballet dance in Bloomington, Indiana. After seeing "Symphony in C," Farrell decided she wanted to dance with that company, where she felt she would fit in. The company seemed more alive and energetic than other companies.

One day Diana Adams, a scout from the School of American Ballet in New York, observed Farrell and invited her to audition for entrance to the school. In 1960, at age 15, Farrell was one of 12 students to be awarded a full Ford Foundation scholarship into their preparatory program for professional dancers. Without money or housing, her family moved to New York, a strange city to them, and lived in a one-room apartment. Farrell's mother worked 20-hour shifts as a night nurse to support them.

As a "small fish in a big pond," Farrell realized that only she was in charge of her life. The program's major goal was to develop the technical strength and the unique creativity of each student. George Balanchine, head of the school, stressed that what they did with the technique was important. Having it was not enough. Within a year, Farrell joined the company while attending high school at Rhodes. She made her corps de ballet debut in Todd Bolender's "Creation of the World" and George Balanchine's "Stars

and Stripes." At 19, she was the youngest principal dancer to dance a solo while in the corps. She was the Dark Angel in "Serenade." Two years later she performed in the world premiere of "Jewels," a signature work.

## Balanchine

One cannot talk about Suzanne Farrell without discussing her relationship with Balanchine. Very early, he began to give her opportunities to learn ballets and parts, sometimes superseding more veteran dancers. He collaborated with her on choreography by pushing her to take risks and allowing her to express herself through the choreography. Until she left four years after becoming a star, she was central to him and he to her. Often referred to as his "muse," she attributed this to her strong belief in him and what he was doing. He trained and perhaps molded her as he wanted. Farrell embodied his ideal and this became the norm for the company. Long-legged, gorgeous, and extraordinarily musical, she became known for her backbends, high extensions, and versatility.

Balanchine had not separated his art from life in the past and Farrell, who was immature, was very focused on her dancing. Pleasing him on stage was all she thought about, and in fact she said later that it was like the child for whom time and distance do not shake the ties he has with his parents. She described him as a feminist celebrating the independence of women while he had them on a pedestal. Some say some of his choreography, such as "Don Quixote" and "Meditation," were autobiographical, reflecting the blending of their private and professional lives. Farrell

was referred to as the "5th Mrs. B" since Balanchine had previously married four of his ballerinas. They never married but other company members resented their relationship and some resigned from the company. Farrell became isolated. Despite this friction, she danced with and appreciated the uniqueness of each of her many outstanding partners, claiming that each brought out something different in her dancing. They included Balanchine, Jacques d'Amboise, Peter Martins, Edward Villela, and Jean-Pierre Bonnefeux. She performed in numerous premiers, including "Tzigane," "Caconne," "Union Jack," and "Vienna Waltzes," as well as in "Meditation," "Mozartiana," "Don Quixote," "Four Temperaments," and "Apollo," to mention only a few which are considered to be some of the most dazzling ballets of this century.

## Self-imposed Exile

In 1969 her marriage to Paul Mejia, a young company dancer from Peru, created some confusion for her and affected his career. (They divorced in the mid-1990s.) He felt Balanchine was not casting him appropriately and finally, in mid-season in May of that year, they left the company with their three cats, Top, Bottom, and Middle. Maurice Bejart had seen Farrell perform the first full length "Swan Lake" with the National Ballet of Canada and sent her a telegram inviting her to join his company. They joined his Brussels-based Ballet of the Twentieth Century the following year. They both enjoyed touring and the experience of working with a style and approach which in its theatrically and reputation for being avant-garde was a dramatic departure from Balanchine's classicism. Even though Farrell performed in over 30 ballets which were composed or revived for her, she referred to this time as "exile."

A series of knee and hip injuries which had begun 20 years before developed into severe and increasingly limiting arthritis. By the 1970s doctors predicted that Farrell would never again dance. After a hip replacement and the emotional, psychological, and physical struggle involved in a prolonged hospitalization and rigorous program of physical therapy, she did in fact return to perform on pointe.

## Reconciliation and Return to New York

After seeing the New York City Ballet perform again in 1974, she asked to return and did so in 1975. She also reconciled with Balanchine, and from it came the late masterworks created for Farrell: "Chaconne," "Davidsbundlertanze" and "Mozartiana." Farrell demonstrated her versatility by dancing leads in ballets choreographed by Jerome Robbins, Jacques d'Amboise, and Stanley Williams and to choreographically innovative ballets with a variety of scores, such as serial music of Stravinsky and "chance" music of Xanakis.

Blanchine died in 1983 and Farrel gave her last performance six years later, at the age of 44, on November 26, 1989, in a performance of "Vienna Waltzes" and "Sophisticated Lady." Farrell made her last bow to "Mr. B" in the presence of Lincoln Kirstein and Peter Martin. She commented that it was easy to get there but difficult to stay there or to hold on to the air. She now restages Balanchine ballets all over the world. Their famously unconsummated relationship lives on in an Oscar-nominated *Suzanne Farrell: Elusive Muse*—a relationship so consuming, that she says she considered suicide.

According to Arlene Croce, she was thought of as "the supreme classicist of our time." She had a reputation for versatility, having performed 75 roles in 70 ballets, starred in three feature-length ballet films, and performed in the Dance in America series and nationally telecast concert at the Kennedy Center in honor of Balanchine. In 1965 she was the recipient of the Merit Award of *Mademoiselle* magazine and the Award of Merit in Creative and Performing Arts at the University of Cincinnati. In 1979 Farrell received New York City's Award of Honor for Arts and Culture for a record of distinguished achievement in the world of dance, and in 1980 Brandeis University's Creative Arts Award.

## Further Reading

*Holding On To The Air* (1954) by Suzanne Farrell with Toni Bentley is the only book about her. Objectivity is a problem, particularly where Balanchine is involved. A sense of overwhelming debt to him pervades the book and may cloud her account. □

# Dianne Feinstein

**Politician and public official, Dianne Feinstein (born 1933) was elected San Francisco's first female mayor in 1979 and became one of the nation's most visible and publicly recognized leaders. In 1992 she was elected to the Senate, becoming along with Barbara Boxer the first female senator from California.**

Born in San Francisco on June 22, 1933, to a Jewish physician father (Leon Goldman) and a Catholic Russian-American mother (Betty Rosenburg Goldman), Dianne laid claim to having been brought up in both religious traditions. She attended a Roman Catholic school and a Jewish temple during her youth, which cultivated in her a deep respect for religious diversity. After having graduated from San Francisco's Sacred Heart High School she enrolled at Stanford where she studied history and political science and was active in student government. She was awarded a B.S. degree in 1955.

Combining marriage and family with a career, Feinstein was employed by a public affairs foundation interested in criminal justice. She worked as an administrative assistant for California's Industrial Welfare Commission and was appointed in 1962 to a four-year term on the state's Women's Board of Paroles. When her first marriage broke up, Feinstein withdrew temporarily from public life but emerged again on a county advisory committee on adult detention and on San Francisco's Mayor's Commission on Crime. During that period she also became the mother of one daughter, divorced her first husband, and organized her household tasks with a professional housekeeper in order to

be free to concentrate on her public career. A second husband died in 1978, and she later married Richard Blum, an investment banker.

## Early Public Career

Introduced to politics by a kindly uncle who began taking her to San Francisco Board of Supervisors (city council) meetings when she was 16, Feinstein recalled later that this was a catalyst that would turn her toward a career in public service. She won election to San Francisco's Board of Supervisors in 1969 and served on the board through the 1970s. Politically ambitious, Feinstein ran twice for the mayoralty, being defeated by Joseph Alioto in 1971 and finishing a poor third in George Moscone's 1975 election. In 1975 she was an early and firm supporter of presidential candidate Jimmy Carter, and when he won the White House, she lobbied actively for a cabinet post in Washington. Turned down in her quest for higher office, discouraged by the deaths of her father and her second husband, and afflicted by illness while abroad, Feinstein told writer Jerome Brondfield: "I decided I would not again be a candidate—for anything."

Concluding that her series of political and personal reversals had exhausted her future political prospects, Supervisor Feinstein scheduled a press conference to announce the same on what would become one of the most fateful days of her career, November 27, 1978. A half an hour before the anticipated announcement, a disgruntled former supervisor, Dan White, fatally shot Mayor George Moscone and Supervisor Harvey Milk, a homosexual political activist. This grisly assault propelled board president Feinstein into the position of acting mayor, and a month later the board selected her to serve out the balance of Moscone's term. As mayor, Feinstein sought to calm the political turbulence and violence, balance the demands of conflicting pressure groups (she appointed another gay to replace Milk), and sought what she called an "emotional reconstruction" of the city's agitated polity.

## Mayor in Her Own Right

Feinstein was elected to a full four-year term as mayor beginning in 1979. During her early tenure she followed an even-handed course which incorporated some off-beat cultural politics as well as conventional politics to appeal to the varied constituencies in the community. She also focused her attention on the problem of crime, took a keen interest in police staffing and policies, and succeeded in reducing the crime rates. The biggest challenge that she first faced was fiscal—the problem of balancing the budget exacerbated by cutbacks in state and federal spending for cities. A proponent of "management by objectives" and utilizing a high-powered group of business and labor leaders in the Mayor's Fiscal Advisory Committee, Feinstein brought the city budget under control, inaugurated enlightened management and personnel policies, and supported downtown development and economic expansion.

Her occasional indulgence in whimsy delighted and amused the citizenry. She once appeared at a ribbon cutting ceremony for a reclamation project in a black wool, knee-length, old fashioned bathing suit, prompted by a wager with the contractor. At a testimonial dinner at which she was guest of honor she applied the Heimlich maneuver to save a guest from choking on a piece of meat. Yet the city's colorful and dynamic mayor occasionally stumbled, as she apparently did in pushing through an ordinance banning handguns, which led to an attempt at recall. Arrayed against her was an anti-ban group that attracted other dissidents, including the homosexual interest group. This part of the community was angered by Feinstein's veto of a measure extending medical and welfare benefits to gays and live-in companions of unmarried city employees. Although the recall movement gathered sufficient signatures, the threat quickly dissipated when Mayor Feinstein easily survived the challenge by polling an 83 percent favorable vote in April and handily winning her second and last full term in the November 1983 election (mayors were limited to two terms by the city charter).

Although beginning her career as a liberal, Mayor Feinstein was considered a moderate on matters of lifestyle tolerance and a conservative on fiscal issues. In 1984 her city hosted the Democratic National Convention, which many of the mayor's backers hoped might lead to the nomination for the vice presidency, but it did not.

In 1990 Feinstein ran for governor of California against Republican candidate Pete Wilson. Although she ran a tough campaign, and one that was well-financed by her investment banker husband, she lost to Wilson by a narrow margin. Feinstein immediately re-focused and in early 1991 announced her intention to run for Pete Wilson's former Senate seat in the 1992 election. Along with fellow Democrat Barbara Boxer, Feinstein was elected to the Senate in 1992; the two became the first women Senators ever elected in California. Their election was part of a new women's revolution, since prior to January 1993 only 15 women had ever served in the Senate, and certainly there had never been more than two serving at any given time. After her re-election in 1996, Feinstein shared the floor with 8 fellow women Senators, representing a spectrum of political viewpoints. Of the change, Senator Tom Harkin said, "Just by being on the Senate floor, they've changed the male mindset."

As Senator, Feinstein took a firm stand on a range of issues: she was outspoken against President Clinton's certification of Mexico as being an ally in the drug war, she argued that China should be granted Most Favored Nation status, and argued against the leasing of a former Navy base to China's state-owned shipping company.

**Further Reading**

For her political career, see Jerome Brondfield, "She Gives Her Heart to San Francisco," in *Readers Digest* (July 1984); M. Holli and P. Jones, *Biographical Dictionary of American Mayors* (1981); and biographical materials from the Office of the Mayor. For the assassination and its aftermath, see *New York Times* and *Chicago Tribune,* November 28, 1978, and *United States News and World Report,* June 6, 1979. For the recall election, see *Chicago Tribune,* April 27, 1983.

For further reading on her race against Pete Wilson for Governor, see Celia Morris's book *Storming the Statehouse: Running for Governor with Ann Richards and Dianne Feinstein* (1992). For a discussion of her role as Senator, see *Year of the Woman,* by Linda Witt, Karen Paget, and Glenna Matthews. □

# Edna Ferber

**American author Edna Ferber (1887-1968) wrote popular fiction and collaborated on several successful Broadway plays.**

B orn in Kalamazoo, Mich., Edna Ferber at an early age moved with her family to Appleton, Wis., where she spent most of her childhood. When her father lost his vision, she was forced to forsake her acting ambitions and, at the age of 17, began full-time work as a reporter for the *Appleton Daily Crescent.* Shortly afterward she joined the staff of the *Milwaukee Journal* and later the *Chicago Tribune.* During this period she wrote several short stories, some of which were published in *Everybody's Magazine.* She discarded a novel which her mother salvaged and had published in 1911 as *Dawn O'Hara.* Two short-story collections followed, *Buttered Side Down* (1912) and *Roast Beef Medium* (1913), and the novels *Fanny Herself* (1917), *The Girls* (1921), and *Gigolo* (1922).

Ferber won her first popular success with the novel *So Big,* the story of a young widow on a truck farm in Illinois

who sacrifices everything for her son's happiness. She was awarded the Pulitzer Prize for it in 1924. *Show Boat* (1926), perhaps her best novel, tells the story of a showboat performer's love for an unscrupulous gambler. The novel was adapted as a successful Broadway musical the following year. *Cimarron,* another best seller, dealt with the spectacular Oklahoma land rush of 1889. In the early 1920s Ferber began a fruitful collaboration with playwright George S. Kaufman, producing such plays as *Minick* (1924), *The Royal Family* (1927), *Dinner at Eight* (1932), and *Stage Door* (1936).

In her later novels Ferber continued to explore various geographical and historical settings. *American Beauty* (1931) describes Polish immigrants in Connecticut; *Come and Get It* (1935) is about Wisconsin lumbermen; and *Great Son* (1945) depicts four generations of a Seattle family.

Many of Ferber's novels have been made into movies, including *Saratoga Trunk* (1941), which is set in New Orleans and Saratoga Springs, N.Y., and deals with the founding of railroad dynasties; *Giant* (1950), a story of oil fortunes in contemporary Texas; and *Ice Palace* (1958), about Alaska, from exploration to the fight for statehood.

Ferber published her first autobiography, *A Peculiar Treasure,* in 1939 and her second, *A Kind of Magic,* in 1963. Her often energetic and pleasantly nostalgic work was immensely popular with both the reading public and movie- and playgoers, making her one of America's best-known authors. She died on April 16, 1968, in New York City.

## Further Reading

Miss Ferber's fiction is reviewed in Robert Van Gelder, *Writers and Writing* (1946), and W. Tasker Witham, *Panorama of American Literature* (1947).

## Additional Sources

Gilbert, Julie Goldsmith., *Ferber, a biography,* Garden City, N.Y.: Doubleday, 1978. □

# Geraldine Ferraro

**Sixty-four years after American women won the right to vote Geraldine Ferraro (born 1935) became the first woman candidate for the vice presidency of a major political party. She had previously served three consecutive terms in the U.S. House of Representatives.**

Geraldine Ferraro was born on August 26, 1935. She was the third child of Dominick and Antonetta Ferraro. The Ferraro's had only one surviving son, Carl, at the time of Geraldine's birth—the other, Gerard, had been killed in a family automobile accident two years earlier. Dominick Ferraro, an Italian immigrant, operated a night club in Newburgh, a small city north of New York City reputed to be wide-open to organized crime.

In 1944, when Ferraro was eight years old, her father was arrested and charged with operating a numbers racket. He died of a heart attack the day he was to appear for trial. The Ferraro family was forced to move, first to the Bronx, and then to a working-class neighborhood in Queens. Here Antonetta Ferraro worked in the garment industry, crocheting beads on wedding dresses and evening gowns in order to support herself and her children.

As a young girl Ferraro attended Marymount School in Tarrytown, New York. She consistently excelled at school, skipping from the sixth to the eighth grade and graduating from high school at 16. She won a full scholarship to Marymount Manhattan College, where she was the editor of the school newspaper. While still at Marymount Ferraro also took education courses at Hunter College. In this way she prepared herself to teach English in the New York City Public School system after she graduated college. While teaching, Ferraro attended Fordham University's evening law classes. She received her law degree in 1960. The week she passed the bar exam she married John Zaccaro, an old sweetheart, but kept her maiden name in honor of her mother.

## Attorney and Congresswoman

From 1961 to 1974 Ferraro practiced law, had her three children—Donna, John Jr., and Laura—and worked in her husband's real estate business. In 1974, with her youngest child in the second grade, Ferraro agreed to serve as an assistant district attorney in Queens County. As an assistant DA, she created two special units, the Special Vic-

tims Bureau and the Confidential Unit. As chief of these units, Ferraro specialized in trying cases involving sex crimes, crimes against the elderly, family violence, and child abuse. From 1974 to 1978 she also served on the Advisory Council for the Housing Court of the City of New York and as president of the Queens County Women's Bar Association.

In 1978 Ferraro decided to run for Congress. In the primary campaign, in an intensely ethnic area of Queens, she faced Thomas Manton, an Irish city councilman, and Patrick Deignan, an Irish district leader. Outspending both opponents, Geraldine Ferraro won the nomination. Against a conservative Republican in the general election Ferraro chose to wage a campaign stressing law and order. Her slogan, "Finally, a Tough Democrat," appealed to voters, and she was elected with 54 percent of the vote.

In Congress Ferraro balanced the conservative demands of her constituency with her own feminist and liberal politics. She voted, for example, against school busing and supported tax credits for private and parochial school parents. Yet she was also a prime mover in opposing economic discrimination against housewives and working women. Ferraro easily won her re-election in 1980 and 1982 and was elected secretary of the Democratic Caucus in her second term. As secretary, she sat on the Democratic Steering and Policy Committee.

In 1982 she received an appointment to the powerful House Budget Committee, which sets national spending priorities. In the House she also served as a member of the House Committee on Public Works and Transportation. Coming from a district with two major airports close by, Ferraro was a strong advocate of air safety and noise control. As a member of the Select Committee on Aging she worked to combat crimes against the elderly and to expand health care and provide senior citizen centers. As a member of the Congressional Caucus for Women's Issues Ferraro helped lead the successful battle for passage of the Economic Equity Act and the unsuccessful campaign for the Equal Rights Amendment. She was the author of those sections of the Equity Act dealing with private pension reform and expanding retirement savings options for the elderly.

### A Leader in the Democratic Party

Ferraro continued her active role within the Democratic Party. She served as a delegate to the Democratic Party's 1982 mid-term convention and was a key member of the Hunt Commission, which developed delegate selection rules for the 1984 convention. Then, in January of 1984, Ferraro was named chair of the Democratic Party Platform Committee for the 1984 national convention.

During the years between the mid-term convention and the national convention Ferraro worked hard to achieve national recognition and to correct any impression that she lacked real foreign policy experience and expertise. In 1983 she travelled to Central America and to the Middle East, and, as nomination time approached, she talked frequently about these trips and about her other international experience, including her membership in congressional groups on United States-Soviet relations.

After a grueling series of interviews—climaxing perhaps the most thorough vice-presidential search in history—Geraldine Ferraro was chosen by Democratic presidential nominee Walter F. Mondale as his running-mate. Thus, 64 years to the day that American women won the right to vote, the first woman candidate for the vice presidency was named by a major party.

### The 1984 Campaign

Politically, Ferraro was seen to have several assets as a candidate. Democrats hoped that she would help to exploit the gender gap—that is, the clear difference in voting patterns between men and women that seemed to have emerged in the 1970s and 1980s, with women voting in greater numbers than men and voting for Democratic candidates and peace issues more consistently than men. A national poll taken in July of 1984 had reported that men favored Reagan 58 percent to 36 percent, but that women favored Mondale 49 percent to 41 percent. Widespread efforts on the part of organized feminists to register large numbers of new women voters also promised to widen the gender gap and increase the value of a woman candidate. Ferraro was also politically appealing as a candidate from a strong working-class and ethnic background and district. Democratic strategists felt it was essential for Mondale to win among such voters.

President Reagan's popularity with the voters, however, resulted in a solid re-election victory. Reagan-Bush received 59 percent of the popular vote and 525 of the 538 electoral votes; Mondale-Ferraro received only 41 percent of the popular vote and 13 electoral votes (Minnesota and the District of Columbia). Mondale was hurt most by his perceived ties to "special interests," his plan to raise taxes, and his lack of a clearly defined economic program. Ferraro's chief problem as a candidate was the investigation of her husband John Zaccaro's real estate business and tax records, begun during the campaign months.

The gender gap had not made the difference that the Democrats had hoped. Although women voted for the Democratic ticket in slightly larger numbers than men, the difference had fallen to 4.5 percentage points in 1984, from 8.5 percentage points in 1980. Instead, in one of the most polarized elections in the history of the United States, the vote split first along racial lines, with Blacks voting 91 to 9 percent for the Mondale-Ferraro ticket and whites voting 66 to 34 percent for Reagan-Bush, and secondly, along economic lines, with those making under $12,500 voting for Mondale-Ferraro 53 to 46 percent, and those in the over $35,000 range voting for Reagan-Bush 67 to 31.5 percent.

### Keeping the Liberal Faith

After Ferraro's term as a congresswoman expired in January of 1985, she wrote a book about the vice-presidential campaign. For a time, she chose to to keep a low political profile. In 1986, she passed up the opportunity to challenge Alphonse D'Amato, the incumbent Republican senator from New York. Still under public scrutiny her husband pleaded guilty to overstating his net worth in getting a loan and was sentenced to community service. Also, police affidavits surfaced detailing a 1985 meeting between Zacarro and Robert DiBernardo, a captain and porno kingpin for mob boss John Gambino. Later, Ferraro's son John, a college student, was arrested for possessing cocaine.

In 1990 Ferraro campaigned aggressively on behalf of female Democratic candidates in New York. She launched her own political comeback in 1992, when she entered the New York Democratic primary as a candidate for the Untied States Senate. Competing against three other candidates in the primary, including New York state comptroller and former congressional representative Elizabeth Holtzman, Ferraro faced a tough battle. Typically optimistic to the end, Ferraro finished second, fewer than 10,000 votes behind Holtzman, who ultimately was defeated in the general election.

Undaunted, Ferraro tested support for possible campaigns for mayor of New York City in 1997 or for Senator or governor of New York in 1998. Meanwhile, she remains true to her Liberal faith and continues to speak out for Liberal policies. In 1993, she published a book demanding more power for women. Beginning in 1996, she appeared every other week on "Crossfire," a half-hour political talk show on Cable News Network—the same show that made Pat Buchanan nationally famous. Occupying the liberal chair opposite John Sununu, President Bush's Chief of Staff, Geraldine Ferraro continued to press for increased government spending and more federal programs on behalf of those she considers "underprivileged."

## Further Reading

Most of the written work on Ferraro is in the popular press. Articles appeared in *US News and World Report* on July 16 and 23, 1984; *Time* on June 4, 1984; *MS* for July 1984; *New York Magazine* on July 16,1984; *Working Woman* for October 1984; and *McCall's* for October 1984. In 1985 she wrote, with Linda Bird Francke, *Ferraro: My Story* (Bantam Books), which was favorably reviewed.

Geraldine, Ferraro *Changing History: Women, Power, and Politics* (Moyer Bell, 1993). Lee Michael Katz, *My name is Geraldine Ferraro: An Unauthorized biography.* (New American Library, 1984). Eugene Larson, "Geraldine Ferraro," *Great Lives from History*, Frank N. Magill ed. Vol. 2. (Salem Press, 1995). Jan Russell, "Geraldine Ferraro" *Working Woman* , November 1996, pages 28-31. Linda Witt, Karen M. Paget, and Glenna Matthews. *Running as a Woman; Gender and Power in American Politics* (Free Press, 1993). ☐

# Minnie Maddern Fiske

**The first important "realistic" actress in the United States, Minnie Maddern Fiske (1865-1932) became known primarily for her portrayals of the heroines of the Norwegian playwright Ibsen.**

M innie Maddern Fiske was born Mary Augusta Davey in New Orleans on December 19, 1865. Her father was the theatrical manager Thomas Davey, and her mother, Lizzie Maddern, was an actress

whose surname the young "Minnie" adopted for her own stage name.

A true child of the theater, Minnie was brought upon the boards as an infant and continued to perform as soon as she could speak. As a child actress she drew attention as early as the age of four, when she made her first New York appearance. She ran the gamut of the so-called "infant prodigy" roles, which included that of Prince Arthur in *King John*, then gracefully graduated to those of the young ingenue by the age of 15. She starred in *Featherbrain, In Spite of All* (with Richard Mansfield), and *Fogg's Ferry*. She was happy to be pronounced a "new Lotta" by one critic for her work in the latter production, as Lotta Crabtree had been her idol.

In 1882 Fiske fell in love with and married Legrand White, a vaudeville musician. Their quarrels over the financing of *Caprice* initiated the break-up of their brief union. It was in this production that Fiske sang "In the Gloaming," popularizing the tune, and created another theatrical innovation by staying "in the setting"—that is, remaining seated by the hearth for the song rather than going to the edge of the stage, as was the custom.

At the age of 25 Fiske married Harrison Grey Fiske (1861-1942), four years her junior and the editor of the *New York Dramatic Mirror*. Harrison Fiske provided life-long support of all of his wife's theatrical ventures, serving in a variety of capacities: business manager, director, producer, dramaturg, critic. He remained her devoted "righthand man" until her death.

Upon her marriage, Fiske declared that she would give up the stage. However, she was drawn back to it four years later, after writing some of her own plays (several of which were produced) and studying a number of the socalled "new" dramas—in particular those of Ibsen, whose work was to have a profound effect upon her subsequent production and acting style. Fiske first played Nora in Ibsen's *A Doll's House* in 1894 and followed this success with the critically acclaimed *Tess of the D'Ubervilles* in 1897. The latter was performed at the only theater in New York City which was not controlled by the Syndicate, which acquired a virtual monopoly of the professional theatrical circuit both in New York and nation-wide. The Fiskes fought the Syndicate, even though it meant playing in opera and vaudeville houses and in the cruder accommodations that were afforded in burlesque halls and the basements of churches.

Finally, in 1901, the Fiskes were able to lease the Manhattan Theatre, and popular productions during their tenacy included Ibsen's *Hedda Gabler* (with Minnie in the title role), as well as his *Pillars of Society* and *Rosmersholm.* Later they produced Langdon Mitchell's *The New York Idea,* a sophisticated comedy about divorce; then Edward Sheldon's *Salvation Nell,* which included real-life slum residents in its cast and a famous ten-minute silent stare of Minnie, who portrayed the heroine.

By 1911 Fiske had sold his interest in the *Mirror* (which had been forbidden reading material for any actor who signed on with the Syndicate) and turned to producing fulltime. Fiske joined her husband in the role of producer, and they proved to be a compatible team. She also made a few adjustments of her artistic concerns and focussed the remainder of her career on classic and light contemporary comedy. Only occasionally would she return to serious roles, as she did in 1926 with a performance as Mrs. Alving in Ibsen's *Ghosts.* Stand-outs among her characterizations in her later years were as the title character in Harry James Smith's *Mrs. Bumstead-Leigh,* Mistress Page in *The Merry Wives of Windsor,* and another popular revival, Mrs. Malaprop in Sheridan's *The Rivals.*

Fiske's sensitivity was evident both on and off the stage. The intensity of her performances was such that she was easily distracted by any noise in the house and thus found it necessary to forbid the presence of babies and the eating of peanuts in her audiences. Outside of the theater she was well known for her support of the American Society for the Prevention of Cruelty to Animals, and she often cared for stray animals herself. She was devoted to a number of humane causes throughout her life, and she was a protester against the killing of animals solely for their fur, against bullfighting, and against President Theodore Roosevelt's hunting expedition to Africa. She also helped to save the egret from extinction.

Fiske has been considered to be the first important realistic actress in the United States, as she was the first major performer in the roles of Ibsen's female protagonists and implemented naturalistic detail and innovation in her interpretations of the contemporary problem play. A pioneer in "psychological realism" years before the work of Stanislavski was evident in America, Fiske was known for a naturalness and simplicity in her acting and production style which countered the stage tricks and artificiality still prevalent on the early 20th-century stage. For each role she assumed she undertook an extremely detailed character study in order to appear unstudied and simple in performance. Her skillful employment of suggestion rather than overt display taught much to the new generation of actors who worked with her and watched her perform. Her subtleties were perhaps better suited for the emerging medium of film; however, that possibility was never explored as movies with sound did not appear until Minnie Fiske's dark beauty was beginning to fade.

She remained as contrary to the so-called "star system" as she had been to the powerful Syndicate, and she emphasized the importance of ensemble work in each production. Quietly and virtually single-handedly, she ushered in a new era of theater in America. Hers was a style different from that which was popular at the time, and much of the acknowledgment of her work by other actors and many critics did not come until the end of her career. A seemingly indefatigable performer, Fiske never really retired, working right up until several months before her death on Valentine's Day, 1932.

## Further Reading

For additional information on Fiske see Archie Binns, *Mrs. Fiske and the American Theatre* (1955). □

# Ella Fitzgerald

**Ella Fitzgerald (1918-1996) was one of the most exciting jazz singers of her time and, because of the naturalness of her style, had a popular appeal that extended far beyond the borders of jazz.**

Ella Fitzgerald was born on April 25, 1918, in Newport News, Virginia, but spent her formative years in Yonkers, New York, and received her musical education in its public schools. When only 16, she received her first big break at the Apollo Theater in Harlem, when she won an amateur night contest and impressed saxophonist-bandleader Benny Carter. He recommended her to drummer-bandleader Chick Webb, who hired her in 1935. She soon became a recording star with the band, and her own composition "A-tisket, A-tasket" (1938) was such a smash hit that the song became her trademark for many years thereafter. When Webb died in 1939, Fitzgerald assumed leadership of the band for the next year.

By 1940 Fitzgerald was recognized throughout the music world as a vocal marvel—a singer with clarity of tone, flexibility of range, fluency of rhythm, and, above all, a talent for improvisation that was equally effective on ballads and up-tempo tunes. Although for a long time her reputation with musicians and other singers outstripped that with the general public, she corrected the imbalance soon after joining Norman Granz's Jazz at the Philharmonic (JATP) in

1946. She made annual tours with the group and was invariably the concert favorite. Three of her unfailing show-stoppers were "Oh, Lady Be Good," "Stomping at the Savoy," and "How High the Moon." Each would begin at a medium tempo and then turn into a rhythmic excursion as Fitzgerald moved up-tempo and "scatted" (that is, sang harmonic variations of the melody in nonsense syllables). The huge JATP crowds always responded tumultuously.

By the early 1950s Fitzgerald's domination of fans' and critics' polls was absolute. In fact, she won the *Down Beat* readers' poll every year from 1953 to 1970 and became known as "The First Lady of Song." In 1955 she terminated her 20-year recording affiliation with Decca in order to record for Norman Granz's Verve label and proceeded to produce a series of superlative "Songbook" albums, each devoted to the compositions of a great songwriter or song-writing team (Jerome Kern and Johnny Mercer; George and Ira Gershwin; Cole Porter; Richard Rodgers and Lorenz Hart; Irving Berlin; Duke Ellington). The lush orchestrations induced Fitzgerald to display the classy pop-singer side of herself; even in the two-volume Ellington set her jazzier side deferred to the melodist in her.

Under Granz's personal management Fitzgerald also began to play choice hotel jobs and made her first featured film appearance, in "Pete Kelly's Blues" (1955). In 1957 she worked at the Copacabana in New York City and gave concerts at the Hollywood Bowl. In 1958, in the company of the Duke Ellington Orchestra, she gave a concert at Carnegie Hall as part of an extended European and United States tour with the band. In the early 1960s she continued to work the big hotel circuit—the Flamingo in Las Vegas, the Fairmont Hotel in San Francisco, and the Americana in New York City—and to tour Europe, Latin America, and Japan with the Oscar Peterson trio, which was three-fourths of Granz's JATP house rhythm section. In 1965 and 1966 she was reunited with Ellington for another tour and record date.

Fitzgerald was always blessed with superb accompanists, from the full orchestral support of Chick Webb and Duke Ellington to the smaller JATP ensembles. In 1968 she teamed up with yet another, the magnificent pianist Tommy Flanagan, who headed a trio that served her into the mid-1970s. In 1971 Fitzgerald had serious eye surgery, but within a year she was performing again. Her singing, however, began to show evidence of decline: the voice that was once an instrument of natural luster and effortless grace became a trifle thin and strained. Nevertheless, so great was her artistry that she continued to excite concert audiences and to record effectively. She appeared after the mid-1960s with over 50 symphonic orchestras in the United States.

A large, pleasant-looking woman with a surprisingly girlish speaking voice, Ella Fitzgerald had a propensity for forgetting lyrics. This endeared her to audiences, who delighted in her ability to work her way out of these selfpainted corners. Unlike some other great jazz singers (Billie Holiday, Anita O'Day), Fitzgerald had a private life devoid of drug-related notoriety. She was twice married: the first marriage, to Bernie Kornegay in 1941, was annulled two years later; the second, to bassist Ray Brown in 1948, ended in divorce in 1952 (they had one son).

Was Ella Fitzgerald essentially a jazz singer or a pop singer? Jazz purists say that she lacked the emotional depth of Billie Holiday, the imagination of Sarah Vaughan or Anita O'Day, and the blues-based power of Dinah Washington and that she was often facile, glossy, and predictable. The criticisms sprang partly from her "crossover" popularity and ignored her obvious strengths and contributions: Fitzgerald was not only one of the pioneers of scatsinging, but, beyond that, she was an unpretentious singer whose harmonic variations were always unforced and a supreme melodist who never let her ego get in the way of any song she sang.

Fitzgerald died on June 15, 1996 at the age of 78. She left a legacy that won't soon be forgotten. In her lifetime she was honored with no less than 12 Grammys, the Kennedy Center Award, as well as an honorary doctorate in music from Yale University. In 1992 she was honored by President George Bush with the National Medal of Freedom. Fitzgerald's impressive financial estate was left in a trust, including the $2.5 million in proceeds from the sale of her Beverly Hills home.

## Further Reading

There is no biography of Ella Fitzgerald, but there are excellent chapters on her in Leonard Feather's *From Satchmo to Miles* (1972) and Henry Pleasants' *The Great American Popular Singers* (1974). Also see *Jet* (December 28, 1992). □

# Frances FitzGerald

**Frances FitzGerald (born 1940) wrote one of the most influential books on the Vietnam War to appear while the conflict was still in progress.**

Frances FitzGerald was not quite 32 years of age when her first book, *Fire in the Lake: The Vietnamese and the Americans in Vietnam* (1972), was published to immediate and extraordinary praise. *Fire in the Lake* was hailed for its "stunning clarity" by one reviewer and as "one of the best descriptions and analyses of Vietnam ever published in English" by another. *TIME* magazine was impressed that she had achieved "so fresh a blend of compassion and intelligence," and even the conservative *National Review*, which loathed it, predicted accurately that her book would "become gospel for the anti-war movement."

The young woman whose career had just taken such a remarkable turn was a journalist with a remarkable family and personal background. Her father, Desmond FitzGerald, was a deputy director of the Central Intelligence Agency (CIA) and an expert on Southeast Asia. Her mother, Mary Endicott Peabody FitzGerald Tree, was a former American ambassador to the United Nations. FitzGerald herself had graduated from Radcliffe College with a BA, *magna cum laude,* in 1962. Five years later she won the first of many honors, an Overseas Press Club award for best interpretation of foreign affairs.

FitzGerald prepared herself for the work to come by visiting Vietnam twice as a free-lance journalist, for a total of 16 months, and by studying Chinese and Vietnamese history and culture under Paul Mus, to whom, as also to the memory of her father, she would dedicate *Fire in the Lake*. Its publication resulted not only in superb reviews but in a whole series of honors including a Pulitzer Prize for contemporary affairs writing, a National Book Award, and the Bancroft Prize for historical writing—all in 1973. The Vietnam War was still strongly affecting America's political and cultural life at this time, and a good book on it was bound to win unusual attention. The Bancroft Prize, for example, is normally given to a professional scholar rather than a journalist.

But while the times partly explain her book's success, FitzGerald had earned it also, not by disclosing new information, but by viewing Vietnam from a different perspective. More than half of her book was devoted to explaining how the National Liberation Front (NLF or the Viet Cong, to most Americans) had adapted itself to Vietnam's unique culture and traditions. As she explained it, Marxism did not clash with local values. Rather, it was highly compatible with Confucianism, the basis of Vietnam's way of life, with the Communist party replacing the emperor as the source of wisdom and leadership. FitzGerald greatly admired the NLF. Although she acknowledged that it had committed atrocities and that land "reform" in North Vietnam entailed considerable brutality, she minimized the NLF's actions. Her book is not even-handed by any means, but for a work of advocacy is reliable.

Nevertheless, *Fire in the Lake* is a partisan book that aims to show the NLF in the best possible light. Despite admitted shortcomings, the Communists are portrayed as fundamentally decent, faithful, and true lovers of the peasantry and champions of the people. At one point FitzGerald says that in NLF controlled areas farm production actually rose. This might well have been true in selected cases, but North Vietnam, had crippled agriculture by ruthlessly imposing collective farming upon their unhappy peasants. That this would happen in South Vietnam too when the Communists won was a foregone conclusion.

Critics also resented her argument that because free elections have no place in Vietnamese culture, the absence of them means nothing. People who honor authoritarian regimes have always argued, as FitzGerald did, that voting is not a part of the national heritage in question, or that decisions are arrived at by consensus, making disputed elections unnecessary. FitzGerald pointed out that in South Vietnam the Communists were trying to attract support and respected local sentiments accordingly. What she didn't say, and perhaps did not believe, was that in North Vietnam, where the Communists were in power, they ignored public opinion. In 1973 the North's present was the South's future, a tragedy for both regions.

FitzGerald devoted the other half of her book to the evils of South Vietnam's various anti-Communist regimes and the folly of America's support for them. American intervention in South Vietnam was a ghastly mistake, not because the NLF was a band of political saints, but because, owing to the outrageous corruption and incompetence of the ruling elite in Saigon, there was no way to save the country.

FitzGerald's next book, *America Revised: History Textbooks in the Twentieth Century* (1979), is a trenchant critique of this debased educational medium, though to some readers it appeared that what FitzGerald objected to most was that textbooks did not give what she saw as the correct version of American history. The contrary objection was raised by her third book, *Cities on a Hill: A Journey Through Contemporary American Cultures* (1987), which described four different communities ranging from a retirement village in Florida to the followers of Bhagwan Shree Rajneesh in Oregon. Though her intent was to explore the effect of the 1960s on American culture, some critics held that while her book was delightfully descriptive, as analysis it did not seem to go anywhere.

Thus, in the years after *Fire in the Lake* appeared FitzGerald continued to write, producing books that invariably strike reviewers as well-written and thoughtful.

### Further Reading

For additional FitzGerald writing on Vietnam see "Life and Death of a Vietnamese Village," *New York Times Magazine* (September 4, 1966) and "The Tragedy of Saigon," *Atlantic Monthly* (December 1966). Probably the best full-length book on the Vietnamese conflict is Stanley Karnow's *Vietnam: A History* (1983). □

# Hallie Flanagan

**Hallie Flanagan (1890-1969) was a director, playwright, and educator who headed the Federal Theater Project, America's first national, federally-funded theater organization, from 1935 to 1939.**

Born in South Dakota on August 27, 1890, and raised in Iowa, Hallie Flanagan attended Grinnell College where she subsequently taught drama. She first gained notice as a playwright when she won a regional contest sponsored by the Des Moines Little Theatre Society with her play *The Curtain*. Her successful productions at Grinnell College eventually led her in 1923 to a position as production assistant in Professor George Pierce Baker's creative Workshop 47 at Harvard University, where she also completed a Master's degree. Returning to Grinnell, she directed for its experimental theater. Her productions there continued to win her recognition as an innovative director and led to her appointment as professor of drama and director of the experimental theater at Vassar College in 1925. A year later she received a prestigious honor—a grant from the Guggenheim Foundation (the first to be awarded to a woman).

On the Guggenheim fellowship Flanagan travelled to Europe and the U.S.S.R. to observe the exciting new developments on the continental stage of the early 1920s and wrote of her experiences in *Shifting Scenes of the Modern European Theatre* (1928). Besides being stimulated by the modernist experiments in staging that she saw in Europe, Flanagan was also strongly influenced by European dramatic forms and themes steeped in folklore, mythology, and history—the classic theater of Greece, popular puppet shows, robust folk plays, expansive verse dramas. In particular, the theaters of the Russian directors Vsevolod Meyerhold and Alexander Tairov impressed Flanagan with their vitality and strength and solidified her own goals to create theater that truly responded to and challenged its audience.

Returning to Vassar in 1926, Flanagan began to put these varied ideas and influences into practice and to build Vassar Theatre's reputation as one of the nation's leading experimental stages. The repertoire at the theater was richly diverse, ranging from contemporary plays dealing with current topics to experiments in form to classic texts daringly reinterpreted for the present. One of Flanagan's most celebrated productions was *Can You Hear Their Voices?* (1931). Co-authored by Flanagan and Margaret Ellen Clifford, the play was a carefully documented dramatization of a recent Arkansas drought that was controversial in both form and content as it revealed a rural world of hunger and privation neglected by governmental bureaucracy. Flanagan remained at Vassar until 1942, at which time she left for a similar teaching and directing position at Smith College in Massachusetts. She retired from academia in 1955.

Undoubtedly, Flanagan's greatest contribution to American theater was as director of the Federal Theater Project from 1935 to 1939. As a program of the Works Progress Administration, the Federal Theater Project was the first nation-wide, federally-sponsored theater in the United States. It was created to provide employment to professional theater artists in socially useful jobs during a time of severe economic depression. Committed to theater that serves as a dynamic artistic and social force for people, Flanagan sought to make the Federal Theater Project a regionally-rooted, popular, educational art theater that reached the entire nation. In many respects, Flanagan succeeded.

At its peak the Federal Theater employed over 10,000 people; operated theaters in 40 states; published a nationally distributed theater magazine; conducted a play and research bureau that served not only its own theaters but 20,000 schools, churches, and community theaters throughout the country; charged admission for less than 35 percent of its performances; and played to audiences totalling many millions.

Flanagan organized an ambitious program of classic and modern plays, dance drama, musical comedy, children's plays, religious plays, marionette shows, and series of plays by established playwrights and by young, new dramatists. Critical reaction to the artistic quality of the project's work grew increasingly positive beginning in 1936.

One of the Federal Theater's major achievements was the Living Newspaper, a compact, cinematic production style that dramatized immediate social and economic issues such as agriculture, flood control, and housing. *Triple A Plowed Under, Power,* and *One-Third of a Nation* represent pioneer productions in this art form.

Other important programs of the project included the development of a Black theater which presented significant productions of *Macbeth, Haiti,* and *The Swing Mikado;* classical revivals of miracle and morality plays and numerous Elizabethan productions; an international cycle of plays from Euripides to Ibsen; simultaneous production in 21 cities of Sinclair Lewis' anti-Fascist *It Can't Happen Here;* nation-wide productions of plays by Elmer Rice, Eugene O'Neill, and George Bernard Shaw; and regional productions such as *The Sun Rises in the West* in Los Angeles and *The Lost Colony* in North Carolina which were specifically geared to speak to local concerns and history.

Following Flanagan's vision of theater as an arena for vital exchange between artists and audiences, the Federal Theater was clearly a people's theater addressing national and regional issues in powerful, dramatic terms. Indeed, its consistently candid questioning of economic policies, especially in the Living Newspapers, ultimately brought the project criticism from witnesses before the House Committee on Un-American Activities and before the subcommittee of the House Committee on Appropriations. Although all major film, stage, and radio organizations as well as many community and sponsoring agencies spoke in favor of the Federal Theater, the Congress heatedly debated the continuation of the project. The House voted to dissolve the theater; the Senate voted to maintain it. On June 30, 1939, the Federal Theater was ended by congressional action.

Throughout her career Hallie Flanagan was a prolific contributor on the subject of theater to many leading American journals. She died in 1969.

## Further Reading

Besides *Shifting Scenes of the Modern European Theatre* (1928), Flanagan's own books on the theatre include *Dynamo* (1943), an account of her work with the Vassar Experimental Theater, and *Arena* (1940), a personal chronicle of the joys and struggles of the Federal Theater Project. Jane DeHart Mathews' *The Federal Theatre 1935-1939: Plays, Relief, and Politics* (1967) is an excellent study of the project's brief history as a national institution.

## Additional Sources

Bentley, Joanne, *Hallie Flanagan: a life in the American theatre,* New York: Knopf: Distributed by Random House, 1988. □

# Alice Cunningham Fletcher

**The American anthropologist Alice Cunningham Fletcher (1838-1923) was a pioneer in the scholarly development and professional organization of the discipline of anthropology in the United States.**

Born in Cuba of American parents on March 15, 1838, Alice Fletcher was privately educated and traveled widely in her youth before settling near Boston. Her interest in North American archeology and ethnology began prior to 1880, when she became informally associated with the Peabody Museum of Harvard University. In 1886 she was listed among the official personnel of the museum. She specialized in the ethnology of the Omaha Indians and other Plains Indian tribes, contributed to the early study of comparative ethnomusicology, and sought to justify aspects of Federal Indian policy of the late 19th century on the basis of anthropological theory.

Fletcher's first field work was undertaken in 1881, when on a camping trip with a missionary party she visited some Native American settlements in Nebraska and South Dakota. She then took up concentrated research of the Omaha tribe, who remained her primary interest, although she studied other Plains groups and published important works on them. Her best-known work, *The Omaha Tribe* (1911), was written with the assistance of Francis La Flesche, an educated member of the tribe.

## Scholarly and Professional Activities

Fletcher's concern for the welfare of Native Americans preceded her serious study of ethnology. She believed that private property, agrarian economic pursuits, and assimilation into white society would quickly alleviate their socioeconomic distress. These convictions were bolstered by the cultural evolutionary theories current in her day and led her to justify "scientifically" and to promote vigorously the Omaha Allotment Act of 1882 and the General Allotment Act of 1887, which divided reservations into small, subsistence family farmsteads. Ironically, the measures in which Alice Fletcher placed so much faith further complicated the problems Native Americans faced, obstructing them in efforts to make rational adaptations of their land resources to opportunities offered by an increasingly industrialized society based on corporate rather than individual enterprise.

At a time when many professions were reluctant to accept women, prominent anthropologists were convinced that women were equally necessary to their discipline to obtain complete and accurate accounts of different societies. This cordiality extended to organizational activities as well. Alice Fletcher, for example, had charge of the Native American exhibit of the New Orleans Industrial Exposition of 1884-1885. In 1893, on the occasion of the World's Columbian Exposition in Chicago, she and several other women participated on equal terms with their male colleagues in the special Anthropological Congress. Matilda Stevenson had founded the Women's Anthropological Society in 1885, and Miss Fletcher served as president in 1893. This group disbanded in 1899, when the members were admitted to the heretofore all-male Anthropological Society of Washington, and by 1903 Alice Fletcher was president of the Washington society. Even earlier, in 1896, she had been vice president of the prestigious American Association for the Advancement of Science. In 1905 she served as president of the American Folklore Society. She died in Washington, D.C., on April 6, 1923.

## Further Reading

Alice Fletcher's correspondence and other papers are deposited in the archives of the Bureau of American Ethnology, Smithsonian Institution, Washington, D.C. An extensive account of Fletcher is in the chapter by Nancy Oestreich Lurie, "Women in Early American Anthropology," in June Helm, ed., *Pioneers of American Anthroplogy* (1966), which compares her career with those of Erminnie Platt Smith, Matilda Stevenson, Zelia Nuttall, Frances Densmore, and Elsie Clews Parsons. J. O. Brew, *One Hundred Years of Anthropology* (1968), is recommended for general background.

## Additional Sources

Mark, Joan T., *A stranger in her native land: Alice Fletcher and the American Indians,* Lincoln: University of Nebraska Press, 1988. □

# Elizabeth Gurley Flynn

**Elizabeth Gurley Flynn (1890-1964) devoted her life to the cause of the working class. She organized workers, defended the civil liberties of radicals, and was a leading figure in socialist and communist circles.**

Elizabeth Gurley Flynn was born in Concord, New Hampshire, on August 7, 1890, to Thomas and Annie Gurley Flynn. From her parents she absorbed principles of socialism and feminism that would inform the rest of her life. After several moves, in 1900 the family settled in the Bronx in New York City, where Flynn attended public schools. At the age of 16 she gave her first public address to the Harlem Socialist Club, where she spoke on "What Socialism Will Do for Women." Her striking appearance and dynamic oratory made her an enormously popular speaker. Upon her arrest for blocking traffic during one of her soapbox speeches she was expelled from high school, and in 1907 she began full-time organizing for the Industrial Workers of the World (IWW).

In the IWW Flynn met Jack Archibold Jones, a miner and organizer, and they married in 1908. The marriage lasted little more than two years, during which their work separated them for much of the time. Their first child died shortly after its premature birth in 1909; the second, Fred, was born in 1910. Motherhood did not interrupt Flynn's career; she moved back to the Bronx, where her mother and sister cared for her son while she travelled on behalf of workers. Flynn did not remarry, but she carried on a long love affair with Italian anarchist Carlo Tresca, who lived with the Flynn family in New York.

Flynn's efforts for the IWW took her all over the United States, where she led organizing campaigns among garment workers in Minersville, Pennsylvania; silk weavers in Patterson, New Jersey; hotel and restaurant workers in New York City; miners in Minnesota's Mesabi Iron Range; and textile workers in the famous Lawrence, Massachusetts, strike of 1912. She spoke in meeting halls, at factory gates, and on

street corners in cities and towns across the country from Spokane, Washington, to Tampa, Florida. As she participated in the IWW campaigns against laws restricting freedom of speech she was arrested ten times or more, but was never convicted.

Many of the workers whom Flynn sought to organize were women and children, and Flynn combined her class-based politics with recognition of the particular oppression women experienced because of their sex. She criticized male chauvinism in the IWW and pressed the union to be more sensitive to the needs and interests of working class women. She was a strong supporter of birth control, and she reproached the IWW for not agitating more on that issue. While Flynn considered the women's suffrage movement largely irrelevant to working-class women and opposed mobilization of workers on its behalf as diversionary and divisive, she believed that women should have the right to vote and never opposed suffrage publicly as did some of her colleagues. Her feminist consciousness grew when she joined the Heterodoxy Club, a group of independent women who met regularly to discuss issues of concern to women.

By the later 1910s Flynn was devoting more and more of her time to defending workers' rights, which came under intensive attack during and after World War I. She was a founding member of the American Civil Liberties Union (ACLU) and chaired the Workers Defense Union and its successor, International Labor Defense. Besides making speeches, Flynn visited political prisoners, raised money, hired lawyers, arranged meetings, and wrote publicity on behalf of dozens of radicals, including Sacco and Vanzetti, whose defense went on for seven years.

In 1926 Flynn's health failed, and she spent the next ten years recovering in Portland, Oregon, where she lived with Dr. Marie Equi, an IWW activist and birth control agitator. In 1936 Flynn returned to New York and joined the Communist Party, on which she would focus her work for the rest of her life. Although she had announced her new affiliation to the ACLU and had been elected unanimously to a three-year term on its executive board, in the wake of the Nazi-Soviet pact of 1940 the ACLU expelled her for her party membership.

During World War II Flynn organized and wrote for the party with a special emphasis on women's affairs and ran on its ticket for congressman-at-large from New York. She joined other women leaders in advocating equal economic opportunity and pay for women and the establishment of day care centers and publicized women's contributions to the war effort. Fully supporting the war effort, she favored the draft of women and urged Americans to buy savings stamps and to re-elect Franklin D. Roosevelt in 1944. Flynn rose in party circles and was elected to its national board.

With other Communist leaders, Flynn fell victim to the anti-Communist hysteria that suffused the United States after the war. After a nine-month trial in 1952, she was convicted under the Smith Act of conspiring to teach and advocate the overthrow of the United States government. During her prison term from January 1955 to May 1957 at the women's federal penitentiary at Alderson, West Virginia, she wrote, took notes on prison life, and participated in the integration of a cottage composed of African-American women. Upon her release Flynn resumed party work and became national chairman in 1961. She made several trips to the Soviet Union. Falling ill on her last visit, she died there on September 5, 1964, and was given a state funeral in Red Square.

## Further Reading

Flynn published two books about her life: *The Rebel Girl, An Autobiography: My First Life* (1906-1926; revised edition, 1973) and *The Alderson Story: My Life as a Political Prisoner* (1955). A summary of Flynn's IWW and labor defense activities can be found in Rosalyn Fraad Baxandall, "Elizabeth Gurley Flynn: The Early Years," in *Radical America* (January-February 1975). The following books provide discussions of Flynn in the context of women activists and labor radicals: Melvyn Dubofsky, *We Shall Be All: A History of the Industrial Workers of the World* (1969); Meredith Tax, *The Rising of the Women: Feminist Solidarity and Class Conflict, 1880-1917* (1980); and June Sochen, *Movers and Shakers: American Women Thinkers and Activists, 1900-1970* (1973).

## Additional Sources

Camp, Helen C., *Iron in her soul: Elizabeth Gurley Flynn and the American Left,* Pullman, Wash.: WSU Press, 1995. □

# Jane Fonda

**Jane Fonda (born 1937) was a member of a famous American theatrical family and recipient of the industry's highest awards. Her numerous radical activities during the period of the Vietnam War brought animosity from some and adoration from others. In the post-Vietnam era, her multi-faceted career included films, television, exercise videocassettes, and writing.**

Jane Fonda, her father Henry, and her brother Peter comprise the "Fantastic Fondas" of the theater. Jane was born in New York City on December 21, 1937, to Henry and Frances Seymour Brokaw Fonda. Born into wealth, her maternal lineage can be traced to the American Revolution leader Samuel Adams. She herself became something of a revolutionary.

When Fonda was 13 her mother committed suicide after learning of her husband's interest in a much younger woman, Susan Blanchard. Told that her mother died from a sudden heart attack, Fonda learned the truth a year later from a magazine story. Both she and Peter had difficulty coping, although Fonda believes Blanchard, whom her father married, did much to provide a stable home life for them. Fonda attended schools in New York and Vassar College, where she admittedly "went wild." Thereafter, she

engaged in a whirlwind of studies in Paris and New York. Her first stage appearance was in 1954, but she did not seriously decide on an acting career until four years later while visiting her father, who lived next door to Lee Strasberg, director of the Actors Studio in Malibu, California. Friends urged her to go into the profession; Strasberg accepted her as his student, and she paid for her acting lessons with a brief but successful modeling career.

Fonda probably inherited some theatrical genius; certainly hers was a meteoric rise to stardom. A number of persons influenced her career, including her godfather, Joshua Logan, first husband, Roger Vadim, and director Sidney Pollock. She received many of the industry's highest awards, including two Academy Awards for Best Actress (*Klute,* 1971, and *Coming Home,* 1979). Both came before her famous father received one and after she was a controversial figure for her lifestyle, her rejection of many American traditional beliefs, and her outspoken anti-Vietnam War views.

Fonda became a heroine of the New Left for her activities in such causes as constitutional rights for American servicemen, Black Panthers, Native American rights, the Vietnam War, the anti-nuclear movement, and women's rights. Her life reflected the uncertainties, confusion, and rapidly changing values which began to rock America in the mid-1960s. To many she seemed mercurial, contradictory, and driven as the fighter for justice and peace. To others, she was naive, irritating, and an anti-American fool. Her causes were so numerous and undiscriminating that Saul Alinsky, fellow American radical, claimed that Fonda was "a hitchhiker on the highway of causes."

Fonda's first act of civil disobedience came in 1970 when she was arrested for illegally talking to soldiers against the military. Her radicalization was completed by what she saw and the people she met on a cross-country journey. Having left California as a left-wing liberal, she arrived in New York where she announced that she was a revolutionary woman, ready to support all struggles that were radical.

Fonda's support and fund-raising for the sometimes violent Black Panthers, including her relationship with Panther leader Huey Newton, led the FBI to place her under surveillance. Meanwhile, many differences with her father became public. As a life-long liberal, he sympathized with many of her views, but emphatically rejected her methods. Jane, in turn, rejected his idea that changes could be effected by electing the right officials into public office.

As her activities increased, government surveillance grew to at least six agencies at one time. Returning from Canada, she was infuriated when U.S. customs officials in Cleveland confiscated vials thought to be drugs. They proved to be vitamins and non-prescription food concentrates which she used to stabilize her weight.

Critics decried Fonda's exaggerations of American atrocities in Vietnam, which even supporters admitted were inflated. Many were astonished when she spoke as if she had visited Vietnam and witnessed the horrors she described. Ultimately, supporters arranged for her to go to Hanoi. When she publicly denounced American involvement there, she was labeled a "Communist" and "Hanoi

Jane" by many back home. The State Department rebuked her, letters of protest filled newspapers, and at least one congressman demanded her arrest for treason. Yet Fonda seemed unperturbed by it all.

As the Vietnam War was ending, Fonda's radicalism diminished. Reconciliation with her father came in the early 1980s as they filmed *On Golden Pond,* a story which paralleled their own relationship in many ways. By the mid-1980s Fonda's popularity in films and television was such that to speak ill of her in Hollywood was to invite professional suicide. Her exercise salon, books, and videotapes became so popular that she may be remembered as much for them as for her films.

By 1985 she rarely spoke for radical causes. Rather, she seemed to have mellowed considerably. On a *CBS Morning News* television program she spoke of a new spiritual awareness during the filming of *Agnes of God,* and on CBS's *America* her comments and dress were quite subdued as she "plugged" her latest exercise videotape. She had moved from the radical to the respectable Jane Fonda.

Her personal life seemed stable as she and husband, former activist Tom Hayden, lived with her daughter Vanessa and their son Troy. Hayden sought a Senate seat from California in 1986, apparently both thinking that changes could be made by electing the "right" officials. Although her interests seemed to lie with her multi-faceted career and family, it seemed likely that Fonda could return to her former radical activism if she perceived that conditions demanded it.

In 1988 the "Hanoi Jane" issue raised its head again during filming of *Stanley and Iris,* which was being shot in a small Connecticut town. Old resentments among the townspeople about Fonda's role in Vietnam flared, leading her to issue her first public apology for her activities during the Vietnam War. She admitted that she'd been misinformed about aspects of the war, as well as some of her other causes at the time.

Fonda and Hayden were divorced in 1989. In 1991 she married media mogul Ted Turner, and settled into a much more domestic phase of her life. She announced that she was leaving her film career behind, and in 1996 confirmed that statement in a *Good Housekeeping* interview: "After a 35-year career as an actress, I am out of the business. That's a big change. Work, in many ways, defined me." Although she left behind her acting and producing career, Fonda was far from idle. In 1996 she published a cookbook, *Jane Fonda: Cooking for Healthy Living.* She also created a new series of workout tapes with the help of a physiologist called *The Personal Trainer Series.* Her goal with the new series was to design a program that anyone could stick with, stating in *Good Housekeeping,* "Anybody can do 25 minutes."

## Further Reading

Although both are unauthorized biographies, *Jane Fonda: The Actress in Her Time* by Fred L. Guiles (1982) and *Jane: An Intimate Biography of Jane Fonda* (1973) by Thomas Kiernan provide interesting additional insights into the life of Jane Fonda and the sub-title of each accurately describes the contents. James Brough's *The Fabulous Fondas* (1973) gives considerable attention to Jane's life, but she shares space there with her father Henry and brother Peter. Also see Christopher Anderson's *Citizen Jane: The Turbulent Life of Jane Fonda* (1990) and *Good Housekeeping* (February 1996, page 24) ☐

# Dian Fossey

**Dian Fossey (1932-1985) was the world's leading authority on the mountain gorilla before her murder, probably at the hands of poachers, in December of 1985.**

Dian Fossey's short life was characterized in equal parts by tragedy, controversy, and extraordinary courage and dedication to the animals she made her life work. That dedication drew her back to Africa over and over despite broken bones, failing health, and threats to her life. All and all, she spent 18 years studying the mountain gorillas and working for their survival as a species.

An unlikely chain of circumstances led Fossey to study the mountain gorilla and to her eventual demise high in the fog enshrouded mountains of eastern Africa. Born in San Francisco on January 16, 1932, Fossey was fascinated with animals from an early age. She entered the University of California at Davis to study pre-veterinary medicine but found it difficult to master courses in chemistry and physics. Instead she completed a B.A. in 1954 from San Jose State University in occupational therapy. In 1956 she took a job at Kosair Crippled Children's Hospital in Louisville, Kentucky, where she could pursue her interest in horses during her free time.

In 1963 Fossey obtained a bank loan for $8,000, took a leave from her job as a physical therapist, and went to Africa to seek out paleontologist Louis Leakey, who had mentored Jane Goodall in her pioneering work with chimpanzees. She hoped that Leakey could help her find a job studying gorillas. Later in her life Fossey explained this change in her life course by saying that she felt extraordinarily drawn to Africa and particularly to the mountain gorillas of Rwanda and Zaire (now Congo). This interest was fueled in part by reading the work of George Schaller, who had spent 1959 doing the first comprehensive study of these animals.

Fossey appeared at Leakey's dig site at Olduvai Gorge in Tanzania without an invitation. He mistook her for a tourist and charged a fee to view the excavation. Despite this inauspicious beginning, Fossey clearly made an impression. Nearly six feet tall, with long black hair and a husky voice—the result of chain smoking—she must have been a startling apparition. While walking through the site, she tripped and fell, breaking her ankle and a newly excavated fossil in the process. Leakey's wife Mary bound up her ankle and she proceeded onwards to the mountains of Zaire (now Congo), where she caught her first glimpse of the mountain gorilla.

Her funds exhausted, Fossey returned to Louisville and to her job. In 1966 it was Leakey who sought her out. He wanted her to study the gorillas on a long-term basis and had found a patron who would support the research. Leakey was interested in studies of primates because he believed their behavior would shed light on the behavior of the early hominids whose fossilized bones he was excavating at Olduvai Gorge. He believed that Fossey would be an ideal person to carry out the study because of her intense interest and because he thought that women were more patient and better observers than men and, therefore, made better naturalists.

Fossey accepted Leakey's invitation eagerly. Since she had no formal training she made a brief stop at Jane Goodall's research center at Gombe to learn Goodall's revolutionary methods of fieldwork and data collection. She then proceeded onward to Schaller's old camp in Congo.

The gorillas that Fossey was to study inhabit a narrow strip of forest that covers the sides of several extinct volcanoes on the borders between Rwanda, Congo, and Uganda. Much of their habitat is rain forest at an altitude of 10,000 feet or more. The mountain gorillas can be distinguished from other types of gorillas partly by their adaptions to the climate and altitude: thick coats, broad chests, and large hands and feet. Mature males stand between five and six feet when upright and far outweigh a human being of equivalent size.

Fossey's research in Congo was interrupted July 10, 1967, when she was held for two weeks by soldiers. After escaping from her captors, she relocated to the Rwanda side of the mountains in the Parc National des Vulcans. This would become the Karasoke Research Center where she would carry out her work for the next 17 years.

At Karasoke Fossey studied 51 gorillas in four relatively stable groups. Despite their menacing appearance, Fossey found the gorillas to be quite shy and retiring. She gained their trust through quiet and patient observation and by imitating the gorillas' behavior until she could sit amongst them and could move about or touch the animals without frightening them.

When Fossey first began her research, the number of these gorillas was less than 500 and rapidly diminishing due to the encroachment of farmers and predation from poachers. She was particularly distressed by the practice of killing an entire group of adult gorillas in order to obtain young gorillas to be sold to zoos. In 1978, after the death of Digit, one of her most beloved silverback males, she began taking up unconventional means to protect the gorillas from poachers and from encroaching cattle farmers. She held poachers prisoner, torturing them or frightening them or kidnapping their children, with the idea that this would give them a sense of what gorillas were experiencing at their hands.

On December 24, 1985, Fossey was killed in her cabin at Karasoke, her skull split by a *panga,* the type of large knife used by poachers. Her murderer has not been identified.

## Further Reading

Fossey has described her own work in *Gorillas in the Mist* (1983). A film of the same name was released in 1988 starring Sigourney Weaver. Biographical information can be found in Farley Mowat's *Woman in the Mists* (1987), Sy Montgomery's *Walking with the Great Apes* (1991), and Donna Haraway's *Primate Visions* (1989). Fossey also wrote a number of articles for *National Geographic Magazine* . Additional information on gorillas can be found in Allan Goodall's *The Wandering Gorillas* (1979) and Michael Nichols' *Struggle for Survival in the Virungas* (1989). □

# Abigail Kelley Foster

**American reformer Abigail Kelley Foster (1810-1887) was a pioneer in the abolitionist movement and contributed to the developing suffragist principles of her time.**

The daughter of Irish Quakers, Abby Kelley was born in Pelham, Mass., on Jan. 15, 1810. She was raised in Worcester and educated at the Friends' School in Providence, R.I. She became a schoolteacher and showed gifts of eloquence and public presence. Abolitionists William Lloyd Garrison and Theodore D. Weld urged her to join their cause. In 1837 she became an antislavery lecturer—the first woman to do so after the Grimké sisters, and the first woman to face mixed and often hostile audiences under the same conditions as men.

Though denounced and ridiculed, Kelley entered alien environments in Connecticut and Pennsylvania, meeting antagonism with oratorical power and a firm grasp of her subject. As a symbol of Garrisonian extremism, she roused criticism among moderate abolitionists who were outraged by Garrison's determination to involve women in decision making. At the 1840 annual meeting of the American Anti-Slavery Society in New York, Kelley was elected to the business committee. At this point the moderates withdrew to form the rival American and Foreign Anti-Slavery Society.

In 1845 Miss Kelley married Stephen Symonds Foster. He too had endured many mob actions, was noted for his denunciations of slavery, and had authored *The Brotherhood of Thieves: A True Picture of the American Church and Clergy* (1843). The couple was honored by James Russell Lowell in his ''Letter from Boston'' (1846). Lowell, like others, had noticed the contrast between their personal mildness and decorum and the violent language they employed in public address.

Such was Abby's reputation that as late as 1850 the managers of the Woman's Rights Convention doubted whether she should be allowed onto the platform. When she appeared, she began with the words, ''Sisters, bloody feet have worn smooth the path by which you come here!''

The Fosters settled on a farm near Worcester and, though engaged in rural pursuits, maintained their war against social discriminations. They refused to pay taxes to a state which deprived Abby of her right to the vote, and twice they had their property sold at auction to satisfy that debt. The friends who purchased back the farm for them were ultimately reimbursed. Their last cause was in helping get passage of the 15th Amendment to the Constitution, which gave the vote to former slaves, though not to women. Abby, surviving her husband, died on Jan. 14, 1887.

## Further Reading

Information on Abby Foster is in Inez H. Irwin, *Angels and Amazons: A Hundred Years of American Women* (1933); Lillian O'Connor, *Pioneer Women Orators: Rhetoric in the Ante-Bellum Reform Movement* (1954); and Alma Lutz, *Crusade for Freedom: Women of the Antislavery Movement* (1968). □

# Helen Frankenthaler

**The American painter Helen Frankenthaler (born 1928) was a central figure in the development of color-field abstraction during the late 1950s and the 1960s.**

Helen Frankenthaler was born on December 12, 1928, in New York City. As a painter her earliest training was with the Mexican artist Rufino Tamayo at the Dalton School in New York. She studied with Paul Feeley at Bennington College, where she received her bachelor of arts degree in 1948. She then lived in New York

City, although she traveled extensively throughout Europe. She was married to the painter Robert Motherwell.

In the early 1950s Frankenthaler participated in several important group shows and had her first solo exhibition in 1951. She exhibited regularly during this decade and by 1960 had begun to receive national and international recognition. Large exhibitions of her work were held at the Jewish Museum in New York City in 1960 and at Bennington College in 1962. In 1969 she enjoyed a major retrospective at the Whitney Museum of American Art.

Frankenthaler's style developed in ways counter to the better-known trends of abstract painting during the 1950s. Inspired by Jackson Pollock's black-and-white paintings of 1951, she began to stain thinned pigment into unprimed canvas. The paintings which resulted possessed a delicate, liquid appearance, and their surfaces were devoid of any hint of physical pigment. By contrast, most abstract painting of this time took inspiration from Willem de Kooning's work and emphasized dense surface face textures and aggressive brushwork. But Frankenthaler's direction gradually became influential. In 1953 she introduced the stain technique to Morris Louis and Kenneth Noland, both of whom adopted and developed it within the personal structures of their own painting. Along with Frankenthaler, these two painters profoundly influenced the direction of nonpainterly color abstraction in the 1960s.

The painting which Frankenthaler showed to Louis and Noland is called *Mountains and Sea* (1952). It clearly reveals the advantages of the staining technique, particularly

in the flowing spontaneity of the color areas. Because the thinned pigment soaks naturally into the canvas ground, passages from one color to the next are experienced within a continuous optical field rather than as abrupt jumps from one discrete plane to another. In other words, the space is generated within the acknowledged limits of the two-dimensional canvas surface.

As its title suggests, *Mountains and Sea* bears a lingering resemblance to a natural landscape. In 1989 the editor-in-chief of *American Artist* referred to *Mountains and Sea* as one of the four "landmark paintings in the history of contemporary art." In her work after the early 1950s, Frankenthaler became more abstract in her imagery and devoted increasing attention to the development of her lyrical color sensibility.

During the 1960s and 1970s, Frankenthaler continued to develop her own style, one which emphasizes the notion of beauty. She explored the use of acrylic paints, and her work during this era tended to be larger, simpler, and more geometric than previous pieces. Still, her goal was to capture emotion through the use of color without using scenes or subjects. In the late 1970s she explored cubist ideas of space that she had learned in art school.

During the late 1980s critics began to realize more fully how significantly Frankenthaler's work had contributed to the art world. They credit her with many technical achievements and approaches to the use of color during her four decades of creativity. Retrospective exhibitions of her work began to tour museums, even as she continued to create. In late 1996 Eric Gibson noted in *ARTnews* that her latest round of prints, *Spring Run Monotypes*, "convey a wide array of sentiments that were barely noticeable in her earlier works."

Critics consider Frankenthaler one of the most highly regarded painters of the 20th century. Though she has experimented with a variety of techniques, her style has remained truly individual. She told *Newsweek* in 1989, "I continue to do the work I do." This beautiful and poetic work has assured her a place among the masters of contempory art.

### Further Reading

For Helen Frankenthaler's position in relation to postwar American painting see Barbara Rose, *American Art since 1900: A Critical History* (1967). Two excellent retrospectives of her work are John Elderfield, *Frankenthaler,* Harry N. Abrams, Inc., 1997; and Ruth E. Fine, *Helen Frankenthaler: Prints,* Harry N. Abrams, Inc., 1993. Interviews with Frankenthaler are featured in Bradley W. Bloch, "Pigments of the Imagination," *New Leader,* September 4, 1989; and Carter Ratcliff, "Living Color," *Vogue,* June 1989. □

# Aretha Franklin

**Aretha Franklin (born 1942) had a modest beginning as a gospel singer in Detroit before becoming known as the "Queen of Soul."**

When asked by Patricia Smith of the *Boston Globe* how she felt about being called the "Queen of Soul," Aretha Franklin's reply was characterized by grace but no false modesty. "It's an acknowledgment of my art," she mused. "It means I am excelling at my art and my first love. And I am most appreciative." Since she burst onto the public consciousness in the late 1960s with a batch of milestone recordings, Franklin has served as a standard against which all subsequent soul divas have been measured.

The combination of Franklin's gospel roots and some devastating life experiences have invested her voice with a rare—and often wrenching—authenticity. "It was like I had no idea what music was all about until I heard her sing," confessed singer-actress Bette Midler, as cited in *Ebony*. Though Franklin's work in later decades has rarely matched the fire—or the sales figures—of her most celebrated singles, she has remained an enduring presence in contemporary music. The release of several CD retrospectives and the announcement in 1995 that she would publish an autobiography and start her own record label seemed to guarantee that her influence would continue unabated.

Franklin was raised in Detroit, the daughter of famed minister C. L. Franklin and gospel singer Barbara Franklin, who left the family when Aretha was small and died shortly thereafter. The singer told *Ebony*'s Laura B. Randolph, "She was the absolute lady," although she admits that memories of her mother are few. The Reverend Franklin was no retiring clergyman; he enjoyed the popularity and, to some degree, the lifestyle of a pop star. He immediately recog-

nized his daughter's prodigious abilities, and offered to arrange for piano lessons. However, the child declined, instead teaching herself to play by listening to records.

## Gospel Roots

Franklin's talent as a singer allowed her to perform with her father's traveling gospel show. She sang regularly before his congregation at Detroit's New Bethel Baptist Church as well, where her performance of "Precious Lord," among other gospel gems, was captured for posterity. She was 14 years old but already a spellbinding performer. Producer Jerry Wexler—who shepherded Franklin to greatness on behalf of Atlantic Records some years later—was stunned by the 1956 recording. "The voice was not that of a child but rather of an ecstatic hierophant [a priest in ancient Greece]," he recalled in his book *Rhythm and the Blues.*

Franklin's life was no church social, however. She became a mother at age 15 and had her second child two years later. "I still wanted to get out and hang with my friends," she recollected to *Ebony*'s Randolph, "so I wanted to be in two places at the same time. But my grandmother helped me a lot, and my sister and my cousin. They would babysit so I could get out occasionally."

Although first inspired by gospel music, Franklin soon became interested in non-religious music. After receiving her father's encouragement, she traveled to New York in 1960, embarked on vocal and dance lessons, and hired a manager. She then began recording demonstration tapes. Like singer-songwriter-pianist Ray Charles, who has often been credited with the invention of "soul music," Franklin brought the fire of gospel to pop music, her spiritual force in no way separated from her earthy sexuality.

## Collaborations Launched Career

Celebrated Columbia Records executive John Hammond was so taken by Franklin's recordings that he signed her immediately. Her first Columbia album was issued in the fall of 1960. While a few singles made a respectable showing on the charts, it was clear that the label wasn't adequately showcasing her gifts, either in its choice of material or production. "I cherish the recordings we made together," remarked Hammond in *Rhythm and the Blues,* "but, finally, Columbia was a white company [that] misunderstood her genius."

Franklin's manager at the time, Ted White, was also her husband; they agreed that she should pursue other options when her contract expired. Wexler leapt at the opportunity to sign her to Atlantic, and eventually he, Arif Mardin, and Tom Dowd produced Franklin's first Atlantic sides.

Wexler brought Franklin to the Florence Alabama Music Emporium (FAME) studios in Muscle Shoals, Alabama, to record with a unique group of musicians adept in soul, blues, pop, country, and rock. This crew was stunned by Franklin's power and prowess. Accompanying herself on piano, she deftly controlled the tone and arrangement of the songs she performed. Backing vocals were provided either by her sisters Carolyn and Erma or by the vocal group the Sweet Inspirations, which featured Cissy Houston, mother of future singing star Whitney Houston. Wexler also brought

in young rock guitarists Duane Allman and Eric Clapton for guest spots.

Unfortunately, only one of two songs—"I Never Loved a Man (the Way I Love You)"—was finished when White and one of the musicians had a drunken row; White grabbed Franklin and they vanished for a period of weeks. Wexler balanced jubilation with anxiety, as radio programmers around the country embraced "I Never Loved a Man," and distributors clamored for an album. But the artist was nowhere to be found. At last she surfaced in New York, where she completed the unfinished "Do Right Woman, Do Right Man," and in Wexler's words, "the result was perfection."

Franklin's first album for Atlantic, *I Never Loved a Man (the Way I Love You),* was released in 1967, and several hit-filled LPs followed. During this crucial period she enjoyed a succession of smash singles that included the rollicking "Baby I Love You," the pounding groove "Chain of Fools," the supercharged "Think," (which she wrote), the tender "(You Make Me Feel Like a) Natural Woman," and a blistering take on Otis Redding's "Respect." The latter two would become Franklin's signature songs.

## R-E-S-P-E-C-T

Franklin's version of "Respect," coming as it did at a crucial point for black activism, feminism, and sexual liberation, was particularly potent. Wexler noted that Franklin took Redding's more conventional take on the song and "turned it inside out, making it deeper, stronger, loading it with double entendres." What's more, he noted, "The fervor in Aretha's magnificent voice" implied not just everyday respect but "sexual attention of the highest order," as implied by the "sock it to me" backup chorus she and her sisters devised.

Writer Evelyn C. White, in an *Essence* piece, referred to "Respect" as a revolutionary force in her own life. Franklin's "impassioned, soulful licks and sly innuendos about sexual pleasure made me feel good about myself," she wrote, "both as a black American and as a young girl about to discover sex." Eventually, the song would become an American pop standard. At the time of its release, however, it served primarily as a fight song for social change, and went on to score two trophies at that year's Grammy Awards.

Franklin's voice was crucial to the soundtrack of the era, and not just as a record playing on the radio. Franklin's father was a close friend of civil rights leader Rev. Martin Luther King, Jr. and his family. When the crusading minister was assassinated in 1968, Franklin was enlisted to sing at his funeral. Wexler described her performance of "Precious Lord" as "a holy blend of truth and unspeakable tragedy."

Franklin also sang the National Anthem at the Democratic Party's riot-marred 1968 convention in Chicago. Yet even as her soulful wail soothed a number of difficult national transitions and transformations, Franklin's own changes were hidden from view. "I think of Aretha as 'Our Lady of Mysterious Sorrows,'" Wexler wrote. "Her eyes are incredible, luminous eyes covering inexplicable pain. Her depressions could be as deep as the dark sea. I don't pretend to know the sources of her anguish, but anguish surrounds Aretha as surely as the glory of her musical aura."

Despite her inner turmoil, Franklin enjoyed phenomenal commercial success during these years. A number of other blockbuster Atlantic albums followed her debut on the label, and she proceeded to take home Grammys every year between 1969 and 1975. Instead of slowing down after all her overwhelming success, she continued to explore rock and pop records for new material and recorded cover versions of songs by the Beatles, Elton John, the Band, Paul Simon, Jimi Hendrix, and many others. "She didn't think in terms of white or black tunes, or white or black rhythms," noted Wexler. "Her taste, like her genius, transcended categories."

In 1972 Franklin sang at the funeral of gospel giant Mahalia Jackson, which suggested her stature in the gospel world; it was no surprise when *Amazing Grace,* an album of church music she recorded with Wexler, soared up the pop charts that year. At the inauguration of President Jimmy Carter in 1977, she provided an *a capella* rendition of "God Bless America."

### Triumphed Despite Turmoil

Having parted ways with husband/manager Ted White some years earlier, Franklin married actor Glynn Turman in 1978. They divorced six years later. By the end of the 1970s, her record sales had dwindled, but she took an attention-getting turn in the *Blues Brothers* movie, in which she both acted and sang. The film and the Blues Brothers albums, recorded by *Saturday Night Live* funnymen and blues and soul fanatics Dan Aykroyd and John Belushi, helped fuel a new mainstream interest in 1960s soul.

In 1980 Franklin elected to leave Atlantic and sign with Arista Records. The label's slick production and commercial choice of material earned greater sales than she had enjoyed for some time, particularly for the single "Freeway of Love." She earned three more Grammys during the decade. Nonetheless, Dave DiMartino of *Entertainment Weekly* grumbled that most of her hits at Arista "have been assembled by big-name producers like Narada Michael Walden and might have easily featured another singer entirely—like, say, label mate Whitney Houston" ; DiMartino also objected to the relentless pairing of Franklin with other stars for much-hyped duets, remarking, "Like . . . Aretha Franklin needs a *gimmick?*"

In 1979 Franklin's father was shot by a burglar in his home and fell into a coma. He died several years later, having never regained consciousness. As *Ebony'* s Randolph wrote, "When you've said as many goodbyes as Aretha, it's impossible not to be palpably shaped by loss." The singer cited a point during her father's hospitalization as the most difficult decision of her life. "We had to have a trach [a tracheotomy, a procedure that involves cutting through the vocal chords]," she confided, "and we were afraid it would affect his voice, which was certainly his living."

But beyond this and other painful incidents, further triumphs lay ahead for Franklin. She was the first woman inducted into the Rock and Roll Hall of Fame, won a

Grammy for best soul gospel performance, was the subject of an all-star documentary tribute broadcast on public television, sang at the inauguration of another president, Bill Clinton, in 1993, and won a lifetime achievement Grammy in 1995. Franklin might not have been the commercial powerhouse that some of her younger acolytes, like Whitney Houston and Mariah Carey, but she definitely had become an institution.

Franklin—who moved back to the Detroit area in the mid-1990s—announced plans for an autobiography and also made public her intention to start a record label, which would be called World Class Records. "I'm looking for space," she told the *Boston Globe.* "I'm the CEO." She continued to perform, her band by that time featuring two of her sons, Kecalf Cunningham and Teddy Richards.

Other projects, including film and television appearances, were also in the works. "I just strive for excellence pretty much across the board, whether it's as a producer, songwriter or singer," Franklin proclaimed to *Boston Globe* writer Smith. "I give people what I feel is best, not just what everyone says is 'hot.' I want to do things that are going to be meaningful and inspiring to them one way or another." Asked by the *Detroit Free Press* if she ever got tired of singing "Respect," the Queen of Soul replied, "Actually, no. I just find new ways of refreshing the song." Similarly, Franklin's voice continues to refresh new listeners.

### Further Reading

Rees, Dafydd, and Luke Crampton, *Rock Movers & Shakers,* Billboard, 1991.
Wexler, Jerry, and David Ritz, *Rhythm and the Blues: A Life in American Music,* Knopf, 1993.
*Boston Globe,* June 14, 1991, p. 39; March 21, 1994, p. 30; September 29, 1995, p. 55.
*Detroit Free Press,* June 10, 1994, p. 3D; June 18, 1994, p. 2A.
*Ebony,* April 1995, pp. 28-33.
*Entertainment Weekly,* May 15, 1992, p. 64.
*Essence,* August 1995, pp. 73-77.
*Jet,* August 21, 1995, p. 33.
*People,* February 19, 1996, p. 22. □

# Betty Friedan

**Betty Friedan (born 1921) was a women's rights activist, author of *The Feminine Mystique,* and a founding member of the National Organization for Women, the National Abortion Rights Action League, and the National Women's Political Caucus.**

B etty Friedan appeared suddenly in the national limelight with the publication of her first book, *The Feminine Mystique,* in 1963. It became a national best seller and propelled Friedan to a leadership position in the burgeoning movement for women's liberation. In that book Friedan identified a condition she claimed women suffered as the result of a widely accepted ideology that placed them first and foremost in the home. Attacking the notion that "biology is destiny," which ordained that women should devote their lives to being wives and mothers at the expense of other pursuits, Friedan called upon women to shed their domestic confines and discover other meaningful endeavors.

Friedan was herself well situated to know the effects of the "feminine mystique." She was born Betty Naomi Goldstein in 1921 in Peoria, Illinois, the daughter of Jewish parents. Her father was a jeweler, and her mother had to give up her job on a newspaper when she married. The loss of that potential career affected her mother deeply, and she urged young Betty to pursue the career in journalism that she was never able to achieve. The daughter went on to graduate *summa cum laude* from Smith College in 1942. She then received a research fellowship to study psychology as a graduate student at the University of California at Berkeley. Like her mother, she did some work as a journalist, but unlike her mother she did not end her career to build a family. She married Carl Friedan in 1947, and during the years that she was raising their three children she continued her freelance writing. After her husband established his own advertising agency they moved to the suburbs, where Friedan experienced what she later termed the "feminine mystique" first hand. Although she continued to write she felt stifled in her domestic role.

In 1957 Friedan put together an intensive questionnaire to send to her college classmates from Smith 15 years after graduation. She obtained detailed, open-ended replies from 200 women, revealing a great deal of dissatisfaction with their lives. Like Friedan herself, they tried to conform to the

prevailing expectations of wives and mothers while harboring frustrated desires for something more out of life. Friedan wrote an article based on her findings, but the editors of the women's magazines with whom she had previously worked refused to publish the piece. Those refusals only spurred her on. She decided to investigate the problem on a much larger scale and publish a book. The result of her effort was *The Feminine Mystique,* which became an instant success, selling over three million copies.

Friedan began her book by describing what she called "the problem that has no name." In words that touched a sensitive nerve in thousands of middle-class American women, she wrote, "the problem lay buried, unspoken, for many years in the minds of American women. It was a strange stirring, a sense of dissatisfaction, a yearning that women suffered in the middle of the 20th century in the United States. Each suburban wife struggled with it alone. As she made the beds, shopped for groceries, matched slipcover material . . . she was afraid to ask even of herself the silent question—'Is this all?'"

With the publication of *The Feminine Mystique* Betty Friedan rose to national prominence. Three years later in 1966 she helped found the first major organization established since the 1920s devoted to women's rights, the National Organization for Women (NOW), and became its first president. Under Friedan's leadership NOW worked for political reforms to secure women's legal equality. The organization was successful in achieving a number of important gains for women. It worked for the enforcement of Title VII of the 1964 Civil Rights Act, which prohibited employment discrimination on the basis of sex. As a result of the organization's efforts, the Equal Opportunities Commission ruled that airlines could not fire female flight attendants because they married or reached the age of 35, nor could employment opportunities be advertised according to male or female categories.

NOW also lobbied for passage of the Equal Rights Amendment (ERA), which had remained dormant since it was first introduced in Congress by Alice Paul in 1923. In addition, the organization called for federally funded day care centers to be established "on the same basis as parks, libraries and public schools." NOW also worked to achieve the legalization of abortion and the preservation of abortion rights. Friedan was among the founders of the National Abortion Rights Action League in 1969. Finally in 1973 the Supreme Court legalized abortions. Deaths of women resulting from abortions dropped by 60 percent.

In 1970 Friedan was one of the most forceful opponents of President Nixon's nomination of G. Harrold Carswell to the Supreme Court. She argued before the Senate Judiciary Committee that in 1969 Carswell defied the Civil Rights Act by ruling in favor of the right of employers to deny jobs to women with children. That same year, at the annual meeting of NOW, she called for a Women's Strike for Equality, which was held on August 26—the 50th anniversary of the day women gained the right to vote. Women across the country commemorated the day with demonstrations, marches, and speeches in 40 major cities. Friedan led a parade of over 10,000 down Fifth Avenue in New York City.

The following year Friedan was among the feminist leaders who formed the National Women's Political Caucus. During the next several years she moved away from central leadership in the movement to concentrate on writing and teaching. She wrote a regular column for *McCall's* magazine and taught at several colleges and universities, including Temple University, Yale University, Queens College, and the New School for Social Research.

Friedan became an influential spokeswoman for the women's movement nationally as well as internationally. In 1974 she had an audience with Pope Paul VI in which she urged the Catholic Church to "come to terms with the full personhood of women."

As the women's movement grew and new leaders emerged with different concerns, Friedan's centrality in the movement dwindled. Nevertheless, she remained an outspoken feminist leader for many years. In 1977 she participated in the National Conference of Women in Houston, Texas, and called for an end to divisions and a new coalition of women. Her writing, teaching, and speaking continued throughout these years, as her ideas concerning the feminist movement evolved. In 1976 she published *It Changed My Life: Writings on the Women's Movement,* which was followed by her 1981 book, *The Second Stage.* In that publication Friedan called for a shift in the feminist movement, one that would address the needs of families and would allow both men and women to break from the sex-role stereotypes of the past.

In 1993, Friedan released *The Fountain of Age,* in which she began to explore the rights of the elderly and aging, just as she had once become attuned to women's issues. Friedan's focus is not on mere economics, but rather on helping the elderly find fulfillment in their latter years. In *The New York Times* she said, "Once you break through the mystique of age and that view of the aged as objects of care and as problems for society, you can look at the reality of the new years of human life open to us."

In 1996 new scholarship arose about Friedan's life when Daniel Horowitz published a controversial article in *American Quarterly.* Horowitz, who teaches at Friedan's alma mater, Smith University, draws a link between Friedan's feminism and her undergraduate years at Smith during the 1940s. Horowitz presents a new outlook on the work of Friedan, who has often said her feminism first emerged during the 1960s; in his article, Horowitz makes a strong case that it can be traced to the 1940s. But regardless of the time that Friedan's feminism first surfaced, she remains a significant influence on societal expectations and equality for women.

## Further Reading

Betty Friedan's own writings are the best source of information on her life and work. She wrote extensively in popular magazines and was interviewed numerous times after 1963. She published four books: *The Feminine Mystique* (1963), *It Changed My Life: Writings on the Women's Movement* (1976), and *The Second Stage* (1981), and *The Fountain of Age* (1993). □

# Sarah Margaret Fuller

**Sarah Margaret Fuller (1810-1850), an American feminist, cultural critic, and transcendentalist, fought for equality of the sexes.**

Not long after her birth on May 23, 1810, in Cambridgeport, Mass., Margaret Fuller's father started to educate her as a wonder child. She was introduced to Latin at 6 and was reading literary classics when she might still have been playing children's games. By the time she was in her 20s, she could impress such transcendentalist leaders as Ralph Waldo Emerson and Bronson Alcott.

Fuller loved to talk, so she seized on the lyceum as a way to support herself and put forth her ideas. When she ran into masculine protest against a woman speaking to mixed audiences, she developed what she called "conversations." These systematic discussions with some of the most intelligent women in the Boston area were held from 1839 to 1844. Fuller had already begun publishing, but her most significant book, *Woman in the Nineteenth Century* (1845), developed from such "conversations." It proposed plans for relieving women's social restrictions and using their abilities to the fullest.

When the transcendentalists set up a journal, the *Dial*, in 1840, they chose Fuller as editor. Her incisive and decisive criticism of literature and the arts attracted the attention of Horace Greeley, editor of the *New York Tribune*, who brought her to New York as a critic for his paper in 1844.

Fuller's reviews for the *Tribune* demonstrated a first-rate esthetic intelligence. Though she found these duties satisfying, a trip to Europe so impressed her that in 1847 she settled in Rome. There she met and lived with a poor but handsome young Italian marquis, Angelo Ossoli, demonstrating her belief in love and in freedom for women. When the son she had by Ossoli in 1849 was a year old, they announced their marriage.

In the late 1840s, when the people of Rome were trying to shake off papal rule to form a city-state, Ossoli fought for the Roman Republic, while Fuller worked in the military hospitals. Throughout her stay abroad she had been writing for the *Tribune;* her descriptions of the Roman revolution were her most vivid work. When the revolution failed, the family fled, finally settling in Florence. Here she wrote the manuscript of a history of the revolution.

In May 1850 Fuller and her family embarked for New York. The ship was wrecked off Fire Island: wife, husband, and son all drowned on July 19, 1850, and in the catastrophe her manuscript was lost.

## Further Reading

The most recent biography of Margaret Fuller is Arthur W. Brown, *Margaret Fuller* (1964). It should be supplemented by Mason Wade, *Margaret Fuller: Whetstone of Genius* (1940). Joseph Jay Deiss, *The Roman Years of Margaret Fuller* (1969), illuminates one of her most important periods. □

# NAME INDEX

Abbott, Berenice
American artist
Volume I: 1

Abbott, Grace
American activist
Volume I: 3

Abzug, Bella Stavisky
American activist
Volume I: 4

Adamson, Joy
Austrian naturalist
Volume IV: 743

Addams, Jane
American activist
Volume I: 6

Albright, Madeleine
American diplomat
Volume I: 7

Alcott, Louisa May
American author
Volume I: 8

Allen, Florence Ellinwood
American politician
Volume I: 9

Allen, Paula Gunn
American author
Volume I: 10

Allende, Isabel
Chilean author
Volume IV: 745

Alvarez, Julia
American author
Volume I: 13

Andersen, Dorothy
American scientist
Volume I: 15

Anderson, Judith
Australian actress
Volume IV: 747

Anderson, June
American singer
Volume I: 16

Anderson, Marian
American singer
Volume I: 17

Andrews, Fannie Fern
American educator
Volume I: 19

Angelou, Maya
American poet
Volume I: 20

Anthony, Susan Brownell
American activist
Volume I: 21

Apgar, Virginia
American scientist
Volume I: 22

Aquino, Corazon
Filipino president
Volume IV: 748

Arbus, Diane Nemerov
    American artist
    Volume I: 24

Arden, Elizabeth
    Canadian business leader
    Volume IV: 750
Arendt, Hannah
    German philosopher
    Volume IV: 751

Ash, Mary Kay Wagner
    American business leader
    Volume I: 26

Ashley, Laura
    British business leader
    Volume IV: 753

Ashrawi, Hanan Mikhail
    Palestinian activist
    Volume IV: 754

Aung San Suu Kyi
    Myanmar activist
    Volume IV: 755

Austen, Jane
    British author
    Volume IV: 757

Baca-Barragan, Polly
    American politician
    Volume I: 29

Baez, Joan
    American singer
    Volume I: 31

Bailey, Florence Merriam
    American scientist
    Volume I: 33

Baker, Ella Josephine
    American activist
    Volume I: 34

Baker, Josephine
    American singer
    Volume I: 36

Baker, Sara Josephine
    American scientist
    Volume I: 38

Balch, Emily Greene
    American activist
    Volume I: 39

Ball, Lucille
    American actress
    Volume I: 41

Bambara, Toni Cade
    American author
    Volume I: 42

Bandaranaike, Sirimavo
    Sri Lankan politician
    Volume IV: 759

Barnes, Djuna
    American author
    Volume I: 43

Barton, Clara
    American activist
    Volume I: 46

Bates, Katharine Lee
    American author
    Volume I: 47

Battle, Kathleen
    American singer
    Volume I: 49

Beard, Mary Ritter
    American activist
    Volume I: 50

Beecher, Catharine
    American educator
    Volume I: 52

Bell Burnell, Susan Jocelyn
    Irish scientist
    Volume IV: 761

Benedict, Ruth Fulton
    American scientist
    Volume I: 54

Bernstein, Dorothy Lewis
    American scientist
    Volume I: 55

Berry, Mary Frances
    American activist
    Volume I: 56

Bethune, Mary McLeod
    American educator
    Volume I: 59

Bhutto, Benazir
    Pakistani politician
    Volume IV: 762

Bishop, Bridget
    American barmaid
    Volume I: 60

Bishop, Elizabeth
    American author
    Volume I: 62

Black, Shirley Temple
    American diplomat and actress
    Volume I: 64

Blackburn, Elizabeth Helen
    American scientist
    Volume I: 66

Blackwell, Elizabeth
    American activist
    Volume I: 67

Blandiana, Ana
    Romanian author
    Volume IV: 763

Blanding, Sarah Gibson
    American educator
    Volume I: 68

Bloomer, Amelia Jenks
    American activist
    Volume I: 69

Bloor, Ella Reeve
    American activist
    Volume I: 70

Blume, Judy
    American author
    Volume I: 72

Bly, Nellie
    American activist
    Volume I: 73

Bok, Sissela Ann
    American philosopher
    Volume I: 74

Boleyn, Anne
    English queen
    Volume IV: 765

Bombal, Maria Luisa
    Chilean author
    Volume IV: 766

Bonnin, Gertrude Simmons
    American activist
    Volume I: 76

Booth, Evangeline Cory
    American activist
    Volume I: 78

Borgia, Lucrezia
    Italian schemer
    Volume IV: 767

Bourgeoys, Marguerite
    French religious leader
    Volume IV: 770

Bourke-White, Margaret
    American artist
    Volume I: 80

Boxer, Barbara
    American politician
    Volume I: 81

Bradley, Marion Zimmer
    American author
    Volume I: 84

Bradstreet, Anne Dudley
    American author
    Volume I: 86

Brice, Fanny
    American entertainer
    Volume I: 86

Bronte, Charlotte
    British author
    Volume IV: 771

Bronte, Emily
    British author
    Volume IV: 772

Brooks, Gwendolyn
    American author
    Volume I: 88

Brothers, Joyce
American psychologist
Volume I: 89

Brown, Charlotte Eugenia
American educator
Volume I: 91

Brown, Helen Gurley
American journalist
Volume I: 92

Brown, Rachel Fuller
American scientist
Volume I: 93

Brown, Tina
American journalist
Volume I: 94

Browner, Carol M.
American government official
Volume I: 95

Browning, Elizabeth Barrett
British author
Volume IV: 773

Brownmiller, Susan
American author
Volume I: 97

Brundtland, Gro Harlem
Norwegian politician
Volume IV: 774

Buck, Pearl S.
American author
Volume I: 98

Burke, Selma
American artist
Volume I: 99

Burnett, Frances Hodgson
American author
Volume I: 100

Butler, Octavia E.
American author
Volume I: 102

Byrne, Jane
American politician
Volume I: 103

Cabrini, St. Frances
American religious leader
Volume I: 105

Caesar, Shirley
American singer
Volume I: 106

Calamity Jane
American frontier figure
Volume I: 107

Caldicott, Helen Broinowski
Australian activist
Volume IV: 777

Caldwell, Sarah
American musician
Volume I: 108

Callas, Maria
American singer
Volume I: 109

Cannon, Annie Jump
American scientist
Volume I: 112

Capriati, Jennifer
American athlete
Volume I: 112

Caraway, Hattie Wyatt
American politician
Volume I: 115

Carey Thomas, Martha
American educator
Volume I: 117

Carnegie, Hattie
American artist
Volume I: 117

Carr, Emily
Canadian artist
Volume IV: 779

Carroll, Anna Ella
American author
Volume I: 118

Carson, Rachel Louise
American scientist
Volume I: 121

Cassatt, Mary
American artist
Volume I: 122

Catherine of Aragon
English queen
Volume IV: 780

Catherine of Siena
Italian saint
Volume IV: 782

Catherine the Great
Russian empress
Volume IV: 783

Catt, Carrie Chapman
American activist
Volume I: 123

Chamorro, Violeta
Nicaraguan politician
Volume IV: 785

Chanel, Coco
French business leader
Volume IV: 787

Chavez, Linda
American activist
Volume I: 124

Chicago, Judy
American artist
Volume I: 126

Chiepe, Gaositwe Keagak
Botswanan politician
Volume IV: 788

Child, Julia McWilliams
American chef
Volume I: 128

Child, Lydia Maria Francis
American author
Volume I: 129

Childress, Alice
American author
Volume I: 130

Chinn, May Edward
American scientist
Volume I: 132

Chisholm, Caroline
Australian author
Volume IV: 788

Chisholm, Shirley
American politician
Volume I: 133

Chopin, Katherine
American author
Volume I: 135

Christie, Agatha
British author
Volume IV: 791

Christina of Sweden
Swedish queen
Volume IV: 793

Christine de Pisan
French activist
Volume IV: 795

Chung, Connie
American journalist
Volume I: 138

Ciller, Tansu
Turkish politician
Volume IV: 796

Cisneros, Sandra
American author
Volume I: 138

Claiborne, Liz
American business leader
Volume I: 140

Clapp, Margaret Antoinette
American author
Volume I: 141

Cleopatra
Egyptian queen
Volume IV: 797

Cline, Patsy
American singer
Volume I: 142

Clinton, Hillary Rodham
American first lady
Volume I: 144

Cochran, Jacqueline
American aviator
Volume I: 146

Coleman, Bessie
American aviator
Volume I: 148

Colette, Sidonie Gabrielle
French author
Volume IV: 799

Collins, Eileen
American astronaut
Volume I: 149

Collins, Marva
American educator
Volume I: 152

Colwell, Rita R.
American scientist
Volume I: 154

Comaneci, Nadia
Romanian athlete
Volume IV: 800

Comnena, Anna
Byzantine author
Volume IV: 801

Conway, Jill Kathryn Ker
American historian
Volume I: 155

Cori, Gerty T.
Czech scientist
Volume IV: 802

Cotten, Elizabeth
American singer
Volume I: 156

Crandall, Prudence
American educator
Volume I: 158

Curie, Marie Sklodowska
French scientist
Volume IV: 805

Cushman, Charlotte
American actress
Volume I: 159

Daly, Mary
American philosopher
Volume I: 161

Dandridge, Dorothy
American actress
Volume I: 163

Davis, Angela
American activist
Volume I: 165

Davis, Bette
American actress
Volume I: 166

Day, Dorothy
American activist
Volume I: 168

de Beauvoir, Simone
French author
Volume IV: 809

Dee, Ruby
American actress
Volume I: 169

Deer, Ada E.
American activist
Volume I: 172

de Mille, Agnes
American dancer
Volume I: 175

Devlin, Bernadette
Irish politician
Volume IV: 810

Dewson, Mary Williams
American politician
Volume I: 176

Diana, Princess of Wales
British princess
Volume IV: 812

Dickinson, Emily
American author
Volume I: 177

Dinesen, Karen Blixen-Fineck
Danish author
Volume IV: 816

Dix, Dorothea Lynde
American activist
Volume I: 179

Dodge, Grace Hoadley
American activist
Volume I: 180

Doi Takako
Japanese politician
Volume IV: 817

Dole, Elizabeth
American politician
Volume I: 181

Doolittle, Hilda
American author
Volume I: 184

Dorr, Rheta Childe
American journalist
Volume I: 184

Douglas, Mary Tew
British scientist
Volume IV: 819

Dove, Rita Frances
American author
Volume I: 186

Drexel, Katherine
American religious leader
Volume I: 188

Dudley, Barbara
American activist
Volume I: 189

Duncan, Isadora
American dancer
Volume I: 190

Dunham, Katherine
American dancer
Volume I: 191

Earhart, Amelia Mary
American aviator
Volume I: 195

Earle, Sylvia A.
American scientist
Volume I: 196

Eddy, Mary Baker
American religious leader
Volume I: 198

Edelman, Marian Wright
American activist
Volume I: 198

Eisenhower, Mamie Doud
American first lady
Volume I: 200

Elders, Joycelyn
American scientist
Volume I: 201

Eleanor of Aquitaine
French queen
Volume IV: 821

Elion, Gertrude B.
American scientist
Volume I: 204

Eliot, George
British author
Volume IV: 822

Elizabeth I
English queen
Volume IV: 824

Elizabeth II
British queen
Volume IV: 827

Elizabeth Bagaaya Nyabongo
Ugandan politician
Volume IV: 829

Elizabeth of Hungary
Hungarian saint
Volume IV: 831

Elizabeth Petrovna
Russian empress
Volume IV: 833

Ephron, Nora
American author
Volume I: 206

Evers-Williams, Myrlie
American activist
Volume I: 207

Falletta, JoAnn
American musician
Volume I: 211

Farmer, Fannie Merritt
American chef
Volume I: 213

Farrell, Suzanne
American dancer
Volume I: 213

Faye, Safi
Senegalese filmmaker
Volume IV: 835

Feinstein, Dianne
American politician
Volume I: 215

Ferber, Edna
American author
Volume I: 216

Ferraro, Geraldine
American politician
Volume I: 217

First, Ruth
South African activist
Volume IV: 836

Fiske, Minnie Maddern
American actress
Volume I: 219

Fitzgerald, Ella
American singer
Volume I: 220

FitzGerald, Frances
American author
Volume I: 221

Flanagan, Hallie
American author
Volume I: 222

Fletcher, Alice Cunningham
American anthropologist
Volume I: 223

Flynn, Elizabeth Gurley
American activist
Volume I: 224

Fonda, Jane
American actress
Volume I: 226

Fonteyn, Dame Margot
British dancer
Volume IV: 837

Fossey, Dian
American activist
Volume I: 227

Foster, Abigail Kelley
American activist
Volume I: 228

Frank, Anne
Dutch author
Volume IV: 838

Frankenthaler, Helen
American artist
Volume I: 229

Franklin, Aretha
American singer
Volume I: 230

Franklin, Rosalind Elsie
British scientist
Volume IV: 839

Franklin, Stella Maraia
Australian author
Volume IV: 841

Fraser, Lady Antonia
British author
Volume IV: 841

Freud, Anna
Austrian scientist
Volume IV: 843

Friedan, Betty
American author
Volume I: 232

Fry, Elizabeth
British activist
Volume IV: 845

Fuller, Sarah Margaret
American activist
Volume I: 234

Gage, Matilda Joslyn
American activist
Volume II: 237

Gandhi, Indira
Indian politician
Volume IV: 849

Garbo, Greta
American actress
Volume II: 239

Garland, Judy
American actress and singer
Volume II: 240

Garrett (Anderson), Elizabeth
British scientist
Volume IV: 850

Gaskell, Elizabeth
British author
Volume IV: 853

Gayle, Helene Doris
American scientist
Volume II: 241

Geller, Margaret Joan
American scientist
Volume II: 242

Gibson, Althea
American athlete
Volume II: 243

Gilbreth, Lillian
American business leader
Volume II: 244

Gilman, Charlotte Anna P.
American author
Volume II: 246

Gilpin, Laura
American artist
Volume II: 247

Ginsburg, Ruth Bader
American jurist
Volume II: 248

Ginzburg, Natalia Levi
Italian author
Volume IV: 854

Giovanni, Yolande Cornelia
American author
Volume II: 250

Glasgow, Ellen
American author
Volume II: 252

Goeppert-Mayer, Maria
German scientist
Volume IV: 855

Goldberg, Whoopi
American actress
Volume II: 253

Goldman, Emma
American activist
Volume II: 256

Goldmark, Josephine
American author
Volume II: 257

Goncharova, Natalia
Russian artist
Volume IV: 858

Goodall, Jane
British scientist
Volume IV: 860

Goodman, Ellen Holtz
American journalist
Volume II: 258

Gordeeva, Ekaterina
Russian athlete
Volume IV: 861

Gordimer, Nadine
South African author
Volume IV: 863

Gordon, Pamela
Bermudan politician
Volume IV: 864

Graham, Katharine Meyer
American journalist
Volume II: 259

Graham, Martha
American dancer
Volume II: 260

Granville, Evelyn Boyd
American mathematician
Volume II: 262

Graves, Nancy Stevenson
American artist
Volume II: 263

Gray, Hannah Holborn
American educator
Volume II: 265

Green, Constance
American author
Volume II: 267

Green, Edith Starrett
American politician
Volume II: 268

Greer, Germaine
British author
Volume IV: 866

Grimke, Angelina Emily
American activist
Volume II: 269

Grimke, Sarah Moore
American activist
Volume II: 269

Grossinger, Jennie
American business leader
Volume II: 270

Guerin, Veronica
Irish journalist
Volume IV: 868

Guisewite, Cathy Lee
American cartoonist
Volume II: 271

Hagen, Uta Thyra
American actress
Volume II: 275

Hale, Sarah Josepha
American journalist
Volume II: 276

Haley, Magaret A.
American activist
Volume II: 277

Hamer, Fannie Lou
American activist
Volume II: 278

Hamilton, Alice
American scientist
Volume II: 280

Hanks, Nancy
American fund raiser
Volume II: 281

Hansberry, Lorraine
American author
Volume II: 282

Hansen, Julia Butler
American politician
Volume II: 283

Harand, Irene
Austrian activist
Volume IV: 871

Hardy, Harriet
American scientist
Volume II: 284

Harjo, Suzan Shown
American activist
Volume II: 285

Harper, Frances Ellen W.
American author
Volume II: 287

Harriman, Pamela
American politician
Volume II: 289

Harris, Barbara Clementine
American religious leader
Volume II: 291

Harris, LaDonna
American activist
Volume II: 292

Harris, Patricia Roberts
American politician
Volume II: 294

Hatshepsut
Egyptian queen
Volume IV: 877

Hayes, Helen
American actress
Volume II: 296

Hayworth, Rita
American actress
Volume II: 297

Head, Edith
American designer
Volume II: 299

Healy, Bernadine Patricia
American scientist
Volume II: 302

Hearst, Patricia
American heiress
Volume II: 303

Heckler, Margaret Mary
American government official
Volume II: 304

Hellman, Lillian Florence
American author
Volume II: 305

Hepburn, Audrey
British actress
Volume IV: 878

Hepburn, Katharine
American actress
Volume II: 306

Hepworth, Barbara
British artist
Volume IV: 880

Hesse, Eva
German actist
Volume IV: 881

Hesse, Mary B.
British philosopher
Volume IV: 883

Higgins, Marguerite
American journalist
Volume II: 308

Hill, Anita
American attorney
Volume II: 310

Hills, Carla Anderson
American government official
Volume II: 313

Himmelfarb, Gertrude
American author
Volume II: 314

Hinton, Susan Eloise
American author
Volume II: 317

Hobby, Oveta Culp
American business leader
Volume II: 317

Hodgkin, Dorothy Crowfoot
British scientist
Volume IV: 884

Holiday, Billie
American singer
Volume II: 320

Holm, Hanya
American dancer
Volume II: 321

Holzer, Jenny
American artist
Volume II: 322

hooks, bell
American author
Volume II: 324

Hopper, Grace
American scientist
Volume II: 327

Horne, Lena
American singer
Volume II: 330

Horner, Matina Souretis
American educator
Volume II: 332

Horney, Karen Danielsen
American scientist
Volume II: 333

Howe, Florence Rosenfeld
American author
Volume II: 334

Howe, Julia Ward
American activist
Volume II: 335

Huerta, Dolores
American activist
Volume II: 336

Hunter, Madeline Cheek
American educator
Volume II: 339

Hurston, Zora Neale
American author
Volume II: 340

Hutchinson, Anne Marbury
American religious leader
Volume II: 341

Hyman, Libbie Henrietta
American scientist
Volume II: 343

Hypatia of Alexandria
Egyptian scientist
Volume IV: 886

Ibarruri, Dolores Gomez
Spanish activist
Volume IV: 889

Imaoka, Shinichiro
Japanese religious leader
Volume IV: 891

Ireland, Patricia
American activist
Volume II: 347

Irene of Athens
Byzantine empress
Volume IV: 892

Isabella I
Spanish queen
Volume IV: 895

Jackson, Helen Hunt
American author
Volume II: 349

Jackson, Shirley Ann
American scientist
Volume II: 350

Jacobs, Harriet A.
American author
Volume II: 351

Jemison, Mae C.
American astronaut
Volume II: 354

Jewett, Sarah Orne
American author
Volume II: 355

Jiang Qing
Chinese politician
Volume IV: 897

Joan of Arc
French saint
Volume IV: 900

Johnson, Betsey
American artist
Volume II: 356

Johnson, Marietta Louise
American educator
Volume II: 358

Johnson, Virginia E.
American scientist
Volume II: 359

Joliot-Curie, Irene
French scientist
Volume IV: 902

Jones, Mary Harris
American activist
Volume II: 360

Jong, Erica Mann
American author
Volume II: 361

Jordan, Barbara Charline
American politician
Volume II: 364

Jordan, June
American author
Volume II: 365

Juana Ines de la Cruz, Sister
Mexican religious leader
Volume IV: 904

Julian of Norwich
English religious leader
Volume IV: 904

Julias of Rome
Roman empress
Volume IV: 905

Kahlo, Frida
Mexican artist
Volume IV: 909

Karan, Donna
American business leader
Volume II: 369

Karle, Isabella
American scientist
Volume II: 371

Kassebaum, Nancy
American politician
Volume II: 372

Keller, Helen Adams
American author
Volume II: 374

Kelley, Florence
American activist
Volume II: 375

Kellor, Frances
American activist
Volume II: 375

Kelly, Petra
German politician
Volume IV: 910

Keohane, Nannerl Overholser
American educator
Volume II: 377

King, Billie Jean
American athlete
Volume II: 379

King, Coretta Scott
American activist
Volume II: 380

Kingston, Maxine Hong
American author
Volume II: 381

Kirkpatrick, Jeane J.
American politician
Volume II: 383

Klein, Melanie
Austrian psychologist
Volume IV: 911

Knopf, Blanche Wolf
American business leader
Volume II: 385

Kollwitz, Kathe
German artist
Volume IV: 912

Krasner, Lee
American artist
Volume II: 386

Kreps, Juanita Morris
American author
Volume II: 387

Kubler-Ross, Elisabeth
American scientist
Volume II: 388

Kunin, Madeleine May
American politician
Volume II: 390

La Flesche, Susette
American activist
Volume II: 393

Lange, Dorothea
American artist
Volume II: 394

Larsen, Nella
American author
Volume II: 395

Lauder, Estee
American business leader
Volume II: 396

Lazarus, Emma
American author
Volume II: 398

Leakey, Mary Douglas
British scientist
Volume IV: 915

Lease, Mary Elizabeth
American activist
Volume II: 398

Lee, Mother Ann
American religious leader
Volume II: 399

Le Guin, Ursula K.
American author
Volume II: 402

Leibovitz, Annie
American artist
Volume II: 403

Leigh, Vivien
British actress
Volume IV: 916

L'Engle, Madeleine
American author
Volume II: 406

Lessing, Doris
British author
Volume IV: 918

Levi-Montalcini, Rita
American scientist
Volume II: 408

Liliuokalani, Lydia Kamakaeha
Hawaiian queen
Volume IV: 919

Lin, Maya Ying
American artist
Volume II: 409

Lindbergh, Anne Morrow
American author
Volume II: 411

Livia
Roman empress
Volume IV: 920

Lloyd-Jones, Esther
American educator
Volume II: 412

Long, Irene D.
American scientist
Volume II: 413

Lonsdale, Kathleen
Irish scientist
Volume IV: 923

Lorde, Audre
American author
Volume II: 414

Loren, Sophia
Italian actress
Volume IV: 925

Love, Susan M.
American activist
Volume II: 416

Lovelace, Ada Byron
British author
Volume IV: 927

Low, Juliette Gordon
American activist
Volume II: 418

Lowell, Amy
American author
Volume II: 419

Lowell, Josephine Shaw
American activist
Volume II: 420

Luce, Clare Boothe
American politician
Volume II: 420

Luhan, Mabel Doge
American author
Volume II: 422

Luxemburg, Rosa
Polish activist
Volume IV: 929

Lynd, Helen Merrell
American educator
Volume II: 423

Lyon, Mary
American educator
Volume II: 425

Maathai, Wangari Muta
Kenyan activist
Volume IV: 931

Macdonald, Eleanor
    American scientist
    Volume II: 429

MacKillop, Mary
    Australian religious leader
    Volume IV: 933

Madison, Dolly
    American first lady
    Volume II: 430

Madonna
    American singer
    Volume II: 432

Mahal, Hazrat
    Indian activist
    Volume IV: 934

Mandela, Winnie
    South African activist
    Volume IV: 936

Mankiller, Wilma
    Native American chief
    Volume II: 434

Mansfield, Katherine
    New Zealand author
    Volume IV: 938

Marcos, Imelda
    Filipino first lady
    Volume IV: 940

Margulis, Lynn
    American scientist
    Volume II: 436

Maria Theresa
    Austrian archduchess
    Volume IV: 941

Marie Antoinette
    French queen
    Volume IV: 943

Markievicz, Constance
    Irish activist
    Volume IV: 944

Marshall, Paule Burke
    American author
    Volume II: 437

Martin, Agnes
    American artist
    Volume II: 438

Martin, Lynn Morley
    American government official
    Volume II: 440

Martin, Mary
    American actress and singer
    Volume II: 441

Martinez, Vilma Socorro
    American activist
    Volume II: 443

Mary I
    English queen
    Volume IV: 947

Mary Queen of Scots
    Scottish queen
    Volume IV: 948

McCarthy, Mary T.
    American auhor
    Volume II: 445

McClintock, Barbara
    American scientist
    Volume II: 447

McCullers, Carson
    American author
    Volume II: 448

McDaniel, Hattie
    American actress
    Volume II: 450

McMillan, Terry
    American author
    Volume II: 453

McMurray, Bette Clair
    American business leader
    Volume II: 454

McQueen, Butterfly
    American actress
    Volume II: 455

Mead, Margaret
    American scientist
    Volume II: 458

Medici, Catherine de
French queen
Volume IV: 950

Meitner, Lise
Austrian scientist
Volume IV: 953

Menchu, Rigoberta
Guatemalan activist
Volume IV: 956

Mendenhall, Dorothy Reed
American scientist
Volume II: 460

Midgely, Mary Burton
British philosopher
Volume IV: 958

Mikulski, Barbara
American politician
Volume II: 460

Millay, Edna St. Vincent
American author
Volume II: 463

Millett, Kate
American artist
Volume II: 464

Min
Korean queen
Volume IV: 959

Mink, Patsy Takemoto
American politician
Volume II: 465

Mintz, Beatrice
American scientist
Volume II: 467

Mistral, Gabriela
Chilean author
Volume IV: 959

Mitchell, Margaret
American author
Volume II: 468

Mitchell, Maria
American educator
Volume II: 469

Modersohn-Becker, Paula
German artist
Volume IV: 960

Molinari, Susan
American politician
Volume II: 470

Monroe, Marilyn
American actress
Volume II: 471

Montessori, Maria
Italian educator
Volume IV: 961

Moore, Charlotte E.
American scientist
Volume II: 472

Moore, Marianne
American author
Volume II: 473

Morgan, Julia
American artist
Volume II: 475

Morgan, Robin
American activist
Volume II: 476

Morrison, Toni
American author
Volume II: 477

Morton, Nelle Katherine
American religious leader
Volume II: 479

Mosely-Braun, Carol
American politician
Volume II: 481

Moses, Grandma
American artist
Volume II: 482

Motley, Constance Baker
American politician
Volume II: 483

Mott, Lucretia Coffin
American activist
Volume II: 485

Muldowney, Shirley
    American race car driver
    Volume II: 485

Murdoch, Iris
    Irish author
    Volume IV: 963

Naidu, Sarojini
    Indian author
    Volume IV: 965

Nation, Carry Amelia Moore
    American activist
    Volume III: 489

Natividad, Irene
    American politician
    Volume III: 490

Navratilova, Martina
    American athlete
    Volume III: 492

Naylor, Gloria
    American author
    Volume III: 495

Nefertiti
    Egyptian queen
    Volume IV: 966

Neufeld, Elizabeth
    American scientist
    Volume III: 496

Nevelson, Louise
    American artist
    Volume III: 497

Nicolson, Marjorie Hope
    American educator
    Volume III: 498

Nightingale, Florence
    British activist
    Volume IV: 966

Nin, Anais
    French author
    Volume IV: 967

Noether, Emmy
    German mathematician
    Volume IV: 969

Norman, Jessye
    American singer
    Volume III: 499

Novello, Antonia
    American scientist
    Volume III: 501

Oakley, Annie
    American frontier figure
    Volume III: 505

Oates, Joyce Carol
    American author
    Volume III: 506

Ochoa, Ellen
    American scientist
    Volume III: 508

O'Connor, Flannery
    American author
    Volume III: 509

O'Connor, Sandra Day
    American jurist
    Volume III: 510

Ogot, Grace Emily Akinyi
    Kenyan author
    Volume IV: 973

O'Hair, Madalyn Murray
    American activist
    Volume III: 512

O'Keefe, Georgia
    American artist
    Volume III: 512

Onassis, Jacqueline Kennedy
    American first lady
    Volume III: 514

Oppenheim, Meret
    Swiss artist
    Volume IV: 974

Ovington, Mary White
    American activist
    Volume III: 516

Owen, Ruth Bryan
    American politician
    Volume III: 517

Pagels, Elaine Hiesey
American historian
Volume III: 521

Pandit, Vijaya Lakshmi
Indian politician
Volume IV: 977

Park, Maud Wood
American activist
Volume III: 522

Parker, Dorothy Rothschild
American author
Volume III: 523

Parks, Rosa
American activist
Volume III: 523

Patrick, Jennie R.
American scientist
Volume III: 525

Patrick, Ruth
American scientist
Volume III: 526

Payne-Gaposchkin, Cecilia
British scientist
Volume IV: 978

Peabody, Elizabeth Palmer
American educator
Volume III: 527

Perkins, Frances
American politician
Volume III: 528

Peron, Eva Duarte de
Argentine first lady
Volume IV: 980

Pesotta, Rose
American activist
Volume III: 528

Peterson, Edith R.
American scientist
Volume III: 529

Piaf, Edith
French singer
Volume IV: 981

Picasso, Paloma
Spanish artist
Volume IV: 983

Plath, Sylvia
American author
Volume III: 530

Pocahontas
Native American princess
Volume III: 532

Poniatowska, Elena
Mexican author
Volume IV: 985

Popova, Liubov Sergeevna
Russian artist
Volume IV: 986

Porter, Katherine Anne
American author
Volume III: 532

Post, Emily Price
American author
Volume III: 534

Potter, Beatrix
British author
Volume IV: 987

Price, Leontyne
American singer
Volume III: 535

Prichard, Diana Garcia
American scientist
Volume III: 536

Priest, Ivy Maude Baker
American politician
Volume III: 536

Proulx, E. Annie
American author
Volume III: 537

Quimby, Edith H.
American scientist
Volume III: 541

Rankin, Jeannette
American politician
Volume III: 543

Ray, Dixy Lee
    American scientist
    Volume III: 545

Redgrave, Vanessa
    British actress
    Volume IV: 991

Reno, Janet
    American government official
    Volume III: 546

Rice, Anne
    American author
    Volume III: 548

Rich, Adrienne
    American author
    Volume III: 549

Richards, Ann Willis
    American politician
    Volume III: 550

Richards, Ellen H.
    American scientist
    Volume III: 551

Richier, Germaine
    French artist
    Volume IV: 992

Ride, Sally
    American astronaut
    Volume III: 554

Riefenstahl, Leni
    German film director
    Volume IV: 993

Ringgold, Faith
    American artist
    Volume III: 556

Rivlin, Alice M
    American government official
    Volume III: 557

Robinson, Harriet Hanson
    American author
    Volume III: 559

Robinson, Joan
    British scientist
    Volume IV: 995

Robinson, Julia
    American mathematician
    Volume III: 563

Robinson, Mary Bourke
    Irish politician
    Volume IV: 996

Rogers, Edith Nourse
    American politician
    Volume III: 564

Rohde, Ruth Bryan Owen
    American politician
    Volume III: 565

Roosevelt, Eleanor
    American first lady
    Volume III: 566

Ros-Lehtinen, Ileana
    American politician
    Volume III: 568

Ross, Betsy
    American patriot
    Volume III: 570

Ross, Diana
    American singer
    Volume III: 571

Ross, Mary G.
    American scientist
    Volume III: 572

Ross, Nellie Tayloe
    American politician
    Volume III: 573

Roybal-Allard, Lucille
    American politician
    Volume III: 575

Rubenstein, Helena
    American business leader
    Volume III: 576

Rudkin, Margaret Fogarty
    American business leader
    Volume III: 578

Rudolph, Wilma
    American athlete
    Volume III: 579

Ruether, Rosemary Radford
American historian
Volume III: 581

Russell, Elizabeth Shull
American scientist
Volume III: 583

Sabin, Florence Rena
American scientist
Volume III: 585

Sacajawea
Native American interpreter
Volume III: 588

Sachs, Nelly
German author
Volume IV: 999

Sadat, Jihan
Egyptian first lady
Volume IV: 1000

Sagar, Ruth
American scientist
Volume III: 591

St. Denis, Ruth
American dancer
Volume III: 592

Salomon, Charlotte
German artist
Volume IV: 1000

Sand, George
French author
Volume IV: 1001

Sanger, Margaret Higgins
American activist
Volume III: 593

Sappho
Greek author
Volume IV: 1003

Sarandon, Susan
American actress
Volume III: 594

Savage, Augusta Christine
American artist
Volume III: 596

Schapiro, Miriam
American artist
Volume III: 598

Schiess, Betty Bone
American religious leader
Volume III: 600

Schlafly, Phyllis
American activist
Volume III: 602

Schniederman, Rose
American activist
Volume III: 603

Schroeder, Patricia Scott
American politician
Volume III: 604

Schussler Fiorenza, Elisabeth
American theologian
Volume III: 606

Seaman, Elizabeth Cochrane
American journalist
Volume III: 607

Seibert, Florence B.
American scientist
Volume III: 609

Selena
American singer
Volume III: 611

Seton, Elizabeth Ann Bayley
American religious leader
Volume III: 612

Sexton, Anne
American author
Volume III: 613

Seymour, Jane
English queen
Volume IV: 1004

Shabazz, Betty
American activist
Volume III: 614

Shaw, Anna Howard
American activist
Volume III: 616

Shaw, Mary
    American scientist
    Volume III: 617

Shelley, Mary
    British author
    Volume IV: 1005

Siebert, Muriel
    American business leader
    Volume III: 618

Silko, Leslie
    American author
    Volume III: 620

Silkwood, Karen
    American activist
    Volume III: 621

Sills, Beverly
    American singer
    Volume III: 623

Singer, Maxine
    American scientist
    Volume III: 624

Sisulu, Nontsikelelo
    South African politician
    Volume IV: 1007

Sitwell, Dame Edith
    British author
    Volume IV: 1009

Slye, Maud
    American scientist
    Volume III: 626

Smeal, Eleanor
    American activist
    Volume III: 627

Smith, Bessie
    American singer
    Volume III: 628

Smith, Dora
    American educator
    Volume III: 630

Smith, Lillian Eugenia
    American author
    Volume III: 632

Smith, Margaret Chase
    American politician
    Volume III: 633

Snowe, Olympia
    American politician
    Volume III: 634

Song Sisters
    Chinese activists
    Volume IV: 1010

Sontag, Susan
    American author
    Volume III: 635

Spark, Muriel Sarah
    British author
    Volume IV: 1012

Stanton, Elizabeth Cady
    American activist
    Volume III: 636

Steel, Danielle
    American author
    Volume III: 637

Steel, Dawn
    American business leader
    Volume III: 639

Stein, Edith
    German philosopher
    Volume IV: 1014

Stein, Gertrude
    American author
    Volume III: 641

Steinem, Gloria
    American activist
    Volume III: 643

Stevens, Nettie Maria
    American scientist
    Volume III: 644

Stone, Lucy
    American activist
    Volume III: 646

Stopes, Marie
    British scientist
    Volume IV: 1016

Stowe, Harriet Beecher
American author
Volume III: 646

Strang, Ruth May
American educator
Volume III: 648

Streisand, Barbra
American singer
Volume III: 649

Suttner, Bertha von
Austrian author
Volume IV: 1017

Suzman, Helen
South African politician
Volume IV: 1019

Switzer, Mary E.
American activist
Volume III: 651

Szold, Henrietta
American activist
Volume III: 652

Taeuber-Arp, Sophie
Swiss artist
Volume IV: 1021

Talbert, Mary
American educator
Volume III: 655

Tallchief, Maria
American dancer
Volume III: 657

Tan, Amy
American author
Volume III: 658

Tarbell, Ida Minerva
American journalist
Volume III: 659

Taussig, Helen Brooke
American scientist
Volume III: 659

Taylor, Elizabeth Rosemond
American actress
Volume III: 661

Taylor, Susie King
American activist
Volume III: 663

Teresa, Mother
Indian religious leader
Volume IV: 1022

Tereshkova, Valentina
Soviet astronaut
Volume IV: 1024

Tharp, Marie
American scientist
Volume III: 664

Tharp, Twyla
American dancer
Volume III: 665

Thatcher, Margaret Hilda
British prime minister
Volume IV: 1026

Thompson, Dorothy
American journalist
Volume III: 666

Tower, Joan
American musician
Volume III: 667

Trotter, Mildred
American scientist
Volume III: 669

Truth, Sojourner
American activist
Volume III: 670

Tubman, Harriet Ross
American activist
Volume III: 671

Tucker, C. DeLores
American activist
Volume III: 672

Turner, Tina
American singer
Volume III: 674

Tyler, Anne
American author
Volume III: 676

Uhlenbeck, Karen
    American mathematician
    Volume III: 679

Van Duyn, Mona
    American author
    Volume III: 681

Vaughan, Sarah Lois
    American singer
    Volume III: 682

Velazquez, Nydia Margarita
    American politician
    Volume III: 683

Victoria
    British queen
    Volume IV: 1029

von Furstenberg, Diane
    American business leader
    Volume III: 686

vos Savant, Marilyn
    American author
    Volume III: 687

Wald, Lillian
    American activist
    Volume III: 689

Walker, Alice
    American author
    Volume III: 690

Walker, Madame C.J.
    American business leader
    Volume III: 692

Walker, Maggie Lena
    American activist
    Volume III: 693

Walker, Margaret
    American author
    Volume III: 694

Walters, Barbara
    American journalist
    Volume III: 695

Warren, Mercy Otis
    American author
    Volume III: 696

Waters, Maxine
    American politician
    Volume III: 697

Wattleton, Faye
    American activist
    Volume III: 699

Wauneka, Annie Dodge
    American activist
    Volume III: 701

Webb, Beatrice Potter
    British activist
    Volume IV: 1033

Weil, Simone
    French philosopher
    Volume IV: 1034

Wells, Mary Georgene
    American business leader
    Volume III: 703

Wells-Barnett, Ida B.
    American journalist
    Volume III: 704

Welty, Eudora
    American author
    Volume III: 705

Westheimer, Ruth Karola
    American psychologist
    Volume III: 707

Westwood, Vivienne
    British business leader
    Volume IV: 1036

Wexler, Nancy
    American psychologist
    Volume III: 708

Wharton, Edith
    American author
    Volume III: 709

Wheatley, Phillis
    American author
    Volume III: 710

Whitman, Christine Todd
    American politician
    Volume III: 711

Whitmire, Kathryn Jean
American politician
Volume III: 713

Widnall, Sheila E.
American scientist
Volume III: 714

Wilder, Laura Ingalls
American author
Volume III: 716

Willard, Emma Hart
American educator
Volume III: 718

Willard, Frances Elizabeth
American activist
Volume III: 719

Wilson, Harriet E.
American author
Volume III: 720

Winfrey, Oprah
American entertainer
Volume III: 721

Winnemucca, Sarah
American author
Volume III: 724

Wong, Anna May
American actress
Volume III: 726

Woodhull, Victoria C.
American activist
Volume III: 728

Woodward, Ellen S.
American activist
Volume III: 729

Woolf, Virginia
British author
Volume IV: 1037

Wright, Frances
American activist
Volume III: 730

Wu Tse-t'ien
Chinese empress
Volume IV: 1038

Xiang Jingyu
Chinese activist
Volume IV: 1041

Yalow, Rosalyn S.
American scientist
Volume III: 733

Yard, Mary Alexander
American organizer
Volume III: 734

Zaharias, Mildred Didrikson
American athlete
Volume III: 737

Zia, Helen
American activist
Volume III: 738

Zwilich, Ellen Taaffe
American musician
Volume III: 739

# NATIONALITY INDEX

## American

Abbott, Berenice
activist
Volume I: 1

Abbott, Grace
activist
Volume I: 3

Abzug, Bella Stavisky
activist
Volume I: 4

Addams, Jane
activist
Volume I: 6

Albright, Madeleine
diplomat
Volume I: 7

Alcott, Louisa May
author
Volume I: 8

Allen, Florence Ellinwood
politician
Volume I: 9

Allen, Paula Gunn
author
Volume I: 10

Alvarez, Julia
author
Volume I: 13

Andersen, Dorothy
scientist
Volume I: 15

Anderson, June
singer
Volume I: 16

Anderson, Marian
singer
Volume I: 17

Andrews, Fannie Fern
educator
Volume I: 19

Angelou, Maya
author
Volume I: 20

Anthony, Susan Brownell
activist
Volume I: 21

Apgar, Virginia
scientist
Volume I: 22

Arbus, Diane Nemerov
artist
Volume I: 24

Ash, Mary Kay Wagner
business leader
Volume I: 26

Baca-Barragan, Polly
politician
Volume I: 29

Baez, Joan
singer
Volume I: 31

## American (continued)

Bailey, Florence Merriam
scientist
Volume I: 33

Baker, Ella Josephine
activist
Volume I: 34

Baker, Josephine
singer
Volume I: 36

Baker, Sara Josephine
scientist
Volume I: 38

Balch, Emily Greene
activist
Volume I: 39

Ball, Lucille
actress
Volume I: 41

Bambara, Toni Cade
author
Volume I: 42

Barnes, Djuna
author
Volume I: 43

Barton, Clara
activist
Volume I: 46

Bates, Katharine Lee
author
Volume I: 47

Battle, Kathleen
singer
Volume I: 49

Beard, Mary Ritter
activist
Volume I: 50

Beecher, Catharine
educator
Volume I: 52

Benedict, Ruth Fulton
scientist
Volume I: 54

Bernstein, Dorothy Lewis
scientist
Volume I: 55

Berry, Mary Frances
activist
Volume I: 56

Bethune, Mary McLeod
educator
Volume I: 59

Bishop, Bridget
barmaid
Volume I: 60

Bishop, Elizabeth
author
Volume I: 62

Black, Shirley Temple
politician
Volume I: 64

Blackburn, Elizabeth Helen
scientist
Volume I: 66

Blackwell, Elizabeth
activist
Volume I: 67

Blanding, Sarah Gibson
educator
Volume I: 68

Bloomer, Amelia Jenks
activist
Volume I: 69

Bloor, Ella Reeve
activist
Volume I: 70

Blume, Judy
author
Volume I: 72

Bly, Nellie
activist
Volume I: 73

Bok, Sissela Ann
philosopher
Volume I: 74

## American (continued)

Bonnin, Gertrude Simmons
activist
Volume I: 76

Booth, Evangeline Cory
activist
Volume I: 78

Bourke-White, Margaret
artist
Volume I: 80

Boxer, Barbara
politician
Volume I: 81

Bradley, Marion Zimmer
author
Volume I: 84

Bradstreet, Anne Dudley
author
Volume I: 86

Brice, Fanny
entertainer
Volume I: 86

Brooks, Gwendolyn
author
Volume I: 88

Brothers, Joyce
psychologist
Volume I: 89

Brown, Charlotte Eugenia
educator
Volume I: 91

Brown, Helen Gurley
journalist
Volume I: 92

Brown, Rachel Fuller
scientist
Volume I: 93

Brown, Tina
journalist
Volume I: 94

Browner, Carol M.
government official
Volume I: 95

Brownmiller, Susan
author
Volume I: 97

Buck, Pearl S.
author
Volume I: 98

Burke, Selma
artist
Volume I: 99

Burnett, Frances Hodgson
author
Volume I: 100

Butler, Octavia E.
author
Volume I: 102

Byrne, Jane
politician
Volume I: 103

Cabrini, St. Frances
religious leader
Volume I: 105

Caesar, Shirley
singer
Volume I: 106

Calamity Jane
frontier figure
Volume I: 107

Caldwell, Sarah
musician
Volume I: 108

Callas, Maria
singer
Volume I: 109

Cannon, Annie Jump
scientist
Volume I: 112

Capriati, Jennifer
athlete
Volume I: 112

Caraway, Hattie Wyatt
politician
Volume I: 115

## American (continued)

Carey Thomas, Martha
educator
Volume I: 117

Carnegie, Hattie
artist
Volume I: 117

Carroll, Anna Ella
author
Volume I: 118

Carson, Rachel Louise
scientist
Volume I: 121

Cassatt, Mary
artist
Volume I: 122

Catt, Carrie Chapman
activist
Volume I: 123

Chavez, Linda
activist
Volume I: 124

Chicago, Judy
artist
Volume I: 126

Child, Julia McWilliams
chef
Volume I: 128

Child, Lydia Maria Francis
author
Volume I: 129

Childress, Alice
author
Volume I: 130

Chinn, May Edward
scientist
Volume I: 132

Chisholm, Shirley
politician
Volume I: 133

Chopin, Katherine
author
Volume I: 135

Chung, Connie
journalist
Volume I: 138

Cisneros, Sandra
author
Volume I: 138

Claiborne, Liz
business leader
Volume I: 140

Clapp, Margaret Antoinette
author
Volume I: 141

Cline, Patsy
singer
Volume I: 142

Clinton, Hillary Rodham
first lady
Volume I: 144

Cochran, Jacqueline
aviator
Volume I: 146

Coleman, Bessie
aviator
Volume I: 148

Collins, Eileen
astronaut
Volume I: 149

Collins, Marva
educator
Volume I: 152

Colwell, Rita R.
scientist
Volume I: 154

Conway, Jill Kathryn Ker
historian
Volume I: 155

Cotten, Elizabeth
singer
Volume I: 156

Crandall, Prudence
educator
Volume I: 158

## American (continued)

Cushman, Charlotte
actress
Volume I: 159

Daly, Mary
philosopher
Volume I: 161

Dandridge, Dorothy
actress
Volume I: 163

Davis, Angela
activist
Volume I: 165

Davis, Bette
actress
Volume I: 166

Day, Dorothy
activist
Volume I: 168

Dee, Ruby
actress
Volume I: 169

Deer, Ada E.
activist
Volume I: 172

de Mille, Agnes
dancer
Volume I: 175

Dewson, Mary Williams
politician
Volume I: 176

Dickinson, Emily
author
Volume I: 177

Dix, Dorothea Lynde
activist
Volume I: 179

Dodge, Grace Hoadley
activist
Volume I: 180

Dole, Elizabeth
politician
Volume I: 181

Doolittle, Hilda
author
Volume I: 184

Dorr, Rheta Childe
journalist
Volume I: 184

Dove, Rita Frances
author
Volume I: 186

Drexel, Katherine
religious leader
Volume I: 188

Dudley, Barbara
activist
Volume I: 189

Duncan, Isadora
dancer
Volume I: 190

Dunham, Katherine
dancer
Volume I: 191

Earhart, Amelia Mary
aviator
Volume I: 195

Earle, Sylvia A.
scientist
Volume I: 196

Eddy, Mary Baker
religious leader
Volume I: 198

Edelman, Marian Wright
activist
Volume I: 198

Eisenhower, Mamie Doud
first lady
Volume I: 200

Elders, Joycelyn
scientist
Volume I: 201

Elion, Gertrude B.
scientist
Volume I: 204

NATIONALITY INDEX

## American (continued)

Ephron, Nora
author
Volume I: 206

Evers-Williams, Myrlie
activist
Volume I: 207

Falletta, JoAnn
musician
Volume I: 211

Farmer, Fannie Merritt
chef
Volume I: 213

Farrell, Suzanne
dancer
Volume I: 213

Feinstein, Dianne
politician
Volume I: 215

Ferber, Edna
author
Volume I: 216

Ferraro, Geraldine
politician
Volume I: 217

Fiske, Minnie Maddern
actress
Volume I: 219

Fitzgerald, Ella
singer
Volume I: 220

FitzGerald, Frances
author
Volume I: 221

Flanagan, Hallie
author
Volume I: 222

Fletcher, Alice Cunningham
anthropologist
Volume I: 223

Flynn, Elizabeth Gurley
activist
Volume I: 224

Fonda, Jane
actress
Volume I: 226

Fossey, Dian
activist
Volume I: 227

Foster, Abigail Kelley
activist
Volume I: 228

Frankenthaler, Helen
artist
Volume I: 229

Franklin, Aretha
singer
Volume I: 230

Friedan, Betty
author
Volume I: 232

Fuller, Sarah Margaret
activist
Volume I: 234

Gage, Matilda Joslyn
activist
Volume II: 237

Garbo, Greta
actress
Volume II: 239

Garland, Judy
actress and singer
Volume II: 240

Gayle, Helene Doris
scientist
Volume II: 241

Geller, Margaret Joan
scientist
Volume II: 242

Gibson, Althea
athlete
Volume II: 243

Gilbreth, Lillian
business leader
Volume II: 244

## American (continued)

Gilman, Charlotte Anna P.
author
Volume II: 246

Gilpin, Laura
artist
Volume II: 247

Ginsburg, Ruth Bader
jurist
Volume II: 248

Giovanni, Yolande Cornelia
author
Volume II: 250

Glasgow, Ellen
author
Volume II: 252

Goldberg, Whoopi
actress
Volume II: 253

Goldman, Emma
activist
Volume II: 256

Goldmark, Josephine
author
Volume II: 257

Goodman, Ellen Holtz
journalist
Volume II: 258

Graham, Katharine Meyer
journalist
Volume II: 259

Graham, Martha
dancer
Volume II: 260

Granville, Evelyn Boyd
mathematician
Volume II: 262

Graves, Nancy Stevenson
artist
Volume II: 263

Gray, Hannah Holborn
educator
Volume II: 265

Green, Constance
author
Volume II: 267

Green, Edith Starrett
politician
Volume II: 268

Grimke, Angelina Emily
activist
Volume II: 269

Grimke, Sarah Moore
activist
Volume II: 269

Grossinger, Jennie
business leader
Volume II: 270

Guisewite, Cathy Lee
cartoonist
Volume II: 271

Hagen, Uta Thyra
actress
Volume II: 275

Hale, Sarah Josepha
journalist
Volume II: 276

Haley, Magaret A.
activist
Volume II: 277

Hamer, Fannie Lou
activist
Volume II: 278

Hamilton, Alice
scientist
Volume II: 280

Hanks, Nancy
fundraiser
Volume II: 281

Hansberry, Lorraine
author
Volume II: 282

Hansen, Julia Butler
politician
Volume II: 283

## American (continued)

Hardy, Harriet
scientist
Volume II: 284

Harjo, Suzan Shown
activist
Volume II: 285

Harper, Frances Ellen W.
author
Volume II: 287

Harriman, Pamela
politician
Volume II: 289

Harris, Barbara Clementine
religious leader
Volume II: 291

Harris, LaDonna
activist
Volume II: 292

Harris, Patricia Roberts
politician
Volume II: 294

Hayes, Helen
actress
Volume II: 296

Hayworth, Rita
actress
Volume II: 297

Head, Edith
designer
Volume II: 299

Healy, Bernadine Patricia
scientist
Volume II: 302

Hearst, Patricia
heiress
Volume II: 303

Heckler, Margaret Mary
government official
Volume II: 304

Hellman, Lillian Florence
author
Volume II: 305

Hepburn, Katharine
actress
Volume II: 306

Higgins, Marguerite
journalist
Volume II: 308

Hill, Anita
educator
Volume II: 310

Hills, Carla Anderson
government official
Volume II: 313

Himmelfarb, Gertude
author
Volume II: 314

Hinton, Susan Eloise
author
Volume II: 317

Hobby, Oveta Culp
business leader
Volume II: 317

Holiday, Billie
singer
Volume II: 320

Holm, Hanya
dancer
Volume II: 321

Holzer, Jenny
artist
Volume II: 322

hooks, bell
author
Volume II: 324

Hopper, Grace
scientist
Volume II: 327

Horne, Lena
singer
Volume II: 330

Horner, Matina Souretis
educator
Volume II: 332

## American (continued)

Horney, Karen Danielsen
scientist
Volume II: 333

Howe, Florence Rosenfeld
author
Volume II: 334

Howe, Julia Ward
activist
Volume II: 335

Huerta, Dolores
activist
Volume II: 336

Hunter, Madeline Cheek
educator
Volume II: 339

Hurston, Zora Neale
author
Volume II: 340

Hutchinson, Anne Marbury
religious leader
Volume II: 341

Hyman, Libbie Henrietta
scientist
Volume II: 343

Ireland, Patricia
activist
Volume II: 347

Jackson, Helen Hunt
author
Volume II: 349

Jackson, Shirley Ann
scientist
Volume II: 350

Jacobs, Harriet A.
author
Volume II: 351

Jemison, Mae C.
astronaut
Volume II: 354

Jewett, Sarah Orne
author
Volume II: 355

Johnson, Betsey
artist
Volume II: 356

Johnson, Marietta Louise
educator
Volume II: 358

Johnson, Virginia E.
scientist
Volume II: 359

Jones, Mary Harris
activist
Volume II: 360

Jong, Erica Mann
author
Volume II: 361

Jordan, Barbara Charline
politician
Volume II: 364

Jordan, June
author
Volume II: 365

Karan, Donna
business leader
Volume II: 369

Karle, Isabella
scientist
Volume II: 371

Kassebaum, Nancy
politician
Volume II: 372

Keller, Helen Adams
author
Volume II: 374

Kelley, Florence
activist
Volume II: 375

Kellor, Frances
activist
Volume II: 375

Keohane, Nannerl Overholser
educator
Volume II: 377

## American (continued)

King, Billie Jean
athlete
Volume II: 379

King, Coretta Scott
activist
Volume II: 380

Kingston, Maxine Hong
author
Volume II: 381

Kirkpatrick, Jeane J.
government official
Volume II: 383

Knopf, Blanche Wolf
business leader
Volume II: 385

Krasner, Lee
artist
Volume II: 386

Kreps, Juanita Morris
author
Volume II: 387

Kubler-Ross, Elisabeth
scientist
Volume II: 388

Kunin, Madeleine May
politician
Volume II: 390

La Flesche, Susette
activist
Volume II: 393

Lange, Dorothea
artist
Volume II: 394

Larsen, Nella
author
Volume II: 395

Lauder, Estee
business leader
Volume II: 396

Lazarus, Emma
author
Volume II: 398

Lease, Mary Elizabeth
activist
Volume II: 398

Lee, Mother Ann
religious leader
Volume II: 399

Le Guin, Ursula K.
author
Volume II: 402

Leibovitz, Annie
artist
Volume II: 403

L'Engle, Madeleine
author
Volume II: 406

Levi-Montalcini, Rita
scientist
Volume II: 408

Lin, Maya Ying
artist
Volume II: 409

Lindbergh, Anne Morrow
author
Volume II: 411

Lloyd-Jones, Esther
educator
Volume II: 412

Long, Irene D.
scientist
Volume II: 413

Lorde, Audre
author
Volume II: 414

Love, Susan M.
activist
Volume II: 416

Low, Juliette Gordon
activist
Volume II: 418

Lowell, Amy
author
Volume II: 419

## American (continued)

Lowell, Josephine Shaw
    activist
    Volume II: 420

Luce, Clare Boothe
    politician
    Volume II: 420

Luhan, Mabel Doge
    author
    Volume II: 422

Lynd, Helen Merrell
    educator
    Volume II: 423

Lyon, Mary
    educator
    Volume II: 425

Macdonald, Eleanor
    scientist
    Volume II: 429

Madison, Dolly
    first lady
    Volume II: 430

Madonna
    singer
    Volume II: 432

Mankiller, Wilma
    Native American chief
    Volume II: 434

Margulis, Lynn
    scientist
    Volume II: 436

Marshall, Paule Burke
    author
    Volume II: 437

Martin, Agnes
    artist
    Volume II: 438

Martin, Lynn Morley
    government official
    Volume II: 440

Martin, Mary
    singer
    Volume II: 441

Martinez, Vilma Socorro
    activist
    Volume II: 443

McCarthy, Mary T.
    author
    Volume II: 445

McClintock, Barbara
    scientist
    Volume II: 447

McCullers, Carson
    author
    Volume II: 448

McDaniel, Hattie
    actress
    Volume II: 450

McMillan, Terry
    author
    Volume II: 453

McMurray, Bette Clair
    business leader
    Volume II: 454

McQueen, Butterfly
    actress
    Volume II: 455

Mead, Margaret
    scientist
    Volume II: 458

Mendenhall, Dorothy Reed
    scientist
    Volume II: 460

Mikulski, Barbara
    politician
    Volume II: 460

Millay, Edna St. Vincent
    author
    Volume II: 463

Millett, Kate
    artist
    Volume II: 464

Mink, Patsy Takemoto
    politician
    Volume II: 465

## American (continued)

Mintz, Beatrice
scientist
Volume II: 467

Mitchell, Margaret
author
Volume II: 468

Mitchell, Maria
educator
Volume II: 469

Molinari, Susan
politician
Volume II: 470

Monroe, Marilyn
actress
Volume II: 471

Moore, Charlotte E.
scientist
Volume II: 472

Moore, Marianne
author
Volume II: 473

Morgan, Julia
artist
Volume II: 475

Morgan, Robin
activist
Volume II: 476

Morrison, Toni
author
Volume II: 477

Morton, Nelle Katherine
religious leader
Volume II: 479

Mosely-Braun, Carol
politician
Volume II: 481

Moses, Grandma
artist
Volume II: 482

Motley, Constance Baker
politician
Volume II: 483

Mott, Lucretia Coffin
activist
Volume II: 485

Muldowney, Shirley
race car driver
Volume II: 485

Nation, Carry Amelia Moore
activist
Volume III: 489

Natividad, Irene
politician
Volume III: 490

Navratilova, Martina
athlete
Volume III: 492

Naylor, Gloria
author
Volume III: 495

Neufeld, Elizabeth
scientist
Volume III: 496

Nevelson, Louise
artist
Volume III: 497

Nicolson, Marjorie Hope
educator
Volume III: 498

Norman, Jessye
singer
Volume III: 499

Novello, Antonia
scientist
Volume III: 501

Oakley, Annie
frontier figure
Volume III: 505

Oates, Joyce Carol
author
Volume III: 506

Ochoa, Ellen
scientist
Volume III: 508

## American (continued)

O'Connor, Flannery
author
Volume III: 509

O'Connor, Sandra Day
jurist
Volume III: 510

O'Hair, Madalyn Murray
activist
Volume III: 512

O'Keefe, Georgia
artist
Volume III: 512

Onassis, Jacqueline Kennedy
first lady
Volume III: 514

Ovington, Mary White
activist
Volume III: 516

Owen, Ruth Bryan
politician
Volume III: 517

Pagels, Elaine Hiesey
historian
Volume III: 521

Park, Maud Wood
activist
Volume III: 522

Parker, Dorothy Rothschild
author
Volume III: 523

Parks, Rosa
activist
Volume III: 523

Patrick, Jennie R.
scientist
Volume III: 525

Patrick, Ruth
scientist
Volume III: 526

Peabody, Elizabeth Palmer
educator
Volume III: 527

Perkins, Frances
politician
Volume III: 528

Pesotta, Rose
activist
Volume III: 528

Peterson, Edith R.
scientist
Volume III: 529

Plath, Sylvia
author
Volume III: 530

Pocahontas
Native American princess
Volume III: 532

Porter, Katherine Anne
author
Volume III: 532

Post, Emily Price
author
Volume III: 534

Price, Leontyne
singer
Volume III: 535

Prichard, Diana Garcia
scientist
Volume III: 536

Priest, Ivy Maude Baker
politician
Volume III: 536

Proulx, E. Annie
author
Volume III: 537

Quimby, Edith H.
scientist
Volume III: 541

Rankin, Jeannette
politician
Volume III: 543

Ray, Dixy Lee
scientist
Volume III: 545

## American (continued)

Reno, Janet
government official
Volume III: 546

Rice, Anne
author
Volume III: 548

Rich, Adrienne
author
Volume III: 549

Richards, Ann Willis
politician
Volume III: 550

Richards, Ellen H.
scientist
Volume III: 551

Ride, Sally
astronaut
Volume III: 554

Ringgold, Faith
artist
Volume III: 556

Rivlin, Alice M.
government official
Volume III: 557

Robinson, Harriet Hanson
author
Volume III: 559

Robinson, Julia
mathematician
Volume III: 563

Rogers, Edith Nourse
politician
Volume III: 564

Rohde, Ruth Bryan Owen
politician
Volume III: 565

Roosevelt, Eleanor
first lady
Volume III: 566

Ros-Lehtinen, Ileana
politician
Volume III: 568

Ross, Betsy
patriot
Volume III: 570

Ross, Diana
singer
Volume III: 571

Ross, Mary G.
scientist
Volume III: 572

Ross, Nellie Tayloe
politician
Volume III: 573

Roybal-Allard, Lucille
politician
Volume III: 575

Rubenstein, Helena
business leader
Volume III: 576

Rudkin, Margaret Fogarty
business leader
Volume III: 578

Rudolph, Wilma
athlete
Volume III: 579

Ruether, Rosemary Radford
historian
Volume III: 581

Russell, Elizabeth Shull
scientist
Volume III: 583

Sabin, Florence Rena
scientist
Volume III: 585

Sacajawea
interpreter
Volume III: 588

Sagar, Ruth
scientist
Volume III: 591

St. Denis, Ruth
dancer
Volume III: 592

## American (continued)

Sanger, Margaret Higgins
activist
Volume III: 593

Sarandon, Susan
actress
Volume III: 594

Savage, Augusta Christine
artist
Volume III: 596

Schapiro, Miriam
artist
Volume III: 598

Schiess, Betty Bone
religious leader
Volume III: 600

Schlafly, Phyllis
activist
Volume III: 602

Schniederman, Rose
activist
Volume III: 603

Schroeder, Patricia Scott
politician
Volume III: 604

Schussler Fiorenza, Elisabeth
theologian
Volume III: 606

Seaman, Elizabeth Cochrane
journalist
Volume III: 607

Seibert, Florence B.
scientist
Volume III: 609

Selena
singer
Volume III: 611

Seton, Elizabeth Ann Bayley
religious leader
Volume III: 612

Sexton, Anne
author
Volume III: 613

Shabazz, Betty
activist
Volume III: 614

Shaw, Anna Howard
activist
Volume III: 616

Shaw, Mary
scientist
Volume III: 617

Siebert, Muriel
business leader
Volume III: 618

Silko, Leslie
author
Volume III: 620

Silkwood, Karen
activist
Volume III: 621

Sills, Beverly
singer
Volume III: 623

Singer, Maxine
scientist
Volume III: 624

Slye, Maud
scientist
Volume III: 626

Smeal, Eleanor
activist
Volume III: 627

Smith, Bessie
singer
Volume III: 628

Smith, Dora
educator
Volume III: 630

Smith, Lillian Eugenia
author
Volume III: 632

Smith, Margaret Chase
politician
Volume III: 633

## American (continued)

Snowe, Olympia
politician
Volume III: 634

Sontag, Susan
author
Volume III: 635

Stanton, Elizabeth Cady
activist
Volume III: 636

Steel, Danielle
author
Volume III: 637

Steel, Dawn
business leader
Volume III: 639

Stein, Gertrude
author
Volume III: 641

Steinem, Gloria
author
Volume III: 643

Stevens, Nettie Maria
scientist
Volume III: 644

Stone, Lucy
activist
Volume III: 646

Stowe, Harriet Beecher
author
Volume III: 646

Strang, Ruth May
educator
Volume III: 648

Streisand, Barbra
singer
Volume III: 649

Switzer, Mary E.
activist
Volume III: 651

Szold, Henrietta
activist
Volume III: 652

Talbert, Mary
educator
Volume III: 655

Tallchief, Maria
dancer
Volume III: 657

Tan, Amy
author
Volume III: 658

Tarbell, Ida Minerva
journalist
Volume III: 659

Taussig, Helen Brooke
scientist
Volume III: 659

Taylor, Elizabeth Rosemond
actress
Volume III: 661

Taylor, Susie King
activist
Volume III: 663

Tharp, Marie
scientist
Volume III: 664

Tharp, Twyla
dancer
Volume III: 665

Thompson, Dorothy
journalist
Volume III: 666

Tower, Joan
musician
Volume III: 667

Trotter, Mildred
scientist
Volume III: 669

Truth, Sojourner
activist
Volume III: 670

Tubman, Harriet Ross
activist
Volume III: 671

## American (continued)

Tucker, C. DeLores
activist
Volume III: 672

Turner, Tina
singer
Volume III: 674

Tyler, Anne
author
Volume III: 676

Uhlenbeck, Karen
mathematician
Volume III: 679

Van Duyn, Mona
author
Volume III: 681

Vaughan, Sarah Lois
singer
Volume III: 682

Velazquez, Nydia Margarita
politician
Volume III: 683

von Furstenberg, Diane
business leader
Volume III: 686

vos Savant, Marilyn
author
Volume III: 687

Wald, Lillian
activist
Volume III: 689

Walker, Alice
author
Volume III: 690

Walker, Madame C.J.
business leader
Volume III: 692

Walker, Maggie Lena
activist
Volume III: 693

Walker, Margaret
author
Volume III: 694

Walters, Barbara
journalist
Volume III: 695

Warren, Mercy Otis
author
Volume III: 696

Waters, Maxine
politician
Volume III: 697

Wattleton, Faye
activist
Volume III: 699

Wauneka, Annie Dodge
activist
Volume III: 701

Wells, Mary Georgene
business leader
Volume III: 703

Wells-Barnett, Ida B.
journalist
Volume III: 704

Welty, Eudora
author
Volume III: 705

Westheimer, Ruth Karola
psychologist
Volume III: 707

Wexler, Nancy
psychologist
Volume III: 708

Wharton, Edith
author
Volume III: 709

Wheatley, Phillis
author
Volume III: 710

Whitman, Christine Todd
politician
Volume III: 711

Whitmire, Kathryn Jean
politician
Volume III: 713

## American (continued)

Widnall, Sheila E.
scientist
Volume III: 714

Wilder, Laura Ingalls
author
Volume III: 716

Willard, Emma Hart
educator
Volume III: 718

Willard, Frances Elizabeth
activist
Volume III: 719

Wilson, Harriet E.
author
Volume III: 720

Winfrey, Oprah
journalist
Volume III: 721

Winnemucca, Sarah
author
Volume III: 724

Wong, Anna May
actress
Volume III: 726

Woodhull, Victoria C.
activist
Volume III: 728

Woodward, Ellen S.
acivist
Volume III: 729

Wright, Frances
activist
Volume III: 730

Yalow, Rosalyn S.
scientist
Volume III: 733

Yard, Mary Alexander
organizer
Volume III: 734

Zaharias, Mildred Didrikson
athlete
Volume III: 737

Zia, Helen
activist
Volume III: 738

Zwilich, Ellen Taaffe
musician
Volume III: 739

## Argentinian

Peron, Eva Duarte de
first lady
Volume IV: 980

## Australian

Anderson, Judith
actress
Volume IV: 747

Caldicott, Helen Broinowski
activist
Volume IV: 777

Chisholm, Caroline
author
Volume IV: 788

Franklin, Stella Maraia
author
Volume IV: 841

MacKillop, Mary
religious leader
Volume IV: 933

## Austrian

Adamson, Joy
naturalist
Volume IV: 743

Freud, Anna
scientist
Volume IV: 843

Harand, Irene
activist
Volume IV: 871

## Austrian (continued)

Klein, Melanie
    psychologist
    Volume IV: 911

Maria Theresa
    queen
    Volume IV: 941

Meitner, Lise
    scientist
    Volume IV: 953

Suttner, Bertha von
    author
    Volume IV: 1017

## Bermudan

Gordon, Pamela
    politician
    Volume IV: 864

## Botswanan

Chiepe, Gaositwe Keagak
    politician
    Volume IV: 788

## Byzantine

Comnena, Anna
    author
    Volume IV: 801

Irene of Athens
    empress
    Volume IV: 892

## Canadian

Arden, Elizabeth
    business leader
    Volume IV: 750

Carr, Emily
    artist
    Volume IV: 779

## Chilean

Allende, Isabel
    author
    Volume IV: 745

Bombal, Maria Luisa
    author
    Volume IV: 766

Mistral, Gabriela
    author
    Volume IV: 959

## Chinese

Jiang Qing
    politician
    Volume IV: 897

Song Sisters
    activists
    Volume IV: 1010

Wu Tse-t'ien
    empress
    Volume IV: 1038

Xiang Jingyu
    activist
    Volume IV: 1041

## Czech

Cori, Gerty T.
    scientist
    Volume IV: 802

## Danish

Dinesen, Karen Blixen-Fineck
    author
    Volume IV: 816

## Dutch

Frank, Anne
    author
    Volume IV: 838

## Egyptian

Cleopatra
    queen
    Volume IV: 797

## Egyptian (continued)

Hatshepsut
queen
Volume IV: 877

Hypatia of Alexandria
scientist
Volume IV: 886

Nefertiti
queen
Volume IV: 966

Sadat, Jihan
first lady
Volume IV: 1000

## English

Ashley, Laura
business leader
Volume IV: 753

Austen, Jane
author
Volume IV: 757

Boleyn, Anne
queen
Volume IV: 765

Bronte, Charlotte
author
Volume IV: 771

Bronte, Emily
author
Volume IV: 772

Browning, Elizabeth Barrett
author
Volume IV: 773

Catherine of Aragon
queen
Volume IV: 780

Christie, Agatha
author
Volume IV: 791

Diana
princess
Volume IV: 812

Douglas, Mary Tew
scientist
Volume IV: 819

Eliot, George
author
Volume IV: 822

Elizabeth I
queen
Volume IV: 824

Elizabeth II
queen
Volume IV: 827

Fonteyn, Dame Margot
dancer
Volume IV: 837

Franklin, Rosalind Elsie
scientist
Volume IV: 839

Fraser, Lady Antonia
author
Volume IV: 841

Fry, Elizabeth
activist
Volume IV: 845

Garrett (Anderson), Elizabeth
scientist
Volume IV: 850

Gaskell, Elizabeth
author
Volume IV: 853

Goodall, Jane
scientist
Volume IV: 860

Greer, Germaine
author
Volume IV: 866

Hepburn, Audrey
actress
Volume IV: 878

Hepworth, Barbara
artist
Volume IV: 880

## English (continued)

Hesse, Mary B.
philospher
Volume IV: 883

Hodgkin, Dorothy Crowfoot
scientist
Volume IV: 884

Julian of Norwich
religious leader
Volume IV: 904

Leakey, Mary Douglas
scientist
Volume IV: 915

Leigh, Vivien
actress
Volume IV: 916

Lessing, Doris
author
Volume IV: 918

Lovelace, Ada Byron
author
Volume IV: 927

Mary I
queen
Volume IV: 947

Midgely, Mary Burton
philosopher
Volume IV: 958

Nightingale, Florence
activist
Volume IV: 966

Payne-Gaposchkin, Cecilia
scientist
Volume IV: 978

Potter, Beatrix
author
Volume IV: 987

Redgrave, Vanessa
actress
Volume IV: 991

Robinson, Joan
scientist
Volume IV: 995

Seymour, Jane
queen
Volume IV: 1004

Shelley, Mary
author
Volume IV: 1005

Sitwell, Dame Edith
author
Volume IV: 1009

Spark, Muriel Sarah
author
Volume IV: 1012

Stopes, Marie
scientist
Volume IV: 1016

Thatcher, Margaret Hilda
politician
Volume IV: 1026

Victoria
queen
Volume IV: 1029

Webb, Beatrice Potter
activist
Volume IV: 1033

Westwood, Vivienne
business leader
Volume IV: 1036

Woolf, Virginia
author
Volume IV: 1037

## Filipino

Aquino, Corazon
politician
Volume IV: 748

Marcos, Imelda
first lady
Volume IV: 940

## French

Bourgeoys, Marguerite
religious leader
Volume IV: 770

Chanel, Coco
business leader
Volume IV: 787

Christine de Pisan
activist
Volume IV: 795

Colette, Sidonie Gabrielle
author
Volume IV: 799

Curie, Marie Sklodowska
scientist
Volume IV: 805

de Beauvoir, Simone
author
Volume IV: 809

Eleanor of Aquitaine
queen
Volume IV: 821

Joan of Arc
religious leader
Volume IV: 900

Joliot-Curie, Irene
scientist
Volume IV: 902

Marie Antoinette
queen
Volume IV: 943

Medici, Catherine de
queen
Volume IV: 950

Nin, Anais
author
Volume IV: 967

Piaf, Edith
singer
Volume IV: 981

Richier, Germaine
artist
Volume IV: 992

Sand, George
author
Volume IV: 1001

Weil, Simone
philosopher
Volume IV: 1034

## German

Arendt, Hannah
philosopher
Volume IV: 751

Goeppert-Mayer, Maria
scientist
Volume IV: 855

Hesse, Eva
artist
Volume IV: 881

Kelly, Petra
politician
Volume IV: 910

Kollwitz, Kathe
artist
Volume IV: 912

Modersohn-Becker, Paula
artist
Volume IV: 960

Noether, Emmy
mathematician
Volume IV: 969

Riefenstahl, Leni
film director
Volume IV: 993

Sachs, Nelly
author
Volume IV: 999

Salomon, Charlotte
artist
Volume IV: 1000

## German (continued)

Stein, Edith
philosopher
Volume IV: 1014

## Greek

Sappho
author
Volume IV: 1003

## Guatemalan

Menchu, Rigoberta
activist
Volume IV: 956

## Hawaiian

Liliuokalani, Lydia Kamakaeha
queen
Volume IV: 919

## Hungarian

Elizabeth of Hungary
saint
Volume IV: 831

## Indian

Gandhi, Indira
politician
Volume IV: 849

Mahal, Hazrat
activist
Volume IV: 934

Naidu, Sarojini
author
Volume IV: 965

Pandit, Vijaya Lakshmi
politician
Volume IV: 977

Teresa, Mother
religious leader
Volume IV: 1022

## Irish

Bell Burnell, Susan Jocelyn
scientist
Volume IV: 761

Devlin, Bernadette
politician
Volume IV: 810

Guerin, Veronica
journalist
Volume IV: 868

Lonsdale, Kathleen
scientist
Volume IV: 923

Markievicz, Constance
activist
Volume IV: 944

Murdoch, Iris
author
Volume IV: 963

Robinson, Mary Bourke
politician
Volume IV: 996

## Italian

Borgia, Lucrezia
schemer
Volume IV: 767

Catherine of Siena
saint
Volume IV: 782

Ginzburg, Natalia Levi
author
Volume IV: 854

Loren, Sophia
actress
Volume IV: 925

### Italian (continued)

Montessori, Maria
    educator
    Volume IV: 961

### Japanese

Doi Takako
    politician
    Volume IV: 817

Imaoka, Shinichiro
    religious leader
    Volume IV: 891

### Kenyan

Maathai, Wangari Muta
    activist
    Volume IV: 931

Ogot, Grace Emily Akinyi
    author
    Volume IV: 973

### Korean

Min
    queen
    Volume IV: 959

### Mexican

Juana Ines de la Cruz, Sister
    religious leader
    Volume IV: 904

Kahlo, Frida
    artist
    Volume IV: 909

Poniatowska, Elena
    author
    Volume IV: 985

### Myanmar

Aung San Suu Kyi
    politician
    Volume IV: 755

### New Zealander

Mansfield, Katherine
    author
    Volume IV: 938

### Nicaraguan

Chamorro, Violeta
    politician
    Volume IV: 785

### Norwegian

Brundtland, Gro Harlem
    politician
    Volume IV: 774

### Pakistani

Bhutto, Benazir
    politician
    Volume IV: 762

### Palestinian

Ashrawi, Hanan Mikhail
    activist
    Volume IV: 754

### Polish

Luxemburg, Rosa
    activist
    Volume IV: 929

### Roman

Julias of Rome, The
    empress
    Volume IV: 905

Livia
    empress
    Volume IV: 920

## Romanian

Blandiana, Ana
    author
    Volume IV: 763

Comaneci, Nadia
    athlete
    Volume IV: 800

## Russian

Catherine the Great
    empress
    Volume IV: 783

Elizabeth Petrovna
    empress
    Volume IV: 833

Goncharova, Natalia
    artist
    Volume IV: 858

Gordeeva, Ekaterina
    athlete
    Volume IV: 861

Popova, Liubov Sergeevna
    artist
    Volume IV: 986

Tereshkova, Valentina
    astronaut
    Volume IV: 1024

## Scottish

Mary Queen of Scots
    queen
    Volume IV: 948

## Senegalese

Faye, Safi
    filmmaker
    Volume IV: 835

## South African

First, Ruth
    activist
    Volume IV: 836

Gordimer, Nadine
    author
    Volume IV: 863

Mandela, Winnie
    activist
    Volume IV: 936

Sisulu, Nontsikelelo
    politician
    Volume IV: 1007

Suzman, Helen
    politician
    Volume IV: 1019

## Spanish

Ibarruri, Dolores Gomez
    activist
    Volume IV: 889

Isabella I
    queen
    Volume IV: 895

Picasso, Paloma
    artist
    Volume IV: 983

## Sri Lankan

Bandaranaike, Sirimavo
    politician
    Volume IV: 759

## Swedish

Christina
    queen
    Volume IV: 793

## Swiss

Oppenheim, Meret
    artist
    Volume IV: 974

Taeuber-Arp, Sophie
    artist
    Volume IV: 1021

## Turkish

Ciller, Tansu
   politician
      Volume IV: 796

## Ugandan

Elizabeth Bagaaya Nyabongo
   politician
      Volume IV: 829

# OCCUPATION INDEX

## Activist

Abbott, Grace
  American
  Volume I: 3

Abzug, Bella Stavisky
  American
  Volume I: 4

Addams, Jane
  American
  Volume I: 6

Anthony, Susan Brownell
  American
  Volume I: 21

Ashrawi, Hanan Mikhail
  Palestinian
  Volume IV: 754

Baker, Ella Josephine
  American
  Volume I: 34

Balch, Emily Greene
  American
  Volume I: 39

Barton, Clara
  American
  Volume I: 46

Beard, Mary Ritter
  American
  Volume I: 50

Berry, Mary Frances
  American
  Volume I: 56

Blackwell, Elizabeth
  American
  Volume I: 67

Bloomer, Amelia Jenks
  American
  Volume I: 69

Bloor, Ella Reeve
  American
  Volume I: 70

Bly, Nellie
  American
  Volume I: 73

Bonnin, Gertrude Simmons
  American
  Volume I: 76

Booth, Evangeline Cory
  American
  Volume I: 78

Caldicott, Helen Broinowski
  Australian
  Volume IV: 777

Catt, Carrie Chapman
  American
  Volume I: 123

Chavez, Linda
  American
  Volume I: 124

Christine de Pisan
  French
  Volume IV: 795

## Activist (continued)

Davis, Angela
American
Volume I: 165

Day, Dorothy
American
Volume I: 168

Deer, Ada E.
American
Volume I: 172

Dix, Dorothea Lynde
American
Volume I: 179

Dodge, Grace Hoadley
American
Volume I: 180

Dudley, Barbara
American
Volume I: 189

Edelman, Marian Wright
American
Volume I: 198

Evers-Williams, Myrlie
American
Volume I: 207

First, Ruth
South African
Volume IV: 836

Flynn, Elizabeth Gurley
American
Volume I: 224

Fossey, Dian
American
Volume I: 227

Foster, Abigail Kelley
American
Volume I: 228

Fry, Elizabeth
English
Volume IV: 845

Fuller, Sarah Margaret
American
Volume I: 234

Gage, Matilda Joslyn
American
Volume II: 237

Goldman, Emma
American
Volume II: 256

Grimke, Angelina Emily
American
Volume II: 269

Grimke, Sarah Moore
American
Volume II: 269

Haley, Margaret A.
American
Volume II: 277

Hamer, Fannie Lou
American
Volume II: 278

Harand, Irene
Austrian
Volume IV: 871

Harjo, Suzan Shown
American
Volume II: 285

Harris, LaDonna
American
Volume II: 292

Howe, Julia Ward
American
Volume II: 335

Huerta, Dolores
American
Volume II: 336

Ibarruri, Dolores Gomez
Spanish
Volume IV: 889

Ireland, Patricia
American
Volume II: 347

Jones, Mary Harris
American
Volume II: 360

## Activist (continued)

Kelley, Florence
American
Volume II: 375

Kellor, Frances
American
Volume II: 375

King, Coretta Scott
American
Volume II: 380

La Flesche, Susette
American
Volume II: 393

Lease, Mary Elizabeth
American
Volume II: 398

Love, Susan M.
American
Volume II: 416

Low, Juliette Gordon
American
Volume II: 418

Lowell, Josephine Shaw
American
Volume II: 420

Luxemburg, Rosa
Polish
Volume IV: 929

Maathai, Wangari Muta
Kenyan
Volume IV: 931

Mahal, Hazrat
Indian
Volume IV: 934

Mandela, Winnie
South African
Volume IV: 936

Mankiller, Wilma
American
Volume II: 434

Markievicz, Constance
Irish
Volume IV: 944

Martinez, Vilma Socorro
American
Volume II: 443

Menchu, Rigoberta
Guatemalan
Volume IV: 956

Morgan, Robin
American
Volume II: 476

Mott, Lucretia Coffin
American
Volume II: 485

Nation, Carry Amelia Moore
American
Volume III: 489

Nightingale, Florence
English
Volume IV: 966

O'Hair, Madalyn Murray
American
Volume III: 512

Ovington, Mary White
American
Volume III: 516

Park, Maud Wood
American
Volume III: 522

Parks, Rosa
American
Volume III: 523

Pesotta, Rose
American
Volume III: 528

Sanger, Margaret Higgins
American
Volume III: 593

Schlafly, Phyllis
American
Volume III: 602

Schniederman, Rose
American
Volume III: 603

## Activist (continued)

Shabazz, Betty
American
Volume III: 614

Shaw, Anna Howard
American
Volume III: 616

Silkwood, Karen
American
Volume III: 621

Smeal, Eleanor
American
Volume III: 627

Song Sisters
Chinese
Volume IV: 1010

Stanton, Elizabeth Cady
American
Volume III: 636

Stone, Lucy
American
Volume III: 646

Switzer, Mary E.
American
Volume III: 651

Szold, Henrietta
American
Volume III: 652

Taylor, Susie King
American
Volume III: 663

Truth, Sojourner
American
Volume III: 670

Tubman, Harriet Ross
American
Volume III: 671

Tucker, C. DeLores
American
Volume III: 672

Wald, Lillian
American
Volume III: 689

Walker, Maggie Lena
American
Volume III: 693

Wattleton, Faye
American
Volume III: 699

Wauneka, Annie Dodge
American
Volume III: 701

Webb, Beatrice Potter
English
Volume IV: 1033

Willard, Frances Elizabeth
American
Volume III: 719

Woodhull, Victoria C.
American
Volume III: 728

Woodward, Ellen S.
American
Volume III: 729

Wright, Frances
American
Volume III: 730

Xiang Jingyu
Chinese
Volume IV: 1041

Yard, Mary Alexander
American
Volume III: 734

Zia, Helen
American
Volume III: 738

## Actress

Anderson, Judith
Australian
Volume IV: 747

Ball, Lucille
American
Volume I: 41

## Actress (continued)

Black, Shirley Temple
American
Volume I: 64

Cushman, Charlotte
American
Volume I: 159

Dandridge, Dorothy
American
Volume I: 163

Davis, Bette
American
Volume I: 166

Dee, Ruby
American
Volume I: 169

Fiske, Minnie Maddern
American
Volume I: 219

Fonda, Jane
American
Volume I: 226

Garbo, Greta
American
Volume II: 239

Garland, Judy
American
Volume II: 240

Goldberg, Whoopi
American
Volume II: 253

Hagen, Uta Thyra
American
Volume II: 275

Hayes, Helen
American
Volume II: 296

Hayworth, Rita
American
Volume II: 297

Hepburn, Audrey
English
Volume IV: 878

Hepburn, Katharine
American
Volume II: 306

Leigh, Vivien
English
Volume IV: 916

Loren, Sophia
Italian
Volume IV: 925

McDaniel, Hattie
American
Volume II: 450

McQueen, Butterfly
American
Volume II: 455

Monroe, Marilyn
American
Volume II: 471

Redgrave, Vanessa
English
Volume IV: 991

Sarandon, Susan
American
Volume III: 584

Streisand, Barbra
American
Volume III: 649

Taylor, Elizabeth Rosemond
American
Volume III: 661

Winfrey, Oprah
American
Volume III: 721

Wong, Anna May
American
Volume III: 726

## Anthropologist

Benedict, Ruth Fulton
American
Volume I: 54

## Anthropologist (continued)

Fletcher, Alice Cunningham
American
Volume I: 223

Mead, Margaret
American
Volume II: 458

## Artist

Abbott, Berenice
American
Volume I: 1

Arbus, Diane Nemerov
American
Volume I: 24

Bourke-White, Margaret
American
Volume I: 80

Burke, Selma
American
Volume I: 99

Carnegie, Hattie
American
Volume I: 117

Carr, Emily
Canadian
Volume IV: 779

Cassatt, Mary
American
Volume I: 122

Chicago, Judy
American
Volume I: 126

Frankenthaler, Helen
American
Volume I: 229

Gilpin, Laura
American
Volume II: 247

Goncharova, Natalia
Russian
Volume IV: 858

Graves, Nancy Stevenson
American
Volume II: 263

Hepworth, Barbara
English
Volume IV: 880

Hesse, Eva
German
Volume IV: 881

Holzer, Jenny
American
Volume II: 322

Johnson, Betsey
American
Volume II: 356

Kahlo, Frida
Mexican
Volume IV: 909

Kollwitz, Kathe
German
Volume IV: 912

Krasner, Lee
American
Volume II: 386

Lange, Dorothea
American
Volume II: 394

Leibovitz, Annie
American
Volume II: 403

Lin, Maya Ying
American
Volume II: 409

Martin, Agnes
American
Volume II: 438

Millett, Kate
American
Volume II: 464

Modersohn-Becker, Paula
German
Volume IV: 960

## Artist (continued)

Morgan, Julia
American
Volume II: 475

Moses, Grandma
American
Volume II: 482

Nevelson, Louise
American
Volume III: 497

O'Keefe, Georgia
American
Volume III: 512

Oppenheim, Meret
Swiss
Volume IV: 974

Picasso, Paloma
Spanish
Volume IV: 983

Popova, Liubov Sergeevna
Russian
Volume IV: 986

Richier, Germaine
French
Volume IV: 992

Ringgold, Faith
American
Volume III: 556

Salomon, Charlotte
German
Volume IV: 1000

Savage, Augusta Christine
American
Volume III: 596

Schapiro, Miriam
American
Volume III: 598

Taeuber-Arp, Sophie
American
Volume III: 1021

## Astronaut

Collins, Eileen
American
Volume I: 149

Jemison, Mae C.
American
Volume II: 354

Ride, Sally
American
Volume III: 554

Tereshkova, Valentina
Russian
Volume IV: 1024

## Athlete

Capriati, Jennifer
American
Volume I: 112

Comaneci, Nadia
Romanian
Volume IV: 800

Gibson, Althea
American
Volume II: 243

Gordeeva, Ekaterina
Russian
Volume IV: 861

King, Billie Jean
American
Volume II: 379

Muldowney, Shirley
American
Volume II: 485

Navratilova, Martina
American
Volume III: 492

Rudolph, Wilma
American
Volume III: 579

Zaharias, Mildred Didrikson
American
Volume III: 737

## Author

Alcott, Louisa May
American
Volume I: 8

Allen, Paula Gunn
American
Volume I: 10

Allende, Isabel
Chilean
Volume IV: 745

Alvarez, Julia
American
Volume I: 13

Angelou, Maya
American
Volume I: 20

Austen, Jane
English
Volume IV: 757

Bambara, Toni Cade
American
Volume I: 42

Barnes, Djuna
American
Volume I: 43

Bates, Katharine Lee
American
Volume I: 47

Bishop, Elizabeth
American
Volume I: 60

Blandiana, Ana
Romanian
Volume IV: 763

Blume, Judy
American
Volume I: 72

Bombal, Maria Luisa
Chilean
Volume IV: 766

Bradley, Marion Zimmer
American
Volume I: 84

Bradstreet, Anne Dudley
American
Volume I: 86

Bronte, Charlotte
English
Volume IV: 771

Bronte, Emily
English
Volume IV: 772

Brooks, Gwendolyn
American
Volume I: 88

Browning, Elizabeth Barrett
English
Volume IV: 773

Brownmiller, Susan
American
Volume I: 97

Buck, Pearl S.
American
Volume I: 98

Burnett, Frances Hodgson
American
Volume I: 100

Butler, Octavia E.
American
Volume I: 102

Carroll, Anna Ella
American
Volume I: 118

Child, Lydia Maria Francis
American
Volume I: 129

Childress, Alice
American
Volume I: 130

Chisholm, Caroline
Australian
Volume IV: 788

Chopin, Katherine
American
Volume I: 135

## Author (continued)

Christie, Agatha
English
Volume IV: 791

Cisneros, Sandra
American
Volume I: 138

Clapp, Margaret Antoinette
American
Volume I: 141

Colette, Sidonie Gabrielle
French
Volume IV: 799

de Beauvoir, Simone
French
Volume IV: 809

Dickinson, Emily
American
Volume I: 177

Dinesen, Karen Blixen-Fineck
Danish
Volume IV: 816

Doolittle, Hilda
American
Volume I: 184

Dove, Rita Frances
American
Volume I: 186

Eliot, George
English
Volume IV: 822

Ephron, Nora
American
Volume I: 206

Ferber, Edna
American
Volume I: 216

FitzGerald, Frances
American
Volume I: 221

Flanagan, Hallie
American
Volume I: 222

Frank, Anne
Dutch
Volume IV: 838

Franklin, Stella Maraia
Australian
Volume IV: 841

Fraser, Lady Antonia
English
Volume IV: 841

Friedan, Betty
American
Volume I: 232

Gaskell, Elizabeth
English
Volume IV: 853

Gilman, Charlotte Anna P.
American
Volume II: 246

Ginzburg, Natalia Levi
Italian
Volume IV: 854

Giovanni, Yolande Cornelia
American
Volume II: 250

Glasgow, Ellen
American
Volume II: 252

Goldmark, Josephine
American
Volume II: 257

Gordimer, Nadine
South African
Volume IV: 863

Green, Constance
American
Volume II: 267

Greer, Germaine
English
Volume IV: 866

Hansberry, Lorraine
American
Volume II: 282

## Author (continued)

Harper, Frances Ellen W.
American
Volume II: 287

Hellman, Lillian Florence
American
Volume II: 305

Himmelfarb, Gertude
American
Volume II: 314

Hinton, Susan Eloise
American
Volume II: 317

hooks, bell
American
Volume II: 324

Howe, Florence Rosenfeld
American
Volume II: 334

Hurston, Zora Neale
American
Volume II: 340

Jackson, Helen Hunt
American
Volume II: 349

Jacobs, Harriet A.
American
Volume II: 351

Jewett, Sarah Orne
American
Volume II: 355

Jong, Erica Mann
American
Volume II: 361

Jordan, June
American
Volume II: 365

Keller, Helen Adams
American
Volume II: 374

Kingston, Maxine Hong
American
Volume II: 381

Kreps, Juanita Morris
American
Volume II: 387

Larsen, Nella
American
Volume II: 395

Lazarus, Emma
American
Volume II: 398

Le Guin, Ursula K.
American
Volume II: 402

L'Engle, Madeleine
American
Volume II: 406

Lessing, Doris
English
Volume IV: 918

Lindbergh, Anne Morrow
American
Volume II: 411

Lorde, Audre
American
Volume II: 414

Lovelace, Ada Byron
English
Volume IV: 927

Lowell, Amy
American
Volume II: 419

Luhan, Mabel Doge
American
Volume II: 422

Mansfield, Katherine
New Zealand
Volume IV: 938

Marshall, Paule Burke
American
Volume II: 437

McCarthy, Mary T.
American
Volume II: 445

## Author (continued)

McCullers, Carson
American
Volume II: 448

McMillan, Terry
American
Volume II: 453

Millay, Edna St. Vincent
American
Volume II: 463

Mistral, Gabriela
Chilean
Volume IV: 959

Mitchell, Margaret
American
Volume II: 468

Moore, Marianne
American
Volume II: 473

Morrison, Toni
American
Volume II: 477

Murdoch, Iris
Irish
Volume IV: 963

Naidu, Sarojini
Indian
Volume IV: 965

Naylor, Gloria
American
Volume III: 495

Nin, Anais
French
Volume IV: 967

Oates, Joyce Carol
American
Volume III: 506

O'Connor, Flannery
American
Volume III: 509

Ogot, Grace Emily Akinyi
Kenyan
Volume IV: 973

Parker, Dorothy Rothschild
American
Volume III: 523

Plath, Sylvia
American
Volume III: 530

Poniatowska, Elena
Mexican
Volume IV: 985

Porter, Katherine Anne
American
Volume III: 532

Post, Emily Price
American
Volume III: 534

Potter, Beatrix
English
Volume IV: 987

Proulx, E. Annie
American
Volume III: 537

Rice, Anne
American
Volume III: 548

Rich, Adrienne
American
Volume III: 549

Robinson, Harriet Hanson
American
Volume III: 559

Sachs, Nelly
German
Volume IV: 999

Sand, George
French
Volume IV: 1001

Sappho
Greek
Volume IV: 1003

Sexton, Anne
American
Volume III: 613

## Author (continued)

Shelley, Mary
English
Volume IV: 1005

Silko, Leslie
American
Volume III: 620

Sitwell, Dame Edith
English
Volume IV: 1009

Smith, Lillian Eugenia
American
Volume III: 632

Sontag, Susan
American
Volume III: 635

Spark, Muriel Sarah
English
Volume IV: 1012

Steel, Danielle
American
Volume III: 637

Stein, Gertrude
American
Volume III: 641

Steinem, Gloria
American
Volume III: 643

Stowe, Harriet Beecher
American
Volume III: 646

Suttner, Bertha von
Austrian
Volume IV: 1017

Tan, Amy
American
Volume III: 658

Tarbell, Ida Minerva
American
Volume III: 659

Tyler, Anne
American
Volume III: 676

Van Duyn, Mona
American
Volume III: 681

vos Savant, Marilyn
American
Volume III: 687

Walker, Alice
American
Volume III: 690

Walker, Margaret
American
Volume III: 694

Warren, Mercy Otis
American
Volume III: 696

Welty, Eudora
American
Volume III: 705

Wharton, Edith
American
Volume III: 709

Wheatley, Phillis
American
Volume III: 710

Wilder, Laura Ingalls
American
Volume III: 716

Wilson, Harriet E.
American
Volume III: 720

Winnemucca, Sarah
American
Volume III: 724

Woolf, Virginia
English
Volume IV: 1037

## Aviator

Cochran, Jacqueline
American
Volume I: 146

## Aviator (continued)

Coleman, Bessie
American
Volume I: 148

Earhart, Amelia Mary
American
Volume I: 195

## Business Leader

Arden, Elizabeth
Canadian
Volume IV: 750

Ash, Mary Kay Wagner
American
Volume I: 26

Ashley, Laura
English
Volume IV: 753

Chanel, Coco
French
Volume IV: 787

Claiborne, Liz
American
Volume I: 140

Gilbreth, Lillian
American
Volume II: 244

Grossinger, Jennie
American
Volume II: 270

Hobby, Oveta Culp
American
Volume II: 317

Karan, Donna
American
Volume II: 369

Knopf, Blanche Wolf
American
Volume II: 385

Lauder, Estee
American
Volume II: 396

McMurray, Bette Clair
American
Volume II: 454

Rubenstein, Helena
American
Volume III: 576

Rudkin, Margaret Fogarty
American
Volume III: 578

Siebert, Muriel
American
Volume III: 618

Steel, Dawn
American
Volume III: 639

von Furstenberg, Diane
American
Volume III: 686

Walker, Madame C.J.
American
Volume III: 692

Wells, Mary Georgene
American
Volume III: 703

Westwood, Vivienne
English
Volume IV: 1036

## Cartoonist

Guisewite, Cathy Lee
American
Volume II: 271

## Chef

Child, Julia McWilliams
American
Volume I: 128

Farmer, Fannie Merritt
American
Volume I: 213

## Dancer

de Mille, Agnes
American
Volume I: 175

Duncan, Isadora
American
Volume I: 190

Dunham, Katherine
American
Volume I: 191

Farrell, Suzanne
American
Volume I: 213

Fonteyn, Dame Margot
English
Volume IV: 837

Graham, Martha
American
Volume II: 260

Holm, Hanya
American
Volume II: 321

St. Denis, Ruth
American
Volume III: 592

Tallchief, Maria
American
Volume III: 657

Tharp, Twyla
American
Volume III: 665

## Designer

Head, Edith
American
Volume II: 299

## Educator

Andrews, Fannie Fern
American
Volume I: 19

Beecher, Catharine
American
Volume I: 52

Bethune, Mary McLeod
American
Volume I: 59

Blanding, Sarah Gibson
American
Volume I: 68

Brown, Charlotte Eugenia
American
Volume I: 91

Carey Thomas, Martha
American
Volume I: 117

Collins, Marva
American
Volume I: 152

Crandall, Prudence
American
Volume I: 158

Gray, Hannah Holborn
American
Volume II: 265

Hill, Anita
American
Volume II: 310

Horner, Matina Souretis
American
Volume II: 332

Hunter, Madeline Cheek
American
Volume II: 339

Johnson, Marietta Louise
American
Volume II: 358

Keohane, Nannerl Overholser
American
Volume II: 377

Lloyd-Jones, Esther
American
Volume II: 412

## Educator (continued)

Lynd, Helen Merrell
American
Volume II: 423

Lyon, Mary
American
Volume II: 425

Mitchell, Maria
American
Volume II: 469

Montessori, Maria
Italian
Volume IV: 961

Nicolson, Marjorie Hope
American
Volume III: 498

Peabody, Elizabeth Palmer
American
Volume III: 527

Smith, Dora
American
Volume III: 630

Strang, Ruth May
American
Volume III: 648

Talbert, Mary
American
Volume III: 655

Willard, Emma Hart
American
Volume III: 718

## Filmmaker

Faye, Safi
Senegalese
Volume IV: 835

Riefenstahl, Leni
German
Volume IV: 993

## First Lady

Clinton, Hillary Rodham
American
Volume I: 144

Eisenhower, Mamie Doud
American
Volume I: 200

Madison, Dolly
American
Volume II: 430

Marcos, Imelda
Filipino
Volume IV: 940

Onassis, Jacqueline Kennedy
American
Volume III: 514

Peron, Eva Duarte de
Argentinian
Volume IV: 980

Roosevelt, Eleanor
American
Volume III: 566

Sadat, Jihan
Egyptian
Volume IV: 1000

## Historian

Conway, Jill Kathryn Ker
American
Volume I: 155

Pagels, Elaine Hiesey
American
Volume III: 521

Ruether, Rosemary Radford
American
Volume III: 581

## Historical Figure

Bishop, Bridget
American
Volume I: 60

### Historical Figure (continued)

Borgia, Lucrezia
Italian
Volume IV: 767

Calamity Jane
American
Volume I: 107

Livia
Roman
Volume IV: 920

Oakley, Annie
American
Volume III: 505

Pocahontas
American
Volume III: 532

Ross, Betsy
American
Volume III: 570

Sacajawea
American
Volume III: 588

### Journalist

Brown, Helen Gurley
American
Volume I: 92

Brown, Tina
American
Volume I: 94

Chung, Connie
American
Volume I: 138

Dorr, Rheta Childe
American
Volume I: 184

Goodman, Ellen Holtz
American
Volume II: 258

Graham, Katharine Meyer
American
Volume II: 259

Guerin, Veronica
Irish
Volume IV: 868

Hale, Sarah Josepha
American
Volume II: 276

Higgins, Marguerite
American
Volume II: 308

Seaman, Elizabeth Cochrane
American
Volume III: 607

Tarbell, Ida Minerva
American
Volume III: 659

Thompson, Dorothy
American
Volume III: 666

Walters, Barbara
American
Volume III: 695

Wells-Barnett, Ida B.
American
Volume III: 704

### Judge

Ginsburg, Ruth Bader
American
Volume II: 248

O'Connor, Sandra Day
American
Volume III: 510

### Mathematician

Granville, Evelyn Boyd
American
Volume II: 262

Noether, Emmy
German
Volume IV: 969

## Mathematician (continued)

Robinson, Julia
American
Volume III: 563

Uhlenbeck, Karen
American
Volume III: 679

## Musician

Caldwell, Sarah
American
Volume I: 108

Falletta, JoAnn
American
Volume I: 211

Tower, Joan
American
Volume III: 667

Zwilich, Ellen Taaffe
American
Volume III: 739

## Naturalist

Adamson, Joy
Austrian
Volume IV: 743

## Philosopher

Arendt, Hannah
German
Volume IV: 751

Bok, Sissela Ann
American
Volume I: 74

Daly, Mary
American
Volume I: 161

Hesse, Mary B.
English
Volume IV: 883

Midgely, Mary Burton
English
Volume IV: 958

Stein, Edith
German
Volume IV: 1014

Weil, Simone
French
Volume IV: 1034

## Politician

Albright, Madeleine
American
Volume I: 7

Allen, Florence Ellinwood
American
Volume I: 9

Aquino, Corazon
Filipino
Volume IV: 748

Aung San Suu Kyi
Myanmar
Volume IV: 755

Baca-Barragan, Polly
American
Volume I: 29

Bandaranaike, Sirimavo
Sri Lankan
Volume IV: 759

Bhutto, Benazir
Pakistani
Volume IV: 762

Black, Shirley Temple
American
Volume I: 64

Boxer, Barbara
American
Volume I: 81

Browner, Carol M.
American
Volume I: 95

Brundtland, Gro Harlem
Norwegian
Volume IV: 774

## Politician (continued)

Byrne, Jane
American
Volume I: 103

Caraway, Hattie Wyatt
American
Volume I: 115

Chamorro, Violeta
Nicaraguan
Volume IV: 785

Chiepe, Gaositwe Keagak
Botswanan
Volume IV: 788

Chisholm, Shirley
American
Volume I: 133

Ciller, Tansu
Turkish
Volume IV: 796

Devlin, Bernadette
Irish
Volume IV: 810

Dewson, Mary Williams
American
Volume I: 176

Doi Takako
Japanese
Volume IV: 817

Dole, Elizabeth
American
Volume I: 181

Elizabeth Bagaaya Nyabongo
Ugandan
Volume IV: 829

Feinstein, Dianne
American
Volume I: 215

Ferraro, Geraldine
American
Volume I: 217

Gandhi, Indira
Indian
Volume IV: 849

Gordon, Pamela
Bermudan
Volume IV: 864

Green, Edith Starrett
American
Volume II: 268

Hansen, Julia Butler
American
Volume II: 283

Harriman, Pamela
American
Volume II: 289

Harris, Patricia Roberts
American
Volume II: 294

Heckler, Margaret Mary
American
Volume II: 304

Hills, Carla Anderson
American
Volume II: 313

Jiang Qing
Chinese
Volume IV: 897

Jordan, Barbara Charline
American
Volume II: 364

Kassebaum, Nancy
American
Volume II: 372

Kelly, Petra
German
Volume IV: 910

Kirkpatrick, Jeane J.
American
Volume II: 383

Kunin, Madeleine May
American
Volume II: 390

Luce, Clare Boothe
American
Volume II: 420

## Politician (continued)

Martin, Lynn Morley
American
Volume II: 440

Mikulski, Barbara
American
Volume II: 460

Mink, Patsy Takemoto
American
Volume II: 465

Molinari, Susan
American
Volume II: 470

Mosely-Braun, Carol
American
Volume II: 481

Motley, Constance Baker
American
Volume II: 483

Natividad, Irene
American
Volume III: 490

Owen, Ruth Bryan
American
Volume III: 517

Pandit, Vijaya Lakshmi
Indian
Volume IV: 977

Perkins, Frances
American
Volume III: 528

Priest, Ivy Maude Baker
American
Volume III: 536

Rankin, Jeannette
American
Volume III: 543

Ray, Dixy Lee
American
Volume III: 545

Reno, Janet
American
Volume III: 546

Richards, Ann Willis
American
Volume III: 550

Rivlin, Alice M.
American
Volume III: 557

Robinson, Mary Bourke
Irish
Volume IV: 996

Rogers, Edith Nourse
American
Volume III: 564

Rohde, Ruth Bryan Owen
American
Volume III: 565

Ros-Lehtinen, Ileana
American
Volume III: 568

Ross, Nellie Tayloe
American
Volume III: 573

Roybal-Allard, Lucille
American
Volume III: 575

Schroeder, Patricia Scott
American
Volume III: 604

Sisulu, Nontsikelelo
South African
Volume IV: 1007

Smith, Margaret Chase
American
Volume III: 633

Snowe, Olympia
American
Volume III: 634

Suzman, Helen
South African
Volume IV: 1019

Thatcher, Margaret Hilda
English
Volume IV: 1026

## Politician (continued)

Velazquez, Nydia Margarita
American
Volume III: 683

Waters, Maxine
American
Volume III: 697

Whitman, Christine Todd
American
Volume III: 711

Whitmire, Kathryn Jean
American
Volume III: 713

## Psychologist

Brothers, Joyce
American
Volume I: 89

Klein, Melanie
Austrian
Volume IV: 911

Westheimer, Ruth Karola
American
Volume III: 707

Wexler, Nancy
American
Volume III: 708

## Religious Leader

Bourgeoys, Marguerite
French
Volume IV: 770

Cabrini, St. Frances
American
Volume I: 105

Catherine of Siena, St.
Italian
Volume IV: 782

Drexel, Katherine
American
Volume I: 188

Eddy, Mary Baker
American
Volume I: 198

Harris, Barbara Clementine
American
Volume II: 291

Hutchinson, Anne Marbury
American
Volume II: 341

Imaoka, Shinichiro
Japanese
Volume IV: 891

Joan of Arc
French
Volume IV: 900

Juana Ines de la Cruz, Sister
Mexican
Volume IV: 904

Julian of Norwich
English
Volume IV: 904

Lee, Mother Ann
American
Volume II: 399

MacKillop, Mary
Australian
Volume IV: 933

Morton, Nelle Katherine
American
Volume II: 479

Schiess, Betty Bone
American
Volume III: 600

Schussler Fiorenza, Elisabeth
American
Volume III: 606

Seton, Elizabeth Ann Bayley
American
Volume III: 612

Teresa, Mother
Indian
Volume IV: 1022

## Royalty

Boleyn, Anne
English
Volume IV: 765

Catherine of Aragon
English
Volume IV: 780

Catherine the Great
Russian
Volume IV: 783

Christina of Sweden
Swedish
Volume IV: 793

Cleopatra
Egyptian
Volume IV: 797

Comnena, Anna
Byzantine
Volume IV: 801

Diana, Princess of Wales
English
Volume IV: 812

Eleanor of Aquitaine
French
Volume IV: 821

Elizabeth I
English
Volume IV: 824

Elizabeth II
English
Volume IV: 827

Elizabeth of Hungary
Hungarian
Volume IV: 831

Elizabeth Petrovna
Rusian
Volume IV: 833

Hatshepsut
Egyptian
Volume IV: 877

Irene of Athens
Byzantine
Volume IV: 892

Isabella I
Spanish
Volume IV: 895

Julias of Rome, The
Roman
Volume IV: 905

Liliuokalani, Lydia Kamakaeha
Hawaiian
Volume IV: 919

Maria Theresa
Austrian
Volume IV: 941

Marie Antoinette
French
Volume IV: 943

Mary I
English
Volume IV: 947

Mary Queen of Scots
Scottish
Volume IV: 948

Medici, Catherine de
French
Volume IV: 950

Min
Korean
Volume IV: 959

Nefertiti
Egyptian
Volume IV: 966

Seymour, Jane
English
Volume IV: 1004

Victoria
English
Volume IV: 1029

Wu Tse-t'ien
Chinese
Volume IV: 1038

## Scientist

Andersen, Dorothy
American
Volume I: 15

Apgar, Virginia
American
Volume I: 22

Bailey, Florence Merriam
American
Volume I: 33

Baker, Sara Josephine
American
Volume I: 38

Bell Burnell, Susan Jocelyn
Irish
Volume IV: 761

Bernstein, Dorothy Lewis
American
Volume I: 55

Blackburn, Elizabeth Helen
American
Volume I: 66

Brown, Rachel Fuller
American
Volume I: 93

Cannon, Annie Jump
American
Volume I: 112

Carson, Rachel Louise
American
Volume I: 121

Chinn, May Edward
American
Volume I: 132

Colwell, Rita R.
American
Volume I: 154

Cori, Gerty T.
Czech
Volume IV: 802

Curie, Marie Sklodowska
French
Volume IV: 805

Douglas, Mary Tew
English
Volume IV: 819

Earle, Sylvia A.
American
Volume I: 196

Elders, Joycelyn
American
Volume I: 201

Elion, Gertrude B.
American
Volume I: 204

Franklin, Rosalind Elsie
English
Volume IV: 839

Freud, Anna
Austrian
Volume IV: 843

Garrett (Anderson), Elizabeth
English
Volume IV: 850

Gayle, Helene Doris
American
Volume II: 241

Geller, Margaret Joan
American
Volume II: 242

Goeppert-Mayer, Maria
German
Volume IV: 855

Goodall, Jane
English
Volume IV: 860

Hamilton, Alice
American
Volume II: 280

Hardy, Harriet
American
Volume II: 284

Healy, Bernadine Patricia
American
Volume II: 302

## Scientist (continued)

Hodgkin, Dorothy Crowfoot
English
Volume IV: 884

Hopper, Grace
American
Volume II: 327

Horney, Karen Danielsen
American
Volume II: 333

Hyman, Libbie Henrietta
American
Volume II: 343

Hypatia of Alexandria
Egyptian
Volume IV: 886

Jackson, Shirley Ann
American
Volume II: 350

Johnson, Virginia E.
American
Volume II: 359

Joliot-Curie, Irene
French
Volume IV: 902

Karle, Isabella
American
Volume II: 371

Kubler-Ross, Elisabeth
American
Volume II: 388

Leakey, Mary Douglas
English
Volume IV: 915

Levi-Montalcini, Rita
American
Volume II: 408

Long, Irene D.
American
Volume II: 413

Lonsdale, Kathleen
Irish
Volume IV: 923

Macdonald, Eleanor
American
Volume II: 429

Margulis, Lynn
American
Volume II: 436

McClintock, Barbara
American
Volume II: 447

Meitner, Lise
Austrian
Volume IV: 953

Mendenhall, Dorothy Reed
American
Volume II: 460

Mintz, Beatrice
American
Volume II: 467

Moore, Charlotte E.
American
Volume II: 472

Neufeld, Elizabeth
American
Volume III: 496

Novello, Antonia
American
Volume III: 501

Ochoa, Ellen
American
Volume III: 508

Patrick, Jennie R.
American
Volume III: 525

Patrick, Ruth
American
Volume III: 526

Payne-Gaposchkin, Cecilia
English
Volume IV: 978

Peterson, Edith R.
American
Volume III: 529

## Scientist (continued)

Prichard, Diana Garcia
American
Volume III: 536

Quimby, Edith H.
American
Volume III: 541

Ray, Dixy Lee
American
Volume III: 545

Richards, Ellen H.
American
Volume III: 551

Robinson, Joan
English
Volume IV: 995

Ross, Mary G.
American
Volume III: 572

Russell, Elizabeth Shull
American
Volume III: 583

Sabin, Florence Rena
American
Volume III: 585

Sagar, Ruth
American
Volume III: 591

Seibert, Florence B.
American
Volume III: 609

Shaw, Mary
American
Volume III: 617

Singer, Maxine
American
Volume III: 624

Slye, Maud
American
Volume III: 626

Stevens, Nettie Maria
American
Volume III: 644

Stopes, Marie
English
Volume IV: 1016

Taussig, Helen Brooke
American
Volume III: 659

Tharp, Marie
American
Volume III: 664

Trotter, Mildred
American
Volume III: 669

Widnall, Sheila E.
American
Volume III: 714

Yalow, Rosalyn S.
American
Volume III: 733

## Singer

Anderson, June
American
Volume I: 16

Anderson, Marian
American
Volume I: 17

Baez, Joan
American
Volume I: 31

Baker, Josephine
American
Volume I: 36

Battle, Kathleen
American
Volume I: 49

Brice, Fanny
American
Volume I: 86

Caesar, Shirley
American
Volume I: 106

## Singer (continued)

Callas, Maria
American
Volume I: 109

Cline, Patsy
American
Volume I: 142

Cotten, Elizabeth
American
Volume I: 156

Fitzgerald, Ella
American
Volume I: 220

Franklin, Aretha
American
Volume I: 230

Garland, Judy
American
Volume II: 240

Holiday, Billie
American
Volume II: 320

Horne, Lena
American
Volume II: 330

Madonna
American
Volume II: 432

Martin, Mary
American
Volume II: 441

Norman, Jessye
American
Volume III: 499

Piaf, Edith
French
Volume IV: 981

Price, Leotyne
American
Volume III: 535

Ross, Diana
American
Volume III: 571

Selena
American
Volume III: 611

Sills, Beverly
American
Volume III: 623

Smith, Bessie
American
Volume III: 628

Streisand, Barbra
American
Volume III: 649

Turner, Tina
American
Volume III: 674

Vaughan, Sarah Lois
American
Volume III: 682